Basic Marketing Management

Douglas J. Dalrymple
Indiana University

Leonard J. Parsons
Georgia Institute of Technology

John Wiley & Sons, Inc.
New York   Chichester   Brisbane   Toronto   Singapore

Acquisitions Editor	Tim Kent
Marketing Manager	Debra Riegert
Production Editor	Jennifer Knapp
Designer	David Levy
Manufacturing Operations Director	Susan Stetzer
Photo Editor	Mary Ann Price
Freelance Illustration Coordinator	Edward Starr
Cover Art	Michael McGurl

This book was set in 10/12 Palatino by University Graphics and printed and bound by Malloy Lithographing. The cover was printed by Phoenix Color Corp.

Library of Congress Cataloging-in-Publication Data
Dalrymple, Douglas J.
    Basic marketing management / Douglas J. Dalrymple, Leonard J.
Parsons.
        p.   cm.
    Includes bibliographical references.
    ISBN 0-471-58603-X (paper)
    1. Marketing—Management.   I. Parsons, Leonard J.   II. Title.
HF5415.13.D314   1995
658.8—dc20   94-26246
                                                           CIP

Printed in the United States of America

10 9 8 7 6 5 4 3 2 1

Basic
Marketing
Management

22-95

About the Authors

Douglas J. Dalrymple is professor of marketing in the School of Business at Indiana University. He received his DBA degree from Michigan State University and has taught at the University of California, Los Angeles, the Georgia Institute of Technology, the University of San Diego, and the University of North Carolina, Greensboro. Publications in which his articles have appeared include *The Journal of Personal Selling and Sales Management, Decision Sciences, Industrial Marketing Management*, the *Journal of Business Research, Business Horizons, California Management Review*, and *Applied Economics*. Professor Dalrymple is the coauthor of 17 books including *Marketing Management: Text and Cases* (6th ed.), *Cases in Marketing Management, Sales Management: Concepts and Cases* (5th ed.), *Sales Management Simulation* (3rd ed.), *Retailing: An Economic View*, and *Retail Management Cases*. Professor Dalrymple is a member of the American Marketing Association and the Institute of Management Science.

Leonard J. Parsons is professor of marketing at the Georgia Institute of Technology. He received his SB degree in chemical engineering from MIT and his MSIA and PhD degrees from Purdue's Krannert School. He has taught at Indiana University and the Claremont Graduate School, and has been a visiting scholar at MIT, a Fulbright-Hays Senior Scholar at Katholieke Universiteit Leuven (Belgium), an Advertising Educational Foundation Visiting Professor at Anheuser-Busch (St. Louis), and a visiting professor at INSEAD (France), the Norwegian School of Marketing (Oslo), and UCLA. He has been a consultant to Glaxo, Sherry & Mitchell, I.B.M., and Burnham Van Service among others. He has been an executive council member of the European Marketing Academy, a member of the Graduate Management Admission Council's Research and Test (GMAT) Development Committee, and is currently chair of the American Statistical Association's Section on Statistics in Marketing. He has served as marketing departmental editor of *Management Science* and associate editor of *Decision Sciences*, and has been on the editorial boards of the *Journal of Marketing Research*, the *Journal of Marketing*, and the *Journal of Business Research*. He has coauthored or coedited five books, including *Market Response Models: Econometric and Time Series Analysis*, two programmed learning texts, seven chapters in books, and articles in journals such as the *Journal of Marketing Research, Management Science, Operations Research*, and *Applied Economics*. He has received several awards from the American Marketing Association, including the first place award in its National Research Design Competition, and a grant from the American Association of Advertising Agencies. He is a member of Beta Gamma Sigma and Phi Kappa Phi and is listed in *Who's Who in America*. He is an expert on market response models, and his main interest is in marketing productivity.

Preface

Basic Marketing Management is something new from the Dalrymple/Parsons textbook team. To accommodate instructors who either don't use cases or prefer to select their own, we are now offering a marketing management book that focuses exclusively on text material. In addition, we are publishing this book in paperback form to help keep the price low for students. We have included 17 chapters to provide good coverage of the subject in a compact format. Those who are familiar with our previous marketing management texts will find that we have broadened our coverage with separate chapters on competitive analysis, direct marketing, and sales promotion. Also, all chapters now have boxed inserts to highlight real-world examples. We have expanded and integrated our coverage of international and Canadian applications and issues throughout the text. These references can easily be identified by a global icon in the text margins highlighting these passages.

We begin in Chapter 1 by defining marketing and explaining the role of marketing managers and the marketing concept. Chapter 2 discusses the development of marketing strategies to exploit future opportunities. Satisfied customers are essential for organizational success, and Chapter 3 focuses on identifying customers, their locations, and why they buy. Chapter 4 introduces the concepts of segmentation/ differentiation and explains why organizations market to special groups of customers. Chapter 5 is concerned with evaluating competitors and positioning firms for best results. In Chapter 6 we help students measure the size of markets and forecast future sales levels.

The traditional marketing mix-coverage starts in Chapter 7 with product development. In Chapter 8, we focus on marketing programs for products after they have been introduced. Our emphasis is on managing products across their life cycles and rescuing products in decline. Chapter 9 introduces the reader to the unique strategies associated with selling intangible services. Chapter 10 details a variety of pricing methods to provide the reader with background for making decisions in this area. Chapter 11 talks about selecting distribution channels that maximize sales and minimize costs. In Chapter 12 we are concerned with personal selling and management of field salespeople.

Chapter 13 discusses the growing emphasis on selling directly to customers. Chapter 14 focuses on the size of advertising budgets and the allocation of funds among different media. In Chapter 15 we show students how to design sales promotional programs. Chapter 16 explains the benefits of international trade and the various marketing strategies used to sell in foreign markets. Chapter 17 focuses on the development and implementation of marketing plans.

We believe that *Basic Marketing Management* offers instructors flexibility to emphasize text or their own case materials and to try innovative methods of instruction. Some instructors may want to supplement the book with specialized readings. For those professors who will be utilizing their own selection of cases, we have provided an appendix for students who need guidance in case methods and preparing case analyses. The Case Method, along with the sample Cook Company case and sample write up will enable students unfamiliar with, or lacking experience in reading, analyzing and presenting a case solution, the means to learn or review this important skill.

This book was made possible through the cooperation and contributions of many friends and colleagues. First, we would like to thank our editor, Tim Kent, and assistant editor, Ellen Ford, for their guidance and support. Next, we would like to thank C. L. Abercrombie of Memphis State University, Frank Alpert of the University of Missouri–Saint Louis, Craig Andrews of Marquette University, Joseph Bellizzi of Arizona State University, Terry Bristol of Oklahoma State University, Richard H. Kolbe of Washington State University, Eldon Little of Indiana University, James Mastrulka of Lehigh University, and H. Rao Unnava of the Ohio State University. In addition, we thank the Indiana University secretaries, Brenda, Linda, and Jessica, for typing countless drafts and revisions, and we thank Lori Parsons for her proofreading skills. Finally, we thank our wives, Nancy and Julie, for their help and encouragement.

Douglas J. Dalrymple

Leonard J. Parsons

Contents

Chapter 1

The Role of Marketing in Organizations and Society

The business enterprise has only two basic functions—marketing and innovation.

PETER DRUCKER

Marketing today is not a function; it is a way of doing business.

REGIS McKENNA

The field of marketing in the 1990s is full of challenges and danger. Domestic firms in every country find that they can no longer ignore foreign competition and foreign markets. Organizations that let their costs and prices get out of line with the rest of the world see their market shares plummet. Companies also learn that they cannot ignore emerging technologies and new forms of organizational structure.

Two giants of American business that did not learn these lessons quickly enough were IBM and Sears. IBM once had 80 percent of the U.S. computer market but focused too long on a maturing mainframe business. Smaller companies came in and grabbed large positions in emerging markets for workstations, minicomputers, personal computers, laptop computers, software, and computer services. IBM sustained huge losses for asset writeoffs, and its stock price fell 50 percent in one year. In 1992, IBM lost $5 billion—one of the worst financial reports in American business history. Sears was once the world's largest and most profitable retailer. Today it is selling off divisions and closing stores. Sears lost sight of its customers and let costs creep up. Wal-Mart found a way to make money while offering lower prices, and now it is the market leader.

Marketing executives at IBM and Sears failed to adjust to a changing world and failed to care for their customers. Management paid too much attention to the stock market and not enough attention to target markets. In their mad rush for

1

quarterly profits, customers' needs became secondary. General Electric, on the other hand, recognized that buyers in the 1990s wanted value. GE has reported record profits by emphasizing dependable basic units at prices that can't be beat in products ranging from computed tomography (CT) scanners to jet engines.

Why do some firms seize opportunities and grow while others fade away? We believe that one reason is *vision*. IBM got into trouble because it focused on selling products from the past. GE, on the other hand, identified and followed global marketing strategies for the future. Another reason some organizations grow is that they choose chief executive officers with marketing backgrounds. Research has shown that more top executives come out of marketing than any other field. Indeed, the chief financial officer of Goodyear recently quit because he lacked the marketing expertise needed to move into the top spot. These examples suggest that a marketing emphasis can make the difference between organizational success and disaster. We believe it is essential that you acquire strong marketing skills so that you can operate in today's competitive environment. This book has been specifically designed to show you how to develop and implement marketing strategies and tactics for organizations of the 1990s.

WHAT IS MARKETING?

Marketing is one of the most powerful tools employed by organizations in their never-ending struggle for survival and growth. Marketing can be defined as

> *the process of planning and executing the conception, pricing, promotion, and distribution of ideas, goods, and services to create exchanges that satisfy individuals, organizations, and society.*[1]

This definition points out that the objective of marketing is to satisfy customers' needs. Thus, the first challenge is to find a set of customers and identify their needs so that appropriate goods and services can be developed. Once organizations have a product, marketing personnel design pricing, promotion, and distribution plans to make these items leap into the hands of the customer. Executives have the responsibility to meet organizational goals while ensuring that the customer and the public are not harmed by marketing activities. When we speak of exchanges, we do not restrict ourselves to the one-time, arms-length transaction between a buyer and a seller.

In a single-event transaction, all that counts is the sale.[2] Price is the most important factor. More often, however, there are repeated transactions between parties. This is true for some industrial components and most consumables: frequently purchased consumer goods and business supplies. Advertising and sales promotions are used to gain and retain customers. Concepts such as brand loyalty now have meaning. Nonetheless, there may be little direct contact between the marketer and the customer in many consumer markets. When we examine business-to-business markets, we often see long-term agreements among parties. Frequently, a buyer has a list of qualified vendors. The buyer encourages competition among these vendors, perhaps by using a competitive bidding process, to get the best price. The buyer monitors product quality by inspection on delivery. Thus, while this is a long-term relationship, its basis is adversarial. However, this picture of the marketplace is changing.

Facing new pressures, once contending parties are coming to see the value of cooperation. *Relationship marketing* emphasizes the interdependence between buyer and seller. Quality, delivery, and technical support, as well as price, enter into negotiations. Quality is built into the production process. In today's world, you should develop long-term mutually supportive relationships with your customers—be they channel members or end users. This approach can be extended to embrace suppliers and, at times, competitors as well. In some cases, the relationship takes the form of a partnership or a strategic alliance. For example, the Coca-Cola Company and Nestlé S.A. have a joint venture, Coca-Cola Nestlé Refreshments Company. Among other

TABLE 1-1

Marketing's Role in the Organization

Organizational Level	Role of Marketing	Name
Corporate	To promote a customer orientation by being a strong advocate for the customer's point of view, as called for by the marketing concept. To assess market attractiveness by analyzing customers' needs and requirements, as well as competitive offerings in the markets potentially available to the firm, to assess potential competitive effectiveness. To develop the firm's overall value proposition in terms reflecting customers' needs and to articulate it to the marketplace and throughout the firm.	Corporate marketing
Strategic business unit	To determine how to compete (market segmentation, targeting, and product positioning) in your chosen business through a more detailed and careful analysis of competitors and of the firm's resources and skills for competing in specific market segments. To decide when and how to partner.	Strategic marketing
Operating	To formulate and implement marketing programs based on the marketing mix—products, pricing, distribution, and marketing communications. To manage customer and reseller relationships.	Marketing management

Source: Developed from Frederick E. Webster, Jr., "The Changing Role of Marketing in the Corporation," *Journal of Marketing*, Vol. 56, No. 4 (October 1992), pp. 1–17.

things, this joint venture sells a canned beverage, Nestea Iced Tea. The product is produced and distributed by Coca-Cola bottlers in various countries.

Even for frequently purchased consumer products, you need to move beyond a repeat-transaction mentality to relationship marketing. This has been made possible by the technical ability to create large databases, which identify customers and their needs. You can reach specific customers through direct selling or direct marketing. This approach is known as *database marketing*.

The role marketing plays in an organization varies by organizational level (Table 1-1). At the corporate level, *marketing as culture* is emphasized; at the strategic business unit level, *marketing as strategy*; and at the operating level, *marketing as tactics*. This chapter emphasizes marketing as culture: the basic set of values and beliefs about the central importance of the customer, as articulated by the marketing concept, that guides the organization.

WHO IS THE MARKETING MANAGER?

A marketing manager is anyone responsible for making significant marketing decisions. Except in the case of very small firms, no single person is accountable for all the decisions described in this book. The responsibility for marketing is diffused throughout the organization. Senior managers are continually making pricing and strategic marketing decisions. But engineers are also involved in marketing because they have to design products that meet customers' needs, wants, and quality standards, as are corporate treasurers who oversee the credit terms and credit availability that directly affect buying decisions.

Several managers in an organization specialize in marketing decision making. These include brand and product managers, who make the day-to-day decisions for individual items and prepare the annual marketing plan. There are also line sales managers who guide the implementation of the marketing plan by the field sales force. In addition to these line managers, there are a variety of staff managers. Advertising and promotion managers control the preparation of print ads, TV commercials, direct-mail brochures, and contests that help to boost the sales of goods and services. Larger firms also have managers of product development and marketing information.

WHAT DOES A MARKETING MANAGER DO?

A marketing manager is, first and foremost, someone who has control or direction of an organization or organizational unit. There are fundamental aspects of a manager's job that apply across functional areas. Managers have been shown to play 10 roles: figurehead, leader, liaison, monitor, disseminator, spokesperson, entrepreneur, disturbance handler, resource allocator, and negotiator. These roles can be classified as interpersonal, informational, or decisional. Table 1-2 describes these roles and

TABLE 1-2

The Marketing Manager's Job

Role	Description	Example
Interpersonal		
Figurehead	Performs some duties of a ceremonial nature.	Takes important customer to lunch.
Leader	Assumes responsibility for work of subordinates.	Motivates the sales force.
Liaison	Makes contacts outside the vertical chain of command.	Meets with an account executive from a direct marketing firm.
Informational		
Monitor	Scans the environment for information.	Hears from a supplier about a competitor's new product.
Disseminator	Shares information with others, especially subordinates.	Provides feedback from meetings with prospective clients at their locations.
Spokesperson	Sends some information to people outside the organizational unit.	Makes a speech to lobby for favorable legislative treatment.
Decisional		
Entrepreneur	Seeks to improve the unit, adapting it to changing conditions in the environment.	Assigns a new idea to the product development team.
Disturbance handler	Responds to high-pressure disturbances.	Addresses a consumer boycott initiated by a special interest group.
Resource allocator	Decides who will get what in the organizational unit.	Determines the allocation of promotion budget across brands.
Negotiator	Bargains with others.	Negotiates sales terms with a channel member.

Source: Developed from Henry Mintzberg, *Mintzberg on Management*, New York: The Free Press, 1989, pp. 7–24.

gives examples of how they might apply specifically to a marketing manager. For example, a national account manager for a health and beauty aids company often negotiates sales and promotional terms with the central purchasing offices of large national supermarket chains. As you can see, many of these roles require not only knowledge of marketing concepts and practices, but the exercise of interpersonal skills as well.

The full range of marketing activities in the firm is described in Figure 1-1. Note that the marketing manager is in the center of interactions with a host of people both inside and outside the organization. Marketing talks to customers, research and development, production, finance, suppliers, ad agencies, and marketing research firms. The net result of these interactions is products delivered to satisfied buyers plus profits to fuel innovations for tomorrow. Your most important role is to understand customers.

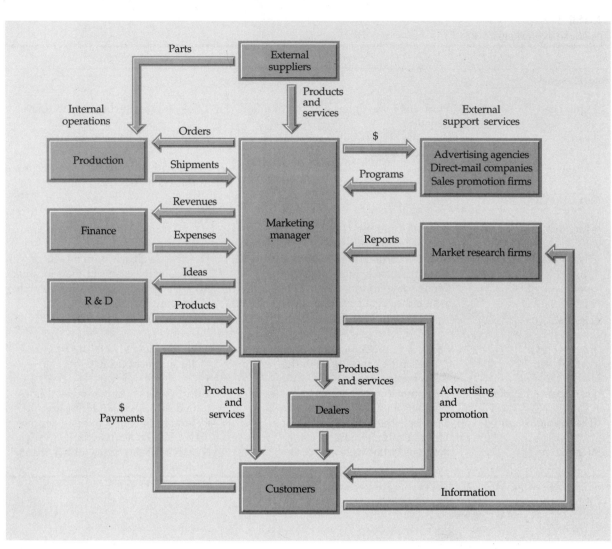

FIGURE 1-1   Operating Areas for Marketing Managers

Customer Contact

Marketing people continually interact with customers. Customers must be your first and most enduring concern. Close attention to their needs is essential for success. Some of the ways that marketing managers relate to customers are shown in Figure 1-1. The diagram shows marketing managers interacting with two types of customers: dealers who resell your products to others and final users. Both types have unique needs that demand specialized marketing programs. Because these customers are typically located some distance from the office, you have to go into the field to talk with them. You also have to set up distribution systems to make goods and

> ## MARKETING IN ACTION 1-1
>
> ### CUSTOMER-DRIVEN FORD MOTOR CO.
>
> Reeling under the onslaught of Japanese cars, Ford Motor Co. realized that it must listen to its customers. At a focus group of car buyers in California in 1980, people of college age said, "I don't own a Ford. I don't know anyone who owns a Ford. I have never been in a Ford." Ford's Chairman sent out the word: "If we aren't customer driven, our cars won't be either." Among the first to get the message were design engineers. They invited more consumers than ever before to evaluate prototypes of the Taurus and Sable, then under development.
>
> Customer feedback has saved Ford from itself. In the mid-1980s, top executives wanted to ditch the boxy Lincoln Town Car. The company kept the sedan after surveys showed that older drivers still liked it. A revamped Town Car won *Motor Trend* magazine's Car of the Year award in 1990.
>
> Ford now surveys some 2.5 million customers a year and invites owners to meet engineers and dealers to discuss quality. It has a user-friendly software system that makes it easy for executives and engineers to use customer satisfaction data. Buyers have rewarded Ford for such efforts by making Taurus the best selling car in America in 1992.
>
> *A large organization may take a decade to become completely customer driven—and keeping it so is a continual battle against complacency.*
>
> Source: "King Customer," *Business Week*, March 12, 1990, pp. 88ff.

services available when and where they are needed. Figure 1-1 also indicates that the marketing manager has responsibility for directing persuasive communications to dealers and ultimate customers and arranging for payment of purchases. In addition, marketing managers have responsibility for collecting information on customer satisfaction and future needs. Managing customer relations is a tremendous responsibility and can represent the difference between achieving the goals of the organization and failing. Some advantages of maintaining customer contacts and being customer driven are illustrated in Marketing in Action box 1-1.

Supplier Contact

An expanding role for marketing managers in the 1990s is more direct contact with suppliers (Figure 1-1). In the 1970s and 1980s the emphasis was on vertical integration, whereby the firm produced all of its own parts. Companies thought that in-house production would lower costs, but it actually raised them. Today some of the most successful firms rely on suppliers for parts and production so that they can focus on core activities such as product design, marketing, and service.[3] Nike, for example, has annual sales of over $3 billion a year, yet they have only one small parts plant. They contract for virtually all footwear production in Taiwan and South Korea. Dell Computer owns no plants and leases two small factories to assemble

---

MARKETING STRATEGIES 1-1

NIKE'S DRIVE TO BE NUMBER 1

Nike is the market leader in America because they concentrate their efforts on things they do well—designing and marketing high-tech, fashionable footwear for sports and fitness. By contracting out production of its shoes, Nike has reduced its fixed investment costs and made itself one of the most profitable U.S. firms as measured by return on assets.

The Nike story begins with a commitment to research and development. They are constantly improving the comfort, durability, and performance of their shoes. The Nike Air Jordan with patented air cushioned insert is a good example. This high-tech shoe has allowed Nike to grab over 50 percent of the basketball shoe market. Nike uses a Japanese kaizen-style process of making continual small improvements in its products. As a result, Nike Air shoes weigh only 12 ounces.

A second strength is marketing. Nike has always employed sports stars to endorse their products. Young people look up to these legends and try to imitate them. Current endorsement icons include Andre Agassi, John McEnroe, and the biggest catch of all, Michael Jordan of the Chicago Bulls. To maintain this stable of stars, Nike spends $240 million or 8 percent of sales a year. These expenditures are backed up with heavy TV advertising. Nike ads with Michael Jordan soaring through the air are creative and memorable.

Nike's drive to be number one is all the more remarkable because they pushed aside two strong market leading German firms, Adidas and Puma, plus Reebok. Having conquered America, Nike is now looking to overseas markets in Europe and other areas. Foreign sales are up 33 percent proving once again that Nike's marketing machine can go the distance.

The structure of the organization is evolving from a hierarchy to a network. Your organizational chart now may resemble a wheel more than a pyramid.

Source: Tim Ferguson, "Nike Seems to Be Doing It Right," *The Wall Street Journal,* July 14, 1992, p. A15.

---

computers from outsourced parts. Both Nike and Dell spend their time and money designing and marketing products to fill customers' needs.

A strategy of focusing on marketing activities with production facilities owned by outsiders has allowed Nike to generate a 16 percent return on assets in 1992 and Dell to earn 35 percent on stockholders equity. These new strategic alliances mean that marketing managers must spend more time with suppliers to make sure product quality is maintained and delivery dates are met. Marketing Strategies box 1-1 provides more details on Nike's marketing success story.

Buying External Services

One of the least understood facts about marketing is that much of the work is assigned to external suppliers (Figure 1-1). In the past, many firms had their own in-house marketing research, advertising, and promotion staffs. Today most companies hire outside advertising agencies to create their advertising and a separate firm to handle direct-mail campaigns. Contests and display materials are developed by special organizations, and market research data are gathered by still another organization. The reliance on outside suppliers means that in your job as marketing manager, you become a buyer of these services. It also means that marketing managers spend a lot of time coordinating the activities of these separate groups and making sure that the work is done on time. Victory in the marketplace often depends on your ability to hire the right service suppliers and to evaluate their output.

Internal Coordination

A third challenge to marketing managers stems from their role as coordinator with other areas of the firm (Figure 1-1). Although marketing is responsible for maintaining good customer relations, as a manager you often do not have formal control over the production of the goods and services customers buy. Thus marketing has to work closely with the production department to make sure that orders are filled on time, at an affordable price, and meet customers' specifications. Sometimes this means that production and marketing personnel have to find ways to modify the product to meet the needs of the market. Less successful firms are often those in which production and marketing are unable to work together to get this job done.

Another key interaction for marketing managers involves their ability to work with the research and development (R&D) department (Figure 1-1). Marketing often comes up with good ideas for new products, but R&D is responsible for turning them into salable products. Thus your success as a marketer may depend on the relationship you develop with the R&D staff.

Marketing managers also have to interact with the financial managers of the firm (Figure 1-1). Marketing activities are often expensive, and marketing managers have to meet with financial managers to prepare budget requests. If funds are tight, marketing managers have to find ways to reorganize their activities to make them more efficient. Some of the areas that require financial support are advertising, product development, maintenance of dealer inventories, and credit lines to finance customers' purchases.

TABLE 1-3
Typical Responsibilities of Marketing Managers

Marketing strategy development
Customer analysis and segmentation
Competitor analysis and positioning
Market analysis and sales forecasting
Product and service development
Pricing
Distribution channel development
Deployment of sales force
Direct marketing
Advertising
Sales promotion
Preparation and implementation of marketing plans

If you take a position in marketing, some of the work-related tasks you will be assigned are listed in Table 1-3. Marketing is much more than a list of things to do; it is a natural sequence of events that leads to greater sales and profits.

THE MARKETING MANAGEMENT PROCESS

Marketing managers plan and implement a sequence of activities that help the firm achieve its goals. The precise actions taken vary with the product or service to be promoted, but a general idea can be obtained from the flowchart shown in Figure

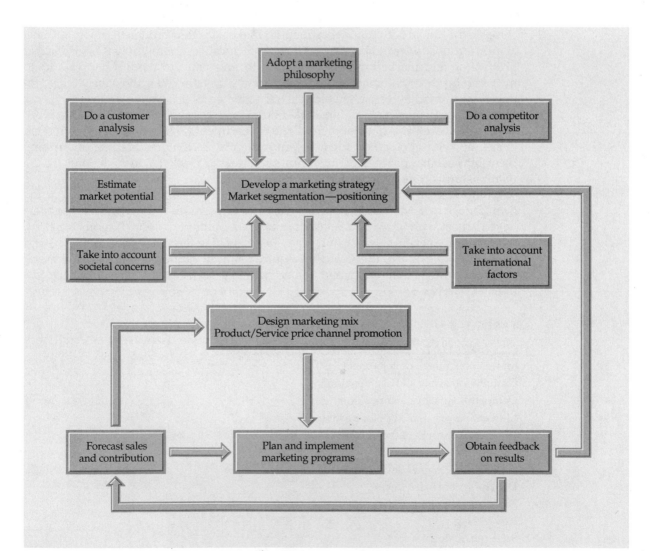

FIGURE 1-2   The Marketing Management Process

1-2. This diagram provides a basic framework for the book. First, managers need to adopt a marketing philosophy. This chapter explains why organizations should be customer driven and in tune with the goals of society. Although you are charged with promoting the sale of goods and services, you must also learn to balance these objectives against the long-term needs of society for a safe and healthy environment. In addition, you need to know which marketing activities are ethical and which violate current business standards.

Second in the management process is a concern with marketing strategy (Chapter 2): our emphasis is on achieving a sustainable competitive advantage for the organization. A problem-solving approach is used throughout the book.

The Marketplace

Before sound marketing strategies can be created (Figure 1-2), you have to know who your potential and/or existing customers are and why they behave as they do (Chapter 3). In developing marketing strategies, the manager must select appropriate market segments to be targets of the marketing effort (Chapter 4). You also have to understand your competitors and where they are going (Chapter 5). A critical decision here is how your organization's offerings should be positioned against those of your competitors. Once you know who you are after, the marketing manager needs to estimate potentials and forecast sales (Chapter 6).

The Marketing Mix

Perhaps the most creative and challenging step in marketing is designing the right mix of marketing activities to tap the target segments. The *marketing mix* is the specific collection of actions and associated instruments employed by an organization to stimulate acceptance of its ideas, products, or services (Table 1-4). The basic functions included in the mix are product development and policy making, pricing, channel selection and control, and marketing communications—personal selling, direct marketing, and advertising. The term *marketing mix* can be used to describe either the activity, such as pricing, or the marketing instrument, such as list price. When trying to determine the best marketing mix for your product, you face a large number of alternatives. The only way to reduce these alternatives to a manageable number is to take a strategic focus. That is one reason why we emphasize strategy in a marketing management book.

Product development activities focus on the conversion of customers' wants into real products or services (Chapter 7). Since existing products and services lose their attractiveness over time, product development is essential to the survival of all organizations. Marketing managers are responsible for designing the systems needed to find, screen, and evaluate new ideas. Product policy (Chapter 8) emphasizes the management of a product over its life cycle. This involves reformulating old products and getting rid of some of them. Since more money is being spent in highly industrialized countries on services than on manufactured goods, the special marketing needs of intangible merchandise are discussed (Chapter 9).

TABLE 1-4
Marketing Mix

Element	Description	Examples
Product	Instruments that mainly aim at the satisfaction of the prospective exchange party's needs	Product characteristics, options, assortments, brand name, packaging, quantity, factory guarantee
Price	Instruments that mainly fix the size and method of payment for goods or services	List price, usual terms of payment, usual quantity discounts, terms of credit
Distribution	Instruments that determine the intensity and manner in which goods or services will be made available	Different types of distribution channels, density of distribution system, trade relation mix, merchandising advice
Marketing communications		
Personal selling	Face-to-face, personal communication efforts	Amount and type of selling, compensation plans
Direct marketing	Other one-to-one communication efforts	Number of direct-mail pieces and telephone calls
Advertising	Mass communication efforts	Theme advertising in various media, permanent exhibits

Source: Based on Walter van Waterschoot and Christophe Van den Bulte, "The 4P Classification of the Marketing Mix Revisited," *Journal of Marketing,* Vol. 56, No. 4 (October 1992), pp. 83–93.

A critical dimension of your job as marketing manager is making decisions on what prices to charge for goods and services to generate desired levels of sales (Chapter 10). Marketing also has the task of organizing brokers, wholesalers, and retailers into channels of distribution so that merchandise and services will be available where customers need and want them (Chapter 11). Personal selling (Chapter 12) is required for many products, and marketing managers have the job of hiring, training, and deploying the right number of salespeople to meet the needs of potential buyers. Direct marketing (Chapter 13) has become increasingly important with the creation of large databases. Direct marketing includes telephone marketing and direct mail. Advertising (Chapter 14) focuses on nonpersonal communication through measured media. This means that you have to choose among newspapers, radio, television, billboards, direct mail, and magazines. The basic marketing mix is supported by sales promotions and public relations (Chapter 15). You must determine budgets for point-of-purchase displays, contests, and other promotional activities.

Building the Plan

After an appropriate marketing mix has been selected, it is your job as marketing manager to prepare and implement a detailed marketing plan. Vital to developing marketing strategies and tactics today is the international dimension (Chapter 16). The production and marketing of many goods are now on a global basis, which leads firms to consider the impact of such things as cultural differences and currency exchange rates on pricing and distribution plans. Responsibility for implementing marketing programs (Chapter 17) rests with brand managers, who continually monitor the results of marketing activities and recommend program improvements.

Although we have shown marketing management as a sequence of steps that follow the chapters of this book, you should realize that brand managers often work on several of these activities at the same time. Also, feedback in terms of results and customer reactions provides continuous input for strategy revisions and updated sales forecasts (Figure 1-2). Marketing management is a highly interactive process, and your success as a marketing professional will depend on your ability to coordinate and work through others.

The marketing management process begins with the adoption of the marketing philosophy. We will now focus on what makes a firm marketing driven.

THE MARKETING CONCEPT

Organizations must adapt to changing economic environments and meet competitive threats to prevent loss of market share, stagnation, and perhaps even bankruptcy. Some companies take an operations orientation. They are primarily concerned with cost cutting and production. Others are technology driven. They want to do something new and exciting. Both may founder because they ignore their customers or their competition.

For example, conservative H. J. Heinz has dominated the U.S. ketchup business for over 100 years. With 53 percent of the market already in hand, Heinz is now looking to international markets for sales growth. However, local competitors have grabbed the number 1 position in France, Sweden, and Japan. The main reason for these setbacks is that Heinz has been slow to adapt to local tastes and trends. In France, BSN S.A. used marketing research to find out that youngsters were more receptive to American products than their parents. BSN's Amora ketchup became the market leader by introducing plastic bottles resembling rocketships and running TV ads featuring children painting smiling faces on fried eggs. Heinz was caught using old-fashioned glass bottles and a stodgy ad featuring an American cowboy on horseback in the desert lassoing a Heinz bottle. Also, Heinz's sweet ketchup recipe did not appeal to some Europeans. The lesson to be learned from these experiences is that market leadership goes to firms that understand and fill customers' needs.

The belief that organizational goals can be reached by satisfying customers has grown so much in importance among managers that it has become known as the *marketing concept*. The marketing concept is a business philosophy that maintains that the key to achieving organizational goals is to determine the needs of target markets and to deliver the desired merchandise more efficiently than do competitors. This idea of focusing a whole organization on attending to customers' needs has gained widespread acceptance among managers. Three important dimensions of the marketing concept that you must understand are:

1. A customer orientation.
2. An integrated company effort.
3. Goal-directed behavior.

Although these three factors interact to help improve marketing activities, they will be discussed separately.

A Customer Orientation

The basic idea of the marketing concept is to give customers what they want. This means that organizations must decide who their target customers are and then find out their wants and needs. The net result should be the creation of goods and services that satisfy customers' expectations. For example, Colgate stole market share from Crest by introducing an easy-to-use pump dispenser and a stand-up squeeze tube. The largest Midas Muffler dealer in the United States offers free pickup and delivery for customers, and the largest Lexus dealer keeps its service department open until midnight. H&R Block's most successful tax office stays open year round to help customers fill out their tax forms. Automobile companies cater to customers' needs by offering options that wash headlights, allow steering wheels to telescope, show road maps on display screens, and remember seat and rear-view mirror positions for several drivers.

The advantages of a customer orientation seem so obvious that it is hard to understand why the concept has not been more widely adopted. However, there have been and still are many organizations that take a very narrow view of their mission, a problem that has been called *marketing myopia*. Banks, for example, once thought of themselves as protectors of their customers' money. They hid behind bars, and their hours were from 10:00 A.M. to 3:00 P.M. a few days per week. Following the marketing concept, banks have added branch locations that are open on Saturdays, have extended weekday hours, and feature drive-up windows. They have also installed 24-hour teller machines that dispense cash and perform other services to serve customers better. An example of what a customer orientation has done for BMW is given in Marketing in Action box 1-2.

An Integrated Company Effort

A second dimension of the marketing concept suggests that marketing activities should be closely coordinated with each other and with the other functional areas of the organization. Under the marketing concept, sales, finance, production, and personnel all work together to satisfy customers' needs. With the production orientation, production emphasized rigid schedules so that costs could be kept low through long production runs. If the sales department said that a customer needed 21-day delivery of 100,000 cases of perfumed, two-color facial tissues in boutique boxes, the answer most likely was that it couldn't be done because it would raise costs. Under the marketing concept, the major task of the production department is to learn how to rearrange schedules to meet customers' needs at an acceptable cost. One result has been the emergence of flexible manufacturing systems.

MARKETING IN ACTION 1-2

BMW ZOOMS AHEAD OF MERCEDES BENZ

For the first time in 30 years, BMW sold more cars in 1992 than its German rival, Mercedes. While BMW was scheduling overtime, Mercedes was laying off workers and extending holiday shutdowns. The main reason for BMW's success is that they paid more attention to customers and designed a broader range of products to fill their needs. One of their best sellers is their sleek new entry level line of cars, the 3-series. BMW introduced the models in 1991 to attract buyers who are unable or unwilling to spend more than $40,000 for a car. They offer five models ranging in price from $23,710 to $36,320 with such features as driver-side airbags and sports suspension. Mercedes' competing car, the 190, comes in only two models and starts at $28,950.

While BMW was gobbling up entry level customers, Mercedes brought out its giant S-class cars costing $69,900 to $139,000 each. These cars have been widely criticized as too big, too heavy, and too expensive. They are so wide that they don't fit into railway cars used by German vacationers who travel by train. Sales of the S-class have been disappointing. In addition to poor design, Mercedes is an inefficient and high cost producer of cars. Mercedes' new plant in Germany, for example, is designed to build 360 cars a day with 5,500 employees. Meanwhile, BMW's new South Carolina plant in America only requires 2,000 workers to build 400 cars a day.

Pay heed to what your customer wants; your product can be ''overengineered'' and thus too expensive for the market.

Source: Krystal Miller and Timothy Aeppel, ''BMW Zooms Ahead of Mercedes-Benz in World-Wide Sales for the First Time,'' *The Wall Street Journal,* January 20, 1993, p. B1.

Authors' note: Mercedes-Benz has outlined dramatic changes aimed at turning the maker of ultra-expensive cars into more of a mass marketer with some smaller cars and a new minivan. Mercedes has also announced plans to build cars in America.

In the past, marketing has emphasized sales goals, production has attempted to minimize costs, and R&D has been concerned with unique ways to apply technology. Although these objectives may be useful performance standards for individual departments, they are not compatible with the marketing concept, and it is unlikely that the goals of the firm will be achieved when they are pursued separately. The objective should be to operate each part of the firm in order to reach overall targets. The marketing concept has been a useful mechanism in helping to unify the independent functional areas to increase customer satisfaction and improve profits.

Goal-Directed Behavior

The third objective of the marketing concept is that behavior should be directed at achieving the goals of the organization. This means that marketing plans and corporate goals must be closely coordinated. For example, during the 1980s, General Motors spent $40 billion on plant and equipment to standardize products and reduce costs. Unfortunately, much of the automated equipment did not work as well as anticipated, and GM became the highest-cost auto manufacturer in the United States. Thus, when the Japanese were forced to raise prices in the United States because of the increase in the value of the yen, GM was not in a position to grab market share. Customers reacted to GM's bland styling, poor quality, and high prices by reducing its market share from 50 percent to 33 percent. GM was faced with the unpleasant task of closing assembly lines to lower costs at the same time that their Japanese competitors were expanding U.S. plants in an effort to steal additional market share.

In the case of nonprofit organizations, objectives are usually stated more broadly. For example, one goal of the U.S. Army is to get recruits and reenlistments, the goal of municipal bus lines is to make their services as convenient as possible to maximize the number of passengers, and the goal of Big Brother–Big Sister programs is to get volunteers to contribute their time.

Organizations often have multiple goals. While community orchestras seek to enhance their audiences' appreciation of music, they also must sell enough seats to meet their operating expenses. This means that they need to offer young people's concerts to make sure that future generations will support the orchestra. Also, community orchestras must balance their programs with a mix of new selections to educate customers and enough traditional favorites to maintain financial support.

Implementing the Marketing Concept

One of the most successful advocates of the marketing concept is the highly profitable, $52 billion, Wal-Mart retail chain. At Wal-Mart, customers come first and are welcomed at the door by *people greeters;* inside, hourly employees (called *associates*) approach customers and ask how they can help, and checkout lines are kept short. The whole operation is designed to be responsive to customers' needs. In addition, most senior managers spend four days a week on the road making sure that the 1300 stores are clean and operating smoothly. Wal-Mart helps to integrate company activities by sharing cost, freight, and profit margin data with department heads and hourly associates. Also, when a store's profit goal is exceeded, the hourly associates share in the additional profit. To help control losses from damage and theft, Wal-Mart has instituted a shrinkage bonus when employees keep store losses below company goals. Group harmony is fostered by encouraging employees with problems to talk about their problems with management. Wal-Mart has shown that when you get employees to work together to meet customers' needs, you are better able to meet company sales and profit goals. Marketing-driven firms must always keep in mind the interests of all the players with which they interact: customers, channel members, competitors, regulators, and society as a whole. The ultimate success of a firm rests on obtaining sustainable competitive advantages based on long-run customer and channel franchises.

MARKETING AND SOCIETY

Some people question whether the marketing concept is an appropriate organizational theme in an era of environmental deterioration, poverty, and neglected social services. Is society better off when firms sell goods to satisfy individual wants and needs or should marketing managers adopt a longer-run goal of maximizing human welfare? Perhaps we should use a broader definition of the marketing concept:

> *The* societal marketing concept *holds that the organization's task is to determine the needs, wants, and interests of target markets and to deliver the desired satisfactions more effectively and efficiently than competitors in a way that preserves or enhances the consumer's and the society's well-being.*[4]

This definition asks marketers to balance customers' wants, company profits, and the public interest. Instead of just maximizing profits, marketing managers are beginning to consider the interests of society when they make decisions. The relative positions of marketing and several environmental variables are highlighted in Figure 1-3. We show marketing plans surrounded by the marketing mix variables under your control. However, most of the factors in the outer ring cannot be changed by individual organizations. You are generally at the mercy of economic conditions and international trade agreements. You also have little control over changes in consumer tastes and the actions of competitors. Two areas that are influenced by marketing

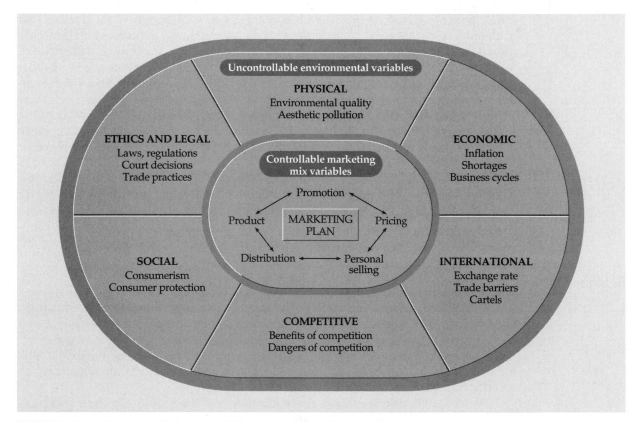

FIGURE 1-3   Societal & Environmental Factors Impacting Marketing Programs

activities are responsible marketing conduct, such as environmental responsibility, and business ethics.

Responsible Marketing Conduct

In our rush to create products that sell, we sometimes select packaging that is bulky and does not degrade over time. Marketing is often blamed for the mountains of trash that are filling up landfills, polluting our rivers, and desecrating the landscape. The "green" movement believes that the answer is for business to produce more environmentally safe products. However, sales of products that help the environment have been slow. One problem is that recycled paper and other green items often cost more. Although people say they will pay 7 to 20 percent more for green merchandise, this sentiment has not held up at the cash register. Also, some people do not like the performance or texture of recycled paper and other household products. Some tissue, for instance, isn't as soft.

The dilemma for marketers is to find ways to help the environment, satisfy customers, and make a profit. A popular solution is to make packages smaller. This is not as easy as it appears because smaller packages are harder to see in the store and offer less space for promotional messages. Procter & Gamble (P&G) has had some success in Europe with refills for cleaners and detergents that come in throwaway pouches. These have not worked in the United States, where the trend is to a reduction in package size. For example, P&G has devised a concentrated Ultra Tide powdered detergent that provides savings for both the manufacturer and the retailer. Consumers get a smaller box to carry around, but the cost per wash is somewhat higher. Other successful green programs include the replacement of Styrofoam hamburger containers with cardboard boxes by McDonald's. Also, P&G has eliminated the cartons from Secret and Sure deodorants, keeping 80 million cartons from going to the landfill. These examples show that creative managers can find ways to balance customer wants, environmental needs and profitability. This approach is known as *green marketing.*

Environmentalism is only one aspect of responsible marketing conduct. Yes, you should design your products for recyclability where possible. Also, products should be reusable without discarding. However, they also must be built with integrity and quality for safety, accessibility by the disabled, longevity, and more. A second problem area is knowing what marketing tactics are ethically acceptable.

Business Ethics

Business ethics is a set of standards governing the conduct of members of the business community. These standards evolve from interactions among businesspeople and reflect how firms expect to be treated by others. In recent years, the drive for short-term profits has been a major threat to American business ethics. When the next quarter's bottom line outweighs all other considerations, ethical shortcuts lead to insider trading and payoffs.

You should understand that companies are not unethical; people are unethical. This implies that if you hire the right employees—people with principles—you are ahead of the game. However, even the right people can go wrong if they are not given proper guidance in moral decision making. A common problem is that standard company solutions simply do not work. Often there are no applicable laws or court decisions to guide you in specific situations, and actions must be taken in the "twilight zone" between the clearly right and the clearly wrong.

SUMMARY

Our book is concerned with showing you how managers develop marketing plans and manipulate marketing variables to fill long-run customer needs in the presence of business rivals. We believe marketing managers are the driving entrepreneurial force that allows organizations to compete successfully in the race for customer acceptance.

This chapter has introduced you to the role of the marketing manager in business and nonprofit organizations. The basic functions of marketing have been described as planning, pricing, promoting, and distributing goods and services to customers. We suggest that organizations must have a marketing focus if they expect to succeed. One such philosophy, called the marketing concept, helps organizations achieve their goals by emphasizing customer satisfaction through close coordination of marketing with the other operating areas of the institution.

Marketing activities must also be coordinated with a number of environmental factors that are largely outside the control of individual organizations. This means that organizations need to spend more time educating their employees about which marketing activities are ethical and making sure that products are safe before they are introduced.

Marketing is a creative and ever-changing occupation with few rules. The position of marketing manager is stimulating because you associate with a wide variety of people in a continuously changing environment. Moreover, marketing management is an excellent training ground for advanced assignments in your or another organization. Marketing managers have to work with so many areas of the firm that they are often tapped for positions as general managers. Research has shown that marketing jobs offer the fastest route to the top. Today organizations are turning away from the financial executives, engineers, and lawyers once favored for CEOs in the 1980s and are looking to marketing managers to provide leadership for the future. We believe that marketing is the path to glory.

NOTES

1. Adapted from the official definition of marketing prepared by the American Marketing Association.
2. This section draws heavily on Frederick E. Webster, Jr., "The Changing Role of Marketing in the Corporation," *Journal of Marketing*, Vol. 56, No. 4 (October 1992), pp. 1–17.

3. Shawn Tully, ''The Modular Corporation,'' *Fortune*, February 8, 1993, pp. 106–115.

4. Philip Kotler, *Marketing Management*, 7th ed., Prentice-Hall, 1991, p. 26.

SUGGESTED READING

Houston, Franklin S. ''The Marketing Concept: What It Is and What It Is Not,'' *Journal of Marketing*, Vol. 50 (April 1986), pp. 81–87.

McGee, Lynn W., and Rosann Spiro. ''The Marketing Concept in Perspective,'' *Business Horizons*, Vol. 31 (May-June 1988), pp. 40–45.

Ruekert, Robert W., and Orville C. Walker, Jr. ''Marketing's Interaction with Other Functional Units: A Conceptual Framework and Empirical Evidence,'' *Journal of Marketing*, Vol. 51 (January 1987), pp. 1–19.

van Waterschoot, Walter, and Christophe Van den Bulte. ''The 4P Classification of the Marketing Mix Revisited,'' *Journal of Marketing*, Vol. 56 (October 1992), pp. 83–93.

Webster, Jr., Frederick E. ''The Rediscovery of the Marketing Concept,'' *Business Horizons*, Vol. 31 (May-June 1988), pp. 29–39.

Webster, Jr., Frederick E. ''The Changing Role of Marketing in the Corporation,'' *Journal of Marketing*, Vol. 56, No. 4 (October 1992), pp. 1–17.

FURTHER READING

Borden, Neil H. ''The Concept of the Marketing Mix,'' *Journal of Advertising Research*, Vol. 4 (June 1964), pp. 2–7.

Drucker, Peter F. *Management: Tasks, Responsibilities, Practices* (New York: Harper & Row, 1973).

Levitt, Theodore. ''Marketing Myopia,'' *Harvard Business Review* (July-August 1960), pp. 45–46.

Mintzberg, Henry. *Mintzberg on Management*. New York: The Free Press, 1989.

QUESTIONS

1. Why has the emphasis in marketing moved from exchanges to relationships?

2. Give another marketing example of each of the 10 roles a manager plays.

3. Avon Products sells cosmetics and jewelry door to door, using 425,000 representatives. In 1992, Avon's sales and number of sales reps both declined. Avon responded by initiating a national TV advertising program, mailing out millions of catalogs to potential customers, and starting to accept phone orders from toll-free 800 numbers. Why is Avon having trouble selling cosmetics door to door? Will Avon's field sales force be happy that the company is sending out catalogs and accepting phone orders?

4. With the decline of communism in Eastern Europe and the Soviet Union, American cigarette companies have been rushing into these markets. Philip Morris and R.J. Reynolds have formed alliances with local firms, set up new plants, redesigned existing packaging, introduced new medium-priced brands, and increased advertising. Why are American cigarette companies so interested in these low-income countries?

5. PepsiCo introduced a new clear cola called Crystal Pepsi. Coca-Cola responded by resurrecting its old Tab diet cola as a new Tab Clear brand. Why did Pepsi bring out its Crystal brand, and why did Coke respond with Tab Clear? Does it make sense for Coke to try to reposition Tab as a clear product instead of bringing out an entirely new brand, as Pepsi did with Crystal?

6. Each year a pace car is selected for the Indianapolis 500 auto race. The manufacturer of the vehicle selected has to supply two specially engineered, high-speed cars to start the race and 118 other cars for use in parades and as courtesy vehicles for celebrities and race officials. In addition, the pace car manufacturer has to buy advertising space in the race program and on the track-side billboards. Why would a manufacturer want to spend the money necessary to gain the designation of official pace car?

7. General Electric's Lighting Division, with annual sales of $3 billion, has formed a 50-50 joint venture with Hitachi of Japan. This venture will give GE access to Hitachi's domestic distribution network, and Hitachi will gain access to GE products and marketing know-how. Why is GE Lighting interested in entering Japan when that country relies almost exclusively on imported fuels to generate electricity?

8. Budget hotels such as Red Roof Inns and La Quinta have been growing rapidly at the expense of full-service hotels like Holiday Inns. Budget hotels keep their single-room rates in the $30 to $40 range by eliminating restaurants and swimming pools. Occupancy rates were recently reported to be 85 percent for Red Roof Inns, 59 percent for La Quinta, and only 45 percent for Holiday Inns. Since Americans have shown great interest in higher-quality merchandise lately, how do you explain the success of reduced-service hotels? What should Holiday Inns do to improve the situation?

9. Liquid detergents account for 37 percent of the home laundry market. Procter & Gamble recently began selling concentrated liquid detergents in refillable bottles. These new detergents are 22 percent more concentrated than ordinary liquids, the packages use 20 percent less plastic, and the refill bottles use 40 percent less plastic than ordinary bottles. Why is P&G introducing concentrated liquid detergents? Who benefits?

10. A U.S. export licensing officer who earned $40,000 a year was convicted of receiving over $100,000 in gratuities in exchange for issuing licenses to ship sophisticated electronic equipment to China. The defendant, who is 35 years old, faces a maximum sentence of 25 years in jail and a fine of $350,000. What are the best ways to prevent middle-level managers from taking bribes and kickbacks?

Chapter 2

Marketing Strategy

Results are gained by exploiting opportunities, not by solving problems.

PETER DRUCKER

Marketing strategy is concerned with finding sustainable ways for organizations to compete in a continuously changing world. For example, the 100-year-old bandage maker Johnson & Johnson (J&J) is reporting record sales and profits. J&J's strategy is to constantly push into new areas to cater to evolving customer needs. J&J is now the leader in disposable contact lenses and pharmaceuticals such as the anti-allergy medicine Hismanal and the dermatological cream Retin A. About one-third of J&J's sales come from products introduced in the last 5 years. This chapter is concerned with helping you select marketing strategies to exploit the opportunities of tomorrow. Organizations that fail to plan for the future will find themselves fading into the sunset.

WHAT IS MARKETING STRATEGY?

A strategy is a plan of action designed to achieve the long-run goals of the organization. Marketing strategies evolve from more general business objectives. Marketing strategies usually include the following dimensions:

1. The product or service market in which you expect to compete.
2. The level of investment needed to grow, maintain, or milk the business.
3. The product line, positioning, pricing, and distribution strategies needed to compete in the selected market.
4. The assets or skills to provide a sustainable competitive advantage (SCA).

Successful marketing strategies are based on *assets* such as brand names that are strong relative to those of competitors. For example, Nestlé, a Swiss company that is the world's largest food company, has performed well in the marketplace with strong brand names including the recently acquired Perrier and L'Oréal lines (see

MARKETING STRATEGIES 2-1

NESTLÉ'S STRATEGY FOR GROWTH

Nestlé is the world's largest food company and is headquartered in Vevey, Switzerland. Its greatest strengths are in chocolate, coffee, and baby food, where its brands are number one or two in most markets. For a while Nestlé's size gave it a sense of complacency and allowed it to get bogged down in procedures. In 1981, a new chief executive took command and Nestlé began to focus more on growth. Personnel and long-term planning departments and headquarters staff were cut back, management layers removed and people told to focus on speed, flexibility, and markets. Funds spun off by cash cows in chocolate and coffee are being used to expand new product lines. In a big coup, Nestlé was successful in a hostile takeover of Source Perrier, the large French bottled water company. Moreover, it now owns 49 percent of L'Oréal, the world's largest cosmetic firm, and has an option to buy the rest of this French company's stock when it becomes available. Nestlé is also planning to move into the pharmaceutical business. It already has a joint venture with Baxter International to produce nutritional products for hospital patients.

One strategy is to be first, be daring, and be different. Cash cows can be milked to fund growth in new areas.

Source: E. S. Browning, "Nestlé Looks to Realms Beyond Food for the Future," *The Wall Street Journal*, May 12, 1992, p. B4.

Marketing Strategies box 2-1). Strategies also spring from *skills* to do a good job in areas such as production or promotion. Marketing strategies take assets and skills and forge them into sustainable competitive advantages.

Searching for SCAs

Organizations are continuously looking for ways to achieve SCAs. Some of the most important SCAs in a survey of 284 businesses are shown in Table 2-1. Note that a wide variety of SCAs are mentioned, and the top few do not dominate the list. The average business reports 4.6 SCAs, suggesting that it is probably foolish to base your marketing strategy on a single SCA. Table 2-1 reveals some interesting differences in SCAs across industries. High-tech firms, for example, favor technical superiority, quality, and customer service. Service companies build their success around quality, good management, name recognition, and customer service. Firms in the ''Other'' category are most interested in SCAs based on quality, name recognition, and low-cost production. On the other hand, technical superiority and low-cost production are not key SCAs for service companies.

Two of the most important SCAs are thought to be differentiation and low costs.[1] Yet these SCAs are ranked fifth and twelfth in Table 2-1. Differentiation strategies enhance profits by developing products with unique design, performance, quality, or service characteristics. The objective is to make your product different from that

TABLE 2-1

Most Important SCAs

Rank	SCA	Type of Firm		
		High-Tech	Service	Other
1	Reputation for quality	**38.2%**	**44.2%**	**43.3%**
2	Customer service/product support	**33.8**	**35.4**	22.4
3	Name recognition/high profile	11.8	**37.2**	**31.3**
4	Retain good management and engineering staff	25.0	**38.1**	7.5
5	Low-cost production	25.9	13.3	**31.3**
6	Financial resources	16.2	23.0	20.9
7	Customer orientation/feedback/ market research	19.1	23.0	13.4
8	Product-line breadth	16.2	20.4	19.4
9	Technical superiority	**44.1**	6.2	13.4
10	Installed base of satisfied customers	27.9	19.5	6.0
11	Segmentation/focus	10.3	19.5	23.9
12	Product characteristics/ differentiation	17.6	13.3	14.9
13	Continuing product innovation	17.6	15.0	9.0
14	Market share	17.6	12.4	13.4
15	Size/location of distribution	14.7	9.7	19.4
16	Low-price/high-value offering	8.8	17.7	9.0
17	Knowledge of business	2.9	22.1	6.0
18	Pioneer/early entrant in industry	16.2	9.7	9.0
19	Efficient, flexible production/oper- ations adaptable to customer	5.9	15.0	6.0
20	Effective sales force	14.7	8.0	6.0
	Number of businesses	68	113	67
	Average number of SCAs	4.63	4.77	4.19

Source: David A. Aaker, "Managing Assets and Skills: The Key to a Sustainable Competitive Advantage," *California Management Review,* (Winter 1989), p. 94.

of your competition. Once customers perceive your product as unique, they are less sensitive to price and you can charge more for the product or service.

Low-cost strategies seek to build volume by achieving an SCA in the areas of production or marketing. Low costs can be captured through economies of scale, access to raw materials, or automated equipment. Firms with low costs can charge low prices to build market share, or they can use the margins to increase profits. Low costs elsewhere may also allow firms to spend more on advertising and promotion.

Two organizations with low-cost SCAs are Goodyear in tires and Whirlpool in appliances. Goodyear has reduced costs through volume and vertical integration and Whirlpool through the use of automated equipment. At the same time, Michelin and

Maytag have had success in the same industries with differentiation strategies. Michelin is well known for the safety of its steel belted radial tires and Maytag for the durability of its appliances. For these firms, differentiation has led to a sustainable price premium.

Other successful marketing strategies include focusing on special classes of customers and preemptive strikes. With focus strategies, a clothes retailer might focus on the needs of hard-to-fit buyers or a limited line of sportswear. A preemptive move stakes out new territory, and it is often difficult for competitors to make an appropriate response. Coca-Cola built a dominant position in the Japanese beverage market by signing up all the best distributors. Pepsi and other firms were preempted and had to make do with weaker sales organizations.

Advantages of Strategic Marketing

A strategic approach to marketing has a number of advantages. First, a strategic emphasis helps organizations orient themselves to key external factors such as consumers and competition. Instead of just projecting past trends, the goal is to build market-driven strategies that reflect customer concerns. Strategic plans also tend to anticipate changes in the environment rather than just react to competitive thrusts.

Another reason strategic marketing is important is that it forces you to take a long-term view of the world. Many people believe that the problems of U.S. automobile and steel companies are due to their obsession with short-term quarterly profits. The Japanese, on the other hand, have had great success in the U.S. electronics and auto markets using a long-run focus. The ability of the Japanese to penetrate U.S. markets also shows that marketing strategy must have an international dimension. Today firms with global marketing strategies are better able to meet customer needs and the growth of international competition.

Strategy-Building Process

The basic dimensions of strategy development are described in Figure 2-1. The first step is to establish a comprehensive mission for the organization. Then a detailed assessment of each strategic business unit must be performed. This usually includes both external and internal analyses of current strengths and weaknesses. Next, appropriate marketing strategies are identified for each business unit. The remainder of Figure 2-1 shows how basic strategies are converted into detailed marketing plans for implementation.

We strongly believe that you first decide what you want to do, your strategy; then you decide how to do it, your tactics.[2] The elements of the marketing mix are highly interrelated, and the best mixes come about when you take a strategic approach. For example, a new product might be positioned as a soap with lotion-like properties or as a lotion with soap-like properties. The appropriate price and advertising appeal depend on this positioning. One price level might cause consumers to perceive the product as a soap, while another price level might cause them to perceive it as a lotion. Of course, market strategy itself must be based on a sustainable advantage on one or more elements of the marketing mix.

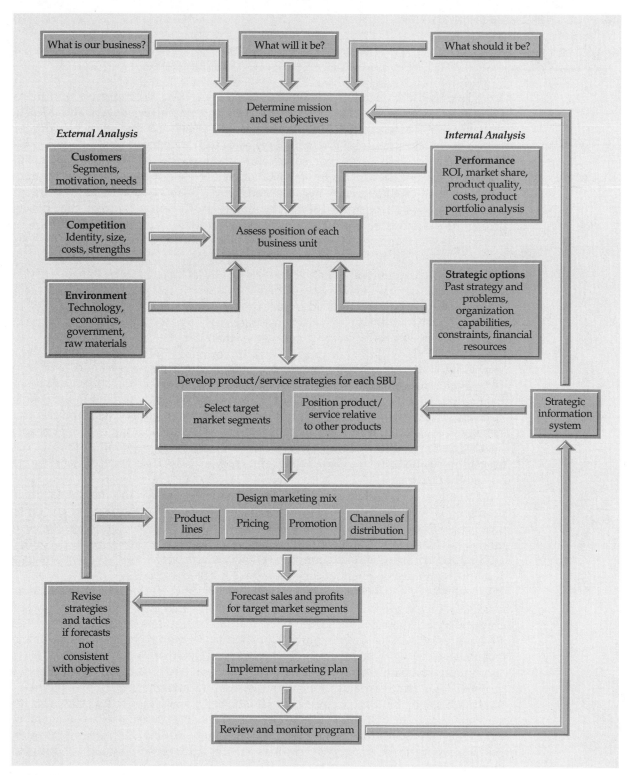

FIGURE 2-1 The Strategy Development Process

WHAT IS OUR MISSION?

A well-defined organization provides a sense of direction to employees and helps guide them toward the fulfillment of the firm's potential. Managers should ask, "What is our business?" and "What should it be?" The idea is to extract a purpose from a consideration of the firm's history, resources, distinctive abilities, and environmental constraints. A mission statement should specify the business domains in which the organization plans to operate. These are usually spelled out in product terms, such as "we are a copy machine company," or more broadly as "we are an office productivity company." The firm should try to find a purpose that fits its present needs and is neither too narrow nor too broad.

Effective mission statements should cover the following areas:

1. Product line definition.
2. Market scope.
3. Growth directions.
4. Level of technology.

Marketing strategies often involve decisions on which products to add, which to drop, which to keep, and which to modify. Thus it is logical to construct mission statements around product dimensions. For example, Famous Amos is in the cookie business rather than in the more general bakery business. Individual products can lose favor, and some firms prefer to define their mission in terms of customer needs. AT&T can be viewed as being in the communications business rather than in the telephone business. Xerox, best known for its copiers, advertises itself as being in the document business.

Organization missions must also be defined in terms of the market for their products or services. This can be expressed in geographical terms or as customer groupings. For example, Coors beer is not pasteurized, so the company has been limited to markets within refrigerated trucking distance of its breweries. Pontiac dealerships, on the other hand, are located everywhere but focus on the performance and sports-minded segment of the automobile market.

Technology has become so important to business success that mission statements need to indicate the types and levels of technology that will be emphasized. For example, American steel mills were slow to adopt continuous casting and to see the advantages of melting scrap in minimills. Their inability to recognize and seize new technology has depressed their profits and growth potential.

Finally, mission statements should give management direction on areas for growth. Some firms expand by penetrating existing markets, others by expanding product lines, by building up present markets, by diversifying, or by growing with new technology or distribution methods. The mission statement tells management what it should not be doing, as well as what it should be doing. Once an organization has a mission, the next step is to focus on the activities of individual business units.

ANALYZING STRATEGIC BUSINESS UNITS

Marketing strategies are designed for use by strategic business units (SBUs) (Figure 2-1). An SBU is any organizational unit that has a business strategy and a manager with sales and profit responsibility. In a small company the SBU would include all operations. SBUs can also be a division of a larger company, product lines, or even selected products. General Electric popularized the SBU concept as a way to foster the entrepreneurial spirit in a diversified firm.

Marketing planners operate on the principle that individual business units should play different roles in achieving organizational objectives. Some units are expected to grow faster than others, some units will be more profitable, and not all units will generate the same cash flow. The concept that the organization is a collection of business units with different objectives is a central belief of modern management. These collections of business units are often described as *portfolios.*

Product Life Cycles

The life-cycle concept helps managers keep track of their product portfolios. This proposition suggests that products are born, grow to maturity, and then decline, much like plants and animals (Figure 2-2). During the introductory period, sales grow rapidly but high expenses keep profits negative. Near the end of the growth stage, the rate of expansion of sales begins to slow down and profits reach a peak. During the maturity phase, sales reach their peak and profits are slowly eroded by increased competition. If something is not done to revive declining products, they eventually have to be dropped from the product line.

The life-cycle concept helps managers think about their product line as a port-

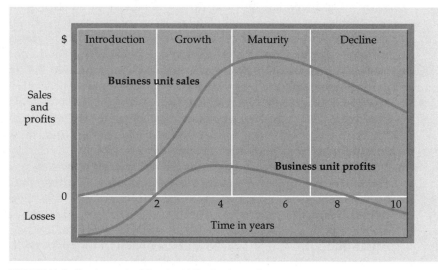

FIGURE 2-2   Impact of Product Life Cycle on Strategy

folio of investments. Ideally, the firm wants to have some business units in each phase of the life cycle. If most of the items are in the mature and declining phases, the company will have trouble reaching its growth objectives. Similarly, if all the products are bunched in the introductory and declining phases, the firm is likely to experience serious cash flow problems. The best plan is to have enough business in the growth and maturity stages spinning off cash to finance the introduction of new products and the reformation of products in decline. The advantage of the product life-cycle analysis is that it makes executives realize that products do not last forever and must eventually be replaced. On the other hand, it is sometimes difficult to know when a product is leaving one stage and entering the next.

Portfolio Matrix

SBUs can be evaluated by positioning them on a diagram that compares relative market shares with market growth rates. Figure 2-3 shows a portfolio matrix developed by the Boston Consulting Group.[4] Each circle in Figure 2-3 represents a business unit in a firm's product portfolio. The size of the circles shows the dollar sales being generated by each unit. The horizontal position of the circles shows their market share in relation to their competitors. A logarithmic scale is used for market share that goes from 1/10 to 10 times the size of the next largest competitor. Thus, business units located to the right of the value 1.0 are smaller than the competition and those to the left are larger.

Portfolio matrices are often divided into four separate quadrants for analysis purposes. The positions of the lines separating the sectors are arbitrary. In Figure 2-3, high growth rates would include all businesses expanding faster than the overall economy. SBUs in each corner of the portfolio matrix have sharply different financial requirements and marketing needs.

Stars   Products that fall into the *star* category have strong market positions and high rates of market growth. The primary objective with stars is to maintain their market positions and to increase their sales volumes. Stars are the keys to the future because they provide growth, technological leadership, and enhanced respect in the business community. Although stars increase revenues to the firm, they tend to use more money than they generate from earnings and depreciation. To maintain their high rates of growth, stars require extra cash for expanded plant and equipment, inventories, accounts receivable, field salespeople, and advertising programs. Thus, stars are both a blessing and a curse because of the strain they put on the firm to constantly expand working capital.

Another problem with stars is that their high growth rates attract competition. The entry of other firms can help expand a market, but eventually the market will become saturated, and growth rates will decline. Apple was the creator and first star of the personal computer market (Product A, Figure 2-3), but IBM came along to grab the biggest share of an expanding market. Eventually the sales of the original Apple and IBM models slowed and they fell into the cash cow category. Apple and IBM were able to replace these stars with their own Macintosh and System/2 models, but then Dell and Compaq gave these products a run for their money.

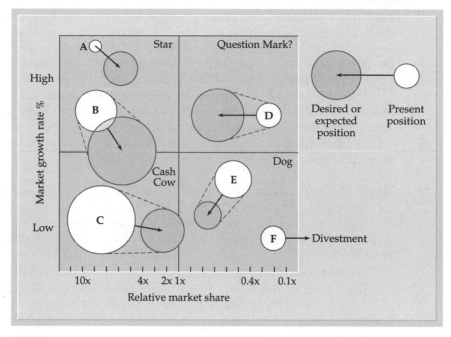

FIGURE 2-3 Balancing the Product Portfolio

Cash Cows Business units described as *cash cows* are low-growth, high-market-share operations (Product C, Figure 2-3). These products are apt to be in the mature stage of their life cycles and do not require extensive funds for production facilities or inventory buildup. Cash cows also have established market positions and do not need large advertising expenditures to maintain their market shares. As a result, their high earnings and depreciation allowances generate cash surpluses that can be used to invest in other growing products, to support research and development, or to buy into new lines of trade. Cash cows thus provide the basic fuel on which portfolio management of business units depends.

For example, at PepsiCo the beverage business provided cash to expand into the related snack and restaurant businesses. Now the sales of its Frito-Lay, Taco Bell, Pizza Hut, and Kentucky Fried Chicken divisions exceed those of beverages and provide 65 percent of the company's profits. Other examples of cash cows include Philip Morris and R.J. Reynolds, which used the profits of their cigarette divisions to finance expansion in beer, soft drinks, dog food, and fruit drinks.

Question Marks Business products with low market shares in fast-growing markets are called *question marks.* These products have the potential to become stars of the future or to fade into oblivion. Question marks have such small market shares that they usually absorb more cash than they generate. Thus, in the short run, question marks just eat money, and when their market growth slows, they become dogs.

The preferred approach with question marks is to increase their market shares and move them into the star category (Product D, Figure 2-3). However, this often takes a pile of cash, sophisticated marketing plans, and a good measure of luck. If the prospects for improving the market position of a business are not attractive, the firm must consider phasing the business out. One popular approach is simply to sell the business to a competitor. Another technique is to withdraw all promotional support and try to make a few dollars as the product withers away.

Over the years, many firms have tried to challenge IBM and most of them have failed. Recently, several relatively smaller companies, including Sun, Compaq, Apple, and Dell, succeeded by emphasizing areas in which IBM was weak. This allowed new firms to slip into the star category by going after segments of the computer market initially ignored by the market leader, IBM.

Dogs Business products that fall into the low-growth, low-market-share quadrant are called *dogs*. These products are often in the decline phase of their life cycles and show little prospect for gaining market position or generating much cash flow. Even worse, dogs can become *cash traps* and absorb more money than they generate as firms try to revive a lost cause. A few years ago, Stroh Brewery tried to revive its dying Schlitz beer with a nostalgic ad campaign. However, sales continued to decline and the ad money was clearly wasted. The usual approach with dogs is to sell them when the opportunity occurs or to deemphasize marketing activities (Products E and F, Figure 2-3).

Corning, for example, recently sold its housewares business to a joint venture with a Mexican glass maker. This 76-year-old business was once the pride of Corning and included such famous brands as Corning Ware, Pyrex, Corelle, and Revere Ware. However, their stodgy design allowed foreign competition to take over the market. As a result, Corning's consumer products division lost market share and produced mediocre earnings. The money Corning received from the sale of the division will be invested in other, higher-growth businesses such as fiberoptics, catalytic converters, and laboratory testing products.

The most common criticism of the portfolio matrix approach is that it does not have enough dimensions to assess a product portfolio accurately. More important, the use of a matrix with its emphasis on market share may interfere with profit maximization.[5] Indeed, while managers believe the matrix approach to be an effective technique, there is no empirical evidence that the BCG matrix is valuable as a decision aid. Despite these limitations, the terms *dog, star,* and *cash cow* have become standard parts of the vocabulary of business planning.

Multifactor Methods

Other approaches to strategic planning include those by Arthur D. Little, Shell Chemical, PIMS (Profit Impact of Marketing Strategy), and future scenario profiles. Arthur D. Little has a 24-sector grid. It uses a four-stage product life-cycle concept and stresses that risks increase as products age and market positions weaken. Shell compares prospects for business sector profitability with company competitive capabilities. PIMS uses historical evidence collected across industries on factors contributing to performance. This information permits assessment of the current performance and

TABLE 2-2

Methods Used for Strategic Planning

| | Users | | | | Satisfied? | |
Approach	Heavy Equipment (32.0%)	Light Equipment (47.4%)	Component Parts (20.6%)	Total (100.0%)	Yes	No
Arthur D. Little	**26.9%**	11.1%	**25.6%**	19.1%	90.0%	10.0%
PIMS	20.9	17.2	18.6	18.7	79.5	20.5
Market attractiveness	10.4	21.2	20.9	17.7	83.8	16.2
Boston Consulting Group	16.4	**23.2**	6.9	17.2	83.3	16.7
Shell	9.0	10.1	16.3	11.5	86.1	13.9
Future scenario profiles	10.4	11.1	9.2	10.5	63.6	36.4
Other (in-house)	6.0	6.1	2.3	5.3	54.5	45.5

Source: Barbara J. Coe, "Most Industrial Firms Report Satisfaction with Strategic Market Planning; 21 to Stop," *Marketing News,* Vol. 14 (May 1, 1981), pp. 1, 6.

future strategy options of a business unit. Future scenario profiles focus on projections of what the future may hold given different strategies that might be adopted by a business unit. In addition, some firms have developed their own in-house approaches.

General Electric, for example, has developed a nine-cell matrix based on industry attractiveness and company strength in each business. Units with the best scores are candidates for further investment, and those with the lowest scores are harvested or sold off. Business units in the middle fall into a hold or cash cow category and are used to finance growth. Business units chosen for additional investments have included microwave ovens and industrial plastics. On the other hand, lamps and large appliances followed a hold strategy, and small appliances were sold off.

One survey of industrial firms found that heavy equipment manufacturers preferred the Arthur D. Little and PIMS approaches, light equipment manufacturers preferred the Boston Consulting Group and market attractiveness approaches, and component parts manufacturers preferred the Arthur D. Little approach (Table 2-2). Arthur D. Little's 24-sector grid has the most satisfied users. One firm where strategic planning has not worked well is Eastman Kodak. Marketing Strategies Box 2-2 describes the problems Kodak has encountered in trying to manage its portfolio of business units.

SELECTING MARKETING STRATEGIES

Once a portfolio of business units has been evaluated, you are ready to assign strategic roles for the future management of each business. This requires creative thinking on your part. You also can consider what businesses like yours usually do by

MARKETING STRATEGIES 2-2

Strategic Problems at Kodak

Four times since 1982 Eastman Kodak has gone through a strategic restructuring where staff has been cut, businesses sold, and remaining businesses realigned. Each new strategic focus promised greater efficiency and better earnings. However, after 10 years, operating profits adjusted for inflation are actually 5.7 percent below what they were when the program started.

Kodak is having trouble with three of its four major divisions. Its main cash cow has always been its film business. However, film sales in January and February of 1992 fell 10 percent from year earlier levels. Apparently the company is losing some of its 80 percent U.S. market share to Fuji, Polaroid, and private label-film sold by mass merchandisers. Kodak's response has been to raise advertising expenditures for film even though it already has a 95 percent name recognition in the U.S. This approach assumes that throwing money at a cash cow will make it a growth business. Experience suggests that when you feed a cash cow you don't get growth, you just get a fat cow. The money is better spent developing some new "film" products. One such idea is Kodak's Photo CD scanning system. Photo CD allows consumers to store photos on compact disks so that they can be viewed and edited on TVs and computers. The product may sell more film if Kodak can get customers to spend $400 to $600 for the necessary equipment and $42 per roll of 24 shots to have the pictures stored on CDs.

Kodak's "problem child" is its Information Systems Division, which makes copiers, printers, microfilm, and graphic art supplies. The division includes a hodgepodge of unprofitable electronics businesses and has been breaking even or losing money on revenue of $4 billion a year. Some believe information systems is a black hole where Kodak has spent a lot of cash flow from businesses at which it is good. Kodak promised to dump problem businesses in this division, but has found few buyers for its dogs.

> **MARKETING STRATEGIES 2-2 (continued)**
>
> Another area where Kodak is having problems is in its health division. In 1987, Kodak bought Sterling Drug to expand its presence in pharmaceuticals. Unfortunately, Sterling has not marketed any new drugs since it was purchased. Kodak recently spent $300 million on a new research facility for Sterling, but it will be years before any new drugs emerge from this pharmaceutical pipeline. The health division may have been better served by spending this money to acquire marketing rights to new drugs developed by other firms or by buying up small firms with new drugs ready for market.
>
> Kodak has done a poor job of picking businesses for expansion and its implementation of its strategies has been weak as well. While a strategic focus has not worked well at Kodak, it has been helpful at other firms such as General Electric.
>
> *You have to pay more than lip service to strategy if you expect to succeed.*
>
> *Source:* Joan E. Rigdon, "Kodak's Changes Produce Plenty of Heat, Little Light," *The Wall Street Journal*, April 8, 1992, p. B4.

examining what are known as *generic marketing strategies*. The objective is to come up with strategies that lead to sustainable competitive advantages.

Creative Strategic Thinking

Managers must be able to step back from the existing situation and view the product and the market from another angle. This is easier said than done. Some approaches that have been suggested to encourage strategic thinking include the following:

1. Challenge the present strategy.
2. Look for strategic windows.
3. Play on the vulnerabilities of competitors.
4. Change the rules of the game.
5. Enhance customer value.

We elaborate on these approaches in later chapters, especially Chapter 5, which stresses looking for strategic windows and playing on competitors' vulnerabilities. Throughout the book we emphasize enhancing customer value.

Generic Marketing Strategies

The nature of marketing strategies may be seen in what companies actually do.[6] Empirical research based on marketing factors—marketing objectives, strategic focus, market targeting, and quality and price positioning—has shown that many businesses follow one of five strategies.

1. Companies have aggressive growth or market dominance goals. The targeting approach aims at the whole market. The *scope* of the target market in this case is

said to be broad. Positioning involves marketing high-quality products at prices similar to those of competitors. This may be considered a differentiation strategy.

2. Companies seek steady sales growth through either market share gain or market expansion. Selected segments are targeted through higher-quality products at higher prices than those of competitors. This may be considered a focused differentiation strategy. *Focus* means narrow market scope.

3. Companies pursue steady sales growth through an emphasis on market share by concentrating on selected segments of the market. Their positioning is average quality at average prices. This may be considered a stuck-in-the-middle strategy, as no real advantage through quality differentiation or low costs is created.

4. Companies strive for steady growth, with a focus on total market expansion or on winning market share by targeting selected segments or individuals. The positioning is higher quality at the same prices. This resembles a variant of a focused differentiation strategy that emphasizes value. It provides a powerful incentive for the expansion of the market as a whole.

5. Companies have defensive objectives, with a focus on cost reduction and productivity improvement. Very selective targeting of individuals is coupled with a positioning of similar quality at similar prices.

While not all firms exactly match one of these profiles, they are usually similar to one of them. As you would expect, differences in deployment of the five strategies correspond to different stages of market maturity (Table 2-3).

Some believe that "All successful strategies are differentiation."[7] The implication is that all strategies are based on some form of differentiation. Where one firm will differentiate on the basis of costs, another will use products, or size of market, or distribution, or some other dimension. If you think of differentiation as the common denominator, then it is easier to see how marketing strategies blend together to achieve the goals of the firm. An example will make this easier to understand.

Hewlett-Packard is a 53-year-old computer manufacturer with annual sales of over $15 billion. A few years ago, this mature company seemed vulnerable to raids on its market share by smaller competitors. However, HP fought back with a strategy of product differentiation and cost leadership. One innovation was a $400 ink jet printer that is quieter and prints sharper images than comparably priced dot matrix printers. This DeskJet 500 quickly became the world's best-seller and is now available in a color version. HP also used high quality and declining prices to grab 56 percent of the laser printer market. A new line of faster and cheaper work stations allowed HP to pick up additional market share. At the same time, HP cut 5000 employees from its labor force and reduced its selling costs as a percentage of sales. The bottom line has been increased earnings to fuel further product innovations. This stellar performance is in sharp contrast to GM's Saturn Division, which boosted sales with high quality and low prices but has had difficulty making money (Marketing Strategies box 2-3). We will pursue our discussion of marketing strategy in more detail after we have covered customer and competitive analysis and the crucial concepts of market segmentation, product differentiation, and product positioning.

TABLE 2-3
Generic Marketing Strategies

	Aggressors	Premium Position Segments	Stuck-in-the-Middlers	High-Value Segmenters	Defenders
Strategic objective	Aggressive sales growth/ domination	Steady sales growth	Steady sales growth	Steady sales growth	Defend/pre-vent/decline
Strategic focus	Win share/ expand market	Win share/ expand market	Win share	Win share/ expand market	Cost reduction/ productivity improvement
Market targeting	Whole market	Selected segments	Selected segments	Selected segments	Individual customers
Competitive positioning	Higher quality/ same price	Higher quality/ higher price	Same quality/ same price	Higher quality/ same price	Same or higher quality/same price
Market type	New, growing; fluid competi-tion; rapid change in cus-tomer needs	Mature and stable	Mature and stable	New, growing	Mature and stable
Corporate attitudes	Pro-active NPD;* marketing important; take on any competition	Pro-active NPD; marketing important; take on any competition	Imitate/lead in NPD; take on/ avoid competition	Pro-active NPD; take on/ avoid competition	Follower in NPD; market-ing of limited importance; take on/ avoid competition
Performance	Best across finan-cial and mar-keting based criteria	Good across most criteria	Mediocre	Mediocre, esp. on profit criterion	Worst perfor-mance overall

*NPD = new product development.
Source: Graham J. Hooley, James E. Lynch, and David Jobber, "Generic Marketing Strategies," *International Journal of Research in Marketing*, Vol. 9, No. 1 (March 1992), p. 87.

SUMMARY

Marketing strategy is concerned with forging assets and skills into a sustainable competitive advantage. Strategies are created for portfolios of business units using multifactor evaluation matrices. Remember, your job is to manage product portfolios so that cash cows generate funds for rising stars and dogs are harvested or sold off.

MARKETING STRATEGIES 2-3

SATURN'S LOW-PRICE/ HIGH-QUALITY STRATEGY

One of General Motors' few successes in recent years has been its new Saturn Division. Saturn started building small cars in 1990 and sells them for $1,000 less than comparable Hondas and Toyotas. The cars also have received rave reviews from J. D. Powers consumer quality ratings. Saturn designed its dealer territories to be several times larger than normal, so the franchises are among the most profitable in the industry. GM has also gained dealer cooperation to refrain from slicing posted sticker prices. This reassures customers that they are not paying more than their neighbor for the same car. Saturn's marketing strategies have been such a success that customers have to wait up to two months to get their cars.

Although Saturn is selling all the cars it can produce, the Division has yet to make any money. Part of the problem is that GM invested $3.5 billion to get the Division started. A more serious problem is that Saturn has yet to learn how to produce cars efficiently. Even with overtime the Saturn plant only ran at 80% of two-shift capacity in 1992. Saturn planned to add a third shift in 1993 and needed to find a way to staff it without hiring a lot of new workers. Currently Saturn requires considerably more labor hours to build a car than does its competition.

It is not enough to have a good marketing strategy; you must also integrate marketing with a good production strategy.

Source: Joseph B. White, "For Saturn, Copying Japan Yields Hot Sales But No Profits," *The Wall Street Journal,* October 1, 1992, p. A10.

NOTES

1. Michael E. Porter, *Competitive Strategy* (New York: The Free Press, 1980), Chapter 2.

2. Who could disagree? Ries and Trout could. We find that Al Ries and Jack Trout's *Bottom-Up Marketing* (New York: McGraw-Hill, 1989) creates confusion rather than clarifies marketing concepts. The example in this paragraph is from A. Charnes, W. W. Cooper, D. B. Learner, and F. Y. Phillips, "Management Science and Marketing Management," *Journal of Marketing*, Vol. 49 (Spring 1985), p. 97.

3. The mission statement is sometimes called a *business statement*.

4. The Boston Consulting Group, "The Product Portfolio," *Perspectives,* No. 66, 1970.

5. J. Scott Armstrong and Roderick J. Brodie, "Effects of Portfolio Planning Methods On Decision Making: Experimental Results," *International Journal of Research in Marketing,* Vol. 11, No. 1 (January 1994), pp. 73–84.

6. This section is taken from Graham J. Hooley, James E. Lynch, and David Jobber, "Generic Marketing Strategies," *International Journal of Research in Marketing,* Vol. 9, No. 1 (March 1992), pp. 75–89. The authors relate their research to that in two other well-known works: R. E. Miles and C. C. Snow, *Organization Strategy, Structure, and Process* (New York: McGraw-Hill, 1978), and Porter, *Competitive Strategy.*

7. William E. Fulmer and Jack Goodwin, "Differentiation: Begin with the Consumer," *Business Horizons,* Vol. 31, No. 4 (September–October, 1988), p. 62.

SUGGESTED READING

Hooley, Graham J., James E. Lynch, and David Jobber, "Generic Marketing Strategies," *International Journal of Research in Marketing,* Vol. 9, No. 1 (March 1992), pp. 75–89.

Prahalad, C. K., and Gary Hamel, "The Core Competencies of the Corporation," *Harvard Business Review,* Vol. 68 (May–June 1990), pp. 79–91.

Williams, Jeffrey R., "How Sustainable Is Your Competitive Advantage?" *California Management Review,* Vol. 34, No. 3 (1992), pp. 29–51.

Wind, Yoram, and Vijay Mahajan, "Designing Product and Business Portfolios," *Harvard Business Review* (January–February 1981), pp. 155–165.

FURTHER READING

Aaker, David A. *Strategic Marketing Management,* 3rd ed. New York: Wiley, 1992.

Barksdale, Hiram C., and Clyde E. Harris, Jr. "Portfolio Analysis and the Product Life Cycle," *Long Range Planning* (December 1982), pp. 74–83.

Buzzell, Robert D., and Bradley T. Gale. *The PIMS Principles: Linking Strategy to Performance.* New York: The Free Press, 1987.

Day, George S. "Diagnosing the Product Portfolio," *Journal of Marketing* (April 1977), pp. 29–38.

Day, George S. *Market Driven Strategy: Processes for Creating Value*. New York: The Free Press, 1990.

Hustad, Thomas J., and Thomas J. Mitchell, "Creative Market Planning in a Partisan Environment," *Business Horizons*, Vol. 25, No. 2 (March–April 1982), pp. 58–65.

Jain, Subhash C. *Marketing Planning and Strategy*, 4th ed. Cincinnati: South-Western, 1993.

Kerin, Roger A., Vijay Mahajan, and P. Rajan Varadarajan. *Contemporary Perspectives on Strategic Market Planning*. Boston: Allyn and Bacon, 1990.

Schnaars, Steven P. *Marketing Strategy: A Customer-Driven Approach*. New York: The Free Press, 1991.

Urban, Glen L., and Steven H. Star. *Advanced Marketing Strategy*. Englewood Cliffs, NJ: Prentice-Hall, 1991.

QUESTIONS

1. In 1992, pharmaceutical giant Bristol-Myers Squibb sold its household products division to S. C. Johnson & Sons for $1.15 billion. Why did Bristol-Myers want to sell such profitable brands as Windex, Drano, and Vanish? Why was Johnson willing to pay two times current sales for the housewares division?

2. A manufacturer of Christmas ornaments has prospered by continuously introducing new products that are superior in quality and cost relative to the competition. This has been accomplished by custom designing its production machinery. Its policy is that "marketing will never be constrained by manufacturing." What is the role of manufacturing as a weapon in the ever-present battle for market share? Give an example.

3. Fujitso of Japan entered the growing U.S. office fax market in 1986 by purchasing Imaging Systems from Burroughs Corporation (now Unisys). Sales of Fujitsu's thermal-print machines reached 67,000 per year, or about 4 percent of the market. This placed Fujitso eighth in a strong field, and the company shut the business down. Why did Fujitso get out of the fax business?

4. Sara Lee Corporation charts its product portfolio (Figure 2-4) in two dimensions—market margin and competitive position. Market margin is found by multiplying the dollar size of the market by the pretax profit percentage. Competitive position is its share in relation to the share of its largest competitor. The size of the circles in Figure 2-4 indicates the size of the operating profit of a business unit in relation to other units of the chart. Shasta Beverages contributes less than 5 percent of both total sales and pretax profit. Would you make a major near-term investment in Shasta? In baked goods? In L'Eggs?

5. Sears has terminated its big catalog business and shut down about 100 mainly rural stores. Sears is also selling off its stock brokerage and real estate businesses and part of its insurance business. Why is Sears making these changes in its portfolio of businesses?

6. What are the advantages and disadvantages of the brand management system? Is the system compatible with the product portfolio concept?

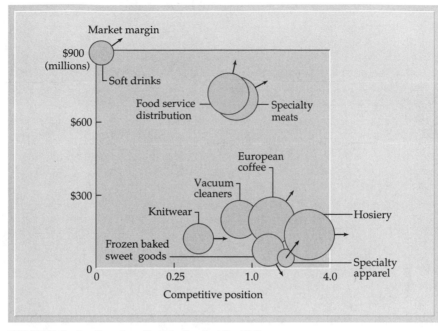

FIGURE 2-4   Sara Lee Corp.'s Product Portfolio

7. Beatrice Foods Company announced divestiture of 50 companies with combined sales of $872 million. Companies targeted for sale were in cyclical, capital-intensive industrial businesses, as well as those without significant market shares. Why did Beatrice Foods sell these firms, consolidate its decentralized businesses, and increase emphasis on marketing? Why did Beatrice Foods buy the 50 firms it is now selling in the first place?

8. Blockbuster Entertainment Corporation, the video store chain, bought 48.2 percent of the common stock of the Spelling Entertainment Group, a television producer and distributor. The Spelling Group has a library of programming that includes more than 50 present and former television series, including *Little House on the Prairie, Dynasty,* and *Beverly Hills, 90210,* and a selection of feature films including *Terminator 2* and the *Rambo* trilogy. Why would Blockbuster make this investment?

Chapter 3

Customer Analysis

The purpose of an enterprise is to create and keep a customer.

THEODORE LEVITT

The most important ingredient in the success of any organization is a satisfied customer. Indeed, some believe that an obsession with customers can lead to a sustainable competitive advantage.[1] This means more than getting close to the customer.

WHY ARE CUSTOMERS IMPORTANT?

Customers are essential because they are where the life of an organization begins. Until customers place orders, nothing really happens. Once customers think enough about your goods or services to buy them, you are in business. Also, when customers stop placing orders, your organization starts to die. Customers thus have a great deal to do with the success or failure of an enterprise. We believe that customers are the engine, the critical driving force, that powers a market economy.

When 433 executives were asked "What is the most important issue managers will face in the 1990s?" customer wants was second only to product quality.[2] The implication is that marketing managers can never know too much about customers and their needs. This chapter is concerned with answering six questions you must ask yourself about your customers, their motivations, and your relationship to your customers:

1. Who are my customers?
2. Where are my customers?
3. When do my customers buy?
4. What do my customers want?
5. How do my customers buy?
6. How does my firm become customer oriented?

Once you understand customers and develop a customer focus, you are ready to design products and marketing programs to fill their requirements.

WHO ARE MY CUSTOMERS?

The question of who customers are seems at first to be an easy one. After all, we can look at current invoices and identify everyone to whom we ship. These firms can be classified by size and industry to give a detailed picture of who buys. However, although customer shipping point data may be useful, they often give a distorted view of who customers really are. The problem is that deliveries often go to fabricators or channel intermediaries, who resell your products to others.

For example, the Ross Modem Company markets electronic devices that make possible the transmission of data to or from a computer via telephone or other communication lines. A breakdown of Ross's customers is shown in Table 3-1. Note that Ross ships to four different "customers," but only 12 percent of its modems are sold directly to final users. Original equipment manufacturers (OEMs) who install modems in computers and other machines order straight from the factory. Ross also sells to distributors who supply retailers and smaller industrial buyers. Some large retailers are sold directly, and final users are contacted via a modest mail order operation. The figures in Table 3-1 show that the relative importance of the four classes of customers has changed over time. Shipments to OEMs and retailers are growing, and sales to distributors and final users are declining. This raises the difficult question of whether your most important customer is the OEM, the distributor, the retailer, or the ultimate user. The results also suggest that it may be useful to distinguish between business and consumer buyers.

Consumer Customers

Consumer buyers include all those who purchase goods for their own or family members' consumption. Firms that sell low-priced products, such as paper towels, often focus their attention on the final buyer. After all, paper towels are branded products that are presold with heavy magazine and television advertising. This suggests that paper towel manufacturers must understand consumer preferences for

TABLE 3-1

Customer Identification at the Ross Modem Company

Year	Proportion of Shipments to:				
	OEMs	*Distributors*	*Retailers*	*Final Users*	*Total*
Current	23%	34%	31%	12%	100%
Last	15	55	16	14	100
Previous	11	60	9	20	100

features such as wet strength, durability, color, number of plys, and price. Firms that accurately measure these preferences are in a better position to create products and ads that will draw customers to the grocery stores.

An alternative argument is that towel *brand loyalty,* or the degree to which customers repurchase, is low. Can you, for example, name five brands of paper towels? The answer is no, and neither can the authors or almost anyone. The truth is, all brands of paper towels are similar and buyers do not have a strong emotional attachment to items in this product class. Under these conditions, the marketing activities of grocery stores may be more important than the preferences of the final buyer. Retail stores determine shelf locations, number of shelf facings, final selling prices, the existence of end-aisle displays, and whether a brand of towels is featured in the weekly store ad. Thus manufacturers who cater to the grocery store buyer with special deals, discounts, display racks, signs, banners, cooperative advertising support, and contests may be able to sell more paper towels than those who just advertise to the final user.

This strategy may work for low-priced paper towels, but does it also apply to higher-priced consumer durables? With durables, the costs of development and manufacturing are so high that companies surely focus on the final users and their preferences. The answer is yes. When manufacturers ask customers to spend $1000 or more, they usually make an effort to tailor the product to their needs. However, customer contact can be expensive, and there may be a cheaper way. For example, a Japanese camera manufacturer wanted to expand its position in the U.S. high-priced camera market. Instead of asking users what they wanted, the firm sent a vice president to America to visit a number of retail camera stores. He observed customers buying cameras and then held long conversations with store managers about what features were desirable. He then returned to Japan and developed a new line of cameras that were very successful in the U.S. market. Why did a focus on retail store employees work so well? The answer is that people do not buy $500 cameras off the shelf; they are sold cameras in this price range by retail salespeople. Thus, a key factor was the manufacturer's ability to include features that the clerks could use to sell the cameras to the final buyer.

Business Customers

The issue of customer identity is even more complicated with products sold to businesses. Remember that business goods and services are used to create merchandise that is then sold to final users. This means that the demand for business products is *derived* from the demand for the final product. Thus, the identity of components and services is often lost when selling to business buyers. As a result, the importance of brands is reduced and the role of specifications, timely delivery, and price is increased. Under these conditions, identifying the right customer is extremely difficult.

A common approach with goods sold to businesses is to treat the purchasing agent as the customer. After all, purchasing agents often select qualified suppliers and negotiate contract terms. However, purchasing agents usually rely on engineers and company scientists for technical expertise. This means that the most important customer may actually be an obscure technician who uses the product in the plant or laboratory. Other key business customers are plant managers and the controller. Production managers typically have some input on the type of equipment installed in their plants. Controllers pay for supplies and equipment, and they have to approve orders before they can be sent out to vendors. Obviously, business marketing involves satisfying a large number of different customers.

Another complication with business markets is that purchasing decisions are frequently made by buying committees. Membership on these committees may be secret, and meetings are usually off-limits to outsiders. Thus, the identity and the buying criteria of key business customers may not be readily available.

An example of business customer identification problems involves firms selling engines for commercial airplanes. The most logical customer for engine manufacturers is the airframe builder such as Boeing or McDonald-Douglas. Engines are a key component and have to be matched carefully with the airframe to give the desired lift, range, and capacity. However, as fuel prices have gone up, engine manufacturers have begun to sell directly to the airlines, using features such as durability and low fuel consumption. As if this situation were not complicated enough, a third customer, the leasing firm, has come into the picture. Airplanes have become so expensive that they are commonly sold to a finance company and then leased to the operating airline. This means that the engine supplier has to satisfy the sometimes conflicting demands of three customers: the airframe manufacturer, the financing company, and the airline.

Nonprofit Customers

Another important class of customer is the nonprofit sector. This includes community orchestras, the United Fund, public radio and TV stations, credit unions, hospitals, and schools. Each of these organizations is managed by a local board of directors. As a result, purchase orders for supplies and equipment often go to firms with offices in the community. In addition, nonprofit groups sometimes place orders with companies associated with friends, relatives, or members of particular political parties. Marketers who expect to sell to nonprofit organizations need a great deal of information on how these customers make purchase decisions.

Choosing the Right Customer

Our discussion has shown that consumer, business, and nonprofit suppliers are often expected to serve multiple customers. This can complicate product design and the creation of marketing programs. Firms that try to be all things to all customers may fail because they lack the resources to get the job done. Some organizations focus on specific groups of customers and succeed by becoming specialists. Most firms need to cater to the ultimate users, as well as dealers and other channel intermediaries. The ability to set priorities helps put the issue of customer identification in proper focus. Perhaps the best solution to the dilemma of customer emphasis is to be guided by the strategic plan. A good strategic plan should identify who the company expects to work with, both now and in the future.

WHERE ARE MY CUSTOMERS?

Knowing where customers are located can be very useful to marketing managers. Existing customers are sometimes traced through invoice data. Service Merchandise catalog stores, for example, make it a point to ask for the address of each customer who makes a store purchase. These addresses are stored in the computer and used to select newspaper and radio media to cover the firm's customer base. They are also used to send catalogs and sales notices directly to customers' homes.

Another way to locate customers is through the use of *warranty cards*. These cards are enclosed with merchandise, and customers are asked to fill them out and return them to the manufacturer. Warranty cards are primarily used to notify customers in case of recalls and safety updates, but they can also be used for marketing purposes. Some firms use these names for telephone solicitations for extended warranties and for mailing direct mail offers. Unfortunately, only about 20 percent of warranty cards are returned, and large numbers of customers are still unidentified. One solution is to use postage-paid warranty cards so that customers are more likely to return them.

Customer location data can be interpreted two ways. Suppose that invoice and warranty card data reveal a locational breakdown of the Ross Modem Company, as shown in Table 3-2. The figures indicate that 97 percent of Ross's customers are located in the United States east of the Rocky Mountains. A conservative reaction would be to focus the efforts of your salespeople, distributors, and advertising on the growing Northeast and Southeast markets. This approach seeks to make money by concentrating on areas that the firm currently dominates.

A more aggressive reaction would be to ask why your organization has no customers on the West Coast and in foreign countries. Is there something wrong with your modems or is it just a marketing problem? Perhaps customers expect local production facilities to ensure quick delivery. Perhaps the firm is using the wrong mix of pricing, distribution, and promotional activities. The absence of sales on the West Coast and overseas may mean that there are no customers there or it may mean that the marketing manager is not serving these areas effectively.

A further complication for marketing managers are customers that operate from multiple locations. For example, a plant manager in Oklahoma may want to buy your modems, but the order may require approval from a parent organization

TABLE 3-2
Location of Ross Modem Customers

Year	Northeast	Southeast	Midwest	West Coast	Foreign	Total
			Proportion of Shipment to:			
Current	34%	41%	22%	1%	2%	100%
Last	30	35	31	3	1	100
Previous	28	33	36	2	1	100

located in New York City. This means that selling efforts have to be coordinated and conducted in two widely separate environments. An even more difficult situation occurs when the Oklahoma plant wants to buy your modem and the Florida plant wants another brand. Under these conditions, the New York parent is likely to demand standardization on one modem, and suppliers will have to sell at three or more locations if they expect to land the order. These examples suggest that sellers need to know where customers are located and that they must be prepared to conduct extensive marketing activities at a variety of sites.

WHEN DO MY CUSTOMERS BUY?

At first glance, the question of when customers buy does not seem to be difficult. For example, sales of Ross Modems by quarter and day of the week are shown in Table 3-3. Sales are low in quarters 1 and 2 and hit a peak in quarter 3 before falling off in quarter 4. Also, sales are highest on Wednesdays, Thursdays, and Fridays. If these are the periods when customers want to order, then the marketing concept suggests that the marketing manager should adapt production and distribution systems to meet these customer demands.

Adapting to Customer Buying Patterns

Demand variation exists for many products. When enough customers want to rent videos at 10 P.M. or on Sundays, alert store managers adjust their hours to fill this need. Similarly, innovative banks have added teller machines so that customers can withdraw cash 24 hours a day, and mail order firms have toll-free numbers so that customers can order at night and on weekends. Even financial service companies have toll-free numbers so that customers can trade securities 24 hours a day. The success of these activities depends on knowing a great deal about when customers want to buy.

One problem due to seasonal variation in customer orders is in the area of forecasting. For example, if second-quarter sales at Ross Modem (Table 3-3) are used to forecast third-quarter revenues, large forecasting errors will result. This can lead to serious problems in scheduling production and in planning advertising and sales

TABLE 3-3
Ross Modem Sales by Quarter and Day of the Week

Year	Quarter					Day of the Week							
	1	2	3	4	Total	Su	M	Tu	W	Th	F	Sa	Total
Current	16%	18%	36%	30%	100%	4%	7%	12%	22%	21%	24%	10%	100%
Past	15	23	33	29	100	1	9	13	20	19	26	12	100
Previous	16	24	29	31	100	0	10	11	21	20	25	13	100

campaigns. Smart organizations maintain detailed historical data on the timing of customer purchases. These figures can then be used to make seasonal adjustments in sales forecasts and marketing plans. A detailed explanation of how to calculate and use seasonal adjustments is provided in Chapter 6.

Changing Customer Buying Patterns

Perceptive marketers not only know when customers buy, they take advantage of those times when they do *not* buy. For example, airlines, resorts, and telephone companies build capacity to meet peak seasonal demands. This means that they have excess capacity sitting idle during the off season. Marketing managers can help utilize this capacity by implementing special pricing and promotional programs to attract new customers when demand is low. The trick is to see the opportunity to expand sales even though customers do not seem to be interested.

A classic example of extending the period during which customers will use a product occurred with that old American favorite, the turkey. Turkeys were traditionally served during the Thanksgiving and Christmas holidays and were not eaten the rest of the year. A whole industry was created to grow and process turkeys for sale during a 2-month period. Although turkey is low in fat and economical, the birds were packaged in 15- to 20-pound units and took a great deal of time and effort to cook. This was not a problem during holidays, when friends gathered to celebrate, but turkey was inconvenient during the week, when members of the family might be working. The key to extending sales beyond the normal holiday season was to make turkey easier for the customer to prepare. Turkeys are now sold year round in pieces, in slices, and as roasts for even the smallest buying unit. This example shows that the time when customers buy products can be extended with careful attention to marketing activities.

WHAT DO MY CUSTOMERS WANT?

Determining customers' wants seems simple enough: just monitor current sales to see what they are buying. A somewhat more sophisticated approach involves recording sales by price range, size, and color so that product offerings can be matched with customer preference. While an analysis of internal sales data is straightforward, what do you do if you are not currently selling the item? This problem can be solved by buying the sales figures for your competitors from independent research firms (e.g., A. C. Nielsen) or sending observers to their stores to count the number of purchases being made.

There is, of course, more to determining customers' wants than just checking out what sells. The main reason is that many new concepts and products have yet to be invented and are not currently for sale. General Motors has such a problem in assessing consumers' interests and concerns about electric vehicles (see Marketing in Action box 3-1).

You must be careful not to let your preconceptions about customers cloud your

---

MARKETING IN ACTION 3-1

GM ELECTRIC VEHICLES

General Motors is plotting how it will meet California's 1998 deadline that at least 2 percent of a carmaker's offerings in the state must have zero emissions of tail pipe pollutants. Under current technology these offerings are limited to electric vehicles. GM must convince consumers to try a technologically advanced product. GM Electric Vehicles is trying to replicate the process a consumer goes through in deciding whether to buy a new car using a system called the MIT Information Accelerator. The interactive system uses a personal computer and video disc; the user controls what information she wants to get and in what order. The technology was first used to measure a test drive's value for the 1985 Buick Park Avenue. The program has been elaborated and refined to deal with a number of other marketing questions, such as the relative importance of word-of-mouth recommendations, advertising, sales experience and showroom environment. The user might check out a published report in an enthusiast magazine or call up views of a car's interior. The video disc allows the user to see a commercial or something like a neighbor's recommendation. At a certain point, the user can take the keys to an electric vehicle and go for a test drive. Afterward, he feeds back impressions. In the course of about two hours, a user will have gone through the shopping process. GM's aim is to get a reading on both the potential market for the product and gauge what marketing strategies work best.

You can use multimedia computers that incorporate your knowledge of buyer behavior to learn about customers' reactions to new product concepts.

Source: Raymond Serafin, "Building Electric Car Is One Thing; Selling Is Another," *The Atlanta Constitution,* February 5, 1993, p. S6.

---

thinking. Experienced managers frequently misjudge what customers really want. For example, the Reflective Products Division of 3M sells reflective materials to a wide variety of city, county, and state governments and to sign and barricade manufacturers. 3M is a major player in this market and has a good idea what product characteristics, delivery times, prices, and services are important. However, when they asked each group of customers to rank these criteria, they were stunned by the results. While all the customers' rankings included the same factors, there was *no* agreement on which one was most important. This meant that the same appeals could not be used for different customers, as had been done in the past. 3M was forced to revise their marketing program to emphasize separate criteria for each customer group. Customer wants in this case were not as generic as the managers believed.

HOW DO MY CUSTOMERS BUY?

By far the most complex issue in customer analysis is figuring how customers buy. The problem for marketers is that much of the decision-making process takes place in the buyer's mind. This makes it difficult to observe exactly how choices are made. Fortunately, extensive research has revealed the basic dimensions of the decision-making process.

A simplified model of this process is shown in Figure 3-1. Note that the procedure is sequential and time constrained. Purchase decisions are also influenced by a variety of internal and external factors. The first step is for the buyer to recognize that a problem or need exists. In a common situation, the buyer is reminded by the computer that the inventory of parts or supplies is low and needs to be replenished. Sometimes needs arise from the breakdown of the old product or from a constant demand for repairs. Advertising or store displays can also make people aware of unfilled wants. Social interaction with friends or associates can often lead to buyer interest in new products. Finally, many consumer needs arise from internally generated desires for food, shelter, and clothing.

The second step in the buying process involves a search for alternative ways of solving the problem or filling the need. The inclusion of a detailed search process in Figure 3-1 indicates that the customer is engaged in extended problem solving. Many routine purchases are much simpler than Figure 3-1 suggests. If you just want a candy bar, for example, you are likely to pick one up from the next available vending machine or candy counter rather than shop around at different stores. In the case of depleted business inventory, the process may be limited to rebuying the item from a regular supplier. If an item is broken, can it be repaired? How much will repairs cost compared to the cost of buying a new unit? If a new product is needed, what

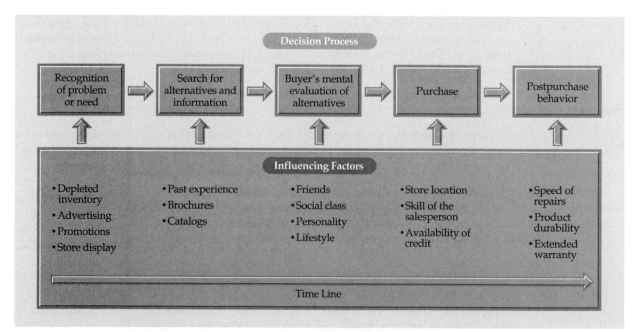

FIGURE 3-1   Customer Buying Process

brands are available? What features are offered by the different models? The information search phase of the process is important because this is where marketing can help the buyer gather necessary data. Marketing helps train the salespeople so that they will have the right information to answer customers' questions. Marketing prepares the tags and brochures that inform buyers about the merchandise. Marketing also designs the point-of-purchase displays, newspaper ads, TV ads, and radio commercials that give customers information on prices, product availability, and desirable product features.

The third step in the buyer's decision process is evaluation of the alternatives. This involves little action for the seller; it occurs primarily in the mind of the customer. The buyer weighs the advantages and disadvantages of the various alternatives and eventually makes a decision. Because this part of purchase behavior is a mental process, it is hard to observe and, consequently, is more difficult for marketing people to influence.

Once the customer has decided to buy, the next step is to complete the purchase transaction. The job of marketing is to make the product conveniently available so that customers do not have to travel great distances or wait in line for it. Marketing can also help complete the purchase by simplifying credit arrangements, packaging, and delivery. It is not enough to interest customers in your product; marketing managers must make the product easily available if they expect to sell in volume.

The final step of the buying process deals with postpurchase behavior. Most products wear out or are used up and have to be replaced. This means that it is important to keep customers satisfied after the purchase so that they will buy the item again. Marketing people carefully watch the postpurchase activities of customers so that interest in the product is maintained. The way customers are treated on returns, repairs, and warranty service will influence the decision process for subsequent purchases. If the firm handles postpurchase doubt and anxiety adequately, it is more likely to build a loyal cadre of repeat buyers.

Problem Recognition

The buyer's decision process begins with problem recognition. This occurs when a person perceives a difference between what he or she has (poor TV reception) and would like (a sharp, clear picture). Problem recognition can be triggered by information on past experiences stored in memory, basic motives, or cues from reference groups (Figure 3-2). *Motives* are enduring predispositions toward specific goals that both start and direct behavior. For example, some people must have the very latest equipment, whereas others like to avoid uncertainty caused by mechanical breakdowns. Problem recognition also can be activated by an outside stimulus such as advertising (Chapter 14).

Not every difference between actual conditions and the ideal state will lead to a purchase. Threshold differences must be exceeded before decision making starts. Buyers often put up with minor inconveniences for a long time before they actually become aware of their needs and start searching for a solution. For example, many people will endure a headache for hours before they go to the drugstore to choose a remedy.

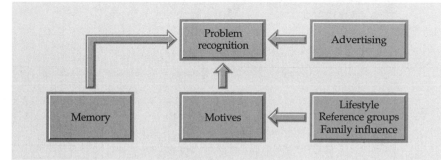

FIGURE 3-2 Factors Influencing Problem Recognition

Motives Needs tend to be arranged in a hierarchy, and consumers usually satisfy their needs on lower levels before they move to higher levels. Once consumers have satisfied their requirements for food and shelter—the first level, they become more concerned with safety and with products such as health insurance and radial tires—the second level. At the third level, a need for belonging is filled by churches, clubs, and family associations. The fourth level in the hierarchy is concerned with status, and some people satisfy this need by buying paintings or jewels. The highest need level, the fifth, is for self-actualization; this implies doing something to develop the talents of the individual, such as taking art lessons or working toward a new occupation.

Although basic needs explain many purchase decisions, we all buy things for other reasons. Some people have an unusually strong concern for their health, for example, and stock up on vitamins and nutrition books. Others are anxious in small groups and purchase quantities of deodorant and mouthwash. Still others crave excitement, and take up skydiving and travel to exotic locales. Marketing managers can also appeal to pride in personal appearance or possessions to sell soap, cosmetics, and house paint. Another powerful motivating factor in buying situations is economy.

One motivating force that is risky to use in marketing communications is *fear*, as illustrated in Marketing in Action box 3-2. The problem is that strong fear may cause consumers to distort advertising messages and thus may actually reduce the sales of the product. To sell antilock brakes, for example, auto manufacturers could use films of cars in accidents being smashed and burned. However, consumers might be so horrified by the pictures that they would refuse to consider that accidents might occur. Lower levels of fear help sales by creating interest in the product message, a facilitating effect. The inhibiting and facilitating effects of fear appeals can balance each other out. In this case, a moderate level of fear is optimal. For example, publication of personal experiences with household fires is very helpful in selling smoke alarms.

Social Interaction One factor that influences the awakening of customers' needs is membership in various *reference groups,* as well as the family. Customers often buy

---

MARKETING IN ACTION 3-2

SLICE OF DEATH

Some commercials are morbid twists on the feel-good slice-of-life commercials used in soft drink and beer advertising. Consider these commercials:

- NAPA automobile parts shows a man in a pick-up truck stalled on a railroad track. While the train bears down on him the announcer tells viewers they're wrong if they think "auto parts are just auto parts."
- Volvo automobiles shows a tin box on camera while the announcer intones: "This is a tin box. It's cute. It's red. Looks like a good place to put things—your valuables, for example. The most exciting thing about it is that it doesn't cost very much." At that point an anvil drops and crushes the box. "Then again, it could cost you a lot," says the announcer.
- Prestone antifreeze shows a woman driving on a frigid street in a desolate section of the city in the middle of the night while the announcer warns: "Don't push your luck. Guarantee it with Prestone."
- American Express Moneygram shows a kid stranded overseas, out of money. "Across the ocean, someone you love doesn't have money," the announcer says. "This is no time to find out that it takes three days to wire it there."

Fear, like sex and hunger, is a basic instinct that advertisers can tap to market their products. You must be careful, however, not to cross the line between high impact and high anxiety or you risk numbing the consumer.

Source: Jeffrey Scott, "Slice of Death," *The Atlanta Constitution,* January 20, 1990, pp. C-1, C-6.

---

products similar to those their friends and business associates own, so it is important to study membership in social groups. For example, cellular telephones are now very popular in business organizations because managers want to have the latest gadget to keep up with their friends.

For consumer goods, buyers are sometimes grouped into social classes based on occupation, source of income, type of housing, and residence location. The important thing to remember is that social class membership often determines when people buy products and what they buy. Research has shown that the middle classes are good markets for insurance and travel and that the lower classes are prime customers for appliances and automobiles. The upper class is small in number, but it controls a lot of wealth that can be steered into various investment opportunities.

The role and influence of *family* members in consumer decision making vary, depending on the product and family characteristics. For example, the six major stages of the family life cycle are (1) young single people, (2) young married couples with no children, (3) young married couples with dependent children, (4) older married couples with dependent children, (5) older married couples with no dependent children, and (6) older single people. The consumer's arrival at each stage of the life cycle initiates needs for new classes of products. When single persons move into a separate apartment, they need to buy basic household equipment. When these persons marry, there is a need for more furnishings. The arrival of children triggers a host of baby-related purchases. Thus, each stage of the family life cycle opens new vistas of needs that can be met by marketing managers who watch for these opportunities.

Joint decision making by the husband and wife tends to decline over the family life cycle as each partner becomes more aware of what the other considers acceptable. Usually, one partner will be responsible for decisions concerning a given product class. For example, the husband may be an expert on autos, whereas the wife may be more knowledgeable about insurance. This division of responsibility is based on relative expertise. Joint decision making is more important when large expenditures are involved.

Search for Alternatives

Once buyers become aware of their needs, the next step in the decision process is to gather information on products and alternative solutions to the customer's problem. A diagram explaining the search process is shown in Figure 3-3.

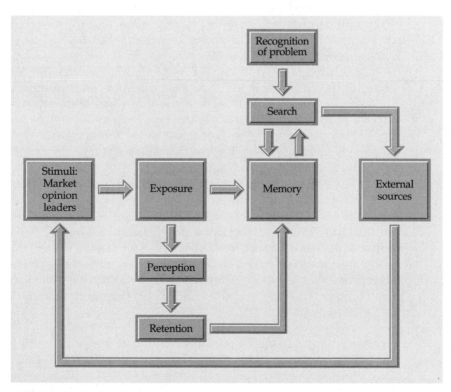

FIGURE 3-3 The Search Process

Memory   The search usually begins when buyers search their memories for information that might solve their current problem. Previous experiences of the buyer with similar merchandise can be reviewed to see what product solutions worked in the past. Memory can also be consulted for recommendations of friends, articles, and advertisements.

External Sources   If memory does not provide enough information, buyers start to consult outside. This includes both marketing sources, such as newspaper ads and salespeople, and nonmarketing sources, such as articles in *Consumer Reports* magazine and conversations with friends.

Opinion Leaders   The search for nonmarket information often involves talking to friends, neighbors, relatives, or people at work or school. Individuals who provide others with information for the buying process are called *opinion leaders* or *influentials*. These nonmarket sources can have a positive effect on purchase, or they can discourage people from buying a product. Research has shown that interpersonal communications are influential in the purchase of durable goods, food items, soaps, motion picture selection, makeup techniques, farming practices, clothing, selection of doctors, retail stores, and new products.[3]

The term *opinion leader* must be used carefully because it is often interpreted as meaning that influence trickles down from members of higher social classes to members of lower social classes. However, influence usually occurs horizontally within strata. Influentials tend to be more gregarious and to possess more knowledge in their area of influence. Often this knowledge has been obtained through greater exposure to relevant mass media.

According to the two-step theory of communication, the firm directs its advertising at the influentials in its product category, and these people influence their followers by word of mouth. The amount of word-of-mouth communication varies according to adopter categories. The purchaser of a product can be classified into one of five groups on the basis of time of adoption in relation to that of other buyers, as shown in Figure 3-4. The five categories are innovators, early adopters, early majority, late majority, and laggards.

Innovators are important in new product introductions because they affect later adopters and retail availability. However, innovators are usually not influentials. They are too innovative to be credible. They do help create awareness of a new product, however, and perform a product testing function that is observed by the influentials. The most important group of opinion leaders are the 13 percent classified as early adopters (Figure 3-4). These people are highly respected and have the most extensive social networks. The early majority also have some value as opinion leaders. However, the late majority and laggards are slow to adopt and have no value as influentials.

Exposure   For outside sources to be effective, buyers have to be exposed to their messages. This means that the buyer has to own a radio or TV set, subscribe to magazines and newspapers, read trade journals, see billboards, and be close enough to visit and talk with dealers.

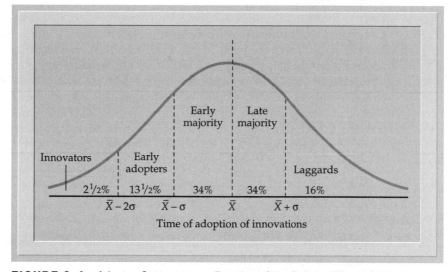

FIGURE 3-4 Adopter Category as a Function of the Relative Time of Adoption

After the buyer is exposed to market information, some of the information is sent directly to memory, where it is processed for decision making. However, most of the information goes through a series of filters, where it is often distorted or discarded. This process of interpreting information is called *perception*.

Perception In a marketing setting, *perception* refers to values attached to communications about products received from salespeople, friends, advertisements, and independent test reports. Variations in the behavior of buyers can be explained partly by individual differences in the way products and services are perceived.

The perceptual process controls both the quantity of information received through attention and the quality or meaning of information as it is affected by bias. *Attention* is the mechanism governing the receptivity of the buyer to ads and other stimuli to which the buyer is exposed. *Bias,* on the other hand, is distortion of incoming data caused by previous exposure to the product, other promotional material, or family background. Two aspects of the perceptual process that have important marketing implications are selective attention and perceptual bias.

In *selective attention*, consumers have frames of reference that they use to simplify the information they are continually receiving from friends and marketing communications. Although the sorting-out process prevents consumers from being overwhelmed by their experiences, it does mean that they are sensing only part of their environment. For example, people can sit in front of a TV set and read in a room full of children. When they are called to dinner, they often do not hear the summons because they have effectively tuned out all sound messages and are receptive only to what they see in the magazines or newspaper. In addition, they are likely to notice only some of the ads, depending on their preferences for articles or news coverage.

An example of *perceptual bias* can be described by referring to some research showing that brand names influence taste perception. One brewer asked consumers to explain their preferences for beer and found that the answers centered on the physical attributes of the product, such as flavor. Then an experiment was conducted to determine whether the beer drinkers could distinguish among major brands when they were not labeled. The consumers failed this test, and when these same drinkers were subsequently asked to rate labeled beers, their ratings differed from those in the unlabeled experiment. These results suggest that brand names influence preference and that the success of a brand of beer may be highly dependent on the effectiveness of its marketing effort. The sense of taste is especially subject to bias and distortion. Product development for items in which flavor is important must be designed with this in mind.

Evaluation of Alternatives

The evaluation phase of the customer decision model is the most complex and the least understood part of the process. Many factors influence individual decision making, and, as noted earlier, it is impossible to observe what is going on inside the buyer's mind. However, a general outline of the evaluation phase is shown in Figure 3-5. Sometimes evaluation occurs as the buyer is searching for information, such as when flipping through a rack of clothes. In other cases, evaluation takes place after the search process is complete.

Evaluative Criteria The first stage involves a comparison of the search information with the buyer's evaluative criteria. The buyer asks whether various brands would deliver the benefits sought in the product. The outcome of this process is a set of beliefs about the brands available for purchase. These beliefs are stored in memory

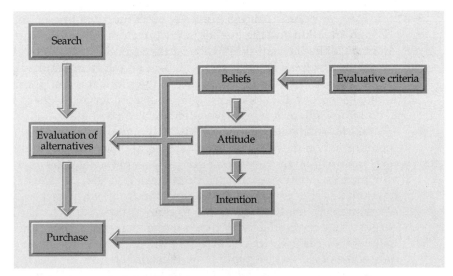

FIGURE 3-5 Alternative Evaluation

and tell the buyer the consequences of different purchases based on the evaluative criteria. As a rule, you should view the buyer's evaluative criteria as a given and learn to adapt your product, price, promotion, and distribution elements to these key buying determinants.

Attitudes   The next step occurs when the buyer's beliefs and evaluations are added together to form attitudes (Figure 3-5). *Attitude* is a mental state of readiness, organized through experience, exerting a directive influence on the individual's response to objects and situations with which it is related. This definition implies that attitude is a hypothetical construct that intervenes between marketing communications and product purchase. Most discussions of attitude recognize three components: cognitive (perceptual), affective (like–dislike), and conative (intentions).

An interesting synthesis of the relationships among the components of attitude and behavior suggests that at least three alternative sequences of cognitive, affective, and conative (behavioral) change may exist. These may be summarized as follows.

1. The Standard Learning Hierarchy

     Sequence of Change: Cognitive   →   Affective   →   Conative
                             (Perceptual)   (Like–Dislike)   (Purchase)
     Conditions: Buyers are highly involved.
                             Alternative products are clearly differentiated.
                             Mass media promotion is heavy.
                             Product is in the early stage of its life cycle.

2. The Dissonance-Attribution Hierarchy

     Sequence of Change: Conative   →   Affective   →   Cognitive
                             (Purchase)   (Like–Dislike)   (Perceptual)
     Conditions: Buyers are highly involved.
                             Products are similar.
                             Personal selling is more important than mass media
                                 promotion.
                             Product is in the early maturity stage of its life cycle.

3. The Low-Involvement Hierarchy

     Sequence of Change: Cognitive   →   Conative   →   Affective
                             (Perceptual)   (Purchase)   (Like–Dislike)
     Conditions: Buyers have low involvement.
                             Products are similar.
                             Broadcast media are important.
                             Product is in the late maturity stage of its life cycle.

Learning   Buyer evaluation of product alternatives is enhanced through learned behavior. *Learning* can be defined as changes in response tendencies due to the effects of experience. Learning occurs when buyers respond to a stimulus and are rewarded with need satisfaction or penalized by product failure. For example, a consumer might see an ad for beverages on a hot day and respond by trying different brands such as 7 Up, Slice, or Sprite. If Sprite satisfies the consumer's taste, then on future occasions he or she will buy Sprite again. The customer has learned. Theories that explain this adaptive behavior include problem solving, stimulus–response, and reinforcement.

Advertising programs are often built on *stimulus–response theory*. For example, a TV picture of a pleasant outdoor boy-girl situation is shown as a stimulus to the prospect. The idea is to elicit a pleasant emotional response that can be remembered when the brand name Sprite is presented in a voice over the commercial.

Marketers also use a learning theory called *operant conditioning*, which says that the probability of a favorable response (reading the ad) can be increased by following up with reinforcement or a reward. A print ad might show a person performing an unpleasant household chore (cleaning the oven) with a new spray product. People who read the ad are rewarded with a 50-cents-off store coupon that is placed at the end of the ad copy.

Consistency Paradigm *Consistency* is another useful concept that helps explain how customers make decisions. Buyers attempt to maintain consistency in their attitudes, behaviors, and the interaction of the two. Exposure to conflicting information produces internal strain. Customers seek to find solutions that minimize this tension. Conflict reduction alternatives include (1) changing behavior to conform to new information, (2) changing attitudes, (3) discrediting the source of the conflict-causing new information, (4) acquiring additional information to reinforce the original position, (5) avoiding the information sources that contribute to the dissonance (selective exposure), (6) distorting the new information, and (7) forgetting the content of the new information (selective recall).

Consistency theory also provides insight in planning new-product prices. Often a new product is temporarily offered at a low introductory price. This is done to encourage consumers to try it. Although many marginal users will be lost when the price is raised, it is hoped that some of these consumers, who would not have tried the product at the regular price, will be retained. Although this reasoning seems plausible, consistency theory suggests that the effort may be counterproductive leading to lower rather than higher eventual sales.

The higher the price consumers pay for a new product, the greater will be the pressure on them to justify their purchase by liking the product. The greater liking will, in turn, produce greater repeat purchases. On the other hand, consumers who buy the product on a cents-off promotion can justify the purchase as a bargain and need not alter their attitude toward the product.

Thus, attempts to change attitudes by first changing behavior must involve commitment to product trial. This suggests that sampling a new product would be ineffectual in cases where consumers have established preferences. In one case, homemakers resisted cold-water detergents and stated that they would not use a free sample. Some commitment was achieved by using cents-off coupons in the initial advertising and forcing the consumer to pay most of the purchase price.

In general, prospects will purchase items when attitudes are favorable toward the product. If attitudes are negative, the purchase is likely to be postponed. Also positive attitudes are associated with a strong intention to act. Measurement of intentions is important because it tells you the probability that a purchase will be made. However, attitudes may be positive, yet no sales may result. You probably have extremely positive attitudes toward Rolls Royce cars and Steinway pianos, but do not own either and probably never will. The situation is even worse than this. Scanner data, which provide irrefutable evidence of buyer choice behavior, show direct contradictions to attitude measurements. For example, those consumers who have the highest positive attitude toward healthful living and diet are the same people buying fattening, creamy desserts. "If you want to know what your favorite product is, look through your trash can."[4] Since the link between attitude and behavior is tenuous, attitude research is giving way to behavior research.

Purchase

Once consumers have selected a product alternative, the next step in the behavioral model is to complete the purchase (Figure 3-6). The purchase part of the transaction is influenced by the buyer's intentions and other special conditions that exist in the marketplace. A buyer may intend to purchase a Sony TV, but if this brand is out of stock, he or she may end up with an RCA. Also, the buyer may want the remote control console model but may only have enough money for a portable TV.

Marketplace Conditions   A number of other in-store conditions can influence purchase decisions. The buying process is helped if the product or service is readily available. Consumers may prefer your product, but if they have to travel 50 miles to the nearest dealer, they are not apt to buy it. Similarly, dealers who are open at night and on weekends have an advantage over stores in which customers must wait in

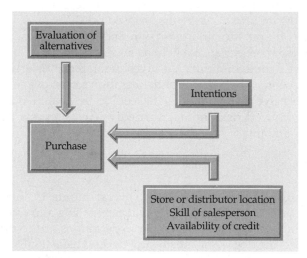

FIGURE 3-6   The Purchase Decision

line and in which credit or check-cashing services are not offered. For example, emergency medical clinics that do not require appointments and are open on evenings and weekends have siphoned off substantial business from regular doctors and hospital emergency rooms.

In-store displays are another special condition that influences buyer choice. When customers encounter a large display of a new soft drink and are given a free sample, they are more likely to try the new item. The display provides new information so that the consumer reevaluates established beliefs and the intention to buy is modified.

A special price in the store is also a strong inducement to get customers to switch brands. Price change is particularly effective when the buyer believes that all brands in a product category are about equal in quality. Under these conditions, a price reduction may temporarily shift customer choice; then it will revert back when the raided brand makes a counter price adjustment. For example, automobile tires, batteries, and shock absorbers fail on a random basis, and the buyer rarely has time to shop for preferred brands. Thus, the buyer frequently buys the item that is on sale when a replacement is needed.

Knowledgeable and helpful personnel at the point of sale are often the key factor in choosing a particular brand. Salespeople who can explain product features and demonstrate benefits are often able to trade customers up to higher profit merchandise. One study revealed that three-fourths of those interviewed in five cities said that the quality of salespeople was a factor in the choice of a shopping center. Clearly, retailers and manufacturers who do the best job of selecting and training salespeople enhance their customer purchase probabilities.

Perceived Risk The amount of risk buyers believe is associated with a purchase decision also affects behavior. The degree of risk varies with the cost and with the buyers' degree of certainty that the outcome of the decision will be satisfactory. The costs of a bad decision include monetary loss, time loss, ego loss, social risks, and losses related to the failure to satisfy the aroused need.

Individuals often pursue different risk reduction strategies. Some buy only for cash; others buy the most expensive item as an assurance of quality; still others buy the least expensive item to minimize the investment. Some risk reduction actions are inconsistent. Frequently, the amount of deliberation for an expensive product is *less* than for an inexpensive one. Some buyers seem to be unable to live with decisions involving high perceived risk and act hurriedly. This suggests that perceived risk interacts with the amount of *time* that can be used for decision making.

Postpurchase Behavior

Customer postpurchase activity provides several inputs to our model of buyer behavior (Figure 3-7). A major concern is that purchasing allows customers to learn more about products or services. Customer expectations are compared with actual product experience; the degree of satisfaction or dissatisfaction is assessed; and possible further customer behavior is projected. Highly satisfied customers, for example, will alter their beliefs about a product in a favorable direction. These satisfied con-

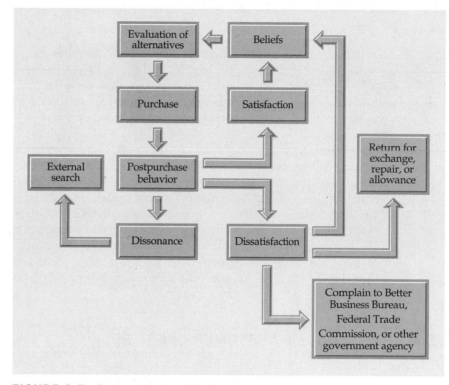

FIGURE 3-7 Postpurchase Behavior

sumers are apt to become repeat buyers and may become advocates of the product in their conversations with others.

Dissatisfaction   Products or services that do not live up to the buyer's expectation for durability or performance result in customer dissatisfaction (Figure 3-7). The most common reaction to product problems is for the customer to return to the dealer and ask for an exchange, a refund, or a repair. If the problem is handled carefully by the dealer, the buyer's positive beliefs in the product will be restored, and the customer will probably buy again. When customer complaints are rebuffed, a negative belief structure is formed, and the probability of repeat purchase will decline. In the case of low-value goods, dissatisfied customers usually do not go back to the dealer for an adjustment; they simply express their resentment by not buying again.

When complaints are not handled adequately, customers may appeal to outside agencies. The ensuing publicity can lead to lawsuits, product recalls, loss of goodwill, and reduced market share. For example, research has shown that customer dissatisfaction is high for places and services such as employment agencies, auto repairs, nursing homes, moving and storage, and appliance repairs. This suggests that some firms could benefit by improving the quality of their services and providing better methods for handling complaints. Firms that fail to deal with dissatisfied customers may end up having to deal with increased government regulation and decreased revenue.

Cognitive Dissonance   Another area of postpurchase behavior that is important is *cognitive dissonance* or *postpurchase doubt* (Figure 3-7). A purchase decision usually does not eliminate dissonance, for the consumer remains aware of the favorable features of the unchosen brands and must reconcile this knowledge with his or her own decisions. The process of reconciliation often involves a search for new information.

The likelihood that consumers will search for information after a purchase increases with the importance of the decision, with the number of negative attributes of the chosen product, and with the number of positive attributes of the unchosen alternatives. The kind of information sought depends on the consumer's confidence in the initial decision. The more certain consumers are that they have made the correct decision, the more likely they will try to find differing information and refute it. On the other hand, the less confident consumers are, the more likely they will seek only information that supports their decision. You should engage in activities designed to give buyers more product information, reduce postpurchase doubt, and turn customers into product advocates.

HOW DOES MY FIRM BECOME CUSTOMER ORIENTED?

Many firms say they are customer oriented, but often they provide only slogans and window dressing. Some managers profess to be interested in customers just to protect their own departments and chances for promotion. For example, managers of a flow controls company gathered to discuss declining sales, earnings, and market share.[5] The president suggested that the only way to solve their problems was to become more customer driven. Everyone agreed and proceeded to give their version of a customer orientation. First, the sales vice president said that they needed more sales-people to get closer to the customers. Then the manufacturing vice president said that they needed more automatic machinery so that they could deliver better quality. The research and development vice president called for more expenditures on research to generate more new products. One division manager asked for separate sales forces for each division, and another wanted a special engineering group to tailor designs to customers' needs. While all of the managers displayed a customer orientation, they were primarily interested in using this theme to protect their own functional areas rather than to integrate a customer mentality throughout the firm.

In today's competitive environment, everyone in the firm is involved in marketing. Factory workers, people who answer phones, service people, and clerks in the back room all contribute to customer satisfaction. Thus, one job of marketing is to make sure that these employees understand their roles in building sales and profits. An Australian public transportation company used the inverted pyramid organization chart in Figure 3-8 to emphasize this new approach.[6] This structure places

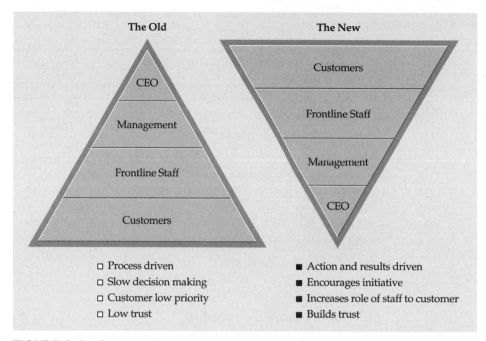

FIGURE 3-8 Customer Focused Marketing. (From Peter Daw, "Empowering Employees Drives Australian Transportation Customer Service," *Services Marketing Today*, American Marketing Association, [July–August 1992], p. 4)

the customer on top, followed by the front-line staff and management and the CEO at the bottom. By empowering front-line staff to make decisions, marketing managers were free to concentrate on strategy development and implementation. This plan also focused everyone on satisfying customers. After the new program was initiated at the transportation company, customer complaint letters dropped by 30 percent.

Customer Checklist

After the president of the controls firm pointed out the need to work together, the managers concluded that they needed more information about present and potential customers. They also prepared a checklist to monitor how well they were doing in their drive to be more customer oriented (Table 3-4). The most common way to gather data for the items on this checklist is customer surveys. Questionnaires can be prepared and distributed to representative samples of customers, and the results summarized in reports. Useful information can be obtained from surveys, but success often depends on asking the right questions. This means that you must know a great deal about your customers before you can conduct a survey. Also, surveys take time to complete, and it is always possible that the people who return them may not be truly representative customers.

A quicker and more personal way to gather customer information is through

TABLE 3-4
Customer Orientation Checklist

1. *Are we easy to do business with?*

    Easy to contact?

    Fast to provide information?

    Easy to order from?

    Make reasonable promises?

2. *Do we keep our promises?*

    On product performance?

    Delivery?

    Installation?

    Training?

    Service?

3. *Do we meet the standards we set?*

    Specifics?

    General tone?

    Do we even know the standards?

4. *Are we responsive?*

    Do we listen?

    Do we follow up?

    Do we ask "why not," not "why"?

    Do we treat customers as individual companies and individual people?

5. *Do we work together?*

    Share blame?

    Share information?

    Make joint decisions?

    Provide satisfaction?

Source: Benson P. Shapiro, "What the Hell Is Market Oriented?" *Harvard Business Review*, Vol. 88, No. 6 (November–December 1988), p. 125.

some form of direct contact. One of the simplest methods is to listen in on your toll-free 800 customer call-in number. In some firms, cassette recordings of customer calls are routinely distributed to a wide range of executives. If managers are adventurous, they may even try to answer a few customer calls themselves. An extension of this method is to use the phone to make regular calls on customers. For example, at Castle Company executives find a 5 × 7 inch sheet of paper with the name and phone number of a customer who has purchased a new piece of equipment on their desk three mornings a week. The executives are expected to call these people to see if they are satisfied with the company's hospital sterilizers. This lets customers know they are important and helps uncover problems before they become serious.[7] You can also call recently lost customers and others who have not purchased for several years.

Ask them why they are not buying and what can be done to bring them back as regular customers.

Plant Tours and Customer Visits

Another good way to learn about customers is to invite them in for a tour of your facilities and some informal discussions. The idea behind these "How are we doing for you?" sessions is to get customers to talk about issues that are important to them. One electrical connector company makes it a point to have the customers outnumber company personnel so that they will feel free to speak up. Customers are generally delighted to be invited and often provide many new insights on their needs. A variation of this idea is to have executives visit customers' plants. This was the approach used by the controls firm mentioned earlier. They sent out 10 executives in groups of 2 to visit 20 major customers. These visits are more informative if you get to talk to operating personnel or actually work for short periods in selected customer operations. Customers can also be contacted at trade shows. Hospitality suites at trade shows are often used to get customers to talk about their problems and needs.

It is not enough to run one survey or call a few customers to establish a customer orientation for your company. Learning about customers is a continuous process that reflects the changing business environment. A knowledgeable consultant suggests that senior line managers should spend at least 30 percent of their time with customers. He also recommends that accountants, manufacturing managers, and management information systems people spend 10 percent or more of their time learning about customers' needs.[8] There is no one best way to interact with customers. The most important issue is to make sure that customer contacts are maintained across time.

SUMMARY

Marketing managers must understand customers' needs in order to recognize new product opportunities, to identify meaningful bases for market segmentation, and to improve existing marketing activities. This means that you should know who your customers are and where they are located. In addition, you need to know when they buy and why. Managers who understand how customers make purchase decisions are in a better position to design products and more effective marketing programs.

NOTES

1. Tom Peters and Nancy Austin, *A Passion for Excellence* (New York: Warner Books, 1985), p. 45.
2. *The Wall Street Journal* (November 15, 1988), p. 31.

3. James F. Engle and Roger D. Blackwell, *Consumer Behavior*, 4th ed. (New York: Dryden Press, 1982), p. 355.

4. Rodman A. Sims, "Positive Attitudes Won't Make Cash Register Sing," *Marketing News* (June 7, 1993), pp. 4–5.

5. Benson P. Shapiro, "What the Hell Is Market Oriented?" *Harvard Business Review*, Vol. 88, No. 6 (November–December 1988), pp. 119–125.

6. Peter Daw, "Empowering Employees Drives Australian Transportation Customer Service," *Services Marketing Today*, American Marketing Association (July–August 1992), p. 4.

7. Peters and Austin, *A Passion for Excellence*, p. 11.

8. Ibid., p. 127

SUGGESTED READING

Bagozzi, Richard P. "The Rebirth of Attitude Research in Marketing," *Journal of the Marketing Research Society*, Vol. 30 (April 1988), pp. 163–195.

Germain, Richard, and M. Bixby Cooper. "How a Customer Mission Statement Affects Company Performance," *Industrial Marketing Management*, Vol. 19, No. 1 (February 1990), pp. 47–54.

Shapiro, Benson P. "What the Hell Is Market Oriented?" *Harvard Business Review*, Vol. 88, No. 6 (November–December 1988), pp. 119–125.

QUESTIONS

1. One of your jobs as a marketing manager is to scan the environment. You are relaxing at home, reading *Billboard* magazine, which calls itself the international newsweekly of music, video, and home entertainment. You come across the information given in Table 3-5. What insights do you draw?

2. An MRCA Information Services survey in the United States revealed that women bought 78 percent of men's sweaters, 71 percent of men's socks, and 70 percent of men's sport shirts. If you were a men's apparel manufacturer, how would you use these results? An apparel department manager in a retail store?

3. Technology has allowed firms to gather large amounts of data about potential customers. Ford Motor Company has a mailing list of 50 million names, and General Foods has a database of 25 million. What would you recommend these companies do to take advantage of this information?

4. "In the United States, the customer is king; in Japan, the customer is god." What are the marketing implications of this statement?

5. When should a firm introducing a new product attempt to identify innovators and influentials for the product category? How can the firm use this knowledge about their identities?

TABLE 3-5

Hits of the World: Top Five Record Albums

	Country				
Rank	France	Italy	Japan	United Kingdom	United States
1	The Bodyguard Soundtrack	Gli Spari Sopra Vasco Rossi	Bokutachino Shippai Moritadouji	Are You Gonna Go My Way? Lenny Kravitz	Unplugged Eric Clapton
2	Dutronic au Casino Jacques Dutronic	Supersanremo Vari	Steps Keizo Nakanishi	Unplugged Eric Clapton	Ten Summoner's Tales Sting
3	Pochette Surprise Jordy	Ten Summoner's Tales Sting	The Bodyguard Soundtrack	Ingenue K. D. Lang	The Bodyguard Soundtrack
4	Regagner les Plaines Pow Pow	T'Innamorerai Marco Masini	Sola Stardust Revue	The Dark Side of the Moon Pink Floyd	Breathless Kenny G
5	Are You Gonna Go My Way? Lenny Kravitz	The Bodyguard Soundtrack	Encounter Sing Like Talking	Ten Summoner's Tales Sting	Pocket Full of Kryptonite Spin Doctors

Source: Derived from *Billboard*, March 27, 1993, pp. 55, 90.

6. Prepare a flowchart showing how you made a recent durable-good purchase. Explain how the manufacturer of the product could use your chart.

7. How might attitude research have misled McDonald's into launching its low-fat McLean burger, a flop?

8. Describe the family life cycle and its influence on consumption patterns and consumer decision processes.

Chapter 4

Market Segmentation and Product Differentiation

Small opportunities are often the beginning of great enterprises.

DEMOSTHENES

In today's competitive environment, companies are finding it dangerous to treat customers as a single homogeneous group. Mass markets are breaking up into dozens of minimarkets, each with its own special needs. This approach to marketing is known as *segmentation*, and it is often the key to developing a sustainable competitive advantage (SCA) based on differentiation or a focus strategy.

MARKET SEGMENTATION

Segmentation is the strategy of developing different marketing programs for different customer groups or segments. It recognizes heterogeneity in the market. Each customer segment has its own unique demand function based on price, physical product characteristics, and nonphysical attributes reflecting image and performance. You build volume by appealing to group preferences.

Using separate marketing programs to sell to different market segments contrasts with *global marketing,* in which the same marketing mix is used for all markets (Figure 4-1). Although global marketing may work well for some companies that employ the same ads to sell to everyone, there is money to be made in most industries by following a segmentation strategy. So, you must decide whether to follow a global or mass market strategy, to focus on one segment or niche, or to compete in several segments simultaneously with different marketing mixes.

First, you need to identify the best ways to segment a market and then define the characteristics of each group. Next, you must evaluate the attractiveness of the segments and select the most appropriate target markets. Finally, you need to posi-

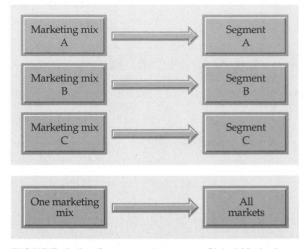

FIGURE 4-1 Segmentation versus Global Marketing

MARKETING IN ACTION 4-1

SELLING ROOT BEER TO A PREMIUM NICHE

Despite the general austerity of the 1990s, it is possible to sell root beer as a luxury product. By carefully picking its market segments, Thomas Kemper Soda Company of Seattle has been able to make money selling root beer for $5 a six-pack, more than twice the price of most competing brands. Kemper's target customers are yuppies (Young Urban Professionals) who are into the microbrew scene. Thomas Kemper root beer was originally produced by a Seattle beer microbrewery that carries the same name. Kemper's high quality root beer is brewed in small batches and takes three days to produce instead of a few minutes to make syrups used for other brands. The current owners took advantage of this heritage and use beer distributors to reach yuppies in bars, corner expresso stands, and high-end coffee bars. With liquor and beer sales flat, many bar owners were looking for non-alcoholic beverages to sell. Much of Kemper's root beer is sold in kegs, so it can be tapped in bars and made into root-beer ice cream floats.

Kemper's success is partially due to the regional preference for upscale coffees, locally brewed beer, and even gourmet potato chips. Seattle customers are willing to pay more for what they perceive as high quality. Kemper has taken advantage of this with a very effective word-of-mouth marketing campaign targeted to yuppies. To make its product more available to its customers, Kemper has expanded distribution to convenience and specialty stores. Kemper's pricey root beer has done so well that it is now stocked in cold cases in 165 Safeway Supermarkets in the Northwest.

Targeting quality products to niche markets can be profitable.

Source: Bill Richards, "Kemper's Shows Even Root Beer Has a Premium Niche," *The Wall Street Journal*, May 18, 1993, p. B2.

tion your product or service relative to competitive offerings within the chosen market segments. An example of successful niche marketing is described in Marketing in Action box 4-1.

Building Customer Segments

Segmentation sounds like a process of breaking large markets into smaller ones. In its extreme form, segmentation involves designing a unique product and marketing program for each buyer. For instance, Computer Designed Swimwear uses a computer and video camera to measure customers nine ways. After buyers pick styles and fabric, the computer prints out a pattern that can be turned into a suit within an hour. Other examples include designing office buildings and insurance plans to meet the needs of individual corporations. However, segmentation is really a process of aggregation. The idea is to pull together groups of customers who resemble each other on some meaningful dimensions.

Although you can consider each buying unit a segment, there are usually some economies if they are grouped into clusters. Buying units are placed into segments, so there is similarity in demand within segments and differences in demand among segments. *The Farm Journal,* for example, groups its 1 million subscribers into 1134 different segments based on location and type of farm. Content varies across editions, and an issue of the magazine might have 150,000 copies for beef farmers, 7000 copies for beef and dairy farmers, and 36 copies for top producers who raise cotton, hogs, and dairy cows. The idea of mailing out 1134 different editions of a magazine is mind-boggling and is possible only because the firm has a computerized bindery. A more typical situation would have a company working with 2 to 12 market segments. One of your jobs as marketing manager is to decide the most appropriate number of segments for your organization.

A variety of statistical methods are available to help you with the grouping task (Table 4-1). While a discussion of these techniques is beyond the scope of this book, you should be aware that the choice of technique depends on the segmentation approach employed and the purpose of the analysis. Segmentation approaches can be partitioned based on whether they are a priori or post hoc. An *a priori* approach is one in which the type and number of segments are completely specified by you,

TABLE 4-1
Statistical Methods for Segmentation

	A Priori	Post Hoc
Descriptive	Contingency tables, log-linear models	Clustering methods: nonoverlapping, overlapping, fuzzy
Predictive	Cross-tabulation, regression, logit and probit models, discriminant analysis	Automatic interaction detector, clusterwise regression

Source: Michel Wedel, *Clusterwise Regression and Market Segmentation* (Wageningen, the Netherlands: Wageningen Agricultural University, 1990), p. 36.

without regard to the data collected; a *post hoc* approach is one in which the type and number of segments are revealed as the result of your analysis of the data. An a priori approach is used when the complexity of the market can be captured by relatively few variables; when you are confident about your understanding of your market; and when the information you mainly need is segment size and perhaps the relative importance of segmentation variables. Otherwise, a post hoc approach is used. The choice of technique also depends on whether you want to identify segments (description) or test the relationship of segmentation variables with purchase behavior (prediction).

Which Characteristics Identify Segments?

The major *bases* for segmentation are geographic, demographic, psychographic, and behavioral. These bases, together with their typical breakdowns, are shown in Table 4-2. Some of these buyer characteristics were discussed in Chapter 3.

Geographic Basis   Markets are often segmented on the basis of nations, states, regions, counties, cities, and population density. Product usage tends to vary among buyers on these dimensions. For example, Maxwell House coffee is sold nationally in the United States but is flavored regionally. Campbell soup also adapts its products and promotions to local conditions. General Motors, Ford, and Chrysler vary their promotions and rebates by geographic regions. The use of regional marketing plans is made easier by the availability of spot TV, spot radio, local newspapers, and regional editions of magazines. Targeting for some consumer products may be as narrow as an individual neighborhood or even a single store, thanks to the information provided by checkout scanners.

Multinational firms often segment markets on the basis of national boundaries. The attractiveness of an international market environment is a function of political stability, market opportunity, economic development and performance, cultural unity, tariff barriers, physiographic barriers, and geocultural distance. In addition, the multinational firm must take into account factors specific to the firm and its industry.

Demographic Basis   Consumer markets can be segmented according to age, sex, stage in the family life cycle, income, education, occupation, and race of the customer. For instance, eye makeup usage rates tend to be higher among the young, the well educated, and working women. Shortening usage rates tend to be higher for those who are older and have larger families. Business markets can be segmented according to total sales, total assets, or number of employees of the firm.

An example showing how income and age can be used to segment new-car buyers is provided in Figure 4-2. The advantage of this graphical approach is that it highlights the positions of your products relative to those of your competitors. Notice that General Motors' Chevrolet, Buick, Oldsmobile, and Cadillac divisions all appeal to older drivers. The only division feeding in young customers is Pontiac. To help attract more first-time buyers, General Motors is promoting their new Saturn and Geo divisions. Figure 4-2 also shows that Buick and Oldsmobile appeal to the same

TABLE 4-2

Alternative Bases for Segmentation

Basis	Typical Breakdown
Geographic	
Country	Canada, England, Mexico, Japan, United States
Region	New England, Metro New York, Mid-Atlantic, East Central, Metro Chicago, West Central, Southeast, Southwest, Pacific
County size	A, B, C, D
SMSA[a] population	Under 50,000; 50,000–99,999; 100,000–249,999; 250,000–499,999; 500,000–999,999; 1,000,000–3,999,999; 4,000,000 or over
Density	Urban, suburban, rural
Demographic	
Age	Under 6; 6–11, 12–17, 18–34, 35–49, 50–64, 65 and over
Sex	Male, female
Family life cycle	Young, single; young, married, no children; young, married, children; older, married, children; older, married, no children; older, single; other
Education	Grade school or less; some high school; graduated high school; some college; graduated college
Occupation	Professional and technical; managers, officials, and proprietors; clerical; sales; artisans; supervisors; operative; farmers; armed services; retired; students; homemakers; unemployed
Race	Black, oriental, white
Manufacturer's industry	Standard Industrial Classification (SIC) Code
Psychographic	
Social class	Lower; working class; lower-middle; upper-middle; upper
Personality	Gregarious, introverted, compulsive
Lifestyle	Cosmopolitan, yuppies
Behavioralistic	
Decision-making unit	Buying committee, purchasing agent, plant or headquarters
Usage rate	Nonuser, light, medium, heavy
Readiness	Unaware, aware, interested, intending to try, trier, repeat purchaser
Benefits sought	Quality, service, value
Occasion	Regular, special
Brand loyalty	Nonloyal, loyal

[a] SMSA, standard metropolitan statistical area.

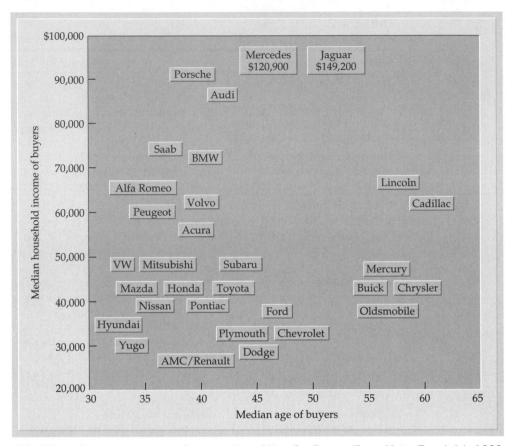

FIGURE 4-2 Income and Age Segmentation of New-Car Buyers (From *Motor Trend*, July 1988, p. 44)

market segment. The unpleasant result is that these cars tend to steal market share from each other rather than from competitors. General Motors is currently running some youth-oriented ads for Oldsmobile to try to differentiate these products in the minds of the customer. Another interesting finding is the hole in the middle of Figure 4-2. This suggests that there is untapped potential for cars designed for 50-year-old customers with $60,000 annual incomes. When data from Figure 4-2 are combined with information on education and occupation, auto firms have precise profiles on customer segments that can be used for market programming.

Although marketing has become more precisely targeted, demographics do not explain enough. While demographics tell you what a customer looks like and does for a living, it does not tell why the customer does things.

Psychographic Basis Psychographics provide a useful supplement to demographics. Psychographics focus on general buyer habits, social class, lifestyles, and attitudes as they might relate to a specific product class. *Lifestyle* is concerned with the activities, interests, and opinions concerning leisure time, work, and consumption of the buyer, either alone or with others, with respect to both general behavior and the specific product class. Researchers find, for example, that buyers of Isuzu Motors' line of Trooper sport utility vehicles tend to be more environmentally conscious and outdoor-minded than other consumers. Lifestyle research at Carnation Company led to the creation of the Contadina line of fresh pastas targeted at two-income couples who like freshly prepared foods but have little time to cook.

Among the best-known psychographic classifications of consumers is SRI International's Values and Life Styles (VALS) program. Consumers are classified into eight categories, as shown in Table 4-3. How can this information be used? A pack-

TABLE 4-3
The World According to VALS 2

Actualizers	*Fulfilleds*
Value personal growth	Moderately active in community and
Wide intellectual interests	politics
Varied leisure activities	Leisure centers on the home
Well informed; concerned with social	Value education and travel
issues	Health conscious
Highly social	Politically moderate and tolerant
Politically active	
Achievers	*Experiencers*
Lives center on career and family	Like the new, offbeat, and risky
Have formal social relations	Like exercise, socializing, sports, and the
Avoid excess change or stimulation	outdoors
May emphasize work at expense of	Concerned about image
recreation	Unconforming, but admire wealth,
Politically conservative	power, and fame
	Politically apathetic
Believers	*Strivers*
Respect rules and trust authority figures	Narrow interests
Enjoy settled, comfortable, predictable	Easily bored
existence	Somewhat isolated
Socialize within family and established	Look to peer group for motivation and
groups	approval
Politically conservative	Unconcerned about health or nutrition
Reasonably well informed	Politically apathetic
Makers	*Strugglers*
Enjoy outdoors	Limited interests and activities
Prefer ''hands-on'' activities	Prime concerns are safety and security
Spend leisure time with family and close	Burdened with health problems
friends	Conservative and traditional
Avoid joining organizations, except	Rely on organized religion
unions	
Distrust politicians, foreigners, and big	
business	

Source: SRI International.

ager of travel tours, for example, might focus on adventure when talking to the experiencer but emphasize luxury and service with the achiever.

Lifestyle segmentation has some limitations. Although lifestyle segmentation greatly increases survey costs, lifestyles explain only a small proportion of brand behavior. Many individuals assume multiple roles in life. How, then, can one lifestyle label be applied to such individuals? Even where lifestyle segments have been identified, the results frequently have not been actionable.

Behavioral Basis   A common way to segment a market is by volume. Marketing managers obviously distinguish between users and nonusers of their product or service. However, users consume different amounts. A small proportion of users might account for a large share of sales. Thus, the importance of a buyer is represented by the volume purchased. Strategies based on the heavy half are easier to implement if these users have clearly defined demographic profiles. Besides the usage rate, markets can be segmented by the decision-making unit, the end use, buyers' purchasing strategies, the degree of brand loyalty, the response to changes in your own and your competitors' marketing mixes, and the readiness stage.

Rather than segment a market on the basis of descriptive factors such as geographic, demographic, or volume, causal factors related to the reasons for purchase might be more appropriate. These causal factors are the benefits sought by the buyer. Once the benefit segments have been constructed, they can be characterized using conventional descriptive factors. As an example, consider the toothpaste market. Four benefit segments can be identified: (1) flavor and product appearance, (2) brightness of teeth, (3) decay prevention, and (4) price. These segments have different demographic strengths, special behavioral characteristics, brands disproportionately favored, and personality and life-cycle characteristics. This information suggests how copy directions and media choices might be tailored to reach different target segments.

The most common way of segmenting a business market is by end use. An industrial marketer might want to segment the pollution-control market. Some of the ways this market could be segmented are by type of pollutant (e.g., odors), medium being polluted (e.g., water), source of the pollution (e.g., municipality), entity requiring the control products (e.g., federal government), and type of control product (e.g., biological organisms). The attributes of a product or service must also be matched to the needs of potential customers. For example, one type of medical equipment can be used in the emergency room of a hospital and another type in the office of a physician in private practice. Some attributes of the equipment are more important in one market than in another. Cost and ease of operation are more important to the individual doctor than to the hospital. The physician must collect fees from individual patients and use the equipment without help, whereas the hospital collects fees from medical insurance companies and employs technicians.

A customer might have different reasons for selecting from a product category, depending on the motivational circumstance. This gives rise to occasion-based segmentation. For example, the occasion is often a prime factor in wine selection. A wine's status is more important if the wine is served to guests than if it is to be consumed alone. The social occasion may make the buyer willing to pay more, more sensitive to brand image, and more attentive to label graphics.

Customer sensitivity to marketing actions is an important aspect of buying behavior. For example, Signode used sensitivity to price and service changes to help it identify buying behavior microsegments (Marketing Strategies box 4-1). Firms can shape the buying behaviors of potential customers by tactically altering marketing mix variables. Your next task is deciding how to balance the costs of segmentation against the potential benefits.

MARKETING STRATEGIES 4-1

FINE-TUNING SIGNODE'S SEGMENTATION STRATEGY

The packaging division of Signode Corporation produces and markets a line of steel strappings used for packaging a diverse range of goods such as brick, steel, cotton, and many manufactured items. Signode has been the market leader for more than 25 years by bundling its strapping with other services. It provides engineering advice on customer packaging needs, as well as parts and service for repair of packaging equipment at user firms. All other competitors offer only steel strapping. Despite its success, Signode's market share was being eroded by stiff price competition.

(*continued on next page*)

MARKETING STRATEGIES 4-1 (continued)

Signode traditionally segmented its customers by size—small, medium, large, and national accounts—and within each of these segments by SIC code. It did not use a buyer-behavior-based segmentation scheme. However, market pressures made customer behavior in terms of tradeoffs between price and service an important additional segmentation criterion. Since Signode could not do an in-depth analysis of the buying behavior of all its customers, it focused on its 174 national accounts whose purchases of Signode's products exceeded $100,000 annually. These national accounts generated nearly 40% of Signode's sales revenues.

To gather information on the customer buying behavior of these key accounts, key informants were used because extensive surveys of multiple members of complex decision-making units have been found to be impractical. The key informants were Signode's five national account managers and 20 national account sales representatives. They provided input on 12 variables. Four buying behavior microsegments were then identified by performing cluster analysis on these variables. These segments were called programmed buyers, relationship buyers, transaction buyers, and bargain hunters. Knowledge of segment behavior helped Signode to redirect marketing resources.

Segmentation analysis can be used proactively to influence customers' movements to segments.

Source: V. Kasturi Rangan, Rowland T. Moriarty, and Gordon S. Swartz, "Segmenting Customers in Mature Industrial Markets," *Journal of Marketing*, Vol. 56 (October 1992), pp. 72–82.

Evaluating Market Segments

Once you have identified some appropriate market segments, you must determine whether a segmentation policy makes sense. Segmentation has a somewhat negative image, as it implies that brand managers deliberately abandon part of the market to the competition. However, mass markets do not have to be ignored. Usually the timing of a brand's entry determines whether a firm should segment a market or treat it as a whole. Original entrants should try to dominate the entire market, whereas latecomers might do better by going after identifiable submarkets or niches. To determine whether segmentation is a good idea, you need a set of evaluation criteria.

Evaluation Criteria   A number of factors that have been suggested to help evaluate segmentation strategies are shown in Table 4-4. Segmentation works only when you have groups of customers with common needs or wants. If every buyer wants the product tailored to unique specifications, segmentation will fail. You must also be able to identify customers in each market segment. This is fairly easy if segments are based on demographic factors such as male/female, age, or income. These characteristics can be observed and measured with some accuracy. However, segments based on lifestyle are much more difficult to use. For example, you might decide to

TABLE 4-4
Requirements for Effective Segmentation

1. Customers with common wants exist.
2. Segment members are identifiable/measurable.
3. Segment members are accessible.
4. The segment responds to marketing efforts differently than does the market as a whole.
5. Specialized communications media are available.
6. The seller has a competitive edge in target segment.
7. The segment is large enough to make a substantial profit.

focus your efforts on marketing to cosmopolitan customers. The problem with this segment is how to measure cosmopolitanism. Worldliness is made up of many traits and is not as easy to scale as age or income.

One of the key requirements for effective segmentation is that group members must respond differently to marketing initiatives. When prospects are uneducated or illiterate or speak foreign languages, they are not likely to understand or react to ads and other promotional communications. Encouraging segment members to buy is helped if specialized promotional media are available. This means that you must have access to spot TV, as well as regional editions of magazines and newspapers. Other special media that can be useful include ethnic and foreign language radio stations.

Direct mail is also effective with segmentation strategies. Toyota, for example, used direct mail to build awareness when introducing its Lexus line of luxury automobiles. Since these cars sell for high prices, Toyota needed an economical way to reach a limited number of prospects without the use of mass media. Their approach was to build a mailing list from people who attended auto shows and appeared on executive referral lists and hit them with multiple mailings about the new model. Toyota included locations of the dealers for the luxury cars so that prospects would be encouraged to go to the showrooms to look at them.

Segment Size   Although a project may score well on the first six criteria in Table 4-4, segmentation will not work unless the market is big enough to make the venture profitable. Even if initially profitable, a small niche may soon be saturated, as in the case of the hand-held vacuum cleaner market described in Marketing Strategies box 4-2. The main reason to worry about size is that segmentation strategies cost more than selling to everyone. Special ads, brochures, and promotions have to be created for individual groups of customers. Also, segmentation leads to smaller expenditures in a wide variety of promotional media, with a resulting loss in quantity discounts. You have to balance these increased costs against the profits produced by selling to relatively small groups of buyers. This issue is especially true with micromarketing.

Micromarketing   Store-specific marketing, often called *micromarketing,* has become possible for many consumer products because of the detailed marketing information

MARKETING STRATEGIES 4-2

DIRT DEVIL FLOODS NICHE

Royal Appliance Manufacturing struck gold in 1984 with a new idea: the bright red Dirt Devil hand-held electric vacuum cleaner, which outperformed battery-operated models. Sales grew exponentially from about $6 million in 1982 to $273 million in 1991. By making the great achievement of enlisting Kmart and Wal-Mart as its sales agents, Royal has been able to have its product in front of about 85% of America. Recently, however, demand has slackened for the hand-held Dirt Devil. They may have exhausted their best impulse customers by achieving impressive distribution. The company is now on its second wave of buyers, who are a tougher sale. The Dirt Devil is a product many households can use but hardly anyone needs. Therefore, Royal must drive demand with advertising. But as sales have slowed, advertising expenses have consumed a greater share of sales dollars, putting pressure on profits.

You must be aware of the size of your niche.

Source: Valerie Reitman, ''Royal Appliance Slips After Flooding Its Niche Market,'' *The Wall Street Journal*, July 30, 1992, p. B3.

now available. For example, one market research company in the United States, Market Metrics, collects statistics such as store size, volume, space devoted to various departments, and shopper sociodemographic profiles on 30,000 supermarkets, which it combines with consumption pattern studies. This permits the research company to rank specific stores based on how well they should sell a specific product. Borden, for instance, used micromarketing for its Classico pasta sauce. Classico carries a premium price—40 cents more than Prego and Ragu. The Classico target market is those who earn at least $35,000, live in dual-income households in metropolitan areas, and are interested in gourmet-style pasta sauces. A mass market approach would have been inappropriate; instead, a list of the best stores for the Classico consumers was generated. This permitted Borden to spend its money more efficiently. Some additional targeting examples are given in Table 4-5. Micromarketing not only helps big food companies, it also allows retailers to allocate store shelf space correctly.

TABLE 4-5
Targeting a Product's Best Customers and the Stores Where They Shop

Brand	Heavy User Profile	Lifestyle and Media Profile	Top Three Stores in New York City Area
Peter Pan Peanut Butter	Households with children headed by 18- to 54-year-olds, in suburban and rural areas	Heavy video renters Go to theme parks Below-average TV viewers Above-average radio listeners	*Foodtown Supermarket* 3350 Hempstead Turnpike Levittown, NY *Pathmark Supermarket* 3635 Hempstead Turnpike Levittown, NY *King Kullen Market* 398 Stewart Ave. Bathgate, NY
Stouffers Red Box Frozen Entrees	Households headed by people 55 and older, and upscale suburban households headed by 35- to 54-year-olds	Go to gambling casinos Give parties Involved in public activities Travel frequently Heavy newspaper readers Above-average TV viewers	*Dan's Supreme Supermarket* 69-62 188th St. Flushing, NY *Food Emporium* Madison Ave. & 74th St. NYC *Waldbaum's Supermarket* 196-35 Horace Harding Blvd. Flushing, NY
Coors Light Beer	Head of household, 21–34, middle to upper income, suburban and urban	Belong to a health club Buy rock music Travel by plane Give parties, cookouts Rent videos Heavy TV sports viewers	*Food Emporium* 1498 York Ave., NYC *Food Emporium* First Ave. & 72 St., NYC *Gristedes Supermarket* 350 E. 86th St., NYC

Source: Spectra Marketing Systems, with data from Information Resources Inc., Simmons Market Research Bureau, Claritas Corp., and *Progressive Grocer*; appeared in Michael J. McCarthy, "Marketers Zero in on Their Customers," *The Wall Street Journal*, March 18, 1991, pp. B1, B5.

PRODUCT DIFFERENTIATION

Our discussion of segmentation would not be complete without a consideration of product differentiation. Where segmentation focuses on groups of customers, *differentiation* emphasizes product differences to attract buyers. Both of these strategies are usually employed at the same time to achieve a sustainable competitive advantage (but not always; see Mattel's experience with a Barbie doll specifically tailored for the Japanese market described in Marketing Strategies box 4-3).

Using Differentiation

A diagram showing product differentiation in the coffee market is presented in Figure 4-3. The first change from ground coffee was the introduction of a powdered

MARKETING STRATEGIES 4-3

MATTEL, BARBIE, AND THE JAPANESE MARKET

Mattel, a U.S. toy maker, introduced its Barbie fashion doll to the Japanese consumers more than a decade ago. Mattel changed the look of its doll after its Japanese advisors insisted that a bosomy clotheshorse wouldn't appeal to Japanese girls. As a result, Barbie has sported the dark, doe-eyed look of an ingenue and a decidedly flatter chest than the voluptuous blue-eyed model sold everywhere else. Her limbs do not bend enough to allow her to hop casually into a Barbie-sized Ferrari or climb the steps to a Barbie-sized mansion. Mattel had only limited sales of lucrative accessories.

While market research did indicate that Japanese girls preferred what they had been conditioned to accept, Mattel would have profited from sticking to what works everywhere else. The enormous "World of Barbie" that it sells is one of fantasy and aspiration. In Japan, Mattel was never able to develop the concept because there were never any props. As a consequence, Mattel decided to sell its toys in Japan much as it sells them in the rest of the world, and to sell the same ones rather than specially designed versions.

You must be careful not to lose the original product concept when redesigning products for foreign target markets.

Source: Pauline Yoshihashi, "Now a Glamorous Barbie Heads to Japan," *The Wall Street Journal,* June 5, 1991, pp. B1, B8.

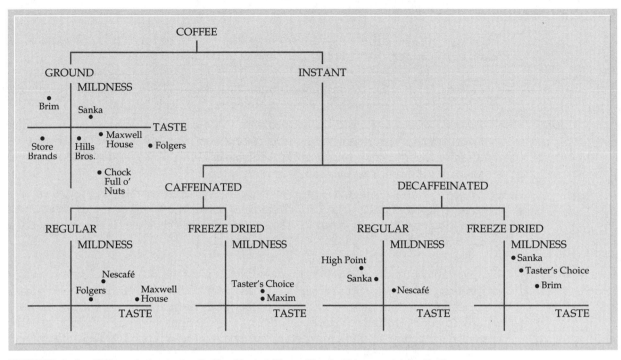

FIGURE 4-3 Differentiation in the Coffee Market (From Glen L. Urban and John R. Hauser, *Design and Marketing of New Products.* Englewood Cliffs, NJ: Prentice-Hall, 1980, p. 94.)

instant coffee for customers in a hurry. Then a way was found to remove the caffeine from coffee for those who do not want their sleep interrupted or who have been told by their doctors to cut down on their coffee consumption. The end result was a proliferation of different types of coffee to appeal to specialized customer segments. A similar explosion of product differences occurred with Coke. Where once there was a single Coke, we now have Classic Coke, Caffeine Free Coke, Diet Coke, Caffeine Free Diet Coke, Cherry Coke, and Diet Cherry Coke. Differentiation is more difficult when you are selling standard items like cement or metal strapping to business buyers. Decisions for these commodities are often based on the lowest bid price. The Lonestar Cement people have partially overcome this problem by developing a fast-drying, superstrong cement targeted at four segments: airport construction and restoration, highway and bridge-deck building and repairs, tunnel work, and precast construction. The cement will harden in just 4 hours instead of the 7 to 14 days required for regular cement to set. Its niche appeal permits Lonestar to charge twice the price of regular cement. Another way to deal with commodities is to broaden the concept of the product in the eyes of the buyer. A cement company could equip its trucks with radios and advertise itself as the on-time cement company.

Costs of Differentiation

Although product differentiation can help improve sales revenues, it is expensive. Some of the added costs of differentiation include the following:

- *Product Modifications.* Adapting products to meet the needs of different segments requires extra payments for R&D, engineering, and special tooling.
- *Shorter Production Runs.* Product proliferation means producing items in smaller lots. Instead of producing 5000 units of one item, you have to manufacture 1000 units of five different products. This increases setup times, and workers have to adapt to different routines.
- *Larger Inventories.* The more products you offer, the larger the inventories needed to meet the demand. This occurs because the safety stock required to meet unexpected variations in demand for several products exceeds the safety stock needed for one product.

The amount of differentiation that you employ should be determined by the impact on profits. For example, not long ago, customers could go into the showrooms of American auto manufacturers and order cars built to their exact specifications with regard to color, upholstery fabric, and 25 other options. However, this raised the costs of production, and the more standardized Japanese cars have been able to grab market share with lower prices. American car manufacturers have found that they can now make more money by offering less product differentiation. The use of a differentiation strategy forces managers to choose between additional revenues and the added costs of serving individual segments.

The high cost of differentiation raises the question of whether it is possible to gain the benefits of segmentation without actually changing the product. The answer is yes, but it requires careful market planning. Mercedes Benz has had a great deal of success selling the same cars to different market segments in Germany and America. In the United States, the Mercedes is sold as a luxury car for the rich and famous. In Germany, the Mercedes has a more popular image and is even used as a taxicab. This example shows that advertising and promotion can be used to position products to appeal to particular buyers.

MUST SEGMENTATION AND DIFFERENTIATION ALWAYS GO TOGETHER?

Market segmentation and product differentiation often are used together. For example, we mentioned that Anheuser Busch and the *Farm Journal* sell to special customer groups with beers and magazine editions that are physically different from one another. However, there are situations where segmentation is used without product differentiation and where differentiation is used without segmentation.

Apple Computer, for example, sells the same basic machines to both educators and businesses. Separate marketing programs are used to reach these segments, and differentiation is a minor issue. Product differentiation without segmentation is shown by P&G's advertising of Charmin toilet paper as softer than competing brands. P&G is attempting to make customers believe that there are differences in softness, but the company really wants to sell Charmin to everyone. The ideal combination of segmentation and/or differentiation strategies varies by products and the competitive environment.

SUMMARY

Segmentation is one of the most powerful strategies available to marketing managers. It requires variation in needs across customers and specialized media to reach the planned target segments. Also, customers have to respond to promotion, and there have to be enough buyers to make segmentation profitable. You must understand how segmentation's focus on customer groups interacts with product differentiation. For segmentation to be successful, your product or service must have a competitive edge.

SUGGESTED READING

Leavitt, Theodore. "Differentiation—of Anything," in *The Marketing Imagination* (New York: Free Press, 1983), pp. 72–93.

Rangan, V. Kasturi, Rowland T. Moriarty, and Gordon S. Swartz. "Segmenting Customers in Mature Industrial Markets," *Journal of Marketing,* Vol. 56 (October 1992), pp. 72–82.

FURTHER READING

Beane, T. P., and D. M. Ennis. "Market Segmentation: A Review," *European Journal of Marketing,* Vol. 21, No. 5 (1987), pp. 20–44.

Berrigan, John, and Carl Finkbeiner. *Segmentation Marketing: New Methods for Capturing Business Markets* (New York: Harper Business, 1992).

Bonoma, Thomas V., and Benson P. Shapiro. *Segmenting the Industrial Market* (Lexington, MA: Lexington Books, 1983).

Dickson, Peter R., and James L. Ginter. "Market Segmentation, Product Differentiation, and Marketing Strategy, *Journal of Marketing,* Vol. 51 (April 1987), pp. 1–10.

Frank, Ronald, William Massy, and Yoram Wind. *Market Segmentation* (Englewood Cliffs, NJ: Prentice-Hall, 1972).

Smith, Wendell R. "Product Differentiation and Market Segmentation as Alternative Marketing Strategies," *Journal of Marketing,* Vol. 21 (July 1956), pp. 3–8.

Wedel, Michel. *Clusterwise Regression and Market Segmentation* (Wageningen, the Netherlands: Wageningen Agricultural University, 1990).

QUESTIONS

1. How do you reconcile market segmentation with economies of scale? Is market segmentation inherently inefficient?

2. Who is more likely to shop in an upscale store: a young couple without children or a mortgage earning $26,000 or a couple with three children, mortgage payments, and future college tuition earning $75,000? Explain your reasoning.

3. Micromarketing permits a manufacturer to tailor in-store signs to different shopper lifestyles. How can you get store operators to sign off on store-specific programs? How can you change the culture of those chains with centralized operations that make buying and store formatting decisions largely at headquarters?

4. The product manager for Mom's Choice salt believes that its market can be segmented by degree of purchase—heavy buyers, average buyers, light buyers, and nonusers. Analysis of data from a consumer purchase panel showed three things. First, 90.9 percent of families made at least one purchase of some brand of salt during the year. Second, 24 percent of Mom's Choice brand buyers were heavy buyers and made 56 percent of the total brand purchases. The data for average buyers were 34 percent and 30 percent, and for light buyers 42 percent and 14 percent. A review of company records revealed some additional information. Annual sales were 1 million cases, packed 24 units of 12 oz each. One-half of the case sales were deal cases with the packages stickered "5 Cents Off." Advertising expenditures for the year were $1,560,000. The average price to the trade is $7.20 per case, with 50 percent of sales for manufacturing, packaging, distribution, and brokerage costs; 15 percent for overhead and taxes; and 5 percent for net profit after tax. Construct a profit and loss statement for each degree of purchase segment.

5. The focus on ever narrower niches places increased importance on database marketing. With this strategy, you can identify an individual customer and meet his or her needs. Discuss the increased responsibility for ethical marketing accompanying database marketing.

6. In 1980, women bought 3.28 million cars, accounting for 36 percent of all sales in the United States. By 1988, women were buying 4.91 million cars, or 47 percent of all cars sold. What implications do these figures have for auto manufacturers in terms of market segmentation and product differentiation?

7. A commercial truck dealership keeps extra trucks on standby in case a customer's truck breaks down. Spare trucks are delivered and loaned out until repairs are complete. In effect, customers do not buy a truck from this dealer, they buy the use of a truck—which is their true need. How does the dealer benefit? Can you think of other examples of bundling a good and a service together to better serve a customer?

8. Many vintners make dollar-a-pint street wines that are targeted at the poor, the homeless, and the skid-row alcoholic. For example, E. & J. Gallo Winery makes Thunderbird. These wines contain cheap ingredients and are fortified with extra alcohol. Discuss the ethical issues raised by the misery market.

9. Honda frets that the average age of Accord buyers is up to nearly 45 years from 35 to 40 in the early 1980s. Lincoln-Mercury wants their newer models to lure younger buyers than luxury divisions usually do. They have had some success. Lincoln-Mercury says that the average buyer of the Mark VIII is 52 years versus 58 years for the Mark VII. On the other hand, Buick is happy with an average buyer age of 60. Buick says, "One way to look at it is that the market is moving our way as the baby boomers age." Who has the right view: Honda and Lincoln-Mercury or Buick?

Chapter 5

Competitive Analysis and Product Positioning

A common problem is the assumption that competitors do things "the same way we do."

ALAN ZAKON

In business environments, domestic and international competitors are constantly attacking existing market positions. Firms that fail to respond to these challenges are destined for the scrap heap. Companies have come to realize that they must focus on global market share, not just domestic share. Toyota's "Global 10" strategy is based on their belief that they need at least 10 percent of the world market to remain strong. Gillette, the American consumer goods company, is the world leader in razor blades and razors. Its Papermate, Waterman, and Parker lines have a 15 percent revenue share of the world pen market; the next biggest competitor is Société BIC, with 8 percent. Gillette's Oral-B toothbrush is the leading seller in the United States and several international markets, and its Braun electric shaver is the top seller in Germany. Gillette sells in 200 countries. A key benefit of big market share is that it gives a company strong bargaining power with suppliers and distributors. Low costs mean that profits can grow faster than revenue.

Competitive analysis flows from customer analysis. To truly know how you stack up against your competitors, you must first understand your customers' wants and needs. Then you must identify current and potential competitors in both your served and unserved markets. Industry analysis is also important. You need to know about the suppliers to your industry, as well as about channel members who serve as intermediaries between you and your competitors and the end users. These actors influence your competitive position. Once you have identified your competitors, it may be possible to group them by factors, such as degree of specialization or degree of globalization, to make it easier to discern patterns of competitive behavior. Now you should be in a position to do an in-depth analysis of your competitors' strategies. You must be careful not to simply focus on what your competitors are doing now. You must consider where your competitors are going.

This chapter focuses on seven issues:

1. Who are your competitors?
2. What are your relations with your competitors?
3. How do you learn about your competitors?
4. Where do you compete?
5. When do you compete?
6. How do you compete?
7. How do you position your product?

In addressing these issues, a firm is examining its *s*trengths and *w*eaknesses, its *o*pportunities and *t*hreats. This is known as *SWOT* analysis.

WHO ARE YOUR COMPETITORS?

You must know which of the many companies in the marketplace you are really competing with for your served market. You should respond most vigorously to those in direct competition. You also must be aware of those potential competitors who are not now in your market but who may be in the future.

Current Competitors

One way of identifying who your competitors are is through *market structure analysis* using perceptual mapping. Products or brands that are perceived to be close together in perceptual space are more in competition with each other than are those far apart.

Perceptual Mapping Every market has a structure based on the strengths of brand attributes. The positioning of products in a market can be illustrated by a perceptual map such as the one shown in Figure 5-1 for automobiles. Perceptual maps are derived from customer data measuring similarities among brands. Customers are asked to rate each pair of brands (e.g., Buick–Porsche) on a scale from "very similar" to "very dissimilar." These ratings are fed into a computer program for doing multidimensional scaling.[1] The program determines the relative positions of the brands and prints out a perceptual map.

The location of the automobiles in Figure 5-1 is a direct measure of similarity across brands. Since Porsche and Plymouth are farthest apart, customers view them as least similar. Notice that Buick and Oldsmobile are seen as the most similar. This result agrees with the findings of Figure 4-2, which showed that these two brands were close in terms of customer age and income. General Motors has a terrible problem with Buick and Oldsmobile—you do not want to compete with yourself. Better positioning has been achieved for Cadillac, which is near Lincoln, and for Chevrolet,

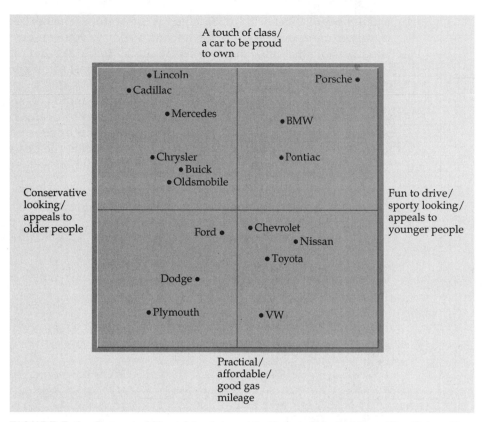

A touch of class/
a car to be proud
to own

• Lincoln   Porsche •
• Cadillac

• Mercedes   • BMW

• Chrysler   • Pontiac
• Buick
• Oldsmobile

Conservative   Fun to drive/
looking/   sporty looking/
appeals to   Ford •   • Chevrolet   appeals to
older people   • Nissan   younger people

                              • Toyota

           Dodge •

• Plymouth   • VW

Practical/
affordable/
good gas
mileage

FIGURE 5-1   Perceptual Map of the Automobile Market. (Adapted from "Car Makers Use 'Image' Map as Tool to Position Products," *The Wall Street Journal*, March 22, 1984, p. 33. Reprinted with permission of *The Wall Street Journal*, © Dow Jones & Company, Inc., 1984. All rights reserved)

which is near Ford. GM executives are sure to be ecstatic that the high-priced BMW is the closest car to Pontiac. This shows that Pontiac's marketing program has been effective in moving it into a desirable market position.

Map Dimensions   Dimensions for perceptual maps are not named by multidimensional scaling programs. Additional information must be gathered from customers to find the critical dimensions and locate them on the maps. Labeling dimensions of perceptual maps and interpreting these diagrams is rather subjective. This does not subtract from the value of perceptual maps, but it does mean that you have to evaluate them carefully.

Dimensions for perceptual maps are often obtained by asking customers to describe the benefits (e.g., economy, durability, ease of service) they associate with each of the brands. These ratings are then fitted to the perceptual space, as shown in Figure 5-1. In this diagram, the vertical axis has been named "A Touch of Class" at the top and ''Practical/Affordable'' at the bottom. The horizontal axis has a conservative/older dimension to the left and a sporty/younger dimension to the right. You may note that these dimensions are similar to the age and income axes of Figure 4-2. Although Figure 5-1 has two labeled dimensions, some perceptual maps have more and some fewer.

Perceptual map dimensions are vital in the preparation of marketing plans. Once you understand the dimensions that customers use to evaluate products, you are better able to design products to fill their needs. This applies both to modifications to strengthen the positions of existing products and to the design of new products to fill gaps in perceptual maps. In addition, map dimensions are useful when you

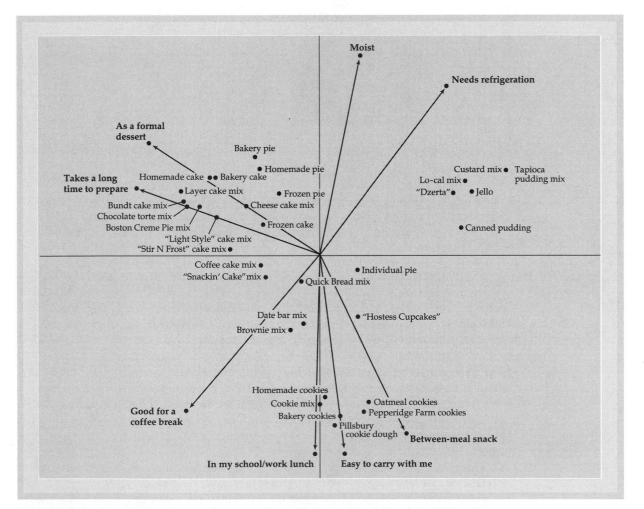

FIGURE 5-2 Mapping the Dessert Category. (From *Marketing News*, May 14, 1982, p. 3)

want to reposition products through the use of advertising. For example, GM has been successful in using advertising to give Pontiac a stronger sporty/youth image. In addition, Oldsmobile has run an ad campaign with the slogan "It's not your father's Oldsmobile" in an effort to attract younger buyers.

Key usage occasions can also be superimposed on a perceptual map. A perceptual map for the dessert category is shown in Figure 5-2. The arrows on the map indicate the relationship between market structure and product attributes and usage occasions. Products toward the bottom of the map are more portable and appropriate for snacks and lunch boxes. Those toward the top take more time to prepare and are more suitable as formal desserts.

Ideal Points   Once you have labeled the dimensions of your perceptual map, the next step is to add information on personal preferences. Each customer can be represented on your map by a point showing that individual's ideal product. Ideal points are person points. Clusters of ideal points indicate where there are sufficient prospects to justify current and new products.

Ideal points evolve from preference data. Customers can be formed into groups by cluster analysis using information on the distances between brands and individual ideal points.[2]

Potential Entrants

While focusing on your current competitors, you must be alert for the emergence of new competitors. The possibility of newcomers to an industry depends on two things: the barriers to entry that exist and expectations about competitive reactions.[3] The barriers to entry include economies of scale, product differentiation, capital requirements, buyer switching costs, access to distribution channels, other cost disadvantages, and government policy. These factors are often interrelated. The need for economies of scale requires capital for plant construction, while overcoming existing brand identification and customer loyalty through product differentiation requires capital for advertising. The costs of motivating a buyer to switch to your product from that of your competitor may be formidable. For example, many new software products are better than those already in use, yet they fail. The problem is not awareness of the product or of its price, but the cost to companies of retraining personnel to use it. A new entrant may find the best distributors already under contract and retailers demanding compensation to provide scarce space. Existing firms may also have proprietary product technology, favorable access to raw materials, favorable locations, government subsidies, or other cost advantages. Governments can limit or prevent entry with regulations such as licensing. An example of this is given in Marketing in Action box 5-1.

Potential entrants may be deterred if they expect a forceful competitive reaction. This may well occur when competitors have a past history of vigorous retaliation, an established position and significant resources to fight back, a commitment to the industry, and slow industry growth.

MARKETING IN ACTION 5-1

COMPETITORS NEED NOT APPLY: THE JAPANESE AUTOMOBILE AFTERMARKET

Potential foreign and domestic competitors alike are largely shut out of the Japanese automobile aftermarket industry for services and parts—a market twice as large as the Japanese telecommunications industry. Government and cultural restrictions pose barriers to entry protecting established repair shops.

The repair and inspection portion of the industry consists of general repairs (27 percent), accident repairs (27 percent), and periodic required inspections (46 percent). Japan's mandatory inspection law has created a huge market of motorists who bring their cars in for routine inspections to confirm road-worthiness and emission control operation. The profitability of the industry is attractive. Profit margins are on the order of 45 percent compared to about 10 percent for new and used car sales.

Why have not more competitors taken advantage of this opportunity? The answer lies in nonmarket, business–government relations. Under the Road Transportation Vehicle Act, the Ministry of Transportation has certified only a limited number of shops. The certification process makes it almost impossible for a new shop with a competitive position to be licensed. License applicants must be in approved zones, have proper equipment, and have a proper percentage of trained mechanics on the premises. Then the applications must be approved by the local and national levels of the Automobile Shop Association. In Tokyo the situation is even worse. The Motor Vehicle Law requires that new repair shops be at least 88 square meters in size. This requirement requires a prohibitively large investment for smaller firms. On the other hand, Tokyo law prohibits repair shops larger than 50 square meters. This excludes larger firms. These "catch-22" provisions obviously protect existing firms.

You must recognize that marketing is a game. Influencing rule making so that the rules of the game favor you is a legitimate activity.

Source: John C. Beck and John C. Pitteger, "Competitors Need Not Apply," *Marketing Management*, Vol. 1, No. 3 (1992), pp. 55–58.

WHAT ARE YOUR RELATIONS WITH YOUR COMPETITORS?

While the primary relationship with your competitors will be a competitive one, it may take some other form. The relationship between competitors is a continuum from conflict to collusion, passing through competition, coexistence, and cooperation along the way.[4]

Conflict

The focus of conflict is your opponent. Confrontation is likely to occur, for example, when you want to increase your market share in a stagnant market. You can gain share only by wresting it from competitors. More generally, conflict may occur when competitors have mutually incompatible objectives. Consider the maturing German ready-made pudding-with-topping market.[5] This market is dominated by four national brands. The remainder of the market is shared by about 30 regional and local competitors. The objectives of the competitors are as follows: Gervais-Danone, the market leader: hold share; Dr. Oetker, a late entrant: increase share; Elite: hold share; Chambourcy: hold share; and other players: increase share. These objectives are mutually inconsistent. They must lead to a fight.

Threats to a company's position may elicit a harsh reaction, especially in Japan.[6] When the president of Yamaha had the temerity to announce that Yamaha would be the domestic leader in motorcycles within one year and the world leader within two, Honda was incensed and adopted the motto "We will crush Yamaha." Honda did just that. It made numerous new product changes (113 changes to Yamaha's 37), increased promotional funds, and slashed prices. Yamaha's share shrank from 37 to 23 percent over the next 18 months. Accepting responsibility for this dismal performance, Yamaha's president resigned.

Competition

Competition is object centered. Competitors strive to win the same prize—the customer. The degree of competition will depend mainly on market attractiveness (market size and growth rate, economic climate, possibilities for economies of scale, technological innovation, differentiation, and segmentation) and industry structure (number of competitors, diversity of competitors and their commitment to the industry, ease of entry and barriers to exit). The competition among brands in an industry is often called the *battle of the brands*. An example of the battle of the brands is given in Marketing in Action box 5-2. Much of the remainder of the chapter will focus on these battles.

Coexistence

Coexistence is working toward a goal independently of others. Coexistence occurs when competitors define different niches of a market to dominate. For example, this happens in distribution, where retail outlets have local monopolies in their core geographic areas.

Cooperation

Cooperation involves working together toward a common goal. A typology of formal forms of cooperation is shown in Figure 5-3. For example, two agribusiness giants that have been longtime competitors are undertaking a joint venture. France's BSN, the world's largest yogurt manufacturer and owner of the Danone brand (Dannon in the United States), is joining forces with the British- and Dutch-owned Unilever, the world's leading ice cream maker, to develop and market an entirely new product combining ice cream and yogurt. Why are they cooperating? To counter the European marketing offensive launched by Grand Metropolitan, the British owner of Häagen-Dazs. The venture should not require extensive investment, as it will draw

BATTLE OF THE HEALTHY FROZEN FOOD BRANDS

The battle is at a boil. Healthy Choice is slugging it out with Lean Cuisine, in the No. 2 spot, and third place Weight Watchers. Each is serving up a medley of low-cholesterol, low-calorie dinners, desserts, and breakfast foods. The three leaders and lesser ranked brands are spending millions of dollars on frenetic promotions and marketing—and all this spending is eating into profits.

ConAgra succeeded in making Healthy Choice a top seller without cannibalizing sales of its other frozen food brands, Banquet and Armour. ConAgra controlled 23.5% of the frozen food market (8.6% for Healthy Choice), followed by Stouffer, a unit of Nestlé, with 21%; Campbell Soup, 15%; Kraft General Foods, a unit of Philip Morris, 13.8%; and Weight Watchers, a unit of H.J. Heinz, 7% (down from 10%). Stouffer, with its Lean Cuisine line, used to be the out-and-out leader until ConAgra leapfrogged them.

Healthy Choice has whetted the appetite of consumers who worry about their health but consider diet a four-letter word. When the brand came onto the market in 1989, it was not only low in calories but also claimed to be low in sodium and fat. A claim neither Weight Watchers or Lean Cuisine could make at the time. Healthy Choice broadened the entire category, bringing in people who'd never eaten frozen foods. Healthy Choice evokes images of joggers, while Weight Watchers conjures up images of fat homemakers.

Weight Watchers believes the battle is shifting to taste and away from fitness because all competitors are now achieving parity on salt, fat, and calorie content. As a

---

MARKETING IN ACTION 5-2 (continued)

result, they are promoting slimming with an added emphasis on taste as a benefit. Their television commercials pitch Weight Watchers with the slogan "Total indulgence, zero guilt," pounding rock music, and delectable close-ups of steaming entrées such as Chicken Kiev and gooey desserts like brownie á la mode.

Stouffer, which until the 1980s was the lean-frozen-food leader with its Lean Cuisine line, has lowered the sodium and fat contents of its entrées, introduced eight new recipes, and increased its marketing budget. Bragging in magazine ads that its products taste better than Healthy Choice, it offers consumers two Lean Cuisine coupons for every Healthy Choice coupon sent to the company. Among the other food giants, Kraft General Foods is concentrating on its Budget Gourmet line of Light and Healthy entrées and Campbell now offers Mrs. Paul's Healthy Treasures frozen-fish entrées as well as its higher priced Le Menu Healthy line.

ConAgra is not relenting. It has introduced Healthy Choice frozen dairy desserts, muffins, breakfast sandwiches, French bread pizza, and pasta entrées. For dieters enrolled in the Ultra Slim Fast program, the company introduced a line of entrées under the Ultra Slim Fast brand name; these dinners are slightly more expensive than Healthy Choice, but come in larger portions. It has also launched a frozen dinner line called Healthy Balance, which is less expensive than Healthy Choice.

Competition can make it difficult to turn a profit.

Source: Gabriella Stern, "Makers of 'Healthy' Frozen Foods Watch Profits Melt as Competition Gets Hotter," *The Wall Street Journal* (February 6, 1992), pp. B1, B6.

---

on the partners' existing research, development, and distribution resources. The frozen treats are to be marketed first in France and Spain, with other countries to follow.

Collusion

Collusion is cooperative behavior designed to injure third parties—customers, suppliers, noncolluding competitors, or the general public. Often collusive behavior is illegal. Collusion may be explicit, involving direct communication among the parties. Such communication may take place at trade association meetings or industry conventions. Sometimes the government is a party to collusion. The intent is to protect existing domestic firms, especially from foreign firms.

Collusion is sometimes indirect, which involves signaling. A firm can make an announcement to test competitors' sentiments. Competitive firms then can reply by making announcements communicating their pleasure or displeasure with competitive developments in the industry. If the industry responds negatively, the firm need not follow through with its intended action.[7]

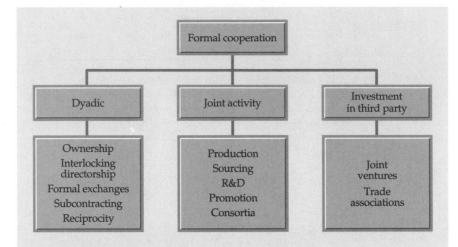

FIGURE 5-3 Typology of Forms of Formal Intercompetitor Cooperation. (From Geoffrey Easton, "Relationships Among Competitors," in *The Interface of Marketing and Strategy*, George Day, Barton Weitz, and Robin Wensley, eds. [Greenwich, CT: Jai Press, 1990], p. 73)

HOW DO YOU LEARN ABOUT YOUR COMPETITORS?

The more and better the competitive information available to you, the sounder will be your marketing decisions. To be helpful, competitive information must be processed in a methodical manner. This involves five steps.[8]

1. Set up an information-gathering system for competitive analysis.
2. Identify your competitors.
3. Gather information through a competitive audit.
4. Evaluate competitive information.
5. Integrate this information into your planning process on a regular basis.

This process forces you to consider competitive actions and reactions in formulating and executing your marketing strategies and tactics.

The *competitive audit* can generate a lot of information about your competitors. You must decide what is worth keeping. Each piece of information has to be evaluated on the basis of source reliability and information accuracy. An example of a competitor profile that comes out of a competitive analysis is given in Table 5-1. This profile is for a competitor of a software company that produces and markets high-quality, high-value products to satisfy the educational and productivity needs of consumers and students in the home and educational marketplaces.

You are now in a position to formulate your marketing strategy by considering three key issues: where to compete, when to compete, and how to compete. We conclude with a discussion of product positioning.

TABLE 5-1
Competitor Profiling

Name	Broderbund
Strengths	• "Hot" products—item merchandisers
	• First mover in "genres"
	• Probably attract free-lance authors
	• "Good enough product"/user accessible
	• 20% tech—80% need of customer
	• 30% mass volume retailers, 70% specialty
	• Not promotional or price oriented
	• Reduced administrative cost from 21% to 13%
	• International dealings, good connection with Japan
Weaknesses	• Lack of franchise on names
	• Milk products
	• Need items
	• Marketing not POS
	• Second-rate packaging
	• Apple is 60% of sales, IBM only 16%
General information	• Planning product line based on hobbies and pursuits
	• Games account for 20% of sales
	• Policies set in stone, they do not bargain and are tough to work with
	• Support distributors, do not sell direct
	• Sales management left, company run by finance people
	• Bought Synapse, may be looking for others

Source: Natalie Tabb Taylor, "Springboard Software," American Case Research Association, 1988.

WHERE DO YOU COMPETE?

Choosing market arenas to seek competitive advantage depends on market attractiveness and organization strengths. Your job as marketing manager is to pick the best of a variety of strategic options. Most firms compete somewhere on a continuum from "avoid competition" to "attack market leader." You also have the choice of playing by the existing rules of the game or changing the rules in your favor. To help clarify these choices, McKinsey[9] has created a strategic game board shown in Figure 5-4. Decisions on where to compete are shown as core market or niche strategies. The choice of how to compete is between strategies based on old or new rules. When competing in an existing core market using existing rules, the firm must do more and better of the same. This may be acceptable if your organization is the market leader. However, other firms must hope that the leader experiences marketing inertia or that some disruption occurs in the marketplace. Consequently, many

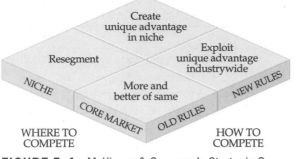

FIGURE 5-4 McKinsey & Company's Strategic Game Board. (From *Advertising Age*, January 21, 1983, p. 22)

firms try to resegment the market and target a niche. This can be successful, at least in the short run. The danger is that the niche may grow and attract other, larger firms.

To achieve a sustainable competitive advantage (SCA), you must try to redefine the rules of competition to create a unique advantage in a niche or an entire industry. For a long time, the profitability of the U.S. blue jeans industry was low. The core market was dominated by Levi Strauss and Blue Bell, maker of Wrangler jeans. Nonetheless, low barriers to entry let almost 100 small jeans manufacturers come into the market. These manufacturers were squeezed by both their suppliers and buyers. Denim was primarily produced by only four large textile companies. The small manufacturer had to accept the price charged by the textile company. Their bargaining position was no better with their buyers. Most jeans were bought by a small number of buyers representing the major retail chains. The small manufacturer had to sell at the price the buyer wanted to pay. Jordache changed the rules of the game by creating designer jeans through the use of heavy advertising. The heavy advertising caused a strong consumer preference, which, in turn, reduced the power of the chain buyer and allowed Jordache to set prices. Jordache established a niche that was defensible against its imitators. The "creative initiative" required *marketing imagination.*

WHEN DO YOU COMPETE?

The ability to compete often depends on *strategic windows* of opportunity. Strategic windows are openings in the competitive map that can be exploited at a point in time. Remember that windows that are open one moment can be closed another. To take advantage of strategic windows, you first have to be able to see them; then you have to be ready to make a move before they close. This requires insight and flexibility.

Table 5-2 provides several examples of strategic windows and shows how four firms reacted. The rapid penetration of microwave ovens into American homes opened a large strategic window for cookware. Metal pans could not be used in these ovens, so everyone buying a microwave oven was an immediate customer for new pots and pans. Corning was in an excellent position to take advantage of this technology change, as it was expert at making ceramic and glass dishes for conventional ovens. However, the company did not interpret this opportunity correctly and failed to push existing items or develop new ones until competitors had grabbed strong market positions. This lack of attention to market conditions for mature product lines is all too common and may explain why Corning spun off its housewares division to a Mexican firm.

In the case of home-delivered pizza (Table 5-2), Pizza Hut and other national chains had strong national positions in restaurant-served pizza long before Domino's came along. However, Domino's was the first to see the open window of the home-delivered-pizza customer and moved rapidly to sew up many of these markets. Dom-

TABLE 5-2

Examples of Strategic Windows

Company	Window Opportunity	Opportunity Seized	Marketing Strategy
Corning Glass Works (microwave cookware)	The microwave oven boom created a major need for "safe" cookware. Corning could immediately meet the needs of this emerging market.	No	Delayed aggressively marketing existing products and developing new products until after competitors had gained important market positions.
Domino's Pizza (home-delivered pizza)	Recognition of consumers' needs for rapid and reliable home delivery of pizza. No major competitive force was present at the time Domino's entered the market.	Yes	Responsive home delivery of pizza from a network of retail outlets. The company emphasizes quality, speed of delivery, courteous employees, and hot pizza.
Lens Crafters (eyewear chain)	Opportunity to develop customer-responsive services in an industry dominated by optometrists.	Yes	Launched a chain of retail shops conveniently located in malls, offering eye exams and one-hour glasses.
United Airlines (air travel)	Deregulation, restructuring, and an opportunity for marketing leadership due to dominant position in U.S. market. Held strong market position at the time of deregulation.	No	Did not expand services and marketing capabilities to strengthen position and gain advantage. United lost market position to more aggressive competitors.

Source: David W. Cravens, "Gaining Strategic Marketing Advantage," *Business Horizons*, Vol. 31, No. 4 (September–October 1988), p. 53.

ino's strategy put Pizza Hut on the defensive and forced it to play an expensive game of catchup. Two different strategies followed by two firms that were the first to see the window of opportunity in the office supply discount business are described in Marketing Strategies box 5-1.

Vulnerability of Market Leaders

Market leaders can be vulnerable to external forces beyond their control. These forces include government or environmental challenge, a random catastrophe, a change in industry technology, and a new personality in the industry. A government or environmental challenge can distract a market leader and weaken brand loyalty. When the Federal Trade Commission (FTC) attacked Listerine's claim that its mouthwash "fought colds," Procter & Gamble launched new brands and ran comparative advertisements. Even more dangerous is a random catastrophe. Tylenol was having no trouble fending off Datril and Anacin II in the analgesic market until several deaths occurred due to criminal tampering with the product. A new personality—a successful firm in a related or even different industry—may be able to transfer its marketing expertise to the market leader's industry.

The technology used in an industry may change because of the expiration of patents or the emergence of new technologies. The expiration of patents is less of a problem than it appears to be. This is because a firm usually builds substantial brand equity during its period of patent protection. This raises a barrier of high marketing costs that any new entrant must overcome. Perhaps the most common challenge to market leaders is the introduction by competitors of new products for market niches. Two market leaders that handled this confrontation differently are Gillette and Schwinn.

Gillette invented the safety razor and has long dominated the U.S. wet shaving market. In 1962, a relatively small company, Wilkinson Sword, Ltd., introduced the first coated stainless steel blade, cutting sharply into Gillette's market share. Gillette swallowed its pride and brought out its own stainless steel blade. This humbling experience taught Gillette several important lessons: (1) Never take a rival for granted, no matter how small it is. (2) Don't concede market niches to competitors because market niches have a way of growing. (3) Don't dally in bringing out new products for fear of cannibalizing old ones; if you don't introduce them, competitors will. Gillette's obsession with defending its core market led to the expenditure of hundreds of millions of dollars on new shaving products. These efforts resulted in the innovative twin-blade Track II in 1972, the pivoting head Atra in 1977, and the hugely successful Sensor, with independently suspended blades, in 1989. The company also rushed out a disposable razor in 1976 to fend off the French rival Bic, even though the cheap throwaways cut into the sales of higher-profit Gillette products. The net result of Gillette's attention to its core shaving business is that it has 64 percent of the U.S. market, 70 percent of the European market, and 80 percent of the Latin American market.

Schwinn, on the other hand, failed to implement strategies to protect its strong position in the U.S. bicycle market. Schwinn started selling bikes in 1895 and for

STRATEGY SELECTION

Since opening in 1986, two firms have dominated the U.S. discount office supply business. Staples of Newton, Massachusetts, and Office Depot of Boca Raton, Florida, now operate over 300 stores with annual sales in excess of $1 billion. These firms were among the first to recognize the potential of the office products discount store. They buy large quantities of office supplies and sell them at 50 percent of retail prices—thus tapping demand among businesses too small to get such discounts on their own.

Although both firms are successful, they have chosen sharply different marketing strategies. Staples follows a strategy of slow growth focused on company-owned distribution centers. Regional distribution centers allow Staples to cut the cost of handling shipments from suppliers and to put up smaller stores without much backup inventory. This strategy has worked well in high-cost urban markets on the East and West Coasts. Office Depot avoids centralization, choosing instead to ship goods directly from suppliers to stores. With reserve stock on the premises, Office Depot outlets are some of the industry's largest. Inventory costs are offset by a policy of expansion in smaller, less expensive cities. Since Office Depot stores are not tied to distribution centers, units can be built quickly and farther apart. This has allowed Office Depot to expand faster and to be first in many markets.

The ability of both Staples and Office Depot to succeed while following sharply different strategies shows that markets, especially expanding new ones, can support more than one strategy. You must know if your competitors are doing business a different way than you are.

Source: Michael Selz, "Office Supply Firms Take Different Paths to Success," *The Wall Street Journal*, May 30, 1991, B2.

years was the dominant U.S. brand. Its market share peaked in the 1960s, with over 25 percent of the market. Schwinn's market position was based on a reputation for quality and a powerful distribution system of exclusive dealers. However, in the 1980s the company made a series of strategic blunders. Customer interest shifted to mountain bikes and exotic frames made of aluminum and carbon fiber. Schwinn refused to spend money to develop new products for these niche markets. It became a follower instead of a product innovator. Unfortunately for Schwinn, the mountain bike niche grew to command 60 percent of the market. Then, in 1981, workers at its main plant in Chicago went on strike. Instead of settling, Schwinn closed the plant and shipped its engineers and equipment to a plant in Taiwan that it did not own. This move cut production costs but led to quality problems and overdependence on foreign suppliers. Schwinn's delays in developing new products and its shift to overseas production resulted in its sale in bankruptcy court in 1993. The lesson to be learned from Gillette and Schwinn is that firms that fail to protect their markets from competitors often regret it.

When there is no strong number two firm in a market, a competitor seeking to fill the vacuum often damages the leader in the process. Ragu held 70 percent of the U.S. spaghetti sauce market compared to Chef Boy-R-Dee's 11 percent. The lack of a strong number two brand attracted Hunt's Prima Salsa and Campbell's Prego into the market. Prego emerged as the new number two brand at the expense of Ragu.

Market leaders may be leery of cutting price because they will lose the most from this strategy. Even in mature markets, new positioning opportunities arise. Dial's standing in the deodorant soap market was endangered by new soaps that used "refreshing" as their appeal. If a market leader is a small firm with limited resources, it is very vulnerable. Tampax, a market leader in the tampon market, has had to face the assaults of Procter & Gamble and Johnson & Johnson, as well as toxic shock syndrome scares. Finally, a strong number two company may not have the same distribution as the leader. The temptation for the number two firm is to expand its coverage into new markets.

A market leader has only itself to blame if it is lethargic, has a significant strategic weakness, or has alienated a key distribution channel. Lethargy may arise because the leader is conservative and fails to make a commitment to raise the stakes for competitors, favors financial goals over marketing goals, is in a market that makes up only a small part of the firm's overall business, fears cannibalism, or is preoccupied elsewhere. Family-owned businesses such as Wrigley in gum are often slow to introduce new products, opening themselves up to competitive initiatives. Vlasic was able to attack and become number one in pickles because pickles were a relatively inconsequential market to Heinz and Borden. Coca-Cola was very slow to take advantage of Coke's tremendous market identification because the company did not want to dilute the Coke name. John Deere was able to wrest the farm equipment leadership away from International Harvester because IH was focusing its attention on trucks. A leader may have a significant weakness in its strategy. Hershey's long-standing policy against national media advertising made it vulnerable to a challenge by Mars. Lastly, the leader may alienate key distributors. This may result in the competition's using the betrayed channel to gain ground or the channel itself may emerge as a competitor. For example, Lee jeans took advantage of the opportunity that arose when Levi Strauss stopped using jeans stores exclusively to add new mass merchandising outlets. These examples suggest that followers must be sensitive to market leaders' problems so that they can be exploited to gain share.

HOW DO YOU COMPETE?

In the battle with competitors, organizations must decide what dimensions to attack or defend. This decision is based, in part, on the size of the firm relative to its competitors. It also depends on the strategies that are viable in a particular industry.

Attack Strategies

The guiding principle for attack is to concentrate strength against the competitor's relative weakness. Attack strategies include (1) frontal attack, (2) flanking attack, (3) encirclement attack, (4) bypass attack, and (5) guerrilla warfare. These strategies are diagrammed in Figure 5-5. A *frontal attack* means challenging a competitor head on. This is one of the most difficult and dangerous of all marketing strategies. To be successful, the firm must have a substantial marketing advantage or deep pockets. For instance, the firm might have a similar product but be able to sell it at a lower price. A *flanking attack* is used in segments of the market where customers' needs are not being fully met. This may simply mean fighting in geographical regions of a country, or of the world, where the competition is weak. More likely, it means bring-

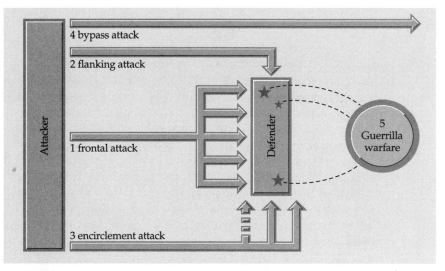

FIGURE 5-5 Attack Strategies. (From Philip Kotler and Ravi Singh, "Marketing Warfare in the 1980's," *Journal of Business Strategy* [Winter 1981], reprinted in *McKinsey Quarterly* [Summer 1981], pp. 62–81)

ing out new products for emerging segments of the market. Flanking addresses gaps in existing market coverage of the competition. An *encirclement attack*, known also as an *envelopment attack*, involves forcing the competitor to spread its resources thin by probing on many fronts at once. Again, superior resources are required. The intent is to break the competitor's will. A *bypass attack* is one of nonconfrontation. The firm diversifies into unrelated products or diversifies into new markets for existing products. *Guerrilla warfare* entails small, intermittent attacks on a competitor. One goal might be to slice off small amounts of share while evoking a minimal competitive reaction.

One of the most common attack strategies includes flanking rivals with new products. Research suggests that product pioneers have higher market shares than late entrants.[10] Those who challenge incumbent businesses believe that a new brand can achieve an SCA based on one or more of the following:

1. Price differentiation.
2. Improved quality.
3. Product line width.

4. Segmentation.
5. Improved services.
6. Distribution innovation.

For example, in the 1980s, Minolta was number two behind Canon in the U.S. 35mm camera market. Minolta decided to try a new product strategy to regain the top spot. After a major engineering effort, Minolta introduced the computerized Maxxum camera. This camera had a number of advanced focusing features and was sold at a premium price. Within a year, the new strategy had secured the number one market position for Minolta and other firms were scrambling to catch up.

Defense Strategies

Defense strategies exist to counter each attack strategy. The six main defense strategies are (1) position defense, (2) mobile defense, (3) preemptive defense, (4) flank positioning defense, (5) counteroffensive defense, and (6) strategic withdrawal. These are diagrammed in Figure 5-6. The *position defense* requires that the firm fortify its existing position. The main risk in this strategy is marketing myopia. A *mobile defense* is a defense in depth. The firm engages in market broadening. Unattacked markets can subsidize the firm's activities in more competitive markets. A *preemptive defense* involves attacking first. This first-strike strategy can use any of the attack strategies previously mentioned. The *flank positioning defense* extends the firm's offerings into new segments to protect the positioning of the firm's existing products. The *counteroffensive defense* involves amassing resources and counterattacking whenever threatened. Sometimes a strategic withdrawal is necessary. With this approach, firms consolidate their positions by competing only where they have competitive advantages.

Defensive Tactics   Most defensive strategies are built around three classes of defensive tactics: raising structural barriers, increasing expected retaliation, and lowering

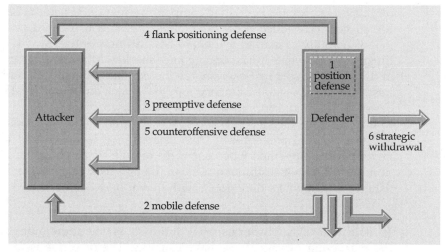

FIGURE 5-6 Defense Strategies. (From Philip Kotler and Ravi Singh, "Marketing Warfare in the 1980's," *Journal of Business Strategy* [Winter 1981], reprinted in *McKinsey Quarterly* [Summer 1981], pp. 62–81)

the inducement for attack. The emphasis is on deterring a competitor from taking action against you. Market leaders can raise *structural barriers* by filling product or positioning gaps, blocking channel access, raising buyer switching costs, raising the cost of gaining trial, increasing scale and capital requirements, or encouraging government policies that create barriers. Product or positioning gaps can be filled by flanking brands and fighting brands. Channel access can be blocked by the use of exclusive dealerships; the proliferation of products, brands, varieties, and sizes; and aggressive trade promotions. Buyer switching costs can be raised by providing special services. The cost of gaining trial can be raised by customer sales promotions. Scale economies and capital requirements can be increased by increasing advertising expenditures, introducing new products, extending warranty coverage, and providing below-market credit financing.

A market leader must let its competitors know that there will be *retaliation* for any attacks on it. A firm can signal its intentions through public statements at trade meetings and in the business press. In particular, the firm can resolve to match or beat any competitive move. Actual attacks can be blunted by disrupting market tests or introductory markets. A market leader can *lower the inducement* for attack by reducing its own profit targets or by manipulating competitors' assumptions about the future of the industry.

A number of promotional tactics can be used to protect the market positions of established brands from new product introductions. The idea is to attack new brands when they are vulnerable by foregoing short-run profits to retard or block the entry of competitive items. A classic approach is to introduce additional brands in the same product class to preempt shelf space and to deprive actual or potential competitors of profits or resources needed to compete in a market. Procter & Gamble, for example, has successfully added other detergents to protect its leading brand, Tide.

The ability of market leaders to fend off new entrants with defensive tactics is illustrated by events in the orange juice market. Minute Maid, made by Coca-Cola, and Tropicana, sold by Seagram, are the dominant deep-pocket players in this business. Procter & Gamble launched a frontal attack on the two market leaders with its Citrus Hill brand. P&G advertised heavily, used cents-off coupons, added calcium to its juice, and tried a screw-top spout. Minute Maid and Tropicana fought P&G's every move and prevented it from establishing needed brand loyalty. Citrus Hill never gained more than 8 percent of the orange juice market, and P&G finally abandoned it after an investment of $200 million. Defensive strategies can work for established brands; where they don't, withdrawal may be necessary.

Withdrawal   The proper use of withdrawal is one of the more delicate maneuvers the marketing manager may have to make. The objective is to cut the company's losses so that resources can be moved to businesses with better prospects for growth. However, many managers are reluctant to give up on a business for fear that the finger pointing will hurt their careers. An example of a typical scenario occurred at Pet, Inc., when the Whitman's Chocolates unit it purchased did not live up to expectations. Pet responded by firing the manager and selling the business. A better job of strategic withdrawal has been done by Johnson & Johnson. It continuously reviews its businesses to make sure they are fit and performing up to company standards. J&J takes the attitude that pruning the business tree of unhealthy units is a natural activity when following a growth strategy. One J&J manager closed down a kidney-dialysis equipment business and a heart surgery equipment business before he became the manager of a successful disposable contact lens business.

HOW DO YOU POSITION YOUR PRODUCT?

You have been introduced to the concepts of segmentation and differentiation. We will now consider how customers view products relative to the competition. Product positioning focuses on buyers' perceptions about the location of brands within specific market segments. These positions are based on how well perceived product characteristics match the needs of the buyer.

The Majority Fallacy

Marketing managers are often concerned with positioning new products in established markets. Companies that are the first in a market can position themselves to appeal to the majority of customers, but this strategy has less attraction for firms that enter late. Some of the factors influencing this decision can be shown by using the preference distribution described in Figure 5-7. The distribution shows the proportion of customers that prefer each of three different levels of chocolate flavoring for ice cream. Preferences are displayed both as a histogram and as the smooth distribution that would result if many flavors of ice cream had been evaluated by buyers.

This diagram suggests that if three levels of chocolate flavoring were available, 60 percent of the customers would choose medium, 20 percent would select light, and 20 percent would choose heavy. With these preferences known, the first company to enter the market would maximize revenue by selling ice cream with a medium level of chocolate flavoring. However, if three companies divide the medium-chocolate-flavored market equally, then the optimum position for succeeding entries is not immediately clear. If a new firm compared customer preferences for a light level of flavoring with the medium-level brands already on the market, the medium-chocolate ice cream would be preferred by most customers. Unfortunately, the firm might interpret these results to mean that the best way to enter the market would be with a medium-chocolate-flavored ice cream. A new medium flavor might be expected to capture one-fourth of the 60 percent in the middle or only about 15 percent of the total market. The potential for a new light flavor, by comparison, is a full 20 percent of the customers. This example shows how the *majority fallacy* can lead an unwary firm to merely duplicate existing characteristics. The fallacy is that competition is ignored. Obviously, the majority of consumers do not have to prefer a particular product for it to be successful.

One product category that illustrates the majority fallacy is spaghetti sauce. A few years ago, relatively little product variation existed and most brands imitated the dominant brand, Ragu. Ragu occupied a position near the center of a continuum from heavy, rich, spicy sauces on one end to light, thin, sweet sauces on the other. Hunt tried to exploit differences in spaghetti sauce by introducing its Prima Salsa

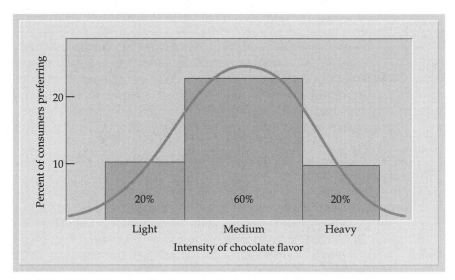

FIGURE 5-7 Customer Preferences for Chocolate Flavoring of Ice Cream

brand, which was much thicker and zestier than Ragu sauce. Hunt compared its new thick sauce directly with Ragu, using personal testimonials and a heavy schedule of TV and print ads. Prima Salsa's initial success attracted Campbell Soup, which introduced more spaghetti sauce variations under its Prego label. Prego was helped by a *Consumer Reports* article that rated its salt-free flavor as the best available. As a result, Ragu was forced to add various new products of its own. Today Ragu and Prego continue to bring out new flavors of spaghetti sauce to appeal to special segments of the market.

Repositioning Strategies

Perceptual maps with dimensions and clusters of customer ideal points are valuable for the management of new and existing products. Two frequent problems are deciding whether to reposition a product and in what direction to move. These issues usually involve a trade-off between maintaining the benefits of the existing position and possible sales gains associated with new positions. When your current position is weak, it is easier to make a case for repositioning. For example, in the early 1970s, Miller beer was sold as the "Champagne of bottled beers" to the high-income lighter beer drinking segment. When Philip Morris bought the brand, it had only 3.4 percent of the market, and the company decided to reposition Miller to appeal to heavier-drinking blue-collar buyers. The "Miller Time" campaign featuring working men enjoying a Miller at day's end successfully moved the brand up to 22 percent of the market.

Creating Gaps   Repositioning decisions are more difficult when there is something to lose. For example, Chrysler interpreted the perceptual map shown in Figure 4-5 to suggest that its cars needed a more youthful image. The company also concluded that Plymouth and Dodge needed to move up on the luxury scale. If Chrysler is successful in its efforts to appeal to a more youthful market, then it is giving up the conservative older market to Buick and Oldsmobile. Further, if Plymouth and Dodge are repositioned as luxury cars, what will Chrysler have to sell to buyers interested in practical, low-priced cars? These examples suggest that you must ensure that repositioning does not create new markets to be exploited by your competition.

In addition, you should realize that a gap in a perceptual map does not necessarily mean that there is an attractive market waiting to be exploited. Customers' preferences change over time, and a gap may mean that few buyers are currently interested in that combination of product attributes. This suggests that you need to know the number of potential buyers involved before you rush in to fill a gap in a perceptual map.

Serving Multiple Segments   Another problem is how to keep one set of customers happy while attracting new segments needed to build future sales. Philip Morris built Miller Lite into the best-selling low-calorie beer with an advertising campaign featuring retired jocks. These commercials did not go over well with young people, and Miller Lite had only 16.6 percent of young drinkers. Anheuser-Busch attacked this weakness with the Spuds MacKenzie "party animal" campaign to grab 23 percent of the younger light-beer market. Miller Lite then had the delicate task of pleasing young drinkers without alienating its older loyalist segment. Any firm that expects to survive in the long run must find a way to capture a share of the entry-level buyers.

Cannibalism   A common reason for repositioning is the discovery that you have two brands occupying the same location on a perceptual map. This generally leads to an unacceptable level of cannibalism. For example, Procter & Gamble found that customers perceived two of its detergents as being identical. In this particular case, P&G dropped one brand rather than attempt repositioning. However, merging Buick and Oldsmobile is not a very attractive alternative to General Motors. It has spent millions of dollars establishing name recognition and dealer networks for each of these brands. GM is naturally reluctant to throw this money away. Instead, it is trying to separate these two cars in the minds of the customer with styling changes and some youth-oriented advertising for Oldsmobile.

SUMMARY

Successful marketing strategies are often based on differentiation, market focus, and lower costs. Firms must identify windows of opportunity and select appropriate attack and defense strategies if they expect to reach organizational goals. Measure performance against your corporate mission; this will prevent you from overreacting to competitors.

Strategic marketing involves selecting a target market and positioning your product relative to competitive products. Various elements of the marketing mix are selected to be consistent with the chosen strategy. This is one of the most fundamental concepts of marketing.

NOTES

1. Mark L. Davison, *Multidimensional Scaling* (New York: Wiley, 1983).
2. For a discussion of cluster analysis, see Girish Punj and David W. Stewart, "Cluster Analysis in Marketing Research: Review and Suggestions for Application," *Journal of Marketing Research*, Vol. 20 (May 1983), pp. 134–148.
3. This section is based on Michael E. Porter, *Competitive Strategy* (New York: Free Press, 1980), pp. 7–17.
4. This section borrows heavily from Geoffrey Easton, "Relationships Among Competitors," in *The Interface of Marketing and Strategy*, George Day, Barton Weitz, and Robin Wensley, eds. (Greenwich, CT: Jai Press, 1990), pp. 57–100.
5. Reinhard Angelmar, "Gervais-Danone," in Douglas J. Dalrymple and Leonard J. Parsons, *Marketing Management*, 5th Ed. (New York: Wiley, 1990), pp. 405–413.
6. David B. Montgomery, "Understanding the Japanese as Customers, Competitors, and Collaborators," *Japan and the World Economy*, Vol. 3 (1991), pp. 61–91.

7. You must be able to distinguish between market signals that are truthful indications of a competitor's intentions and those that are bluffs. See Michael E. Porter, *Competitive Strategy* (New York: Free Press, 1980), pp. 75–87.

8. These steps are from K. Michael Haywood, "Scouting the Competition for Survival and Success," in *Marketing: The Art and Science of Business Management*, A. Dale Timpe, ed. (New York: Facts on File, 1989), pp. 129–141. The many kinds of information you should consider collecting are listed in his Figure 1.

9. Roberto Buaron, "New Game Strategies," *The McKinsey Quarterly* (Spring 1981), pp. 24–40.

10. William T. Robinson and Claes Fornell, "Sources of Market Pioneer Advantages in Consumer Goods Industries," *Journal of Marketing Research*, Vol. 22 (August 1985), pp. 305–317.

SUGGESTED READING

Day, George S., and Robin Wensley, "Assessing Advantage: A Framework for Diagnosing Competitive Superiority," *Journal of Marketing*, Vol. 52 (April 1988), pp. 1–20.

FURTHER READING

Abell, Derek F. "Strategic Windows," *Journal of Marketing*, Vol. 42, No. 3 (July 1978), pp. 21–26.

Duro, Robert. *Winning the Marketing War: A Practical Guide to Competitive Advantage* (New York: Wiley, 1989).

Easton, Geoffrey. "Relationships Among Competitors," in *The Interface of Marketing and Strategy*, George Day, Barton Weitz, and Robin Wensley, eds. (Greenwich, CT: Jai Press, 1990), pp. 57–100.

Haywood, K. Michael. "Scouting the Competition for Success," in *Marketing: The Art and Science of Business Management*, A. Dale Timpe, ed. (New York: Facts on File, 1989), pp. 129–141.

Oxenfeldt, Alfred R., and William L. Moore, "Customer or Competitor: Which Guideline for Marketing?" *Management Review* (August 1978), pp. 43–48.

Porter, Michael E. *Competitive Strategy* (New York: Free Press, 1980).

Porter, Michael E. *Competitive Advantage* (New York: Free Press, 1985).

QUESTIONS

1. Dun & Bradstreet's A. C. Nielsen division is the world's largest market research firm, with annual revenues of over $1 billion. A new entrant, Information Resources Incorporated (IRI), has achieved sales of over $200 million a year by focusing on the sale of checkout scanner data from a sample of 2400 stores. Why did Nielsen let IRI run off with the scanner data market niche?

2. Jug wines made from a blend of inexpensive grapes have 64 percent of the U.S. table wine market. However, the sales of jug wines are falling 4 percent per year. To combat this slump, Vintners International plans to introduce a new line of fine varietal wines to compete with traditional fine wines. Most of Vintners' current business is in jug wines sold under the Paul Masson label. The new wines are made from 75 percent of a particular grape and will be called Vintners Selections. They also will have new bottles and a new advertising campaign and will sell for $5 to $6 per bottle. Fine varietal wines currently have 5 percent of the market and sell for $7 to $50 per bottle. What marketing strategy is Vintners International pursuing? Would it be easier for it to sell its new varietal wines under its established Paul Masson label?

3. The leading cigarette in America, Marlboro, sold by Philip Morris, recorded a 5 percent decline in sales in 1992. Some believe the decline was related to seven Marlboro price increases that occurred over a two-year period. Marlboro now sells for over $2 a pack, and its competitor, R. J. Reynolds's off-price Monarchs, sells for $1. Others believe that Marlboro's sales decline was caused by cannibalism by Philip Morris's own low-priced Cambridge cigarettes. Philip Morris makes an estimated 55 cents on the sale of each pack of Marlboro and 5 cents a pack from Cambridge. Why did Philip Morris continue to raise Marlboro's price in the face of new low-priced competitors, and what should it do with its Marlboro and Cambridge brands?

4. The perceptual map for six antidepressant drugs is shown in Figure 5-8. Which two drugs are most similar? Most dissimilar? Rank Segment 5 on drug preferences from most preferred to least preferred.

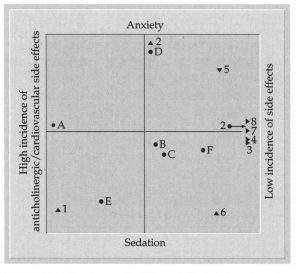

FIGURE 5-8 Perceptual Map of Six Antidepressant Drugs. (Circles represent products; triangles represent segments.)

5. A group of U.S. airlines were found to have violated antitrust laws by engaging in an unlawful conspiracy to fix prices for domestic air transportation. They also allocated certain airline markets and airports. As a result, prices for airline tickets on such flights were higher than they otherwise would have been. Why would the airlines engage in indirect tacit signaling behavior to control prices?

6. How might packaging be used to position a product?

7. The Sharper Image traditionally has positioned itself for the upscale market. Through its retail stores (75 percent of sales) and catalogs, it has sold unique "pricey playthings for yuppie boys and girls"—products such as a $649 model of a Ferrari Testarossa and a $1295 high-tech stationary bike. In the 1990s, however, conspicuous consumption is out. Moreover, Sharper Image's prime target is the segment of the affluent market most susceptible to downturns in the economy. How can The Sharper Image reposition itself without losing its image of uniqueness?

Chapter 6

Measuring and Forecasting Market Opportunities

The pace of events is moving so fast that unless we can find some way to keep our sights on tomorrow, we cannot expect to be in touch with today.

DEAN RUSK

Now that we have discussed the advantages of market segmentation, it is time to measure the size of market opportunities. Part of your job as a marketing manager is to evaluate the many markets available and choose the best targets for exploitation. This means that you need to know how to measure the size, growth, and potential of various customer groups.

IMPORTANCE OF DEMAND ESTIMATES

Demand projections provide vital inputs for many areas of business planning. They are used by personnel to make sure that the right number of workers are hired; by manufacturing to plan capacity and production schedules; and by finance to ensure that necessary cash is available to pay for parts and wages. The impact of demand estimates on the budgetary process is shown in Figure 6-1. If your estimates of demand are off the mark, then expenses are apt to get out of control throughout the organization.

Inaccurate demand predictions can have disastrous effects on profitability. For example, for two quarters in a row in 1989, Hewlett-Packard was unable to predict the proper mix of products demanded by its customers. It had unexpected high

117

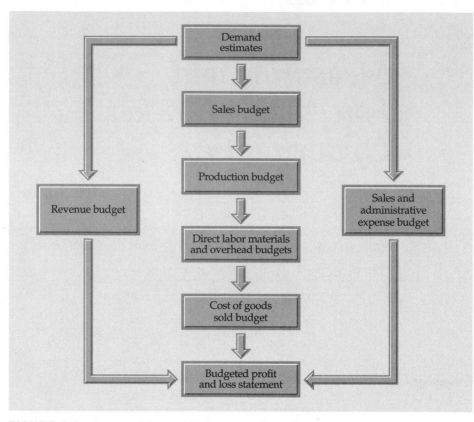

FIGURE 6-1   Impact of Demand Estimates on Budgeting

demand for low-end printers and workstations and low demand for commercial computers. As a result, earnings were 14 percent less than analysts expected. The stock market was dismayed with Hewlett-Packard's forecasting problems and knocked the company's stock down 5 percent in one day.[1] More recently, Compaq grossly underestimated the demand for its ProLinea group of low-cost computers introduced in June 1992. This forecasting failure meant that the company had to scramble to find parts, losing good will with customers and dealers. Compaq also was prevented from making further price cuts or distribution changes to keep customers from switching to new low-cost machines from IBM.[2]

In this chapter, we show how to measure current and future levels of demand. First, you must know the language of demand estimation.

DEMAND ESTIMATION TERMINOLOGY

Many terms are used in discussions of demand measurement. Managers talk casually about *potentials*, *forecasts*, *predictions*, *targets*, and *estimates*. Frequently, these terms mean the same thing. The key terms you should remember are *market potential, market demand, company demand*, and *company forecast*.

Market Potential

Market potential is an estimate of maximum demand for a product when industry marketing expenditures approach infinity. It is calculated for a particular point in time and a specific area. For example, to estimate market potential for compact disk players, we could begin with the total number of households in the United States (Figure 6-2). However, not everyone has the income, interest, or stereo amplifier and speakers needed to become a buyer of a compact disk player. Thus the maximum number of CD players that can be sold may represent only 60 percent of U.S. house-

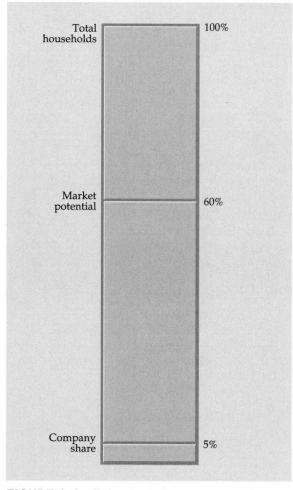

FIGURE 6-2 Estimating Market Potential for Compact Disk Players in the U.S.

holds (Figure 6-2). The actual number of CD players sold by individual firms would be less than this amount. In this example, we have shown one company with its CD players in 5 percent of U.S. households.

Market Demand

Although market potential is rarely achieved, market demand represents an amount that can actually be sold in an industry. Market demand is defined as the number of units of a product that can be sold in an area with a specified marketing program. With market demand, the emphasis is on units sold in response to industry price, promotion, and distribution decisions.

Market demand is deliberately shown below market potential in Figure 6-3. The difference between these two measures is known as the *basic demand gap*. In the case of CD players, this gap is large. Although we have suggested that 60 percent of U.S.

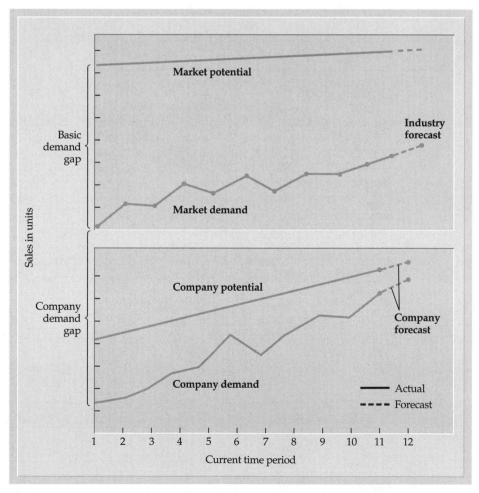

FIGURE 6-3   Market Potential, Market Demand, and Company Demand

households could buy a CD player, only 20 percent had purchased one by 1990. Apparently consumers view CD players as nonessential luxury items. When a basic demand gap is of this size, manufacturers need to stress the advantages of CD players compared to other recording and playback systems. You must first educate buyers about CD players before you promote individual brands of players.

Company Demand

Company demand is invariably less than market demand and company potential (Figure 6-3). It is the amount a firm can sell by following its own marketing program. Company potential, on the other hand, is the maximum volume the firm could sell based on its manufacturing capacity, a very large marketing budget, and optimum execution of its marketing plan. The difference between company demand and market demand is known as the *company demand gap*. This gap measures how well a firm is doing relative to its competitors.

The company shown in Figure 6-3 is selling close to its potential and does not appear to have much room to grow. Although the firm is increasing its market share, the real problem is the large basic demand gap. The data suggest that many prospects are still waiting to be converted into buyers. Thus, the firm needs to focus on introducing people to the product concept and needs to build industry sales before its own position can improve over time.

Company Forecast

Whereas market potential, market demand, and company demand focus on what is happening today, sales forecasts deal with the future. In Figure 6-3, demand and potential are shown as solid lines. Forecasts, however, are shown as dotted lines because they are guesses about what will occur in the future. Some people believe that the marketing plan evolves out of the sales forecast. In reality, company forecasts result from an assumed marketing program for tomorrow.

Sales forecasts are often extensions of current trends and plans and are not tied directly to potentials. We will describe a variety of techniques used to project the future later in this chapter.

MEASURING CURRENT DEMAND

There are several different ways to estimate current demand. We will review procedures that can be used to measure total market and geographic market potentials.

Market Potential

Market potential represents the maximum sales in dollars or units that can be obtained by an industry with a specified marketing effort. A simple way to estimate potential is as follows:

$$MP = N \times P \times Q \tag{6.1}$$

where

$$MP = \text{market potential}$$
$$N = \text{number of possible buyers}$$
$$P = \text{average selling price}$$
$$Q = \text{average number purchased by each buyer}$$

Assume, for a moment, that there are a million people who own CD players in an area, CDs sell for $12, and average buyers purchase four disks a year; thus, the market potential for CDs will be $48 million (1,000,000 × $12 × 4). The success of this approach depends on the accuracy and stability of your assumptions. For example, the purchase rate (Q) for CDs can change with disposable income and the availability of alternative recording formats. Also, the number of potential buyers (N) is often hard to pin down. While you can start with population figures, you have to subtract the number of people who are too young, too old, or too poor to purchase the product. Errors in making these adjustments can lead to unreliable market potential estimates.

Chain ratio procedures provide another way to measure market potential. This approach calculates potential by applying a series of ratios to an aggregate measure of demand. A firm could start with population figures and multiply by ratios that discard nonusing segments of the market.

An example showing how a firm estimated demand for replacement thermostat timers is given in Table 6-1. First, the number of year-round housing units in populated colder areas of the country was multiplied by the proportion of owner-occupied homes. These numbers were then adjusted by the proportion of homeowners between 21 and 65 years of age. The firm believed that very young and older people would not be attracted to this product. Next, an adjustment was made for the targeted income bracket. Low-income people could not afford this item, and high-income residents were not interested in such a gadget. The next adjustment eliminated homes that lacked a central thermostat. These calculations produced a total market potential of 5,762,000 households. The company estimated that 5 percent of

TABLE 6-1
Using Chain Ratios to Estimate Market Potential for Thermostat Timers

Region	Year-Round Housing Units (000)	Owner-Occupied Proportion	Between 21 and 65 Years of Age Proportion	Income Between $15,000 and $30,000 Proportion	Central Thermostat Proportion	Market Potential (Multiply All Columns, 000)
New England	4,278	0.61	0.78	0.55	0.67	750
Middle Atlantic	13,724	0.57	0.78	0.55	0.67	2,047
East North Central	14,489	0.68	0.76	0.57	0.69	2,965
Total						5,762

Source: Adapted from Charles W. Gross and Robin T. Peterson, *Marketing: Concepts and Decision Making* (St. Paul, MN: West, 1987), Chapter 8.

these households would purchase a thermostat timer each year. Thus, the industry annual sales potential was projected to be 288,100 units per year (5,762,000 × 0.05). The final step in the analysis converted industry potential into company sales potential. This was done by multiplying the industry potential of 288,100 units per year by the estimated company market share of 20 percent (288,100 × 0.20 = 57,620). By multiplying an aggregate measure of housing units by a series of ratios, the company was able to derive an estimated annual company market potential of 57,620 units.

Area Market Potential

Part of your job as marketing manager is to allocate your budget across geographic areas to maximize profits for the firm. This job is easier if you have data on market potentials for each sales territory. One way to get this information is with the help of programs that display market data on computer screens. Dun's Marketing Services is one firm that provides Census Business data in convenient computer formats. Examples of firms that have used these packages include a metals manufacturer that wanted to know the size of a neglected market segment on a state-by-state basis and an office products manufacturer that used the statistics to assign sales potentials to target markets and to forecast demand for production scheduling. Other companies have found the potentials data indispensable in setting up sales territories and assigning quotas. We will describe three ways to estimate geographic market potentials: the Buying Power Index, the SIC buildup method, and the scrappage method.

Buying Power Index Market potentials are often estimated by constructing indexes from basic economic data. Perhaps the most popular multifactor index of area demand is the Buying Power Index (*BPI*) published in July or August of each year by *Sales & Marketing Management* magazine. This index combines estimates of population, income, and retail sales to give a composite indicator of demand in specific metropolitan areas, counties, and cities in the United States.

The Buying Power Index for a particular area (*i*) can be calculated using the formula

$$BPI_i = \frac{5I_i + 3R_i + 2P_i}{10} \qquad (6.2)$$

where

I_i = percentage of U.S. disposable personal income in area *i*

R_i = percentage of U.S. retail sales in area *i*

P_i = percentage of U.S. population in area *i*

Some of the figures used to calculate Buying Power Indexes are shown in Table 6-2. Note that the state of California has 13.2 percent of U.S. income, 12.1 percent of retail sales, and 12.2 percent of U.S. population and a Buying Power Index of 12.7. That is, California has 12.7 percent of U.S. sales potential—considerably more than average for a state. The figures also show that Sacramento county has 0.451 percent

TABLE 6-2
Data Used to Calculate Buying Power Index

	1991 Effective Buying Income		1991 Total Retail Sales		Total Population		Buying Power Index
	Amount ($000,000)	Percentage of United States	Amount ($000,000)	Percentage of United States	Amount (000)	Percentage of United States	
Total United States	$3,728,967	100.0%	$1,821,385	100.0%	53,629	100.0%	100.0
California	490,750	13.2	220,871	12.1	30,975	12.2	12.7
Sacramento metro	24,204	0.6491	11,512	0.6320	1,569.8	0.6189	0.6383
Sacramento county	16,821	0.4511	8,301	0.4557	1,098.8	0.4332	0.4491
Sacramento city	5,538	0.1485	2,945	0.1617	389.8	0.1537	0.1535

Source: "1992 Survey of Buying Power," *Sales & Marketing Management,* August 24, 1992, pp. B-2, B-3, B-4, C-23, C-28. Copyright © 1992 by *Sales & Marketing Management.* Reproduced by permission.

of the U.S. income, 0.456 percent of U.S. retail sales, and 0.433 percent of the U.S. population. These three numbers are weighted as follows to give a Buying Power Index for Sacramento county:

Percentage of U.S. income	$0.451 \times 5 = 2.255$
Percentage of U.S. retail sales	$0.456 \times 3 = 1.368$
Percentage of U.S. population	$0.433 \times 2 = \underline{0.866}$
	$4.489/10 = 0.449$ *BPI*

Thus, an area with only 0.433 percent of the U.S. population has 0.449 percent of the national sales potential because of higher than average retail sales and income. When retail sales for an area exceed the income and population bases, as in this example, there is strong evidence that people are driving from surrounding counties to shop in that area. This suggests that managers must spread their promotional dollars over a fairly wide area if they expect to reach all the customers who shop in Sacramento county. Buying Power Index values are used to help managers allocate selling efforts across geographic regions. That is, the Buying Power Index suggests that Sacramento county, with 0.449 percent of the U.S. sales potential, should receive about 0.449 percent of the personal selling and advertising budgets for products in national distribution.

The Buying Power Index expresses sales potential in relative rather than absolute terms, but specific estimates of area potential can be obtained by multiplying the Buying Power Index (expressed as a fraction rather than a percentage) times projected national sales figures. For example, if an automobile manufacturer expects national sales of 1,000,000 units, then Sacramento county should be able to sell 4490 cars ($1,000,000 \times 0.00449 = 4490$). If actual sales are only 3000 units, then the company should add more salespeople, dealers, or promotional efforts to this area.

SIC Buildup Method   Although the Buying Power Index is widely employed as a measure of sales potential for consumer goods, it is not especially useful in the business market. Business market potential can be built up from data made available through the U.S. Census of Manufacturers. The Census of Manufacturers combines businesses to form Standard Industrial Classifications (SIC) according to products produced or operations performed.

The first step in estimating potentials from census data is to identify all the SIC codes that use your product or service. This is usually accomplished by using judgment to pick likely codes from the SIC manual and running surveys of different types of firms to see where products are employed. Next, you must select an appropriate data base for estimating the amount of the product that will be used by firms in each SIC code. A food machinery manufacturer, for example, could review past sales data to determine the relationship between the number of its machines in use and the number of production workers in a particular industry. If the manufacturer found that seven machines were used for every 1000 grain milling employees, 10 for every 1000 bakery workers, and 2 for every 1000 beverage workers, then the market potential for North Carolina could be determined, as shown in Table 6-3. Because

TABLE 6-3

Estimating the Market Potential for Food Machinery in North Carolina

SIC Code	Industry	*(1)* *Production* *Employees[a]* *(1000)*	*(2)* *Number of* *Machines Used* *per 1000* *Workers[b]*	*Market* *Potential* *(1) × (2)*
204	Grain milling	1.5	8	12.0
205	Bakery products	4.8	10	48.0
208	Beverages	2.1	2	4.2
				64.2

[a]From *1987 Census of Manufacturers*, Geographical Area Series, North Carolina, p. NC 11.
[b]Estimated by manufacturer from past sales data.

grain milling (SIC No. 204) has 1500 workers and eight machines are used per 1000 workers, the market potential would be 1.5 × 8 or 12 machines. Similar calculations for other codes yield a total market potential of about 64 machines for the state of North Carolina. The potential built up for North Carolina would then be added to estimates derived for other states to give national figures. These figures can be converted into annual measures of market potential by adjusting for the average life of the machines. If the machines last an average of 10 years, then 10 percent of the North Carolina potential of 64 units, or 6.4 machines, would be replaced each year. Estimates of company potential would be derived by multiplying annual demand potential by the firm's current market share.

Scrappage Method   Estimating market potential for durable goods such as appliances and machinery often depends on the rate at which owners scrap products due to wearing out or obsolescence. You can derive scrappage rates for forecasting purposes from data on the age of trade-ins or from service records sorted by geographic area. The scrappage approach is most useful for mature products for which replacement demand is important. This method does not work for new products to which customers are still being introduced.

An example showing how durable demand potential can be estimated from scrappage rates is presented in Table 6-4. Industry sales for this product are stable and have averaged 109,500 units a year for the past five years. Of the 110,000 units sold in 1993, 10 percent, or 11,000 units, were lost the first year due to scrappage, leaving 99,000. Twenty percent of these units are expected to be replaced in 1994, generating 19,800 units of potential demand. Similar calculations for other years give an estimate of replacement demand from past sales of 109,310 units. However, some of the units sold in 1994 will be replaced as well. If 10 percent of first-year units are scrapped as the result of damage, then the estimate of replacement potential will be about 120,000 units. Remember that the actual scrappage rate depends on economic conditions, interest rates, price concessions, and advertising, as well as on the frequency of machinery breakdowns, fires, floods, and other natural disasters. You may wonder if actual sales will be more or less than the 120,000 units of potential that

TABLE 6-4
Estimating Replacement Demand for 1994

Year Machine Sold	Industry Sales	Number Still Operating in 1994	Historical Annual Scrappage Rate	1994 Replacement Demand from Past Sales
1993	110,000	99,000	0.20	19,800
1992	112,000	78,400	0.35	27,440
1991	110,500	55,250	0.60	33,150
1990	106,000	21,200	0.85	18,020
1989	109,000	10,900	1.00	10,900
				109,310

we have estimated. Managers may repair their old machinery and keep it longer than indicated by the scrappage rates used in the table. Or managers may be attracted by the greatly improved productivity of new machines and replace equipment sooner.

MEASURING FUTURE DEMAND

Predicting future levels of demand for products is not easy because of continuous changes in customer preferences and market conditions. A host of supply, price, and competitive factors can increase or decrease sales without warning. Thus, it is important that you understand the strengths and weaknesses of each forecasting technique so that you can choose methods that are appropriate to your situation.

Types of Demand Forecasts

There are basically two forecasting approaches. You can start by estimating industry demand and then break out company or product line sales. This is called *top-down forecasting*. A second approach is the *buildup method*, whereby you forecast sales for individual products or geographic areas and then aggregate them to produce a prediction for the company.

Top-down and *buildup* forecasts can utilize opinions of customers or managers, or they can be extrapolated from test market data. A third procedure uses numerical techniques to extend past sales accomplishments into the future (Figure 6-3). We will discuss the most popular forecasting procedures used with each of these approaches.

Customer Surveys

A simple way to predict the future is to ask a sample of customers (via personal interviews, telephone calls, or mail questionnaires) what products and amounts they expect to purchase in a future period. Responses are then aggregated, and estimates of total demand for each product are prepared. Sales forecasts for individual firms are derived from total demand, using market share estimates. Intentions to buy and industry surveys are quite popular and together were mentioned by 31 percent of the firms shown in Table 6-5. American Airlines used this method to discover that its market share could be improved by targeting older travelers as a distinctive market niche. Despite these advantages, buyer surveys are time-consuming and expensive, and there is always the question of whether the persons interviewed will actually buy what they say they intend to purchase. User surveys have been most successful in business markets in which there are limited numbers of customers with specific needs and these firms tend to follow through on purchase intentions.

Sales Force Composite

A favorite forecasting technique for new and existing products is the *sales force composite* method. With this procedure, salespeople project volume for customers in their own territory, and the estimates are aggregated and reviewed at higher management levels. Some sales force systems use subjective probabilities and expected values. Note that the sales force composite method was used regularly by 45 percent of the firms in a U.S. survey (Table 6-5). This technique is popular with industrial concerns

TABLE 6-5

Utilization of Sales Forecasting Methods of 134 Firms

Methods	Percentage of Firms That Use Regularly
Subjective	
Sales force composite	44.8%
Jury of executive opinion	37.3
Intention to buy survey	16.4
Industry survey	14.9
Extrapolation	
Naive	30.6
Moving average	20.9
% Rate of change	19.4
Leading indicators	18.7
Unit rate of change	15.7
Exponential smoothing	11.2
Line extension	6.0
Quantitative	
Multiple regression	12.7
Econometric models	11.9
Simple regression	6.0
Box-Jenkins	3.7

Source: Douglas J. Dalrymple, "Sales Forecasting Practices: Results from a United States Survey," *International Journal of Forecasting*, Vol. 3 (1987), p. 382.

because they have a limited number of customers, and salespeople are in a good position to assess customers' needs. Forecasts prepared by salespeople may be biased, however, because the projections are often used to set quotas and salespeople hesitate to predict more volume than they can deliver. One benefit of the sales force composite method is that participation in the forecasting process may increase the salesperson's confidence in his or her sales quota and may provide a greater incentive to achieve it. However, participation by every salesperson and several levels of supervisors can make the sales force composite method slower than other techniques for long-range forecasts. An example showing how salespeople can be used to forecast is given in Marketing In Action box 6-1.

Executive or Expert Opinion

This technique involves soliciting the judgment of a group of experts or experienced managers to give sales estimates for proposed and current products. Jury of executive opinion was used by 37 percent of the firms described in Table 6-5. The main advantages of this method are that it is fast and it allows the inclusion of many subjective factors such as competition, economic climate, weather, union activity, and so forth. Helene Curtis, for example, relied on the judgment of its executives when they forecasted that Finesse hair conditioner would generate strong sales if introduced. In this

---

MARKETING IN ACTION 6-1

FORECASTING INDUSTRIAL SALES

Metier Management Systems grew from start-up to a $100 million market leader in eight years as the result of a carefully designed sales forecasting procedure. Metier sold project management systems, costing an average of $300,000, to large industrial and government buyers. The product included specialized computers and associated software, and the sales cycle lasted from 3 to 18 months. Because of the unique nature of each sale, Metier needed accurate data on the status of prospects to make efficient use of their sales resources. Also, orders had to come in on time to achieve their goal of remaining self-financed.

The key to their success was a four- to six-hour monthly prospect review meeting with each salesperson. During this meeting, sales managers went through a detailed checklist for all significant prospects. If a sales rep didn't know the answer to crucial questions, such as who controlled budgets or when the project was to start, the meeting was stopped and the rep made phone calls to get the answers. These meetings were long, boring, and dreaded by the salespeople. They were also the basis for very accurate three-month sales forecasts. The system was made more effective by tying sales managers' compensation to the accuracy of their forecasts as well as the volume of business they generated.

The sales force composite method can lead to accurate forecasts.

Source: William E. Gregory, Jr., "Time to Ask Hard-Nosed Questions," *Sales & Marketing Management* (October 1989), pp. 88–93.

case they were right, and Finesse has become a very profitable product for the firm. The continued popularity of the jury of executive opinion shows that most managers prefer their own judgment to other, less well-known mechanical forecasting procedures. However, available evidence does not suggest that the jury of executive opinion method leads to more accurate forecasting. Perhaps the main problem with the method is that it is based on experience, and it is difficult to teach someone how to forecast using this method.

Test Markets

When you are trying to predict sales of new products, test marketing can be useful. This technique places new items in retail stores and measures how fast they sell. Test results can then be projected to give national sales forecasts. The main drawback of test marketing is that it takes a lot of time. An alternative is to use *simulated test markets*. With this approach, a store environment is set up in a laboratory and customers are sent through on shopping trips. Simulated store tests are quick and cannot be observed by competitors.

Leading Indicators

Where sales are influenced by basic changes in the economy, *leading indicators* can be a useful guide in the preparation of sales forecasts. For example, 19 percent of the firms in Table 6-5 regularly use leading indicators in sales forecasting. The idea is to find a general time series that is closely related to company sales, yet is available several months in advance. Changes in the series can then be used to predict sales directly, or the series can be combined with other variables in a forecasting model. For example, General Electric has found that sales of dishwashers are closely related to the number of housing starts that occur several months earlier. Obviously, the key issue is finding indicators that have forecasting value for particular products. Some of the more useful leading indicators include prices of 500 common stocks, new orders for durable goods, new building permits, contracts and orders for plant and equipment, and changes in consumer installment debt.

Seasonal Adjustments

Sales forecasts are often prepared monthly or quarterly, and seasonal factors are frequently responsible for many of the short-run changes in volume. Thus, an apparently good forecast may turn out to be a poor one because of a failure to consider seasonal factors. When historical sales figures are used in forecasting, the accuracy of predictions can often be improved by making adjustments to eliminate seasonal effects.

The first step in seasonally adjusting a time series is to collect past sales figures for several years. Next, sales for months or quarters are averaged across years to build a seasonal index. In Table 6-6, four years of quarterly sales are averaged to give a rough indication of seasonal effects.[3] The quarterly averages are then divided by mean sales for all quarters to give seasonal index numbers. For example, when

TABLE 6-6

Calculating a Seasonal Index from Historical Sales Data

Quarter	Year				Four-year Quarterly Average	Seasonal Index
	1	2	3	4		
1	49	57	53	73	58.0	0.73[a]
2	77	98	85	100	90.0	1.13
3	90	89	92	98	92.3	1.16
4	79	62	88	78	76.8	0.97

Four-year sales of 1268 ÷ 16 quarters = 79.25 average quarterly sales

[a]Seasonal index is 58.0 ÷ 79.25 = 0.73.

average sales of 58.0 for quarter 1 are divided by the mean for all quarters of 79.25, a seasonal index of 0.73 is obtained. This number says that seasonal factors typically lower first-quarter sales by 27 percent.

Once seasonal index numbers are developed for each time period, it is easy to adjust seasonally a set of sales data. Actual sales, such as those shown in Table 6-6, are simply divided by the appropriate index numbers to give a set of deseasonalized sales figures (Table 6-7). Sales forecasts are then prepared using the deseasonalized data. These forecasts must be multiplied by the seasonal index for the forecast period to make them comparable with regular sales figures. The mechanics of using seasonal adjustments will be demonstrated by working through some examples using time series procedures.

Some students assume that because seasonal adjustments complicate the forecasting process, they are not worth the time and effort required. However, there are two truths about seasonal adjustments that you should remember:

1. Seasonal adjustments are widely used in business.
2. Seasonal adjustments reduce forecasting errors.

TABLE 6-7

Deseasonalized Sales Data

Quarter	Year			
	1	2	3	4
1	67[a]	78	73	100
2	68	87	75	89
3	78	77	79	84
4	81	64	91	80

[a]Calculated by dividing actual sales from Table 6-6 by the appropriate seasonal index: (49 ÷ 0.73 = 67, 77 ÷ 1.13 = 68).

Naive Forecasting

Time series forecasts rely on past data to provide a base for making projections about the future. The *naive forecast* is the simplest technique and is often used as a standard for comparison with other procedures. It assumes that nothing is going to change and that the best estimate for the future is the current level of sales.

For example, actual sales of 49 units observed in quarter 1 in Table 6-6 can be used to predict sales in quarter 2. Since actual sales in quarter 2 were 77, the error is

$$\text{Percentage error} = \frac{\text{forecast} - \text{actual}}{\text{actual}} \times 100\% \qquad (6.3)$$

$$= \frac{49 - 77}{77} \times 100\% = -36\%$$

A seasonally adjusted naive forecast starts with deseasonalized sales figures, such as those in Table 6-7. The seasonally adjusted sales in the first quarter of 67 would be used to forecast sales in the second quarter, which is done by multiplying the seasonally adjusted sales of 67 by the seasonal index for quarter 2 to give a forecast of 76 (67 × 1.13 = 75.7). Seasonally adjusted naive forecasts for the last three quarters of year 1 would be as follows:

		Quarter		
	1	2	3	4
Seasonally adjusted sales	67	68	78	81
Seasonally adjusted naive forecast		76	79	76
		(67 × 1.13)	(68 × 1.16)	(78 × 0.97)

Because actual sales in period 2 were 77, the percentage error in the seasonally adjusted naive forecast is

$$\text{Percentage error} = \frac{76 - 77}{77} \times 100\% = -1.3\%$$

The example indicates that the seasonally adjusted naive forecast (1.3 percent error) was much more accurate than the nonadjusted forecast (36 percent error). When you want to compare forecasting accuracy across several time periods, the *mean absolute percentage error (MAPE)* formula should be used.

$$MAPE = \frac{\sum_{i=1}^{n} (\text{forecast} - \text{actual})/\text{actual}}{n} \times 100\% \qquad (6.4)$$

where n is the number of forecasts to be made.

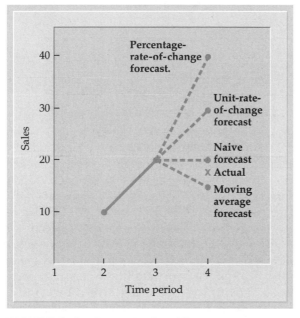

FIGURE 6-4   Comparing Trend Forecasting Methods

Trend Projections

The use of trends to project sales is a popular technique among business firms. With this method, you estimate a trend from past data and add this figure to current sales to obtain a forecast. For example, in Figure 6-4 sales increased from 10 units in period 2 to 20 units in period 3, suggesting a trend of 10 units per period. A *unit rate of change forecast* for period 4 would combine current sales of 20 plus 10 units of trend for a total of 30. Expressed as a percentage, the 10 units of trend would be divided by 10 units of sales to give a 100 percent growth rate. A 100 percent growth rate applied to current sales of 20 units would give a forecast of 40 units for period 4. Note that the percentage and unit rate of change methods give different sales forecasts. When sales are increasing, forecasts prepared with the percentage rate of change approach will normally be higher than those obtained by other projective techniques. A third projective technique is the *line extension* forecast. With this method, you draw a line to extend the trend shown by recent sales data. Research reported in Table 6-5 shows that the percentage rate of change method is the most popular projective forecasting technique, followed by the unit rate of change. The line extension method is not widely used by business firms.

Moving Averages

One of the easiest ways to follow trends in sales data is with the *moving average*. The analyst computes the average volume achieved in several recent periods and uses it as a prediction of sales in the next period. The formula takes the form

$$F_{t+1} = \frac{S_t + S_{t-1} + \cdots + S_{t-n+1}}{n} \qquad (6.5)$$

where

$$F_{t+1} = \text{forecast for the next period}$$
$$S_t = \text{sales in the current period}$$
$$n = \text{number of periods in the moving average}$$

This approach assumes that the future will be an average of past achievements. For example, if sales in the last two periods went from 10 to 20, then a two-period moving average forecast would be 15 (Figure 6-4). Thus, when there is a strong trend in a time series, a moving average forecast lags behind. This lag can be an advantage, however, when a series changes direction. If actual sales decline to 17 units in period 4, as shown in Figure 6-4, then the forecast will be more accurate than the trend projection methods. Businesspeople regularly use moving averages, and it was the second most popular extrapolation method in the survey reported in Table 6-5.

Remember that a moving average really does move. Table 6-8 shows how to calculate two- and three-period moving average forecasts using sales figures from Table 6-6. At least two periods of data are needed for a moving average, so the first forecast that can be produced is for period 3. This forecast averages period 1 season ally adjusted sales of 67 with period 2 sales of 68 and multiplies by the seasonal index of 1.16 to give a forecast of 78.3. Then period 1 sales are dropped, and period 3 sales are averaged with period 2 and multiplied by the index of 0.97 to give a forecast for

TABLE 6-8
Forecasting with Moving Averages

	Time Period[a]					
	1	2	3	4	5	6
Actual sales	49	77	90	79	57	98
Seasonally adjusted sales	67	68	78	81	78	87
Two-period moving average forecast seasonally corrected			78.3	70.8	58.0	89.8
Three-period moving average forecast seasonally corrected				68.9	55.2	89.3

Two-period moving average forecast

$$F_3 = \left(\frac{S_1 + S_2}{2}\right) \times I_3$$

$$= \left(\frac{67 + 68}{2}\right) \times 1.16^b$$

$$= 78.3$$

Three-period moving average forecast

$$F_4 = \left(\frac{S_1 + S_2 + S_3}{3}\right) \times I_4$$

$$= \left(\frac{67 + 68 + 78}{3}\right) \times 0.97$$

$$= 68.9$$

[a]Actual sales are from Table 6-6 years 1 and 2; seasonally adjusted sales are from Table 6-7.[b]Index numbers are from Table 6-6.

period 4 of 70.8. At each step, one old piece of data is dropped and one new piece is added as the moving average moves through the figures. The procedure is similar for a three-period moving average, and the first forecast that can be made is for period 4. Note that you cannot use a moving average to predict time periods that were included in the calculation of your forecast.

A characteristic of moving averages that reduces their ability to follow trends is that all time periods are weighted equally. This means that information from the oldest and newest periods is treated the same way in making up a forecast. A popular technique which overcomes this problem is known as *exponential smoothing*.

Exponential Smoothing

An important feature of exponential smoothing is its ability to emphasize recent data and systematically discount old information. A simple exponentially smoothed forecast can be derived using the formula

$$\overline{S}_t = \alpha S_t + (1 - \alpha)\overline{S}_{t-1} \tag{6.6}$$

where

$\overline{S}_t$ = smoothed sales for period t and the forecast of period $t + 1$
α = the smoothing constant
S_t = actual sales in period t
$\overline{S}_{t-1}$ = smoothed sales for period $t - 1$

The formula combines a portion (α) of current sales with a discounted value of the smoothed average calculated for the previous period to give a forecast for the next period.

An example of how exponential smoothing forecasts are derived by using seasonally adjusted data is shown in Table 6-9. First, smoothed sales for period 2 are obtained by multiplying a constant of 0.2 times current seasonally adjusted sales of 68 units and adding this to 80 percent of smoothed sales for the prior period. Because smoothed sales are not available for period 1, actual seasonally adjusted sales of 67 units is used as a proxy to get the process started. The forecast for period 3 is calculated by multiplying smoothed sales for period 2 (67.2) times the seasonal index for period 3 (1.16). Notice that the smoothed sales figure obtained for period 2 is then used to calculate the value of smoothed sales for the next period (Table 6-9). This means that a portion of all past sales is included in each exponentially smoothed forecast.

The main decision made with exponential forecasting is the selection of an appropriate value for the smoothing constant (α). Smoothing factors can range in value from 0 to 1, with low values providing stability and high values allowing a more rapid response to sales changes. Using a smoothing constant of 1.0 gives the same forecasts that are obtained with the naive method. Forecasts produced with a

TABLE 6-9
Forecasting with Exponential Smoothing ($\alpha = 0.2$)

	Time Period					
	1	2	3	4	5	6
Actual sales	49[a]	77	90	79	57	98
Seasonally adjusted sales	67	68	78	81	78	87
Smoothed sales ($\overline{S}_t$)		67.2	69.4	71.7	73.0	75.8
Sales forecast (F_{t+1})			77.9	67.3	52.3	82.5

$\overline{S}_t = \alpha S_t + (1 - \alpha)\overline{S}_{t-1}$

$F_{t+1} = \overline{S}_t \times I_{t+1}$

$\overline{S}_2 = 0.2(68) + 0.8(67)$ $\overline{S}_4 = 0.2(81) + 0.8(69.4)$

$= 67.2$ $= 71.7$

$F_3 = 67.2 \times 1.16^b$ $F_5 = 71.7 \times 0.73$

$= 77.9$ $= 52.3$

$\overline{S}_3 = 0.2(78) + 0.8(67.2)$ $\overline{S}_5 = 0.2(78) + 0.8(71.7)$

$= 69.4$ $= 73.0$

$F_4 = 69.4 \times 0.97$ $F_6 = 73.0 \times 1.13$

$= 67.3$ $= 82.5$

$$MAPE = \frac{(77.9 - 90)/90 + (67.3 - 79)/79 + (52.3 - 57)/57 + (82.5 - 98)/98}{4}$$

$$= 13.1\%$$

[a]Actual sales from Table 6-6; seasonally adjusted sales from Table 6-7.
[b]Index numbers from Table 6-6.

low smoothing constant, such as 0.2, lag when there is a trend in the data, and forecasts generated with high values, such as 0.8, will likely overestimate sales at turning points. For example, the use of a smoothing constant of 0.2 in Table 6-9 produced a *MAPE* of 13.1 percent for periods 3 through 6. Note that an α of 0.2 tended to lag changes in the data and gave lower forecasts than did the two-period moving average described in Table 6-8. The moving average *MAPE* for periods 3 through 6 was only 8.6 percent. However, when a smoothing constant of 0.8 is used, the exponential forecasting error for periods 3 through 6 declines to 7.9 percent. This suggests that the best way to select a smoothing constant is to take some representative sales data and measure the forecasting errors produced by smoothing constants of different sizes. The optimum smoothing factor would be the one that gives the smallest forecasting error.

Trend Regression

In simple *trend regression*, the relationship between sales (Y) and the independent variable time (X) can be represented by a straight line. The equation of this line is $Y = a + bX$, where a is the intercept and b shows the impact of the trend. The key step in deriving trend regression equations is finding values for the coefficients (a, b) that give the best fit to the data. These are usually obtained with computer programs that

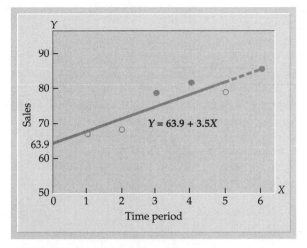

FIGURE 6-5 Fitting a Trend Regression to Seasonally Adjusted Sales Data

minimize the sum of the squared differences between actual and predicted sales observations. An example of a trend regression derived from seasonally adjusted data is shown in Figure 6-5. This equation says that sales will be 63.9 plus 3.5 units for every time period. A forecast for period 6 would be

$$
\begin{aligned}
F_6 &= [63.9 + 3.5(6)] \times I_6 \\
&= 84.9 \times I_6 \\
&= 84.9 \times 1.13 \\
&= 95.6
\end{aligned}
$$

The forecast of 84.9 is multiplied by the period 6 index of 1.13 to give a final forecast of 95.9. One of the benefits of trend regression is that you can predict as many periods into the future or the past as you like by simply entering the number of the period in the forecasting equation. Regression equations with two variables can be calculated using some pocket calculators or desktop and laptop computers using Lotus 1-2-3 or other programs. Some commercial forecasting programs are shown in the Marketing Tools box 6-1.

Trend regressions do a poor job of forecasting when series change direction. The usual procedure is to include all data points to provide stability. However, short regressions do a better job of tracking changes. Research has shown that short regressions are more accurate than all data regressions for forecasting up to 8 months ahead.[4]

Multiple Regression

With *multiple regression*, a computer is used to build forecasting models based on relationships between sales and *several* independent variables. Sales predictions are

MARKETING TOOLS 6-1

COMMERCIAL FORECASTING PROGRAMS

Vendor	Package	Description	Mem	Price	Hardware/Sys
Application Consulting Group	ACG Forecast Window	Integrated sales forecasting with automated statistical calculations, reporting and graphics, esp. for consumer packaged goods cos.; requires pcEXPRESS	640K (hard disk)	$30,000	IBM PC full range; any DOS
Applied Decision Systems	ADDATA Forecasting System	Forecasts for product code level of detail; expert choice between four techniques; report generator	500K (hard disk)	$1000+ (SU), $55,000 (MU)	IBM PC-AT and up, math co-processor; DOS 3.3+
Applied Decision Systems	SIBYL	Research tool; 18 distinct time series forecasting techniques	384K	$495	IBM PC full range; DOS 3.0+
Business Forecast Systems	ForeCALC	Forecasting for Lotus 1-2-3; uses Lotus base to establish variables	640K (need Lotus)	$149	IBM PC full range; OS/2
Concurrent Technologies	Probe PC	Statistical analysis and forecasting program; time series; direct link to many database modules avail.	384K (hard disk)	$1,600	IBM PC full range; DOS 2.0+
JIAN	Operations Integrator	Excel spreadsheet model to structure, modify, evaluate, and balance the financial impact of sales forecasts with a variety of manufacturing and service opportunities	640K or 1MB (need Lotus)	$149	IBM PC full range; any DOS; Mac & up; and MOS

MARKETING TOOLS 6-1
(continued)

MarketWorks	Sales Forecaster	Produces three types of sales forecasts; most likely, expected value and risk analysis	256K	$349	IBM-PC full range; DOS 2.0+
Palo Alto Software	Sales & Market Forecasting Tool 2	Real-world sales forecasting using leading spreadsheets and a choice of methodologies from market share to whole market penetration, etc.	256K (need Lotus)	$149.95	IBM PC full range; any DOS; Mac full range; any DOS
Scientific Computing Assoc. Inc.	PC-UTS	Forecasting and time series analysis using Box-Jenkins methodology; multiple regression; statistical functions	640K (hard disk)	$745	IBM PC full range; DOS 2.1+; Mac II series
SmartSoftware	SmartCasts II 2.15	Forecasting tool for sales/marketing managers with expert system graphics and data analysis; projects sales, demand, costs, revenues; time-series analysis; multivariate regression	256K	$495	IBM PC full range; DOS 2.1+

Source: Sales & Marketing Management (December 1990), p. 97.

obtained by estimating values for the independent variables for the forecast period and then plugging these numbers into the regression equation. For example, suppose that a manufacturer of aluminum siding collected data on sales, interest rates, incomes, and numbers of marriages in 20 territories (Table 6-10). If these numbers are run through a multiple regression program, a forecasting equation will be obtained in the form

$$Y = 204.8 - 87.12 \log_{10} X_1 + 1.930X_2 - 0.018X_3 \qquad (6.7)$$

where

$$Y = \text{sales of aluminum siding}$$
$$X_1 = \text{interest rate}$$
$$X_2 = \text{family income}$$
$$X_3 = \text{number of marriages}$$

The equation suggests that siding sales increase with income and decline with growth in the interest rate and the number of marriages. Because the relationship between sales and the interest rate appeared to be nonlinear, logarithms of the interest rates were used instead of the actual values shown in Table 6-10. When sales are associated with relative rather than absolute changes in a variable, the use of logs will give a better forecast.

A sales forecast for a new territory in which the interest rate is 10 percent, family income is $15,000, and 100,000 marriages are performed annually can be prepared by inserting these values in equation (6.7). Because the logarithm of the interest rate is 1, we have [204.8 − 87.12(1) + 1.930(15) − 0.018(100)], or a sales estimate of 1,448,300 ft^2 of siding for the new territory.

Using multiple regression in sales forecasting presents a number of problems. First, a computer is needed to help calculate the necessary equations. Second, a lot of historical data have to be gathered to ensure that the model will forecast accu-

TABLE 6-10

Economic Indicators and Sales of Aluminum Siding in 20 Territories

Average Interest Rate on Home Mortgage[a] (%)	Average Family Income[a] ($1000)	Marriages per Year[a] (1000)	Sales of Aluminum Siding[b] (1000 ft^2)
8.50	14.3	62.0	142
9.40	9.5	55.5	138
6.43	17.8	76.5	177
7.40	11.5	45.8	156
6.50	13.0	90.3	158
10.40	11.6	35.0	144
7.41	14.7	93.1	150
10.60	11.1	33.5	136
8.00	13.1	90.0	140
7.05	16.9	75.2	157
7.80	11.2	97.0	153
7.95	12.7	75.6	147
6.75	16.5	99.5	170
6.30	18.4	89.5	165
6.75	16.0	110.9	160
6.56	13.3	30.6	153
7.25	13.8	21.2	146
9.85	9.6	25.1	140
6.85	18.2	52.7	173
6.50	14.8	50.0	167

[a]Data derived from business and census publications.
[b]Company sales records.

rately. Generally, five observations are needed for every independent variable in the equation. Third, estimates are needed of the independent variables for the time period into which you are forecasting. This means that the best variables for multiple regression forecasting are leading indicators that are available today. When these are not available, independent variables have to be forecast first before you use them to predict tomorrow. Despite the complexities of multiple regression forecasting, Table 6-5 shows that about 13 percent of surveyed firms use this technique to predict sales.

SELECTING FORECASTING METHODS

When you pick a forecasting method from among those we have discussed, you should consider factors such as accuracy, time available, need for a computer, cost, pattern of the data, and company experience. Remember that accuracy tends to vary with the length of the forecast. Moving average and exponential smoothing work well for short-range forecasts, but simple and multiple regression methods are more desirable for longer forecasts.

Accuracy is one of the most important criteria in your selection of forecasting procedures. Management expects you to find methods that work well for the type of products under your control. Research has shown that simple procedures such as naive forecasting, moving average forecasting, and exponential smoothing often have lower forecasting errors than other, more complex methods.[5] This suggests that you should start with the basic procedures we have described and move to more sophisticated models only when they are needed.

The existence of trend, horizontal, seasonal, or cyclical patterns in a time series also influences the choice of forecasting method. Thus, if a series is basically horizontal, a moving average method could be used. If it showed a trend, regression might be employed. Historical data for business and economic time series are often limited, which can restrict the choice of techniques that can be used. Even though you might like to use the complex Box-Jenkins procedures (Table 6-5), you may have only enough data for exponential smoothing.

SUMMARY

An important part of your job as marketing manager is to prepare estimates of current market potential and to make forecasts for the future. Estimates of potential are based on projections of the number of users and the expected purchase rate. Geographical measures of potential can be obtained by using the chain ratio, Buying Power Index, and SIC code or scrappage procedures. Forecasts of the future may be extensions of historical data or, in the case of new products, based on test markets or judgment. Examples of subjective forecasting methods include sales forecast composite, jury of executive opinion, customer surveys, and leading indicators. When you are working with historical data, you can often improve the accuracy of your forecasts by seasonally adjusting the data.

A variety of numerical sales forecasting techniques are available. You need to understand how they work and where they should be employed. Detailed explanations have been presented for naive, moving average, exponential smoothing, and regression procedures. Your choice among these and other methods is a function of the length of the forecast, pattern of the data, cost accuracy, and ease of understanding. Possibly the ideal forecasting procedure combines a numerical analysis of past data with your own interpretation of current developments.

Since no one forecasting technique is best for all situations, some analysts employ several methods and then take the average of these projections as their final forecasts. Research shows that predictions based on averages of several procedures have lower errors than single-technique forecasts. However, this approach forces you to balance possible improvements in accuracy against the greater costs and complexity associated with preparing multiple forecasts. You must select techniques that can be sold to management. If managers cannot understand how forecasts are prepared, they are apt to reject the techniques in favor of their own judgmental forecasting methods.

NOTES

1. G. Pascal Zachary, "Hewlett to Post About Flat Net for 3rd Period," *The Wall Street Journal*, August 15, 1989, p. 10.
2. Kyle Pope, "Compaq Remains Unable to Meet Demand for New ProLinea Line," *The Wall Street Journal*, September 1, 1992, p. B8.
3. The seasonal indexes derived in Table 6-6 are easy to explain, but most computer programs use a more sophisticated procedure known as *ratio to moving average*. See Spyros Makridakis, Steven C. Wheelwright, and Victor E. McGee, *Forecasting: Methods and Applications* (New York: Wiley, 1983), pp. 137–141.
4. Douglas J. Dalrymple, William M. Strahle, and Douglas B. Bock, "How Many Observations Should Be Used in Trend Regression Forecasts," *Journal of Business Forecasting*, Vol. 8, No. 1 (Spring 1989), pp. 7–9.
5. Spyros Makridakis, A. Andersen, R. Carbone, R. Fildes, M. Hibon, R. Lewandowski, J. Newton, E. Parzen, and R. Winkler, "The Accuracy of Extrapolation (Time Series) Methods: Results of a Forecasting Competition," *Journal of Forecasting*, Vol. 1, No. 2 (April–June 1982), pp. 111–153; and Steven P. Schnaars, "Situational Factors Affecting Forecasting Accuracy," *Journal of Marketing Research*, Vol. 21 (August 1984), pp. 290–297.

SUGGESTED READING

Reisberg, Gerald. "Using Data to Increase Marketing Effectiveness," *Sales & Marketing Management* (June 1990), p. 132.

Gilbert, Samuel. "Who Your Potential Customers Are: A Marketing Application," *Sales & Marketing Management* (June 1990), pp. 136–148.

FURTHER READING

Armstrong, J. Scott. *Long Range Forecasting*, 2nd ed. (New York: Wiley, 1985).

Makridakis, Spyros. *Forecasting, Planning, and Strategy for the 21st Century* (New York: Free Press, 1990).

Makridakis, Spyros, A. Andersen, R. Carbone, R. Fildes, M. Hibon, R. Lewandowski, J. Newton, E. Parzen, and R. Winkler. "The Accuracy of Extrapolation (Time Series) Methods: Results of a Forecasting Competition," *Journal of Forecasting*, Vol. 1, No. 2 (April–June 1982), pp. 111–153.

Makridakis, Spyros, Steven C. Wheelwright, and Victor E. McGee. *Forecasting: Methods and Applications*, 2nd ed. (New York: Wiley, 1983).

Wheelwright, Steven C., and Spyros Makridakis. *Forecasting Methods for Management*, 5th ed. (New York: Wiley, 1989).

QUESTIONS

1. Why do marketing managers need projections of market potential? How are they obtained?

2. Secure a copy of the computer FORECAST program from your instructor. Using this program and the following data, forecast sales for periods 4 through 7 using naive, trend projections, moving average, and simple exponential smoothing. Compare the *MAPE*s across these methods for time periods 4 to 7. What length of moving average and smoothing constant works best? What are your forecasts for periods 8 and 9?

Period	1	2	3	4	5	6	7	8	9
Sales	18	24	26	20	35	30	40	?	?

3. Quarterly sales (thousands of dollars) for the Chester Furniture Company for the past four years have been as follows:

			Year		
Quarter	*1*	*2*	*3*	*4*	*5*
1	230	240	264	328	?
2	245	266	290	344	?
3	193	259	221	275	?
4	174	218	202	281	?

   Using the FORECAST program, calculate seasonal indexes and adjust the data. Run seasonally adjusted naive, moving average, exponential smoothing, and lin-

TABLE 6-11
Company Sales and Other Variables (Semiannual)

Period	Company Sales (thousands of dollars)	Personal Disposable Income (millions of dollars)	Dealers Allowances (thousands of dollars)	Price (dollars)	Product Development Budget (thousands of dollars)	Capital Investments (in thousands of dollars)	Advertising (thousands of dollars)	Sales Expenses (thousands of dollars)	Total Industry Advertising Budget (thousands of dollars)
1	5540.39	398	138	56.2058	12.1124	49.895	76.8621	228.80	98.205
2	5439.04	369	118	59.0443	9.3304	16.595	88.8056	177.45	224.953
3	4290.00	268	129	56.7236	28.7481	89.182	51.2972	166.40	263.032
4	5502.34	484	111	57.8627	12.8916	106.738	39.6473	258.05	320.928
5	4871.77	394	146	59.1178	13.3815	142.552	51.6517	209.30	406.989
6	4708.08	332	140	60.1113	11.0859	61.287	20.5476	180.05	246.996
7	4627.81	336	136	59.8398	24.9579	-30.385	40.1534	213.20	328.436
8	4110.24	383	104	60.0523	20.8096	-44.586	31.6456	200.85	298.456
9	4122.69	285	105	63.1415	8.4853	-28.373	12.4570	176.15	218.110
10	4842.25	277	135	62.3026	10.7301	75.723	68.3076	174.85	410.467
11	5740.65	456	128	64.9220	21.8473	144.030	52.4536	252.85	93.006
12	5094.10	355	131	64.8577	23.5062	112.904	76.6778	208.00	307.226
13	5383.20	364	120	63.5919	13.8940	128.347	96.0677	195.00	106.792
14	4888.17	320	147	65.6145	14.8659	10.097	47.9795	154.05	304.921
15	4033.13	311	143	67.0228	22.4940	-24.760	27.2319	180.70	59.612
16	4941.96	362	145	66.9049	23.3698	116.748	72.6681	219.70	238.986
17	5312.80	408	131	66.1843	13.0354	120.406	62.3129	234.65	141.074

18	5139.87	433	67.8651	8.0330	121.823	24.7122	258.05	290.832
19	4397.36	359	68.8892	27.0486	71.055	73.9126	196.30	413.636
20	5149.47	476	71.4177	18.2208	4.186	63.2737	278.85	206.454
21	5150.83	415	69.2775	7.7422	46.935	28.6762	207.35	79.566
22	4989.02	420	69.7334	10.1361	7.621	91.3635	213.20	428.982
23	5926.86	536	73.1628	27.3709	127.509	74.0169	296.40	273.072
24	4703.88	432	73.3650	15.5281	-49.574	16.1628	245.05	309.422
25	5365.59	436	73.0500	32.4918	100.098	42.9984	275.60	280.139
26	4630.09	415	74.9102	19.7127	-40.185	41.1346	211.25	314.548
27	5711.86	462	73.2007	14.8358	68.153	92.5180	282.75	212.058
28	5095.48	429	74.1615	11.3694	87.963	83.2870	217.75	118.065
29	6124.37	517	74.2838	26.7510	27.088	74.8921	306.80	344.553
30	4787.34	328	77.1409	19.6038	59.343	87.5103	210.60	140.872
31	5035.62	418	78.5910	34.6881	141.969	74.4712	269.75	82.855
32	5288.01	515	77.0938	23.2020	126.420	21.2711	328.25	398.425
33	4647.01	412	78.2313	35.7396	29.558	26.4941	258.05	124.027
34	5315.63	455	77.9296	21.5891	18.007	94.6311	232.70	117.911
35	6180.06	554	81.0394	19.5692	42.352	92.5448	323.70	161.250
36	4800.97	441	79.8485	15.5037	-21.558	50.0480	267.15	405.088
37	5512.13	417	80.6394	34.9238	148.450	83.1803	257.40	110.740
38	5272.21	461	82.2843	26.5496	-17.584	91.2214	266.50	170.392
39	?	485	81.6257	20.0000	40.000	85.0000	275.00	180.000

Source: Steven C. Wheelwright and Spyros Makridakis, *Forecasting Methods for Management*, 4th ed. (New York: Wiley, 1985), pp. 181–182.

ear regression forecasts through the data to see which method has the lowest *MAPE*. Select the best method and forecast sales for quarters 1 through 4 in year 5.

4. Pacific Gas and Electric Company serves central and northern California. This region had a population of about 10 million. The company estimated the demand for household durables. The regression equation for washing machines is

$$Q = 210{,}739 - 702.59P + 69H + 20Y$$
$$(t\text{-statistic}) \quad (-6.34) \quad (4.61) \quad (5.39)$$

where

Q = annual retail sales of washing machines

P = average installed price

H = new single-family housing units connected to utilities

Y = California per capita income.

The R^2 was 0.95 and the standard error was 5773. What is your interpretation of the regression results? How could Pacific Gas and Electric make use of these results?

5. You are the marketing manager for a manufacturer, and you have been asked to forecast company sales for the next six months. You have collected data on company sales and other variables for the last 38 semiannual time periods (Table 6-11). In addition, you have estimates for period 39 for most of your variables. You also have access to a FORECAST program that has multiple regression. Calculate a correlation matrix and explain what it tells you about your variables. Create an equation to predict sales using all or a subset of your variables. Explain why you have included each variable and discuss the power of your equation. Forecast sales for period 39 using your multiple regression model.

6. The first optical scanner was installed in a U.S. supermarket in the second quarter of 1974. The number of optical scanners installed in each quarter through the third quarter of 1979 is given. Using the FORECAST program, predict scanner sales for the last six quarters with a variety of techniques. What method works best? What is different about forecasting scanners? Estimate the number of scanners that were installed in the fourth quarter of 1979.

Year	Quarter 1	2	3	4
1974	0	1	3	1
1975	3	4	7	12
1976	10	15	17	19
1977	27	25	31	23
1978	47	67	95	137
1979	143	196	235	?

Chapter 7

Product Development and Testing

No war, no panic, no bank failure, no strike or fire can so completely and irrevocably destroy a business as a new and better product in the hands of a competitor.

F. RUSSELL BICHOWSKY

New product development (NPD) is the process of finding ideas for new goods and services and converting them into commercially successful product line additions. The quest for new products is based on the assumptions that customers want new items and that the introduction of new products will help achieve the goals of the firm. This chapter will explain each step of the development process from the search for new ideas to the introduction of products to the marketplace.

The Product Development and Management Association's (PDMA) *Best Practices Study* found that only 56.4 percent of responding companies have a specific new product strategy and only 54.5 percent have a well-defined NPD process.[1] Incredibly, 32.8 percent had neither one! Clearly, many firms have room to improve their NPD management.

WHY DEVELOP NEW PRODUCTS?

The basic reason organizations develop new products is to increase the sales and profits of the firm. Not-for-profit organizations also develop new programs to better serve the needs of their constituents. We define *new products* as goods and services that are basically different from those already marketed by the organization. Thus, museums add exhibits, zoos acquire new animals, and theaters produce new plays in an effort to maintain interest and attract more patrons. Successful new programs and products can make substantial contributions.

New Products Boost Profits

There is a positive correlation between the introduction of new items and the achievement of the goals of the firm. One study has shown a simple correlation of +0.59 between research and development (R&D) spending and profits for 24 industries. For aerospace, electronics, office equipment, computers, and telecommunications the correlations are even higher. Another study found a U-shaped relationship between product innovativeness and return on investment (ROI).[2] High ROIs for noninnovative products are a result of their low investments. Moderately innovative products performed by far the worst. An example of how being less innovative than their competitors hurt General Motors is given in Marketing in Action box 7-1.

MARKETING IN ACTION 7-1

LACK OF AIR BAGS HURTS GENERAL MOTORS

A fleet of 2,000 cars at McDonald's corporate headquarters used to be exclusively General Motors. In 1993, the fast-food giant still bought 1,000 Oldsmobiles a year, but also bought 1,000 Ford Tauruses and Mercury Sables. USG, the gypsum-mining company, was another long-time GM customer, purchasing 1,100 cars a year. Now the fleet includes 350 Fords. The reason they both diversified: the limited availability of air bags on GM cars, either as standard or optional equipment. None of GM's midsize cars, the biggest chunk of the U.S. market, came with an air bag and you couldn't order one. Meanwhile companies were demanding air bags to protect their employees and lower insurance rates. Lack of air bags was also hurting sales to individuals.

The U.S. government ordered carmakers to install automatic seat belts or air bags on all cars beginning in fall 1989. Luxury carmakers—such as Lexus, Infiniti, and Mercedes-Benz—opted for air bags. So did Chrysler, then struggling to stay afloat. Putting in bags was a good marketing move at a time Chrysler had nothing else to push. GM chose to put in automatic seat belts in most of its cars. One reason was that automatic belts are easier and cheaper to install—an average of $100 versus $500 to $900 for a driver-side air bag. Studies by GM's marketing experts said consumers were only willing to spend a few hundred dollars more for air bags, meaning that GM would lose money on each air bag it installed. A second reason was GM's skepticism about buyers' acceptance. GM had offered air bags as an option in the mid-seventies. Few were purchased.

Even if GM had recognized the trend, its product development system was so ponderous that it couldn't have reacted quickly. In the 1980s, it took GM four to seven years to bring a completely new car to market. Generally, the key decisions about a car's basic design were made within the first 24 months. If air bags were not designed into the car then, they could not be added later because the whole project would have to be delayed.

The lack of air bags is a reason GM's car sales did not share in an auto-industry rebound. At a time when car sales were up 11% at Ford and 32% at Chrysler, GM's were down 2.7%.

Clinging to your beliefs long after customers have changed theirs can be costly.

Source: Michelle Maynard, "GM Lagging in Air-Bag Installations" *USA Today,* June 29, 1993, pp. B1–B2.

The Product Life Cycle

Perhaps the most important concept supporting product development activities is the life-cycle hypothesis. This proposition suggests that products follow patterns of birth, growth, and decline much like those observed for plants and animals (Figure 7-1). Sales of Brand A grow rapidly during the introductory period and eventually decline owing to the appearance of competitive products and ensuing price cutting. Profits for Brand A are negative at the start of the cycle because of introductory expenses, and they also come under pressure later because of price reductions and advertising designed to maintain market shares. The life-cycle hypothesis suggests that the firm in Figure 7-1 needs to introduce new items such as Brand B if it expects to maintain and/or improve profits. The PDMA *Best Practices Study* found that 32 percent of company sales came from new products introduced during the previous five years.

Competitive Obsolescence   Product life cycles, like those shown in Figure 7-1, are becoming shorter in some lines of trade. Competitors have been increasingly quick to copy new items and introduce their own brands at low prices. This can lead to rapid declines in profit margins and market shares for innovators. For example, the microprocessor-applied industries in Japan such as calculators, electronic character recognition devices, plain paper copiers, and small business computers are experi-

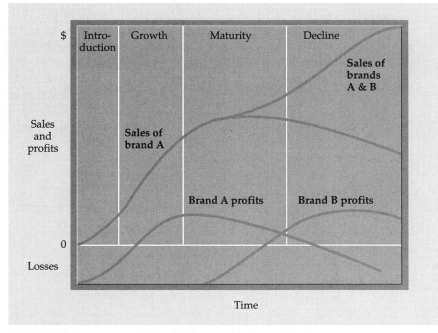

FIGURE 7-1   Impact of New Products on Sales and Profits

encing an accelerated life cycle. The model life for facsimile machines is down to less than four months and for audio components less than six months. Each of these industries has become almost a fashion industry. If the life expectancy of new products continues to decline, firms will need to develop even greater numbers of new items to maintain their market positions.

Chances for Success   Given the high costs of product development, you need to know the proportion of new products that succeed. The PDMA *Best Practices Study* reports that about 60 percent of products introduced are classified as successful. Many new products are lost in the screening and development stages, and these help account for the high failure rates reported in the trade press. Overall, about one new *idea* in 11 is converted into a successful new product. This means that a great deal of money is spent developing products that never reach the marketplace. Research has shown that strength in R&D, engineering, and production helps increase the number of new products. In addition, the average success rate of new products (60 percent) is related to strength in marketing, sales force/distribution, and promotion. These data suggest that most new products succeed and that careful attention to marketing activities can make a difference.

NPD STRATEGY

NPD strategy must integrate technology and marketing strategies. *Technology strategy* can be described in terms of technological breadth and technological capability, while related *marketing strategy* can be described in terms of product mix and customer development.[3] *Technological breadth* refers to the extent to which new product research and development (R&D) is mainly within an established area of technology or combines technology by bridging different areas of knowledge. *Technological capability* refers to the extent to which R&D is completely self-reliant versus dependent on outside resources. *Product mix* refers to the extent to which the firm concentrates on developing products that are essentially variations of existing products versus those that fall outside the established product line. *Customer development* refers to the extent to which new products are aimed at tying existing customers closer to the company versus getting new customers.

Open NPD strategies emphasize synergistic technology use, external technological inputs, product diversification, and new customers. These strategies are most appropriate in rapidly changing and uncertain environments. By contrast, closed NPD strategies focus the firm's efforts more efficiently and work better in stable predictable environments.

SEARCH AND SCREENING

The management of product development has been described as a sequential process that converts ideas into commercially successful product line additions. The procedure is essentially a series of go, no-go decisions in which the best ideas emerge as finished products. The five steps of the product development process are highlighted in Figure 7-2. Product development begins with screening and then moves on to revenue and cost analysis, followed by laboratory development and market testing and concludes with commercialization. Large numbers of new product ideas are passed into the system at one end, and months or years later, a few successful items reach the market. Ideas that fail to meet development criteria along the way are either dropped or sent back for more testing. The developmental process demands a steady stream of new ideas from which a few choice projects can be selected for more intensive development.

Sources of Product Ideas

The most common source of ideas for new products lies within the company itself. A survey revealed that 60 percent of industrial and 46 percent of consumer new product ideas came from the research staff, engineers, salespeople, marketing research personnel, and other employees and executives of the firm.

Another 26 percent of industrial new product ideas and 30 percent of consumer new product ideas came from users. Lead users are an especially good source.[4] In addition, consumers are often studied by using depth and focus group interviews to find opportunities for new items in individual product categories. Market structure maps such as those discussed in Chapter 4 can reveal gaps that suggest ideas for new products.

The frequent dependence on internally contributed ideas suggests that many firms do not pay enough attention to external sources for new projects. Company-generated ideas seem to gain acceptance easily, and there is a widespread suspicion about products that are "not invented here." An inventor developed a new type of mercury vapor light bulb that uses much less electricity and lasts considerably longer than incandescent light bulbs. The inventor took this attractive new product to several lighting companies, and they all turned him away. Apparently, the companies wished to protect their investments in regular light bulbs and were not interested in gaining access to new technology. Firms that carelessly reject new product ideas that appear promising are likely to suffer in the long run in terms of lost opportunities and reduced market shares. There is an almost endless number of external sources of new product ideas, some of which are shown in Figure 7-2.

Imitation

Rather than creating an innovation, a firm may find it expedient to imitate competitive offerings. In the survey mentioned earlier, 27 percent of industrial new product ideas and 38 percent of consumer new product ideas came from the analysis of competitors. Adapting an existing product created elsewhere is less expensive and time-consuming than creating an innovation.

Even the most innovative firm will not come up with all the new products generated in its industry. As a consequence, every firm should have a policy to guide its responses to the innovations of competitors. The firm may observe the market

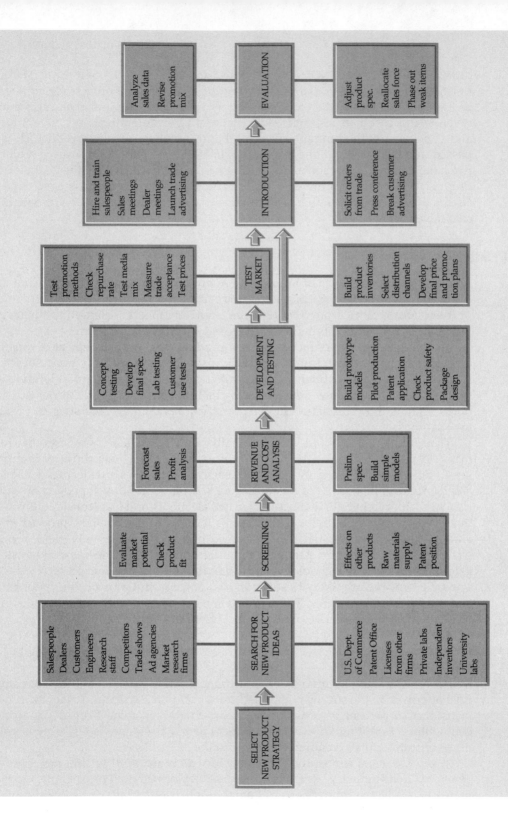

FIGURE 7-2 Flowchart of the Product Development Process

performance of the innovative product before launching its own product. Nonetheless, the rewards tend to go to early entrants. As a result, a firm should ensure itself against a competitor's new product being successful by spending R&D money on "reverse R&D," working backward from what the competitor has done and trying to do the same thing itself, for the more promising competitive new products.

Acquisition

One of the most attractive ways of acquiring new products is to buy other companies that have developed new items. This procedure has the advantages of eliminating all the costs of search, screening, testing, and commercialization, and it involves fewer risks because someone else has already built up a satisfied group of customers and dealers. For example, Johnson & Johnson bought the Playtex tampon brand to strengthen its position in the tampon business. Before this acquisition, it was a minor player in the market, with its O.B. tampon holding 9.5 percent of the U.S. market. Despite considerable effort, Johnson & Johnson has been unable to increase the market share of the O.B. brand. The problem appears to be customer resistance to inserting the tampons without an applicator. Although such tampons are big sellers in Europe, U.S. women prefer applicators. By purchasing the Playtex brand, Johnson & Johnson grabbed an additional 30 percent of the market and is now second to the market leader, Tambrands.

The main problems with this approach to product development are finding available brands to acquire and paying the sometimes high asking prices. Johnson & Johnson paid $726 million for Playtex tampons, and had to take Playtex nursers, gloves, and Tek toothbrushes as well. Some analysts believe that today it is much easier to buy into a consumer market than to try to create your own brands.

Licensing of New Products

Obtaining new product ideas through licensing offers several advantages for firms that wish to avoid the high cost of product development yet lack enthusiasm for acquiring going concerns. Probably the most important attraction is that there are more firms willing to license their ideas than there are firms willing to sell successful new products. Also, most license agreements involve the payment of royalties on a unit or percentage of sales basis so that initial costs are low and subsequent payments are due only when the product is actually sold. Furthermore, it is unusual for royalties paid on products obtained by licenses to exceed the savings achieved in R&D expenses. Licensing can also reduce lead time compared with the months or years that may be required to develop similar products in the company's own laboratories.

New Product Scouts

Product scouts are employees or consultants whose primary job is to find ideas that offer commercial potential for their sponsoring companies. The primary advantage of scouts is that the cost of locating an externally developed product by systematic investigation is usually less than 2 percent of the cost of internal development. Product scouts search through a wide variety of leads for new product ideas, ranging from such obvious sources as trade publications or more obscure personal contacts with inventors and patent attorneys. The astute product scout also maintains close contact with the major university and independent research laboratories, as well as with other manufacturers who may have unusual products for sale or lease. Some new product scouts publish newsletters describing recent innovations. The process of matching buyers and sellers of new technology is also aided by the sponsorship of special trade shows and conferences.

One other area where product scouts can be used to advantage is a search through the maze of government agencies and publications for spinoffs from federal projects. Product scouts can be used to help monitor the activities of the U.S. Patent Office. Occasionally, good ideas can be obtained from the Register of Patents available for licensing or sale and the listing of government-owned or dedicated patents. Another good source is the *Official Gazette*, a weekly publication of the Patent Office, which lists patents added to the Register plus new patents granted. Once the flow of new product ideas has been started, procedures must be established to select the most promising projects for more intensive analysis and development.

Screening Procedures

The objective of the screening process is to eliminate those new product ideas that are inconsistent with the goals or resources of the firm. Screening can be viewed as a filtering process. First, a fairly quick judgment is made on whether the idea is compatible with the company's plans, technical skills, and financial capabilities. This evaluation is made by knowledgeable managers and staff specialists who weed out the obviously unsuitable ideas so that valuable resources will not be wasted reviewing impractical proposals. The second phase of the new product screening process is more detailed and is designed to establish a ranking for the remaining ideas. This ranking is based on an evaluation of the factors that are considered relevant for the product development in a particular firm. A checklist shows the relative importance of the criteria and combines the factor evaluations into a single index number for each product. The main value of a new product index is its ability to separate quickly the best proposals so that priorities can be established for succeeding stages of development. The main problem with such scoring models is that they rely on the subjective ratings of managers; hence, data input may not be very reliable.

A better scoring model would take into account the information available in the success or failure of a large number of past new product launches. One such model is *NewProd*, a software-based new product screening, evaluation, and diagnostic tool.[5] NewProd was benchmarked initially by a statistical analysis of almost 200 projects from 100 companies. Managers were asked to rate their own project on about 50 potentially useful screening criteria. These characteristics were further reduced to 13 underlying dimensions using factor analysis. A regression was run relating these dimensions to degree of commercial success. Eight factors were linked to product outcomes, with the results shown in Table 7-1. The regression is used to predict an overall project rating from factor-analyzed screening questions on a new product. Thus, NewProd combines empirically identified rating factors and associated statis-

TABLE 7-1

NewProd Screening Model

Key Dimensions (factor name)	Regression Coefficient (weight of factor)	F-Value	Variables or Items Loading on Factor
Product superiority, quality, and uniqueness	1.744	68.7	Product: is superior to competing products has unique features for user is higher quality than competitors' does unique task for user reduces customers' costs is innovative—first of its kind
Overall project/resource compatibility	1.138	30.0	A good "fit" between needs of project and company resource base in terms of: managerial skills marketing research skills salesforce/distribution resources financial resources engineering skills production resources
Market need, growth, and size	0.801	12.5	High need level customers for product class Large market ($ volume) Fast growing market
Economic advantage of product to end user	0.722	10.2	Product reduces customers' costs Product is priced lower than competing products
Newness to the firm (negative)	−0.354	2.9	Project takes the firm into new areas for the firm such as: new product class to company new salesforce/distribution new types of users' needs served new customers to company new competitors to company new product technology to firm new production process to firm
Technological resource compatibility	0.342	2.5	A good "fit" between needs of project and company resource base in terms of: R&D resources and skills engineering skills and resources
Market competitiveness (negative)	−0.301	2.0	Intense price competition in market Highly competitive market Many competitors Many new product intros into market Changing user needs
Product scope	0.225	0.9	Market-driven new product idea Not a custom product, i.e., more mass appeal A mass market for product (as opposed to one or a few customers)
Constant	0.328		

Source: Robert G. Cooper, "Selecting New Product Projects: Using the NewProd System," *Journal of Product Innovation Management*, Vol. 2, No. 1 (March 1985), p. 39.

tically determined factor weights with subjective factor ratings on a new product provided by management.

NewProd validation studies in North America, the Netherlands, and Scandinavia have shown correct predictions for 75–85 percent of the new products studied.[6] For example, Procter & Gamble used a modified version of NewProd to assess 60 projects. Of the projects that NewProd predicted to be successes, 80 percent succeeded in test market and 60 percent were rated as financial successes when expanded nationally. On the other hand, of those it predicted to be failures, 25 percent were successful in test market but only 5 percent were financially successful when expanded nationally. NewProd predicts success and failure before development even begins.

REVENUE AND COST ANALYSIS

The business analysis phase of the product development cycle includes a detailed study of the potential profitability of new product ideas. The objective is to eliminate marginal ventures before extensive development and market testing expenses are incurred. Profit potentials are evaluated several times during the product development cycle. An initial analysis is done before projects are approved for lab testing, and additional reviews are conducted at the pilot plant and test market stages of the process. A wide variety of techniques has been created to measure the profitability of product development projects. A number of these measures will be reviewed later in the pricing chapter.

The procedures for analyzing the profitability of new products are fairly simple and enjoy widespread acceptance by the business community. Because of the different types of information provided by each method, most firms calculate break-even, payback, and ROI rates for each new product being evaluated. The main limitations of these methods are that they do not allow for interactions among marketing variables and they do not adequately handle risk.

DEVELOPMENT

Development and testing are concerned with establishing physical characteristics for new goods and services that are acceptable to customers. The objective is to convert ideas into actual products that are safe, provide customer benefits, and can be manufactured economically by the firm. Usually, development includes concept testing, consumer preference tests, laboratory evaluations, use tests, and pilot plant operations (Figure 7-2).

Concept Testing

The first step in the development process often includes measuring customers' reaction to descriptions of new products. Promising ideas are converted into concept statements, which are printed on cards and shown to small focus groups of customers. Sometimes pictures or preliminary models of the product are included, together with the written descriptions. Participants are asked if they would buy the item and are requested to give reasons for their decisions. Modifications are then made in the product concept, and the revised statement is tested with another group of customers. When the product concept appears well defined in terms of customer acceptance, a real product is developed to go along with the concept.

Product Design

The success of new products is often related to how well they are designed. Attractive products catch the attention of customers, and good design makes items easier to use. In addition, products should be designed so that they are easy to manufacture.

Braun A G, the German subsidiary of Gillette, entered the coffee maker market in 1972 with an attractive model that quickly won many design awards. However, its tower construction required two heating elements, and it was expensive to manufacture. As a result, selling prices were high and sales suffered. In 1981, Braun began to redesign the coffee maker with a single heating element, less expensive plastic, and fewer parts. After three years of effort, Braun was able to cut production costs by 50 percent. The new model was introduced in 1984, with production running at 2000 units a day. By 1988, the lower-priced model had found a broader market and production had expanded to 12,000 units a day. This example suggests that new products are accepted best when they are both attractive to you and economical to manufacture.

Preference Tests

Preference tests are employed to compare reactions to different product attributes or quality levels. Consumers usually are given two samples of the product with different characteristics to taste or use, and are then asked which they prefer and why. The idea is to isolate the most desirable characteristics and quality levels so that they can be built into the new product. Consumer preference tests are often helpful in determining specifications for new items because product standards developed by laboratory technicians can be different from the more general standards used by consumers.

A variety of methods has been developed to identify product features that are important to consumers and to estimate the numbers of persons who prefer different variations or quality levels. Perhaps the simplest approach is to interview potential customers and ask them to rate product features on a scale from 1 (unimportant) to 5 (very important). This makes it possible to compare the relative values of product attributes and to construct distributions of customer preferences. Another method submits a full range of sample products to groups of consumers, using a forced-choice, paired-comparison technique. Whatever the method employed, marketing managers need accurate preference data so that they can set product specifications to achieve the best possible market positions.

Product Attributes

A method for examining several product attributes at the same time is conjoint analysis. *Conjoint analysis* determines numerical values, which are known as *utilities* or *part-worths*, for each level of each product attribute. In addition, conjoint analysis reveals the relative importance of each of the product attributes to the customer. This information helps us understand the trade-offs a customer makes in rendering marketplace decisions.

Suppose that a firm wants to bring out a new spot remover for carpets and upholstery. R&D has come up with a core product that will handle tough, stubborn spots. We now want to design the tangible product. Factors believed to affect consumer preference are package design, brand name, price, a Good Housekeeping seal of endorsement, and a money-back guarantee.

Three applicator-type package designs (shown in Figure 7-3) are being considered. Three brand names—K2R, Glory, and Bissell—are being evaluated. One is the brand name we have chosen for the new product, and the other two are names of existing competitive products. Three possible prices—$1.19, $1.39, and $1.59—are being tested. The use of the Good Housekeeping seal or a money-back guarantee, or both, is being assessed. If we tested all possible combinations of features, the consumer would have to rank $3 \times 3 \times 3 \times 2 \times 2 = 108$ potential products. Fortunately, a special experimental design permits most of the desired information to be captured by having the consumer rank only the 18 product configurations shown in Figure 7-3.

The results of the conjoint analysis are shown in Figure 7-4. The best combination tested was number 18, with a numerical score of 3.1 $(0.6 + 0.5 + 1.0 + 0.3 + 0.7)$. However, if we modify this configuration by replacing package design C by package design B, we would have an even more desirable product from the customer's point of view. Also, note that if we want to reassure this customer, we would be better off using a money-back guarantee rather than the Good Housekeeping seal.

Use Tests

Once a firm has established a viable product concept and a set of specifications, the next step in the development process is to test samples of the product to see if they meet the needs of the customer. Usually, this is done through a combination of laboratory and field testing. Lab tests offer the advantage of controlled conditions, and they can often simulate usage of the product and obtain results faster than field trials can. Car doors, for example, can be slammed thousands of times in the lab to see if they are designed to last the lifetime of the automobile. Despite these advantages, laboratory tests are artificial, and most new products are also subjected to testing by potential customers.

Customer-use tests are designed to determine how a product performs under the realistic conditions encountered in the home or factory. General Electric, for example, tested its electric slicing knife among 800 persons in 26 different cities before introducing it to the marketplace. In another case, a food manufacturer offered 738 women from four cities sample bottles of a new pourable mayonnaise. After 10 days,

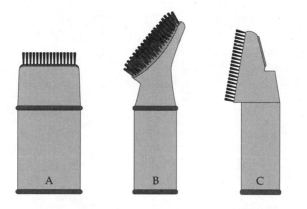

Array	Package Design	Brand Name	Price	Good Housekeeping Seal?	Money-back Guarantee?	Respondent's Evaluation (rank number)
1	A	K2R	$1.19	No	No	13
2	A	Glory	1.39	No	Yes	11
3	A	Bissell	1.59	Yes	No	17
4	B	K2R	1.39	Yes	Yes	2
5	B	Glory	1.59	No	No	14
6	B	Bissell	1.19	No	No	3
7	C	K2R	1.59	No	Yes	12
8	C	Glory	1.19	Yes	No	7
9	C	Bissell	1.39	No	No	9
10	A	K2R	1.59	Yes	No	18
11	A	Glory	1.19	No	Yes	8
12	A	Bissell	1.39	No	No	15
13	B	K2R	1.19	No	No	4
14	B	Glory	1.39	Yes	No	6
15	B	Bissell	1.59	No	Yes	5
16	C	K2R	1.39	No	No	10
17	C	Glory	1.59	No	No	16
18	C	Bissell	1.19	Yes	Yes	1[a]

[a]Highest ranked.

FIGURE 7-3 Experimental Design for the Evaluation of a Carpet Cleaner (Reprinted by permission of *Harvard Business Review*, an exhibit from Paul E. Green and Yoram Wind, "New Ways to Measure Consumers' Judgments," Vol. 53, July–August 1975, p. 108. Copyright © 1975 by the President and Fellows of Harvard College. All rights reserved.)

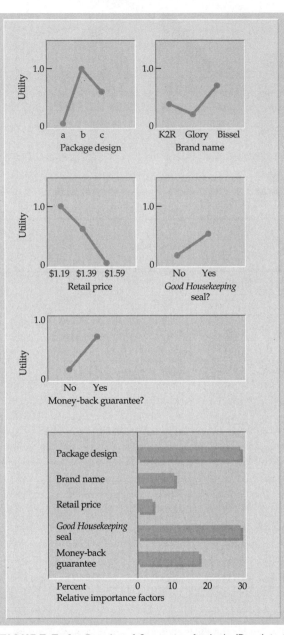

FIGURE 7-4 Results of Computer Analysis (Reprinted by permission of *Harvard Business Review*, an exhibit from Paul E. Green and Yoram Wind, "New Ways to Measure Consumers' Judgments," Vol. 53, July–August 1975, p. 108. Copyright © 1975 by the President and Fellows of Harvard College. All rights reserved.)

personal interviews were conducted to gauge customer reactions and to give the women a chance to purchase some of the product at the regular price. Women who bought samples of the new pourable mayonnaise were contacted three additional times to see whether they wanted more of the item. In addition, the respondents were asked to keep a diary to show how they used the product. This research indicated that although consumers liked pourable mayonnaise, they tended to use it as a liquid salad dressing rather than as a mayonnaise. Thus, the use test suggested that some changes were needed in packaging and promotional appeals if the firm expected the item to compete with more traditional mayonnaise products.

Selecting a Name

New products and services are given names so that they can be easily identified and promoted to consumer and industrial buyers. The best names tend to be short, distinctive, and easy to pronounce and remember. Also, desirable names often suggest action (i.e., Drano, Sinex, U-Haul).

Suggestions for names are frequently provided by the advertising agency that writes the promotional material for the product and by computers programmed to make up nonsense words. Sometimes consumers are interviewed to find out what images are associated with prospective brand names and to measure preferences for alternative names. Words that are made up, such as the Exxon name adopted by Standard Oil of New Jersey, are likely to have fewer negative connotations than words that are already in use. Moreover, fanciful words with no preexisting meaning but created for a specific product have the most legal protection of four grades of trademarks. Some examples of the picking of car names are presented in Marketing in Action box 7-2.

A growing problem with naming new products is that it seems that most of the good names have already been trademarked by other firms. Most names belong to someone else, but this is usually not a problem if the product categories are unrelated. A California automobile security firm challenged Chrysler Corporation over the name Viper. Directed Electronics, Inc., owned a trademark for a line of automobile security alarm systems before Dodge claimed it for its muscle car. The two companies reached an out-of-court settlement, agreeing to coexist peacefully.

You should realize that the names you pick do not have to be spelled the same way to cause problems. Toyota coined the word *Lexus* as a play on the word *luxurious* for a new line of high-priced sedans. However, Mead Corporation thought the name had infringed its trademarked Lexis name for computer database systems. Mead won the first round by getting an injunction that stopped Toyota from advertising its new cars. This action hurt Toyota and slowed down the introduction of the vehicle. Toyota appealed and had the initial ruling reversed. These examples show that you have to be careful with names to avoid lawsuits and delays in getting products to market.

Sometimes brand names become so popular they are used by the public to describe a whole class of products (e.g., Scotch Tape). When this occurs, the manufacturer can lose the rights to the name, as happened in the case of *aspirin* and *escalator*. One way to avoid this problem is to insert the word *brand* after the name, as in Scotch Brand Cellophane Tape, to show that the word *Scotch* is not a generic term.

MARKETING IN ACTION 7-2

WHAT'S IN A NAME?

What's in a name? is a time-consuming and costly question. Selecting, researching, and legally claiming a name, called a *marque*, for a new automobile can cost as much as $200,000. Here is how some cars got their names:

- *Acura:* A computer-generated name, or neologism, that doesn't mean anything but connotes precision. Created with the understanding that one of Honda's desired hallmarks for the brand was precise engineering.
- *Altima:* A neologism that hints at ultimate or best. Replaced the Stanza, a name that never caught on with the public in a decade of use.
- *Geo:* A morpheme—the smallest meaningful language unit—that means world in many languages. Used for a lineup of small vehicles sold in Chevrolet dealerships.
- *Mitsubishi:* Means three pebbles in Japanese, but the company portrayed it as three diamonds, which is Mitsubishi's logo.
- *Mondeo:* Means world in Italian. Ford's "world car" designed and engineered in North America and Europe for sale on both continents.
- *Taurus:* The vice president of Ford car product development and one of his top engineers determined that both their wives were born under the Taurus sign of the Zodiac. Was the project code name that eventually became the name of the car.
- *Windstar:* Ford's successor to its Aerostar minivan. The goal was to keep a family relationship with the Aerostar while being different enough to persuade buyers that it was a new vehicle.

Before Villager was picked as the name for Mercury's minivan, the name Columbia was a finalist. Mercury liked the name because of the symbolism of the space shuttle. It was scrapped when consumer research suggested a link with drugs, as in Colombia's cocaine trade.

It is very difficult to find a name that is crisp, appropriate, inoffensive, and not owned by someone else.

Source: Alan L. Adler, "Marque of a Winner," *Atlanta Constitution*, May 7, 1993, pp. S1, S6.

Packaging

The main concern in designing packages for new products is to protect the merchandise on its journey from the factory to the customer. This is particularly true for industrial goods and appliances whose sales are made from display models. When consumers select products from store shelves, however, packaging becomes an important promotional tool. Sales are enhanced by packages that are visible, informative, emotionally appealing, and workable.

An example of how packaging can boost sales is provided by the new Tropicana orange juice container. Most ready-to-use juice comes in boxy cartons that are hard to open, hard to pour, and impossible to reseal. Tropicana decided to get ahead of the competition by selling its premium juice in a 96-ounce plastic container. The new package has a screw-on cap, and the juglike container is easier to handle and pour. The new package proved to be so successful that Minute Maid responded by introducing a more rounded 64-ounce plastic container for its orange juice. Minute Maid's package came with a smooth handle that was placed low to lower the center of gravity for easier pouring.

Good packaging helps sell because items with high *visibility* are easier to find when they are displayed on store shelves. Designs with good *informational value* tell the consumer at a glance what the package contains. In addition, packages are required by U.S. law to provide information on food additives, flammable materials, net weight, name of the manufacturer or distributor, and other factors. In the United States, the Fair Packaging and Labeling Act also has provisions designed to help standardize package sizes and make comparative shopping easier for the consumer.

The *emotional factor* in packaging refers to the image that consumers form after viewing a product. Emotional appeals can be measured by asking respondents to rate packages by using simple scaling techniques. Thus, consumers could be asked to indicate whether a package was "very modern" at one extreme or "old-fashioned" at the other. Emotional reactions can be critical in the case of certain prestigious products. For example, the bottles used to hold Liz Taylor's White Diamonds perfume are so pleasing visually that many of them have become collector's items.

Workability in packaging means that the container not only protects the product but is also easy to open and reclose, is readily stored, and has utility for secondary uses once the product is used up. Examples of package designs that have these characteristics include tear-top pudding cups, reclosable pop bottles, and the drinking mugs used to hold margarine. The pump dispenser, aseptic packaging, squeezable and recappable bottles, ultralight plastic, and plastic pouches are consumer packaging approaches that have combined convenience with cost effectiveness. The global marketplace is a good source of innovative designs.

MARKET SIMULATIONS

Once the basic dimensions of a new product have been established, marketing executives often forecast future sales levels to see whether a project should be continued. The idea is to obtain some customer reactions to the new item without incurring the cost and publicity associated with a full market test. These projections are usually based on concept and product tests, historical data regressions, laboratory test markets, controlled store tests, and sales wave experiments.

Projections Based on Concept and Use Tests

With this approach, customers are presented with the idea or physical product, and sales are estimated from purchase intentions. An estimate of first-year trials is obtained by multiplying the percentage of prospective buyers who say that they "definitely will buy" by the percentage incidence of prospective buyers in the population. General Foods, in testing a frozen vegetable line, found that 21 percent of its sample of prepared-vegetable users would definitely buy. The prepared-vegetable segment was thought to represent 50 percent of the total population. The estimate of first-year trials was then calculated as 10.5 (0.21 × 0.50 × 100%) percent.[7] This score was compared with data for previous vegetable products. Repeat purchases were estimated using concept fulfillment scores and posttrial attitude scores. This method does a fairly good job of predicting trials for product extensions, but it is not as accurate for repeat purchases of more innovative items.

Computer models have been developed to integrate information from concept tests and other custom marketing research with information from secondary source materials, related product experiences, and informed judgments to make new product forecasts. One such model, called NEWS/Planner, forecasts consumer awareness, trial, repeat purchase, usage, sales, and market share. The model was developed for the clients of a leading advertising agency, BBDO. A more widely available model is Burke's BASES.

Projections Based on Historical Data

Market response can also be simulated using *historical data regressions* (Table 7-2). Equations are constructed that relate the success of past new products to such factors as category penetration, promotional spending, relative price, and distribution. Once

TABLE 7-2
Market Simulation Procedures

	Historical Data Models	*Laboratory Test Markets*	*Sales Wave Test*
Measures of trial	Use past data	Uses observed current data	Uses purchase intentions
Measures of first repeat	Uses repurchase intentions	Uses repurchase intentions	Uses observed current data
Measures of adoption	Uses a decay function model applied to first repeat	Uses a decay function model	Uses observed current behavior
Measures of purchase frequency	Uses past data on other products in category	Uses past data on other products in category	Uses observed current data
Tests price?	No	Yes	Yes
Tests advertising?	No	TV commercials only	Rough concepts only
Tests promotion?	No	In-store promotion only	No
Tests distribution?	No	No	No
Applicable to?	Line extensions and me-too products	New products falling into existing categories	New products not easy to classify into existing product categories

Source: C. J. Chaterji, Ronald T. Lonsdale, and Stanley F. Stash, "New-Product Development: Theory and Practice," in Ben M. Enis and Kenneth J. Roering, eds., *Review of Marketing 1981* (Chicago: American Marketing Association, 1981), p. 150.

an equation is derived based on past experience, values are estimated for the predictor variables for the new item and plugged into the regression equation. The regression procedure works well in predicting trial but is not as accurate for items that fail to fit existing product categories. Some marketers believe that even a small amount of consumer research data collected for the new brand will lead to more insight and thus better new product decisions than will data collected on other brands.

Laboratory Test Markets

Laboratory test markets (Table 7-2) expose consumers to commercials for new and existing products and then allow them to make purchases from the product category in a simulated store. The new item is then taken home and used, and a follow-up interview measures satisfaction and repurchase intent. Frequently, repeat purchases are measured by offering consumers a chance to buy the product again after initial home placement. Although the exposure to ads and the store purchases are somewhat artificial, the method has proved to be a quick, inexpensive, and fairly accurate predictor of future sales levels. The method might not work well for highly seasonal products, emerging ill-defined categories, or therapeutic products for infrequent symptoms. Even so, Johnson & Johnson ran a test market simulation of Sundown Sunscreen that proved to be within 5 percent of its equilibrium market share in a concurrent test market.

A computer model called ASSESSOR combines executive judgments on marketing strategy with laboratory data using preference and trial and repeat purchase models of behavior. Although this model has proved to be an accurate predictor of market shares, the method can be used only when new brands seek to enter well-defined product categories. Situations in which innovative products create product categories, or in which products require long periods of usage before benefits are realized, are best evaluated by using extended sales wave tests or regular test markets.

Sales Wave Tests

Product adoption and purchase frequency can also be estimated by using *sales wave* experiments (Table 7-2). This approach measures repeat purchase behavior by observing a sample of consumers who receive the new product through a home placement and then are offered a series of opportunities to purchase it at a special price. Forcing the consumer to pay for repeat purchases on several occasions (four to six) simulates the wear-out and adoption process that normally occurs in the marketplace. An advantage of sales wave experiments is that they can be used to forecast performance of category-creating new products. The main problem with these experiments is that they take more time and are more expensive than the other methods that have been discussed. Also, the continual recontact with the customer cannot be duplicated in the marketplace with normal advertising programs.

The market simulation procedures that we have discussed share several advantages that have made then widely used by marketing managers. First, they allow you to keep the existence and the special features of new products secret from your competitors. This provides an element of surprise and often allows you to grab and keep a larger share of the market. Second, these simulations take less time to run than traditional test markets and you can get products to the market faster. Third, market simulations are cheaper, and they allow you to develop more new product ideas.

TEST MARKETING

Test marketing involves placing your new product in selected retail stores and measuring customer purchase rates in response to regular promotional activities. It is most often used when new products are radically different and companies do not know how to promote them or whether customers will buy them. Low-cost consumer items are the most common products placed in test markets. High tooling costs make it impractical to test-market appliances or automobiles. Industrial goods manufacturers work closely with their customers and rely on feedback from use tests to determine when a new product is ready for national distribution.

Test Procedures

One of the first steps in designing a test market is selecting a representative group of test cities. One rule of thumb is that two or more test areas with a minimum of 3 percent of all households are needed for national projectability. Each market should have at least 0.2 percent of these households but no more than 1.5 percent.[8] The objective is to find stable communities in which key demographic statistics are typical of the anticipated buyers of the product. Test cities must also have cooperative merchants and good media coverage to facilitate promotional activities. In addition, test cities should be isolated from each other so that promotional campaigns run in one city do not influence sales in other test areas. The three best-matched markets in terms of demographic profiles, media coverage, and market isolation are reputed to be Erie, Pennsylvania; Fort Wayne, Indiana; and Tucson, Arizona.

Test markets typically vary in length from a few months to one or two years. A key factor in determining the length of a particular study is the repurchase cycle of the product. Some items, for example, are used infrequently and may be repurchased only every three or four months. A test market cycle must be long enough to measure repeat buying as well as trial purchases. Other factors influencing the length of a study are the availability of research funds and the threat of retaliation by competitors.

Limitations of Test Markets

Perhaps the most serious drawbacks of test marketing are that it is expensive and that potential sales are lost because of delays in getting the product to the marketplace. In addition, it is often difficult to interpret sales results produced by test markets. Because the products are new, there are no absolute standards of performance that can be used for comparison. Except for situations where sales are unusually high or low, test results may simply reflect the basic uncertainty that prevailed when the study was initiated. In addition, the small number of test cities used and the artificial nature of the testing process make it hazardous to project results into national sales figures. A compounding factor is the realization that some products succeed in test markets and then fail when introduced nationally, and vice versa.

For example, Holly Farms developed a roasted chicken to appeal to busy customers. This convenient precooked product scored well in a year of test marketing. Holly Farms found that 22 percent of Atlanta women had tried the roasted chicken and 90 percent said they would buy it again. Based on these enthusiastic results, Holly Farms built a $20 million plant to produce the chickens and spent $14 million in advertising to gain national distribution. Despite strong customer acceptance, the national rollout went poorly and the roasted chickens gained distribution in only 50 percent of U.S. stores. Holly Farms found that poor sales were due to the short (14-day) shelf life of the product and to the fact that it took up to 9 days to get the chickens to the stores. Although grocery buyers described the product as outstanding, they were not reordering because of the limited time they had to sell it. Problems with the new roasted chickens were so severe that Holly Farms' profits were expected to decline by 20 percent. An even more insidious problem is the response that competitors can make to test market activity. One possibility is a direct attempt to wreck the test by introducing price cuts or coupons that upset normal sales patterns. A more probable reaction is that competitors will audit your test markets and use the results to develop their own product. For example, a health and beauty aids firm developed a deodorant containing baking soda. A competitor observed the product in the test market and was able to create and roll out its own version of the deodorant nationally before the first firm completed its testing. To add insult to injury, the second firm successfully sued the product's originator for copyright infringement when it launched its deodorant nationally! The moral of the story is that firms that allow easily copied items to languish in test markets for extended periods may find that competitors have stolen their ideas, their advertising copy, and their markets.

Test markets are also inappropriate for most industrial products and for items that require extensive tooling and unique production equipment. It is simply too expensive to test-market lift trucks, automobiles, and large appliances; alternative measures of customer acceptance must be developed for these items. One possibility is to try out new products with regional market introductions. This involves promoting and selling the product in a few markets and then expanding distribution if the product is successful. Although regional introductions are more expensive than test markets, this method is cheaper than introducing a product nationally. Also, if successful items are moved quickly from regional to national distribution, competitive responses are likely to be weak and ineffectual.

Remember that test marketing is not a cure-all for product development problems. It is simply one of many ways to gather data on new items.

COMMERCIALIZATION

The next step in the product development process is the introduction of new items to the dealers and then to the ultimate buyers of the product. The objective of *commercialization* is to get the dealers to stock the item and persuade the ultimate consumer to purchase it for the first time. Previous stages have eliminated undesirable projects and have established the specifications, prices, and promotional arrangements most desirable for the new venture. Now you must weld these elements into a new product introduction plan that will achieve your objectives. Commercialization is concerned with implementing this plan. Marketing in Action box 7-3 describes how a clever plan allowed a small company to successfully introduce a new frozen pasta line without the $10 to $20 million usually required for promotion and advertising.

The Importance of Timing

The success or failure of many products often depends on when the product is introduced. If it is too soon, customers may reject the product because it is not fully developed or because it is too far ahead of its time. For example, First Nationwide Financial Corporation opened 170 mini-bank branches in K-Mart stores in 12 states. After three and one-half years of extensive efforts, the branches were all closed. K-Mart customers proved to be reluctant to do their banking at the same store where they bought jeans, light bulbs, and motor oil. The new service required customers to change their habits radically. In this case, the strategic window of opportunity had not yet opened. A more common error is to introduce a product too late—after competitors have captured a dominant market position. Motorola moved too slowly on its 68040 microprocessor and yielded the field to Intel's 80386 and 80486 chips.

While a few *market pioneers*, such as Crisco shortening and Coca-Cola soft drink, are long-lived market share leaders, the first firm to sell in a new product category usually does not maintain this leadership very long—about five years. On the other hand, the firm known as the *early leader*, that is, the market share leader during the early growth phase of the product's life, is generally still the market leader today. For example, Trommer's Red Letter was the first entrant in light beer, but Miller Lite, introduced 14 years later, quickly became the dominant brand. Researchers believe that early leaders are successful because of their ability to spot a market opportunity and their willingness to commit large resources to develop the market.[9]

Another problem is timing new products so that they do not merely replace the sales of existing company products. Many firms develop a number of new product ideas and then keep them in "cold storage" until they are needed.[10] This allows new items to be released as interest in current products declines (product saturation) or when competitors come out with an innovation.

New product introductions also vary with the business cycle.[11] The number of new product announcements is low when the business cycle is high and slowing. New product introductions increase when firms anticipate that the economy will improve. New product introductions thus lead the business cycle. Once the impor-

MARKETING IN ACTION 7-3

INTRODUCING MICHELINA'S FROZEN PASTA

In 1991, a small Minnesota firm decided to go up against three of the biggest players in the frozen food business—Conagra, Nestlé's Stouffer unit, and Philip Morris's Kraft unit. At the time there was intense competition in frozen entrees among the three giants and the prospects for a new brand were dismal. Also Luigino's planned to enter this market without spending a penny on media advertising or couponing. Without advertising to build awareness, there appeared to be no chance for Luigino's to break into the frozen entree market.

Luigino's introductory plan was based on the use of a small sales force and trade promotions. This allowed stores to feature the products in their ads and use them as in-store specials. By emphasizing trade promotion, Michelina's entrees sold for about $1 retail and sometimes as low as 69 cents. These prices were one half or less than those of their competitors. After two years Michelina's had 4.7 percent of the product category and annual sales of about $100 million. Also its competitors were forced to bring out new lower priced entrees.

Successful product introduction does not have to be expensive.

Source: Richard Gibson, "Michelina's Frozen Entrees Trip Up Giants," *The Wall Street Journal*, September 21, 1993, p. B7.

tance of timing is understood, the question becomes how to manage product development activities so that products arrive on the market at the right competitive moment.

Coordinating Product Introductions

Timing is crucial during commercialization because goodwill and sales can be lost if the product fails to reach the market on schedule. The introduction of General Motors' Cavalier compact car provides a classic example of the problems that can occur. GM announced a spring availability date for the new car with a lavish advertising campaign. Customers were told to go to their dealers and test-drive it. However, when they arrived, there were no cars because last-minute production delays had greatly reduced the supply of engines. When the cars finally arrived months later, customers found them to be underpowered and first-year sales were far below expectations. In this case, failure to coordinate production and advertising cost GM millions in lost revenues.

Using PERT   Optimum coordination of commercialization activities can be achieved by monitoring the introduction of new products by using a PERT (program evaluation and review technique) type of control procedure. This approach helps identify critical operations, and the status reports produced by the system keep the project director informed of delays in completion times. The first step in the application of PERT techniques is the development of a detailed activity network. This is based on a listing of all activities that must be performed and a careful analysis of the sequential and concurrent relationships among activities. Estimates of completion times are then used to derive a product development network, as shown in Figure 7-5.

This diagram is made up of a series of arrows that represent activities or jobs to be completed. Each activity is labeled, and begins and ends at points called *events* (circles with letters in them). The relationship of the arrows to the events indicates the sequential and frequently parallel character of different product development activities. The most important path through the network is known as the *critical path*. This represents the longest sequence of activities to be completed in the development cycle, and it determines the earliest date that the project can be completed. The critical path is obtained by adding and comparing activity completion times for all possible routes through the network. In Figure 7-5, the critical path is shown by the broken line connecting activities A, D, F, and G. The critical path is important because delays in completing activities on this route will mean slippages in the schedule for the entire project. Also, if competitive pressure makes it necessary to speed up the introduction of a new product, the critical path will show the activities that will have to be expedited or omitted entirely.

Saving Time   Three approaches can be used when competitive pressure or slippages in critical path activities make it necessary to save time on a project. One is to convert sequential activities into projects that can be run in parallel. A second approach is to eliminate certain activities entirely. This method has the advantage of saving both time and money. In one application, network analysis indicated that it would take

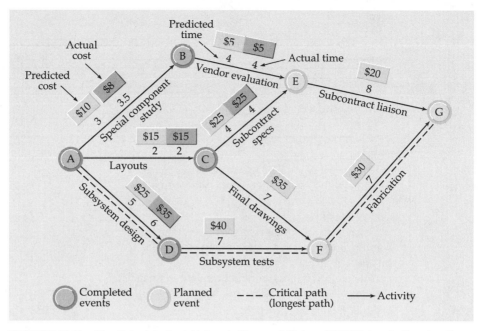

FIGURE 7-5 The Schedule-Cost Network: Plan and Status, PERT Network Showing Precedence of Activities (Tasks) (From Edgar A. Pessemier, *Product Management Strategy and Organization* [New York: Wiley, 1982], p. 48)

two years for an improved product to reach national distribution. A simulation was run with the test market removed, and the length of the development schedule was reduced to nine months. Management was willing to accept a greater risk of failure in order to get its product on the market quickly. A third way to speed the completion of activities in development networks is to apply additional resources such as money, human resources, materials, machines, or space.

Although network analysis has been effectively used in product development by Lever Brothers, Diamond Alkali, American Cyanamid, Sealtest, and other companies, there are limits to what this or any other control technique can accomplish. Network analysis is a fairly expensive procedure, and potential benefits must be significant if the technique is to pay its way. Because of the cost and problems of implementing network analysis, this method is probably not justified unless a project involves the investment of $1 million.

ACCELERATING NPD

An average company in the PMDA's *Best Practices Survey* took about three years to develop more innovative types of new products. The respondents described the new product activities that were part of their organization's product development process

TABLE 7-3

NPD Usage and Time Spent

Activity	Percent Using	Months Spent
Concept search	89.9	3.51
This includes brainstorming and other creativity-stimulating techniques, preliminary discussions about the product's design, and identifying new product opportunities.		
Concept screening	76.2	2.96
This may include scoring and ranking concepts according to some criteria and eliminating unsuitable concepts.		
Concept testing	80.4	3.63
This covers preliminary market research to determine market need, niche, and attractiveness.		
Business analysis	89.4	2.58
An evaluation of the product concept in financial terms as a business proposition.		
Product development	98.9	14.37
The technical work to convert a concept into a working model.		
Product use testing, field testing, and/or market testing	86.8	6.04
Offering the product to a preselected group of potential buyers to determine its suitability and/or marketability.		
Commercialization	96.3	6.46
Launching the new product into full-scale product and sales.		
Other process activities	20.1	8.59
Includes regulatory approval/registration and patent filing.		

Source: Alan L. Page, ''Assessing New Product Development Practices and Performance: Establishing Crucial Norms,'' *Journal of Product Innovation Management*, Vol. 10, No. 4 (September 1993), p. 281.

and how long it typically took for each activity to be completed. This information is shown in Table 7-3.

Facing shorter product life cycles and realizing that being early to market can provide a significant competitive advantage, businesses are trying to reduce the development cycle time for new products. Leading firms are making major gains in accelerating NPD:

• AT&T now takes one year to design a new phone, down from two years.

• Honda turns out new models in less than four years from drawing board to show room compared with five years for most U.S. manufacturers.

- Honeywell now takes 12 months to design and build a new thermostat, a process which used to take four years.
- HP took 22 months to develop its new printer, down from 4½ years.
- Xerox cut its development time from six years to three.[12]

Actions that you can take to accelerate NPD include simplifying, eliminating delays, eliminating steps, speed up, and parallel processing. These actions are detailed in Table 7-4.

MARKETING INTERFACES WITH R&D AND PRODUCTION

Cooperation and communication among marketing, R&D, engineering, and manufacturing yield more successful new products. This section focuses on managing relations among these groups and, in particular, on using quality function deployment (QFD) to encourage joint consideration of marketing and technology issues.

Managing Relations

Managing NPD requires balancing the appropriate involvement of top management with empowerment of project teams.[13] This balancing is accomplished by using four mechanisms: the NPD committee, the project steering committee, phase reviews, and structured development methodology. The NPD committee is made up of senior managers whose role is to control the flow of new products by approving, canceling, or redirecting projects at specific points in their development. The project steering committee or task force is a small, cross-functional group which is solely responsible for taking a project from concept through launch. Phase reviews allow the NPD committee to impact major project decisions without micromanaging. Structured development methodology provides the "rules of the game" by defining deliverables for each phase review and setting objective measures with which to assess the progress of a project. Some guidelines for improving relations between R&D and marketing are given in Table 7-5.

A large division of a digital telecommunications manufacturer balanced its NPD, with impressive results. Time to market plunged and products were aligned with the marketplace, leading to significant increases in market share and revenue. Quality improved and manufacturing costs decreased, substantially improving product margins. With the same resources, the company now has significantly more development projects under way than ever before. Product development has become challenging and rewarding for both management and individual contributors.

Quality Function Deployment

QFD is a key total quality management technique for the NPD process. Interfunctional teams use a series of matrices, which look like "houses," incorporating the

TABLE 7-4

NPD Acceleration Approaches

Approaches	How	Benefits	Limitations
Simplify	Focus product requirements and minimize user education requirements	Makes technology and design more understandable Applies to external, human corporate relationships Streamlines reports, documents, and controls Flatter organizations	Reentry problems of "project dedicated" team members back into their functional groups at project completion Not meeting customer requirements Higher costs if external vendors are used to augment NPD process Not meeting product design requirements Lack of project status detail Lack of control if reporting not adequate Use of trust to simplify NPD process can lead to inadequate critical thinking
Eliminate delays	Reduce marketing plan and launch delays	Fosters clearer up-front thinking—vision Encourages early technological investigation of long-lead items	Hurried acceptance of NPD vision Early capital appropriations/alternative technologies may result in poor estimates Early launch may lead to inadequate product documentation
Eliminate steps	Utilize "lead user" ideas and minimize formal market testing	Authorizing signature elimination moves authority down the organizational hierarchy Helps eliminate the "not invented here" attitude	If external vendors are used, cost, quality, propriety advantages may be lost Senior management may be reluctant to decentralize NPD decision making Requires vendors supplying component parts to adopt high quality standards to minimize in-house testing
Speed up	Use small groups to generate ideas	Forces use of new technologies "Smarter" and "shorter" testing algorithms Switch from matrix to project organization structure increases focus on NPD	Higher stress Danger of inadequate NPD project documentation Higher risks may occur if some phases, such as testing, are shortened
Parallel processing	Concurrent marketing	Simultaneous engineering, testing, and market research Increased knowledge of other functions Fosters teamwork	Potential for confusion Higher stress levels NPD participants must work with greater uncertainty More frequent communication required More resources required Need for teamwork training

Source: Adapted from Murray R. Millson, S. P. Raj, and David Wilemon, "A Survey of Major Approaches for Accelerating New Product Development," *Journal of Product Innovation Management*, Vol. 9, No. 1 (March 1992), pp. 53–69.

TABLE 7-5
Guidelines for Improving Relations Between R&D and Marketing

1. *Break large projects into smaller ones.* The smaller number of individuals and organizational layers on small projects permits increased face-to-face contacts, increased empathy, and easier coordination.

2. *Take a proactive stance toward interface problems.* Aggressively seek out and face potential and actual interface problems; openly criticize and examine behaviors.

3. *Eliminate mild problems before they grow into severe problems.* Severe disharmonies are extremely difficult to overcome.

4. *Involve both parties early in the life of the project.* Make R&D and marketing joint participants in all decisions, from the start of the project to its completion. This lessens feelings of distrust and lack of appreciation.

5. *Promote and maintain dyadic relationships.* A dyad is a very powerful symbiotic, interpersonal alliance between two individuals who become intensely committed to each other and to the joint pursuit of a new product idea. Foster dyads by assigning persons with complementary skills and personalities to work together and give them significant autonomy.

6. *Make open communication an explicit responsibility of everyone.* Require quarterly information meetings between R&D and marketing, day-long and week-long exchanges of personnel, periodic gripe sessions, and the constant encouragement of personnel to visit their counterparts. Formally charge every employee to participate in this open-door policy.

7. *Use interlocking task forces.* A steering committee, which includes, among others, the project coordinator, as well as the R&D and marketing task force leaders, should oversee the entire NPD project. However, the R&D and marketing task force memberships may change as the project passes through the various NPD stages.

8. *Clarify the decision authorities.* A well-developed charter, which details who has the right to make what decision in which circumstances, should govern and guide the R&D/ marketing venture. For example, marketing might have sole authority and responsibility for defining users' needs, while R&D might have ultimate authority and responsibility for selecting the technical means to meet these needs.

Source: William E. Souder, "Managing Relations Between R&D and Marketing in New Product Development Projects," *Journal of Product Innovation Management*, Vol. 5, No. 1 (March 1988), pp. 6–19.

"voice of the customer" throughout design, manufacturing, and service delivery.[14] Firms using QFD include Campbell's Soup, Colgate, General Motors, Hancock Insurance, Hewlett-Packard, IBM, Kodak, Mitsubishi, Procter & Gamble, Toyota, and Xerox. An example is given in Marketing in Action box 7-4.

QFD uses houses for visual-data presentation. The first house, shown in Figure 7-6, is known as the "House of Quality" and links customer needs to design attributes, engineering measures of product performance. The second house links these design attributes to actions the firm can take. The third house links these actions to implementation decisions. The final house links implementation to production planning. The goal of QFD is customer satisfaction.

THE VOICE OF THE CUSTOMER: PURITAN-BENNETT'S RENAISSANCE SPIROMETRY SYSTEM

Puritan-Bennett's (PB's) PB900A was a major player in the market for spirometers, a medical instrument that measures lung capacity—an important indicator of general health. However, its share slipped from 15 percent to 7 percent as a result of a new product by Welch Allyn (WA). WA's PneumoCheck was introduced at a dramatically lower price ($1995 vs. $4500 for PB). WA's lower cost was made possible by lower functionality. The PneumoCheck measured a person's ability to exhale, while the PB900A measured both exhaling and inhaling. PB considered a cost-reduction program but felt that the basic design of the PB900A would make it impossible to come close to the WA price. Instead, they started the design from scratch based on QFD and the voice of the customer.

An interfunctional team drawn from marketing, customer service, sales, engineering, R&D, manufacturing, and management began with qualitative interviews and focus groups to identify customer needs. PB structured customer needs into a hierarchy, measured importances, and measured customer perceptions of both PB and competitive products. Needs identified included these:

- Product is affordable
- Easy to operate
- Easy to clean
- Convenient-sized output
- Sanitary
- Quick service response
- Provides accurate readings
- Eliminates technician variability
- Good printout quality
- Reliability
- Diagnostic information meets needs
- Easy-to-interpret diagnostic information
- Fast to use

- Easy to hold
- Right size for patient
- Easy to set up for first time
- Easy to calibrate
- Availability of machine parts
- Good training/education
- Sleek appearance
- Good printer quality
- Low cost of repairs/service
- Portability
- Effective data storage/retrieval
- Environmentally safe

By focusing on these needs, PB designed within a year an entirely new modular spirometry system that could be customized by each user segment (hospitals, large laboratories, small clinics, and general practitioners). For example, affordability was achieved with the modular prices and effective data storage and retrieval by plug-in patient data cards. Each customer need was met at a level that matched or exceeded that of the competition. A screening system for occasional use was priced $405 below WA's, but heavy users could increase functionality and productivity with a system of three spirometers, two base stations, two charging stations, two memory cards, and a Canon Bubblejet printer at a cost of $4088.

Design teams allow firms to meet customers' needs at lower costs.

Source: Abbie Griffin and John R. Hauser, "The Voice of the Customer," *Marketing Science*, Vol. 12, No. 1 (Winter 1993), pp. 1–27.

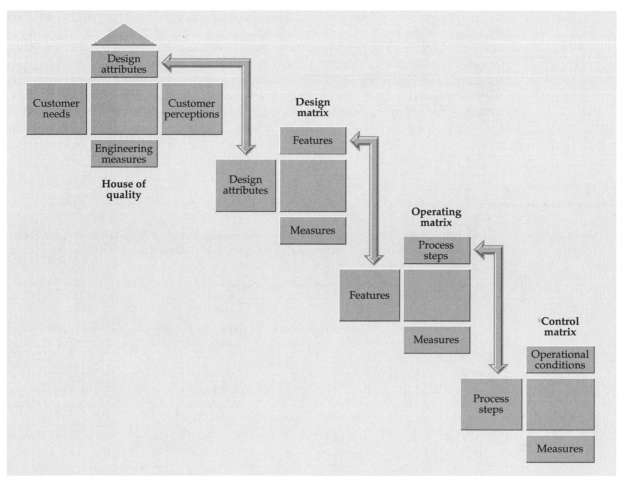

FIGURE 7-6   Linked Houses Convey the Customer's Voice (From Abbie Griffin, "Evaluating Development Processes: QFD as an Example," *Journal of Product Innovation Management*, Vol. 9 [September 1992], p. 173)

SUMMARY

Product development is an exciting, creative process that converts ideas into commercially viable goods and services. Product development is also expensive. The likelihood of increasing sales and profits from new items is enhanced by careful attention to the organization and control of this activity. A key ingredient is a full-time director of product development to expedite and coordinate the many jobs and individuals necessary to produce new merchandise. Flow diagrams and PERT-type control procedures are particularly useful in making sure that projects reach the market on time and at an acceptable cost. In addition, the firm must foster a climate that is receptive to new ideas and develop screening criteria that are appropriate to its own objectives and resources. Also, new products need to be carefully tested so that they reflect the attributes and quality levels actually desired by the ultimate customer. This means concept tests to gauge customer reactions to product ideas, preference tests to select product attributes, and use tests to evaluate packaging and long-run customer acceptance. Where new products are radically different, sales tests may be needed to measure repurchase rates and alternative promotional appeals. Finally, products must be introduced to the marketplace so that dealers and customers will become aware of the new items and begin to purchase them on a regular basis.

NOTES

1. Albert L. Page, "Assessing New Product Development Practices and Performance: Establishing Crucial Norms," *Journal of Product Innovation Management*, Vol. 10, No. 4 (September 1993), pp. 273–290.

2. E. J. Kleinschmidt and R. G. Cooper, "The Impact of Product Innovativeness on Performance," *Journal of Product Innovation Management*, Vol. 8, No. 4 (December 1991), pp. 240–251.

3. This section taken from Harry Nyström, "Product Development Strategy: An Integration of Technology and Marketing," *Journal of Product Innovation Management*, Vol. 2, No. 1 (March 1985), pp. 25–33.

4. Eric von Hippel, *The Sources of Innovation* (Oxford: Oxford University Press, 1988); and Cornelius Herstatt and Eric von Hippel, "Developing New Product Concepts Via the Lead User Method: A Case Study in a 'Low-Tech' Field," *Journal of Product Innovation Management*, Vol. 9, No. 3 (September 1992), pp. 213–221.

5. Robert G. Cooper, "Selecting New Product Projects: Using the NewProd System," *Journal of Product Innovation Management*, Vol. 2, No. 1 (March 1985), pp. 34–44.

6. Robert G. Cooper, "The NewProd System: The Industry Experience," *Journal of Product Innovation Management*, Vol. 9, No. 2 (June 1992), pp. 113–127.

7. General Foods' Americana Recipe Vegetables (B) case written by Lawrence J. Ring, University of Virginia.

8. Edward M. Tauber, "Improve Test Market Selection with These Rules of Thumb," *Marketing News*, Vol. 15 (January 22, 1982), pp. 8–9.

9. Peter N. Golder and Gerald J. Tellis, "Pioneer Advantage: Marketing Logic or Marketing Legend," *Journal of Marketing Research*, Vol. 30, No. 2 (May 1993), pp. 158–170.

10. For some examples, see William P. Putsis, Jr., "Why Put Off Until Tomorrow What You Can Do Today?" *Journal of Product Innovation Management*, Vol. 10, No. 3 (June 1993), pp. 195–203.

11. Timothy M. Devinney, "New Products Over the Business Cycle," *Journal of Product Innovation Management*, Vol. 7, No. 4 (December 1990), pp. 261–273.

12. Murray R. Millson, S. P. Raj, and David Wilemon, "A Survey of Major Approaches for Accelerating New Product Development," *Journal of Product Innovation Management*, Vol. 9, No. 1 (March 1992), p. 54.

13. This section taken from Michael T. Anthony and Jonathan McKay, "Balancing the Product Development Process: Achieving Product and Cycle-Time Excellence in High-Technol-

ogy Industries," *Journal of Product Innovation Management*, Vol. 9, No. 2 (June 1992), pp. 140–147.

14. John R. Hauser and Don Clausing, "The House of Quality," *Harvard Business Review*, (May–June 1988), pp. 63–73; Abbie Griffin, "Evaluating QFD's Use in U.S. Firms as a Process for Developing Products," *Journal of Product Innovation Management*, Vol. 9, No. 3 (September 1992), pp. 171–187; and Abbie Griffin and John R. Hauser, "The Voice of the Customer," *Marketing Science*, Vol. 12, No. 1 (Winter 1993), pp. 1–27. QFD/Capture, software to perform QFD on your personal computer, is available from International TechneGroup, Inc.

SUGGESTED READING

Masten, David L. "Packaging's Proper Role Is to Sell the Product," in *Marketing*, A. Dale Timpe, ed. (New York: Facts on File, 1989), pp. 43–46.

Hauser, John R. and Don Clausing. "The House of Quality," *Harvard Business Review* (May–June 1988), pp. 63–73.

FURTHER READING

Crawford, C. Merle. "The Dual-Drive Concept of Product Innovation," *Business Horizons*, Vol. 34, No. 3 (May–June 1991), pp. 32–38.

Day, Ronald G. *Quality Function Deployment: Linking a Company with Its Customers* (Milwaukee: ASQC Quality Press, 1993).

Eppen, Gary D., Ward A. Hanson, and R. Kipp Martin. "Bundling—New Products, New Markets, Low Risk," *Sloan Management Review*, Vol. 32, No. 4 (Summer 1991), pp. 7–14.

Hall, John H. *Bringing New Products to Market: The Art and Science of Creating Winners* (New York: AMACOM, 1992).

Moore, William L., and Edgar A. Pessemier. *Product Planning and Management: Designing and Delivering Value* (New York: McGraw-Hill, 1993).

Pine, Joseph B., II. *Mass Customization* (Boston: Harvard Business School Press, 1993).

Wheelwright, Steven C., and Kim B. Clark. *Revolutionizing Product Development: Quantum Leaps in Speed, Efficiency, and Quality* (New York: Free Press, 1992).

Zangwill, Willard I. *Lightening Strategies for Innovation: How the World's Best Firms Create New Products* (New York: Lexington Books, 1993).

QUESTIONS

1. In 1900, there was legislation in the United States to close the Patent Office. The country was convinced that everything that could be invented had been invented. Are we ever going to run out of ideas?

2. "Real entrepreneurs don't do market research." Comment on this saying.

3. Sports drinks are designed to replenish fluid, minerals, and carbohydrates lost during exercise. Primarily water, the beverages typically include sweeteners and such electrolytes as potassium and sodium. Gatorade dominates the U.S. market, with about a 90 percent market share in supermarkets. Gatorade is Quaker Oats's most important product, accounting for more than 15 percent of its sales. Quaker vigorously defends its turf. Gatorade's promotional expenditures run about $25 million and feature basketball star Michael Jordan as the drink's chief spokesman. Coca-Cola is bringing out PowerAde. PowerAde has 33 percent more carbohydrates for energy than Gatorade. Coke claims that PowerAde is lighter, goes down quickly, and does not have a heavy salt flavor. PowerAde will be the official sports drink at the 1996 Olympic Games in Atlanta, Coke's home town. Assess PowerAde's chances.

4. Consider the following quotations from *Financial World* about a company in the restaurant business:

    - ''World's biggest chain of highway restaurants'' (May 20, 1964, p. 5)
    - ''Pioneer in restaurant franchising'' (April 5, 1967, p. 6)
    - ''Most strongly entrenched factor and highest quality investment'' (April 5, 1967, p. 6)
    - ''Most fabulous success story in restaurant chains'' (September 8, 1965, p. 5) What restaurant do these statements bring to mind? What does this example say about the pioneer advantage?

5. Sophisticated Data Research illustrates conjoint analysis with the example of a bath/beauty bar soap. We have to choose the color (red, blue, yellow), the shape (cubic, cylindrical, spherical), and the aroma (scented, unscented). Rather than ask users to rank all 18 combinations, we ask them to rank 9 combinations chosen by following sound experimental design procedures. The results for a typical consumer are as follows:

Possible Product	Rank
Red-cubic-scented	8
Red-cylindrical-unscented	2
Red-spherical-scented	4
Blue-cubic-unscented	9
Blue-cylindrical-scented	5
Blue-spherical-scented	6
Yellow-cubic-scented	7
Yellow-cylindrical-scented	3
Yellow-spherical-unscented	1

where 1 = most preferred and 8 = least preferred. Conjoint analysis yields the following utilities or part-worths:

Attribute/Level	Utility
Color	
Red	0.214
Blue	−1.072
Yellow	0.857
Shape	
Cubic	−1.929
Cylindrical	1.072
Spherical	0.857
Aroma	
Scented	−0.482
Unscented	0.482

Which of the 18 possible product configurations would be most preferred by this consumer? For a given shape, is this consumer better off with a yellow-scented bar or a red-unscented bar?

6. PepsiCo has launched a clear, colorless cola called "Crystal Pepsi." The product is designed to cash in on consumer interest in New Age beverages. The product's main appeal is image. With clear bottles and silver cans with labels tinted blue, the product is designed to convey good health, purity, and icy cold water. Procter & Gamble has concocted a version of its Ivory bar soap that won't float. What risks are these firms taking in removing attributes from products that consumers have come to expect?

7. The three marketers of nicotine patches bombarded smokers so relentlessly with ads that promise a new and better way to kick the habit that widespread patch shortages developed. This created problems not just for potential new users, but also for current users who need patches to complete the recommended six- to eight-week cycle. What should the patch marketers do?

8. From a manufacturing point of view, "quality is conformance," that is, the product meets specifications. How is this definition helpful? Lacking? What do you think the dimensions of quality are?

Chapter 8

*Product
and Brand
Management*

Nothing is more profitable than adding a few share points to an existing product.

WILLIAM TRAGOS

This chapter emphasizes the management of products and services from the time they are introduced until they are removed from the marketplace. Our focus is on the specific plans and strategies needed during each phase of the product life cycle to improve the competitive position of the firm. The objective is to show how marketing executives work to control the destinies of products and services on a day-to-day basis.

You must first understand what products are and how they fit into the offerings of your organization. In addition, you need to know the advantages of identifying products by national and distributor brand names. Finally, it is your job to decide when to rescue declining products and when to bury them.

WHAT IS A PRODUCT?

Products can be defined as goods and services that fill customers' needs. We most often think of products as *physical objects* such as computers, cars, lipstick, or wine. However, marketers are also concerned with promoting *service-oriented* products such as insurance, banking, movies, and resort locations. In addition, products include *people* such as political candidates and *events* such as the Super Bowl. Another category of products is the *organization* such as the American Cancer Society and Friends of the Opera. Even *ideas* can be marketed, as in the case of recycling or seat belt usage. These examples suggest that the term *product* is broadly defined and can include physical goods, services, events, organizations, people, and ideas.

Product Components

Every product is made up of a set of tangible and intangible characteristics. The most obvious are features such as color, shape, and price. More subtle components include styling and quality levels. Most products are marketed under brand names that help identify them for promotional purposes. Packaging is an important characteristic of physical products. Not only does packaging protect products, but it helps catch the attention of the buyers in retail stores. Packaging has the added advantage of making products easier to use. We now see ketchup and salad dressings packaged in plastic squeeze bottles that simplify dispensing of the products.

Beyond the basic product characteristics are a host of intangible supporting factors. These include such things as after-sale service and installation. Some firms just sell the product; others make sure that it is installed correctly and performs up to specifications. Warranties are a vital characteristic as products become more complicated and difficult to repair. Customers often prefer products with the best guarantees and will sometimes buy extended warranties to gain peace of mind. Favorable credit terms and delivery are also valuable characteristics that help sell merchandise. One national retail chain, for example, charges $20 to deliver major appliances, but competitors are gaining market share by offering free next-day delivery.

Product Classifications

Marketing managers often group products into categories based on their attributes. The idea is that different types of products should be marketed according to their special needs. For example, *nondurable* consumer goods such as shampoo are used up quickly and purchased often. This suggests that they should be made available in many locations and promoted with advertising to induce trial and to build preference. *Durables*, on the other hand, last longer and are replaced less frequently. With durables such as tape decks and computers, you need to provide personal selling and after-sale service. Distribution with durables tends to be selective, and warranties are more important.

Another way to classify products is by customer shopping habits. *Convenience* goods are purchased frequently, with a minimum of effort. Examples include gasoline, typewriter ribbons, and newspapers. Your objective with convenience goods is to make them readily available at multiple locations so that it is easy for customers to buy them. A special class of consumer goods are *impulse* items that are purchased on the spur of the moment. These goods include candy, gum, and cigarettes. You want them near checkout counters so that customers will be reminded of the need to buy.

Shopping goods are items for which customers compare price and quality at several dealerships before they buy. Furniture and appliances are examples of shopping merchandise. With these items, the dealer with the widest assortment and the best-trained salespeople is most likely to get the sale. *Specialty* goods have unique characteristics or brand names that draw customers to retail stores. If you want to buy a Porsche, convenience is not as important as whether the dealer will keep his promises on delivery and service.

PRODUCT MIX STRATEGY

One of your key jobs as marketing manager is to select a mix of compatible products that promotes efficiency in selling, production, pricing, promotion, and distribution. This set of merchandise that your firm offers to customers is called the *product mix*. In a small organization the product mix may be just a few items, but in a large firm it may contain thousands of products.

Assortment Dimensions

Product assortments are usually described in terms of width, length, and depth. *Width* refers to the number of different product lines that are marketed by a single firm. Product lines are groups of similar items that are used together, sold to the same customer, or handled through the same distribution channels. For example,

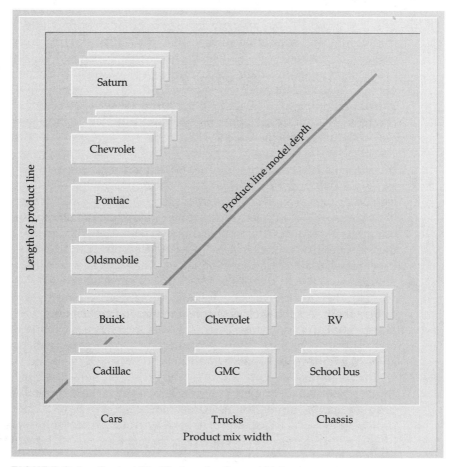

FIGURE 8-1   Product Mix Strategy for General Motors

among other things, General Motors sells cars, trucks, and chassis, and each of these can be thought of as a product line (Figure 8-1). *Length* refers to the number of items sold by a company within each product line. Thus, length in General Motors' automobile line is represented by the six Cadillac, Buick, Oldsmobile, Pontiac, Chevrolet, and Saturn divisions. The third axis in Figure 8-1 has been labeled the *depth* dimension. This suggests that each of the car, truck, and chassis categories at GM is available in different shapes and model designations. Thus, the Chevrolet buyer can purchase a family Lumina or a sporty Corvette. Similarly, a truck buyer can select from pickup, panel, or flatbed designs.

The three dimensions of the product mix provide useful starting points for determining product strategies for a firm. Companies can use them to expand in three basic directions. First, they can add new product lines to serve a broader range of customers. Second, they can deepen their model offering by adding product variations. Third, they can lengthen their product line.

Optimizing the Product Mix

The best product mix strategy for a particular firm depends on the engineering, production, and marketing skills available; the financial resources; and the objectives of the organization. Well-managed firms with limited product lines can often increase profits by expanding their product offerings. Mature organizations with extensive product assortments can make money by dropping items. When times are hard and a firm is looking for a boost in short-run profits, the strategy of trimming back the product mix can be effective. By weeding out slow-selling products, costs can be reduced and profits increased.

Advantages of Growth   Companies that are interested in long-term growth are advised to expand their product mix continuously. One of the most successful American advocates of product line expansion has been Procter & Gamble. It started with bar soap in 1879 and over the years has added lines of detergents, toothpaste, shampoo, paper products, disposable diapers, coffee, cooking oils, cake mixes, and cosmetics. One reason the strategy of expanding product lines has worked so well for Procter & Gamble is that most of its new items can be sold through the same grocery distribution channels with the same promotional activities.

Another advantage of complete product lines is that they give salespeople more opportunity to fill customers' needs. If you have only one model of personal computer, you can't take care of as many customers as a company that has 10 different models from which to choose. Manufacturers of cars, copiers, boats, and other durables like to have inexpensive models for first-time buyers and more elaborate models for customers who are ready to trade up to something better.

An alternative strategy is to market only the most profitable items within each product line. A number of appliance manufacturers have found that it is no longer profitable to market a full line of items. General Electric, Motorola, and Westinghouse have dropped several small appliances so that they can concentrate on products with higher returns.

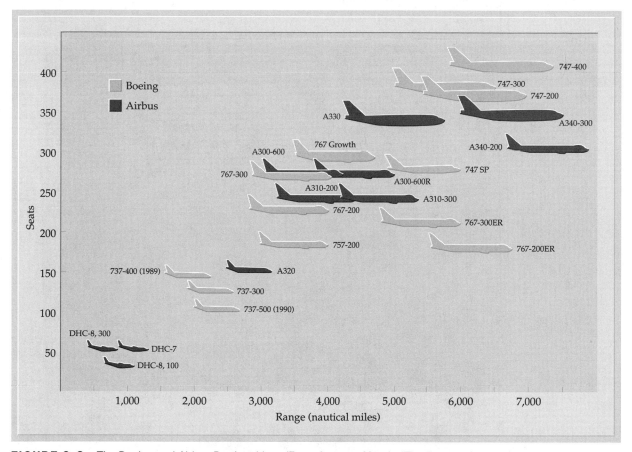

FIGURE 8-2 The Boeing and Airbus Product Lines (From Artemus March, "The Future of the U.S. Aircraft Industry," *Technology Review* [January 1990], p. 36)

Another product line strategy is to concentrate on the highest-volume products or emphasize items that can be most easily manufactured with the skills and equipment of the firm. Although the strategy of supplying a maximum of product variation seems desirable from a customer-oriented standpoint, there is no assurance that this is the most profitable approach for all firms. Most firms must search for the degree of product specialization that optimizes profits for their own particular manufacturing and marketing capabilities. The product lines of two commercial aircraft manufacturers are shown in Figure 8-2 and discussed in Marketing Strategies box 8-1.

Effects of Time The optimum product mix for a firm tends to vary across time. Gerber, for example, advertised for years that baby food and related products were its sole business. The recent decline in the birth rate, however, suggests that a more diversified product line would offer Gerber a measure of protection against changes

AIRBUS VERSUS BOEING

Boeing Co., an American manufacturer, dominates its industry with about a 60% share of the global market for commercial aircraft. However, Airbus Industrie, a European consortium, has made inroads. Airbus patiently develops advanced products targeted against holes in Boeing's fleet (Figure 8-2). For example, in comparison with Boeing's 737-400, the Airbus A320 has 15% to 20% advantage in range, an ability to fly further out of high-altitude airports, advanced "fly-by-wire" electronic controls, and a heavily computerized cockpit. In addition, by designing different models with common features, Airbus cuts down on production costs. While Boeing merely stretched a 1960s design for the 737 once more and added some technical improvements, Airbus started with a clean sheet of paper. Boeing figured that airlines flying thousands of other 737 models would still want it for fleet commonality savings, such as not having to retrain flight and maintenance crews. Instead Boeing has put its resources into developing a big new 777 twinjet. If Boeing keeps losing ground, it might consider the ultimate cost-saving move for a company famous for offering the only full jetliner "family." Boeing might stay on the sidelines for the next big jetliner project: a super jumbo with more than 600 seats.

You don't have to have a product in every segment of the market.

Source: Jeff Cole, "Boeing's Dominance of Aircraft Industry Is Beginning to Erode," *The Wall Street Journal*, July 10, 1992, pp. 1, 6.

in lifestyle. When the Japanese first started selling cars in America, they carried a very limited number of models, colors, and styles. This allowed them to lower unit costs and improve their quality. Once they had established themselves in the marketplace, they proceeded to add new lines, new divisions, and new models to expand their coverage of the market. It is common for firms to go through cycles of extending product lines for growth and then periodically contracting them to boost profits. These examples suggest that the search for the best product mix is a continuous process for every organization.

BRAND STRATEGY

Brand strategy is concerned with deciding which products should be branded and whether they should be sold under one's own label or under labels controlled by other firms. *Brands* include all names, terms, symbols, or designs that are used to identify and differentiate the goods of one seller from those of the competitors. Brands allow the customer to recognize products and increase the chances for repeat sales. Brands also encourage the use of preselling and reduce the need for personal contact at the retail level. In addition, brands facilitate the development of permanent price-quality images for products. Brands also simplify the introduction of new products and allow the manufacturer some control over the channel of distribution. Not all products can be branded; many raw materials such as wheat and coal are bought according to specifications, and individual brands are meaningless. Branding is easiest where identifying tags or symbols can be attached directly to the product and where the customer is willing to use brand designations to differentiate among products.

Brand Equity

A strong brand is a valuable asset. A petroleum jelly factory is much more valuable if its output can be called "Vaseline." With the cost of establishing a new brand name estimated at $50 to $150 million and the chances for success so low, companies are looking at alternative ways to use their established brands to sell new products. This has given rise to the emphasis on brand extension and brand leveraging.

Brand asset management includes not only issues such as brand positioning, but also the visual presentation of the brand image through its trademark and trade dress. A brand's *trade dress* is its nomenclature, symbol, type style, and colors and the way these are put together on the product package. Misuse or inconsistent use of the trademark or trade dress by its owner may have adverse legal (loss of trademark rights) and financial (devaluation of the brand) implications. Trade dress issues are especially critical with globalization of markets. Effective trade dress such as Coca-Cola and Eastman Kodak can be used consistently across borders. Thus, brand asset management is mandatory as you introduce new and restaged brands and enter global markets.[1] We will now look at some of the issues involved in more detail.

Family Brands

Family brands are groups of products sold under one label by a single firm. Heinz, Del Monte, and General Electric are companies that endorse a wide array of products with their own corporate name. Other firms, such as Procter & Gamble, as illustrated by Marketing Strategies box 8-2, prefer to use separate brand names for each product.

MARKETING STRATEGIES 8-2

PROCTER & GAMBLE'S HEAVY-DUTY DETERGENT PORTFOLIO

Procter & Gamble (P&G) has *eleven* brands in the heavy-duty detergent category in the United States. All brands are formulated to offer good cleaning, but each offers different benefits to meet different consumer needs. The company controls more than half of the $3.2 billion detergent market in supermarkets (nearly $5 billion in all retail outlets). Even small brands are important when 1 share point represents $40 million to $50 million. P&G seems bullish on its smaller brands. Gain has gone from a 0.6% share in the mid-1980s to about a 3% share. Line extensions include Gain with Odor Removing Bleach powder and Ultra Liquid Gain. Other recent product initiatives include Ultra Ivory Snow, a concentrated version, and Oxydol powder, upgraded with a bleach boosted formula. P&G has also taken a regional approach for some brands. Ariel, the No. 1 detergent in Mexico, is aimed mainly at Hispanics and is sold primarily in Los Angeles, San Diego, San Francisco, south Texas, and Miami. Solo is sold mainly in the Northeast, a strong liquid detergent market.

Brand	Positioning	Share
TIDE	Tough, powerful cleaning	31.1%
CHEER	Tough cleaning & color protection	8.2
BOLD	Detergent + fabric softener	2.9
GAIN	Sunshine scent & odor removing formula	2.6
ERA	Stain pre-treated & stain removed	2.2
DASH	Value brand	1.8
OXYDOL	Bleach-boosted formula, whitening	1.4
SOLO	Detergent+fabric softener in liquid form	1.2
DREFT	Outstanding cleaning for baby clothes, safe for tender skin	1.0
IVORY SNOW	Fabric & skin safety on baby clothes and fine washables	0.7
ARIEL	Tough cleaner, aimed at Hispanics	0.1

Source: Nielsen Marketing Research.

If you have a small brand, you should concentrate your efforts in stronghold markets.

Source: Jennifer Lawrence, "Don't Look for P&G to Pare Detergents," *Advertising Age*, May 31, 1993, pp. 3, 42.

Family brands have the advantage that advertising for one brand promotes the sales of all items carrying that particular label. Family brands also make it easier to introduce new products to distribution channels and the customer. On the other hand, it is more difficult to create and maintain an identify for each item using a family brand strategy. One possible compromise is to use separate brand names for each product and then tie them together with a unifying trade name. This is the strategy used by General Motors; cars are promoted under their own names, and the GM symbol is used as a common point of reference.

National versus Distributor Brands

Manufacturers have the choice of marketing products under their own labels or selling all or part of their output under brands controlled by distributors. Distributors' brands (e.g., A&P's Ann Page) have limited dissemination and are available only in stores that share a common wholesaler. National brands typically receive national advertising support, enjoy wide distribution, and are frequently stocked by competing retailers. In addition, some stores sell generic products that are plainly wrapped, with no brand identification. Generics are usually priced 10 to 35 percent below national brands and 10 to 20 percent below private label brands.

Private Labels   Private label shares exhibit wide variation across categories. For example, private labels represent 65 percent of the sales of frozen green and wax beans and 25 percent of liquid bleach but only 1.1 percent of personal deodorants. Private labels do well in categories where they offer high quality comparable to that of national brands. They do much worse in categories where multiple national manufacturers are investing a lot of money in national advertising.[2]

Private brands are more sensitive to changes in personal income than are

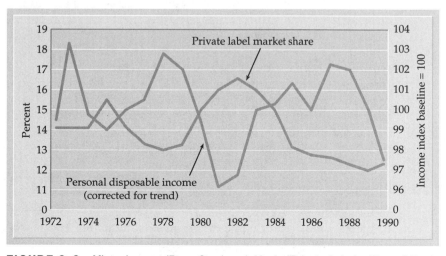

FIGURE 8-3   Mirror Images (From Stephen J. Hoch, "Private Label a Threat? Don't Believe It," *Advertising Age*, May 24, 1993, p. 19)

national brands. The proportion of grocery sales held by store brands hit its peak at the bottom of the 1982 recession (Figure 8-3). One reason for the decline of private labels since then is the escalating competition for shelf space. Where store labels were once given three years to build a following, they are now dropped after six months if they fail to perform. Also, national brands have gone heavily into coupons that reduce the gap between the price of advertised brands and that of private brands. In addition, *Consumer Reports* research has shown that 80 percent of its readers preferred national brands because they perceived them to be of higher quality.

Store brands offer retailers a number of advantages, especially in large categories with high margins. Retailers can set prices and promotional programs to maximize profits for the store as a whole rather than stress the sales of individual items. Distributor brands also tend to be family brands that help build store loyalty and assist in the introduction of new items. In addition, private brands usually offer 10 to 15 percent higher margins than national brands, and they can be sold at lower prices. This means that retailers can broaden their market penetration by using private labels to appeal to price-conscious customers. Retailers can stock private labels and national brands next to each other and take advantage of the price comparison to increase sales of their own brands.

Limitations of Private Labels   Although store brands account for a significant proportion of sales in cheese, orange juice, sugar, and soft drinks, retailers have to be careful that they do not carry too many private labels. Marketers believe that the downfall of the once giant A&P grocery chain was due to its excessive dependence on private labels. When store brands reached 35 percent of A&P's sales, customers could not find their favorite national brands and they began to shop elsewhere. More recently, Sears has cut back drastically on the number of its own Kenmore appliances and now features many popular national labels, such as GE, RCA, Sony, and Zenith. Also, mass merchandisers like K-Mart and Target like to feature national brands in their weekly newspaper inserts to draw people to their stores. This suggests that customers rely on national brands and that retailers who fail to carry them are following a risky strategy.

National Brands   The message for national brands from Figure 8-3 is to take a long-term perspective and not overreact to temporary economic conditions. The Micro-Marketing Project at the University of Chicago found that national brands were not very sensitive to the price gap with private labels. They concluded that the national brand should not try to narrow the gap through trade promotions, but would be better off spending the money on brand advertising and new product development.[3]

New Brands versus Brand Extensions

When a new item is added to the firm's product line, the firm must decide whether to create a new brand name or use an existing name. For instance, when Coca-Cola first developed a diet cola drink, it chose to use a new name, Tab, rather than capitalize on its existing consumer franchise by using the name Diet Coke. However, when PepsiCo came out with Diet Pepsi, Coca-Cola countered with Diet Coke, which now outsells Tab. Sometimes a firm will want to draw on its investment in a brand name and consequently will direct its product development to products that fit its existing image.

The various possibilities for products and brands are shown in Figure 8-4. When the firm simply adds another variant to an existing brand in an existing product category, the firm has a *line extension*. At the other extreme, a firm can introduce a new brand in a new category, and it has a completely new product.

Flanker Brands   When a firm markets another brand in a category in which it already had a presence, the firm is protecting its market position and the product is said to be a flanker brand. A special case of a flanker brand is a fighting brand. When a firm has a high relative market share, it is usually not in its best interest to cut price because it will be hurt most by the price cut if primary demand does not expand to offset the cut. This makes a dominant brand susceptible to having share sliced away by aggressive pricing by smaller firms. To discipline such firms, a fighting brand is created for which no money is invested in advertising, and the product is sold on price. American Express sells premium-priced products in the form of its green, gold, and platinum charge cards. Facing new entrants in the credit card business, such as AT&T, and intensified competition from veterans, including Visa and MasterCard, American Express brought out a credit card called Optima as a fighting brand.

You have to decide whether to bring out a new item as a line extension or as a new brand. Generally it is better to employ a line extension strategy when parent brand penetration is high and a new brand strategy when parent brand penetration is low. This is true even though a line extension will cannibalize parent brand sales much more than a new brand will. To maintain profit margins, a rule of thumb is that a new product must gain two share points for each point lost by the original

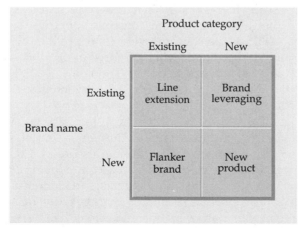

FIGURE 8-4   Brand Types (From Edward M. Tauber, "Brand Franchise Extension: New Product Benefits from Existing Brand Names," *Business Horizons*, Vol. 24 [March–April 1981], p. 37)

brand. Usually, half of the gain will come from users of competitors' products and half from new users being drawn into the market.

Brand Leveraging   Using an existing brand name to enter a new product category is called *brand leveraging*. For example, Mr. Coffee has long been the best-selling brand in the drip-coffee maker market. With over 40 million machines sold, a Mr. Coffee coffee is being test-marketed. This is logical leveraging of Mr. Coffee's brand franchise.

Brand leveraging is potentially very attractive. It makes use of existing customer awareness and goodwill. As a result, the advertising expenditures needed to introduce the product to the market are minimized. Although the introduction of Always sanitary napkins, an entirely new brand name, cost Procter & Gamble about $100 million, the introduction of Liquid Tide cost a relatively modest $30 to $40 million because of existing name recognition.

The Limits of Product Proliferation

There are risks to using one brand name on many products, as demonstrated by Marketing Strategies box 8-3. The image conveyed by the brand name may become too diffuse as the specific customer benefit for which the brand name stands is lost. Care must be taken not to extend the brand name to categories where it cannot provide its inherent customer benefit. In addition, as the number of linked products increases, the ability to reposition an individual item decreases. Finally, a bad product can tarnish the other products sharing a common brand name.

At some point, the number of brands and products in a category become greater than customers' need for variety and creates duplication. Too many sizes and too many me-too products just add to distribution costs. Consumers feel that they don't require 16 barbecue potato chip products to satisfy their need for variety. A Food Marketing Institute study found that retailers can reduce stock-keeping units (skus) by 5–25 percent without hurting sales or consumers' perception of variety offered by the store. As a result of the concern over brand proliferation, the prediction is that only the No. 1 and No. 2 brands will be assured of distribution. The No. 3 brand will probably need to go to value positioning to remain viable. Lesser-ranked brands will likely disappear. Even the leaders will need to rationalize the lines and reduce the number of skus. The U.S. leader in salty snacks, Frito-Lay, has dropped about 100 sizes and flavors. Borden, the No. 2 company, had 3200 line items to Frito-Lay's 400 because of using three regional brands. Borden is simplifying its business by consolidating the regional brands under the Borden brand. Procter & Gamble has exhibited various responses to the pressure to accommodate retailers who want to consolidate the number of products. In detergents, P&G is continuing product innovation and differentiation even for secondary brands, reducing skus—mainly package sizes—rather than eliminating brands and strengthening secondary brands in regional markets where they sell best. On the other hand, P&G has put Puritan cooking oil under the Crisco label and has discontinued the White Cloud toilet tissue brand by turning it into a Charmin extension called Charmin Ultra. The new tissue is 30 percent thicker than White Cloud and 50 percent thicker than regular Charmin, P&G's leading brand.

EXTENDING THE 7UP BRAND

The Dr Pepper/Seven Up Co. did all the right things before tackling its first brand extension, Cherry 7Up. It conducted a brand image study to determine the leveraging opportunities for its core brands (7Up and Diet 7Up) and did substantial concept and product testing. After Cherry 7Up was introduced, the company's total sales volume greatly increased. They thought "This is great. It works. Let's do it again." That is why 7Up Gold was brought to market.

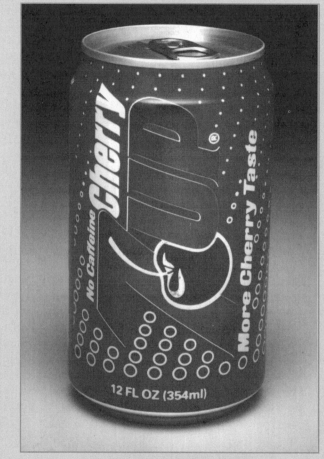

However, 7Up Gold was a different story. Not only did the product not sell well, but sales for the company's core brands also declined. With lackluster sales, 7Up Gold's brand share was essentially nonexistent within six months. Basically, they took their eye off the ball. They took resources away from their core brands to support their brand extensions. This caused their core brands to decline.

You should extend your brand only to the point where you can support the brand itself without taking resources away from core brands.

Source: Elinor Selame and Greg Kolligian, "Brands Are a Company's Most Important Asset," *Marketing News*, September 16, 1991, p. 14.

PRODUCT QUALITY

The ability of a firm or a country to compete is often influenced by the quality of the products it offers for sale. Some American firms have been complaisant about product quality deterioration, and their share of some markets has declined sharply. These changes are related to the ability of foreign firms to produce higher-quality products and sell them at lower prices in the United States.

Research has shown that most quality problems are a result of poor design (40 percent), errors in the manufacturing process (30 percent), and defective supplier goods (30 percent).[4] Thus careful monitoring of customers' complaints and tough standards for suppliers can lead to improved quality. Moreover, high quality does not necessarily mean higher costs. The potential impact of higher quality on the performance of the firm has been shown by the Strategic Planning Institute. They examined 525 American business units and found that those with low relative product quality earned 17 percent; medium quality, 20 percent; and high quality, 27 percent. This suggests that continuous improvements in product quality can raise profits.

Quality is important, but how do you go about raising it? Many firms focus on total quality management (TQM). TQM calls for a comprehensive master plan for continuously improving quality in an organization. Concepts stressed in TQM are "continuous improvements," "zero defects," "do it right the first time," "faster is better," and "empowerment—employees closest to the situation know best how to improve it." Going further, a good approach is to adhere to a set of quality standards endorsed by more than 50 countries, including those of the European Community and the United States. In the late 1980s, the International Organization for Standardization created a set of five standards, known collectively as *ISO 9000*, to offer a uniform way of determining whether manufacturing plants and service organizations implement and document sound quality procedures. To register, a company must undergo a third-party audit of its manufacturing and customer service processes, covering everything from how it designs, produces, and installs its goods to how it inspects, packages, and markets them. This is not cheap. It may cost $250,000 and take 9 months to certify a plant. Nonetheless, ISO registration is rapidly becoming the passport to success in the international marketplace.[5]

Impact of Quality on Sales

Our discussion of product quality concludes with two stories. One concerns a U.S. vacuum cleaner manufacturer and the other a German shoe company. Regina Company grabbed 11 percent of the U.S. vacuum cleaner market by heavy use of rebates, low prices, and an allocation of 20 percent of revenues for TV advertising. Unfortunately, it neglected product quality, and up to 20 percent of its vacuums were returned by customers for broken belts, handles, and beater bars. Meanwhile, their competitors (Hoover and Eureka) kept their returns at less than 1 percent of sales and remained profitable. Regina's profits plummeted, and the company was almost destroyed by low quality.

Our second story describes the effort of Lenwest to make and sell shoes in the

Soviet Union. This company is a joint venture with a German firm that provided all the machinery, training, and factory managers. The Russians supplied the labor and most raw materials. The German managers were very careful in how they trained the workers, and they set strict standards on raw materials and demanded the highest possible quality. The result was that the Russians snapped up every shoe the company could make, and Lenwest is now expanding production and enlarging its network of retail stores. These examples suggest that high quality helps build repeat sales and long-run profitability. Firms that let quality decline may be risking long-term survival for short-term gains.

PRODUCT WARRANTIES AND SERVICE

When customers are concerned about product quality, warranties are often used to help reduce anxiety. Warranties represent commitments on the part of the seller to repair and adjust products that fail to perform after purchase. The main objectives of product warranties and services are to encourage sales by reducing customers' worries about postpurchase problems and to build repeat business from satisfied customers. The linkages between consumers' attitudes about product performance and subsequent buying behavior were described earlier in Chapter 4.

Warranties Can Sell

Historically, warranties have been written statements that tell the buyer what steps the seller will take if the product fails within a specific period of time. They were usually designed to limit the liability of the seller in case damage claims were filed by the buyer. In recent years, however, the courts have ruled that warranties do not have to be written and that they do not limit the liability of the seller. As a result, marketing managers have become more concerned with the promotional aspects of product warranties. For example, a warranty that offers "double your money back" is clearly designed to boost sales by having the buyer try the product at little or no risk. Under these conditions, a warranty becomes a competitive tool designed to build customer confidence and to woo customers away from firms with weaker warranty policies.

After high-quality Japanese products stole a significant portion of the U.S. car market, American manufacturers responded by offering longer warranties. When the standard Japanese warranty was 36 months or 36,000 miles, GM offered 60 months or 60,000 miles and Chrysler offered 70 months or 70,000 miles. The objective was to show buyers that American firms had improved auto quality and stood behind their products. The evidence suggests that longer warranties helped Chrysler but did not increase GM's market share.

Service Strategies

Service strategies are concerned with establishing procedures for repairing merchandise after the product has been sold to the customer. Over the years, product complexity and high wages for service personnel created service problems for many manufacturers. Consumers have found that it is difficult to get products repaired, and the cost is often out of proportion to the value of the product. As a result, consumers are now demanding and receiving better repair service from manufacturers. Many firms have expanded their regional repair centers and have installed "cool lines" so that customers can call directly when they encounter repair problems.

In the past, some manufacturers considered service a necessary evil and attempted to keep expenditures as low as possible. This raised profits in the short run, but eventually consumers began to rebel at the absence of local repair facilities. The failure of Fiat and Renault to penetrate U.S. auto markets is often attributed to the lack of adequate service facilities.

An alternative service strategy is to consider repair work as a profit-making opportunity. If most of the products owned by customers are out of warranty and require periodic repair, then the active solicitation of service work can be a lucrative business. Automobile manufacturers, for example, profit from the sales of fenders and other parts to their dealers and independent service facilities. However, too great a reliance on service profits may stifle product improvements and allow competitors to grow by introducing new items.

A more desirable market-oriented strategy for service emphasizes fast, economical repairs, with the objective of building long-run sales. Although a liberal factory service policy may cost more than other strategies, it can help protect the brand names owned by manufacturers and reduce problems caused by poor dealer service. Implementation of this strategy often requires extensive training of dealer repair personnel and the establishment of regional service centers run by the company. In recent years, the appliance industry has adopted a factory service policy of this type.

Manufacturers have used product service in a variety of ways to help promote the sales of merchandise. Sears, for example, emphasizes the nationwide availability of its service, so that even if customers move to another area, repair service will be available. Maytag, on the other hand, takes a more whimsical approach and shows its repair personnel with nothing to do, suggesting that Maytag appliances rarely break down. One of the most aggressive manufacturer service policies offers a lifetime of free service repairs. At the other extreme, service costs can be minimized by making the product disposable—for example, cigarette lighters that can be simply thrown away when they break or run out of fuel. These examples suggest that the choice of an optimum service strategy depends on the cost, complexity, and life expectancy of the product; the importance of repairs to the customer; and the manufacturer's concern for maintaining a satisfied group of repeat buyers.

EXPLOITING THE PRODUCT LIFE CYCLE

Most successful products follow a life cycle that includes introduction, growth, maturity, and decline stages (Figure 8-5). At the start, products are unknown, so the emphasis in the marketing mix is on promotion to acquaint customers with the product and gain product trial. As sales increase during the growth phase, emphasis shifts

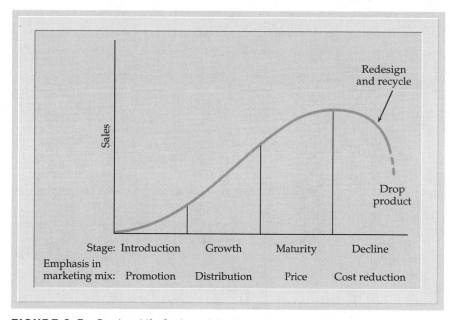

FIGURE 8-5   Product Life Cycle and the Marketing Mix

to opening new distribution channels and retail outlets. When a product reaches maturity, competition increases and marketing managers emphasize price, deals, coupons, and special promotions to draw attention to their merchandise.

The main danger during the growth and maturity stage of the product life cycle is marketing inertia. If a firm becomes too complacent with its success, it may lose touch with its customers and ignore competition. Thus, when the market changes, the firm may fail to react quickly enough—or perhaps not at all—to the changed circumstances.

One way of increasing customer interest during the growth and maturity phases of the product life cycle is to expand product lines and offer greater variety. Another possibility is to follow a strategy of market segmentation and sell the product under a variety of brands owned by distributors or other manufacturers. A third alternative is to engage in clever promotional campaigns devised to catch the eye of selected groups of customers.

Products in decline often need to be redesigned or reduced in cost so that they can continue to make a contribution to the company. When items become unprofitable, the company must decide whether the product should be carried at a loss or phased out to make room for more profitable lines. The effect of the product life cycle on the marketing strategies of a toothpaste that periodically reenters the market with a "new and improved" version is illustrated in Figure 8-6.

Product life cycles vary in length from a few weeks for fashion merchandise to up to 50 years or more for appliances and food items. The amount of time a product stays in any one stage of the life cycle depends on customer adoption rates and the

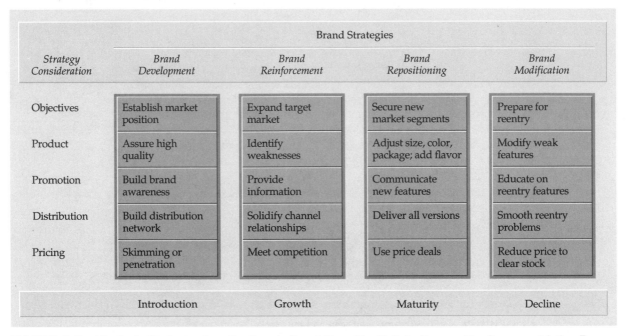

Strategy Consideration	Brand Strategies			
	Brand Development	Brand Reinforcement	Brand Repositioning	Brand Modification
Objectives	Establish market position	Expand target market	Secure new market segments	Prepare for reentry
Product	Assure high quality	Identify weaknesses	Adjust size, color, package; add flavor	Modify weak features
Promotion	Build brand awareness	Provide information	Communicate new features	Educate on reentry features
Distribution	Build distribution network	Solidify channel relationships	Deliver all versions	Smooth reentry problems
Pricing	Skimming or penetration	Meet competition	Use price deals	Reduce price to clear stock
	Introduction	Growth	Maturity	Decline

FIGURE 8-6 Life Cycle Strategies for a Toothpaste Brand (From Ben M. Enis, Raymond La Garce, and Arthur E. Prell, "Extending the Product Life Cycle," *Business Horizons*, Vol. 20 [June 1977], p. 53)

amount of new product competition. Because businesses invest a great deal of money to gain consumer acceptance, it makes sense to extend the life of their products as long as possible. Three methods that can be employed to stretch product markets are (1) promotion of more frequent and varied usage among current users, (2) finding new uses for the basic material, and (3) creating new users for the product by expanding the market.

Ciba-Geigy AG has extended the life cycle of its aging antiarthritis drug, Voltaren, by formulating a spate of new versions. To hold off the inevitable erosion caused by generic competition as its patents expire on the original tablet form of Voltaren, Ciba-Geigy now sells it in the form of eyedrops, as intravenous solutions, as time-release pills, and as emulgel—a cross between a cream and an ointment. The last product is so novel that it earned Ciba-Geigy a new 20-year cycle of patent coverage. As a result of these actions, Voltaren continues to be a blockbuster pharmaceutical.

PRODUCTS IN DECLINE

The theory of the product life cycle suggests that products are born, grow to maturity, and then enter a period of decline. The length of the decline phase is determined by changes in consumer preferences, activities of competitors, and the product elimination policies of the firm. Although usually little can be done about basic shifts in consumer preferences and the entry of competitive items, the firm has a wide range of alternatives that can be exercised for products with falling sales.

Strategies for Reviving Products

Perhaps the most important task of product review procedures is to separate the items that can benefit from a redesign of the package or promotional plans from those that are on an irreversible slide toward extinction. Too often vast sums of money are wasted in trying to save products that have no future.

What Is the Problem?   The job of identifying candidates for rescue operations is not easy, and specific reasons for sales declines must be identified. The first step is to determine the contribution to the sales loss of buyers versus the amount they buy (see Figure 8-7). Although customers are purchasing less of the brand shown in Figure 8-7, the number of buyers is holding up and the product may be salvageable. The next step is to assess the underlying causes of such losses. If the quality is found to be inadequate and customers are shifting to improved versions, there may be little hope for the product. The best rescue situation occurs when most people have positive memories of the brand and the product still has a small group of loyal fans.

The easiest solution to declining sales is to move the product into new foreign or domestic markets. This may require the addition of new distributors or the enlargement of the existing sales force. An alternative to greater breadth of market coverage is finding and promoting new uses among existing customers. Manufacturers of packaged food products are particularly skilled at devising new recipes that

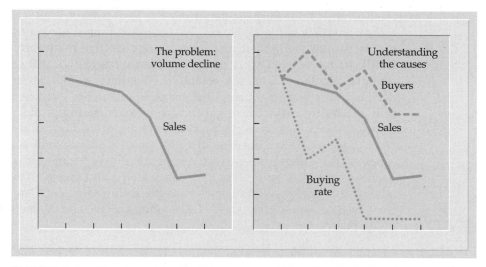

FIGURE 8-7   What Is Causing My Brand's Losses? (From NPD Research, Inc., *Marketing News* advertisement, March 23, 1979, p. 5)

help extend the life of old products. Since it costs millions to introduce a new brand, it can be cheaper to reformulate an existing product.

What Can Be Done? A classic turnaround occurred with Kraft's Cheez Whiz. The processed cheese had been on the market for 36 years and was losing 3 to 4 percent of its sales each year. The marketing manager thought up the idea of repositioning Cheez Whiz as a sauce for the microwave oven. New ads were created emphasizing its use in microwave ovens, and the ad budget was tripled. Cheez Whiz was also repackaged in multipacks of 4-ounce cups designed for microwave heating. As a result of these activities, sales spurted 35 percent.

Frito-Lay nearly dropped its Tostitos tortilla chip after sales slumped 50 percent from a peak. Instead, hoping to latch on to the Tex-Mex food craze, it reformulated Tostitos into a restaurant-style chip—doubling its size, changing its shape from circular to triangular, and substituting white corn for yellow. Packaged in a new clear bag with big, bolder graphics, Tostitos Restaurant Style Chips set new revenue records. This proves that consumers crave what's old and familiar. You just have to freshen it up.

Despite the successful revivals that we have mentioned, however, not every aging brand can be saved. Also, spending money on weak products often takes energy and resources away from your leading brands. This suggests that fading brands such as Carnation powdered milk, Seratan laxative, and Del Monte canned peas do not deserve expensive new promotional programs. Marketing expenditures on declining products are risky and are justified only when there is good reason to believe that the item can be saved.

Strategies for Dropping Products

A variety of strategies can be employed for products that firms expect to drop from their product lines. Perhaps the simplest is to do nothing and wait until there are no longer any orders for the item. This approach cannot be recommended because it ties up capital, equipment, and human resources that might produce greater profits if utilized to promote other items. Experience has shown that company profits can often be increased despite substantial reductions in sales revenues resulting from discontinuing weak products. The business press periodically features stories of how individual firms have cut their product lines and raised profits. The trick is to find a way to make money as the product is being phased out of production. One successful approach has been to drop all promotional activities and rely solely on repeated purchases from current customers. Where promotional expenditures have been substantial, sales are apt to decline slowly, and the savings from discontinued advertising may make the item profitable in the short run. An example of an unusually successful phase-out for GM's aging Cavalier model is described in Marketing in Action box 8-1.

Sharing the Risks Another useful strategy for declining products is to continue to sell the item but to contract with another company for manufacturing. An alternative is to continue to make the product but license others to sell it. A third possibility is

---

MARKETING IN ACTION 8-1

CAVALIER'S LAST HURRAH

A clever product elimination strategy employed by General Motors shows how firms can make money while they are phasing out a product. Cavalier has been one of GM's leading small cars with peak sales of 431,000 in 1985, but by 1992 its dated styling produced sales of only 212,000 units. Rather than invest in a redesign of the 12-year-old model, GM decided to slash prices and promote it with a special value package. For 1993 the base price of the VL model was cut to $8,520 from $8,899 in the 1992 model year without removing any equipment from the car. GM was able to lower prices because production had been consolidated at a single Ohio plant that operated on three shifts instead of the normal two. They also reduced the number of colors offered and simplified the optional equipment packages. Antilock brakes were made standard on all Cavalier models and advertising was increased. One of the best TV ads shows a Cavalier coupe weaving through a line of pylons as enticements such as a 3-year warranty and a $500 rebate offer flashed on the screen. The clincher line comes as the car stops in front of the camera: "The lowest-priced car in America with antilock brakes." On top of a $500 rebate, GM also offered a $400 discount for first-time buyers.

The sales impact of GM's phase-out program for an aging car that comes without an airbag has been astonishing. In April of 1993, Cavalier actually outsold the market leading Ford Taurus by 300 cars. GM only had a 34 day supply of Cavaliers in May of 1993 and car rental companies were snapping them up for their rental fleets, making it difficult for regular dealers to meet consumer demand. The company now faces a decision on what to do with the Cavalier when a replacement model goes into production in the fall of 1994. The phenomenal success of the Cavalier value phase-out is likely to keep the old model on the market longer than originally planned.

Well designed product phase-outs can generate high profits.

Source: Joseph B. White and Oscar Suris, "GM, Pitching Value, Scores Cavalier Upset," *The Wall Street Journal*, May 11, 1993, p. B1.

---

to sell the product to another firm and let that firm worry about manufacturing and marketing it. This procedure is attractive because it allows the seller to profit from the liquidation and may provide the buyer with a unique opportunity as well. For example, a 2 percent annual decline in distilled spirits sales has prompted Seagrams to focus its attention on the premium end of the liquor business. This has led to the discontinuation of 13 rum, vodka, scotch, and gin brands and the sales of trademark rights to 12 other brands. These include such old-line whiskey names as Carstairs Blend, Paul Jones Blend, Nikolai and Crown Russe vodkas, and Benchmark Bourbon. Smaller firms can buy up these brands and make money because they require little promotion and no fixed investment in facilities. The new buyer profits by milking the brand loyalty of existing customers.

Helping the Dealers   In situations in which nothing can save a declining product, the firm should dispose of the product with a minimum of inconvenience to the interested parties. This means notifying dealers in advance and helping them clear out old stock. Frequently, special discounts are offered to dealers to stimulate the sale of discontinued items. It may even be necessary for the manufacturer to buy back the unsold merchandise. Dealers should also be informed about replacement items that are being promoted to take the place of the discontinued items, which may affect consumer goodwill, and arrange to provide service and parts for recent buyers.

SUMMARY

In this chapter we have described some of the strategies used to manage products during the introductory, growth, maturity, and decline phases of the life cycle. New products are especially vulnerable to competitive pressures, and you must know how to manipulate product lines, brands, promotions, warranties, and repair services to optimize profits and social benefits. Finally, a variety of strategies for products with declining sales has been explained. We believe that the effective management of products in decline is an important activity for marketing managers and can increase sales and profits for the firm. Too often marketing executives become obsessed with the glamour of new products and fail to realize the profits that can be made in the declining portion of the product life cycle.

NOTES

1. From Elinor Selame and Greg Kolligian, "Brands Are a Company's Most Important Asset," *Marketing News* (September 16, 1991), pp. 14, 19.
2. From Stephen J. Hoch, "Private Label a Threat? Don't Believe It," *Advertising Age* (May 24, 1993), p. 19.
3. Ibid.
4. *Marketing News* (June 20, 1988), p. 15.
5. From Cyndee Miller, "U.S. Firms Lag in Meeting Global Quality Standards," *Marketing News*, Vol. 27, No. 4 (February 15, 1993), pp. 1, 6.

SUGGESTED READING

Keller, Kevin Lane. "Conceptualizing, Measuring, and Managing Customer-Based Brand Equity," *Journal of Marketing*, Vol. 57, No. 1 (January 1993), pp. 1–22.

FURTHER READING

Aaker, David A. *Managing Brand Equity* (New York: Free Press, 1991).
Arnold, David. *The Handbook of Brand Management* (Reading, MA: Addison-Wesley, 1992).

Cortada, James W. *TQM for Sales and Marketing Management* (New York, McGraw-Hill, 1993).

Moore, William L., and Edgar A. Pessemier. *Product Planning and Management: Designing and Delivering Value* (New York: McGraw-Hill, 1993).

Shocker, Allen D., Rajendra K. Srivastava and Robert W. Ruekert, Eds., "Special Issue on Brand Management," *Journal of Marketing Research*, Vol. 31 (May 1994), pp. 149–304.

QUESTIONS

1. The Driscoll Strawberry Associates, Inc., of Watsonville, California, has been growing and shipping strawberries and raspberries since 1940. Given the success of Dole and Del Monte in branding fresh produce, should Driscoll launch branded berries for consumers? If so, how can they nurture the perception that among consumers that their strawberries and raspberries are something different, something better, that is, suggest a positioning statement for them.

2. Should product lines be managed to maximize sales, profits per unit, or profit per unit of scarce resources?

3. At one time, disposable diapers came in small, medium, large, and extra-large sizes. Now they are made to fit babies at every stage of development, from newborns with sensitive umbilical cords to toddlers ready for toilet training. And some are no longer unisex. Some diapers for boys are blue and have padding up the front, while others for girls are pink and have padding in the middle. Some brands have fastener tabs with Disney cartoon characters; others feature the Muppets. Procter & Gamble makes a dozen kinds of Pampers and a dozen kinds of Luvs. And each kind comes in "boy" and "girl" styles and various packages. P&G has about 52 percent of the disposable-diaper market. Are there any risks to P&G's strategy?

4. Are warranties primarily designed to protect consumers and manufacturers against loss or to boost sales of goods and services?

5. The chief engineer for the Chevrolet Corvette is locked in a struggle to keep the Corvette alive. The next generation of the Corvette must overcome a number of hurdles. The first is sharply declining sales for Corvette and other two-seaters in the specialty car segment. Sales for the current-generation Corvette peaked at about 38,000 in 1987. In 1992, fewer than 20,000 Corvettes were sold. The second problem is the enormous tooling costs to create a unique body, powertrain, electronics, braking, and suspension. The third is high engineering costs for sophisticated performance systems. Image builder or not, Corvette must make money if it is to survive. What suggestions do you have for Corvette's chief engineer?

6. In what situations does a firm have a responsibility to keep selling a declining product?

Chapter 9

Services Marketing

If you can sell green toothpaste in this country, you can sell opera.

SARAH CALDWELL

One of the most important marketing developments in your lifetime has been the explosive growth of services in the U.S. economy. Today over 55 percent of all personal consumption in the United States goes to purchase services.[1] If consumption is more broadly defined to include industrial goods, then services account for 71 percent of the nation's output.[2] This growth is associated with declines in the manufacturing sector and is spurred by additional wealth, an expansion in leisure time, and increases in the number of dual-career families. With their extra money, people are renting cellular phones, paying bills by computer, traveling more, renting cars, and turning to a host of special cleaning and child-care services. Growth in services is not limited to the United States; many firms are finding new markets overseas. Marketing Strategies box 9-1 describes three small service companies that have successfully exported their service know-how.

Now that the world is becoming more service oriented, it is essential for you to know how to market these items. This chapter will acquaint you with the nature of services, their special characteristics, managing service marketing, and managing service quality.

NATURE OF SERVICES

Most physical products include some service elements as part of the offering. For example, a common service is the warranty to replace or repair durables such as compact discs, computer programs, or books that are defective. Goods with a low service component are positioned in Sectors 3 and 6 of Figure 9-1. Goods with a higher service component are shown in Sectors 2 and 5. Hotels are a classic example because, while rooms are a service, customers also consume food and take advantage of flower and gift shops that sell goods. Pure services such as mail delivery, medicine, and engineering are shown in Sectors 1 and 4 of Figure 9-1. Thus the service com-

SERVICES GO GLOBAL

Prompted by a sluggish economy at home, many small U.S. service companies are seeking business overseas. Also the current trade talks under GATT are helping open the door to small firms in foreign markets. The most active small service companies are in accounting, finance, information processing, insurance, education and restaurants. For example, in 1990 the Tokyo city government gave New York architect Rafael Vinoly a $50 million contract to design a $1 billion International Forum complex. In addition, Fuji Bank gave Vinoly a $700,000 line of credit without asking for any collateral soon after he won the contract.

The growth in the world economy has opened up opportunities for small service companies. Information Systems Experts of Washington, DC, is now working with companies in 19 European countries to create technology to distribute and sell marketing software. Business is so good that the chairman has to spend half of his time in Europe to oversee his operations there. Another small firm, Macro Systems, is helping the Steel Authority of India Ltd. to design and implement quality systems for its five steel plants. To reduce marketing costs, Macro Systems has joined forces with the Total Quality Institute in the city of Gyor to help promote its services in Hungary. The use of joint ventures has provided Macro Systems with a safe, low-cost entry method and helps them relate to local culture, language, and regulations.

Small companies can compete in overseas services markets.

Source: Udayan Gupta, "Small Service Companies Find High Profits Overseas," *The Wall Street Journal*, March 29, 1991, p. B-2.

ponent of a product can range from very low to very high, and marketing programs vary for each type of product.

Many of the examples in this chapter are concerned with pure services. For purposes of discussion, *pure services* will be defined as intangible activities and benefits that satisfy customers' wants without the ownership of goods. This definition includes services such as insurance policies and stock brokerage but excludes home-delivered pizza. Our emphasis on pure services is deliberate because we want you to understand the special character of services so that you can do a better job of marketing.

Recent Trends

A number of changes in the economic environment in the last few years have increased the importance of marketing in service industries.[3] We will discuss the impact of these changes and show how marketing can help organizations adapt to the new climate.

Less Regulation   Service industries have traditionally been highly regulated. Government agencies often mandated price levels, constrained distribution areas, and

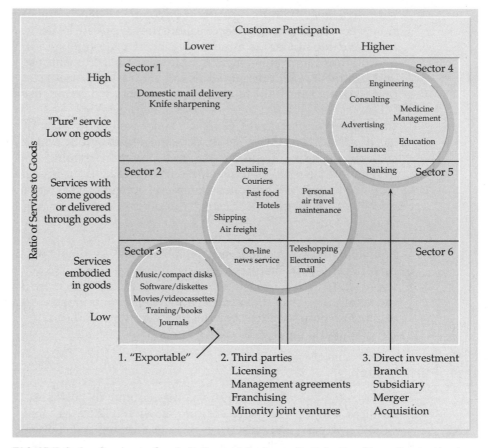

FIGURE 9-1 Service to Goods Ratios and Customer Participation (From Sandra Vander-merwe and Michael Chadwick, "The Internationalization of Services," *The Services Industry Journal* [January 1989], pp. 79–93)

even regulated possible product features. However, the trend in the United States and throughout the world is toward deregulation of major services. This means that there are fewer constraints on competitive activity in airlines, railroads, trucking, banking, securities, insurance, and telecommunications. Barriers to entry by new firms have been dropped, geographical restrictions on service delivery have been reduced, and there is more freedom to adjust prices. Substantial relaxation of trade regulation of services is occurring in the European Community, and rules are being eased in Japan as well.

A related trend has been a move to force professional associations to remove bans on advertising and promotional activities. Professions that now allow more competitive activity include accounting, architecture, medicine, law, and optometry. This had led to more use of informational advertising and more price competition.

Privatization   With the growth of government deficits, there has been a trend to return government-owned service industries to private investors. In England, France, Italy, and Japan there is a move to convert telecommunications, national airlines, and utilities to private ownership. Municipal governments are also selling airports and contracting with private firms to haul trash. The new result is more emphasis on cost cutting and more interest by new owners in meeting customers' service needs.

Creation of Service Profit Centers   Many well-known firms in the computer and electrical industries have set up separate service profit centers. Ancillary services, such as consulting, credit, leasing, transportation, training, and maintenance, once designed to help sell equipment, are now offered as profit-seeking services in their own right. General Electric, for example, no longer makes computers, yet it has developed a huge business leasing computers and other equipment to outside organizations.

Financial Pressure on Nonprofit Organizations   Declining public support for museums, libraries, and charities has forced nonprofit agencies to take a more businesslike approach to fund-raising and management. We now see more use of money-making museum shops, mail-order catalogs, and restaurants in these organizations. They are also being more selective about the market segments they target, and are more market oriented in their pricing and promotional activities.

Customer Participation

Services can also be classified by the amount of customer participation that is required. High-participation services shown in Figure 9-1 include banking and education; low-participation services include shipping and couriers. When you are having a couch reupholstered, you do not have to be present. This means that the upholstery firm can be located in an old building without a waiting room, while a dentist needs to offer a convenient location, comfortable seating, pleasant views, and soothing music.

The degree of customer participation and the ratio of services to goods have an impact on international marketing strategies. Figure 9-1 groups products into three strategy clusters. Cluster 1 includes low-participation, low-service products that are best exported. Products with intermediate values in cluster 2 should be handled by third-party arrangements with overseas businesspeople through licensing or franchising. For pure services with high customer participation, you need to consider direct international investment in sales branches or subsidiaries.

Public or Private

Another factor that affects the marketing of services is whether the organization is publicly or privately owned and whether it is seeking profits. Many tax-supported services such as libraries, zoos, and museums are turning to marketing to help make ends meet. Any marketing activities of a private golf club are likely to differ from those of a city-owned course or a public course run to make a profit.

Major Service Industries

To grasp service marketing concepts fully, you must appreciate the many different types of services that are available to buyers. A good way to understand the breadth of this sector is to look at how the government classifies services for the Census of Business. Table 9-1 lists the major categories of service industries and gives examples that fall into each group. These include communications, consulting, educational, financial, health, household operations, housing, insurance, personal, and transportation. Note that retailing and restaurants are not considered to be major service industries even though they provide a service element in their product offerings.

TABLE 9-1

Major Service Industries

SIC Code	Industry	SIC Code	Industry
48	*Communications* Telephone Radio broadcasting TV broadcasting	49	*Household Operations* Electrical companies Sewer companies Laundries Cleaning
73	*Consulting* Advertising agencies Outdoor advertising Direct mail Employment agencies Testing laboratories Temporary help Auditing	65	*Housing* Apartment buildings Rental agents Hotels Trailer parks
82	*Educational* Colleges & professional schools Libraries Technical institutes	63	*Insurance* Insurance agents Life insurance Health insurance Fire & casualty
60	*Financial* Banks Savings & loans Credit unions Commodity dealers Security exchanges	72	*Personal* Beauty & barber shops Motion picture theaters Bowling alleys Skating rinks
80	*Health* Hospitals Medical laboratories Physicians & surgeons	4	*Transportation* Suburban transit Airlines Motor freight Automobile rental

Services Are All Around

One of the most striking things about Table 9-1 is how many of the services are routinely used by consumers and businesses on a daily or weekly basis. Consider a day in the life of Paula, an assistant product manager. When she wakes up in her rented apartment, one of the first things she does is switch on the lights to get ready for work. Soon she jumps in her leased BMW and turns on the radio to catch the traffic report. Parking the car in the pay lot at the subway station, she notices an outdoor ad for a movie she wants to see at a local theater. When she arrives at the office, she picks up the phone to talk with the advertising agency that handles one of her brands. Later that day, she calls her insurance agent about the liability coverage on her sailboat. On the way home, she stops at a teller machine to pick up some cash and then spends some of it on repairs for her watch. Back home, she flips on the TV to catch the evening news. As Paula prepares dinner, she checks the mail and reads a direct mail piece for a vacation trip to Hawaii. After dinner she heads out to her marketing class at the local university.

All of this businesswoman's daily activities have involved contact with service organizations. But why did Paula select certain companies? The implication is clear. For your service company to succeed, you must understand how to market your benefits to customers. A choice of service suppliers is available to buyers, so you must consider what factors are important to them.

SERVICE MARKETING CHARACTERISTICS

Services have special characteristics that affect how marketing programs are created. Managers need to be aware of these attributes if plans are to succeed. These features include intangibility, perishability, inseparability, variability, and client relationships.

Intangibility

The most obvious problem with marketing services is that they are intangible. Buyers cannot touch, smell, see, taste, or hear services before they are purchased. When they buy goods, customers get something to take home. When they buy services, they receive only a ticket stub or a piece of paper. With services, consumers buy a performance rather than a physical product.

Since services are abstract, the marketer must find a way to dramatize the concept for the customer. Several clever solutions to this problem are offered in Figure 9-2. To overcome the lack of a physical product, marketers need to develop a tangible representation of the service. One of the best examples is the use of plastic cards to symbolize bank credit. Ads can then be created showing customers using their bank cards to pay for real products such as meals or souvenirs of exotic locations.

Another dilemma with intangibles is that it can be hard for buyers to grasp service concepts mentally. One solution is to use physical symbols in the advertising that are more easily understood by the customers (Figure 9-2). For example, the phone company has had good luck with "Let your *fingers* do the walking," and

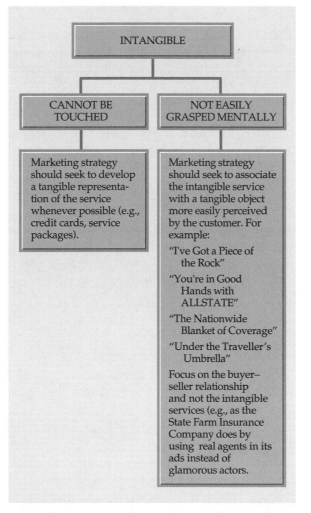

FIGURE 9-2 Marketing Intangible Services (From James H. Donnelly, Jr., "Intangibility and Marketing Strategy for Retail Bank Services," *Journal of Retail Banking* [June 1980], pp. 39–43)

Travelers Insurance is well known for its *umbrella*. Insurance companies convey security by association with familiar rocks, hands, umbrellas, and blankets.

A third approach focuses on the service provider (actor, lawyer, professor), who is more tangible than the actual service (screen role, courtroom appearance, education). In this case, advertising emphasizes the skills and technical competence of the person who is in contact with the buyer. Insurance agents are shown as family counselors and loan officers as friendly neighbors; the Maytag repairman is depicted as someone with little to do. Thus, the service being offered becomes more tangible because of the fellowship with the provider.

Perishability

Services cannot be stored or carried in inventory. If they are not used when offered, they go to waste. The empty classroom or hospital bed represents revenue that is lost forever. Most of the problems with perishability are related to inaccurate forecasts of demand. When demand is steady, service organizations are able to provide staff to meet customers' requests. However, unpredictable demand can lead to serious difficulties. For example, during the stock market boom of the 1980s, Wall Street hired extra staff to process orders. After the crash of 1987 cut trading volume, many clerks and brokers were laid off.

The best way to avoid service perishability is to do a better job of matching supply with demand. This can be done by adjusting supply or by smoothing out demand. Some suggestions for supply-side management include the following:

- Perform maintenance at night when services are not in demand. Examples include airplanes and transit buses.
- Encourage customers to perform part of the service, such as filling out forms in doctors' offices or at the car rental counter.
- Hire temporary help to meet peak demands. An example is the use of Manpower and Kelley Services in offices.

Demand can be managed by the following methods:

- Differential pricing to shift demand from peak to off-peak periods. An example is low weekend rates at urban hotels.
- Advertising campaigns that focus on the solitude of island beaches during off-season periods.
- Offering complementary services to those who are waiting. Theaters sell popcorn and candy and rent videotapes to people waiting to see a movie.
- Reservation systems guarantee services to customers who cannot be handled during peak periods. These extra customers can be told of available service times and kept from going to competitors.

Inseparability

A tangible product is first manufactured by a firm; next, it is distributed to dealers who sell it; and finally, the product is consumed. With services, however, the sale comes first. Then the service is produced and consumed at the same time. For example, a customer buys an opera ticket; then, on the night of the performance, the opera is presented and viewed by the audience. Simultaneous production and consumption forces services to be delivered directly to the customer. This close relationship with buyers makes the image of the service provider more important in the purchase decision. In addition, services must be easily accessible to customers.

Outlet Accessibility   Since services cannot be stored or transported, they have to be delivered to customers by local sales agents. This means that the revenue of service marketers is often limited by the number of service outlets they maintain. While customers may be willing to drive 50 miles to an airport, they will travel only a few miles to go to a bank, stockbroker, insurance agent, or bowling alley. Service marketers have to balance the revenues produced by additional outlets against the costs of maintaining the facilities. Service marketers have tried various strategies to reduce the costs of getting close to customers. H&R Block opens hundreds of temporary offices during the tax season and then closes them. Century 21 uses a system of franchising local offices to expand its coverage and enhance revenues. One of the best ways to expand coverage is through the use of machines. Ticketmaster machines dispense theater and sports tickets at locations that are close to customers. Banks have been very successful at providing low-cost services by placing teller machines in outlying areas that would not support a full service outlet.

Image Is Important   Since the buyer must be present to obtain certain services, marketers should be aware of the image projected by their facility. Doctors' and lawyers' offices are often luxuriously decorated to instill a feeling of confidence in the client. Attractive furnishings imply that the business is doing well and suggest professional competence.

    The same concept applies to auto repairs. If you visit a shop and find the floor strewn with broken parts, tools, and grease, you are apt to wonder about the ability of the mechanics to fix your car. Clearly, successful service suppliers maintain the quality of their customer contact facilities so that buyers will come again.

Variability

As most services are produced by people, service quality tends to vary considerably from one transaction to the next. Products, on the other hand, are produced in factories where inspectors can ensure uniformity from item to item. The lack of standardization by service providers means that you may be satisfied with your haircut, your dry cleaner, or your dentist on one visit and be dissatisfied on your next visit. As one hotel executive put it:

> *When you buy a box of Tide, you can reasonably be 99 and 44/100% sure that this stuff will work to get your clothes clean. When you buy a Holiday Inn room, you're sure at some lesser percentage that it will work to give you a good night's sleep without any hassle, or people banging on the walls and all the bad things that can happen to you in a hotel.*[4]

Service buyers face greater uncertainty in the marketplace and try to reduce that risk. One result is that customers are more likely to seek a friend's advice when they are selecting a doctor than when they are buying a microwave oven.

    Another way of reducing risk is to provide warranties such as those used for physical products. One warranty program for auto repairs says that if Ford doesn't fix the car correctly, the customer does not have to pay. Customers will be more willing to take their cars to Ford service departments if they know that the company stands behind its repair work.

Perhaps the best way to reduce variability in services is to hire and train employees very carefully. For example, Disney World's success is clearly related to the enthusiasm and courtesy of its employees. Disney is selective in hiring and spends a great deal of time making sure that its employees know how to act on the job. If Disney can build a loyal and dedicated team of customer contact people, so can other service organizations.

Firms that expect to reduce service variability need to monitor service production to detect when problems exist. Information on customer satisfaction can be obtained through suggestion boxes, phone surveys, and mail questionnaires. Once a firm identifies rude, discourteous, and uninformed personnel, these employees can either be retrained or terminated.

Client Relationships

Relationships between service organizations and customers are often close and long-lasting. Under these conditions, service providers should work to develop client rapport. When you are dealing with clients, try to associate on a first-name basis and include customers in social activities (assuming this is appropriate to the culture). Clients are not afraid to deal on a first-name basis with the person who cuts their hair, buys stock for them, and creates their advertising. This means that service providers who are attempting to steal clients from competitors need to have a clearly superior product. Also, existing service customers need to be rewarded with extra perks and benefits. For example, it is not uncommon for stockbrokers to host cocktail parties and intimate dinner parties for clients. Even airlines have had success with "presidential lounges" for preferred groups of customers.

The objective of creating a client relationship is to make it easier to sell new services. The longer you provide a service to customers, the more confidence they will have in your recommendations. After all, it is easier for all of us to accept new hair styles, new investments, and new vacation ideas from people we like and respect. The task for the service company is to build an ongoing relationship so that customers will resist the blandishments of competitors and come back to buy again and again.

MANAGING THE SERVICE MARKETING SYSTEM

Services marketing is complicated because services are created and consumed simultaneously. This also means that you must produce services and sell them at the same time.

Service organizations usually have an operations person in charge of facilities, hiring, and customer contact personnel. As a result, marketing activities do not always get the attention they deserve. When marketing managers are employed, they usually advise staff on services development, pricing, promotion, and delivery. Thus service organizations often lack a strong marketing orientation that focuses on determining and filling customers' needs.

Systems for Service Marketing

A better structure for services marketing integrates the activities of the operations and marketing supervisors. The relationships between these two managers are highlighted in Figure 9-3. A service marketing system should be made up of three interrelated parts: services operations, services delivery, and marketing support.

Services operations is responsible for facilities, equipment, and personnel. In a hotel, the operations manager runs the building and hires, trains, and supervises the employees. Only half of the services operations are visible to the customer. Hotel guests see the rooms and talk to the desk clerk and waitresses in the dining room, but they do not come in contact with the kitchens, laundries, garage, and office areas behind the scenes.

Services delivery is concerned with the interface between the provider and the customer (Figure 9-3). The goal is to promote pleasant exchanges with customers so that they will return. Companies can encourage this trend by giving the marketing manager some control over service delivery. For example, in a hotel, marketing can operate the reservation service, convention scheduling, and the information booth

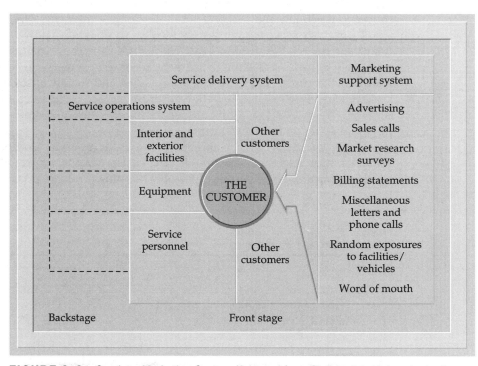

FIGURE 9-3 Services Marketing System (Adapted from Christopher H. Lovelock, *Services Marketing*, 2nd ed. [Englewood Cliffs, NJ: Prentice-Hall, 1991], p. 16)

in the lobby. These activities solicit future business and take care of special needs of customers. If these tasks are handled efficiently, the flow of new business will be enhanced. Successful service delivery systems demand the coordinated efforts of marketing and operations personnel to make sure that customers are satisfied. A good marketing manager will handle inquiries and complaints to make sure that the quality of the services offered is maintained.

Managing Service Quality

Firms that consistently deliver high-quality services can expect higher returns than organizations with poor customer relations. Table 9-2 shows how the top third of a sample of business units in terms of service quality outperformed the bottom third. These data, from the Strategic Planning Institute, reveal that high-service businesses were able to charge higher prices, grow faster, and make more profits on sales than their low-service competitors. Other research has shown that service quality is an antecedent of customer satisfaction.[5] These results suggest that service organizations must pay attention to quality.

While it is easy to talk about delivering quality services, there are a number of problems that must be overcome. First, service quality is harder to define than product quality. What constitutes good service from a doctor is clearly more complex than good service from a detergent. Remember, services are delivered by highly variable humans, while products are produced on assembly lines that are more easily checked and monitored.

To manage service quality successfully, you have to know what level of service customers expect. When clients call a securities firm, they do not expect to be put on hold for 5 minutes and bombarded with recorded excuses and Musak. Thus part of your job is to run surveys, analyze complaints, and review customer comment cards to determine exactly what buyers want from service companies. Southwest Airlines is making money today, while others are not, because customers know that Southwest planes fly on time and fares are low.

Once you know what customers want from a service company, you are in a better position to deliver. Frequently the easiest way to improve service quality is by providing front-line people with more training. This gives customer contact rep-

TABLE 9-2

Service Quality and Performance

	Top Third in Service Quality	Bottom Third in Service Quality
Prices relative to competitors	7%	−2%
Change in market share per year	6%	−2%
Sales growth	17%	8%
Return on sales	12%	1%

Source: Phillip Thompson, Glenn Desoursa, and Bradley T. Gale, "The Strategic Management of Service and Quality," Quality Progress (June 1985), p. 24.

MARKETING STRATEGIES 9-2

SERVICE QUALITY GURUS

Until recently few companies in the service sector employed people with the word "quality" in their titles. A survey of 52 large firms revealed that half had created executive level quality posts since 1988. One of these people is Darla Mendales, who is vice president of quality management for Fidelity Investments. Fidelity is America's largest mutual fund company, and most of its business is done through the mail and over the phone. Mendales' job is to slash response times and cut red tape to improve customer service.

Her first task was to avoid trivializing her mandate by turning down suggestions from top officials to use a system of "logos, buttons, and mugs." Mendales spends her days promoting service programs, planning front line staff training, and editing summaries of service problems for top executives. A key theme is shifting Fidelity's focus to standards set by customers rather than managers. One successful project involved simplifying its automated phone prompts, recording softer voiced instructions, and expanding its toll-free numbers from two to five. Brochures were rewritten so "service" became "account assistance" and "sales" became "product information." As a result, 33% more customers got where they wanted to be by pushing numbers rather than waiting for operators to direct them.

(*continued on next page*)

> **MARKETING STRATEGY 9-2** (*continued*)
>
> Fidelity also merged its back-room and phone operations to reduce call transfers and delays. However, it is not easy to get representatives to be more personable when the number of calls they answer per hour is being monitored. Bonuses were cut back and base salaries increased as quality standards were raised. Phone reps complained that the company was talking quality but they were still measuring productivity. Mendales is allowing reps more flexibility in handling calls and productivity standards are being eased to handle the problem.
>
> Mendales is encouraging employees to suggest ideas for service improvements using newsletters, hallway signs, cash prizes and other gifts. She feels that "recognition" is a big part of quality improvement programs at service companies.
>
> *Service quality can be improved by appointing expeditors.*
>
> *Source:* Gilbert Fuchsberg, "Gurus of Quality Are Gaining Clout," *The Wall Street Journal*, November 27, 1990, p. B-1.

resentatives more background to solve problems and complete transactions more quickly. Another technique that can improve quality is to provide additional automated equipment. Some firms have boosted their quality by adding more toll-free phone lines, switching to 24-hour automated access to account data, and using computers to schedule doctors' appointments.

Although service quality can be managed to satisfy customers, there is still the question of cost. Your problem is to give good service without bankrupting the firm. This means that you cannot sacrifice everything just to make the customer happy. There has to be a balance between the level of service and the cost of providing this service. For example, Citibank tries to answer phone calls within 10 seconds and customers' letters within 2 days. While Citibank has the resources to give this high level of service, it may not be feasible for everyone. Some of the trade-offs between service levels and productivity are discussed in Marketing Strategies box 9-2.

Managing Service Demand

Most services cannot be stored in inventory. When demand is high, there is usually no backup stock to help fill orders, and potential business is lost. When demand is low, service capacity is wasted. With manufactured goods, it is much easier to match production with demand and to draw down inventories when demand is unusually high. Service organizations need extra help to manage demand.

The first step is to list the major factors that affect sales. Does demand vary by the hour, day, week, or month? What are the underlying causes of demand changes? In some situations, service demand is affected by work schedules, pay dates, climate, and school schedules. Once managers know why customers use services, adjustments can be made to smooth fluctuations over time.

An example of the impact of demand variation on services is shown in Figure 9-4. In sector 1 of the diagram, demand exceeds maximum service capacity and customers are lost. When demand is greater than optimum capacity (sector 2), the

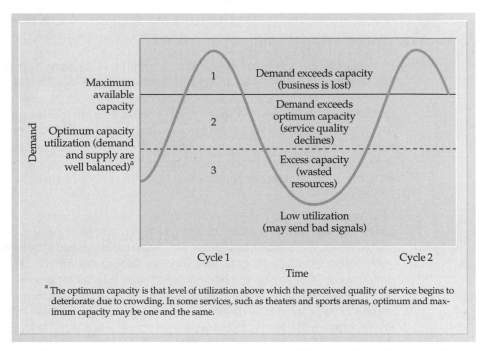

FIGURE 9-4   Impact of Demand Variation on Service Utilization (From Christopher H. Lovelock, *Services Marketing*, 2nd ed. [Englewood Cliffs, NJ: Prentice-Hall, 1991], p. 132)

quality of service deteriorates. This is undesirable because customers who wait in line for service may never return. With low demand (sector 3), service capacity is wasted and investors and customers may get the impression that the business is poorly run.

Inventorying Demand   Although most services cannot be carried in inventory, astute marketers can inventory demand. The idea is to get customers to wait in line for services or to make appointments for a future slack period. Both of these approaches can help shift peak demand (Figure 9-4, sector 1) to periods with excess capacity.

The use of queues to manage demand is simplified if you know how long customers will wait. Amusement parks understand customer time constraints and sometimes use clocks to show how long it will take to get on a particular ride. They also provide covered ramps to keep the sun off and refreshment stands to make waiting easier. Other ways to make queues more enjoyable include providing seating, reading material, and numbered tags to show people their positions in line.

Using Price   A common method for balancing a limited service supply with varying levels of demand is through the use of pricing. The usual procedure is to raise prices during high-demand periods to encourage thrifty customers to shift to off-peak times. High prices help allocate demand and increase profits at the same time. In a similar manner, low prices attract customers during periods of low demand (Figure 9-4, sector 3). Since many service costs are fixed, low prices can improve profits if demand is sufficiently elastic.

One of the best examples of using pricing to manage demand is provided by telephone companies. They charge high rates during the day for inflexible business buyers and much lower rates in the evening for students and people with limited resources. This successful strategy of pricing to shift phone usage is based on a thorough understanding of the price elasticity of demand for each market segment. Service providers also have to ensure that the low priced off-peak services do not attract too many peak customers. Airlines solve this problem by attaching enough restrictions to their excursion fares so that they cannot be used by full-fare business travelers.

Using Advertising   Another effective technique to shift peak demand to slack periods is through advertising. Appropriate signs and advertising messages can encourage prospective customers to buy services during slack periods. Off-season promotions by resorts have been effective because some customers prefer vacations when beaches are less crowded and there are no lines at the tennis courts. Suggestions to avoid the rush are also successful when aimed at movie theater and transit customers. When intermediaries such as travel agents are used, they can tell customers when the best slack-demand periods occur.

Managing the Mix of Service Customers

The selection of customers is much more important for service organizations than for manufacturers. While many manufactured goods are consumed in the privacy of customers' homes, service clients are often part of the product. In addition, service providers face fixed capacity constraints, whereas factories can easily schedule overtime to meet surges in demand. As a result, service managers must be careful about the customers they choose to serve.

Customer Compatibility   Many services require customers to come to a central location and mingle with one another. Customers can quickly see who the other buyers are and decide whether they fit in terms of age, income, and lifestyle. This means that service firms must think about who they want to attract and how these people dress and behave.

A classic segmentation dilemma occurs when a resort hotel is offered a convention of 200 high school cheerleaders. On the one hand, the firm is attracted by the guaranteed booking of 100 rooms and the positive impact on meal and recreation revenues. This must be balanced against the reaction of regular business and family customers, who may take offense at the late-night noise and commotion caused by the teenagers. The revenue gain from the cheerleading convention could easily be less than the ultimate loss in future business if regular customers fail to return.

Finding a solution to the customer compatibility problem does not require a focus on homogeneous groups. Simply throwing out large numbers of potential customers because they do not mix well with others is unlikely to lead to profit maximization. One approach is to institute dress and behavior codes so that all clients know what is expected. However, this requires management to assume the role of police officer. A better technique is to separate the groups physically from one another—either in time or in space. For example, the convention of cheerleaders could be accepted if the teenagers can be housed in a separate building with its own lounge, pool, and restaurant. Another approach would be to book the convention during the off season. Additional examples of separation include the division of airplane cabins into first-class and economy sections and the use of adult buildings in condominium projects. These solutions allow the service provider to appeal to more than one class of customer.

Customer Profitability Service organizations typically have a high ratio of fixed to variable costs because of expensive facilities, equipment, and a cadre of full-time personnel. Under these conditions, there is a strong incentive to fill all the available

TABLE 9-3

Segmentation of the Financial Services Market

Segment	Percentage of Segment	Benefits Desired	Characteristics	Behavior
1. Planners and dealers	33	Profits Investment counsel Not convenience	Optimistic Well informed High income Self-confident	Multiple investments Use of nonbank services (e.g., money markets with nonbank institutions) Savings accounts
2. Conservators	20	Privacy One-stop shopping Service	Cautious Older	Savings accounts
3. Service seekers	16	Service Social interaction	Less educated Lower income Widows	Savings accounts
4. Uninvolved	19	None	Less self-esteem Pessimistic Suspicious of banks	Little use of bank services
5. Hopefuls	13	Financial security Personal attention	Young adults Black Female Less educated Lower income	High bank loyalty

Source: Adapted from ''Measuring Markets by Hopes and Fears,'' *The Wall Street Journal,* June 3, 1982, p. 27. Reprinted by permission of *The Wall Street Journal,* © Dow Jones & Company, Inc. (1982). All rights reserved.

seats in a plane or theater. The assumption is that the higher the usage rate, the greater the profit.

A common measure of performance in service firms is the percentage of capacity sold. Airlines talk of their "load factor" and hotels of their "occupancy rate." Although these percentages tell us something about how a company is run, they say very little about profits because the customers may have been obtained by aggressive price cutting. This suggests that success depends on knowing how much each customer segment will pay for services at different points in time.

Some characteristics of the financial services market are described in Table 9-3. In this case, customers are broken into five segments based on benefits desired and behavior. The information in Table 9-3 could be used to estimate how the different groups will respond to alternative prices. In addition, the data show the number of potential customers in each group, so that the profitability of different plans can be projected.

In pricing services, one measure of success compares the average price obtained per unit with the maximum price that might have been charged.[6] When this ratio, called the *yield percentage*, is multiplied by capacity utilization, the result is an index of asset revenue-generating efficiency (*ARGE*).

Suppose that a hotel has 200 rooms with a posted price of $100. On a particular night, 80 rooms are sold for $100 and 40 for $70. The yield percentage would be

$$\frac{\dfrac{(80 \times \$100) + (40 \times \$70)}{120} = \$90}{\text{Posted price} = \$100} = 0.90 \tag{9.1}$$

When this ratio is multiplied by the utilization factor of $120 \div 200 = 0.60$, an *ARGE* value of 0.54 is obtained ($0.90 \times 0.60 = 0.54$). *ARGE* can also be calculated by looking at the actual revenues relative to the maximum revenues that could be obtained:

$$ARGE = \frac{(80 \times \$100) + (40 \times \$70)}{(200 \times \$100)} = 0.54 \tag{9.2}$$

These results show that the simple utilization ratio of 0.60 was lowered to a more meaningful *ARGE* of 0.54 by some price cutting. The ARGE ratio is a handy yardstick for evaluating how well a firm manages the desired customer mix.

Planning the Customer Mix   One of the tricks of service marketing is recognizing the opportunity costs associated with accepting business from different groups of customers. For example, should a hotel book a block of rooms at a low price or hold them in case some transient guests show up to pay full rates? The answer might be that it depends on the probability of transient customers arriving. In reality, the solution is much more complicated. The reason is that customer demand is also influenced by personal selling and advertising. As both of these factors are under the control of management, marketing managers must carefully plan how to allocate service capacity among different customer segments at particular times.

A hotel room allocation plan is shown in Figure 9-5. A set number of rooms is reserved for airline flight crews for both the high- and low-demand periods. Notice that room renovations are scheduled for the slow season. Also, during off-peak times, the largest block of rooms is saved for conventions and groups. This block is greatly reduced during high-demand periods. In the high seasons, allocations triple for executive guests and transient customers who pay full rates. Since business guests do not stay over weekends, a special weekend package is offered to fill these rooms.

Once a capacity plan is created, the sales and advertising staffs are charged with achieving this goal. The success of a capacity allocation plan depends on how well it is implemented. In the case of a hotel, reservation personnel must keep track of whether the sales goals for different segments are being met. When convention rooms are sold out for a particular date, the system *must* stop accepting new reservations. This type of monitoring requires well-designed computer programs and the active attention of marketing personnel. At the completion of each planning period, an *ARGE* value can be calculated to measure how well the capacity plan has worked.

One of the most successful capacity management systems is employed by airlines in allocating seats to different classes of passengers. Airlines use a sophisticated reservation system that allows them to change prices and seat allotments as the time of a flight approaches. For a flight taking place in three months, Bouncy Airlines

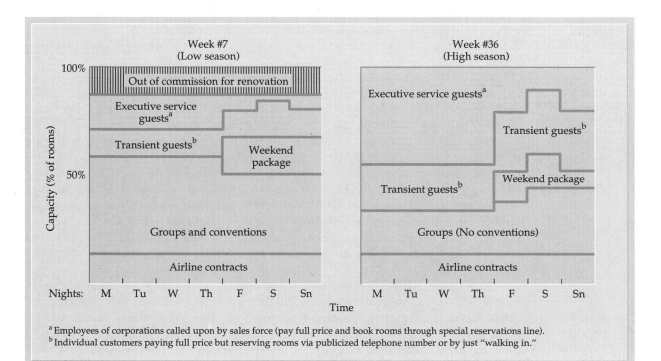

FIGURE 9-5 Allocating Hotel Capacity to Different Market Segments (From Christopher H. Lovelock, *Services Marketing*, 2nd ed. [Englewood Cliffs, NJ: Prentice-Hall, 1991], p. 124)

might plan 50 seats for super saver fares and 100 for tourist customers. If it sells 30 super saver seats in the first month, Bouncy might cut the allocation to 40 seats, with the expectation that the extra 10 seats will be sold to higher-paying tourist passengers as the time of the flight approaches. Airlines change the capacity allocations for different market segments on a daily basis to make sure that their planes are as full as possible and revenues are maximized.

Managing Productivity

Service organizations are highly labor-intensive, and many tasks are difficult to automate. This means that when wages increase, prices have to be raised and service growth tends to slow down. As a result, service managers are continually looking for ways to make operations more efficient.

The types of problems managers face are illustrated by employees answering customer-service calls at mutual fund companies. Phone reps are in relatively low-paid, low-glamour, high-turnover positions. At Fidelity a few years ago, a phone rep took 3 minutes and 188 keystrokes to complete a transaction. Now an advanced software package allows the transaction to be completed with 33 keystrokes in just 1 minute and 9 seconds. This allows Fidelity to handle more calls with fewer people and reduces customer waiting times. An even more advanced program is in the works that will allow phone reps to call up short bulletins on taxes, IRAs, and optimum fund allocations. These programs make it easier to train personnel, and phone reps will soon carry out most of the services offered by full-service brokers. An example of productivity gains at a car rental company is presented in Marketing Productivity box 9-1.

Another way to increase productivity in service industries is to move the work to lower-wage offshore locations. Recent advances in telecommunications technology and improved educational systems have made it easier to move backroom operations abroad. In Jamaica, 3500 people work at office parks connected to the United States by satellite dishes. There they make airline reservations, process tickets, handle calls to toll-free numbers, and do data entry work. More than 25,000 documents a day are scanned electronically in the United States, and copies are transmitted to Montego Bay for processing. In Ireland, multilingual workers answer questions on computer software programs for customers in the United States and Europe. Metropolitan Life has 150 workers in Ireland analyzing U.S. medical insurance claims. Offshore service workers tend to be more productive and cost 35 percent less than U.S. workers. In addition, foreign governments often grant tax concessions, and workforce turnover is usually very low.[7]

An example showing how service productivity can be improved is described in Figure 9-6. In this case, Rocky Resort's advertising had created more demand for tennis playing time in July and August than the existing facilities could deliver. Management decided to set a service level that allowed any guest who wanted to play 1 hour of court time per day. To achieve this goal, Rocky Resort considered doubling the number of courts and building a new clubhouse at a separate location. Management felt that it had to expand the tennis capacity or the future of the resort might be in jeopardy.

MARKETING PRODUCTIVITY 9-1

IMPROVING CAR RENTAL EFFICIENCY

One of the most difficult management problems in the service industry is finding ways to minimize customer waiting time when there are sudden surges in demand. Nowhere is this problem more evident than at airport car rental desks. Customers pour off flights all at once and rush to car rental counters to wait in long lines to provide information they have given countless times before. Finding ways to reduce this bottleneck is the most important operational question facing car rental companies today.

Hertz has designed a new No. 1 Gold Service program that allows customers to bypass the rental counter entirely. With Gold Service, customers pay an annual $50 fee and complete a one-time rental agreement that is stored on a computer. Members can then dial a special toll-free number to make reservations. Once at their destination, they take a courtesy bus to the service center, where a lighted sign steers them to a parking space containing a car with its trunk open, engine running, climate control set, and completed rental agreement waiting inside. At the gate, the member flashes a driver's license and rental agreement and is on his way.

(*continued on next page*)

> **MARKETING PRODUCTIVITY 9-1 (*continued*)**
>
> Efforts to take the bureaucracy out of renting cars have also been adopted by National with its Emerald Aisle program and Budget with Budget Express. However, most rental car companies lack the computer power to provide faster service to all customers. Thus these programs are generally limited to the most frequent rental customers. Car rental companies have also speeded up procedures to return cars. Now it is common to have attendants roaming the return lanes with portable computers that give you a receipt in seconds. These examples show that there are ways to solve customer queuing problems if you have some imagination.
>
> *Computers can improve service productivity.*
>
> *Source:* Johnnie L. Roberts, "Car Companies Move to Eliminate Dreaded Bottleneck: The Rental Counter," *The Wall Street Journal*, January 24, 1989, p. B-7

The actual solution used to remedy the problem was both imaginative and cost effective. First, in its promotional literature, the resort warned about possible congestion in July and August, encouraging some guests to schedule their visits during off-peak times. Then the resort set up a reservation system to manage the available playing time better. Court fees were changed so that four people could play for the price of two. Tennis mixers were also scheduled early in the week to help match up players.

Tennis capacity was expanded by adding lights to some courts and by opening courts two hours earlier in the morning. The resort also increased its promotion of sailing, surfing, and nature walks that were operating below capacity. As a result of all these efforts, only a few new courts had to be built. The new facilities were operated only during peak months and were staffed with part-time students. By managing demand and capacity effectively, the resort was able to turn a profit on its tennis program with a minimum of additional investment.

SUMMARY

Consumption of services is growing rapidly, so you need to understand how to market these intangible products. Marketing of services is tricky because services are perishable and often require the presence of a buyer. Since services are created and consumed at the same time, the delivery channel can be vital to your success. Other special characteristics of services include greater variability and stronger client relationships than for durables. Services have a high ratio of fixed to variable costs and require careful management to avoid losses during slack times. Successful managers know how to use reservation systems, pricing, and promotion to shift demand from peak to off-peak periods. Those who master the subtleties of service marketing are likely to satisfy customers, improve bottom-line performance, and reap financial rewards.

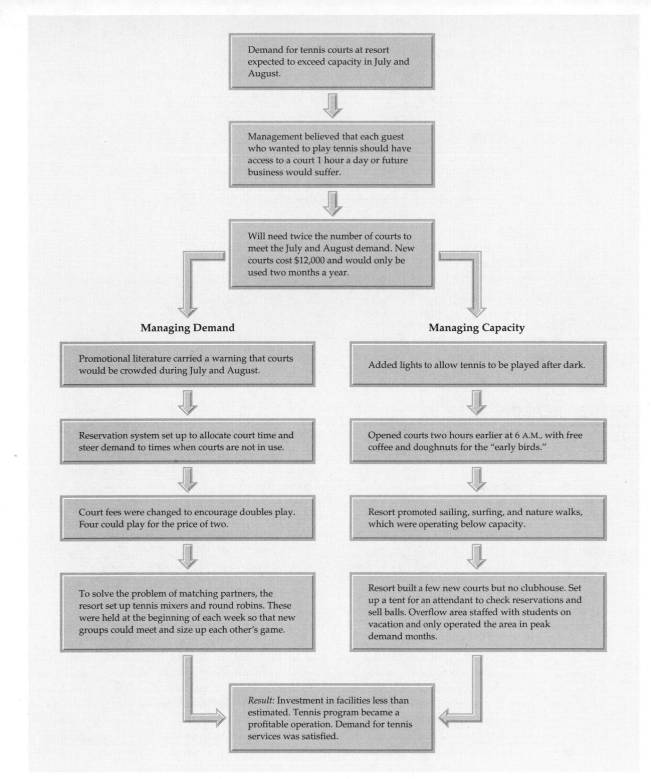

FIGURE 9-6 Managing the Supply of and Demand for Tennis Services (Adapted from an example in W. Earl Sasser, "Match Supply and Demand in Service Industries," *Harvard Business Review*, Vol. 54 [November–December 1976], p. 139)

NOTES

1. *Survey of Current Business*, Vol. 72, No. 8 (August 1992), p. 2.
2. *The Wall Street Journal*, March 21, 1988, p. 1.
3. Christopher H. Lovelock, *Services Marketing*, 2nd ed. (Englewood Cliffs, NJ: Prentice-Hall, 1991), pp. 2–5.
4. Gary Knisely, "Greater Marketing Emphasis by Holiday Inns Breaks Mold," *Advertising Age*, January 15, 1979, p. 47.
5. J. Joseph Cronin and Steven A. Taylor, "Measuring Service Quality: A Reexamination and Extension," *Journal of Marketing*, Vol. 56 (July 1992), p. 55.
6. Lovelock, *Services Marketing*, p. 122.
7. Brian O'Reilly, "Your New Global Work Force," *Fortune*, December 14, 1992, p. 62.

SUGGESTED READING

Bertrand, K. "In Service, Perception Counts," *Business Marketing* (April 1989), pp. 44–50.

FURTHER READING

Bateson, John E. G. *Managing Services Marketing*, 2nd ed. (Chicago: Dryden, 1992).

Bloch, T. M., G. D. Opah, and V. A. Zeithaml. *Service Marketing in a Changing Environment* (Chicago: American Marketing Association, 1985).

Donnelly, J. H., L. L. Berry, and T. W. Thompson. *Marketing Financial Services: A Strategic Vision* (Homewood, IL: Dow Jones-Irwin, 1985).

Lovelock, Christopher H. *Services Marketing*, 2nd ed. (Englewood Cliffs, NJ: Prentice-Hall, 1991).

Rathmell, J. M. *Marketing in the Service Sector*. (Cambridge, MA: Winthrop, 1974).

QUESTIONS

1. To increase customer satisfaction, British Airways recently installed some Video Point Booths at Heathrow Airport. These allowed disgruntled customers to tape their complaints. As a result, the airline had to refund $200,000 to passengers on a flight that failed to depart on time. Is this the best way to make service quality pay?

2. A marketing consultant to the legal profession has said: "Law firms are finding that the most effective way to get new business is to hire lawyers who already have it." Does this mean that the $45 million a year that lawyers spend on TV advertising is wasted? Should lawyers spend money on Yellow Pages advertising, entertainment, brochures, seminars, and newsletters?

3. Video rental is one of the fastest-growing departments in supermarkets. Sales are increasing 11 percent per year. Should supermarkets devote more space to the sale of other services?

4. An automatic teller machine (ATM) costs an average of $50,000 a year to service and maintain. This is twice the cost of a human teller. Why are banks and savings and loans installing ATMs, and how do they make them pay? Why do people use ATMs for withdrawals but not for deposits? How could this behavior be changed?

5. Today 91 percent of U.S. hospitals have marketing programs costing over $1.6 billion. About $500 million of this money is spent each year on advertising. A survey of customers revealed that hospital advertising is considered boring, unclear, and uninformative. Respondents were turned off by "mushy" image-enhancing advertising slogans. Does this mean that hospitals should spend less on advertising? What would you recommend?

6. In 1933, Congress passed the Glass-Steagall Act, which prohibits banks from selling their own mutual funds. Despite this law, Chase Manhattan Bank is spending $4 million on a national advertising campaign to promote its Vista Mutual Funds and other financial services. Although the mutual funds carry Chase's Vista label, they are actually sponsored by MFS Financial Services of Boston. Why has Chase decided to act as a distributor of mutual funds?

7. The cruise industry is attracting more passengers by adding exercise equipment, conference centers, small TVs in cabins, movie theaters, Las Vegas–style shows, financial seminars, shopping arcades, and casinos. They have also had great success with "theme" cruises that appeal to jazz enthusiasts, stamp collectors, bridge players, and pastry chefs. Does this mean that segmentation is the salvation of all service businesses?

8. The Health Services Marketing Association recently gave out 27 gold, silver, and bronze awards in categories such as product achievement, pricing, distribution, and communications. What does the association expect to gain by giving out these annual awards?

9. A relaxation of rules on the marketing of professional services has led to more interest in the use of promotions to boost sales. For example, an orthopedic surgeon who wanted to specialize in joint replacement came up with a brochure designed to appeal to older people and distributed it by direct mail to retirement communities. This appeal was so successful that the surgeon had to open two more offices and find a partner. In another case, a dentist who doubled the size of his Yellow Pages ad found that demand for his services doubled as well. How should professionals allocate their marketing budgets across different promotional alternatives to maximize sales?

10. You have been selected to be the training manager for a group of representatives selling financial services. What subjects in your training classes will be the same as those used for durable goods and what subjects will be different? Why?

11. Affinity credit cards that support special causes have fallen on hard times. A Memphis bank, for example, has had trouble signing people up for its Elvis

Presley MasterCard. The Elvis card has a portrait of the King, a $36 annual fee, and an interest rate that is lower than that of other cards. Some of the income from the Elvis card goes to music scholarships. Direct mail has not worked for the Elvis card, but the bank has had some success by promoting it through record and tape clubs. What does this example say about the use of segmentation in the credit card industry?

12. Georgia Power Company has 110 field representatives scattered throughout the state. Most of the reps are electrical and mechanical engineers who work with customers as energy consultants. Why is Georgia Power so interested in marketing its services when it has a quasi-monopoly on electricity sales in Georgia?

Chapter 10

Pricing

The art of pricing is to have the price be an equate to the value of the product to the customer—anything less than that represents a sacrifice in potential profits.

E. RAYMOND COREY

Pricing goods and services is a critical job in the successful operation of for-profit and not-for-profit organizations. Price is the one element of the marketing mix that generates revenue; the rest are costs. Many marketing executives are under great pressure to increase prices to boost short-term profits. Stock markets in the United States, for example, are sensitive to quarterly earnings reports, and managers often raise the prices of cash cows to maintain earnings growth. However, high earnings tend to attract competitors—and even investigations from government agencies.

Low prices can be used as a weapon to build market share. Prices that undercut competitors attract new customers and allow for greater utilization of facilities. However, low prices squeeze margins and often reduce net profits. Thus your challenge as a marketing manager is to find a pricing strategy that balances your need for sales growth against your demand for profits.

In many firms, the struggle to find the right price is not handled well. Too often organizations rely too heavily on costs to set prices and ignore the effects of demand. Other firms fail to integrate pricing with their market positioning strategy. Moreover, some organizations do not vary the price enough across market segments and leave money on the table. Our goal is to show you how to resolve these problems and build an optimal pricing strategy.

This chapter will answer two basic pricing questions: How should you set prices for new and existing products and services? How and when should prices be changed?

FINDING THE RIGHT PRICE

Setting prices for new and existing products appears simple enough. All you apparently have to do is estimate your costs, add a margin for overhead and profit, and

233

you have your selling price. However, the amount you can sell varies with the price you set. Moreover, costs change with volume, so profits depend on price.

A second issue is that customers compare prices with the perceived quality of your goods and services. Some customers are value oriented and want to pay low prices for acceptable quality. At the other extreme are buyers who want high quality and are willing to pay more to get it. Thus your price must be congruent with the prospective buyers you choose to target.

A third complication involves your competitors. The prices they set often limit what you can charge. Furthermore, when you sell several items, you have to consider how the price of one product affects the sales of others in your line.

The setting of initial prices for goods and services is influenced by a variety of factors. We explain them using a four-step pricing procedure: (1) determine pricing goals, (2) measure demand, (3) estimate costs, and (4) choose a pricing method.

Determining Pricing Goals

Your first pricing task is to select an overall pricing goal for the firm and then determine objectives for individual product lines. If your company is the first to enter a particular market with a patented product, you are in a good position to follow a premium pricing strategy. On the other hand, firms that enter third often use price to buy market share. For example, in 1988 Anheuser-Busch, the largest American brewer, began to move its Eagle Snacks from a niche player into national distribution. They offered retailers up to $500 a linear foot for shelf space and engaged in heavy consumer promotions. By 1991 they had 4 percent of the market, behind Frito Lay with 40 percent and Borden with 10 percent. However, this strategy produced losses of $21 million in the Eagle division in 1991. In the long run, Eagle has to find a way to sell snacks at prices that produce a profit.

Selection of pricing goals sometimes is determined by prior business and positioning decisions. Toyota, the largest Japanese car manufacturer, created its Lexus division to compete in the U.S. luxury car market. Thus all Lexus cars are priced higher than cars sold by the regular Toyota dealerships. The distinction between the divisions became more pronounced with the decision to drop the highest-priced regular Toyota, the Cressida. Individual Lexus product lines are priced from $28,000 to over $50,000 to take advantage of different segments of the demand curve.

These examples suggest that different firms emphasize different pricing goals. We discuss four key pricing objectives: profit maximization, revenue maximization, market share maximization, and quality leadership.

Profit Maximization Many organizations need profits to satisfy stockholders and provide funds for expansion and product development. To maximize profits, you need data on the number of units that can be sold at different prices plus estimates of fixed and variable costs. The relationship between profits and price for a company manufacturing battery-operated vacuum cleaners is shown in Figure 10-1. The variable costs for producing the vacuum cleaner are $20 per unit, and the fixed costs are $15,000. As prices rise, profits increase until they hit a maximum of $49,000 at a price of $60 (the mathematics of this relationship are explained in the Marketing Tools box

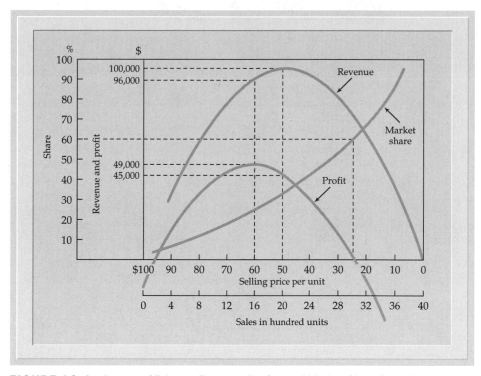

FIGURE 10-1   Impact of Price on Revenue, Profits, and Market Share for a Battery-operated Vacuum Cleaner

10-1). At prices above $60, fewer customers are interested in buying, so profits decline. The goal of profit maximization thus leads the firm to charge a fairly high price ($60) and to restrict output to only 1600 units.

A slightly different approach occurs when a company starts with a high price to "skim" the market. This profit goal is often used with new products that cannot be easily copied. The idea is to charge high prices to early buyers and then slide down the demand curve with lower prices to capture successive layers of more price-sensitive buyers. The price-skimming goal tries to maximize profits by extracting the highest possible price from each market segment. The major problem with any profit-maximizing goal is that the high profits attract competitors, who try to steal away your customers with similar products offered at lower prices.

An example of the pursuit of a profit-maximizing goal occurred with Ford's 1993 model year cars. Ford, the second largest American car manufacturer, had lost a record $2.26 billion in 1991 and was desperate for cash to help update and modernize its product lines. In the summer of 1992, Ford announced price increases of 4 percent to more than 6 percent on its cars and trucks in the U.S. market. These increases exceeded inflation and succeeded only because Japanese manufacturers announced even higher prices. The Japanese needed bigger margins due to a strong yen, weak sales at home, and a protectionist sentiment in the U.S. Congress. The

MARKETING TOOLS 10-1

MAXIMIZING PROFITS

Suppose that in the process of making price adjustments you have learned the shape of your demand curve for battery-powered vacuum cleaners. The basic relationship is negative and the quantity purchased, Q, increases as the price, P, declines. This relationship can be expressed as

$$Q = 4000 - 40P \tag{10.1}$$

If fixed costs for tooling and overhead are estimated at \$15,000 and variable costs for the vacuum cleaner are \$20 per unit, then the total cost, C, will be

$$C = \$15,000 + \$20Q \tag{10.2}$$

where, assuming that supply equals demand, the number of units produced in also Q. Because costs are subtracted from revenues (or turnover) to get profits, it is handy to have an equation that expresses total revenue, R, as a function of price. This can be obtained by noting that revenue is equal to price times quantity. Because equation (10.1) expresses quantity in terms of price, a revenue function can be obtained as follows:

$$\begin{aligned} R &= PQ \\ &= P(4000 - 40P) \\ &= 4000P - 40P^2 \end{aligned} \tag{10.3}$$

Now that we have equations for demand, costs, and revenue, it is a simple matter to express profits, K, in terms of price.

$$\begin{aligned} K &= R - C \\ &= (4000P - 40P^2) - (\$15,000 + \$20Q) \\ &= (4000P - 40P^2) - (\$15,000 + \$20[4000 - 40P]) \\ &= -\$95,000 + 4800P - 40P^2 \end{aligned} \tag{10.4}$$

This equation can be solved, using calculus, to show that profits hit a maximum of \$49,000 at a selling price of \$60. Figure 10-1 shows that the optimal price of \$60 can also be found by plotting the profit curve and finding the high point.

---

base price for the Escort subcompact was held constant, while prices for the popular F-Series pickup trucks were raised 6.5 percent and those for the top-of-the-line Lincoln Town Car 9.5 percent.

Revenue Maximization   An alternative pricing objective is to maximize revenue. When the price of the battery-operated vacuum cleaner is set at \$60 to maximize profits, revenues of \$96,000 are generated (Figure 10-1). The diagram indicates that if prices are cut \$10, revenue will hit a peak of \$100,000. At a price of \$50, volume increases to 2000 units and profits decline. Managers who are looking for sales growth are often willing to trade a little profit for higher volume. Also, because it is difficult to measure demand, some managers may believe that it is easier to maximize sales than the more abstract profit factor. The lower prices associated with revenue maximization could also be used to keep competitors out of a market.

Market Share Maximization   A third pricing goal is to maximize market share subject to a minimum profit constraint. This objective trades profits and revenue for market position. If our vacuum cleaner manufacturer sets a price of $25, market share will expand to 60 percent while profits fall to nothing (Figure 10-1). An absence of profits means that market share maximization must have other long-run objectives. This approach is frequently used to break into new markets. Some retailers and wholesalers demand that you obtain a certain market share in other markets before they will stock your product (and you must keep a minimum share for them to continue to carry it). Market share maximum unit volume is especially important in situations where unit sales data and market share figures are made available to the public, as in the case of automobiles. Under these conditions, a firm is under pressure to maintain its share of the total business to bolster its image, regardless of the effects on profits. Market share maximization is best employed when a firm has a cash cow in another line of trade that can be used to cross-subsidize product improvements and expansion of production facilities.

Quality Leadership   Another pricing goal is to support an image as the quality leader in a market. Some customers use price as an indicator of quality. Buyers tend to prefer higher-priced products when price is the only information available, when they believe that the quality of available brands differs significantly, and when the price difference among brands is large. Consequently, a premium price may allow you to build a perception in customers' minds that your product is of high quality. On the other hand, if customers believe that the quality is high, you can often charge a premium price. For example, Maytag builds very durable washing machines and advertises their lonely repairman. A survey by *Consumer Reports* showed that Maytag is the second best company for repairs. The magazine also reported that Maytag washers are only average on performance, yet cost $140 more than the top-rated Sears washers. Maytag buyers are willing to pay more to get a repair-free washer. A premium price can be used to fund the manufacture of a quality good or the delivery of quality service. Buyers determine the value of a product by comparing its perceived quality with its price.

Research has shown that the variable costs for General Motors, the largest American car manufacturer, of producing Cadillacs are only slightly higher than the costs of building full-sized Chevrolets. However, customers believe that Cadillacs are higher in quality, and this allows General Motors to price them at twice the price of Chevrolets. These examples show that quality leadership can lead to improved profits in the long run. Once you have decided on a pricing goal, you need to look at demand.

Measuring Demand

Each price you charge for your goods or services is associated with a different level of sales. Let us assume that in the process of making price adjustments you have learned the general shape of the demand curve for battery-powered vacuum cleaners. This tells you how many units you can expect to sell at alternative prices (Figure 10-2). The basic relationship is usually negative: the quantity purchased increases as the price declines, and vice versa. When the price is set at $60, demand is 1600 units and profits are maximized. If the price is cut to $25 per unit, demand expands to 3000 units. When you know the shape of your demand schedules, you can set prices to reach any of a variety of goals.

Sometimes raising prices results in increased sales. The usual explanation is that the initial price has been set so low that buyers believe that the product is inferior and refuse to purchase it. This occurred with a panty hose manufacturer who could not sell his product at 69 cents and did better at $1.39. In such cases, the price changes the perceived product. Thus, you do not have a rising demand schedule; rather, you are moving from a demand schedule for one perceived product to a demand schedule for a different perceived product—and all the while, the actual physical product has not changed!

Today many firms have estimates of their demand schedules. The usual way to obtain these data is to vary prices in a laboratory or in the store and measure how much customers purchase.[1]

Price Elasticity of Demand   The preferred way to express customer sensitivity to price is with a ratio known as the *price elasticity of demand*. This is obtained by dividing

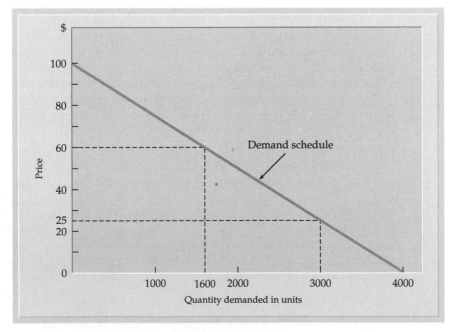

FIGURE 10-2   Demand for Vacuum Cleaners

percentage changes in the quantity sold by associated changes in price. The formula for price elasticity is

$$\text{Price elasticity of demand} = \frac{\%\text{ change in quantity demanded}}{\%\text{ change in price}} \tag{10.5}$$

Price elasticities are negative. When a relative change in volume is more than the relative change in price, demand is described as *elastic*. If the price is cut by 1 percent and demand increases by 5 percent, the elasticity is -5. When demand is this sensitive to price, it almost always pays to cut prices. You will more than make up in volume what you lose in margin per unit. When the quantity response is the same as the percentage change in price, elasticity is -1 and revenues collected by the firm stay the same whether prices are raised or lowered.

When a relative change in the quantity sold is less than the relative change in price, demand is said to be *inelastic*. Thus, if a price increase of 10 percent results in a 3 percent reduction in sales, price elasticity will be -0.3. In situations where elasticity is between 0 and -1, revenues increase as prices are raised. This suggests that when demand is inelastic, profits can be improved by raising prices. Demand is most likely to be inelastic when the product is infrequently purchased or it has few substitutes or competitors.

You should understand that although an industry's price elasticity may be inelastic, an individual brand's elasticity is usually elastic. Thus, while the industry elasticity for gasoline is -0.3, the demand for Shell and Texaco brands across the street from one another is much more elastic. Brand studies have shown that the price elasticity of cars is -1.5; that of coffee, -5.3; and that of confectionery, -2.0.[2] Other reviews of published research have found average price elasticities of -2.5 for U.S. brands and -1.6 for major British brands.[3]

Price elasticities tend to vary over the product life cycle. Real prices for brands often decline over time—even in the face of improvements to product quality. Products that are inelastic when introduced may become more elastic as they mature.[4]

An important part of your job as marketing manager is to make your brands less elastic, allowing you to charge higher prices. This can be done with advertising or by bundling your basic product or service with other products or services. For example, Technimetrics markets financial databases. It commands premium prices by bundling free consultations, research reports, and other services with its database products.

Estimating Costs

Our discussion of demand provides a ceiling price that the organization can charge for goods and service. At the other extreme, costs determine the price floor. Organizations must charge enough to cover their total costs in the long run and have enough left over to pay the stockholders or buy replacement animals for the zoo.

Types of Costs Costs come in two basic forms, fixed or variable. *Fixed costs* include expenditures for overhead such as plant, equipment, and executive salaries. These

costs do not vary with the level of output. In the case of the vacuum cleaner manufacturer, the fixed costs of tooling and other overhead amounted to $15,000 (Figure
10-3). These costs are the same at all output levels.

Variable costs represent the direct labor, materials, and commissions needed to
produce and sell each unit of merchandise. The unit variable costs for the vacuum
cleaner are $20. Variable costs are so named because their total varies with produc-
tion levels (Figure 10-3). When you look at per unit costs, you notice that variable
costs for this product are constant across different levels of production (Figure 10-4).

Total costs are the sum of the fixed and variable costs at various levels of output.
Note that total unit costs for the vacuum cleaner decline sharply as the fixed costs
are spread over more units of production (Figure 10-4). Most of the economies of
scale that occur when plants are run at capacity are due to a decline in allocated
fixed costs per unit. Unit variable costs may also decline if volume purchases lead
to quantity discounts on raw materials. Managers who have a decreasing unit-cost
curve are in a strong position to lower prices to expand market shares. An alternative
approach to costing used by the Japanese is explained in Marketing Tools box 10-2.

Costs and the Experience Curve   There is convincing evidence that the cost of manufacturing products also declines as workers gain experience in their jobs. An example of an experience curve is shown in Figure 10-5. Note that both axes are expressed
in logarithmic form and that experience is measured as cumulative increases in vol-

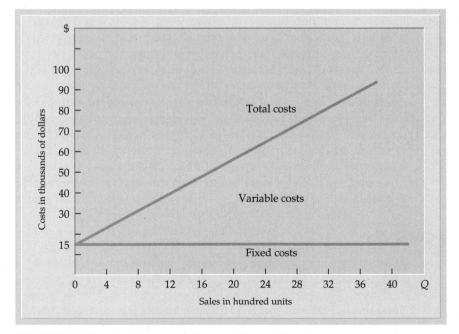

FIGURE 10-3   Cost Curves for Vacuum Cleaner Manufacturer

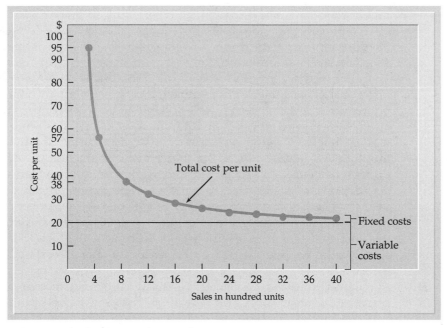

FIGURE 10-4 Vacuum Cleaner Costs per Unit

MARKETING TOOLS 10-2

TARGET COSTING

When American firms develop new products, they begin by finding what customers want and then design in these characteristics to meet customers' needs. Next, engineering develops models of the product, which are sourced to suppliers to determine component costs. These costs are added up, and a profit margin is included to give a selling price. The Japanese do it differently. They look at the product characteristics important to customers, evaluate competitive offerings, and come up with a planned selling price for the new product. Next, they subtract the desired profit to give a target cost. Then the product is designed and engineered to achieve the target cost. This system focuses on getting costs out during the planning and design stages. With the Japanese approach of target costing, you are more apt to reach your profit goals than with the American buildup plan, in which cost overruns are common with new products. The success of the Japanese approach requires a close, cooperative relationship with component suppliers, which is not always available in the United States.

Focusing on cost during product development increases profits in the long run.

Source: Ford S. Worthy, "Japan's Smart Secret Weapon," *Fortune*, August 12, 1991, pp. 72–75.

ume rather than as calendar time. Experience can grow faster than calendar time during periods of rapid growth early in the product life cycle. Also, the cost or price data used for the vertical axis in Figure 10-5 must be free of inflation before experience curves can be observed.

There are two major sources of the cost reductions shown in experience curves. First, workers and managers learn how to do a better job through repetition. Assembly workers develop greater dexterity and better work routines, and machine operators learn how to adjust their equipment for the greatest output. Also, marketing managers learn through experience how to do a better job of introducing and promoting new products. A second source of cost reductions is technology. New production processes are introduced, and products are redesigned to save money.

Experience curves suggest that costs decline continuously over the entire product life cycle. This means that you have the ability to cut prices on a regular basis to meet competitive threats and to achieve sales objectives. Also, during introductory periods, it is common to set prices below current actual costs to help expand demand for the product. Firms expect profits to return later as costs fall faster than selling prices.

During the growth stage of the product life cycle, there is little incentive to cut prices. As a result, prices do not fall as fast as costs and profit margins grow fat

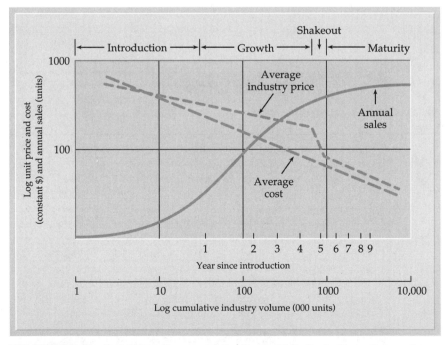

FIGURE 10-5 Experience Curves and the Product Life Cycle (From George S. Day and David B. Montgomery, "Diagnosing the Experience Curve," *Journal of Marketing*, Vol. 47 [Spring 1983], p. 51. Reproduced by permission of the American Marketing Association)

(Figure 10-5). This price umbrella attracts new entrants who are able to make money despite high initial costs. The new firms survive by stealing market share from the market leader. Dominant organizations that allow a price umbrella during the growth stage are actually trading long-run market share for current profits.

At the end of the growth stage of the life cycle, a shakeout occurs and prices drop sharply (Figure 10-5). This may happen because the market leader is attempting to stop the loss of market position or regain previous share levels. During the maturity phase of the life cycle, the margin between costs and prices erodes continuously, and cost savings are harder to find.

Elasticity and Costs   When demand is elastic, it is frequently assumed that organizations can increase profits by lowering the price. Although revenue is sure to increase, the profitability of this action depends on the ratio of fixed to variable costs. For example, Table 10-1 shows a computer manufacturer who is currently selling 100,000 small business computers per year at a factory price of $3000 each. If unit costs are $2700 and fixed costs are $54 million, then this manufacturer will generate a total profit of $30 million for the year. If the price of the computers is reduced $120 ($-4$ percent) and price elasticity is realistically estimated at -1.5, then expected sales will increase by 6000 units ($-0.04 \times -1.5 \times 100,000$). This means that more computers are sold at a lower price and total revenues will increase. However, because most of the costs are variable ($216/$270 \times 100\% = 80\%$ of total costs), the increase in production raises total variable costs by more than the growth in revenues, and profits decline to about $22 million. The price elasticity would have to be greater than -4 just to maintain profits at their original level.

Choosing a Pricing Method

Now that you understand demand and costs, you are ready to select a price. Remember, prices should be high enough to produce some profit but not so high that customers refuse to buy. The primary external constraint on your prices is the actions of competitors. Any pricing procedure that you select must be in line with the prices

TABLE 10-1

Effects of a Price Reduction on the Profits of a Computer Manufacturer When Price Elasticity Is -1.5

	Before Price Reduction (*millions*)		*After 4% Price Reduction* (*millions*)	
Sales	($3000 × 100,000)	$300	($2880 × 106,000)	$305
Variable costs	($2160 × 100,000)	$216	($2160 × 106,000)	$229
Fixed costs		$ 54		$ 54
Total costs		$270		$283
Profit		$ 30		$ 22
Average cost per unit		$2700		$2670

set by competitors. Your task is to find a method that balances demand, costs, and competitive factors for an individual product. We will discuss six pricing procedures: markup pricing, break-even pricing, target return pricing, variable-cost pricing, peak-load pricing, and new-product pricing.

Markup Pricing   Many organizations prefer pricing procedures that are easy to administer and require only limited assumptions about demand. Perhaps the simplest and most popular one is known as *markup pricing*.

With markup pricing, you add a fixed *dollar amount* to the cost of the item to yield a selling price. This amount is the markup designed to cover overhead expenses and produce a profit for the firm. Markups are usually stated as a percentage of the cost or selling price of the item. Setting prices with cost markups usually involves multiplying the markup percentage (expressed as a fraction) by the cost of the item and then adding the result to the cost. This may be simplified by adding 1 to the markup percentage to create a cost multiplier. For example, if an item cost $5 to manufacture and the firm wanted a 300 percent markup on the cost, the selling price would be 4 × $5 or $20. It is not unusual to find companies setting prices by informally multiplying costs by a factor of 3, 4, or 5.

Markups on selling price are more complicated because they cannot be multiplied directly by the cost to give a price. With these markups, costs are divided by 1 minus the markup percentage (expressed as a fraction) to yield the selling price. Thus, if a dealer wanted a 30 percent margin on the selling price and an item cost $7, the selling price would be

$$\text{Selling price} = \frac{\text{cost}}{(1 - \text{markup on selling price})} = \frac{7}{1 - 0.3} = \$10 \qquad (10.6)$$

Cost markups are always larger than markups on the selling price because of the smaller base. Note that markups on cost can be any amount, whereas markups on selling price range between zero and 100 percent. Traditionally, resellers, such as wholesalers and retailers, base markups on selling price, whereas manufacturers tend to favor markups on cost.

The example of markup pricing in Table 10-2 shows how a manufacturer uses a cost markup of 80 percent to convert a factory cost of $6 into a selling price of $10.80 for a barbecue grill. The wholesaler and retailer divide their costs by 1 minus their markup percentages to produce selling prices. Note that although the manufacturer has the highest markup percentage ($4.80/10.80, or 44 percent of the selling price), the retailer has the largest dollar margin ($9). This is a natural result of applying a similar markup to a larger cost.

Markup pricing does not adequately handle demand when the same markup percentage is applied to different classes of goods. If you select this method, you should vary markup percentages according to customers' price sensitivities. For example, supermarkets use markups of 9 percent on baby food and 50 percent on the more inelastic greeting cards. This strategy of varying margins by price elasticities leads to greater profits.

Markup pricing is also flexible and is fully compatible with actions of the firm

TABLE 10-2

Using Markups to Set Factory, Wholesale, and Retail Selling Prices

Components of the Pricing Process	Barbecue Grill (dollars)
Factory cost (including direct labor, materials, and factory overhead)	$6.00
Manufacturing margin (administrative overhead, marketing expenses, and profit)	4.80
Manufacturing selling price ($6.00 × 1.8)	10.80
Wholesale margin	2.70
Wholesale selling price [$10.80/(1 − 20% MUSP)][a]	13.50
Retail margin	9.00
Retail selling price [$13.50/(1 − 40% MUSP)]	22.50

[a]MUSP = markup on selling price.

designed to maximize profits. The size of the markups can be set to accomplish a variety of objectives, and the inherent simplicity of the method makes it easy to pass on pricing decisions to other employees.

Break-Even Pricing   Break-even pricing shows how many units must be sold at selected prices to regain the funds invested in a product. Suppose that the fixed selling, advertising, R&D, and tooling costs for your barbecue grill are $200,000 and the variable costs $6 per unit. At a selling price of $8, the break-even volume is

$$\text{Break-even volume} = \frac{\text{fixed costs}}{\text{price} - \text{variable costs}} = \frac{\$200,000}{\$8 - \$6} = 100,000 \text{ units} \quad (10.7)$$

Profits are generated when volume exceeds the break-even point, and losses occur when volume fails to reach the break-even point. Break-even volumes for factory selling prices of $8, $10, and $12 are shown in Figure 10-6.

Although break-even pricing shows the volume needed to cover your costs, it makes some simplifying assumptions about demand. The total revenue lines in Figure 10-6 are straight, implying that larger volumes can be sold without lowering prices. This is unrealistic, and executives must be able to estimate the number of units that will be sold at each tentative price.

Target Return Pricing   Pricing to achieve a target rate of return on investment (ROI) is a popular method among large businesses. The idea is to build in enough margin to ensure that you earn an adequate ROI. The key steps in this procedure are your estimate of demand and the utilization of facilities.

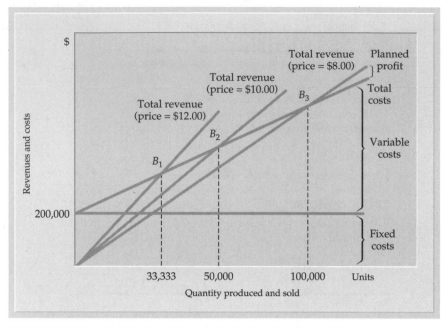

FIGURE 10-6 Multiple Break-Even Analysis for a Barbecue Grill

If plant capacity for barbecue grills is 125,000 units and you expect to operate at 80 percent capacity, then you anticipate sales of 100,000 grills. Since full costs decline as volume increases, 100,000 grills will cost $8 each to produce (Figure 10-7). The $8 represents all the fixed and variable costs of producing and marketing each barbecue grill. The next step is to add a profit margin so that the planned ROI will be achieved. If you have $250,000 tied up in the barbecue grill facilities and inventory and your target ROI is 20 percent before taxes, planned profit is $50,000. A target return price is then

$$\text{Target return price} = \text{full unit cost} + \frac{\text{target ROI} \times \text{invested capital}}{\text{expected sales}} \quad (10.8)$$

$$= \$8 + \frac{0.20 \times \$250,000}{100,000} = \$8.50$$

If you can sell 100,000 grills at $8.50, you will generate the desired ROI. The problem with rate-of-return pricing is that you have to estimate demand before you set your price. This implies that customers are *not sensitive* to the prices charged for the product. Although this may be true for large, dominant firms, such as Kellogg in the ready-to-eat cereal market, it may not hold for smaller firms in more competitive industries. Also, target return pricing can lead to wide fluctuations in profits because the amount earned is directly related to the accuracy of your sales estimate. For example, if only 80,000 grills are sold at a factory price of $8.50, ROI slumps to zero!

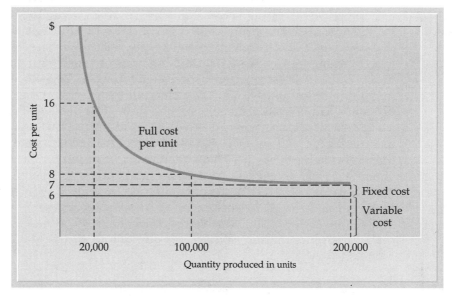

FIGURE 10-7   Effects of Volume on Unit Costs for a Barbecue Grill

Variable-Cost Pricing   Variable-cost pricing is based on the idea that the recovery of full costs is not always realistic or necessary for the short-run operation of organizations. Instead of using full costs as the lowest possible price, this system suggests that variable costs represent the minimum price that can be charged. For example, assume that you have been able to sell 100,000 barbecue grills at $8.50 through your regular discount store channels. A supermarket chain offers to purchase 20,000 barbecue grills at $7 each. The buyer suggests that the grills carry the supermarket's label without the wheels found on the regular model. If the design changes reduce variable costs to $5.75, the order represents a potential profit of $25,000.

Should you accept the offer and price the modified grills at $7.00? Some would say that the order can *never* be approved because the price does not cover the full cost of $7.42 (Figure 10-7). Others would point out that if you cut prices to the supermarket, your regular customers may demand equally low prices. This could lead to losses, as it would be difficult to recover the fixed costs. The important point to remember is that the full cost to manufacture the grills is not constant, but in reality is quite sensitive to changes in volume (Figure 10-7), where unit costs decline as the fixed expenses are spread over a large volume. At a volume of 20,000 units the grills cost $16, but this cost declines to $7.42 at a volume of 120,000 units and to $7 at a volume of 200,000 units. This shows that very low prices can cover full costs if volume expands sufficiently.

Perhaps the most important issue in variable-cost pricing is whether the two markets can be kept separate. If the supermarkets are in different geographic locations or service different income classes, then the additional business looks more attractive.

Variable-cost pricing is common where fixed costs comprise a large proportion of total unit costs. The airlines and railroads are two industries with high fixed costs that have made effective use of the volume-generating aspects of variable-cost pricing. For example, American Airlines one summer slashed fares on advance-purchase tickets by up to 50 percent to boost vacation business. These low fares were matched by other airlines, and within a few days, all the excursion seats allocated to these programs had been sold. This illustration shows that the demand for summer travel is very elastic and that low prices will fill seats on airplanes. However, the airlines had trouble keeping the special low fares out of the hands of their regular customers. Many people were able to exchange higher-priced tickets for the excursion fares, and others who had planned to pay regular fares rushed to take advantage of the low rates. Because of the size of the price cuts and their inability to restrict the low fares to new customers, all the major U.S. airlines lost money with variable-cost pricing that summer. Obviously, variable-cost pricing is not a panacea for all firms, but it can be useful for the sophisticated organization that understands its potential and limitations.

Peak-Load Pricing   Whereas variable-cost pricing is used to encourage demand, peak-load pricing is used to discourage it. Peak-load pricing occurs when there are definite limits to the amount of goods and services a firm can provide and when customer demand tends to vary over time. For example, the telephone company builds capacity to satisfy 97 percent of its customers during the peak periods that occur on weekdays, but this means that there are many unused phone circuits at night and on weekends. Peak-load pricing suggests that phone rates should be raised above average costs during high-demand periods and reduced toward variable costs during off-peak hours. This tends to shift price-sensitive customers to slack times and allows the phone company to operate with less total capacity. In addition, the very low off-peak rates may increase revenues by attracting some customers who normally do not use the phone for long-distance calls. The primary advantage of peak-load pricing, then, is that it depresses peak demands and thereby reduces the total resources needed to fill customers' wants. In addition, it stimulates off-peak consumption and allows more efficient utilization of existing facilities.

New-Product Pricing   One of the most difficult problems that you must resolve is setting prices for new products. These decisions are complicated by the frequent lack of adequate information on both demand and costs. Because new products have not been sold before, price elasticity cannot be estimated from an analysis of historical data. Asking consumers if they are interested in buying a new product at a particular price is not very helpful. The maker of Johnson wax products asked shoppers what they pay for air fresheners. Only 28 percent gave answers within 15 percent of the actual price, and a third of the consumers had no idea what they paid. Also, the desire to prevent competitors from learning about new products may prevent the firm from using test markets to obtain elasticity data. Even the simple expedient of copying a competitor's price is not a practical alternative for new products. Despite these problems, the marketing manager must find a price that will sell the product and still contribute to the profits of the firm. One approach is to attempt to assess the "value in use" of the product to the customer. A more common approach to new-product pricing is to make an intuitive appraisal of the product and apply either a skimming or a penetration price strategy.

Value-in-use pricing stresses understanding price from the customer's point of view. A buyer trades off the price of the product against the perceived benefits, costs, risks, and value in use of the product. This approach requires that you understand the benefits (functional, operational, financial, or personal) that customers perceive as important. In addition, you have to know what costs customers incur beyond the price of the product. These costs may include order handling, freight, installation, and training. Customers also have other costs, such as the fear of late delivery, the need for custom modification of the delivered product, or the impact of product failure on organizational productivity. Thus, you must understand the customer's possible applications of the product. Once a firm assesses customers' benefits and costs in terms of the complete usage system, it is in a position to set the price. The highest price a customer will pay is found by subtracting the costs other than price from the value of the benefits received.

Skimming prices assume that demand is inelastic, so high initial prices are set and then gradually reduced over time. This situation is described by the downward-sloping curve DD in Figure 10-8. The high initial price (P^1) is designed to skim off the segment of the market that is insensitive to price, and subsequent reductions (P^2, P^3) broaden the market by tapping more elastic sectors of the market. The logic of the skimming price strategy is supported by the observation that many new products have few technical substitutes and that the price is not as important as it is for more established products.

A successful application of a skimming price strategy occurred with the intro-

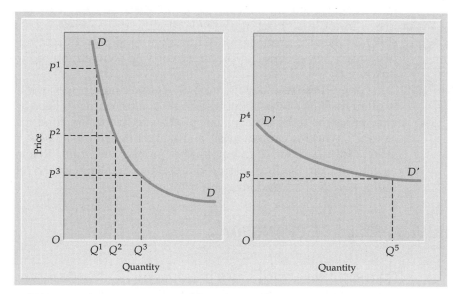

FIGURE 10-8 Demand Curves Assumed by Skimming and Penetration Price Strategies

duction of electronic hand-held calculators. When the sets were first introduced, retail prices were well over $300 and the products were clearly designed for managers and other professionals. As competition increased, prices were reduced gradually to the point where some models now sell for less than $5. The price reductions opened up a vast market in the general population, and the resulting economies of scale led to further cuts.

The main disadvantage of a skimming price policy is that the high margins usually attract competitors into the field. This suggests that a skimming price is best used when the product has strong patent protection or when there are other barriers to entry, such as technical know-how or high capital requirements. Although skimming prices can increase short-term profits, they may not be sustainable in the long run. An example of how price skimming works in the pharmaceutical industry is described in Marketing Strategies box 10-1.

Penetration prices are prices below current costs designed to open mass markets quickly. This pricing strategy is based on the assumptions that (1) there is little prospect of creating or maintaining product superiority, (2) there are few barriers to entry or expansion by competitors, and (3) demand is highly elastic (curve $D'D'$ in Figure 10-8) and low prices will significantly expand the market. In addition, penetration pricing assumes that the high volume associated with low introductory prices (P^5Q^5 in Figure 10-8) will reduce costs, so that a profit can be made during the growth phase of the product life cycle. Thus penetration price strategies are encouraged by the experience curve and by related declines in unit costs over the product life cycle (Figure 10-5). One of the most successful examples of penetration pricing in recent years was Chrysler's introduction of its Neon cars.

Research has shown that for a new product without direct competition and in the presence of imitative consumer demand, an optimum price would be a penetration price substantially below the initial cost.[5] Although penetration prices lead to losses in the first year, by the *fifth* year the discounted cumulative profits will be several times the profits achieved by skimming procedures. High initial prices may produce quick profits, but the rapid entry of competition reduces long-run market positions.

Given these results, why do managers set high prices on new products when it is often in their long-run interests to set the price low to keep competition out? The answer seems to be that current profits are needed to fund growth in production capacity, working capital, R&D, and market development activity. Also, the reward system for managers often emphasizes immediate profits. Remember that if you are or can become the low-cost producer, low initial prices are often the best way to build market share and long-run profits.

WHEN SHOULD PRICES BE CHANGED?

Once you have selected a basic price for your goods and services, there are a number of situations in which adjustments have to be made to account for unique market conditions. We will discuss several price adaptation strategies, including responding

PRICING PHARMACEUTICALS

Normal pricing rules do not apply to pharmaceuticals. New drugs commonly sell at wholesale for three to six times their cost. These generous gross margins provide a lot of money for sales calls and free samples. The relatively high prices charged for drugs are due to several factors. Most new drugs are under patent and have few substitutes. Also, doctors care little about prices, so demand is inelastic. Under these conditions, price wars do not exist and price increases are common.

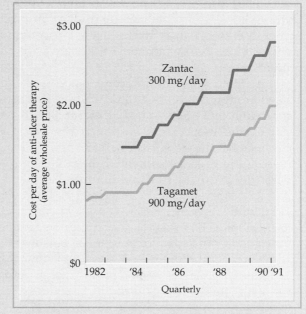

The ulcer drugs Tagamet and Zantac provide a good example of pharmaceutical pricing. Tagamet was the first of the acid blockers to be introduced by Smith Kline, at a price of 80 cents per patient per day. This drug was so effective that ulcer surgery was virtually eliminated. Tagamet produced far more revenue for Smith Kline than ordinary antacids. Zantac was introduced by rival Glaxo at $1.50 per patient per day in 1983. In most market categories, the idea of a second firm choosing to enter with a 50 percent price premium would be described as suicidal. However, Zantac has fewer side effects and Glaxo had a good marketing plan. They formed a marketing alliance with the Hoffman-LaRoche sales force and by 1990 Zantac's world sales were $2.46 billion, or twice Tagamet's sales. What is even more spectacular about this example is that both Smith Kline and Glaxo were able to raise prices continuously over the product life cycle (see the diagram). Thus instead of moving prices down the learning curve, as is done with most products, pharmaceutical manufacturers have learned to milk their cash cows with price increases. However, these premium prices do not last forever, as generic alternatives drive prices down once patents expire. This means that Glaxo must invest some of its Zantac profits in new drugs so that it can continue to grow.

Patented products with low price elasticity can be milked for profits.

Source: John Abbott, "Drugmakers Under Attack," *Fortune,* July 29, 1991, pp. 48–63.

to competitive cuts, geographical pricing, price discounts, product-line pricing, and price discrimination.

Responding to Competitive Cuts

One of the most difficult challenges you will face as a marketing manager is responding to price cuts by competitors. This situation is fraught with danger no matter what you do. If you play it safe and maintain your prices to keep short-run profits up, you risk losing market share and long-run profitability. If you match competitive price cuts to maintain market share, short-term profits and the price of your company's stock will plummet. Price wars with competitors appear to be a no-win situation.

A classic price-cutting scenario occurred a few years ago in the market for personal computers. In 1990, IBM had 15 percent of the world market for personal computers and Compaq had 6 percent. Both companies charged premium prices for state-of-the-art machines. However, competitors such as Dell and AST started selling cheap clones through discount stores and by mail. At first, IBM and Compaq ignored these upstarts and maintained their high-price policies. By 1991 customers were deserting in droves; IBM and Compaq lost market share, and profits declined. Compaq was especially hard hit, posting its first quarterly negative profit in September 1991, while revenue for the year fell 9 percent. Compaq responded to the plunge in its stock price by firing its chief executive, slashing prices on existing products, and introducing a new line of low-priced personal computers. These changes saved the company, but the low-priced machines cannibalized sales of its higher-margin products to corporate customers. In this case, Compaq had little choice, as "either you eat your children or somebody else does." Other examples of price wars are described in the Marketing In Action box 10-1.

The moral of the PC story is that brand loyalty does not last forever when competitors cut prices. If you expect to survive a price war, you must keep your costs under control so that you can continue to make money when prices are pushed down. Some firms are able to avoid price wars by differentiating their products and focusing on customers in niche markets. It is also desirable to have some "fighting brands" available to do battle when price competition heats up. Another approach is to develop computer models to help predict what will happen when competitors cut prices. For example, Research International offers its PriceSolve model to help you plan pricing strategies for the future.

Geographic Pricing

There is often money to be made by charging different prices to customers located in separate geographical areas. These adjustments reflect variation in transportation costs and price elasticities. The most common geographic pricing system is known as *FOB pricing*.

FOB Pricing   With FOB pricing, the manufacturer places goods *free on board* a carrier, and the buyer pays the freight to the destination. The system is fair because

MARKETING IN ACTION 10-1

PRICE WARS

Price wars have become a depressing fact of life in businesses ranging from fast food to credit cards to steel. A growing number of firms are pursuing market share at all costs to protect investments that are too big to write off. PepsiCo and Borden are entering a third year of warfare that has crumbled the margins of their once highly profitable salty snacks business. Pepsi's Frito-Lay has laid off 1800 people and Borden 1000 in an effort to improve profitability.

A frequent cause of price wars is excess production capacity. For example, the consumer electronics industry has too many suppliers and too many retailers. Since 1977 the average price of a TV set has declined 37 percent in real dollars to $301. It is very difficult to show any profit in making or selling TVs. The last American manufacturer, Zenith, has lost money for five of the last six years.

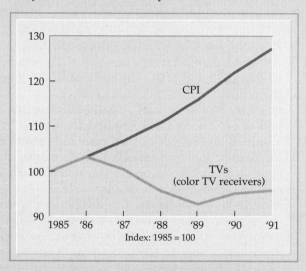

In the laptop computer market, there are 120 competitors and prices decline almost daily. In steel, the problem is excess capacity chasing volume plus large, unfunded pension obligations that make it difficult to close down unneeded facilities. Occasionally, price wars work. Coke and Pepsi have battled for years, with the result of expanded shares for both and smashed rivals. For most firms, the answer to price wars is to cut costs and let prices inch down. Profits generated along the way can be used to open other markets and leave you free to fight another day.

To fight price wars you must be a low-cost producer.

Source: Bill Saporito, "Why the Price Wars Never End," *Fortune,* March 23, 1992, pp. 68–78.

customers near the plant pay the lowest freight charges and those farthest away pay the highest charges. With FOB pricing, buyers tend to purchase from the closest supplier. The main problem with FOB pricing is that it is difficult to build market share by selling in distant markets.

Delivered Pricing Firms that want to expand into other markets often set prices on a delivered basis. Under this plan, an average freight charge is added to the factory price, and everyone pays the same delivered price. A delivered system favors distant customers and allows the use of a single nationally advertised price. However, customers close to the factory pay higher prices, and they may buy from local competitors who use FOB pricing. Delivered pricing tends to sacrifice sales nearby to gain business from more distant buyers. A variation of delivered pricing occurs when the manufacturer absorbs some or all of the freight charge to meet competitive prices. This is an aggressive tactic used to penetrate markets and is not used on a regular basis.

Zone Pricing Under a zone pricing system, markets are divided so that all customers within a zone pay the same price. For example, in the United States it is common to charge higher prices in the West Coast states to reflect higher shipping costs to these markets. Zone pricing can also be used to take advantage of differences in price elasticity across markets. A good example involves the prices charged for Mercedes and BMW cars in Germany and the United States. These cars are sold as prestige automobiles in America and command premium prices. However, these cars are sold to broader segments of society in Germany, and prices are considerably lower. The price differential was once so large that many American tourists used to buy these cars in Germany and have them shipped home. This led to complaints from American dealers, and the German dealers were forced to stop selling to tourists.

Zone pricing can lead to serious problems for border dealers when price differentials are substantial. The most common issue involves customers in high-priced zones who cross the border and buy from dealers in low-priced areas. For example, because of zone pricing and the strength of the dollar, Americans who live near the Canadian border can buy American cars more cheaply in Canada than in America. An even more serious problem occurs when independent dealers start buying products in the low-priced zone and ship them to high-priced markets. These *parallel importers*, as they are called, can quickly destroy company-sponsored distribution networks. This suggests that zone prices must be set carefully if border disruptions are to be kept to a minimum.

Discounts and Allowances

To help field representatives close sales, many firms offer special discounts and allowances. Trade promotions will be discussed further in Chapter 15.

Cash Discounts The most common incentive is a cash discount for paying bills early. For example, an organization might offer terms of "2/10, net 30," which means that the buyer can deduct 2 percent of the price if the bill is paid by the tenth of the month; otherwise, the whole amount is due on the thirtieth. A 2 percent discount may not seem like much incentive, but it encourages buyers to pay 20 days early, and this amounts to 36 percent on an annual basis. Cash discounts improve the cash flow for the seller and reduce collection costs.

Quantity Discounts Another popular buying incentive is the quantity discount. The objective of this plan is to get customers to increase order sizes and to buy from fewer suppliers. Thus, a buyer might be offered neckwear at a regular price of $35 a dozen and a reduced price of $33 in lots of five dozen. To help buyers control their inventory, some firms will ship in small lots and add the shipments together to give the quantity discount. Quantity discounts reflect cost savings associated with longer production runs, reduced selling expenses, and transportation economies.

Seasonal Discounts Consumer purchases in industries such as toys and swimwear are highly concentrated, leading to underutilization of labor and factories in the off-season. To help control this problem, many firms in these industries offer seasonal discounts to get buyers to place orders early. Seasonal discounts are often substantial and can be thought of as an example of variable-cost pricing.

Allowances Allowances for price reductions are designed to compensate buyers for certain activities. Promotional allowances, for example, include cash or free merchandise designed to get dealers to advertise or build in-store displays to promote products. Trade-in allowances are another incentive offered on durable goods to help reduce down payments and get customers to buy. To be legal, discounts and allowances must be made available to all competing channel members.

Product-Line Pricing

When you have several items in your product line, prices often must be set to maximize profits for a whole array of products. This may be difficult because margins vary and some items have interrelated costs. A further complication is that the sales of one product may be influenced by the price charged for a second product. This can be measured by calculating values for *cross-price elasticity*. Suppose that when you raise the price of Bayer Aspirin 5 percent in your store, sales of Tylenol increase 10 percent. In mathematical terms,

$$\frac{\text{Cross-price}}{\text{elasticity}} = \frac{\text{\% change in sales of Tylenol}}{\text{\% change in price of Bayer Aspirin}} = \frac{+10\%}{+5\%} = +2 \quad (10.9)$$

The positive cross-price elasticity of +2 indicates that consumers considered the two items to be substitutes. A negative cross-price elasticity would indicate that the products were complementary and typically were sold together.

Examples of cross-price elasticities for various sizes of eggs are shown in Table 10-3. Large eggs are very price elastic (−3.3), as are private-label eggs (−3.1). All cross-elasticities are positive, suggesting that the different-sized eggs are substitutes. For example, large-egg sales are impacted by the price of medium-sized eggs (1.4).

TABLE 10-3

Price Elasticities and Cross-Price Elasticities

	Egg Size			
	Large	*Private Label*	*Medium*	*20-Pack*
Price for large size	−3.3			
Price for private-label brand		−3.1	2.8	1.4
Price for medium size	1.4	2.0	−2.1	1.4
Price for 20-pack		0.9		−2.0

A 10 percent cut in the price of medium-sized eggs causes a 14 percent fall in the sales of large eggs, a 20 percent fall in private-label sales, and a 14 percent fall in 20-pack sales. Meanwhile, medium-sized egg sales go up 21 percent.

The price elasticities from Table 10-3 were combined with cost data to find the most profitable price level for each brand sold by the company. The results suggest that total profits would increase if you consider cross-price elasticities when you set prices for different sizes and brands of eggs. This success in measuring demand interrelationships suggests that you no longer have to rely on rules of thumb for product-line pricing.

Price Discrimination

Price discrimination is an attractive pricing strategy that can boost volume and profits by taking advantage of differences in customers' price sensitivities. For example, you can segment your market on age and offer lower-priced admission tickets to children. Another approach is to vary price by time. Customers who want to play golf on weekdays are offered low prices, while weekend players are charged high prices. A third way to segment customers is by location. Theater managers and sporting events promoters charge higher prices for front-row seats than for seats in the balcony.

Price discrimination works best when customer segments have different elasticities. Also, a low-price customer must not be able to resell the product to the high-price segment. Moreover, the cost of segmenting and policing the market should not exceed the benefits of price discrimination. You must make sure that the form of discrimination employed does not break the law.

AN EXAMPLE: THE PRICING OF MULTIMETERS

Now that you understand demand, costs, and standard pricing methods, let us consider how prices are set in the real world. The situation involves an electronics manufacturer located in the northwestern United States. One of its product lines, hand-held multimeters, was in the late stages of its product life cycle. Sales were flat, and competitors were stealing market share with added features. The standard pricing procedure used by this firm was a markup method whereby costs were multiplied by 3 to get a selling price. This means that costs represent one-third of the selling price, and the firm has a gross margin of 67 percent.

Responding to Competitive Challenge

To counter the problem of declining market share, the brand manager proposed a product upgrade until new models were available in two years. The product modifications cost $100,000 in engineering expenses plus $5 a unit for audible continuity indicators for the two basic items in the line. Salespeople estimated that revenue would increase 7 percent if the three remodeled multimeters were sold at existing prices. The brand manager felt that customers were becoming increasingly price sensitive and that higher prices for the upgraded multimeters would cut sharply into incremental sales. As a result, the manager recommended keeping the price the same for the upgraded meters.

Pricing Alternatives

If you were the chief marketing executive at this firm, what would you do? One possibility would be to take advantage of the company's fat 67 percent gross margin and slash prices to buy back the lost market share. This approach would save the $100,000 in engineering expenses and put a severe squeeze on competitors' profit margins.

A second approach would be to follow the brand manager's recommendation and keep prices the same for the upgraded multimeters. With this strategy, you would be relying on the increased volume associated with the new features to pay for the engineering expenses and the added variable costs. Another way to recoup the added costs would be to tack on $5 to $10 to the current selling prices of the meters. A more sophisticated strategy would allow different price increases for the three meters in the line. This last method is the most difficult, as you need estimates of price elasticity and cross-price elasticity for each meter.

Selecting the Best Price

Slashing prices does not appear to be a good approach in this case because competitors are stealing customers by emphasizing added features—not price. The impact of three possible pricing strategies for the multimeters is shown in Table 10-4. If prices are kept the same, the contribution margin increases $44,897. This is less than half of the added engineering costs needed to upgrade the line. Better results occur when prices are raised $5 per unit. Contribution margins expand to over $400,000 and sales revenues are maximized. When the prices of the meters are raised $10 per unit, contributions increase but sales are projected to decline. Thus the best way to regain market share and boost profits is to charge $5 more for the redesigned multimeters. To determine whether the three models should have different price

TABLE 10-4

Revenue and Incremental Contribution Margins for Upgraded Multimeters

Model	Current Prices	Plus $5	Plus $10
1010	$41,875	$138,760	$128,455
1020	−39,318	141,322	195,945
1030	42,340	163,112	264,788
Total contributions	44,897	443,194	589,188
Total revenue	$25,258,000	$25,661,440	$25,414,160

Source: "Winkleman Manufacturing Company," case prepared by William L. Weis and Jim Dooley of Seattle University. © William L. Weis and Jim Dooley.

increases, you would have to make some additional assumptions about cross-price elasticities.

This example has shown that real pricing decisions require an understanding of pricing goals, demand, costs, markup, and the actions of competitors. The firm was able to improve sales and profits for its upgraded, higher-priced meters because it was well known in the industry. Customers were willing to pay a little more to buy a better product from the market leader.

SUMMARY

Pricing is a key component of the marketing mix, and it is essential that you understand the different pricing options that are available. Prices must be set that are consistent with your product's positioning and appropriate for your target market segment. Effective pricing is impossible without a keen awareness of price elasticities. When demand is inelastic, you can increase profits by raising prices. When demand is elastic, lower prices increase revenues. You also need to understand markup procedures to help set prices for wholesalers and retailers. No pricing analysis is complete without a review of the fixed and variable costs associated with different product alternatives. Sometimes the prices should be set below current full costs to expand markets and keep out the competition. The ideal pricing system combines estimates of costs and price elasticity to maximize the discounted stream of profits of the firm. Finally, no pricing scheme can last unless it considers the actions of competitors and is within the law.

NOTES

1. A summary of the methods used to measure demand is provided in Thomas T. Nagle, *The Strategy and Tactics of Pricing* (Englewood Cliffs, NJ: Prentice-Hall, 1987), chap. 11.
2. Dominique M. Hanssens, Leonard J. Parsons, and Randall L. Schultz, *Marketing Response Models: Econometric and Time Series Analysis* (Boston: Kluwer, 1990), pp. 187–191.

3. Gerald J. Tellis, "The Price Sensitivity of Selective Demand: A Meta Analysis of Econometric Models of Sales," *Journal of Marketing Research*, Vol. 25 (November 1988), pp. 391–404; Simon Broadbent, "Price and Advertising: Volume and Profit," *ADMAP*, Vol. 16, No. 11 (November 1980), pp. 532–540.

4. Philip Parker, "Price Elasticity Dynamics Over the Adoption Cycle," *Journal of Marketing Research*, Vol. 20 (August 1992), pp. 359–367; Gary L. Lilien and Eunsang Yoon, "An Exploratory Analysis of Industrial Chemical Products," *Issues in Pricing*, Tim M. Devinney, ed. (Lexington, MA: Lexington Books, 1988), pp. 261–287; David J. Curry and Peter C. Reisz, "Price and Price/Quality Relationships: A Longitudinal Analysis," *Journal of Marketing*, Vol. 52 (January 1988), pp. 36–51.

5. Bruce Robinson and Chet Lakhani, "Dynamic Price Models for New-Product Planning," *Management Science*, Vol. 21, No. 10 (June 1975), pp. 1113–1122. For more recent results, see Engelbert Dockner and Steffen Jorgensen, "Optimal Pricing for New Products in Dynamic Oligopolies," *Marketing Science*, Vol. 7 (Fall 1988), pp. 315–334.

SUGGESTED READING

Simon, Hermann, and Martin Fasfnacht, "Price Bundling," *European Management Journal*, Vol. 11 (December 1993), pp. 403–411.

Simon, Hermann, and Eckhard Kugher, "The European Pricing Time Bomb," *European Management Journal*, Vol. 10 (June 1992), pp. 136–145.

FURTHER READING

Gijbrechts, Els. "Prices and Pricing Research in Consumer Marketing: Some Recent Developments," *International Journal of Research in Marketing*, Vol. 10, No. 2 (June 1993), pp. 115–151.

Monroe, Kent B. *Pricing: Making Profitable Decisions* (New York: McGraw-Hill, 1990).

Nagle, Thomas T. *The Strategy and Tactics of Pricing* (Englewood Cliffs, NJ: Prentice-Hall, 1987).

Rao, Vithala. "Pricing Models in Marketing," in *Handbooks in Operation Research and Management Science: Marketing,* Joshua Eliashberg and Gary L. Lilien, eds. (Amsterdam: North-Holland, 1993), pp. 517–552.

Simon, Hermann, *Price Management* (Amsterdam: North Holland, 1989).

QUESTIONS

1. In the mid-1980s, tobacco giant Philip Morris bought Kraft and General Foods and proceeded to raise the prices of its power brands, Velveeta and Miracle Whip, to fatten profit margins. At first, the concept worked, with record results in 1989 and 1990. In 1991, however, food sales growth declined to less than 1 percent and market share slid 4 percent. Why did Philip Morris raise prices so aggressively, and what should it do now?

2. If a retailer has product costs of $42 and plans to make a 40 percent margin on its selling price, what price would it charge?

3. Ford has raised the price of its least expensive Taurus model over 50 percent, or twice the inflation rate since 1986. In 1982 an average family took 25.5 weeks to earn the price of a car; now it takes 32 weeks. What has allowed auto manufacturers to raise prices so aggressively? Was it a good idea?

4. Pathmark grocery stores introduced an all-purpose cleaner under its own label that closely resembled Fantastick, the top seller in the category. Pathmark's Premium had a similar package design and was chemically identical to the national brand. Best of all, Premium cost shoppers only $0.89 compared with $1.79 for Fantastick. However, Premium has sold poorly. What seems to be the problem? What should Pathmark do?

5. Matsushita recently announced an introductory price of $1000 for its new digital compact cassette deck. DCC machines boost quality by storing sound digitally instead of in the analog format used in conventional cassettes. The new players will also play conventional cassettes, but without enhanced sound quality. Why has Matsushita set the DCC price so high?

6. A refrigerator is produced at a cost of $200 to the manufacturer. To this cost is added a margin of 35 percent, and the refrigerator is shipped to an independent wholesaler. The wholesaler then adds a 20 percent margin based on its selling price. What would be the cost to the retailer? If the retailer then charged the consumer $675, what margin was used on the selling price? On the cost?

7. McCain Foods of Canada is the world's largest producer of frozen french fries. However, it has only 11 percent of the U.S. market and just 4 percent of the seasoned and specialty french fry business. Recently, it announced a 10 percent price cut on curled, seasoned, and other specialty products popular in fast-food restaurants. Why did McCain start a price war in an industry burdened with overcapacity and thin margins? Why did it cut the prices of the specialty products?

8. A retailer notes that a line of woks is selling at a rate of 100 per week. When the price is cut from $40 to $35, sales increase to 106 per week. What is the price elasticity of demand? What happens to revenue? What price should the retailer place on the woks?

9. If a retailer wants a markup on cost of 300 percent and a selling price of $48, what is the dollar markup?

10. A markup of 400 percent of cost is equal to what percentage of retail? If an item costs $30 and the dealer wants a 200 percent markup on cost, what is the selling price? The dollar markup?

11. The Taunton Municipal Lighting Company in Massachusetts has introduced a program of leasing compact fluorescent light bulbs for 20 cents per month. These power-saving bulbs screw in like incandescents and last for 10,000 hours. Why does the power company lease these bulbs rather than sell them? Why would a power company promote a product that reduces the demand for electricity?

12. Two partners invest $40,000 to purchase a small production firm. If they make 20,000 units at a total cost of $30,000, what must their selling price be to return 14 percent on their investment? In larger firms, are cost data accurate?

13. A price decrease of $10 on a $200 TV resulted in an increase in volume of 21,000 units. If the original volume was 300,000 units, what is the price elasticity of demand? What does the calculated value for price elasticity suggest you should do with the price of the TV? Why?

Chapter 11

Selecting and Managing Distribution Channels

The art of getting rich consists not in industry, but in a better order, in timeliness, in being at the right spot.

RALPH WALDO EMERSON

A critical task for marketers in the 1990s is the efficient movement of goods and services from the point of production to the points of consumption. Some organizations approach this task by selling directly to customers through the use of the telephone, mail order, or calls by company salespeople. Others employ a host of marketing intermediaries to get their products into the hands of final users. These may include wholesalers and retailers who buy and then resell merchandise. Another approach is to use middlemen who search for customers and negotiate sales but do not take title to the goods they handle. Each approach has its advantages and disadvantages.

Your goal as a marketing manager is to build a distribution network that increases sales and operates at the lowest possible cost. Your ability to organize an effective distribution channel for your products is often the difference between success and failure in the marketplace. Indeed, distribution channels are a key strategic asset that can lead to sustainable competitive advantages. For example, McDonald's dominates the fast-food business because of its ability to push its food through thousands of affiliated retail outlets throughout the world. Steelcase's strong dealer network is the envy of its competitors in the office furniture business. In this chapter, we explain how distribution networks are created and adapted to changing market conditions. The key tasks are selecting the best distribution channels for each firm and finding ways to operate them efficiently.

WHAT IS A DISTRIBUTION CHANNEL?

Distribution channels are groups of related organizations that help make goods and services available for use by customers. Our discussion will explain different activities performed by these channel intermediaries and provide an economic justification for their use.

When Should Intermediaries Be Used?

Industrial firms sell to relatively few customers and usually contact these customers directly. Xerox, for example, developed the first plain paper office copiers and has always sold its machines with its own field sales force. Even today most of its copiers go through this direct channel of distribution. Steel companies also sell directly to final users, and tire manufacturers sell original equipment tires directly to auto manufacturers. However, small firms that want to sell products on a national or international basis quickly realize that they cannot afford all the salespeople and distribution facilities necessary to get merchandise to every user. These organizations are often better off investing their limited capital in R&D and production facilities and leaving distribution to established intermediaries.

Although large organizations are better able to shoulder some of the distribution burden, they also find the costs of owning their channels of distribution to be prohibitive. Ford has a network of 6000 independent dealers who sell its cars in the United States. Ford would have to spend billions of dollars to assume ownership of this channel and has settled instead for a system of franchised dealers. Another problem occurs when your product is sold as part of an assortment supplied by other firms. Mars M&M candies are sold along with other brands of candy in supermarkets, drug stores, theaters, vending machines, and convenience stores all over the world. Instead of owning all these businesses, Mars has decided to work with established wholesalers and retailers.

The most common reason to employ market intermediaries is that they can reduce costs and improve distribution efficiency. Sometimes it is difficult to see how the addition of another dealer, with the attendant margins and delays, can *raise* distribution efficiency. This efficiency can be demonstrated with the channel diagrams shown in Figure 11-1. In Figure 11-1(a), three organizations must make 18 calls to contact six customers. When a distributor is added to the channel (b), however, the number of calls needed to contact wholesale and final customers is reduced to nine. Each organization calls on the distributor, and the distributor represents all of them in contacting the customers. Thus, the addition of a distributor reduces the total amount of work to be done. Intermediaries also provide organizations with a ready-made channel of distribution that is experienced in handling particular product lines. In addition, dealers have established contacts with buyers and often have the special warehouse facilities and repair equipment needed for some items. An example showing how a distributor helped market a unique hair styling device is described in Marketing in Action box 11-1.

Although dealers normally improve distribution efficiency, too many channel

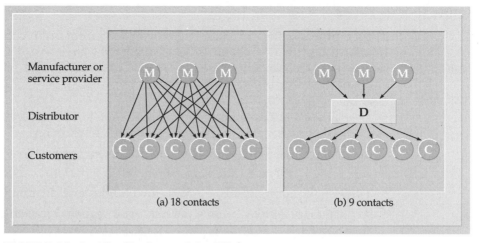

Manufacturer or service provider

Distributor

Customers

(a) 18 contacts

(b) 9 contacts

FIGURE 11-1 Why Distributors Raise Efficiency

members can raise the cost of moving goods to customers. In Japan, for example, an elaborate, multilevel system uses four times the number of wholesalers as in the United States to service the same number of retailers. National wholesalers sell to regional and local wholesalers, with the result that wholesale volume is five times sales in Japan compared to only twice retail volume in the United States. Until Japanese retailers grow large enough to deal directly with manufacturers, consumers will be burdened with a distribution system that employs too many intermediaries.

MARKETING IN ACTION 11-1

DISTRIBUTING TOPSYTAIL

After a creative IBM salesperson, Tomima Edmark, invented a unique hair styling device called Topsytail, she found it difficult to get retailers to carry the product. Topsytail is a patented plastic loop with a pointed handle that is used to convert regular ponytail styles into glamorous variations. Working alone, Edmark was able to sell 250,000 Topsytails by mail order and through retailers in 20 months at $10 apiece. She realized that the product would not be a big success unless she found a way to demonstrate how easy it was to use. After several false starts, Edmark hired a New Jersey–based distributor, T.V. Products, Inc., to promote Topsytail on television. This company put together a two-minute commercial, and managed Topsytail's television marketing and print advertisements and retail distribution. All Edmark had to do was appear in the commercial and supply enough product to meet the demand. In the first six months after the commercial hit the networks, T.V. Products sold 3.6 million Topsytails at $15 apiece. Since Topsytail cost about 50 cents to make, Edmark quickly became a multimillionaire.

Finding the right distribution channel can turn a so-so product into a bonanza.

Source: R. Lee Sullivan, "Unemployment Insurance," *Forbes,* August 2, 1993, p. 134.

Marketing Channel Jobs

The job of marketing channels is to move goods from production sites to customer locations. Distribution channels help conquer the time and distance intervals that divide users from merchandise they need. Channel members initiate and complete many of the following vital activities:

- *Communication:* Dispense product information to customers and report back data on market potentials, competitors, and market conditions.
- *Bargaining:* Negotiate agreements on prices and terms with potential buyers.
- *Reordering:* Transmit orders for merchandising back to manufacturers.
- *Financing:* Acquire funds to finance inventories and distribution facilities.
- *Maintain inventories:* Assume the risk of storage and movement of goods down the channel.
- *Cash settlements:* Collect money from buyers and deliver it to sellers.
- *Ownership:* Transfer title for goods and services from one firm to another.

Some of these activities flow forward (title, inventories) and some move backward (ordering, market data). All of them need to be performed by someone. The choice of who does the work of distribution depends on the costs of different alternative channels and the efficiencies of specialization. If the manufacturer assumes these functions, the selling prices must be adjusted to cover the costs. When distribution functions are shifted to intermediaries, manufacturer costs decline but dealer costs increase. Sometimes distribution activities are transferred to the customer (self-service gasoline) and prices to the buyer are lowered.

Frequently, channel members try to shift distribution costs to someone else. For example, in 1993 K-Mart asked its toy vendors to ship merchandise on consignment.[1] This meant that K-Mart would not have to pay for toys as they were received, and inventory carrying costs would be shifted from the retailer back to the manufacturer. In this case, K-Mart was trying to lower its operating costs at the expense of its suppliers. Usually changes in channel activities reflect a desire to make necessary distribution functions more efficient.

DISTRIBUTION ALTERNATIVES

There are hundreds of ways goods and services can be distributed to customers. These range from direct bulk shipments in railcars or pipelines to the use of complex arrangements of brokers, wholesalers, and retailers. No one distribution system can satisfy the needs of every firm, and many organizations use several distribution channels to reach different market segments. A paper mill, for example, may contact large users directly, whereas smaller customers are serviced by independent wholesalers.

Distribution systems not only vary across firms but also change over time. A channel that works well when a firm is small is likely to be inefficient when the firm expands and needs greater volume. Also, changes in customer needs and transportation methods can cause existing distribution methods to become obsolete.

Direct Distribution

The simplest channel is directly from the producer to the consumer or business buyer (Figure 11-2). Direct contact eliminates the need for dealers, but this method still involves expenditures for salespeople, postage, and advertising. Direct distribution is also used by not-for-profit organizations to disperse literature; and even museum prints, sculpture, and jewelry. Examples of merchandise distributed directly to consumers include the phone sale of flowers, securities, computers, clothing, cards, books, and CDs. Currently, over half of the hardcover books published in the United States are sold by mail.

At one time, marketers believed that only simple, standard items such as tapes and flower seeds could be sold direct. Today, however, even complex electronic equipment is being successfully sold over the phone. Firms run print ads in magazines and send out catalogs that feature toll-free 800 phone numbers. Customers are offered money-back guarantees and toll-free service lines to encourage sales. The net result has been an explosion in the amount of business conducted over the phone. Marketing Strategies box 11-1 describes how Michael Dell revolutionized the mail-order sale of computers with toll-free numbers.

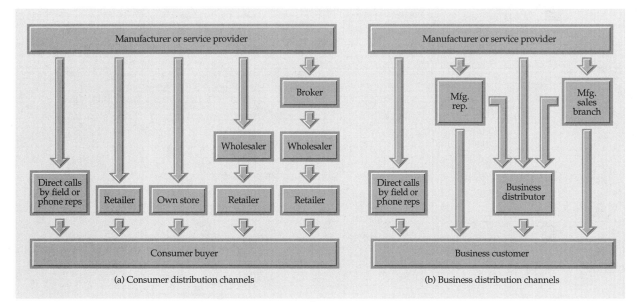

FIGURE 11-2 Consumer and Business Channel Alternatives

MARKETING STRATEGIES 11-1

DELL SELLS DIRECTLY

One of the most successful direct sales organizations in the history of American business is Dell Computer. In the past, direct marketing worked best in the sale of standardized, low-priced items like books, tapes, CDs, and flower seeds. Complex, high-priced items like computers that required after-sale service were thought to be inappropriate for mail-order distribution. Virtually all major PC manufacturers elected to sell through storefront dealers that allowed customers to touch and feel the machines and provided repair service. In the mid-1980s, Michael Dell was the first to realize that PCs were becoming a commodity business. Dell's initial strategy was to cut out the middleman and sell his computers directly to consumers via heavy advertising in the computer press and toll-free numbers. He eliminated the fears and uncertainties of mail-order purchasing by offering unlimited calls to a toll-free technical support line, a 30-day money-back guarantee, and free next-day, on-site service through independent contractors for the first year of ownership.

Some people assume that Dell's success is simply due to its low prices. While Dell's prices are lower than those of its major competitors, they are not the lowest in the industry. Dell succeeds because it builds a quality machine and backs it with the best service in the country. In 1991 Dell won a J. D. Power customer satisfaction award for a PC maker serving small to medium-sized businesses. In addition, Dell builds most of its computers to meet the needs of individual customer orders. This allows Dell to stay abreast of changing market conditions and greatly reduces inventory carrying costs.

> **MARKETING STRATEGIES 11-1 (continued)**
>
> Dell is a very efficient manufacturer and distributor of computers. It operates on a gross margin of only 28 percent of sales. At Dell, selling and administrative costs amount to a mere 14 percent of sales compared to 20 percent at Compaq, 24 percent at Apple, and 30 percent at IBM. Dell's sales organization is primarily made up of 600 phone order takers. About 40 percent of Dell's domestic sales are now made over the phone.
>
> To help expand business beyond the original small business buyer, Dell has set up account teams to sell to *Fortune* 1000 firms and large, privately held corporations. A separate team sells to government entities and educational institutions. Dell has also hired a 25-person sales force to sell to value-added resellers and original equipment manufacturers. Sales of computers through mass merchandisers are growing rapidly and are especially important in the household market. Dell has watched this trend and now sells 15 percent of its computers through mass outlets like Staples and Price Club. Although Dell built its business around mail-order sales, it has been willing to add other channels to reach special market segments. The highest praise of Michael Dell's genius is that *all* of his major competitors (IBM, DEC, Apple, Zenith, and Compaq) have instituted telephone sales operations. Dell will be remembered as the greatest computer marketer of the twentieth century.
>
> *Technical products can be sold successfully over the phone.*
>
> *Source:* Julie Pitta, "Why Dell Is a Survivor," *Forbes,* October 12, 1992, pp. 82–91.

Adding Retailers

Retailers have been a traditional part of distribution channels for hundreds of years. They provide shopping convenience, local inventories, exchange services, and repairs. The use of retailers has proved effective and efficient for both consumers and manufacturers of food, clothing, tires, video rentals, hardware, dry cleaning, and auto sales.

The advantages to the customer of retail stores in a channel of distribution are highlighted by a recent experience of one of the authors. I purchased a set of tires over the phone from a magazine ad because the delivered price was lower than that offered by retailers. The tires arrived in two days. Since the phone order company did not have a local installer, I had a dealer mount the tires. Afterwards I took the car out on the highway and noticed some vibration in the steering wheel at 60 miles per hour. I called the phone tire company, and they said I could drive 250 miles to their central office and have the tires checked out. They indicated that they would not exchange the tires just because I didn't like the way they rode, but only if they found them to be defective. I couldn't take the tires off the car and ship them back, and I didn't want to drive 500 miles to resolve the issue, so I went to a second dealer and had the wheels aligned and the tires rebalanced. The second dealer could find nothing wrong with the tires, but the vibration persisted. Apparently, the mud and snow tread design and the performance characteristics of the tires were poorly matched to the suspension of my car. If I had purchased the tires from a local retailer, I would not have had to spend all the money I had saved by purchasing over the

MARKETING IN ACTION 11-2

HYPERMARKETS: A DISTRIBUTION FAILURE

	Discount Store	Super Center	Hypermarket
Average size (in square feet)	70,000	150,000	230,000
Employees	200–300	300–350	400–600
Annual sales per store (millions)	$10–$20	$20–$50	$75–$100
Gross profit margins	18–19%	15–16%	7–8%
Stock-keeping units (number of different kinds of items stocked)	60,000–80,000	100,000	60,000–70,000

Hypermarkets, the ultimate one-stop shopping experience, have not worked in the U.S. market. These huge stores, which combine groceries, banks, restaurants, sporting goods, clothing, and electronics under one roof, have been rejected by American shoppers. Although hypermarkets have been quite successful in Europe, they have failed to draw the necessary volume to make a profit in the United States. Wal-Mart stopped building hypermarkets after experimenting with four units. K-Mart dropped out after opening three AmericanFare hypermarkets.

The main reason for the poor results is that the 230,000-square-foot stores are simply too big. It takes much longer to walk around a hypermarket than a discount store, and the task can scare off older shoppers. Also, the vast adjoining parking lots keep hypermarkets isolated from complementary stores that might attract more customers. Another problem is that despite their size, the selection of items within a category is not as broad as that of other stores. Hypermarkets have proved to be expensive to operate and need huge volumes to make money on their razor thin 10 percent gross margins.

An alternative to the hypermarket is a new distribution concept called the *super center* or *super store*. These stores are about two-thirds the size of a hypermarket and combine a supermarket with a discount store. Where Wal-Mart's hypermarkets did 70 percent of their business in food, its new super centers sell about 33 percent food and 67 percent general merchandise. Wal-Mart currently operates 38 super stores and expects to have over 200 by 1996. To help make its super centers more profitable, Wal-Mart rolled out 450 new private-label items in 1993. Although Wal-Mart looks to super centers for sales growth, there is some evidence that the United States has become saturated with these new types of stores. In 1993 Wal-Mart's discount stores reported annual sales growth of less than 10 percent for the first time in eight years. Also, sales at Wal-Mart's Sam's Wholesale Club stores actually declined on a same-store basis. Since Sam's generates 23 percent of Wal-Mart's total sales, the stock market knocked 20 percent off the price of Wal-Mart's shares.

Bigger is not necessarily better in retailing.

Source: Laurie M. Grossman, "Hypermarkets: A Surefire Hit Bombs," *The Wall Street Journal,* June 25, 1992, p. B1; Bob Ortega, "Wal-Mart's Challenge: Slow Business," *The Wall Street Journal,* April 16, 1993, p. B4.

phone to have the tires rebalanced. Also, a local dealer would have let me exchange the tires for a different brand if I continued to have problems with them. This experience suggests that my next set of tires will be purchased from a local dealer and that retailers are unlikely to vanish from the channels of distribution systems anytime soon.

The most recent innovations in retailing have been the growth of interactive kiosks at one extreme and superstores, warehouse clubs, and hypermarkets at the other. Interactive kiosks house touch screens that can access photographs and other information stored electronically. Many have video and audio features and can accept and verify credit cards. The kiosks are placed in malls and airports. Their weakness is that most customers want to talk to a live person. Superstores, also known as *category busters,* emphasize low prices (but may encourage customers to buy premium brands) and wide selection within a specialty. Superstores have successfully penetrated the toy, book, office-supply, and home-improvement markets and are now a factor in the pet products industry. Warehouse clubs like Sam's, owned by Wal-Mart, sell large amounts of limited assortments at low prices. They act as wholesalers to small businesses and sell case lots to consumer members. The hypermarket, or super center, combines a discount store and a supermarket under one roof. These stores are large and offer one-stop shopping for food, clothing, general merchandise, pharmaceuticals, dry cleaning, video rental, and film processing. Marketing in Action box 11-2 describes how the hypermarket concept failed in the American retail environment.

Using Wholesalers

When products are sold in different types of retail stores scattered all over the country, wholesalers may be needed to help transfer the merchandise from the manufacturer to retailers (Figure 11-2a). Wholesalers are dealers who buy in large volume and resell to retailers in case lots. They provide retailers with assortments of merchandise, backup stocks, credit, delivery, and promotional assistance. Organizations use wholesalers to get maximum exposure and direct contact with retailers is not justified because of low volume or lack of resources. For example, wholesalers are typically used to distribute beer to the many restaurants, hotels, taverns, liquor stores, supermarkets, drugstores, and corner groceries that sell this product in a given market area. Because specialized beer wholesalers carry several lines, they can perform the store contact work more efficiently than delivery systems operated by individual brewers. Also, the beer wholesaler is likely to do a better job of promotion, inventory control, and stock rotation than would be possible if the product were handled by general-purpose wholesalers.

While wholesalers are a standard component of many distribution systems, they are currently losing market share to factory outlets, mail-order catalogs, warehouse clubs, and mass merchandisers who buy directly from manufacturers. Research suggests that wholesalers' share of producer shipments will fall from the 42 percent achieved in 1992 to 36 percent by the year 2000.[2] Manufacturers battered by a weak economy and shrinking profits have been looking for cheaper and more efficient ways to move their goods. If 300,000 mostly small wholesalers in the United States expect to survive in the future, they will have to find ways to cut costs and improve customer benefits.

Agents and Brokers

Relatively few people understand why manufacturers use brokers and independent representatives to sell goods in a channel of distribution (Figure 11-2). Reps are specialized agents who neither own nor take possession of the merchandise they sell to wholesale, distributor, business, or retail customers. They operate on commission in specified territories and sell where manufacturers cannot handle the job. For example, small food packers with a limited product line often lack the resources to hire their own sales force. By using a rep, the manufacturer avoids the high fixed costs associated with salespeople and branch facilities and gains the benefits of the contacts the rep has already established with the wholesale and retail trade. The choice between company salespeople and independent reps is a difficult make-or-buy decision. A company sales force takes more time to recruit and train, but it sells only for you. Using reps is like purchasing a ready-made sales force that can start producing immediately; however, reps have the disadvantage that their loyalties are spread across several different firms that they represent.

Although reps are a common element in distribution channels, they have begun to lose clout in many markets. Large retail chains like Wal-Mart, the cataloger Fingerhut, and K-Mart's Builders Square are eliminating reps in favor of direct negotiations with executives of supplier organizations. If this trend continues, reps may be relegated to special situations and employment by small manufacturers. This change in emphasis suggests that distribution channels are rarely permanent and that you must continually search for new procedures that lower costs and improve service to customers.

Nonprofit and Service Distribution

Nonprofit programs and services are rarely sold from inventory, and extensive systems of warehouses and retail stores are not needed. Nonprofit programs are often sold through networks of branch offices. Sales offices may be owned and operated by the parent organization or franchised to local independent managers. Service Master and other temporary help companies, for example, operate their branches on a franchise basis, whereas loan companies typically own their local units.

Many nonprofit programs have limited customer appeal and are promoted to relatively small market segments. This often means that special distribution channels must be set up to reach these target markets. The channels used by the National Safety Council to market its defensive driving course include local safety councils and contacts with businesses, service clubs, schools, police, and the courts. These independent agencies are part of the distribution channel, and success depends on the local safety council's ability to get these groups to recommend the driving course.

Channel Ownership

Organizations can sell their goods and services through independent wholesalers and retailers, or they can acquire facilities to perform these activities using their own employees. When an organization extends this operation to the wholesale and retail levels, it has a *vertically integrated channel*. This method of distribution can improve efficiency by eliminating promotion and selling expenses that normally occur between the organization and the wholesaler and between the wholesaler and the retailer. With a completely integrated channel, the main job for marketing executives is to increase demand among the final buyers and to coordinate the activities of different units in the channel. The primary advantage of this system is that it gives maximum control over the selection of products sold in the channel, their prices, and the promotional activities designed to sell them to the final consumer. Examples of completely integrated distribution channels are provided by Sherwin-Williams, which operates 2000 paint stores; Hart Schaffner Marx, which owns more than 200 clothing stores; and Bridgestone, which owns 1500 Expert and Firestone tire stores. Although the completely integrated channel offers manufacturers the most control over the distribution of their products, it also requires the greatest financial investment and good managers to operate the facilities efficiently.

Franchise Distribution

Franchising is a system of distribution whereby independent business managers are given the right to sell products or services in exchange for a fee or agreements on buying and merchandising policies. The main advantage of franchising is that it

TABLE 11-1

Costs of Operating an Ice Cream Franchise

Company (location)	Franchise Fee	Total Estimated Investment Required	Royalty and Advertising Fund	Total Stores in Chain	Total Franchised Stores
Baskin-Robbins USA Co. (Glendale, California)	$ 0	$ 80,000–140,000	2%	(U.S.) 2500	(U.S.) 2438
Ben & Jerry's Homemade, Inc. (Waterbury, Vermont)	15,600	125,000–150,000	4	80	75
Bresler's Ice Cream & Yogurt/Bresler's Division of Oberweis Dairy, Inc. (Des Plaines, Illinois)	10,000	125,000–145,000	9	300	300
International Dairy Queen, Inc. (Minneapolis, Minnesota)	30,000	445,000–675,000	7–9	5005	5000
TCBY Enterprises, Inc. (Little Rock, Arkansas)	20,000	93,000–155,000	7	1075	972

Source: The Wall Street Journal, December 21, 1988, p. B2.

offers the parent organization a low-cost way to expand rapidly. For example, when Prudential Insurance Company opened a chain of real estate agencies, the franchisees put up most of the money and the business was profitable from the start. Prudential estimates that it would have cost over 10 times as much to open its own outlets. Ashland Oil chose franchising to expand its quick-lube business. Ashland wanted to grow from 178 outlets to over 2000 by the mid-1990s. Since each unit costs over $500,000, growth by franchising will save Ashland over $1 billion.

The costs associated with franchising are described for ice cream stores in Table 11-1. Note that the local manager pays a franchising fee of $10,000 to $30,000 and has a total investment of between $80,000 and $675,000. In addition, the local outlets pay a royalty and advertising fee of 2 to 9 percent of sales. This shows how franchisees pay to expand a distribution network for you and then subsidize the advertising needed to make it successful.

SELECTING DISTRIBUTION CHANNELS

Distribution channels must be designed to give customers ready access to goods and services at a minimum cost. This means that you have to balance the costs of employing different types of channels against the revenues generated. Using a wholesaler, for example, reduces the manufacturer's sales and communication costs and may increase profits. However, many of the costs associated with channel choice are lost opportunities and are very difficult to estimate. A model of the channel selection process is shown in Figure 11-3. The choice of distribution method begins with a decision on planned market coverage. Depending on the product and the number of customers, the organization must decide whether it wants broad distribution or more selective coverage with a few dealers.

Intensive Distribution

The intensive distribution approach is used for convenience goods when the firm wants the product available in as many retail outlets as possible. Intensive distribution can be achieved by recruiting large numbers of jobbers and wholesalers to cover every market area. Candy, photographic film, and cigarettes are made available in thousands of stores for easy access and more impulse sales.

Selective Distribution

With selective distribution, several dealers in each area are designated to handle the product, but the merchandise is not made available to every retailer. The idea is that restricted availability will increase the volume per dealer and make the brand more important to them. Also, selective distribution is used when dealers require extensive training and carry large stocks and parts inventories. Selective distribution is common with automobiles and branded clothing. For example, designer jeans and Liz Claiborne dresses are available in department and specialty stores but are kept out of K-Mart.

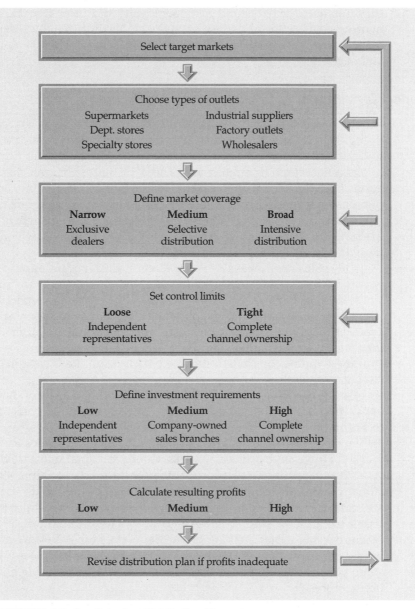

FIGURE 11-3   Selecting Distribution Channels

Exclusive Distribution

With exclusive distribution, the organization appoints a single dealer in each local market area to handle branded goods or services. Exclusive distribution has been used in the sales of luxury automobiles, Schwinn bicyles, Midas mufflers, and soft drink concentrate. By granting dealers local monopolies, the firm expects to gain cooperation on price maintenance, promotion, and inventory levels. Exclusive distribution helps dealers build customer loyalty and allows the dealers to charge higher markups. In addition, the use of exclusive territories allows dealers who invest in marketing activities to capture all the customers who want to buy the firm's goods and services.

Multiple-Channel Distribution

When an organization begins operations, it is common to concentrate its efforts on a single channel of distribution. However, as the firm grows, there are strong incentives to add channels to reach new market segments and to accommodate changes in customer shopping preferences. The net result is that many companies distribute goods and services through several channels at the same time. Frequently, the addition of new channels creates morale problems with existing dealer networks. Firms face the terrible dilemma of choosing between the slow growth offered by traditional distribution channels and faster growth via new channels, which in turn, may cause regular dealers to drop the product.

One solution pursued by Pella, a manufacturer of premium windows and doors, was to introduce a special ProLine of lower-priced items for sale in home supply stores such as Payless, Cashways, and Home Depot. To keep its regular distributors happy, Pella designated them as quality assurance representatives for all ProLine products sold in their territory. Distributors now train local retailers and help with installation and customer service. Pella distributors also earn a commission on every ProLine window the chain outlets sell. As a result, Pella's stagnant sales and profits have improved.[3]

Goodyear Tire & Rubber Company is another company that has had problems expanding its distribution alternatives. Goodyear sells 40 percent of its tires directly to automobile manufacturers for use on new cars and has relied on a network of 2500 independent dealers and 1000 company stores for sales to the replacement tire market. However, by the early 1990s, Goodyear's market share had declined 20 percent; the company is now third in the world market behind Michelin and Bridgestone. Goodyear decided to broaden the distribution of its tires to regain market share. It started selling its tires to Sears, the nation's largest tire retailer. Also, Goodyear tires are now sold at Tire America, a chain of discount stores owned by Sears. Goodyear has started making private-label tires for Wal-Mart, and mail-order firms sell Goodyear tires over the phone. Now that Michelin tires are available at K-Mart, some believe that Goodyear tires will eventually be available in discount and warehouse stores.[4]

By the end of 1992, Goodyear's market share was up 1 percent. However, many of Goodyear's 2500 traditional dealers were furious at the loss of sales to the new channels. While few regular dealers have started to sell Michelin or Bridgestone tires, many are stocking private-label tires manufactured by other firms. One analyst estimates that Goodyear could lose one-third to one-half of the expected increase in Sears orders to smaller sales through its regular dealers.[5] This example shows how difficult it is to keep an existing channel alive when customers want to buy from newer outlets. Marketing in Action box 11-3 describes how new distribution channels have created havoc for American computer manufacturers.

MARKETING IN ACTION 11-3

CHANGING PC DISTRIBUTION CHANNELS

When personal computers were first introduced in the United States, they were sold by traditional dealers who provided installation and repair services. As PCs became more widely accepted, manufacturers began to broaden their distribution channels to include computer superstores, warehouse clubs, and mail-order operations. Although traditional dealers still have two-thirds of corporate PC sales, mail order and superstores are expected to grab 19 percent by 1994 compared to 13 percent in 1991. These new channels emphasize low prices and have also been effective in reaching the home market.

These shifts in the importance of PC distribution channels have created serious problems for manufacturers and for the traditional dealers. Compaq, for example, resisted the trend to mass merchandising, citing its need to supply the dealer channel that nurtured its growth. However, when Compaq brought out its new low-priced, ProLinea computers, they decided to expand into the new, fast-growing channels. Unfortunately, the demand for ProLinea computers has been so intense that Compaq has been forced to allocate production among its new and traditional dealers. Some traditional dealers have hundreds of ProLinea machines on back order and have been forced to buy computers from superstores and mail order companies to satisfy their customers' needs. These actions have devastated profit margins and left the dealers wondering why computers are available by mail and in the superstores while their orders go unfilled. The traditional dealers are concerned about their futures as they see the market growth being grabbed by the new channels. The dealers are not only losing sales, but their long-term relationships with customers are in jeopardy. Some customers refuse to wait for dealers to get restocked and are starting to buy directly at the computer superstores. Compaq claims that it shipped more ProLinea machines to dealers in 1993 than in 1992, but still many orders go unfilled.

Computer manufacturers face a terrible dilemma. If they ship only to the traditional dealers, they lose out on the future sales of the new channels. If they focus on the mass merchandisers, they risk alienating their regular dealers, who still control the largest share of the PC market. Some traditional dealers are already pushing the sales of computers that are available for immediate delivery.

Channels created to introduce a product may not work for more mature product lines.

Source: Kyle Pope, "Dealers Accuse Compaq of Jilting Them," *The Wall Street Journal,* April 7, 1993, p. B1.

International Distribution

Once the firm has established distribution channels for domestic markets, emphasis often shifts to finding ways to sell in foreign countries. Because of the high costs and risks associated with international distribution, most firms start by making arrangements with foreign dealers to handle their products. For example, joint ventures have helped a number of U.S. firms to enter the Japanese market. Black & Decker, the leading U.S. manufacturer of power tools, has been losing market share in the domestic market to Mikita Electric. Its response has been to sign an agreement with Shin-

Daiwa Kogyo to market Black & Decker's tools in Japan.[6] The idea is to take advantage of Shin-Daiwa's extensive sales force, distribution network, and service operations. Chrysler has signed up with the Seibu/Saison group in Japan to gain access to established Japanese car dealerships. In a similar manner, Ford has arranged for 200 local dealers to handle its cars in Japan.

Finding good dealers in foreign countries is sometimes difficult because domestic firms may already have ties to the best distributors. For example, Korea-based Samsung Electronics has 15 percent of the U.S. VCR market and 20 percent of the

MARKETING IN ACTION 11-4

DISTRIBUTING COMPUTERS IN JAPAN

American firms have had a difficult time gaining distribution for personal computers in Japan. PCs need enormous processing power to handle the 10,000 characters that make up the three Japanese alphabets. This power became available with Intel's 386 microprocessor, but American PCs designed for Japan were still slow because of weak operating systems. In 1991, a group of American PC manufacturers introduced a Japanese version of DOS/V that featured an extra-large data "pipeline" that eased the flow of Japanese characters through a PC. DOS/V could also handle the huge library of existing English language DOS software. Also Microsoft has brought out a new Japanese version of its popular Windows software. Programs written for Windows will run on U.S. machines or machines produced by giant NEC, who has 53 percent of the Japanese market. Windows could neutralize NEC's tenfold advantage in software titles.

Once American computer manufacturers had comparable machines, operating systems, and software, they tried to buy their way into the Japanese market by offering extremely low prices. These moves attracted attention, but market share gains have been slow. Although American firms have had some success selling PCs direct to large corporate buyers, they needed to recruit local dealers to sell to smaller firms and to the home market. Progress has been slow because Japanese dealers are reluctant to damage the close relationships they have cultivated with NEC. Compaq, for example, had to delete the names of ten firms that sell its machines from a brochure listing its approved Japanese dealers. Other dealers have set up separate subsidiaries with different names to handle Compaq equipment. One dealer forced Compaq to deliver goods to an out-of-the-way warehouse to avoid NEC snoops who might see the machines come and go from the main warehouse. For every dealer Compaq has signed up to sell its products, NEC has 100.

To overcome the resistance of Japanese dealers and ultimate users, American firms have had to advertise heavily to assure customers that their machines are reliable and strong service and support is available. Low prices are not enough to gain distribution in Japanese markets dominated by large firms with familiar products and large dealer networks.

Building distribution in Japan takes time and money.

Source: Kyle Pope and David P. Hamilton, "U.S. Computer Firms, Extending PC Wars, Charge Into Japan," *The Wall Street Journal,* March 31, 1993, p. A1.

microwave oven market. However, it sells very few of these items in nearby Japan because half of the consumer electronics products are sold by retail stores controlled by Japanese manufacturers. These stores have no intention of stocking Korean goods.

Careful attention to building strong distribution networks is often the key to successful foreign sales. The Germans, for instance, have grabbed 76 percent of the imported car market in Japan due to their strong local dealers. Volkswagen sells its cars in Japan through Yanase & Company, the largest group of foreign car dealers in the country. BMW purchased its own dealer network in Japan and then expanded it. BMW has also set up a service and parts system so that Japanese buyers do not have to worry about repair problems. A discussion of the problems involved in gaining distribution for computers in Japan is presented in Marketing in Action box 11-4. The lesson from these examples is that you cannot ignore distribution problems if you expect to win overseas sales.

MANAGING THE CHANNEL

After a distribution network has been installed, the emphasis shifts to finding ways to improve performance. This is an ongoing process of evaluating results, modifying dealers' incentives, and replacing weak players.

Dealer Incentives

Independent wholesalers and retailers are in business to make money and are obviously interested in stocking and promoting items that will increase their profits. Organizations that sell through these dealers must design products and marketing programs that are equal to or better than competitive offerings if they expect to gain support of these entrepreneurs. A list of incentives available to help organizations build dealer enthusiasm is shown in Table 11-2. The most direct dealer incentives are price concessions granted for volume purchases, advertising support, and seasonal orders. Other, more indirect methods for building dealer excitement include display materials, training programs, sales literature, and the hiring of in-store demonstrators. Perhaps the most enduring technique used to gain dealer cooperation involves the extension of credit. This may take the form of loans to finance inventories of display merchandise, loans for fixtures and equipment, or cash to finance customer purchases.

Another way to encourage dealers' cooperation is to give them exclusive rights to sell particular brands or models. Although Michelin sells a few lines of tires through K-Mart discount stores, its premium tires are available only through its traditional independent dealers. Dell has expanded its distribution channels to include retail outlets and has tailored its new Precision line of computers for warehouse stores such as Sam's Club and Price Club. In a similar fashion, Hallmark sells Ambassador cards through supermarkets and reserves its own name cards for sale through its franchised independent outlets.

Disincentives that damage dealer relations include delayed delivery, shipment

TABLE 11-2
Techniques Used to Gain Dealer Cooperation

I. "Price" Concessions
   A. Discount structure:

Trade (functional) discounts	Prepaid freight
Quantity discounts	Seasonal discounts
Cash discounts	Mixed-carload privilege
Anticipated allowances	Drop-shipping privilege
Free goods	Trade deals
New product, display, advertising allowances (without performance requirements)	

   B. Discount substitutes:

Display materials	Advertising materials
Premarked merchandise	Management consulting services
Inventory control programs	Merchandising programs
Training programs	Sales "spiffs"
Shelf-stocking programs	Technical assistance
Payment of sales personnel and demonstrator salaries	Catalogs and sales promotion literature

II. Financial Assistance
   A. Conventional lending arrangements:

Term loans	Accounts payable financing
Inventory floor plans	Lease and note guarantee programs
Notes payable financing	Accounts receivable financing
Installment financing of fixtures and equipment	

   B. Extended dating:

End of month dating	"Extra" dating
Seasonal dating	Postdating
Receipt of goods dating	

III. Protective provisions
   A. Price protection:

Premarked merchandise	"Franchise" pricing
Agency agreements	

   B. Inventory protection:

Consignment selling	Rebate programs
Memorandum selling	Reorder guarantee
Liberal returns allowances	Guaranteed support of sales events
Maintenance of "spot" stocks and fast delivery	

   C. Territorial protection:

Selective distribution	Exclusive distribution

Source: Bert C. McCammon, Jr., "Perspectives for Distribution Programming," in Louis P. Bucklin, ed., *Vertical Marketing Systems* (Glenview, IL: Scott, Foresman, 1970), pp. 36–37. Copyright © by Scott Foresman & Co. Reprinted by permission of the publisher.

of unwanted products, slow warranty claims, and high prices.[7] An auto dealer study has shown that manufacturers that emphasize information exchange do a better job of improving dealer relations.[8] Firms that discuss the overall strategy of dealer operations and those that make simple requests are able to gain dealer agreements on inventory levels, participation in special programs, number of salespeople, and advertising expenditures. On the other hand, companies that make threats, promises, legalistic pleas, or specific recommendations have a negative impact on dealer cooperation.

Channel Power

Power in a distribution channel is the ability to get people to do things they might not otherwise want to do. Manufacturers who own their distribution channel have the power to set price, inventory, and promotion levels as they see fit. However, many firms distribute their products through independent dealers, and there are limits to what they can be forced to do. Firms that exercise too much channel power are apt to lose shelf space and dealers, be taken to court, or face additional legislation designed to protect channel members.

An example of a power struggle between food manufacturers and grocery stores has developed over slotting allowances. In the old days, large manufacturers could bully grocers into carrying their products, and the manufacturer could dictate prices. However, supermarket chains consolidated into regional giants with immense distribution clout. Supermarkets used their control over shelf space to ask for slotting allowances of $15 to $1000 per store to place new items on their shelves. Manufacturers were told that they had to pay cash to gain retail distribution they once purchased with consumer advertising. Manufacturers grew tired of this game and began to push food sales in discount stores, warehouse clubs, and superstores that were not so greedy. As a result, the share of the food business handled by traditional supermarkets has declined. This example suggests that firms that abuse their power in distribution channels often lose in the long run.

Gray Market Distribution

One of the most difficult distribution control problems facing multinational firms is the so-called gray market issue. The gray market is a system in which retailers import branded goods from foreign countries without approval of the product's manufacturer. These importers purchase branded goods from wholesalers in countries with low taxes and markups and then resell them in countries where markups are high. Gray market goods typically sell for 25 to 40 percent less than imports handled through regular distribution channels. Common gray market merchandise includes cameras, watches, fragrances, cosmetics, electronics goods, liquor, and tires made overseas.

Gray market (or parallel) importation develops when multinational firms sell products at higher prices in one country than in another. Firms often use larger markups to help attract wholesalers and pay for advertising and sales promotion activities. Although high markups help build a strong distribution network, they also attract gray market importers. You may wonder why a company would care whether merchandise flows through the company's authorized channels or the gray market. The reason is that the regular distribution network provides inventory backup, spare parts, repairs, and promotional support that are not provided to customers who buy through gray markets. Thus, the gray market grows under an umbrella of services provided by the regular channel. Parallel importation can seriously damage authorized dealers by siphoning off sales.

The best way to eliminate gray markets is to reduce differentials across countries that allow parallel importation to exist. Japanese camera firms have recently cut their prices in the United States to the point where they are similar to those of the gray importers.[9] Another solution is to buy up the merchandise brought in by gray marketers to protect your regular dealers. This approach could become expensive if it encouraged dealers to bring in even more merchandise. The U.S. Supreme Court has ruled that gray market importation is legal, and the problem is likely to exist for a long time.

ORGANIZING DISTRIBUTION

Once you have selected appropriate distribution channels, the next step is to design and operate a physical handling system that delivers merchandise to customers as cheaply as possible. For many products, distribution costs can be 30 to 40 percent of the product's cost. Firms that learn how to cut these costs can sell at lower prices and steal market share from their competitors. Amazing changes are taking place in physical handling systems, and this area may be the last profit frontier for marketing in the twentieth century.

Customer Service Levels

One of your most difficult distribution jobs is balancing the service needs of customers against the need to control distribution costs. Customer service is often measured in terms of the time it takes to deliver merchandise or the proportion of orders that can be filled from inventories. In general, sales revenues increase as service levels are raised (Figure 11-4). However, improved service levels also raise distribution costs for extra inventory and faster delivery. Thus your task is to determine optimum service levels that balance the increased revenues associated with better customer satisfaction against the costs of providing these services.

An example of an optimum service level developed for a lemon juice item is shown in Figure 11-4. In this case the item had been carried at the manufacturer's warehouse with an in-stock probability of over 99 percent. When the extra revenue generated by the in-stock positions was balanced against the added costs of safety stock needed to meet these service levels, the optimum service level was found to be 93 percent rather than the current 99+ percent (Figure 11-4). A similar analysis was run for other items, and the firm was able to save millions of dollars in inventory carrying costs. Adjusting service levels to reduce costs works well when channel

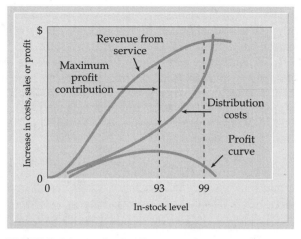

FIGURE 11-4 Setting Customer Service Levels

members are independent firms and deal on an arms-length basis. When channel members are tied together with computer information networks, even greater economies can be realized.

Using Scanner Data

The engine fueling the revolution in distribution efficiency is improved information on customer purchases. These data are gathered by optical scanners that read bar codes on product packaging. Whenever a customer buys anything, data on the purchase goes directly—in real time—to the manufacturer's plant. Computers prepare a manufacturing schedule and instructions on when, how, and where to ship.

This type of system is used by the U.S.'s largest retailer—Wal-Mart. By tying point-of-sale terminals to suppliers' factories, Wal-Mart has made several significant cost savings. Most of the cost of distribution involves keeping inventory in three warehouses: the manufacturer's, the wholesaler's, and the retailer's. With Wal-Mart's system there is no need for factory buffer stock, as the goods are made to order and shipped immediately. Also, some of the orders go directly to the stores, reducing the need for wholesale inventories. Since store shipments replace stock already sold, Wal-Mart needs less safety stock at the store level. Wal-Mart allocates only 10 percent of its square footage for inventory compared to 25 percent at other stores. Another area for savings is reduced order cycle time. Because of direct computer linkages, communication delays are eliminated and it takes less time to get merchandise into Wal-Mart stores. This means that fewer people are needed to process the orders, and quick delivery cuts out-of-stock conditions and boosts sales.[10]

Wal-Mart's direct information ties with suppliers has allowed it to reduce its expense ratio to only 15 percent of sales. This is half of Sears' expense ratio and explains how Wal-Mart was able to use low prices to become the world's largest retailer. No traditional retailer, no supermarket, and no catalog store can compete with Wal-Mart on price. Wal-Mart has successfully employed advanced information technology to achieve a sustainable competitive advantage in distribution costs.

The use of scanner data to improve distribution efficiency at Wal-Mart is not an isolated example. Ito-Yokado uses a similar system to supply its 4300 7-Eleven stores in Japan. Point-of-sale information is linked to factories to control the product mix of major suppliers such as Coca-Cola. The data are used to schedule production and set delivery schedules, including the hour the new goods are to arrive at each store. The savings achieved by Ito-Yokado exceed those of Wal-Mart because in Japan five levels of wholesalers can be eliminated.

Are Warehouses Necessary?

In the past, discussions of warehouses in channels of distribution focused on the number of warehouses required and where they should be located. Today the question is whether they are needed at all. Firms that produce to customers' orders and sell directly do not have to operate any warehouses. Dell Computer, for example, takes orders over the phone, builds machines to these specs, and then ships directly to customers via UPS. Inventories and warehouses are not required in this distribution system. Any storage in the channel is maintained by the shipping company.

MARKETING PRODUCTIVITY 11-1

USING HAND-HELD SCANNERS

Hosiery is sold by a wide variety of retail stores, and many of these are not connected by computer to their suppliers. To help these accounts manage their inventory and place reorders, Hanes Hosiery has equipped their field salespeople with hand-held optical scanners. When Hanes salespeople visit stores, they fill in displays, take inventory, and create a reorder. They are equipped with hand-held Telxon computers equipped with bar code reading wands to check inventory levels. When they complete the inventory, they use a lightweight Kodax 150 battery-powered printer to create a full report. Inventory levels are then checked against the store's target stocks, and a Grid laptop computer is employed to create a new order. Once the orders are approved, they are transmitted electronically to Hanes' main office.

The new system drastically reduces the time needed to restock a store and improves accuracy. Also, reps can compare inventories on the sales floor to that in the back room. Often these reports show that several styles have been buried in the stockroom, while the shelves are empty. This information helps the store manager better control inventories. Hanes has another Electron Re-Order system that gathers data from cash registers equipped with UPC wands. These new systems have cut the time spent on in-store inventories in half. This has allowed Hanes reps to spend more time with customers and to make more calls.

Scanners and computers speed up activities of field salespeople.

Source: Cyndee Miller, ''Hanes Takes the Snags Out of Maintaining Hosiery Inventories,'' *Marketing News*, May 14, 1990, p. 23.

Other firms are also finding ways to reduce the need for warehouses. In one medium-sized supermarket chain, half of the merchandise goes directly from manufacturers to stores.[11] The other half still goes through company warehouses. However, it is not held there: the merchandise is shipped to stores within three hours. These warehouses are *switching yards* instead of storage bins. Any retailer that stores only half of its goods for three hours in a warehouse is saving a great deal on inventory carrying costs.

Firms that serve many small customers that require warehouse distribution have found ways to operate their remaining warehouses more efficiently. Helene Curtis, for example, has built a highly automated and computerized warehouse that can handle twice the volume of the six older warehouses it replaced. The new system helped Helene Curtis cut distribution costs by 40 percent. These savings allowed the company to cut prices to the consumer by 10 percent and increased market share. Mervyn's has built four new automated distribution centers to serve its 247 department stores. These centers cut the average time merchandise spends moving from vendor to store from 14 days to less than 9 days. The results have been spectacular. Mervyn's sales have grown 50 percent, but inventory carrying costs have remained the same as they were five years ago. Manufacturers and retailers that refuse to buy into computerized information systems will have trouble competing in the future. An inexpensive inventory control and reorder system that uses hand-held scanners is described in Marketing Productivity 11-1.

Transportation Alternatives

Transportation represents the largest single distribution cost element, and you must understand how to use this resource to its best advantage. Choosing transportation methods involves a series of trade-offs between cost and service factors. Water, pipeline, and rail tend to be low-cost methods, but they involve higher storage and in-transit inventory costs. Inventory costs are lower for truck and air delivery, but the rates are higher. Telecommunications, based on emerging technologies (fiberoptic cables, wireless microwave broadcasting, and satellite transmission) and computer advances, is the newest form of transportation. Telecommunications can provide instant delivery of certain products and services. The best approach is to select the transportation alternative that minimizes total distribution costs.

You must also consider customers' expectations for speed and dependability of delivery. In some situations, premium transportation is used even though it costs more than other methods. For example, when customers need parts to repair assembly lines, the extra cost of quick delivery may be small compared to the potential savings for the customer.

Each transportation alternative has its own special advantages and disadvantages. The seven primary transportation modes will be described to give you a better view of the distribution choices.

Pipeline   The main advantage of pipeline distribution is that it is the cheapest method of delivery. Pipelines, for example, cost only 1.26 cents a ton-mile to move oil to customers. As a result, pipelines have grown more important and now account for 23 percent of the intercity freight movement in the United States. However, pipelines are the slowest distribution method, and require special facilities to handle oil, gas, coal, and chemicals that are typically hauled with this technique.

Rail   The largest haulers of merchandise in the United States are the railroads, with 38 percent of the intercity ton-miles. Recently, railroads have been able to attract significant business from truck carriers by offering substantially lower rates. Railroads provide a variety of special cars for hauling containers, grain, coal, lumber, and chemicals. Shipping by rail costs about 3 cents a ton-mile, and this method is cost-effective for bulk commodities hauled longer distances. On the other hand, rail tends to be slower than truck or air freight.

Truck   Using trucks is favored for smaller shipments moved shorter distances. The average length of haul for a truck shipment is only 300 miles. Advantages of trucks include door-to-door delivery, good availability of service, and convenience. Disadvantages include higher costs and limits on the size and volume of goods that can be carried. Trucks are fast and dependable, and they have 23 percent of the intercity ton-miles despite a cost of 15 cents a ton-mile.

Water   The primary advantages of water distribution are low cost and the ability to carry large volumes of goods. It costs less than 2 cents a ton-mile to ship by water, and this method is very competitive for hauling sand, salt, coal, oil, and grain. However, water shipment is slower than rail and is confined to areas that have access to ports and the intercoastal waterway system. Also, the availability and dependability of water delivery are strongly influenced by the weather.

Air   For shipments of over 500 miles, air freight is the fastest distribution method. Air delivery is favored for perishable items like cut flowers, spare parts, and other high-value commodities. Advantages of air freight include less damage to merchandise than by rail or truck delivery and less inventory in safety stocks and in transit. Utilization of air freight is constrained by very high costs (three times those of trucks), and air delivery accounts for less than 1 percent of the ton-miles hauled in the United States.

Telecommunications   Information and entertainment services can often be "shipped" electronically. Some newspapers, for example, are available on local, interactive networks. Indeed, these networks provide more news, sports updates, and entertainment articles than can fit into conventional editions of a newspaper. Kiosks are becoming available that will allow record stores to pull an album out of a central computer and print it on a compact disk (Figure 11-5). The same system, combined with fiberoptic telephone or cable TV lines, interactive television, and digital tape machines could someday pipe albums into the home. The implications of the technology for making CDs in store are discussed in more detail in Marketing Productivity 11-2.

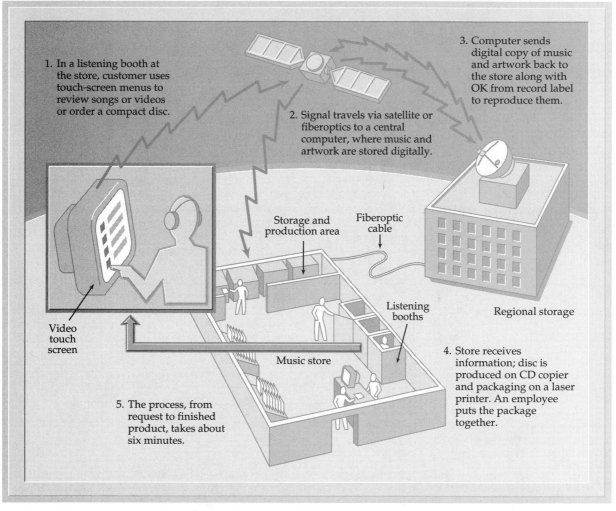

1. In a listening booth at the store, customer uses touch-screen menus to review songs or videos or order a compact disc.

2. Signal travels via satellite or fiberoptics to a central computer, where music and artwork are stored digitally.

3. Computer sends digital copy of music and artwork back to the store along with OK from record label to reproduce them.

Storage and production area

Fiberoptic cable

Video touch screen

Listening booths

Regional storage

Music store

4. Store receives information; disc is produced on CD copier and packaging on a laser printer. An employee puts the package together.

5. The process, from request to finished product, takes about six minutes.

FIGURE 11-5 Making a CD On-Site (Adapted from Marty Baumann, *USA Today* [May 17, 1993], p. B1)

Intermodal Shipping Efficient delivery of merchandise to customers often involves coordinated shipment by several modes of transportation. Trucks may be used for pickup and delivery, and the long-haul movement may be by rail, water, or air carrier. Frequently, goods are packed in large containers at the factory and moved by truck or rail to ports for overseas delivery. The fastest-growing intermodal shipping method is the truck/rail combination. Highway trailers and container volume carried on rail flat cars increased 7.4 percent in 1992, and this rate of growth is expected to continue in the future. Truck/rail shipping is expanding because of efficiency gains resulting from reductions in the size of train crews and improvements

---

MARKETING PRODUCTIVITY 11-2

OVERCOMING THE GROSS INEFFICIENCIES OF MUSIC RETAILING

Record stores haven't changed much since the 1950s. They buy and store many copies of popular albums and few or no copies of older or more obscure recordings. That may shield record stores from getting stuck with inventory that's not selling, but it often means that stores incur an opportunity cost in terms of missed sales. About 60 percent of the people who walk into a record store know what they want. Of these, about 43 percent leave empty-handed. This is about to change with the availability of high-tech kiosks to duplicate compact disks in record stores.

A customer goes into a kiosk and touches buttons on the screen to go through menus. The menus list recordings by artist, album title, or song title. Theoretically, you could find the title of any album ever made. You would have just as much access to obscure independent releases as to megahit major releases. When you decided what you wanted to buy, you would hit a button. The kiosk would be linked to central computers that stored a digital version of all the recordings the record shop was authorized to sell. The computer would send a digital copy of the album back to the kiosk and send payment to the record company that produced the album. Back in the record store, the kiosk, which is connected to a high-speed CD duplicating machine, would copy the music onto a CD for you.

Transportation adds $3 to the cost of a CD. Stores can either pocket what they save by printing their own CDs or slash prices.

Advanced technology permits manufacturing plants and distribution networks to be bypassed.

Source: Kevin Maney, "Revolution in Store for Record Shops," *USA Today*, May 17, 1993, pp. B1–B2.

---

in new railcar technology. By stacking containers two high on low-slung railcars, railroads can move freight at savings of as much as 30 percent compared with over-the-road trucking. Truck/rail hauling is now competitive for distances of over 800 miles, and new equipment is being designed to attract shipments traveling over 250 miles. Picking the right transportation alternative can obviously cut distribution costs.

SUMMARY

This chapter has been concerned with selecting channels of distribution and designing systems to move goods and services efficiently to the point of final consumption. You have to decide whether to sell directly or to organize a channel made up of independent brokers, wholesalers, or retailers. This choice is influenced by the supply of independent distributors and by the amount of money and sales volume the firm has to support its own distribution network. If independent dealers are selected, you must find ways to care for and nourish channel members to ensure their continued cooperation and survival. A common problem today is finding ways to keep your regular dealers happy as you add new distribution channels to build market share.

The last frontier of marketing efficiency is finding ways to reduce the costs of distribution. Some of the most spectacular savings have been achieved by linking optical scanners in retail stores to factories. Others have had success by automating field warehouses and using intermodal transportation systems. American distribution systems are undergoing radical changes, and firms that do not pay attention may not survive.

NOTES

1. Christina Duff, "Nation's Retailers Ask Vendors to Help Share Expenses," *The Wall Street Journal*, August 4, 1993, p. B4.
2. Michael Selz, "Firms Innovate to Get It for You Wholesale," *The Wall Street Journal*, July 24, 1993, p. B1.
3. Ronald Henkoff, "Moving Up Downscaling," *Fortune*, August 9, 1993, p. 72.
4. Dana Milbank, "Goodyear's Go-Getting Gault Just Never Seems to Tire," *The Wall Street Journal*, January 28, 1992, p. B4.
5. Dana Milbank, "Independent Goodyear Dealers Rebel," *The Wall Street Journal*, July 8, 1992, p. B2.
6. *The Wall Street Journal*, September 7, 1988, p. B6.
7. John G. Gaski and John R. Nevin, "The Differential Effects of Exercised and Unexercised Power Sources in a Marketing Channel," *Journal of Marketing Research*, Vol. 22 (May 1985), p. 140.
8. Gary L. Frazier and John O. Summers, "Interfirm Influence Strategies and Their Application within Distribution Channels," *Journal of Marketing*, Vol. 48 (Summer 1984), pp. 43–55.
9. *The Wall Street Journal*, June 1, 1988, p. 30.
10. Rita Koselka, "Distribution Revolution," *Forbes*, May 25, 1992, pp. 54–61.
11. Peter F. Drucker, "The Economy's Power Shift," *The Wall Street Journal*, September 24, 1992, p. A16.

SUGGESTED READING

Dant, Rejiu P., and Patrick L. Schul. "Conflict Resolution Processes in Contractual Channels of Distribution," *Journal of Marketing*, Vol. 56 (January 1992), pp. 38–54.

Frazier, Gary, and Raymond C. Rody. "The Use of Influence Strategies in Interfirm Relationships in Industrial Product Channels," *Journal of Marketing*, Vol. 55 (January 1991), pp. 52–69.

Hallen, Lars, Jan Johanson, and Nazeem Seyed-Mohamed. "Interfirm Adaptation in Business Relationships," *Journal of Marketing*, Vol. 55 (April 1991), pp. 29–37.

O'Callaghan, Ramon, Patrick J. Kaufmann, and Benn R. Konsynski. "Adoption Correlates and Share Effects of Electronic Data Interchange Systems in Marketing Channels," *Journal of Marketing*, Vol. 56 (April 1992), pp. 45–56.

FURTHER READING

Ballou, Ronald H. *Business Logistics Management: Planning and Control*, 4th ed. (Englewood Cliffs, NJ: Prentice-Hall, 1992).

Coyle, John J., and Edward J. Bardi. *The Management of Business Logistics*, 5th ed. (St. Paul, MN: West, 1992).

Nielsen Marketing Research. *Category Management* (Lincolnwood, IL: NTC Business Books, 1992).

Rosenbloom, Bert. *Marketing Channels*, 5th ed. (Chicago, IL: Dryden Press, 1994).

Stern, Louis W., and Adel I. El-Ansary. *Marketing Channels*, 3rd ed. (Englewood Cliffs, NJ: Prentice-Hall, 1987).

QUESTIONS

1. While American firms are consolidating and closing down field warehouses, Matsushita of Japan is constructing five new central inventory warehouses in the United States. Matsushita already has 50 local distribution centers in the United States to handle its Panasonic, Quasar, and Technics brands of electronic goods. Why does Matsushita have so many distribution centers in the United States, and why is it adding more?

2. Medco, of Fair Lawn, New Jersey, is the largest mail-order prescription drug firm in the United States. Sales in 1992 rose to $1.3 billion. Why has Medco been so successful? Why would the pharmaceutical companies sell to Medco when these sales could hurt sales through traditional retail pharmacies?

3. Why was the franchise form of distribution able to expand during the recession years of 1991 and 1992 while the rest of the U.S. economy slumped?

4. The Jones Company was trying to decide whether to continue using independent sales reps or to replace them with company salespeople. The firm produced a line of ceramic dinnerware that was sold by 15 rep organizations employing 55 salespeople to contact 12,100 retail stores. Management felt that the reps were not giving Jones' dinnerware enough attention, particularly in the large department stores. Annual sales of the Jones Company were $5.2 million. The company liked to have its retail accounts contacted every six weeks. The reps were paid 10 percent of sales, although 12 percent was typical for this type of merchandise in other firms.

    Compare the advantages of reps over company salespeople for making personal contacts. How many company salespeople would be needed to call on the retail accounts? Should Jones switch to company salespeople? If not, what should it do to improve the performance of the present reps?

5. SuperValu, Inc., of Minneapolis has purchased Wetterau, Inc., of Hazelton, Missouri, for $643 million. The combined firm is the nation's largest food wholesaler. Before the merger, SuperValu serviced 2600 independent grocery stores in 31 states plus 105 of its own stores, including its deep-discount Cub Foods stores. Wetterau owned 160 retail stores and distributed to 2800 independent grocers. Why are mergers taking place among America's wholesalers?

6. The Carter Company marketed a line of hair dryers and related equipment throughout the United States. Current sales were $25 million a year, and profits were $1 million. The company's distribution channel is shown in Figure 11-6. Carter was having trouble motivating distributor salespeople to push its prod-

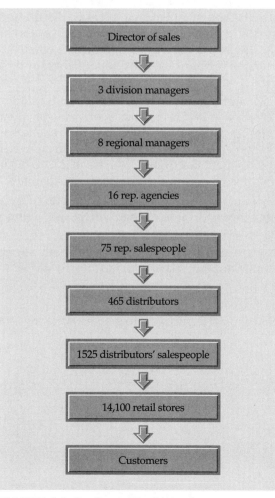

FIGURE 11-6 Carter Distribution System

ucts and service the shelves in retail stores. As a result, Carter's sales were suffering from frequent "stockouts" and sloppy displays of merchandise.

Why did Carter employ such a long, complicated channel of distribution? Should Carter take over and handle the store contact work itself? What should Carter do to motivate distributor salespeople more effectively? Under what conditions are consignment and franchise distribution most appropriate?

7. Apple Computer, Inc., is now selling its lowest-priced personal computers through CompUSA, Inc., the nation's largest chain of computer discount stores. Why is it doing this? Won't the change create problems with Apple's regular computer dealers?

8. During a recent Japanese business recession, growth in the sales of imported American liquor declined from 18 percent a year in 1985–1990 to only 1.3 percent in 1991. Also, gray market exporters are buying American brands in other countries and shipping them directly to Japanese discount stores. Seagram's Chivas Regal can be bought at Sakaiya, a Tokyo discount store, for $30 a bottle compared with $64 at official department and liquor stores. As long as customers are buying Chivas, why should Seagram care whether it comes from gray market importers or regular dealers? Should Seagram do anything about this problem, and if so, what?

9. Hewlett-Packard and Motorola have traditionally sold their high-powered workstations directly to engineers and technicians or to value-added resellers that market complex packages of computer equipment, software, and service. They recently agreed to sell workstations through mass market dealers MicroAge and Intelligent Electronics, which sell PCs to businesses. Explain why they are making this change in their distribution channels.

10. What factors account for the recent productivity gains observed in U.S. channels of distribution? How will these changes affect marketing planning by manufacturers, wholesalers, and retailers?

11. Pet superstores are collaring customers from both supermarkets and small shops. How should supermarkets respond? Small shops?

12. Denny's is a chain of mid-priced family dining restaurants. It was saddled in 1993 with old, drab outlets, financial losses, and findings of bias against black customers. What should Denny's do to get its marketing strategy back on track?

Chapter 12

Personal Selling and Sales Force Management

In the world of business, it is useless to be a creative thinker unless you can sell what you create. Customers cannot be expected to recognize a good idea unless it is presented by a good salesperson.

ANONYMOUS

Informative and persuasive marketing communications encourage customers to buy your goods or services. The three principal means of communications, in order of the strength of their relationship with the customer, are the sales force, direct marketing, and advertising. Supporting activities include sales promotion and public relations. These communication methods interact to build sales. While we discuss them in separate chapters, they must be carefully coordinated to assist the customer—giving rise to the term *integrated marketing communications.*

Marketing goods and services depends on personal contacts made by sales representatives, and these calls represent a key channel of communication for the firm. Personal selling accounts for over 50 percent of the marketing budget, and individual sales calls cost over $200.[1] Thus you need to manage sales resources effectively if you expect to have a successful marketing program.

The sequence of activities that guides *sales managers* in the creation and administration of a sales program is shown in Figure 12-1. This general model divides the sales management process into five major components. First, you must come up with a selling strategy and a plan of action. This selling strategy must, of course, be in close alignment with your company's marketing strategy. Then you have to locate target customers and recruit, train, motivate, compensate, and organize a field sales force. The next phase of the sales management process is concerned with the interactions between customers and salespeople. This dialogue is influenced by the buyer's needs, the salesperson's skills and knowledge, and ethical factors. The results of successful salesperson–customer interactions are orders,

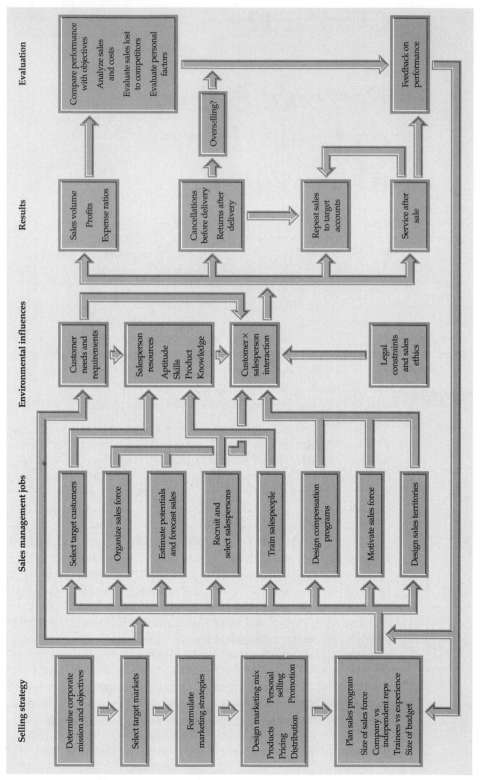

FIGURE 12-1 The Sales Management Process

profits, repeat customers, and after-sale service. When the sales process breaks down, the result can be order cancellations and merchandise returns. Your final management task involves monitoring the performance of the sales organization that has been created. This means that you must design an information system to assemble data on current sales operations and set appropriate standards for control purposes.

THE ROLE OF PERSONAL SELLING

Sales managers help define the role that personal selling plays in marketing programs. In some door-to-door companies, such as Avon and Fuller Brush, personal selling dominates the marketing program almost to the exclusion of other forms of promotion. At the other extreme, book clubs and mail-order firms rely entirely on advertising and employ no field salespeople at all. Thus, you must decide how to balance personal selling with direct marketing, advertising, and sales promotion to achieve the goals of your organization. Next, you have to determine the source of field sales help.

Reps versus Own Sales Force

Your first decision as sales manager is whether to hire your own sales force or to hire salespeople from independent rep organizations. Some firms adopt a strategy of spending all available cash on product development and promotion, so field sales work is left to independent representatives. Because reps are paid a percentage of sales, the companies pay only when sales are made, thereby avoiding the fixed costs of hiring, training, and supervising their own sales force. Furthermore, the firm can capitalize on the reps' already established relationships with the trade.

The use of a company sales force offers several advantages over the use of independent reps. For example, firms can exert more control over the activities of their own field personnel and can train them to sell according to fixed guidelines. In addition, inexperienced people can be hired and paid relatively low salaries, and these fixed costs help to keep expenses down as sales increase over time. A company's own salespeople spend all their time selling the firm's products rather than dividing their efforts among the products of several firms.

The choice between a rep strategy and a hire strategy is made on the basis of a comparison of costs and benefits. When a firm is small, with limited financial and personnel resources, it may make more sense to hire independent reps to do the selling. This approach conserves cash and provides more flexibility for growth. However, as your product line grows, the firm eventually reaches a point where it is financially wiser to hire and train your own salespeople. Thus you must choose between the variable costs, flexibility, and special services offered by reps and the fixed costs and greater control offered by a company sales force.

The Selling Job

Personal selling can be thought of as a sequence of eight tasks (Figure 12-2). Most organizations do not have enough customers, and it is the responsibility of the field sales force to go out and discover who may need your products so as to identify new prospects. Once they are located, they must be qualified to make sure that they can use what you are selling and have the financial resources to pay for it. Then salespeople have to prepare what they will say to the prospect during the sales call. Next, the salesperson must overcome the obstacles erected by secretaries and assistants to gain an audience with the person with buying authority. At this point, the salesperson should try to find out something about the customer's needs. Sometimes hints can be gained ahead of time from trade gossip or talks with shop personnel. This *needs analysis* leads to *application selling*. The salesperson should deliver a sales presentation tailored to fit the special needs of the prospect. This is called *adaptive selling*.

Every sales presentation encounters objections from the prospect, and the salesperson must be ready with counterarguments. Salespeople frequently fail to try to

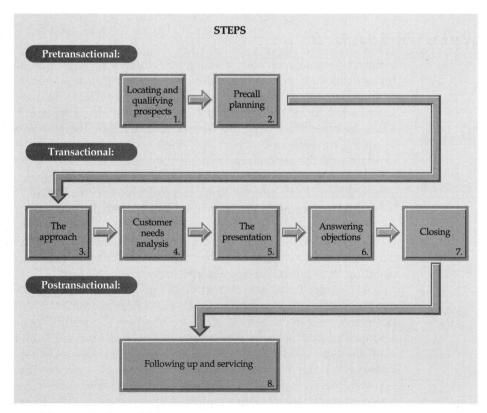

FIGURE 12-2 The Selling Job

close a sale after they have made their presentation. Salespeople do not want to be turned down, and customers can't be expected to volunteer orders. This means that sales managers must train salespeople to ask for the order. The average number of calls needed to close a sale varies by industry and by the method of selling. Relatively few calls are necessary for those who sell to distributors; the highest number are required for those selling directly to industry.

After-sale service is important in cementing relations with customers. Service work is designed to help customers solve problems related to the goods and services sold by the firm. This includes activities such as expediting orders, obtaining repair parts, setting up displays, stocking shelves, taking inventories, and training dealer personnel. Equipment salespeople, for example, often help customers rearrange machinery and personnel to improve efficiency. After the role of personal selling has been determined, managers must decide on the ideal number of salespeople to hire.

HOW MANY SALESPEOPLE?

Finding the right size for a sales force is complicated by variations in salespeople and compensation plans. However, a rough idea of the personnel needed can be obtained by looking at costs and the number of customers.

What Can I Afford?

The size of the sales force is often a compromise between what the firm can afford and the total number of people needed to call on all existing and potential customers. An example of the "What can I afford?" approach suggests that a firm with $20 million in annual volume might be able to allocate 5 percent for field sales, or about $1 million a year. If supervisory expenses ran about 20 percent of selling costs, the firm would have $800,000 to hire salespeople. Assuming that salespeople cost $40,000 a year each for salary and expenses, the company could afford to acquire 20 field salespeople. The size of the sales force is thus a direct function of the amount budgeted for field selling. The main problem with this approach is that it does not consider market potential or customers' needs.

The Workload Approach

The workload method of determining the size of the sales force is based on decisions regarding the frequency and length of calls needed to sell to existing and potential customers. An estimate of the total number of salespeople required using this approach can be made with this formula:

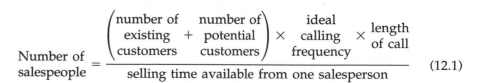

$$\text{Number of salespeople} = \frac{\left(\begin{array}{c}\text{number of}\\\text{existing}\\\text{customers}\end{array} + \begin{array}{c}\text{number of}\\\text{potential}\\\text{customers}\end{array}\right) \times \begin{array}{c}\text{ideal}\\\text{calling}\\\text{frequency}\end{array} \times \begin{array}{c}\text{length}\\\text{of call}\end{array}}{\text{selling time available from one salesperson}} \qquad (12.1)$$

For example, if the firm had 3000 existing customers and 2250 potential clients to be called on five times a year for 2 hours (including travel time) and available selling time per salesperson was 1500 hours, the size of the sales force would be

$$\text{Number of salespeople} = \frac{(3000 + 2250) \times 5 \times 2}{1500} = 35 \qquad (12.2)$$

This estimate of 35 salespeople is based on the assumption that the desired frequency and length of calls are the same for all customers. If it is decided that these should vary according to the size and type of customer, then the formula can be modified accordingly. Note that the number of salespeople based on workload estimates is larger than the number derived using the percentage of sales method. This points out the biggest weakness of the workload approach: its failure to consider the costs and profits associated with different levels of customer service. Because ideal call frequencies are based on executive judgment, you never really know if you have set the number of calls to maximize profits. Procedures used at Loctite Corporation to set the size of the sales force are described in the Marketing in Action box 12-1.

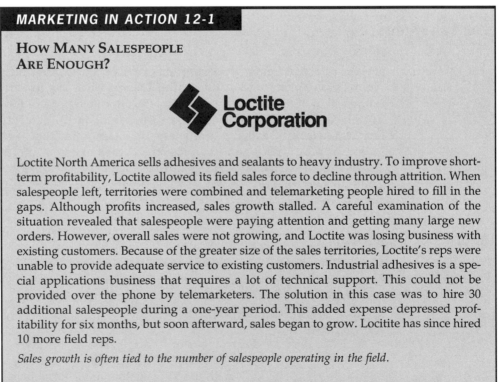

MARKETING IN ACTION 12-1

HOW MANY SALESPEOPLE ARE ENOUGH?

Loctite Corporation

Loctite North America sells adhesives and sealants to heavy industry. To improve short-term profitability, Loctite allowed its field sales force to decline through attrition. When salespeople left, territories were combined and telemarketing people hired to fill in the gaps. Although profits increased, sales growth stalled. A careful examination of the situation revealed that salespeople were paying attention and getting many large new orders. However, overall sales were not growing, and Loctite was losing business with existing customers. Because of the greater size of the sales territories, Loctite's reps were unable to provide adequate service to existing customers. Industrial adhesives is a special applications business that requires a lot of technical support. This could not be provided over the phone by telemarketers. The solution in this case was to hire 30 additional salespeople during a one-year period. This added expense depressed profitability for six months, but soon afterward, sales began to grow. Locitite has since hired 10 more field reps.

Sales growth is often tied to the number of salespeople operating in the field.

Source: "How Lean Is Too Lean?" *Sales & Marketing Management* (January 1988), p. 53.

Sales Force Turnover

The size of the sales force is also influenced by the problem of personnel turnover. If salespeople are constantly leaving, then the number of players on the team is apt to vary as you scramble to fill vacancies. Turnover is calculated by dividing the number of separations during a year by the average size of the sales force. Thus, if 15 people leave each year and the size of the sales force is 150, then the turnover rate is

$$\text{Turnover rate} = \frac{\text{separations per year}}{\text{average size of sales force}} = \frac{15}{150} = 10\% \qquad (12.3)$$

Turnover is important because empty territories mean lost sales, and high turnover raises hiring and training costs. For example, assume that it costs $25,000 to recruit and train each sales force replacement. This means that a turnover of 30 percent in a sales force of 150 people would cost the firm $1,125,000 (0.30 × 150 × $25,000 = $1,125,000).

The high costs of turnover usually mean that sales managers try to keep this factor as low as possible. Turnover can be reduced by balancing territories and by improving the financial rewards paid to salespeople. Another way to lower turnover is to provide several levels of sales positions so that employees have multiple promotion opportunities within the sales organization. A third way is to offer a variety of nonfinancial rewards such as trips, prizes for sales contests, plaques, trophies, and recognition awards. All these techniques are designed to make salespeople feel better about their jobs and to reduce the attractiveness of outside offers.

Although you are often interested in reducing personnel turnover, this factor is a subtle control variable, and it can be too low as well as too high. For instance, when a sales force does not have any turnover, there is immediate suspicion that the salespeople are overpaid or are not being supervised. A lack of turnover may also signal that salespeople are all of the same age. The situation can be serious because they are likely to retire at the same time, and the firm will have to recruit and train an entirely new sales force. The ideal situation, of course, is to have salespeople of various ages so that a few retire each year and new blood can be added on a regular basis. For example, if the average sales career spans 20 years, then 5 percent of the sales force would normally retire each year. Because some people leave the sales force before they retire—because of promotions, resignations, or dismissals, for example—a turnover rate of 10 to 15 percent a year can be considered normal. However, much higher turnover rates are found among first-year employees, and it is not uncommon for direct sales organizations like Amway and Fuller Brush to experience turnover rates of 100 to 250 percent per year. Beyond the problem of size is the issue of how to build an efficient sales organization.

ORGANIZING THE SALES FORCE

In small firms with only a few employees, the sales force usually reports directly to the president of the company. However, when firms grow larger, there is often an opportunity to raise productivity by adding sales managers. An example of a line sales organization employing several sales managers is shown in Figure 12-3. In this case, 12 salespeople report to each district sales manager. The number of people reporting to each sales manager, or span of control, varies from 8 to 1 to 14 to 1 or more, depending on the needs of the firm. Narrow spans of control are used for expensive technical products, and wider spans of control are used for simpler products and by firms that want to minimize supervisory expenses. The district sales manager takes over responsibility for hiring, training, and motivating salespeople; designing sales territories; and evaluating sales performance.

As sales organizations grow larger, it is usually necessary to hire additional staff personnel. For example, Figure 12-4 shows staff recruiters, trainers, and sales analysts reporting to a general sales manager. These staff specialists act as advisors to the general sales manager and interface with the regional and district sales managers.

Field salespeople are usually organized around geographic control units. Each salesperson is given an area, and these areas are grouped into districts and regions headed by sales managers. With a straight geographic orientation, salespeople sell all products to all customers in their territories (Figure 12-4, Western Region). Geographic organization produces the smallest territories and is the most economical way to structure a sales force. Only one person calls on each customer, and there is no cross-travel.

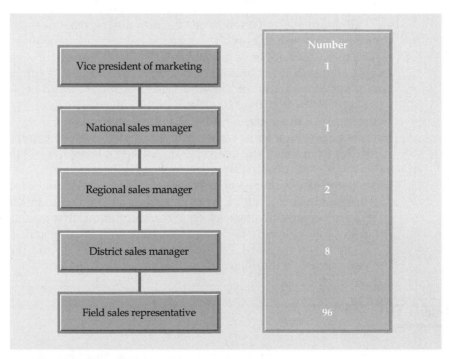

FIGURE 12-3   A Line Sales Organization

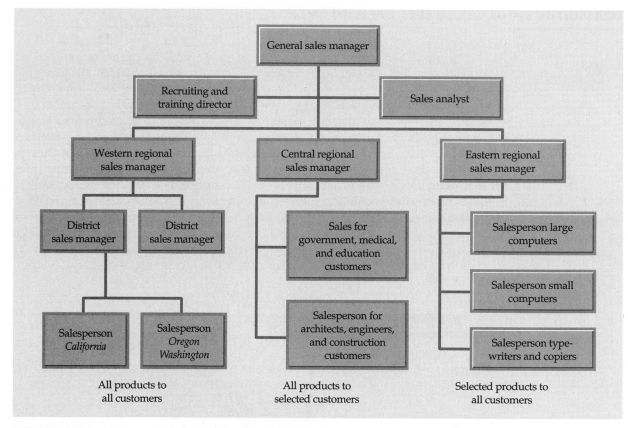

FIGURE 12-4 A Line and Staff Sales Organization Using Geographic, Customer, and Product Specialization

Organizing salespeople around customers makes sense when customers have unique purchasing requirements (Figure 12-4, Central Region). For example, NCR uses a customer approach, with one sales team selling data entry systems to banks and a second group selling to other retailers. When companies have a diverse, highly technical product line, it may be desirable to hire salespeople to sell groups of products (Figure 12-4, Eastern Region). Under this plan, salespeople are product specialists, and it is unlikely that buyers will become bored during sales presentations. Salespeople who focus on groups of customers or products tend to work larger territories, and the resulting cross-travel increases selling expenses. To help control costs, customer and product salespeople often operate out of district sales offices that are organized on a geographic basis. Geographic-, product-, and customer-oriented sales forces have all been used successfully, and some firms switch back and forth, depending on the needs of the times.

RECRUITING AND SELECTING SALESPEOPLE

After a firm has decided on the basic dimensions of the sales organization, you are in a position to hire salespeople. Basically, two recruiting strategies are available. You can recruit experienced salespeople who can be placed in the field immediately, or you can hire inexperienced people and teach them the necessary product knowledge and sales skills. Although experienced salespeople must be paid higher wages, they will begin producing orders sooner and in larger amounts than new trainees. Small firms selling technical products often hire experienced people because they do not have the time, personnel, or facilities to train new employees. Larger companies, on the other hand, have the resources and the desire to train new salespeople to follow directions and act in a prescribed manner with customers. One of the risks of hiring experienced sales personnel is that they may have learned some tricks to advance their own wages at the expense of their new employer. Also, experienced salespeople who have changed jobs in the past are more apt to be hired away by competitors. The issue of whether salespeople are made or born is discussed in Marketing in Action box 12-2.

MARKETING IN ACTION 12-2

ARE SALESPEOPLE BORN OR MADE?

The age-old question of whether good salespeople are born or made has yet to be resolved. When sales and marketing executives are asked directly, they maintain, by a margin of 7 to 1, that good salespeople are made, not born. At the same time, many of these same executives are quick to describe men and women they know who are born salespeople. They point out that it is difficult to teach ego, personal drive, or the persistence that gets the sale. You have to hire for these characteristics.

When the executives were asked what is most predictive of a salesperson's success, half of them said experience. Also, 68 percent said that the first place they look for new blood is their competition. These results show there is a strong tendency to hire people with outstanding selling skills and related experience rather than hiring novices and molding them with training. For example, Information Systems of America sells financial applications software and makes a practice of hiring people with related selling experience. These people are able to master the product line quickly, and training costs have been slashed to $3000 per person.

Hiring experienced salespeople can boost revenue quickly.

Source: Arthur Bragg, "Are Good Salespeople Born or Made?" *Sales & Marketing Management* (September 1988), pp. 74–78.

Determining Qualifications

An important first step in recruiting is to analyze the job and prepare a list of qualifications needed for successful performance of the work. Careful study of customers, amount of travel, number of accounts, amount of paperwork, and so on will allow you to set minimum standards for age, education, experience, and other factors. A common error is to set these standards higher than necessary. For example, firms will often demand that salespeople be college graduates even when the job may be repetitive and offer little chance for advancement. Under these conditions, college graduates are likely to become bored and move on to something more challenging. These problems can be minimized if job qualifications are based on the characteristics of salespeople who have achieved high performance ratings.

Sources of new salespeople vary with the job to be filled, but young trainees are often recruited from schools and colleges, from employment agencies, and from among present employees. Experienced salespeople, on the other hand, are more likely to come from newspaper ads, recommendations by company or business associates, and suggestions by dealers or suppliers. A good way to evaluate sources of sales recruits is to keep track of how well candidates perform after they have been hired. Hiring top salespeople from competitors is tempting, but extensive recruiting from this source can be dangerous. Some stockbrokers and accounting firms have been sued for stealing salespeople from competitors. Also, competitors may retaliate by hiring away some of your salespeople, and everyone will have higher sales expenses.

Screening Procedures

Once you have accumulated a pool of candidates, the next step is to select and hire the best salespersons (Figure 12-5). This job is complicated by a need to fill open territories quickly and by the fear that poorly selected salespeople will permanently damage your firm's relations with important customers. As a result, companies spend more time screening applicants for sensitive industrial sales positions than they do for more routine selling jobs. In the case of retail delivery people, door-to-door salespeople, and insurance agents, turnover is high, and it doesn't pay to spend a lot of time searching for the perfect candidate. With these jobs, the best policy is to place recruits on the job as quickly as possible and let the "sink or swim" policy identify those with the most potential.

There are no hard-and-fast rules guaranteed to match job requirements with the best candidates. You have to weigh the job qualifications against the background of the applicants and make a decision. Normally, candidates fill out application blanks, go through a series of interviews, have references checked, and complete aptitude and psychological tests (Figure 12-5). Note that you have to make an offer before you can schedule a physical examination. The new federal Americans with Disabilities Act prevents you from using information from physical exams in the selection of sales help. You can, of course, reject people who have been offered jobs but fail the physical examination.

Application blanks are a standard screening device for sales positions because

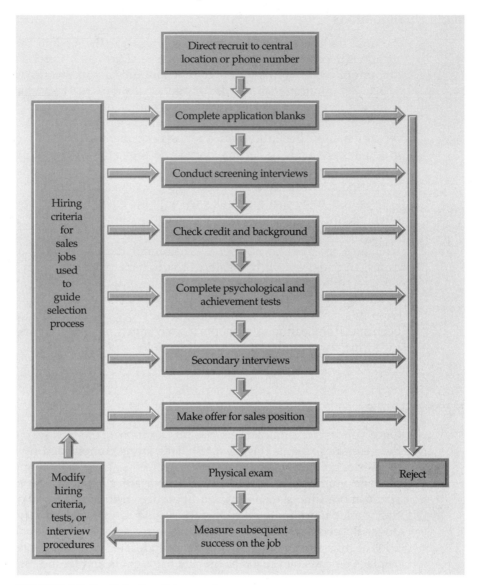

FIGURE 12-5 Selecting Salespeople

it is essential that salespeople be able to read and write. They also provide useful background information on educational level and experience that can be explored during personal interviews. However, federal regulations prohibit questions related to age, sex, race, marital status, financial position, national origin, and other subjects. As a result, sales managers tend to place more emphasis on personal interviews and testing to screen sales candidates. Hiring tests are perfectly legal, but they have to be validated to show a correlation between test scores and job performance.

Another way to evaluate sales candidates is to send out candidates with a regular salesperson to see how they react to actual field selling conditions. In one insurance company, candidates selected after exposure to conditions in the field were much more successful than salespeople selected by other methods.

Recruiting new salespeople is risky, and organizations must expect that some people will not perform up to expectations. Selection criteria must be flexible enough to allow a few mistakes so that good candidates are not rejected because of a minor problem. One way to profit from hiring mistakes is to conduct exit interviews to determine what can be done to improve hiring procedures. In addition, persons who fail in a sales role may be able to perform in a superior fashion if they are transferred to some other division of the company.

MOTIVATING AND COMPENSATING SALESPEOPLE

Salespeople are rewarded with compensation and other benefits to help inspire them to do a better job. The ideal compensation plan motivates salespeople to achieve both their own goals and the company's objectives at the same time. Unfortunately, the natural desire of salespeople to make money for themselves often conflicts with the firm's need to control sales expenses. Thus you have the difficult task of designing compensation programs that motivate the sales force without financially ruining the company.

Straight Salary

Perhaps the simplest reward system for salespeople involves paying a fixed amount each pay period. *Straight salary* rewards people for time spent on job responsibilities and was used by 8.7 percent of the firms reported in Table 12-1. The major benefits of salary are more control over wage levels and generally lower compensation for field salespeople. For example, independent sales reps on salary make an average of $47,700 compared to $185,000 for those on straight commission.[2] With a salary plan, wages are a fixed cost to the firm, and the proportion of wage expense tends to

TABLE 12-1
Use of Compensation Plans by Size of Firm

Company Size	Proportion of Surveyed Firms This Size	Percentage of Companies Using		
		Salary	Straight Commission	Combination
Less than $5MM	39.0	2.0	22.0	76.0
$5–25MM	31.0	19.0	5.0	76.0
$25–100MM	15.0	4.0	4.0	92.0
$100–250MM	6.0	6.0	6.0	88.0
Over $250MM	9.0	12.0	6.0	82.0
Weighted average		8.7%	11.6%	79.7%

Source: Sales Force Compensation (Chicago: Dartnell Corporation, 1989), p. 35.

decrease as sales increase. Another advantage of salary is that it allows maximum control over salespeople's activities. Salaried employees can be directed to sell particular products, call on certain customers, and perform a variety of nonselling jobs for customers. Because a salesperson's income is not tied to the volume of business done with specific customers, it is easier for the sales manager to divide territories and reassign salespeople to new areas. Further, salaried salespeople tend to exhibit higher loyalty to the firm than employees under other plans. Salary plans are common in industrial selling, where service and engineering skills are more important in the long run than having salespeople press for an immediate order. Salary is also effective when salespersons spend their time calling on retailers to set up displays, take inventory, and arrange shelves. Pharmaceutical detail people, for example, are not expected to make direct sales and are paid a salary to strengthen relations with doctors and pharmacists.

Because pay is not tied directly to performance, salary systems are often criticized for failing to provide incentives for extra effort. Some cynical sales managers respond by noting that salary plans have a strong incentive because those who do well keep their jobs. Others point out that semiannual salary adjustments can be used to encourage and reward outstanding performance.

Commission Plans

Salespeople on commission are paid a percentage of the sales or gross profits that they generate. The straight commission plan rewards people for their accomplishments rather than for their time or efforts. Also, salespeople who are paid commissions typically make more money than with other wage programs. A survey of 85 firms revealed that the average maximum commission wage was $99,800 compared to $63,998 for those on straight salary.[3] Higher wages tend to attract better-qualified applicants and provide a strong incentive to work hard. However, Table 12-1 indicates that straight commission plans are used by a relatively small number of firms. In this study, 11.6 percent reported using straight commissions. Some firms combine a draw with straight commission so that salespeople will have some stability of income in the face of an erratic sales pattern.

The advantages of a commission plan are shown in Figure 12-6. Notice that when sales per person are low, the costs of the commission plan are low. In contrast, the fixed-cost salary plan ($24,000) gives higher costs when sales are low. Companies that want to minimize their financial risk can choose variable-cost commission plans. Firms that want to minimize compensation costs as sales grow use fixed-cost salary programs. Thus, in Figure 12-6, when sales are less than $300,000 per year, the commission plan results in lower total costs for the company. But when sales exceed $300,000 a year, the straight salary plan costs less. Thus small firms use the commission plan to get started and then tend to shift to the salary plan when they grow big.

Despite some obvious advantages, straight commission has a number of drawbacks. The major problem is that sales managers have little control over commission salespeople, and nonselling activities are apt to be neglected. Commission salespeople are tempted to sell themselves rather than the company, as well as to service only the best accounts in their territories. Because salespeople's wages are directly related

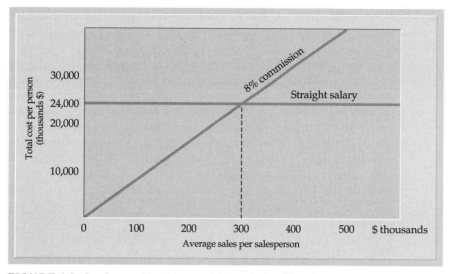

FIGURE 12-6 Comparing Salary and Commission Plans for Field Sales Representatives

to sales to particular accounts, salespeople are often reluctant to have their territories changed in any way.

Combination Plans

The most common compensation plans for salespeople combine a base salary with a commission or bonus (Table 12-1). The base salary provides salespeople with income security and the commission and bonus give added incentives to meet the company's objectives.

A primary benefit of these plans is that they allow wages to be tailored to the needs of a particular firm. If an organization wanted a modest incentive, the plan could be designed so that 80 percent of the compensation was salary and 20 percent was earned by commissions or bonuses. Firms that needed more push to move their products could raise the incentive portion to 40 percent or more.

Another advantage is that commission rates can be manipulated to achieve a variety of goals. Some firms start paying commissions on the first dollar of sales; others establish base points or quotas that must be reached before commissions or bonuses are paid. Many organizations vary commission rates by sales volume or by the profitability of groups of products. For example, one industrial fastener company pays a base salary of about $30,000 a year, plus a commission that varies from 0.3 to 1 percent of sales and a discretionary bonus for reps who show good sales increases.

When products are largely presold by advertising, like many consumer items, it does not make sense to pay a salary plus a commission to push for added volume. Under these conditions, it is cheaper to pay a salary plus a bonus to get the job done. Bonus payments are drawn from a pool of funds based on the overall sales or profitability of the firm and are usually paid at the end of the year.

Gross Margin Plans

The main objective in creating sales compensation programs is to maximize the profits of the firm. However, when incentive payments are based on a percentage of the sales of each product, it is unlikely that salespeople will sell the mix of items that will lead to the most profits. Salespeople usually do not have data on costs and

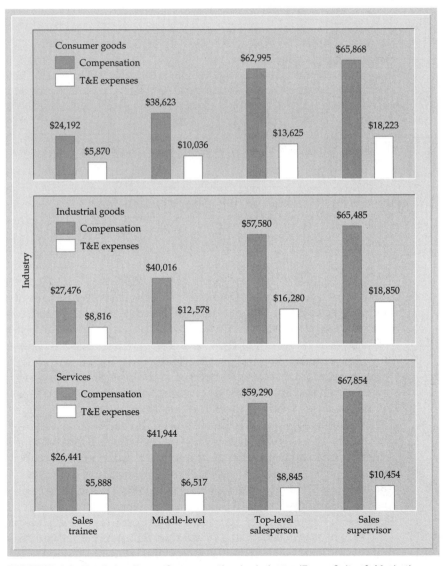

FIGURE 12-7 Sales Force Compensation by Industry (From *Sales & Marketing Management*, [June 22, 1992], p. 67)

economies of scale. In addition, they look at the incentive rates and emphasize those items that are easy to sell and carry the highest commissions.

An alternative approach is to set commission rates as a percentage of the gross margin on each product. When salespeople and the company share the same pool of money (realized gross margin), salespeople earn more and the firm generates optimum profits. Automobile and medical products salespeople are often paid a percentage of the gross margin on each sale so that they will bargain with customers to obtain the highest possible profit for themselves and their employer.

Gross margin plans have not been successful in all industries. Certain-Teed Corporation, for example, tried paying its building materials salespeople a commission on gross margin but was forced to shift to a salary-plus-incentive program. The problem arose because the salespeople were unable to distinguish between making a 10 percent margin on a $1 million order and a 20 percent margin on a $500,000 order. These two orders seem to be equivalent because the company makes $100,000 on each and the salesperson collects 15 percent or $15,000 on both. If the selling time is similar, the salesperson is likely to work for the glory of the million-dollar order. However, the company is better off with the $500,000 sale and its 20 percent gross margin. The smaller order means lower inventory carrying costs and a reduced drain on raw materials and plant capacity.

Travel and Entertainment Expenses

In addition to designing compensation plans, sales managers are expected to build expense reimbursement programs that encourage sales reps to contact and entertain customers. These plans need to be generous enough so that salespeople will go out and meet customers but not so liberal that salespeople become rich. Typical expense payments and wages for several classes of salespeople are shown in Figure 12-7. Note that T&E amounted to 16 percent of wages in service industries, 25 percent in consumer goods, and 30 percent in industrial products. Well-designed expense plans help recruit, motivate, and retain field salespeople.

DESIGNING EFFICIENT SALES TERRITORIES

Dividing customers into geographic territories improves both market coverage and customer relations. Territories encourage salespeople to get to know their customers' needs and allow managers to evaluate sales performance more easily. Sales territories are usually constructed from groups of present and potential customers and assigned to individual salespeople to help ensure adequate customer contact, minimize selling costs, and simplify control. Territory design is a never-ending task because customers, products, and salespeople change regularly and territorial boundaries must be adjusted to meet the new conditions.

The Buildup Method

The most popular technique employed to create sales territories is known as the *buildup* method. This approach can be thought of as a five-part decision program:

1. Select the geographic control unit.
2. Decide on allocation criteria.
3. Choose starting points.
4. Combine adjacent control units.
5. Compare territories on allocation criteria.

The first step is to select appropriate geographic control units that can be combined to form sales territories. These units usually are counties, but they can be states, zip code areas, or census tracts. Control units must be small enough to allow flexibility in setting boundaries, yet not so small that the geographic areas lose their identity. States, for example, are often too large for effective combination into sales territories, and census tracts may be unnecessarily small. The selection of appropriate control units for individual companies depends on the availability of data on population, sales, and prospective customers in each of the areas. This information is readily available for political units, and these areas have the advantage of clearly defined boundaries.

Allocation Criteria   You need some guiding principles to set priorities and simplify the process of grouping control units into territories. An equitable solution would be to divide up the total market to minimize differences in the number of present customers per territory and in the amount of sales potential per territory. Not only is the principle of equal opportunity more acceptable to the American way of life, but it could also lead to better morale and greater productivity to earn an adequate living, and equality among territories can help make this possible. In addition, similar territories make it easier for the sales manager to identify and reward outstanding performance. If territories are essentially the same, differences in productivity can be attributed to individual effort.

Combining Control Units   The process of creating sales territories is straightforward once you decide on a geographic control unit and a set of allocation principles. Suppose that you have the problem of dividing a territory that has become too large for one person to handle. A map of the territory is shown in Figure 12-8a, with the numbers of present accounts in each county labeled. The salesperson currently assigned to the territory lives in Brockton. A logical home base for the second salesperson is Hillsdale, located in the west center of the territory. If these cities are used as starting points, new territories can be constructed by adding and subtracting adjacent counties until all the counties are assigned and the number of customers is the same for both territories.

One solution to this problem is shown in Figure 12-8b. Note that the heavy concentration of customers in the Brockton area has produced one small territory in

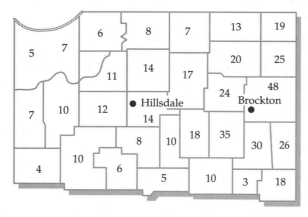

(a)

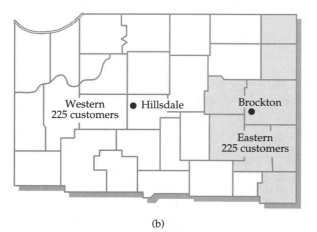

(b)

FIGURE 12-8 Dividing a Large Territory

the eastern region and one very large territory in the west. Although the two new territories have the same number of customers (225), the western territory requires considerably more travel because the customers are more scattered. In addition, the western territory is likely to have greater sales potential than the small eastern territory.

Compare Sales Territories   After the manager makes an initial allocation of control units to starting points, he or she compares territories using other criteria. For example, if a set of territories is designed so that each has the same number of customers, the manager or analyst would then calculate the square miles in each territory to see how they compare. If there is an imbalance, the analyst would look at counties on the borders of the territories to see if some switching could improve the initial allocation. Balancing new territories on several important criteria, such as customers, potential, and size, is often difficult; computers can make the job easier.

Designing Territories by Computer

Computer models are now routinely used to help managers design sales territories. Sales forces that are growing rapidly or have a large number of people can save a great deal of time by building territories with computer programs. Sales managers are generally pleased with the computer territories. They also believe that the solutions are imaginative and realistic and, at the same time, relieve them of a major clerical burden.

Computer models have been used successfully to build territories for pharmaceutical representatives and for salespeople who call on supermarkets. However, although computers can help design efficient sales territories, they sometimes make mistakes when the area to be divided contains natural barriers. The problem is that large rivers, bays, mountain ranges, and swamps are often difficult to cross because of limited numbers of roads and bridges. Computers often assume that roads are there, and this can lead to trouble. One computer-designed sales territory was split down the middle by the Appalachian Trail. This meant that the salesperson would have to spend a great deal of time traveling up and down narrow mountain roads to get from one half of the territory to the other. To avoid these problems, either the

---

MARKETING PRODUCTIVITY 12-1

USING COMPUTERS FOR TERRITORY DESIGN

Dividing up sales territories is a headache for most companies. Stephanie Thompson, manager of marketing programs at Perdue Frederick pharmaceuticals, recalls: "We used to sit down with our district sales managers for days and do a ton of manual calculations to put together our territories." As the company grew in size, it found that it could no longer manage its territories by hand and turned to a microcomputer software package. The mapping software allowed Thompson to reconfigure regions in just half a day instead of the several days she previously needed.

The interactive computer program selected uses data on zip code locations of physicians, current call activities, and major highway routes to build territories. As the territories are put together, they are shown as maps on a computer screen and summarized on spreadsheets. This allows managers to balance territories on potentials and other variables. The computer-generated territories are fine-tuned during meetings with regional and district managers. Although "the software is a wonderful thing, nothing takes the place of a district manager's knowledge," according to Thompson.

Perdue Frederick believes that the computerized system works better than the old approach. Salespeople can see that new assignments are fair because objective criteria are used. The company no longer makes the arbitrary assignments of physicians that were common under the old plan. Also, salespeople now get printed maps and lists of physicians to be called on that were not available with the manual program.

The use of computers can lead to better and quicker territory design.

Source: Tom Eisenhart, "Drawing a Map to Better Sales," *Business Marketing* (January 1990), pp. 59–61.

computer has to be told about the natural barriers or other procedures must be adopted in these areas. An example of territory design by computer is given in Marketing Productivity box 12-1.

Territory Planner Plus, published by TTG, Inc., is an example of a commercial design program.[4] This microcomputer program can be purchased for $2995 and used to reallocate territories and draw maps for salespeople. The program has the advantage that territory maps are tied in with spreadsheets that show current potentials, sales, and target number of calls. Any changes made in allocations of control units to territories are automatically reflected in the spreadsheet data. However, although Territory Planner Plus is an interactive program that helps you create territories, it does not find an optimum design. In contrast, the TERRALIGN program, published by Metron, Inc., finds optimal territory alignments by balancing territories on sales potential and other attributes and minimizes travel time.[5] This program sells for $10,000 and up. These examples suggest that programs with various levels of sophistication of territory design are available, and you need to exercise judgment to choose one that meets your needs. A recent survey, for example, turned up 24 different mapping programs that were available for an average of $495.[6]

ALLOCATING SELLING EFFORT

Once sales territories have been designed, you must decide how to employ the sales force to cover different customers and product lines so that total revenue or gross profit is maximized. This has become more important in recent years because of the increased direct cost of an industrial sales call.

The ideal solution would be to devise a model that considered the cost and revenue aspects of allocating sales resources across all possible territory, customer, and product dimensions. Unfortunately, a general solution is not available, and firms must resolve each selling allocation separately. In addition to deciding what customers to call on, salespeople need to plan their sales tours.

Selecting Sales Routes

Careful scheduling can minimize travel time and expenses. One firm has reported that an analysis of driving patterns reduced the travel of salespeople by 15,000 miles a year and allowed each salesperson to make eight more calls a week. Techniques used to schedule and route salespeople have received considerable attention from management scientists, and the issue has become known as the *traveling salesman problem*. The dilemma is usually stated as a search for a route through the territory that visits each customer and returns to the starting point with a minimum expenditure of time or money. The traveling salesman problem is difficult to solve because there are $(n - 1)!$ possible routes to be considered (where n is the number of customers).

A variety of techniques has been employed to search for the best routes for salespeople, including linear programming, integer programming, nonlinear programming, heuristic programming, and branch-and-bound methods. Although a discussion of these procedures is beyond the scope of this book, they all appear to provide good solutions. One disadvantage of these methods is that they require complicated manipulations of travel costs between cities to find the optimal route. A simpler way to find the best sequence of calls is based on a consideration of the location of points in two-dimensional space.

There are four basic rules that should be followed when designing routes through a sales territory:

1. Tours should be circular.
2. Sales tours should never cross.
3. The same route should not be used to go to and from a customer.
4. Customers in neighboring areas should be visited in sequence.

The idea of circular tours is reasonable because salespeople usually start at a home base and then return at the end of the sales trip. Also, if sales tours cross, the salesperson knows that a shorter route was overlooked. Sometimes a salesperson will be forced to use the same route to go to and from a customer because of local road conditions, but this must be avoided when possible.

EVALUATING SALES PERFORMANCE

The evaluation of sales performance is a complex task because salespeople and territories are all different, and field representatives normally spend most of their time away from their supervisors. In addition, salespeople perform a vast array of jobs, and the diversified nature of their work has spawned a host of control measures that can be used to monitor their activities. A further complication is that salespeople are not above manipulating the reward system to increase their own wages rather than maximizing the profits of the firm. Thus, it is your job to design a performance evaluation system that balances all dimensions of the salesperson's job. A computer program that can help managers monitor salespeople is described in Marketing Productivity box 12-2.

Total Revenues

A logical first step in a *sales analysis* is to look at aggregate sales figures for a company or division. To illustrate the process, sales figures for the Bear Computer Company are provided in Table 12-2. Bear seems to be doing well. Sales have increased from $15 million to $26 million in only six years, which represents aggregate sales growth of 73 percent, or 12 percent annually. However, the rate of growth is declining, as indicated by the figures in column 2. For some reason, Bear has been unable to maintain the sales increases that it achieved in earlier years. One common reason for this situation is that slow growth simply reflects general economic conditions. How-

MARKETING PRODUCTIVITY 12-2

USING COMPUTERS TO ELIMINATE PAPERWORK

Sales departments are often the last area in an organization to take advantage of computers. After reviewing sales statistics at RealWorld Corporation, the national sales manager realized the sales force was becoming stagnant. Further research revealed that salespeople were buried in mountains of paper, with lists and tickler files everywhere. The company decided it was time to introduce a computer system for field sales reps. The objective was to make the salespeople more efficient so that they could make more calls and keep better track of existing proposals and accounts. They also wanted the sales managers to have more control over the field reps.

RealWorld looked for a computer program that included tickler reports, lists, a calendar, personal notepad, word processing, calculator, activity reports, proposals, and the ability to generate orders. Existing packages were unable to fill the bill, so RealWorld

> **MARKETING PRODUCTIVITY 12-2 (continued)**
>
> developed its own system. Next, it ran a field test and found that reps using the new program increased sales 16 percent compared to salespeople operating with the old manual system. This success prompted RealWorld to equip all 35 sales reps with laptop computers.
>
> Since the new computer system was installed at RealWorld, the volume of contracts, number of proposals, and dollar sales have increased 10 to 20 percent due to better organization. Leads are handled more rapidly and are no longer lost in the shuffle. Also, sales managers are better able to track the productivity of each rep and to print reports and graphs to monitor results.
>
> *Giving salespeople laptop computers can increase efficiency.*
>
> *Source:* Sam Licciardi, "Paper Pushing Sales Reps Are Less Productive," *Marketing News*, Vol. 24, No. 23, November 12, 1990, p. 15.

ever, industry sales have been expanding rapidly at the same time that Bear's sales gains have fallen off. The resulting impact on market share is shown in column 4. Because of its relatively slow growth, Bear's market position has fallen from 20 percent in 1990 to only 10 percent in 1995. Thus, although Bear's sales have increased 73 percent, its market share has taken a disastrous plunge. The implication is obvious. A sales increase by itself tells only part of the story. Even though sales performance seems adequate, this computer company has performed miserably.

There could be numerous reasons for the drop in market share at Bear Computer. One possibility is that the product itself may be deficient in terms of performance or reliability. Or perhaps the production department was unable to turn out the machines fast enough. Because personal selling is the primary way of getting computers sold, it is a likely problem area. Bear may not have enough salespeople or sales offices, or the sales force may not be calling on the right prospects. A logical next step is to look at performance in individual territories.

TABLE 12-2
Sales Data for Bear Computer Company, 1990–1995

Year	1 Company Volume ($ millions)	2 Percentage Change from Previous Year	3 Industry Volume ($ millions)	4 Company Market Share (%)
1995	$26	+8.3	$260	10.0%
1994	24	+4.3	200	12.0
1993	23	+9.5	150	15.3
1992	21	+16.7	125	16.8
1991	18	+20.0	95	18.9
1990	15	—	75	20.0

Sales by Territory

A breakdown of Bear Computer's sales by territory is shown for the Eastern Sales Division in Table 12-3. At first glance, things look good because dollar sales are up in all four territories. Also, overall growth is 8.3 percent in the current year, which compares favorably with the performance achieved in 1994. The largest dollar increases in sales were achieved in territories 1 and 3, and the weakest performance was in territory 4. However, these results take on a different meaning if the sales manager looks carefully at the sales potential of the four territories.

If actual sales in territory 1 of $825,000 are divided by planned sales of $943,000, the sales manager finds that this territory is running about 13 percent below expectations. Territory 3 has not achieved planned sales even though it has the largest potential of all (32 percent). Territory 4, which had the lowest dollar increase, was still able to sell 102 percent of the sales plan. Thus, the two territories with large dollar increases in computer sales actually were the two weakest territories when sales are related to potential. The best performance was achieved in territory 2, which had the smallest potential in the division and was third in terms of dollar sales growth. These results suggest that you should consider cutting the size of territory 3 and giving some of this potential to the salesperson who is currently handling territory 2. This change should increase total sales of the division, for the salesperson in territory 3 is not covering this large market adequately.

Sales by Products

Breakdowns by products are also useful in evaluating sales performance (Table 12-4). Industry figures suggest that Bear Computer should sell 60 percent of its volume in basic computers, 20 percent in accessory equipment, and 20 percent in computer software. Actual sales figures in 1995 show that Bear is selling 70 percent computers, 20 percent accessories, and only 10 percent in the software category. This heavy emphasis on machine sales can lead to long-run problems, as customers will not have enough programs to use their computers effectively. Perhaps existing commission rates encourage salespeople to push the sales of higher-priced machines rather than lower-priced software.

TABLE 12-3
Analyzing Territorial Sales in the Eastern Division of the Bear Computer Company, 1994–1995

Territory	Sales 1994 January–September (thousands)	Sales 1995 January–September (thousands)	Dollar Change (thousands)	Market Potential Index (percent)	Planned Sales (thousands)	Percentage of Plan Achieved	Sales Variance (thousands)
1	$ 750	$ 825	+$75	26%	$ 943	87%	−$118
2	500	570	+70	15	543	105	+27
3	1025	1110	+85	32	1160	96	−50
4	960	1000	+40	27	977	102	+23
Total	$3235	$3505	+$270	100%	$3623		

TABLE 12-4

Analyzing Sales by Product Line, Bear Computer Company

Product Line	Industry Sales Ratio (%)	Actual Sales (thousands)	Bear Sales Ratio (%)	Forecast (thousands)	Variance (thousands)
Computers	60%	$18,200	70%	$18,816	−$616
Accessories	20	5,200	20	5,000	+200
Software	20	2,600	10	3,064	−464
Total	100%	$26,000	100%	$26,880	−880

Another product breakdown that provides valuable information for the sales manager is based on the number of units sold (Table 12-5). Unit sales are useful when inflation and other price changes distort dollar sales figures. For example, dollar sales of Bear computers went from $16.8 million in 1994 to $18.2 million in 1995. However, unit sales actually declined from 560 to 520 over the same period, meaning that the average price of a Bear computer went from $30,000 in 1994 to $35,000 in 1995. Although some of the 17 percent increase in computer prices was due to inflation, some other factor is contributing to this change. The data suggest that the sales force is trading customers up to the most expensive computers in the line. Another breakdown of unit sales by individual models of Bear computers would tell you what items are being ignored. A decline in unit sales is a serious problem in an expanding market, and you should make adjustments in the wage and quota systems to achieve more balanced growth in computer sales. Unit sales growth is desirable because it keeps production lines and employees busy.

A somewhat different situation exists with Bear's line of accessory equipment (Table 12-5). Note that dollar and unit sales both increased between 1991 and 1992. However, unit sales grew much more rapidly than dollar sales, and the average unit price dropped from $1200 in 1994 to $1100 in 1995. These results suggest that the sales force is cutting prices to boost unit volume. This push for market share is to be applauded as long as profit margins are not completely destroyed. Bear's software product line also experienced growth in dollar and unit sales. In this case, the sales force was able to sell more units at higher average prices. These efforts are commendable, but Bear's software sales are still far below industry levels.

TABLE 12-5

Sales by Products and Units for Bear Computer Company, 1995 versus 1994

Product Line	1994 Sales Thousands of Dollars	1994 Sales Units	1994 Sales Average Price per Unit	1995 Sales Thousands of Dollars	1995 Sales Units	1995 Sales Average Price per Unit
Computers	$16,800	560	$30,000	$18,200	520	$35,000
Accessories	4,800	4000	1,200	5,200	4727	1,100
Software	2,400	1200	2,000	2,600	1280	2,031
Total	$24,000	5760		$26,000	6527	

Territorial Cost Analysis

Although a sales analysis provides useful data on the operation of a field sales force, it does not tell the whole story. Sales figures show general trends, but they do not reveal the effects of price cutting or the differences in selling costs, potential, and saturation that exist across products or territories. A more complete picture of sales force efficiency can be obtained by comparing actual selling costs with planned performance standards.

An example of a territorial cost review is shown in Table 12-6 for the Bear Computer Company. The analysis begins with net sales for each territory, from which the cost of goods sold and sales commissions are then subtracted. The resulting contribution margin is greatest in territory 4, even though territory 3 had the highest sales. Note that territories 1 and 4 had high contribution percentages compared to territories 2 and 3. Salespeople in territories 2 and 3 are apparently pushing low-margin products and are cutting prices to gain volume.

Another selling cost issue is raised by the activities of the salesperson in territory 1. This territory produced almost as much contribution margin as territory 3 and had an outstanding contribution percentage. However, the profit contribution in territory 1 was $7700 less than that generated in territory 3. The explanation for this difference lies in the various expense categories. Although the salary of the salesperson ($42,000) seems reasonable, the amounts spent on travel, food and lodging, and entertainment appear to be high. While salespeople in the other three territories averaged $9700 for these expenses, the person in territory 1 spent $17,400. The typical response of a sales manager to expenditures of this size would be to pressure the salesperson to cut back so that the profit contribution will increase. However, these

TABLE 12-6

Analyzing Costs and Profits of the Southern District of the Bear Computer Company

	Territory Performance (thousands)			
	1	*2*	*3*	*4*
Net sales	$825	$570	$1110	$1000
Less: CGS and commissions	95	428	777	660
Contribution margin	330	142	333	340
Contribution margin as a percentage of sales	40%	25%	30%	34%
Less: Direct selling costs				
Sales force salaries	42.0	25.0	45.0	55.0
Travel	8.5	4.1	5.5	5.0
Food and lodging	6.5	4.0	4.2	4.5
Entertainment	2.4	0.3	0.5	1.0
Home sales office expense	4.5	2.0	4.0	4.5
	$63.9	$35.4	$59.2	$70.0
Profit contribution	$266.1	$106.6	$273.8	$270.0
Profit contribution as a percentage of sales	32%	19%	25%	27%

above-average expenditures might explain why territory 1 was generating a 40 percent contribution margin on sales. The salesperson is apparently entertaining customers so effectively that they are buying high-margin computers at list price, though it is possible that the salesperson is using the expense account to offer customers under-the-table discounts on the computers. But if these travel, food, and entertainment expenditures are legitimate, the manager might consider asking the other salespeople to spend more on these items.

Profitability Analysis

Up to this point, we have reported profitability in terms of contribution margins and profit contributions (Table 12-6). Two other ways to measure profitability include return on assets managed and residual income analysis.

Return on Assets Managed   A more complete approach to profitability analysis includes a review of the assets employed to generate profit contributions.[7] This method points out that it costs money to maintain assets in a sales organization and that managers should be evaluated on how well they utilize these investments. Return on assets managed (*ROAM*) can be calculated using the following formula:

$$ROAM = \text{profit contribution as a \% of sales} \times \text{asset turnover rate.} \quad (12.4)$$

Since the *asset turnover rate* is sales divided by assets managed, the formula reduces to

$$ROAM = \frac{\text{profit contribution}}{\text{assets managed}}. \quad (12.5)$$

The most difficult job in calculating *ROAM* is deciding what assets to include in the analysis. Different assets can be identified for each level of a sales organization. A typical *ROAM* analysis would include investments in accounts receivable, finished goods inventory, parts, field laptop computers, cellular phones, fax machines, copiers, and samples. Notice that these assets are under the direct control of the sales organization. Assets that are not controlled by sales managers, such as finished goods inventories held at the factory, would not be included.

Table 12-7 presents *ROAM* figures for three districts in the Eastern region of Bear Computer Company. The weakest performance on *ROAM* was the 16.1 percent return observed in District 3. Assets were managed poorly in this district, as shown by the mediocre turnover ratio of 0.9. This manager is apparently using easy credit and a large inventory to boost sales revenues. Although District 3 has the best sales record, *ROAM* is low.

Asset management was considerably better in the other two districts. District 2 had the best asset turnover ratio of 1.5. When this ratio is multiplied by the profit contribution of 20.1 percent, District 2 generated an attractive *ROAM* of 30.1 percent District 1 had a better profit contribution percentage (22.5) but a lower asset turn of 1.2, which led to a *ROAM* of only 27.0 percent. If the manager in District 1 could cut

TABLE 12-7
ROAM for the Eastern Region of Bear Computer Company, 1995

	District 1 (000)	District 2 (000)	District 3 (000)
Net sales	$3505	$4006	$4800
Less CGS and commissions	2360	2604	3360
Contribution margin	1145	1402	1440
Less direct selling costs	355	595	588
Profit contribution	790	807	852
Accounts receivable	2000	1000	3000
Finished goods inventory	500	600	1533
Parts, equipment, supplies	420	400	800
Total assets managed	$2920	$2000	$5333
Profit contribution percentage	22.5%	20.1%	17.8%
Asset turnover ratio	1.2	1.5	0.9
ROAM	27.0%	30.1%	16.0%

$400,000 out of accounts receivable, this district could move into the number one position on overall performance.

ROAM calculations provide a valuable extension to our standard profitability analysis. Asset turnover gives a useful way to measure managers' control over money tied up in inventory and credit. This allows senior managers to improve ROAM through stricter credit and inventory reductions.

Residual Income Analysis   Although ROAM is an improvement over conventional performance measures, it does have several limitations. Some managers may be reluctant to invest in accounts receivable and inventory for new markets for fear that this will lower branch ROAM. Also, ROAM does not include the level of sales or sales growth. Sales appears in the numerator and denominator of the ROAM equation (12.4) and is therefore eliminated from the final return-on-assets figure. This means that sales could grow by 20 percent, but ROAM would remain unchanged. One performance measure that overcomes these problems is residual income analysis (RIA).[8]

RIA focuses on the excess of earnings over the cost of capital. The formula for residual income is

$$\text{Residual income} = \text{profit contribution} - \text{accounts receivable costs} \quad (12.6)$$
$$- \text{inventory carrying costs}$$

This equation suggests that sales growth is desirable as long as profits exceed the cost of acquiring assets.

An example of RIA is described in Table 12-8. The figures shown in the table are from a distributor of hospital supplies with four sales branches. RIA works well for wholesalers because branches are responsible for inventories and accounts receiv-

TABLE 12-8
Residual Income Analysis for a Medical Supply House

	District 1	District 2	District 3	District 4
Performance				
Sales volume	$5,750,000	$5,750,000	$5,250,000	$5,250,000
Growth	15%	15%	5%	5%
ROAM	35%	15%	35%	15%
Operating Results	5 times	4 times	5 times	4 times
Inventory turnover	30 days	40 days	30 days	40 days
A.R. days outstanding	$1,150,000	$1,437,500	$1,050,000	$1,312,500
Accounts receivable	$ 479,167	$ 718,750	$ 437,500	$ 656,258
Assets managed	$1,629,167	$2,156,250	$1,487,500	$1,968,750
Residual Income				
Contribution margin	$ 570,208	$ 323,437	$ 520,625	$ 295,312
Less: Accounts receivable cost	$ 47,917	$ 71,875	$ 43,750	$ 65,626
Less: Inventory cost	$ 178,500	$ 107,812	$ 157,500	$ 98,438
Residual income	$ 349,791	$ 143,750	$ 319,375	$ 131,248
Target residual income	$ 282,792	$ 282,792	$ 282,792	$ 282,792
Over/under target	$ 66,999	$ (139,042)	$ 36,583	$ (151,544)

Source: William L. Cron and Michael Levy, "Sales Management Performance Evaluation: A Residual Income Perspective," *Journal of Personal Selling and Sales Management* (August 1987), p. 63. Reproduced by permission.

able. In situations where shipments were made from one central warehouse, RIA would not be appropriate.

Notice that Districts 1 and 3 had the same *ROAM* and were considerably better than Districts 2 and 4 (Table 12-8). However, closer inspection reveals that District 1 had better sales growth that led to $30,000 more residual income than District 3. The higher ROAM observed for Districts 1 and 3 was due to better control over inventories and accounts receivable. Although Districts 2 and 4 had the same *ROAM*, District 2 outperformed District 4 on residual income due to better sales growth.

Another useful comparison occurs between Districts 2 and 3. District 2 had the highest growth and was second on *ROAM*. District 3 had the highest *ROAM* and was second on sales growth. These results suggest that the two districts were about equal in performance, with perhaps a slight edge to District 2 because of its high growth. However, RIA paints quite a different picture. District 3 had over twice the residual income of District 2 due to its ability to control accounts receivable and inventory. This illustrates the fundamental principle that if the rate of return on sales does not exceed the cost of assets, then selling more volume will not increase short-term profits.

Models for Sales Force Evaluation

The basic model used to evaluate salespeople includes four measures of performance. Individual effort is gauged by the number of days worked and the total number of calls made on customers or prospects. The output of the salesperson is measured by the number of orders and dollar sales that are generated. These factors are combined to give the following equation:

$$\$ \text{ sales} = \text{days worked} \times \frac{\text{calls}}{\text{days worked}} \times \frac{\text{orders}}{\text{calls}} \times \frac{\text{sales } \$}{\text{orders}} \qquad (12.7)$$

This equation indicates that sales can be increased by working more days, making more calls per day, closing more sales with customers, and increasing the size of the average order. If a salesperson is not generating sufficient volume, then the problem must be a deficiency in one or more of these areas. The sales manager can use this model to help identify problem areas and suggest ways to improve efficiency.

Jones versus Smith   An example of the four-factor model in action is presented in Table 12-9. The data show that although Pete Jones had high sales, Ann Smith worked more days, made more calls, had lower expenses, and landed more orders. As a result, Smith made one more call per day and had a 50 percent batting average (orders per calls). Although Jones closed the sale on only 40 percent of his calls, he had a high average-order size. Thus, despite lower values for days worked, calls per day, and batting average, Jones obtained larger orders and the highest total sales volume.

In this case, you might be tempted to encourage Ann Smith to increase the size of her average order. Larger orders should increase total sales but would probably result in fewer and longer sales calls and a reduction in her batting average. Fewer calls per day produced larger orders in Jones's territory, but it is not clear that this strategy would work as well for Smith. Also, Jones's expenses seem high, especially when expressed on a per call or per order basis. However, expenses as a percentage of sales were the same for both representatives. You must therefore exercise caution when comparing performance ratios for salespeople who pursue different selling strategies. That is, you clearly need a way of combining several criteria into a single productivity measure.

TABLE 12-9
Evaluating Individual Performance

Performance Factors	Peter Jones	Ann Smith
Sales	$1,000,000	$650,000
Days worked	210	225
Calls	1,200	1,500
Orders	480	750
Expenses	$22,000	$14,300
Calls per day	5.7	6.7
Batting average (orders per calls)	40%	50%
Average order	$2,083	$866
Expenses per call	$18.33	$9.53
Expenses per sales	2.2%	2.2%

Performance Ranking   One way to simplify sales force comparisons is to convert the performance results into rankings. The rankings can then be added up to give an overall measure of efficiency. For example, Table 12-10 shows how five salespeople ranked on 10 different control factors. The first factor used to evaluate performance is sales per person. Although this variable is a good overall measure, it can be deceiving. Note that Ford, for example, had the highest total sales but was last on sales-to-potential, suggesting that this high volume was due to a large territory. Gold, on the other hand, had low volume and high sales-to-potential, indicating good coverage of a limited market. Sales-to-quota is also popular, showing primarily a salesperson's ability to increase revenue. Sometimes attainment of quotas qualifies salespeople for special commissions or bonuses.

Sales per order is important to some firms because they have found that small orders are unprofitable. Thus, salespeople who sell large quantities to each customer are viewed as the most efficient. Ford, for example, achieves a high sales volume by making a large number of calls and selling small amounts to each customer (Table 12-10). The ratio of orders to calls measures the ability of the salesperson to convert prospects into buyers. Sometimes called the *batting average*, this ratio shows how successful salespeople are at closing sales presentations.

The gross margin percentage achieved by salespeople shows how good they are at controlling prices and selling the right mix of products. Table 12-10 suggests that Ford's low margins are the result of price cutting to open new accounts and boost sales. Direct selling costs include expenses for travel, meals, phone calls, and overnight accommodations. These expenses usually vary with the size of a territory, and salespeople have only limited control over these costs.

The performance of the five salespeople in Table 12-10 varied widely across the 10 factors, and each person ranked first on two criteria and last on at least one factor. If all of the criteria are considered equal in importance, then the ranks can be added across to give a measure of overall performance. This procedure shows that Bell, Shaw, and Mann had total performance scores close to the expected value of 30 points, whereas the scores of Ford and Gold were different enough to warrant special attention. Note that although Ford had the highest sales volume, he actually had the worst overall record, whereas Gold was doing an excellent job despite low sales volume.

TABLE 12-10
Ranking Salespeople on Ten Performance Factors

Salespeople	Dollar Sales	Sales-to-Potential	Sales-to-Quota	Sales per Order	Number of Calls	Orders per Call	Gross Margin Percent	Direct Selling Costs	New Accounts	Number of Reports Turned in
Ford	1	5	5	5	2	4	5	4	1	4
Bell	2	3	4	1	5	2	1	3	4	3
Shaw	3	4	2	4	1	5	3	5	2	1
Mann	4	2	1	3	3	3	4	1	5	5
Gold	5	1	3	2	4	1	2	2	3	2

Performance Matrix   A new model for evaluating salespeople is the performance matrix (Figure 12-9). This diagram plots the position of individual salespeople on the basis of sales revenues and gross margin percentages. Then averages for other control factors are calculated for reps falling into different sectors of the matrix. The matrix shown in Figure 12-9 has nine cells, with descriptive names to highlight comparisons among salespeople.

In our example, building products salespeople on straight commission began their careers by selling a high-margin mix of products and ended it by sacrificing margins for revenues (Figure 12-9). Also, two of the most productive groups of reps, compromisers and eager beavers, made the most calls.

Data from performance matrices can also be used to make career recommendations. Some will look at the contribution dollars produced by the compromisers

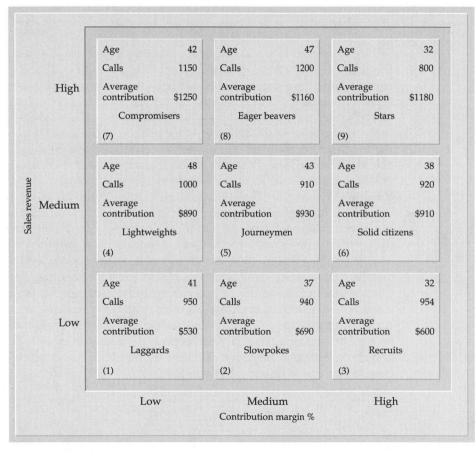

FIGURE 12-9   Performance Matrix Developed for 56 Building Products Salespeople (From Douglas J. Dalrymple and William M. Strahle, "Career Path Charting: Frameworks for Sales Force Evaluation," *Journal of Personal Selling & Sales Management*, Vol. 10, No. 3 [Summer 1990], p. 64)

in cell 7 (Figure 12-9) and suggest that the stars should move in this direction. Others will look at the high margins produced by the stars in cell 9 and say that compromisers should become stars. In this case, the choice between high-contribution dollars (cell 7) and high-contribution margin percentages (cell 9) is not easy to make. After reviewing the data in Figure 12-9, management of the firm changed the compensation plan from straight commission to a salary-commission-bonus program to tie sales efforts more closely to the profitability of the different lines.

Performance matrices allow you to review and compare the accomplishments of your sales force along several dimensions at the same time. The matrix is easy to construct, and it neatly summarizes a variety of sales activities in a readable format. With this procedure, the key task for the manager is to select appropriate performance measures for the review process.

SUMMARY

Selling is basically a personal encounter between the salesperson and customers, and the firm must understand how this relationship works. If salespeople with certain characteristics are more successful than others, it may pay to select or train field representatives to fill these needs. The optimum size of the sales force is obtained by hiring salespeople until the marginal profit from an additional salesperson is equal to the marginal cost of adding another person. In the absence of sales response data, the firm can set the size of the sales force on the basis of what it can afford or the actual workload. The creation of equitable territories for salespeople is important for building morale and improving the efficiency of the sales organization. Sales territories are usually created by combining geographic areas, and the computer has proved to be a great help in speeding up this tedious, recurring task. Once sales territories have been created, you must decide how to deploy the sales force to cover different customers and product lines. In addition, the careful scheduling and routing of salespeople through their territories can reduce expenses and increase the number of calls that can be made. Salespeople also must be rewarded for their services, and the design of compensation plans is one of the most creative jobs performed by sales managers. The idea is to provide a blend of salary, bonuses, commissions, and noncash incentives that stimulates the salespeople to work hard, maximizing the profits of the firm at the same time. This requires decisions on what factors measure success and the subsequent inclusion of these criteria in a sales reporting system that is both easy to use and economical to operate.

NOTES

1. *Sales & Marketing Management* (June 22, 1992), p. 73.
2. *The Wall Street Journal*, September 16, 1986, p. 1.
3. *Sales & Marketing Management* (August 1986), p. 48.

4. Tom Eisenhart, "Drawing a Map to Better Sales," *Business Marketing* (January 1990), pp. 59, 61.

5. TERRALIGN, Metron, Inc., 1481 Chain Bridge Road, McLean, VA 22101.

6. Thayer C. Taylor, "More Software, But Higher Prices," *Sales & Marketing Management* (April 1989), pp. 86–89.

7. J. S. Schiff, "Evaluate the Sales Force as a Business," *Industrial Marketing Management*, Vol. 12 (1983), pp. 131–137.

8. William L. Cron and Michael Levy, "Sales Management Performance Evaluation: A Residual Income Perspective," *Journal of Personal Selling & Sales Management* (August 1987), pp. 57–66.

SUGGESTED READING

Voss, Bristol. "The Electronic Salesperson," *Sales & Marketing Management* (September 1990), pp. 44–52.

"What Skills Do Today's Sales and Marketing Managers Need to Succeed?" *Sales & Marketing Management* (May 1990), pp. 34–37.

FURTHER READING

Brooks, William T. *Niche Selling: How to Find Your Customer in a Crowded Market* (Homewood, IL: Business One Irwin, 1992).

Churchill, Gilbert A., Neil M. Ford, and Orville C. Walker, Jr. *Sales Force Management*, 3rd ed. (Homewood, IL: Richard D. Irwin, 1990).

Dalrymple, Douglas J. *Sales Management: Concepts and Cases*, 5th ed. (New York: Wiley, 1995).

Futrell, Charles. *Sales Management*, 2nd ed. (Chicago: Dryden, 1988).

Ingram, Thomas N., and Raymond W. LaForge. *Sales Management: Analysis and Decision Making*, 2nd ed. (Chicago: Dryden, 1992).

QUESTIONS

1. Sales quotas motivate self-oriented salespeople to meet them. Contests encourage product-driven salespeople to push products. How do you foster a "customer focus"?

2. One furniture salesperson greets a new customer in the showroom by asking, "Can I help you?" Another salesperson begins by asking, "How would you describe your decorating motif?" Which salesperson will be more successful? Why?

3. Representatives in the pharmaceutical sales industry deal with two distinct groups. They call on physicians, attempting to convince them of the product's

superior quality, and they call on pharmacists, who must be convinced to stock the product instead of a competitor's. In recruiting salespeople, some firms hire only pharmacy school graduates, whereas others hire business or liberal arts majors and put them through an intensive training program. What are the advantages and disadvantages of each method? What implications might this have for sales management? Will there be a difference in the number or type of person moving into middle and upper management?

4. Research has shown that firms that pay their salespeople the highest wages have the lowest rates of sales force turnover. Does this mean that you should pay your reps more?

5. Car salespeople tend to be a nomadic breed, switching from one dealership to another, depending on what brand is hot. To combat this problem, Volkswagen pays salespeople their commission in three installments, with the final payment coming two years after the car is sold. Audi pays cash bonuses to top salespeople at the end of the year. Both plans require salespeople to stay to collect the money. Why are dealers using compensation programs in an attempt to cut turnover? Which of the two plans is better and why?

6. Avon Products, Inc., sells cosmetics and jewelry door-to-door using 425,000 representatives. In 1992, Avon's sales and number of sales reps both declined. Avon responded by initiating a national TV advertising program, mailing out millions of catalogs to potential customers, and starting to accept phone orders from toll-free 800 numbers. Why is Avon having trouble selling cosmetics door-to-door? Will Avon's field sales force be happy that the company is sending out catalogs and accepting phone orders?

7. Market Statistics, which produces the Survey of Buying Power, is now offering a computer program to help design sales territories. The basic program sells for $5950 and includes some on-site training. A county data file to use with the program costs $6950, a zip code data file sells for $11,950, and both files are priced at $12,950. Major highway data are available at $450. The program displays county and zip code borders on a computer screen and allows you to draw lines to create sales territories. In addition, the program keeps running totals on several control factors. Additional training and support for the program can be purchased for $600 a day plus travel and expenses. How can sales managers justify expenditures of this size to the presidents of their companies? How will you know whether you have an optimum solution with this program? What determines the amount of money you can spend on computer programs to design sales territories?

8. Purchasing agents often complain that salespeople are just order takers. In today's increasingly competitive market, purchasing agents prefer salespeople who can talk about technical applications and make suggestions to reduce costs. They also like salespeople who prepare proposals that help the buyer make better decisions. However, most sales managers measure performance by looking at output factors such as the number of orders signed. What procedures do you recommend to better evaluate the subjective dimensions of personal sell-

ing? Performance reviews normally turn up a few salespeople who are having trouble in the field. What steps would you follow to improve the performance of a mediocre salesperson? When is termination appropriate?

9. There are 3139 counties in the United States. Fairfax County, Virginia, has the highest household effective buying income (EBI), $54,232. Tunia County, Mississippi, has the lowest EBI, $7953. If you had a map showing EBI by counties, how would you use it to help control your sales force?

10. Sales force turnover rates of instrument and office equipment companies are reported to be 35 percent a year compared with only 12 percent for rubber and plastics and 13 percent for electronics firms. What accounts for these differences? How should you evaluate turnover rates? What is good or bad on this control factor?

11. You work for Media, Inc., which specializes in buying and reselling air time from radio and TV stations. Media pays for air time with travel, recorded jingles, and equipment and then resells the air time to advertisers. You notice that Media also routinely provides clients and prospects with cars, prostitutes, and envelopes filled with cash. Should you report these activities to your boss? The president of the company? The Securities and Exchange Commission? The police? Or should you remain silent?

12. You have recently moved from a field sales position to a new job as sales analyst for a competitor of your old employer. The new job pays 25 percent more, and all relocation expenses were paid by the new company. At a cocktail party during a sales meeting, the general sales manager asks you detailed questions about the wages, costs, price discounts, and customers of your former employer. What should you do?

Chapter 13

Direct Marketing

The 1990s belong to the totally integrated direct marketers.

RICHARD BENCIN

Direct marketing allows you to speak directly to the people who are most likely to buy your product.[1] You ask them to take an immediate action in the form of an order, a donation, an inquiry, or a store visit. You want to establish an ongoing customer relationship. You focus on the profit generated *over the life of the customer*.

Direct marketing usually involves building a database of respondents. A survey of packaged goods marketers found that two-thirds were compiling and using consumer databases. Among those building databases, mail-in premium offers and sweepstakes are the most commonly used methods of information collection, followed by trackable coupons and rebates. More than two-thirds of those using database marketing enhance their data with outside demographic and lifestyle information.[2] Sophisticated database methodologies identify high-potential prospects. Marketing resources are concentrated on these select list segments.

Strategic decisions in direct marketing include program scope (testing versus rollout of the full program), the basic offer (product, incentives, and premiums), the concept and theme, versioning and/or personalization, and media selection. Our focus is cost-effective media selection for the product and situation. Telemarketing and direct mail are two media that are especially appropriate for direct marketing, although general mass media can be used as well.

TELEPHONE MARKETING

The telephone is the third largest medium in the United States, with over 18 million calls being made each day. Telephone marketing uses communication technology as part of a marketing program that prominently features the use of personal selling. Telemarketing works because it is personal, urgent and deadline driven, interactive, and flexible, generates an immediate response, allows for constant improvement through testing, and is cost effective. You can take the initiative in contacting your customer (outbound operations), or you can let your customer contract you (inbound operations).

Outbound Operations

With the average business-to-business sales call costing over $300, many firms are turning to telephone marketing, where the average cost per contact is only $7.[3] A major advantage of telephone marketing over other direct marketing approaches is *flexibility*. Scripts can be changed as events unfold in real time. For example, see Marketing Strategies insert 13-3, discussed later.

The acceptability of telephone marketing varies with the type of product or service being offered. A recent survey shows customer reactions to telephone marketing: 62 percent terminate the call before or during the presentation; 32 percent listen to the entire presentation, and 6 percent comply with the request.[4] When asked what was the impression of the company's last phone call, 42 percent said it was an unpleasant experience; 39 percent a pleasant experience; and 19 percent said neither or that they didn't know. Another survey followed up calls placed 30 days earlier and found that 72 percent didn't mind the call, 2.8 percent objected to all calls, and 95 percent said that their relationship with the firm was unchanged or better.[5] Reasons for a call being unpleasant were a poorly trained caller, a computerized message, inconvenient timing, and poor targeting/no need.

Inbound Operations

The telephone can be used to take customer-initiated orders, requests for information, and complaints. You have to decide whether you want many calls that are free to the caller (800 numbers) or fewer but more qualified calls for which the caller has to pay (900 numbers). The telephone is one way to listen to your customers—what they like about your firm and what they don't like. The Buick Division of General Motors handles 30,000 calls monthly through an 800 number for customer assistance.

Telecommunications technology lets you know the telephone number of a caller before actually talking to the person. With Automatic Number Identification (ANI), the caller's telephone number is sent along with the call. When ANI is coupled on a real-time basis with reverse directory matching, customers can be given more personalized service. With the help of some software, you can have displayed on a computer screen not only the customer's name and address, but also the record of past purchases, credit history, and other information.

DIRECT MAIL

More than 60 billion pieces of mail, from fashion catalogs to ads offering pizza coupons, arrive at U.S. homes each year. About 68 percent of all magazine subscriptions are sold through the mail, and 25 percent of all charitable contributions are raised in the same fashion.

Direct mail involves sending a sales proposition to targeted respondents through the mail. The aim is to create a direct response to the mailing, whether it be by mail, phone, or personal contact. This response can be measured. A 2 percent response rate represents success if the target market is enormous and undifferentiated. One key to improving on this rate is the targeted mailing list. The targeted list makes it possible to establish relatively personal relationships with potential and existing customers.

Target Markets

Your starting point must be the question "Who is my customer?" Target marketing depends on qualified list choices. If you are selling a product for children, the most significant qualifier in a list selection process would be the presence of children on the list. On the other hand, if your product is geared to the agricultural market, you would want lists of farmers and suppliers to the agricultural community. 3Com, a maker of computer network adapters, targeted local area network (LAN) coordinators and management information systems (MIS) managers for its EtherLink III adapter (Marketing Strategies box 13-1). In any case, be sure to test your assumptions about who your customer is. One conservative organization was convinced that medical doctors would contribute to its cause. An order was put in for a 5000-name test list. The prospect package cost 55 cents to mail out but raised only 10 cents per name mailed!

Mailing Lists

Lists may be classified as internal or external. An internal list, called a *house file*, is the organization's own file, which may include buyers, former buyers, subscribers, lapsed subscribers, donors, former donors, prospects, inquiries, employees, salesperson contacts, warranty card respondents, stockholders, and so on. External lists include compiled and direct response lists. *Compiled lists* do not necessarily represent people who have bought by direct mail, but rather those who have common relevant characteristics. There are compiled lists that cover most of the households and businesses in the United States. Households can be selected by demographic, geographic, or other identifiers. Businesses can be selected by SIC code, number of employees, net worth, and many other factors. Some sample records from one list company are shown in Figure 13-1. In addition, there are compiled business lists of executives by name—chairmen, presidents, treasurers, and so on—that can be selected by line of business and other important characteristics. *Direct response lists* contain the names of past direct-mail purchasers. These lists are possible because many firms make their internal mailing lists available to noncompeting firms. Obviously, the most responsive list is the house file. Maximum financial return comes from taking into account the recency, frequency, and dollar amount of past purchases or gifts.

The use of *overlays* has surfaced as a value-added marketing technique. This involves matching the house file against the 85 million households that are classified by key demographic, socioeconomic, housing, and ethnic characteristics. The measurement units are then clustered into groups with similar demographic and lifestyle

BUSINESS-TO-BUSINESS
DIRECT MAIL

3Com, a leader in computer network solutions, launched a new adapter board, EtherLink III. The company's biggest challenge was the commoditylike nature of the network adapter market. Adapters from competing manufacturers typically use price as their only distinguishing feature. In addition, the network adapter market is traditionally a low-involvement category in which purchases are not based on brand name. Adapters are recommended by the value-added reseller (VAR), who installs the board and tests it for hardware and software compatibility. 3Com's objectives were to persuade VARs to recommend 3Com network adapters over the competition and to encourage end users to try 3Com boards.

EtherLink III used direct mail and sales tools featuring bright, colorful visuals and headlines that focused on the benefits of the product rather than technical features. In this marketing effort, EtherLink III adapters were christened "SuperBoards." The initial direct mailing to resellers used short copy, bright colors, and sophisticated illustrations to make the point that EtherLink III network adapters are faster than the competition, yet competitively priced. The resellers were asked to fill out a business reply card or call an 800 number to receive a free sales kit. A direct mail piece sent to LAN coordinators and MIS managers at Fortune 2000 companies used a series of humorous cartoon vignettes to drive home key points about the product and the technology and to grab the prospect's attention.

This product launch elevated EtherLink III above other entries in the crowded 16-bit board market. End users began requesting the board by name.

Creative, nontechnical approaches can be developed to market even the most technical products.

Source: Marcia Kadanoff, "Nontechnical Approach to Marketing High Tech Has Benefits," *Marketing News,* April 26, 1993, p. 10.

COMPANY PROFILE

NAME:	HDB ELECTRONICS
ADDRESS:	2860 SPRING ST
CITY:	REDWOOD CITY

ABI NO. 101952752

PHONE: 415/368-1388
STATE: CA ZIP: 94063

CONTACT: RON HARRIS, President

SALES VOL: E ($5,000,000 - $9,999,999)   NO. OF EMPLOYEES: 11

SIC	YELLOW PAGE CATEGORY	AD SIZE	FRANCHISE & SPECIALTY CODES
505102	WIRE	A	
506519	ELECTRONIC EQUIPMENT & SUPPLIES	B	

COMPANY PROFILE

NAME:	ROBERT'S OLDSMOBILE-CADILLAC
ADDRESS:	631 ORCHARD LN
CITY:	DAYTON

ABI NO. 000351562

PHONE: 513/426-6401
STATE: OH ZIP: 45434

CONTACT: ROBERT M. SPITZ, Owner

SALES VOL: F ($10,000,000 - $19,999,999)   NO. OF EMPLOYEES: 45

SIC	YELLLOW PAGE CATEGORY	AD SIZE	FRANCHISE & SPECIALTY CODES
551102	AUTOMOBILE DEALERS NEW CARS	D	D, O
551103	AUTOMOBILE DEALERS USED CARS	B	
753201	AUTO BODY REPAIRING & PAINTING	A	
753801	AUTOMOBILE REPAIRING & SERVICE	C	

Key: Ad size
    A - Regular listing
    B - Boldface listing
    C - In-column ad
    D - Display ad

Key: Franchise code
    D - Cadillac
    O - Oldsmobile

FIGURE 13-1 Sample List Records (from American Business Information)

characteristics and applied against the internal file. The result is a profile of customers and products.

When you need an external list, you can do your own list research. This may involve some creativity. The Sierra Club gathers the names of environmentally aware young people with tabletop displays at rock concerts, by setting up voter registration booths on college campuses, and by marketing an affinity credit card to college students. Such diverse direct marketing activities attracted 45,000 members at a cost per thousand (CPM) of $9.70, and these members had a net dollar value to the Sierra

Club of $18.80. In contrast, while direct mailings yielded more members, 105,000, the CPM was $27.60 and the net dollar value was only 40 cents.

Getting names yourself, however, is time-consuming and expensive. Why do it when there are thousands of lists available? Within each list, there are segments that can be selected based on interest categories, geographic location, and other elements. Thus, you will probably want the services of a list broker to help you. The list broker serves both parties, the list owner and the list user. The broker's commission (usually 20 percent of the list rental price) is paid by the list owner.

Not everyone on an externally compiled list is a prospect. You want to reach your prospects economically. You will need to develop a model or overlay to identify your prospects from a larger list. To do so, enough offers or appeals must be mailed to an nth of a large compiled list with appended data to ensure a statistically viable response group. This means doing systematic sampling with perhaps 100,000 pieces. Respondents are compared to the file at large by their appended data—information on spending or giving, lifestyle, and any other data available. Once a model for your organization is determined, you can mail sections of compiled lists using your overlay.

Almost all list transactions are on a one-time rental basis. List rental transactions are priced on a per M (per thousand) basis. List rental prices are biased toward mailers who mail entire lists and penalize those who need more narrow segments of lists. The rental of lists involves certain important conditions. First, the names are rented for one-time use only. No copy of the list is to be retained for any purpose. The only names that can be retained are those of persons who respond to the specific mailing. Second, usage must be cleared in advance with the list owner. The mailing piece approved by the list owner is the only one that can be used. Third, no reference to the list being used can appear in the promotional package. And finally, the mailing must be made on the mail date approved by the list owner.

Catalogs

Catalog sales have been increasing rapidly in the United States in recent years and are in excess of $50 billion. The very large catalogers, such as J. C. Penney and Spiegel, continue to perform well, and niche marketers have uncovered audiences for catalogs devoted to everything from African violets to barbeque sauce. Manufacturers can also benefit from having catalogs, as illustrated by Marketing Strategies box 13-2.

Catalog marketing has some characteristics of both direct mail and retail selling. However, unlike most direct-mail selling, customers rarely make an immediate decision based on impulse; rather, they wait until something triggers a buying impulse. The response to many solo mailings comes in just three weeks, whereas the response to a typical catalog comes in over many weeks, perhaps up to six months later. Unlike retail selling, a catalog does not provide an opportunity to touch and feel the merchandise or ask questions of a salesperson (although this last issue can be addressed by an inbound telephone operation).

Catalogers often use multiple catalogs to reach another market segment without compromising their image. Spiegel entered a partnership with Johnson Publishing's *Ebony* magazine to create a new catalog targeting black women. Market research

---

MARKETING STRATEGIES 13-2

A PLACE FOR MANUFACTURERS' CATALOGS

Johnson & Murphy, a leading footwear company, has been producing its own catalog. Its rationale is: "For you to succeed at retail, your product must first pass through the filter of the store buyer. However, with your own catalog, it's not filtered by anyone. You have direct contact with the consumer. You can use that to adjust product development and future styles to match what the consumer is seeking."

The company's latest catalog was designed to highlight its new J. Murphy brand of casual footwear. Targeting men aged 25–45 with individual incomes of $40,000 or more, the first catalog was distributed to 1.5 million consumers. The J. Murphy catalog tries for a more hip look than Johnson & Murphy's regular catalog. Set in a vertical format, the catalog is heavy on fashion photography, including many women giving heartfelt looks of admiration to men wearing J. Murphy shoes. This move was based on company research indicating that men look to women for approval when they buy casual shoes.

Along with the new catalog, Johnson & Murphy introduced a new exchange policy based on company research showing exchange hassles to be consumers' top complaint. To make it easier for shoppers, all catalog orders now come with "Back Packs" that include a preaddressed Federal Express label and packing tape to reseal the box. Dissatisfied customers call a toll-free number, and a Federal Express employee comes and picks up the shoes. If it's an exchange, a new pair of shoes is shipped directly to the shopper via Federal Express at no cost.

If you as a manufacturer have your own catalog, the benefit is that you get direct feedback on how consumers perceive your product.

Source: Cyndee Miller, "Major Catalogers, Niche Players Carve Up Mail-Order Market," *Marketing News*, September 27, 1993, pp. 1–2.

---

indicated that, on average, black women have distinct fit and proportion needs and prefer better-tailored clothing. The new catalog, called E Style, contained 64 pages showing a complete line of apparel and accessories, along with selected merchandise for the home. To promote E Style, Spiegel ran a print ad in an issue of *Ebony* that resulted in the largest response to a single print ad in its history. E Style is also promoted through ads for Spiegel's big book and with cards inserted in the company's other catalogs.

MASS MEDIA

Direct response marketing makes use of mass media—print and broadcast—to make initial contact with customers, especially for single-product appeals, and to support other media approaches. Cable shopping channels and infomercials show that there is an increasing role for mass media as primary direct response media.

Print

Print, or space, media include magazine ads and free-standing inserts (FSIs). Magazines help you efficiently reach groups of people with special interests, such as tennis players or gardeners. Newspaper CPMs are often a fraction of the cost of magazine ads or direct mail. Direct response print ads provide a way for your customer to respond by incorporating a clip-out coupon, coming with a bind-in reply card, or giving an 800 number.

Broadcast

Broadcast media include radio, cable, and broadcast television. A key feature of broadcast media is speed. When coupled with a toll-free telephone number, results can be known in a matter of hours rather than having to wait several weeks, as in the case of direct mail. This provides you with an opportunity to adjust, fine-tune, and improve a broadcast campaign while it is being conducted.

While the price of a direct mailing is relatively stable, broadcast time fluctuates widely from market to market and even from day to day. Because broadcast time is a perishable commodity, a station will frequently reduce prices on unsold inventory. This means that you must continually assess the cost of broadcast.

You can use broadcast as support for another medium or as the primary sales medium. A radio or television spot commercial can tell your prospect to watch for your mailing or look for your ad. In this supporting role, broadcast works more efficiently with print media, with their more predictable delivery dates, than with direct mail, which requires you to run announcements over an extended period of time to bracket anticipated delivery dates. Cable shopping channels and infomericals are two specialized ways of using broadcast as a primary direct response medium.

Cable Shopping Channels   The home shopping industry has annual sales of more than $2 billion in the United States. It is drawing name retailers. Saks Fifth Avenue has shows on the home shopping network QVC.

Who shops by TV? Deloitte & Touche conducted a national survey of home TV shoppers.[6] People who shop regularly by television are younger than was previously thought. Almost half of home shoppers fall into the age range of 25 to 44 years. Their household income is lower than the market average, and the number of children living in their household is higher. They are more likely to watch sporting events but less likely to exercise. These shoppers are more interested in fashion than value or comfort. Additional findings are given in Table 13-1.

Infomercials   An infomercial is a 30-minute (typically) TV commercial that incorporates an 800 number for viewer response. The emphasis is on reality-based commercials with live people. It was originally associated with kitchen gadgets, beauty products, and get-rich schemes on late-night TV. However, most products and services can be sold in the infomercial format and at virtually any time, thanks to cable and independent networks. Infomercials are typically run in off-hours because they are cheaper. Even though HUT (households using television) rates are lower at off-

TABLE 13-1

A Look at Who Shops by TV

Category	TV Shopper	General Population
Married	44%	49%
Widowed	8	8
Single, never married	27	25
Professional	13	18
Business manager	11	12
Factory worker	12	9
Homemaker	11	9
White	55	72
Black	20	14
Hispanic	17	8

Source: Deloitte & Touche (from *The Atlanta Constitution*, March 13, 1993, p. B2).

hours, the ROI is greater. From a marketing perspective, an infomercial is a long form of direct response advertising that pays for itself.

GTE, a leading-edge telecommunications company, launched a new package of services with an infomercial. The services included Personal Secretary, a person's own voice-messaging system for important reminders, and Smart Ring, a service for distinguishing rings on different lines into the same place so that you always know for whom the call is intended. The 30-minute length gave GTE an opportunity to educate and inform its customers about these services. The day after the first program ran, GTE knew it had a success.

INTEGRATED DIRECT MARKETING

Adding media to a marketing program will raise the total response more effectively than simply increasing the level of activity in a single medium because different people are inclined to respond to different stimuli. When a mailing piece that might generate a 2 percent response on its own is supplemented by a toll-free 800-number ordering channel, the response typically rises by 50 percent. A skillfully integrated outbound telemarketing effort can add another 50 percent to the response. Integrated direct marketing builds synergies.

For example, one of Citicorp's primary goals is to break down the traditional geographic restrictions on financial institutions in order to expand its business and consumer customer bases. The key product of one campaign was a fixed-rate home equity loan. Bank research indicated that the same target market segment would also be interested in a flexible revolving credit line vehicle. Thus, more than the immediate sale of a financial instrument was at stake. Each completed transaction produces

TABLE 13-2
Citicorp's Integrated Marketing Test

Test Packages	Accounts Opened	Revenue per Account	Cost Decrease per $1000 Loaned
Basic *control* package: a direct-mail piece with a lengthy application to be filled out and mailed to the bank.	Baseline	Baseline	Baseline
The same mail piece with the addition of an 800 number inviting the customer to call, ask questions, and have the application completed by phone.	+ 7%	+30%	−63%
The same mail package with 800 service plus a business reply card for requesting further information. People who returned the card received a follow-up telephone call.	+13%	+19%	−72%
Newspaper ads featuring an 800 number were run in the test market. These ads were timed to coincide with the mail drop.	+15%	+23%	−71%

Source: Ernan Roman, "Integrated Direct Marketing," in *Resource Report* 506.03A, New York: Direct Marketing Association, July 1989, p. 3.

a new, geographically remote customer for continued solicitation in an ongoing banking relationship. To assess how to market the home equity loan product to territories outside the area where the corporation maintains a branch banking presence, Citicorp tried four test packages involving increasing levels of integration starting from a common direct mail package. The impact of each was carefully tracked, with the results shown in Table 13-2. Based on these figures, Citicorp decided to roll out the fourth package—the combination of all media tested. At a 1 percent higher cost than that of the third test package, the fourth package produced a 15 percent higher market share. An illustration of integrated direct marketing for a nonprofit organization is given in Marketing Strategies box 13-3.

SUMMARY

As lifestyle changes create the need for convenient, time-sensitive, and reliable ways for people to shop, and as increased competition segments the market into ever more distinct niches, traditional mass marketing has become less efficient. Marketing funds are being shifted to database-driven direct marketing. Direct marketing creates a dialogue between you and your customer. The key to exploiting this relationship is the use of a customer database to maintain up-to-date information on your customers and your exchanges with them.

MARKETING STRATEGIES 13-3

Financing the America³ Team

For the Defender Selection Trials for America's Cup, the financing of the America³ Team, the American challenge team skippered by Bill Koch, depended largely on individual donations. This was in contrast to competitor Dennis Connor, who relied on major corporate funding to compete. To encourage current members of the America³ Foundation to upgrade their memberships to higher levels of giving, selected members were invited to become charter members of the Foundation's newly created Masthead Society. As part of the overall marketing strategy, an integrated direct marketing program was executed. Direct mail, a video, and a personal follow-up call were used.

Each person first received a letter telling him or her to watch for a 10-minute, fast-action videotape—featuring live footage of the America³ yacht entries, *Jayhawk* and *Defiant*—in their mail within the next week. They were also given an 800 number to call in case the tape was never delivered. Enclosed with the video was a four-page letter introducing the Masthead Society and inviting the member to be a guest at the Defender Trials by joining at one of three levels. Each level or "club" offered various benefits based on its value. The highest level, the Skipper's Club, entitled the member to two four-day Defender Selection Trial passes, deluxe double accommodations for four

MARKETING STRATEGIES 13-3 (continued)

nights, two invitations to a formal Masthead Society reception, and a personalized commemorative America³ yacht identification flag. Approximately one week after the member received the video, a telephone marketing firm called on behalf of the Foundation to personally invite the member to the Defender trials. The script was straightforward and benefit driven. Members were offered the option of paying by credit card or invoice. If they chose to be billed, they were sent an invoice accompanied by a personalized letter acknowledging the phone conversation, thanking them for becoming members, and restating the many benefits of their membership. Even when members were unable to attend the Defender Trials, they were extremely impressed with the video and with the fact that the Foundation personally called with an invitation. The success of the program went beyond dollars and cents to reinforce the loyalty of the members to the organization.

Subsequently, the Foundation decided to take advantage of the enthusiasm for the races by launching an emergency, last-minute fund-raising campaign during the week of the America's Cup. Members were telephoned starting the day of the first race. Throughout the scripted presentation, communicators referenced the race, specific happenings, and the outcome, adding timeliness, excitement, and authenticity to the appeal. In fact, during the days when the race was actually taking place, a supervisor monitored the race on the cable television sports channel, ESPN, and made up-to-the-minute script changes as events transpired. As a result of this flexible scripting, the Foundation was able to convey its own enthusiasm and engage in a knowledgeable interaction with the member over the phone. (The America³ Team won the America's Cup, four races to one, against the Italians.)

Integrated direct marketing is a powerful marketing approach.

Source: TransAmerica Marketing Services, Inc.

Integrated direct marketing emphasizes the coupling of diverse marketing media to create powerful media interrelationships. While integrated direct marketing increases your up-front investment, more customers are contacted and more orders per thousand contacts are produced.

NOTES

1. Major portions of this chapter have been taken from materials provided by the Direct Marketing Educational Foundation at its Direct Marketing Institute for Professors.
2. *Advertising Age,* April 12, 1992, p. 53.
3. Ted Schwartz, "What Telemarketing Does for America," APAC Teleservices, 1992.
4. Walker Direct Marketing, L.P., 1992.
5. TransAmerica Marketing Services, 1990.
6. *The Atlanta Constitution,* March 13, 1993, p. B2.

SUGGESTED READING

Blattberg, Robert C., and John Deighton. "Interactive Marketing: Exploiting the Age of Addressability," *Sloan Management Review*, Vol. 33, No. 1 (Fall 1991), pp. 5–14.

FURTHER READING

Direct Marketing Educational Foundation, Inc. *Resource Reports* (New York: Direct Marketing Association, 1989).

Hodgsons, Dick. *Complete Guide to Catalog Marketing* (Chicago: Dartnell, 1991).

Hughes, Arthur M. *The Complete Database Marketer* (Chicago: Probus, 1991).

Kobs, Jim. *Profitable Direct Marketing* (Lincolnwood, IL: NTC Business Books, 1992).

Magliozzi, T. L., and P. D. Berger. "List Segmentation Strategies in Direct Marketing," *OMEGA*, Vol. 21, No. 1 (January 1993), pp. 61–72.

Vavra, Terry. *After-Marketing: How to Keep Customers for Life Through Relationship Marketing* (Homewood, IL: Business One Irwin, 1992).

QUESTIONS

1. Many people perceive art galleries as catering exclusively to the more elite members of society. But most art dealers are smaller businesses trying to survive in today's difficult economic climate. They traditionally relied heavily on walk-ins and referrals for business. How might they use direct mail to sell works and build better relationships with customers?

2. What types of industries and products are best suited for database marketing?

3. A Harris-Equifax Consumer Privacy Survey found that 78 percent of the respondents were concerned about threats to their personal privacy. Consumers have two privacy problems with direct marketers. First, some consumers feel that they shouldn't have to deal with pitches flooding their mailboxes and telephones. Second, they are concerned that there is too much information floating around in sophisticated databases, and they want to know how it got there. On the other hand, direct marketers have a right to conduct business. How do you maintain the delicate balance between consumers' right to privacy and direct marketers' use of consumer data?

4. Direct marketers have been using database marketing to chip away at retail stores' share of consumer spending, identifying the best customers, and bombarding them with reasons to keep on buying. To what extent can retailers use customer database marketing?

5. When Sears closed its catalog, it was deriving revenue of $3.3 billion from a list of 14 million at-home shoppers. Where do you think this business went? How could someone go about getting this business?

6. What is the difference between a mailing list and a marketing database?

7. Memberships are an important source of funds to public broadcasting stations. Propose a fund-raising strategy for those stations that use direct response marketing to build membership.

8. Should direct marketers run magazine ads with clip-out coupons in *National Geographic*? Television commercials with 800 numbers during the Super Bowl or the World Cup? Explain your reasoning.

Chapter 14

Designing Advertising Programs

Associating meanings with products in order to turn products into brands is the real value of effective advertising.

CHARLES YOUNG
MICHAEL ROBISON

Advertising communication expenditures have a variety of purposes: to enhance the image of the organization, build brand preferences, promote the sale of particular items, announce a special promotion or sale, and encourage participation in causes. Advertising is employed around the world because it is a very cost-effective method of communicating ideas to mass audiences. It works for promoting disease prevention as well as for selling soap.

Advertising is created in a variety of ways. Small organizations think up their own ads and place them in appropriate media. Larger firms rely on special organizations called *advertising agencies* to develop and execute promotional campaigns. Business firms typically employ an advertising manager to develop a budget, approve agency ads, and handle direct-mail and special promotions. This person also monitors the advertising agency's selection of media and purchases of advertising space.

In your role as marketing manager, you will need to identify the appropriate target market segments and uncover the relevant buying motives. You must then make a series of decisions that establish the scope and direction of your advertising program. These include the following:

- Select advertising objectives.
- Develop an advertising budget.
- Develop campaign themes.
- Pick appropriate media.
- Monitor results.

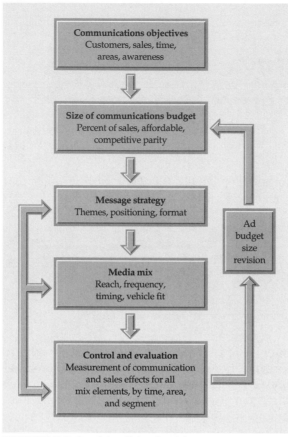

FIGURE 14-1 Advertising Decisions

These decisions are shown in Figure 14-1 and are explained in more detail in the following sections. They are part of an ongoing process, and the market results feed back into the next round's decisions.

THE OPPORTUNITY FOR ADVERTISING

Before setting budgets and doing other advertising planning, you must decide whether to use advertising. The Hershey chocolate bar, for example, became a leading product in the United States on the basis of extensive distribution gained through the use of salespeople, not as the result of consumer advertising. Even so, Hershey now spends heavily on advertising, as indicated in Marketing in Action box 14-1. An appraisal of the opportunity for advertising begins with an assessment of the potential for stimulation of demand.

MARKETING IN ACTION 14-1

HERSHEY DEFENDS POSITION WITH HEAVY AD SPENDING

Hershey, the U.S.'s number one confection marketer, has been losing ground to M&M/Mars since 1990. Hershey's product line includes Hershey's milk chocolate bars, Kit Kat bars, Mounds bars, Reese's peanut buttercups, Rolo, Symphony candy bars, and York peppermint patties, while M&M/Mars' line includes Milky Way, Skittles, Snickers, Starburst, and 3 Musketeers. Some industry experts foresaw the day when M&M/Mars would surpass Hershey in market share. But that does not appear likely anytime soon.

Hershey reported sales of $1.87 billion in 1992 for the 12 months ended November 31, up 5.8% from the previous year, according to Nielsen Marketing Research. M&M/Mars had sales of $1.66 billion for the same period, down 2.7%. That gives Hershey 27% of the $6.9 billion candy market, compared to M&M/Mars' 23.4%.

Hershey had a mission and accomplished it. They went after M&M/Mars, caught them and beat them up. Increased ad spending on core brands and new products fueled Hershey's rise. Hershey increased ad spending to 17% of sales in 1992, a record high and up 2 points from a year earlier. Hershey has also been more successful with bagged and seasonal candy which comprise a growing percentage of sales. Meanwhile, M&M/Mars took its eyes off core brands to promote line extensions, which confused customers and cannibalized sales.

You can defend core brands with marketing muscle, especially heavy advertising.

Source: Christy Fisher, "Hershey Widens Lead Over Mars," *Advertising Age*, February 15, 1993, p. 4.

Foundations of Effective Advertising

The ability to increase demand with advertising varies across product categories. To assess opportunities for advertising, you must understand the factors that account for these differences. Four of the more important factors are these:

- The trend in primary demand is favorable.
- Product differentiation is marked.
- Hidden qualities of the product are important to customers.
- Funds for advertising are available.

The social and environmental factors that underlie the basic trends in product demand are often more important than the amount of advertising expenditure. Advertising can accelerate an expansion in demand that would have occurred without advertising or, correspondingly, can retard an adverse trend. A reversal of a trend by advertising alone, however, is most unlikely. The impact of advertising is believed to decline over the product life cycle.

When demand is expanding, there are frequently opportunities for selective advertising appeals. These selective appeals are more effective if the product has unique attributes. Product differentiation facilitates the establishment of brand preference. This preference enables the product to have a larger gross margin than might have been possible with an undifferentiated product. In turn, a larger gross margin provides more funds for advertising. The firm must have sufficient resources to make an impression on the customer, however, and high advertising costs are a barrier to entry in some markets.

Advertising Strategies

Several advertising strategies have been suggested for implementation by marketing managers:

1. Influence the choice criteria that govern product class selection.
2. Change the relevance of a product attribute (create a salient attribute).
3. Change the ideal amount of an attribute that a brand should possess.
4. Change the perceived amount of an attribute held by the firm's brand.
5. Change the perceived amount of an attribute held by a competitor's brand.

Note that these advertising strategies are substrategies of the more general marketing strategy of positioning.

Strategy 1 attempts to stimulate primary demand by modifying the individual's motivation and choice criteria. Usually, this involves accelerating an environmental trend, such as the use of margarine instead of butter. Compaq encouraged demand for multimedia personal computers with a print advertisement having the headline "Just because you learned the hard way doesn't mean your kid has to." Strategy 2 can take several forms. Sometimes an existing attribute can be made more prominent. At one time, all appliance manufacturers had wheels as an optional feature for their refrigerators so that the homemaker could move the appliance in order to clean under it, but none of the firms advertised this feature. One company with a history of noninnovation decided to advertise this attribute. After the campaign, image studies revealed that the consumer viewed the firm as innovative! Sometimes a new attribute is added to extend the life of a mature product. The low-suds detergent market in Great Britain is dominated by Procter & Gamble, with its Ariel, Bold, Fairy, and Daz brands, and Lever Brothers, with its Persil, Surf, and Wisk brands.[1] During the 1980s, Lever lost share to P&G. To reverse this trend, Lever launched Radion in late 1989. Advertising introduced the concept of odor removal as the ultimate test of a detergent's cleaning power and conferred ownership of this property on Radion. This odor removal proposition was based on a Unilever patented technology, a unique deo-perfume system that deodorizes clothes rather than merely masking odors. Advertising worked to position Radion to complement other Lever brands. The impact of Radion's launch on brand images in the low-suds sector is shown in the image map by Millward Brown (Figure 14-2). The communication of odor removal placed Radion in the modern/efficient quadrant of the map. Moreover, Radion was differentiated from the Lever portfolio, market leader Persil in particular.

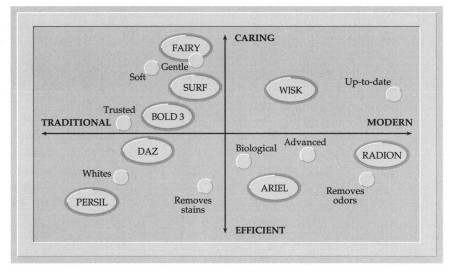

FIGURE 14-2 Detergent Brand Image Map (From "The Case for Radion Automatic: A New Brand in the Lever Portfolio," in *Advertising Works 6*, Paul Feldwick, ed. [Henley-on-Thames: NTC Publications, 1991], p. 220)

The remaining three strategies involve positioning the firm's brand in relation to ideal and competing brands by moving the ideal toward its own brand position (strategy 3), by moving its brand toward the ideal (strategy 4), or by moving competitive brands away from the ideal (strategy 5). Croft Original pale cream Spanish sherry employed strategy 3.[2] When Croft Original was launched, all sweet or cream sherries, including market leader Harveys Bristol Cream, were dark in color. Croft Original's advertising presented paleness as a positive product attribute while also establishing Croft Original as the superior pale cream sherry. Creative executions were based on P. G. Wodehouse's characters, Jeeves and Wooster. The relationship between the likeable but basically inept Wooster and his butler Jeeves, the arbiter of good taste and discernment, provided a platform for projecting the quality of Croft Original and the stylish sophistication of its drinkers. Jeeves leaves no doubt about the fine quality of Croft Original: "One can tell a great deal, sir, just by looking at things. Your Croft Original, for example, with its light, delicate color. One glance at the sherry tells one all one needs to know about the quality." The concept of paleness was later expanded, associating it with modernity (and dark with old-fashioned). The success of this communication strategy is evidenced by the correspondence map by MAS shown in Figure 14-3. Strategy 4 can be illustrated by L&M cigarettes. Liggett & Myers decided that its L&M brand was not properly positioned and that it had to be repositioned in the full-flavor category. Although L&M was reformulated so that it had a new tobacco blend and a new cork filter, the primary repositioning effort was a massive advertising campaign. The first print advertisements showed a rugged, powerfully built man clearing an area and building a cabin in the wilderness. Liggett & Myers was trying to move its brand closer to Marlboro, which was already

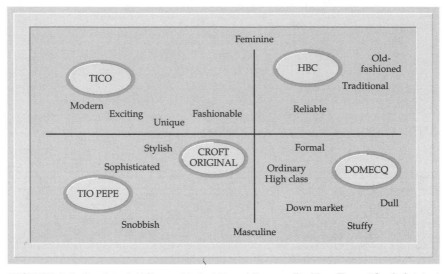

FIGURE 14-3 Spanish Sherry Market Brand Personality Map (From "Croft Original 'One Instinctively Knows When Something Is Right,'" in *Advertising Works 6*, Paul Feldwick, ed. [Henley-on-Thames: NTC Publications, 1991] p. 41)

in the full-flavor category. An example of strategy 5 is a china ad that reads "Royal Doulton, the china of Stratford-on-Trent, England, versus Lenox, the china of Pomona, N.J." Thus, Royal Doulton repositioned Lenox china, a brand that many consumers believed was imported. This advertisement resulted in a 6 percent gain in market share for Royal Doulton.

How Advertising Works

Two theories of what takes place when a person receives an advertisement have been put forth: replacement and accumulation.

Replacement　Existing concepts are replaced in memory by new concepts with increasing exposure to advertising. This theory implies that you can capture your product category by delivering more messages than your competitors. Your aim is to have the highest "share of voice."

Accumulation　Desirable response tendencies increase with advertising exposure and compete with undesirable or incorrect response tendencies, such as positive attitudes toward competing products or misinformation. New information is combined with existing concepts. From an information processing perspective, then, product positioning and message consistency are critical. This model implies that it is necessary to measure the strength of both desirable and competing responses.

Once customers decide that they have enough information to make a purchase, they tend to ignore more information. Traditional split-cable heavy-up tests (which will be explained later) often fail to show a significant sales response to large increases in advertising spending. One reason is that heavily exposed groups are already beyond their saturation limits.

Effects of Advertising on Demand

Advertising can increase the demand for a particular brand within a product category or raise per capita consumption; that is, customers are encouraged "to choose" or "to use." The competitive activity generated when brands attempt to increase their own sales may result in an increase in total demand.

At an operational level, advertising is measured in monetary units and we talk of advertising expenditures or *adspend*. After all, you need this number to budget and to calculate your profits. But this is an internal measure. You also need an external measure that expresses advertising *delivery* to prospects. Here we speak of *opportunity to see (OTS), television rating points (TVR),* or *gross rating points (GRP)*. GRP is calculated by multiplying a program's audience share by the number of times an ad is run. If an ad is shown 14 times a week on two programs we have:

$$
\begin{array}{llr}
\text{4 showings in a time slot with a 12 rating} & = & 48\text{GRP} \\
\text{10 showings in a time slot with a 9 rating} & = & \underline{90\text{GRP}} \\
\text{Total for the week} & & 138\text{GRP}
\end{array}
$$

Since ratings are expressed as percentages, the average person will be exposed 1.38 times. Of course, some people will not see the ad at all and others will be exposed 14 times. Depending on the media mix employed, the same adspend could generate quite different GRPs. A further refinement comes when we do household-level measurement of the actual number of advertising *exposures* received by each household.

The impact of advertising is often spread over several periods. Not everyone who sees an advertisement in a particular week will buy in the same week. Consequently, we allocate advertising delivery in part to when it actually happens and distribute the rest in decreasing amounts to subsequent periods. This new advertising variable is called *adstock*.[3] An example of this process is shown in Figure 14-4.

The sales response function for advertising may be S-shaped. At low levels of advertising, the sales response may be negligible. The advertising does not have sufficient weight to break through the clutter of advertisements. At some *threshold*, the sales response begins to increase at an increasing rate. Finally, additional advertising produces further sales but at a decreasing rate. This is the region of *diminishing returns to scale*. Empirical evidence shows that this is the region in which most major brands operate. Brand A in Figure 14-5, for example, shows diminishing returns to advertising. One way to measure the declining impact of advertising is by calculating advertising elasticities. The formula is

$$
E_a = \frac{\%\ \text{change in sales}}{\%\ \text{change in advertising}} = \frac{10}{100} = .1
$$

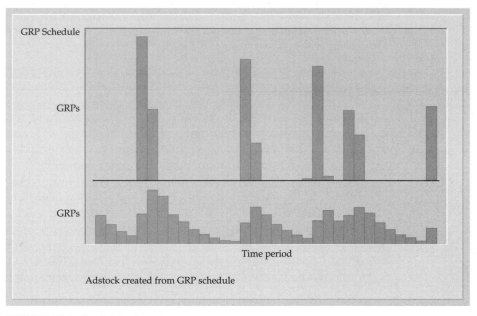

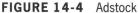

FIGURE 14-4 Adstock

In this case a 100 percent increase in advertising results in only a 10 percent increase in sales. Advertising thus has a positive yet declining impact on sales. Research has shown advertising elasticities typically range in value from .03 to .25.[4]

The sales response functions for two brands in the same product category are shown in Figure 14-5. These are important brands in a very large package-goods category. Data are from the 20 largest U.S. markets covering 1.5 years of weekly scanning and media data—over 1500 observations. The horizontal axis shows television GRPs (or TVRs) that have been adjusted for adstock. The vertical axis is a sales index scaled so that 1.0 corresponds to no advertising. For example, a continuous delivery of 100 GRP stock for Brand A corresponds to an index of about 1.15. This level of stock will increase sales 15 percent over what they would have been with no advertising.[5]

ADVERTISING OBJECTIVES AND GOALS

Under most conditions, the primary objective of a firm is profit. Consequently, you should select the advertising alternative that generates the highest present value for long-term profits. Nonprofit organizations focus on net benefits rather than on profits.

The advertising objectives for a product will depend on the stage of the life cycle that the product is in. New-product advertising makes the customer aware of the new product, forces distribution of the new brand, and provides the customer with

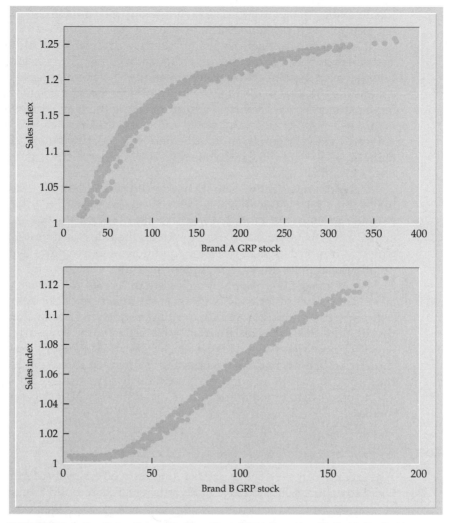

FIGURE 14-5 Sales Response Functions (From Laurence N. Gold, "Let's Heavy Up in St. Louis and See What Happens," *Journal of Advertising Research*, Vol. 33, No. 6 [November–December 1992], pp. 34–35)

a reason for buying the product. Established-product advertising is aimed at maintaining the product's market position.

The task of advertising is also a function of the product category. For more expensive products such as cars and appliances, the decision process of the buyer is deliberate and occurs over a comparatively long time horizon. Buyers usually are able to identify various brands even when the labels are removed. In contrast, many packaged goods such as soaps and detergents are physically almost identical. Furthermore, these products are often of low interest to buyers. Consequently, manufacturers of these products seek to achieve top-of-mind awareness among buyers.

Ideally, they attempt to associate their brand name with the generic product category. An example is Kleenex and facial tissue.

Advertising can increase the number of customers or the usage rate of current customers or both. More customers come from converting customers from competing brands, from holding current customers by developing brand loyalty, and from expanding the total market for the product class. Greater usage comes from reminding customers to use the brand and from telling them about new uses. Encouraging loyal customers to use your brand more is sometimes called *frequency marketing*. Advertising is also aimed at intermediaries in the distribution channel. This advertising seeks to encourage the wholesaler and retailer to stock and promote the advertiser's brand.

Advertising objectives should be coordinated with the objectives set for the other marketing variables. For instance, advertising can be used to solicit sales leads. Salespeople can then contact these prospects. If the product is too complex to explain in an ad, advertising might be used to presell the salesperson rather than the product. Culligan doubled its sales of water conditioners in five years by preselling its salespeople through its slogan "Hey, Culligan Man!"

Sometimes advertising objectives are described as *demand pull* or *demand push* advertising. Pull advertising is aimed at the final user of the product so that the user will go to the distributor and ask for the product, in effect pulling the merchandise through the channel of distribution. Most brand name advertising falls into this category (Timken bearings, Haggar slacks). Push advertising, on the other hand, is directed at brokers and distributors and is intended to presell them on the merits of the product. It is more common to use push advertising with industrial products and to stress direct mail, trade journals, and display materials rather than broadcast media.

Time Horizon

Advertising can have short- and/or long-term effects. Short-term advertising makes a call to action, while long-term advertising seeks to build a brand image.

Calls to Action   You should get an immediate response to action advertising. Response is typically measured as sales transactions (or donations or number of recruits or number of votes), but it can also be tallied in the form of mail-in requests for a brochure, calls to an 800 number, or visits to a dealer.

Television ads hawking low prices are powerful calls to action. About a third of the most popular television commercials in the United States for a recent year feature lower prices. Fast-food restaurants hyperactively promise special deals. Taco Bell leads the way, with "59! 79! 99!" blaring as its sole jingle, slogan, and message. Its screaming-price tactic has outperformed much classier campaigns. Flying in the face of conventional wisdom, Taco Bell does not believe that dwelling on low price has eroded its image; indeed, Taco Bell believes its image is healthier than ever.

Brand Building   With consistent theme advertising, you probably will not detect any sales movement in the short run; rather, you may see increased awareness of advertising claims and advertising memories associated with certain brands. Consistent themes focus on building and maintaining brand equity.

Defining Advertising Goals

Advertisers should specify their advertising objectives and subsequently measure the results. The idea is to measure performance in terms of achievement of a quantitative statement of performance. A goal for a new brand might be to attain 80 percent brand awareness within six months after introduction. This provides a benchmark against which to measure accomplishment. Advertising performance should be measured in terms of sales whenever possible because of the simple accounting equation that relates sales to profits.

The Hierarchy of Effects   The hierarchy-of-effects hypothesis states that advertising guides the consumer through a sequence of steps that culminates in a purchase. Consumers can be classified into seven groups. The first group contains potential purchasers who are *unaware* of the existence of the product. The second group contains consumers who are merely *aware* of the product's existence. The third group contains consumers who *possess knowledge* of the product and its benefits. The fourth group contains customers who *like* the product. The fifth group contains those who have developed a *preference* for the product over all other possibilities. The sixth group contains consumers who are *convinced* that they should buy the product. The final group contains consumers who *purchase* the product. Two variants of this hierarchy-of-effects theory will now be discussed.

Awareness-Interest-Desire-Action (AIDA)   This theory asserts that advertising is a strong market force that propels the prospect through a sequence of steps that culminates in purchase. The theory focuses on new buyers of a brand and does not say much about former buyers.

Awareness-Trial-Reinforcement (ATR)   This theory contends that advertising is a weak market force that is suggestive rather than strongly persuasive. ATR says that advertising can only exert influence at each stage of the process. The first purchase for frequently purchased consumer goods is viewed as a trial purchase. Consequently, advertising plays a role in reducing cognitive dissonance and reinforcing satisfaction. Given brand switching, advertising rekindles brand awareness and retrial by lapsed users. Thus, the *R* in ATR theory stands for *reassurance* and *retrial* as well as reinforcement.

The role of advertising in moving consumers from one group to another tends to vary. A panel survey can provide the data necessary to assess the economic value of causing consumers to change groups. This means that immediate sales results may not have to be the major criterion for measuring advertising effectiveness. Simply measuring the consumer's progress through the intermediate steps may provide a better indicator of the long-term effects of advertising.

The danger with defining advertising goals for measured results *(DAGMAR)* is that rather than defining your goals first and then determining how to measure the results, you may be tempted to decide on what can be easily measured first and then set your goal. Moreover, if you select some intermediate measure of performance, you have to assume that your measure ultimately drives sales—and it may not.

THE BUDGET

You need to understand the various procedures used to determine the size of advertising expenditures. The efficiency of these procedures often depends on a firm's ability to measure the effectiveness of advertising. Judgment-oriented techniques include the subjective approach and the fixed guidelines approach, while data-oriented techniques include the competitive parity approach, the objective and task approach, the experimentation and testing approach, and the modeling and simulation approach. Selection among these methods depends on the extent to which returns from advertising can be identified.

The Subjective Approach

The subjective method sets budgets on the basis of executive judgment and experience. The executive generally has the task of allocating a fixed budget between advertising and other marketing costs. When direct customer contact is viewed as the most important element in the marketing mix, advertising needs are often subordinated.

The Fixed Guidelines Approach

The fixed guidelines approach involves setting the advertising budget in terms of a percentage of sales, a fixed sum per unit, or competitively with other firms. Many companies determine their budgets as a percentage of the sales volume forecasted or anticipated for the period that the advertising budget will cover. A variant of the percentage of sales method sets the budget as a fixed sum per unit. In this approach, the appropriation for advertising is determined by multiplying the projected unit sales volume by a certain number of dollars per unit. The method is used primarily for consumer durables. When applied to convenience goods, the method is called the *case-rate method.* One problem with judgment-oriented approaches is that when a firm is under pressure to lower costs, advertising is usually cut because of the absence of hard data to support the need for promotion.

Competitive Parity Approach

The competitive parity approach sets spending in line with that of major competitors. To some degree, it reflects a belief in collective industry wisdom. The focus is on share of voice. Information on competitive spending comes from sources such as Nielsen Ad Tracker. This system automatically monitors the commercial content of network, national cable, spot TV, and national syndicated programs by recognizing the unique programs signal of each commercial broadcast. Local cable GRPs are estimated.

The Objective and Task Approach

The task approach involves setting objectives, translating these objectives into a series of communication-specific tasks, and then determining the necessary appropriation. Firms using this approach begin by setting specific and measurable objectives for their advertising. The Texasgulf company provides a useful case history.

Texasgulf supplies phosphoric acid to fertilizer manufacturers. Before advertising began, Texasgulf had a market share of about 5 percent, and six large customers accounted for most of the sales. A short-term advertising goal was to increase the awareness of Texasgulf's superior phosphoric acids by 10 percent in one year. The campaign that was employed emphasized that Texasgulf's acid products had fewer impurities than those of the competition and a distinctive green color. The acid products were always referred to as being "clean and green," and the overall campaign theme was "Texasgulf has changed things."

A before-and-after research study found the following: (1) an increase from 15.3 to 35.1 percent in the number of respondents who recognized that Texasgulf made a clear, green acid; (2) an increase from 3.6 to 16.3 percent in the number of respondents who associated Texasgulf with the theme "(Blank) has changed things"; and (3) an increase from 9.4 to 24.3 percent in the number of respondents who thought that Texasgulf made an above-average acid. The results indicate that the advertising campaign met the objectives that were set.

Experimentation and Testing

The experimentation and testing approach involves controlled field experiments. The impact of spending and weight variations in test markets is compared to baseline results from controlled markets.

An example of a controlled field experiment is Du Pont's evaluation of its advertising for Teflon coatings for cookware. Du Pont was following a pull strategy in the hope that advertising could create sufficient consumer demand so that cookware manufacturers would be forced to coat the inside of their utensils with Teflon. Advertising was varied in selected markets to determine the best level of Teflon advertising expenditures between zero and $1 million. The results are shown in Table 14-1. There appeared to be a threshold effect at which $500,000 had little impact but $1 million

TABLE 14-1
Winter Results in Units/1000 Households

			Fall Advertising	
		None	*$500,000*	*$1,000,000*
	None	25	26	32
Winter	$500,000	29	29	35
Advertising	$1,000,000	49	53	70

Source: Malcolm A. McNiven, "Choosing the Most Profitable Level of Advertising: A Case Study," in Malcolm A. McNiven, ed., *How Much to Spend for Advertising* (New York: Association of National Advertisers, 1969), pp. 90–96.

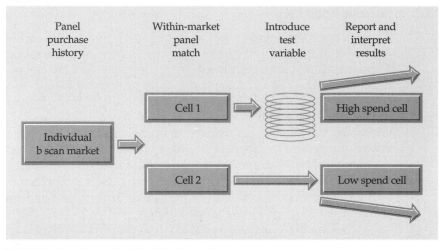

FIGURE 14-6 Split-Cable TV Market Test

gave significantly greater sales. The $1 million expenditure was known to be profitable but not necessarily the most profitable level. Another experiment was conducted in which much higher levels were tested. This second experiment permitted Du Pont to set the advertising level so that the marginal profit from the sale of Teflon was just greater than zero.

Today controlled market testing often involves split-cable markets or electronic test markets and scanning data. This process is illustrated in Figure 14-6.

Modeling and Simulation

Econometric methods can be used to estimate the unknown parameters of an advertising sales response function from historical data.[6] We will discuss this in more detail later in the chapter. Once estimation is complete, the estimated sales response function is embedded in a profit equation. The optimal sequence of advertising expenditures is found by solving the profit model using mathematical programming.

A *simulation* is the representation of the behavior of one system (in our case, the real world) through the use of another system (a computer program designed for that purpose). An example of a microcomputer simulation model is the extended version of PROD II, shown in Figure 14-7.[7] The PROD II system is very flexible inasmuch as it has various options for its component parts. The planner can input alternative GRP levels to assess their impact. Simulation outputs include one-year forecasts of sales volume, brand penetration, average number of brand purchases, market share, awareness, trial-repeat dynamics, and profit payoff.

In conclusion, research has shown a significant movement by medium-sized and large companies toward more professional approaches to advertising budgeting. The objective and task approach, and to a lesser extent experimentation and testing, are being adopted by advertising managers. If you use a data-oriented technique, remember that it generates only suggestions and must be tempered by your judg-

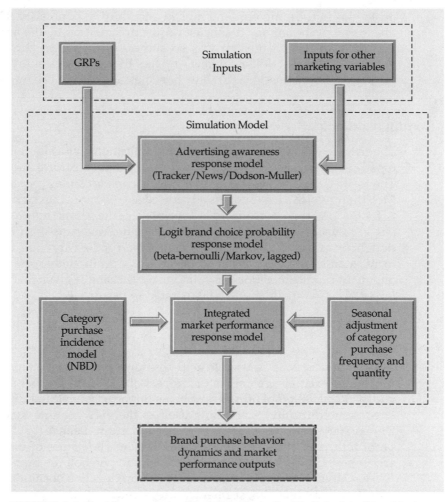

FIGURE 14-7 Microcomputer Simulation (From Fred S. Zufryden, "How Much Should Be Spent for Advertising a Brand?" *Journal of Advertising Research*, Vol. 29, No. 2 [April–May 1989], p. 26)

ment. What you can afford seems to play an important role in determining the degree to which the prescriptions of these more sophisticated techniques can be implemented. The budget-setting process in many organizations is a *political process.*

MESSAGE CONTENT

Message creativity often is a deciding factor in the success of an advertising campaign. For example, one year California raisins had the most popular ads on television despite a budget of only $6.8 million. McDonald's spent a total of $385 million on TV ads in the same year and ranked only third in popularity. The difference was the appeal of the animated dancing raisins dreamed up by the agency Foote, Cone, and Belding. This campaign was so successful that the California Raisin Board received millions of dollars in licensing fees from the sales of toy raisin figures. The purpose of our discussion is to show how message content can impact sales revenues.

Marketing Communications

The message content of marketing communications typically falls into one of three broad categories. The first approach stresses product features and customer benefits. The focus is on *demonstrable differences* or the *unique selling proposition.* For instance, Mrs. Butterworth's Lite Syrup is advertised as "The only Lite syrup made with Grade A Butter." A brand personality is developed in the second approach. The focus is on *image, goodwill, brand franchise,* and *brand equity.* An example is Pillsbury's use of the doughboy. The third approach positions the product through the great idea. The focus is on *strategy.* For instance, Seven-Up is positioned as the "Un-Cola." A taxonomy of product positionings found in advertising is given in Table 14-2. Given its importance, positioning will be illustrated in more detail.

Positioning

Creative strategy can be used to help position a product in the marketplace. Product names, for example, can affect the impact of advertising expenditures. Stolichnaya vodka ($8 per 80-proof fifth) is now being imported from Russia. Stolichnaya encountered some difficulty establishing itself as the only genuine Russian vodka in the United States because surveys show that Americans believe that Smirnoff ($5 per 80-proof fifth) and other U.S. brands are Russian. The names of the U.S. brands often are, or sound like, Russian names and serve to position the brands favorably.

Creative strategy plays a crucial role in product line positioning. Kraft was interested in a multibranded, segmented positioning approach that would maximize its opportunity within the ice cream category. Kraft had been marketing an ice cream called Breyers in the northeastern United States. Breyers ice cream contains no artificial flavoring, added coloring, stabilizers, or emulsifiers. Kraft wanted to take this premium ice cream national by capitalizing on its all-natural positioning through an advertising claim that Breyers was "*The* All-Natural Ice Cream." The only problem was that Kraft already had a premium-quality ice cream, Sealtest, on the market. Blind product testing showed that Sealtest compared favorably in taste with ice cream parlors' ice cream. Given that Sealtest cost half or less of the price of these hand-packed ice creams, Sealtest offered the consumer real value. Sealtest was positioned as "The Supermarket Ice Cream With That Ice Cream Parlor Taste." This appeal was not in conflict with Breyers' natural-ingredient appeal. In the first five years after the start of the new advertising campaigns, total sales of packaged ice cream only rose about 5 percent, but Sealtest sales increased 23 percent and Breyers sales jumped 50 percent. Each brand established its own niche in the marketplace.

TABLE 14-2
Product Positioning Taxonomy

Positioning	Our product is better than or different from others because . . .	Example
Product attributes		
Features	it has some special characteristic.	Cotton swabs: "Q-tips have 50% more cotton at the tip than any other swab."
Benefits	it offers unique gains (direct or indirect) through product use.	Pampers Phases: "Your crawler doesn't stay put for long. That's why we designed a diaper that does."
Surrogates		
Nonpareil	it is the top-quality product.	Ice cream: "Häagen-Daz. It's better than anything."
Parentage	where it comes from, who makes it, who performs it, etc.	Dairy products: "If it's Borden, it's got to be good."
Manufacture	how the product is made—process, ingredients, or design.	Juicy Juice: "100% juice for 100% kids."
Target	the product is made especially for people or firms like you (based on attributes such as end use, demographics, psychographics, or behaviors).	Apéritif: "Compari. Few drinks say so much about you and where you have been."
Rank	it is the best-selling product.	UPS: "The package company more companies rely on."
Endorsement	people you respect use it.	Toothbrush: "Oral-B. The brand name more dentists recommend."
Experience	its long (years) or frequent use (in other markets or by others—the bandwagon effect).	Buick: "90th Anniversary."
Competitor	it is just (or almost) like another product that you know and like.	Hewlett-Packard: "The new HP DeskJet 1200C gives you great-looking print quality, but it's as easy to use as a LaserJet printer."
Predecessor	it is comparable (in some way) to an earlier product that you liked.	Swiss Army Watch: "Built like our Swiss Army Knife."

Source: C. Merle Crawford, "A New Positioning Typology," *Journal of Product Innovation Management*, Vol. 2, No. 4 (December 1985), pp. 243–250.

Segmentation

Many firms make different appeals to different segments. AT&T Long Lines segmented its residential long-distance market and found a group of prospects with reasons to call long distance, but who didn't call because of a perceived price barrier. As a result, AT&T augmented its successful emotional appeal, its "Reach Out and Touch Someone" campaign, with a pragmatic appeal, a "Cost of Visit" campaign. This example will be discussed in more detail later in this chapter.

Where a product's image is important, psychographics are critical. Cosmetic firms, for example, use psychographics to make sure that the image of their products and ads is in sync with their customers' self-image. Marketers tend to reflect their own lifestyle in marketing communications, without paying adequate attention to the lifestyle of the target group. You have to make sure that it's your customers, not yourself, to whom you are talking.

Copy Pretesting

Focus groups are frequently used to evaluate rough commercials. The purpose is to ensure that communication objectives are met—that the message you want to send is the same one being received. This screening procedure prevents spending money on flawed commercials.

A variety of commercial copy-testing services test finished commercials. They differ in whether they conduct on-air or off-air tests, use a pre/posttest or posttest-only (matched-group) design, provide a single exposure or multiple exposures (reexposure), and other details. A major concern in using one of these services is whether their audience corresponds to your target market.

Copy-testing measures fall into six general categories: measures of persuasion, brand salience, recall, communications (playback), overall commercial reaction (liking), and commercial diagnostics. Representative examples are given in Table 14-3.

The Advertising Research Foundation's Copy Research Validity Project studied five pairs of commercials for established packaged goods that had produced significant sales differences in split-cable copy tests.[8] The pairs were commercials that had not previously aired from advertisers making minimal use of print in the test markets. The commercials were the only ones in use during the tests. At least six months

TABLE 14-3
Copy Testing Measures

Measure	Example
Persuasion	Overall brand rating
Brand salience	Top-of-mind awareness
Recall	Recall brand from category cue
Communications (playback)	Main point communication
Commercial reaction (liking)	Impression of commercial (average)
Commercial diagnostics	Told me something new about the product that I did not know before

of sales data were available. The Validity Project found that copy testing is helpful in identifying commercials known to be generating incremental sales. The most surprising finding is a strong relationship between likability of the copy and its effects on sales. On the other hand, the Information Resources Inc.'s "How Advertising Works" study found that the relationship between standard recall and persuasion scores and the sales impact for established brands is tenuous at best.[9]

MEDIA SELECTION

The objective in media planning is to select the set of TV and radio programs, magazines, newspapers, and other media vehicles that will maximize profits within a given budget. Your problem is that the optimum allocation tends to vary for each organization. Computer models have been developed to help evaluate media and audience data. The success of these models depends on understanding the appropriateness of media vehicles and on a knowledge of how media are matched with markets.

Media Vehicle Appropriateness

Media vehicles are not passive conductors of messages and can often influence the effectiveness of the message. Factors that determine the appropriateness of media vehicles include editorial climate, product fit, technical capabilities, comparative advertising strategy, target population receptiveness, and the product distribution system.

A vehicle has an image and a personality that can add to or detract from a message. *Sunset* is regarded as an expert source and *Vogue* as a prestige source. The relative value will depend on the campaign objectives (awareness versus attitude change versus image creation), the target segment, the campaign tactics (image versus reason-why advertising) and the product.

Media are believed to work in different ways. At each stage in the purchase process, one medium may be superior to another. In relation to TV commercials, print advertisements are less able to command attention, are more able to arouse personal involvement, and are more likely to cause conscious, discrete attitude change.

Consumers can pay *no* attention to a print advertisement or can deliberately expose themselves to one. They do the latter when they are seeking information for decision making. Consumers can concentrate longer on an advertising theme and thereby make more personal connections with it. This means that they can become more personally involved in print advertisements for products that possess intrinsic interest. Because attention is voluntary, the consumer is more likely to be consciously influenced. Attitude change under conditions of high involvement occurs through the process of dissonance resolution.

Even when customers do not watch a commercial on TV, they usually listen to it. Their involvement is low, and they are unaware that their attitudes are slowly being modified by the onslaught of repeated exposure to the message. Their attitudes may change more rapidly later when the source of the message is forgotten. This phenomenon is called the *sleeper effect*. When the consumer ultimately faces a purchasing situation, these shifts in attitude move to a more conscious level.

These differences suggest that print and TV advertising may be used most effectively in combination. One may be more suitable than the other for a particular step in the intermediate process. Thus, you need to match the media with company goals. Next, you must match the media with the target audience.

Matching Media with Markets

Advertisers prefer media whose audience characteristics are closest to the profile of the market characteristics of their customers.[10] For example, see Marketing in Action box 14-2. Characteristics by which the target population may be identified include demographic, psychographic, and purchase behavior variables. Matching takes two forms: direct matching, in which media are matched to product usage variables from syndicated product-media research services, and indirect matching, in which media are matched to demographic or psychographic profiles. The latter is useful when target markets are defined using a company's market research survey and media usage is obtained from a syndicated research service. Managers also need methods to help them select media that show the best combination of cost and exposure value.

Cost per Thousand

One method used to select media is to compare the cost per thousand persons reached by different vehicles. For example, a single four-color, one-page ad in *Reader's Digest* costs $153,600 and circulation in the United States is 16,258,476, so the cost per thousand circulation is $9.45. By comparison, *Newsweek* has a lower four-color rate of $120,835 but the circulation is only 3,240,131, so the cost per thousand is $37.29. Cost per thousand figures for all appropriate magazines can be compared and the magazines with the lowest cost per thousand chosen for use in the advertising campaign.[11]

The main problem with cost per thousand is that circulation figures do not include all persons exposed to the ads and thus may not be a good measure of the number of people who are in the market for the product. This deficiency can be overcome by gathering additional data on media readership and making appropriate adjustments. For example, *Reader's Digest* reports a total audience of 48 million readers and *Newsweek* has 22 million, so their costs per thousand readers for a four-color page are much closer, at $3.20 and $5.49, respectively. Further adjustments can be made to the denominator of the cost per thousand ratio for products that appeal to special market segments. Thus, a cost per thousand for women readers could be developed to compare alternative vehicles for products sold only to women.

Although cost-per-thousand calculations are helpful for finding the best vehicle buys within a particular medium, the technique is not appropriate for making comparisons across media. Differences in the form and presentation of ads are so vast among radio, TV, newspapers, and direct mail that cost-per-thousand comparisons

Van Heusen Advertises Men's Shirts to Women

After trying for 111 years, Van Heusen has finally pulled ahead of archrival Arrow to take top spot in the $2.4 billion men's dress shirt market. The Van Heusen brand edged ahead with a 9.9% market share, compared to Arrow's 9.2%, according to MRCA Information Services. This occurred in the face of a dwindling dress-shirt business. Men have been dressing more casually and have been satisfied with department stores' focus on their own brands, which are priced $5 to $10 below the Arrows and Van Heusens. For instance, Nordstrom says that about 90% of its dress shirts are private label.

White on **WHITE** The Dress Shirt.

VAN HEUSEN

One secret of Van Heusen's success—advertising directly to women. About half of Ven Heusen's $8 million ad budget is devoted to women's magazines, such as *Vogue*, *Glamour*, and *Cosmopolitan*. The shirt ads consist of bold two-page spreads featuring a handsome hunk clad in a colored shirt and a polka-dotted tie. Van Heusen's seemingly unorthodox approach stems from a reality of the menswear market. Women wear the pants when it comes to making purchases for the men in their lives.

Even as Van Heusen's new advertising has reinforced brand awareness among women, the company has drastically expanded its retail distribution. Traditionally Van Heusen restricted its sales to department stores. But bowing to the fact that shirts are increasingly sold on discount, it has opened its own network of more than 200 factory outlet stores and began selling to J.C. Penney. Van Heusen is counting on the fact that women tend to be more brand-conscious than men.

You should use the media whose audience characteristics are closest to the characteristics of your target segment.

Source: Teri Agins, "Women Help Van Heusen Collar Arrow," *The Wall Street Journal*, May 22, 1992, pp. B1, B5.

are not meaningful. In addition, restrictions on the distribution or patronage patterns of the advertiser may limit the portion of a media audience that is useful.

A retailer, for example, can buy a six-inch by three-column ad in the morning *Chicago Tribune* during the week for about $6200. Circulation of this paper is 691,941, so the cost per thousand is $8.96. An alternative approach might be to employ a direct-mail campaign where the cost per thousand would run between $400 and $600 for a letter, postage, brochure, and mailing list. If the choice of an advertising medium is based simply on cost per thousand, then obviously the newspaper is the better buy. Retailers typically draw their customers from a restricted market area, however, and the *Tribune* may provide a lot of waste circulation. This means that a dry cleaning store would be better off spending $6200 to send direct-mail literature to 15,500 consumers in the immediate area than to hope that an ad in the *Tribune* will reach them. When ads are placed in more than one medium or vehicle, audience duplication must be taken into account.

Duplication in advertising occurs because some of the individuals exposed to an ad in one vehicle will also see the ad in a second vehicle. For example, suppose that magazine A has an audience of 300,000 and magazine B has an audience of 200,000. If 100,000 of these people subscribe to both magazines, then the unduplicated audience is only 400,000. This suggests that the more media vehicles you buy, the greater the chance for duplication and the more likely you are to have diminishing returns to advertising.

Reach versus Frequency

The total impact of an advertising campaign can be measured by counting the number of exposures that result from *reaching* different people and multiplying by the average *frequency* of ad exposure per person. Thus, we have

$$\text{Total exposures} = \text{Reach} \times \text{Frequency}$$

This implies that high total exposure can be obtained by reaching a large number of people with a few ads or by exposing a small number of potential buyers to many ads. Your problem is to decide which combination of advertising reach and frequency is best for a particular product at a given point in time.

When an advertiser has a message that has to be heard only once, a media schedule that maximizes reach is used. The idea is to have every exposure appeal to a different potential buyer. Most of the retail advertising that emphasizes special sales and prices falls into this category. Also, many of the direct-mail promotions used for book and record clubs are designed to make a sale on the first impression, and reach is crucial to their success. In addition, reach can be important when introducing new products to the marketplace. This is especially true when cents-off coupons are offered to encourage trial and the firm wants each potential buyer to get only one coupon.

Alternatively, some advertisers must repeat ads frequently to get the buyer's attention and bring about attitude changes that precede purchase. In these situations, the emphasis is on the number of exposures per person rather than the reach of the campaign. This approach is based on research that shows that recall of ads and purchase intentions increase with the number of exposures per person. For many consumer products, the best exposure frequency seems to be at least two, and perhaps three, exposures within a purchase cycle. Repetition in advertising is also used to keep the name of the product in the buyer's mind so that when a purchase is planned, the company's brand will be remembered. This is particularly important for frequently purchased consumer goods, for which brand loyalty is low. Reminder ads can also be used to promote the sale of products and services that are bought infrequently. Funeral homes, insurance agents, and car dealers all employ repetition in their advertising to build a favorable image so that they will be considered when the buyer is ready to make a purchase.

Because of differences in products and market conditions, it is probably foolish to generalize about the optimum combination of reach and frequency for an advertising campaign. However, managers usually have better data on the reach of media vehicles than they have on duplication and the effects of repetition on sales. This suggests that media selection will often emphasize reach, with a more subjective adjustment made for frequency.

Computer Media Models

Traditional procedures for media selection that rely on judgment and experience are suspect because of their inability to consider the very large number of vehicle combinations possible. Computer models that help in making better media decisions are currently being developed. However, the original media models were used by advertising agencies more as promotional gimmicks than as tools to aid decision making.

There are two major groups of models. In the first group, enough assumptions are made so that the best media schedule can be found. This schedule is optimal only if the underlying assumptions are true. Optimizing models generally include some type of mathematical programming: linear, dynamic, integer, or nonlinear. In the second group, less restrictive assumptions are made, so that it is unknown whether the best media schedule examined is optimal. Nonoptimizing models involve heuristic problem solving and simulation.

Heuristic models are based on the actual decision rules used by media planners. These rules have evolved through experience and have been found to work satisfactorily. Media planners do not guarantee that they will produce the best solution.

MEASURING ADVERTISING EFFECTIVENESS

The ability of a firm to measure the effectiveness of its advertising is crucial to developing more efficient advertisements, determining the optimal level of expenditures, and allocating available funds to media. As soon as the relationship between advertising pressure and effectiveness is known, a firm can calculate the optimal advertising budget size, compare various media (intermedia optimization), and select vehicles within the same medium (intramedia optimization).

The importance of measuring the effectiveness of advertising can be illustrated by some case histories:

1. An advertiser had a great story. Twenty percent more of those who remembered it bought. Then the campaign was changed, and now only 10 percent more buy. But the advertiser did not realize this because an appropriate measurement was lacking.

2. An advertiser, spending $4 million a year, had a story with enormous pull. Yet this story was hidden in a small box in the ad. Knowledge of this fact would enable the advertiser to make copy changes.

3. An advertiser was spending $7 million a year, but the campaign had no usage pull. People who did not remember the advertising bought just as much as those who did remember it.

These cases suggest that one cannot base advertising decisions on intuition alone.

The four most commonly used measures of advertising effectiveness are changes in sales, number of inquiries received, increases in knowledge of the product, and attitude changes. Although the intermediate measures of effectiveness can provide helpful insights, sales are the best criterion for evaluating advertising results.

The analysis of the influence of advertising on the sales of a product or service is a complex undertaking. The difficulties involved in measuring the influences of advertising may be separated into three major categories: (1) the problem of isolating the effects of advertising from the many other variables that influence sales; (2) the problem of measuring the quantity of advertising, taking into account the fact that advertising dollar expenditures reflect alternative choices of media, psychological appeals, and copy; and (3) the problem of identifying the relationship that reflects the influence of advertising on sales.

You must be aware of the presence or absence of carryover effects. *Carryover* occurs when current marketing expenditures influence sales in future periods. The *delayed response effect* occurs when there is a delay between the advertisement and the resulting purchase. The *customer holdover effect* occurs when the advertisement influences a sequence of purchases. Carryover is represented in the advertising response function by the use of lagged variables.

The methods available for measuring advertising elasticity include controlled experiments and econometric procedures. Controlled field experiments can provide good data, but they are expensive. Econometric methods are more popular for studying the impact of advertising on the sales of existing products. We begin with a discussion of tracking.

Tracking

Consistent theme advertising maintains the saliency of the mental connections that constitute the brand. You should then track the advertising memories of people in connection with brands. One company that does this is Millward Brown.

Andrex toilet paper is closely associated with the benefits of being "soft, strong, and long." These associations were developed, maintained, and enhanced by advertising. Andrex has used a series of puppy ads. One advertisement, known as "little boy," featured a little boy sitting on the toilet and watching a puppy run off with the toilet roll. Millward Brown tracked this advertisement in Great Britain as the ad consolidated the traditional associations and added some more emotional strands.

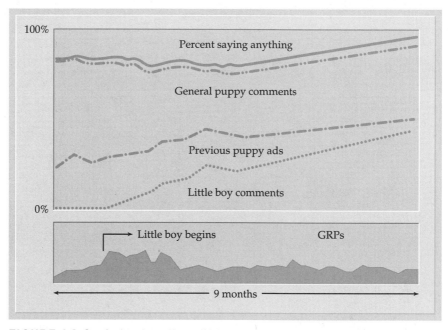

FIGURE 14-8 Andrex Long-Term Ad Awareness (From Jeremy Green, "How Repetition and Consistency Build Mental Connections," in *People, Brands & Advertising*, Millward Brown, 1992, p. 48)

One question they asked consumers was "When you think of all the advertising you've seen for Andrex, what, if anything, do you particularly remember from it?" The results are shown in Figure 14-8. Notice how heavy media weight gradually brings images from the "little boy" ad into people's minds in connection with Andrex. This approach gives us information about when the communications job is done.[12]

Qualitative research in the form of before-and-after brand image maps can indicate whether or not your advertising is working as desired. Silentnight launched a new bed in the United Kingdom.[13] Unfortunately, the launch was bogged down by a serious industrial dispute that hampered production. After the dispute was ended, Silentnight needed to relaunch an improved version of the product. The ultimate Sleep System was a unique combination of mattress and base that offered individual support for two sleepers regardless of the differential in weight, support right up to the edge of the bed to eliminate roll-off, and a posturized zone of extra springs in the central third to provide extra support where body weight is greatest. The creative advertising solution for communicating these features was a unique product demonstration that was sufficiently novel to break through customer apathy and to communicate convincingly the product's principal benefits. The stars of this demonstration were a hippo and a duck! Consumers reacted enthusiastically. The establishment of Silentnight's differential positioning is tracked over 18 months in Figure 14-9a, and the improvement in perception of the brand is tracked over 24 months in Figure 14-9b.

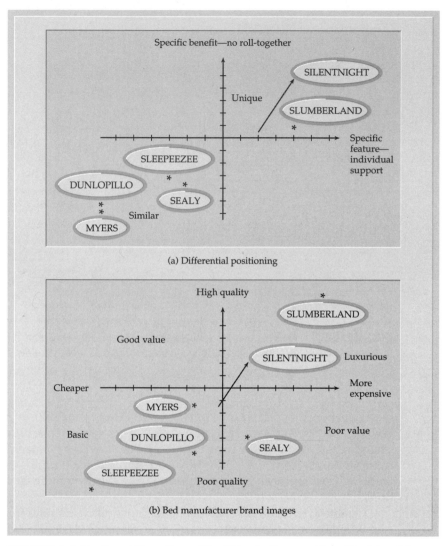

FIGURE 14-9 Brand Maps (From "The Ultimate Success Story," in *Advertising Works 6*, Paul Feldwick, ed. [Henley-on-Thames: NTC Publications, 1991], pp. 59–60)

Experimental Methods

Successful users of field experiments include AT&T, Nabisco, and Campbell Soup. AT&T used a dual-cable television system in conjunction with its own long distance usage tracking system to test the impact of a new "Cost of Visit" campaign against the existing "Reach Out" campaign. Households in test markets are connected to either an "A" or a "B" cable in checkerboard fashion. This allows different ads to be sent to each group. The experimental design executed by AT&T is shown in Table

TABLE 14-4
AT&T Field Experiment

Study Phase	5-Month Preassessment	15-Month Test	6-Month Reassessment
Cable A	"Feelings"	"Reach Out"	"Reach Out"/ local company
Cable B	↓	"Cost of Visit"	↓

14-4. The test results indicated that, over a five-year period, the "Cost of Visit" campaign would generate some $100 million more than the "Reach Out" campaign.[14]

RJR Nabisco was resigned to slow growth from its biscuit division because it was in a mature industry. Nabisco experimented with saturation advertising aimed at small population segments and found that the whole cookie and cracker business was underpromoted. Nabisco heavily advertised its 40-year-old Ritz cracker, in six different geographical markets, representing 3.2 percent of the adult population in America. The buying behavior of this group in the face of heavy TV and store promotions was monitored for one year. The purchases of a control group were also recorded. The experimental group had a 16 percent increase in sales. Nabisco modified its promotional strategy in light of its experimental findings.

Campbell Soup has conducted a series of experiments and subsequent analyses that have shown that budget levels generally have little or no impact on the sales of well-established brands. By contrast, changes in copy strategy, media selection, media mix, and targeting have a substantial payout. The products studied included Campbell's Condensed Soup, Chunky Soups, Franco-American, V-8, and Swanson.[15]

Econometric Methods

Econometric models have been constructed that permit (1) the isolation of the effects of advertising from those of other factors; (2) the characterization of carryover effects, diminishing returns to scale, the relative effectiveness of each medium, and the impact of different campaigns; (3) comparison of various media; and (4) prediction of the behavior of competitive advertising and sales, as well as the behavior of brand advertising and sales.

Single-equation models are suspect in this analysis because they assume a unidirectional flow of influence. Although sales are a function of advertising expenditure, advertising is also a function of sales. Frequently, the demand for a product shifts, whereas the firm's advertising budgeting remains rigid. Under these conditions, advertising budgets that are set as a fixed percentage of sales or in relation to the size of markets will increase with demand. Although it may seem that larger ad budgets produce higher sales, in reality advertising is just reacting to changes in volume. Thus, what appears to be a demand curve showing the relationship between advertising and sales is merely a trace of the advertising budget line. In econometrics, this is known as the *identification problem*. Processes that involve multiple relationships must be represented by a system of equations.

Research has shown that advertising elasticities for established consumer pack-aged goods are surprisingly low. A typical advertising elasticity is probably on the order of 0.10. This means that doubling advertising spending will increase sales volume by only 10 percent.[16] The results of the measurement of advertising effectiveness feed back into the advertising budget process.

The profits for a brand are a function of market responsiveness to advertising and the cost structure of the brand. This is illustrated in Table 14-5, where the impact of a 50 percent increase in advertising expenditures is assessed for various values of

TABLE 14-5

Sales and Profit Outcomes of a 50% Advertising Increase

Variable Cost (as a percent of NSV)[a]	Advertising-to-Sales Ratio	Advertising Elasticity Level	Effect on Sales	Effect on Net Profit (if 5% of NSV)	Effect on Net Profit (if 5% of NSV)
40%	4%	+0.1	+5%	+20%	+10%
50	4	+0.1	+5	+10	+5
60	4	+0.1	+5	No change	No change
40	4	+0.2	+10	+80	+40%
50	4	+0.2	+10	+60	+30
60	4	+0.2	+10	+40	+20
40	4	+0.3	+15	+140	+70
50	4	+0.3	+15	+110	+55
60	4	+0.3	+15	+80	+40
40	6	+0.1	+5	No change	No change
50	6	+0.1	+5	−10	−5
60	6	+0.1	+5	−20	−10
40	6	+0.2	+10	+60	+30
50	6	+0.2	+10	+40	+20
60	6	+0.2	+10	+20	+10
40	6	+0.3	+15	+120	+60
50	6	+0.3	+15	+90	+45
60	6	+0.3	+15	+60	+30
40	8	+0.1	+5	−20	−10
50	8	+0.1	+5	−30	−15
60	8	+0.1	+5	−40	−20
40	8	+0.2	+10	+40	+20
50	8	+0.2	+10	+20	+10
60	8	+0.2	+10	No change	No change
40	8	+0.3	+15	+100	+50
50	8	+0.3	+15	+70	+35
60	8	+0.3	+15	+40	+20

[a]NSV stands for net sales value.

Source: John Philip Jones, *How Much Is Enough* (New York: Lexington Books, 1992), p. 111.

the advertising elasticity and various levels of variable and fixed costs. Note that the point where you start from, expressed as the advertising-to-sales ratio, is also important.

ADVERTISING VERSUS DIRECT MARKETING

While general mass media advertising allows you to target your audience somewhat, ultimately your customers self-select themselves while remaining anonymous. Direct marketing, on the other hand, sells to identifiable customers at their location. As discussed in Chapter 11, direct marketing has the added benefit of delivering your product directly to the customer's door. Advertising is often used as part of direct marketing to generate inquiries and orders. A comparison between direct marketing and general mass-marketing advertising is presented in Table 14-6. The main distinction between direct marketing and general mass marketing is that of a dialogue versus a monologue.

TABLE 14-6

Comparison of Direct Marketing and General Mass-Marketing Advertising

Direct Marketing	General Mass-Marketing Advertising
Selling to individuals, with customers identifiable by name, address, and purchase behavior (personal, targetable, ability to vary the message by segment, measurable, ability to capture data).	Mass selling, with buyers identified as broad groups and sharing common demographic and psychographic characteristics (cost efficient where identity of customers is unknown).
Products have the added value of distribution to the customer's door as an important product benefit.	Product benefits do not typically include distribution to the customer's door.
The medium is the marketplace.	The retail outlet is the marketplace.
Marketing controls product all the way through delivery.	The marketer typically loses control as the product enters the distribution stream.
Uses targeted media.	Uses mass media.
Is hard for competitors to monitor—the stealth factor.	Can be monitored by competitors using syndicated services.
Advertising is used to generate an immediate inquiry or order, with a specific order.	Advertising is used for its cumulative effect over time in building awareness, image, loyalty, and benefit recall. Purchase action is deferred.
Repetition is used within an ad or mailing.	Repetition is used over a period of time.
Consumer feels a high perceived risk—product bought unseen, distant recourse.	Consumer feels less risk—has direct contact with product and direct recourse.

Source: Adapted from DMA's Direct Marketing Institute; and Jim Kobs, *Profitable Direct Marketing* (Lincolnwood, IL: NTC Business Books, 1991), p. 13.

SUMMARY

Advertising can assume an important role in building awareness and providing information about goods and services. Advertising begins with the determination of objectives and goals. Next, you need to set the size of the advertising budget. This can be done using percentage-of-sales methods, the task procedure, or normative approaches. Given a budget, you need to develop appropriate themes and campaign materials. Advertising agencies are often employed to help with this work. The next step is to pick an appropriate set of media vehicles. Computer media models are available to assist in this planning. Finally, you need to measure the effects of advertising expenditures and integrate them with promotional activities.

NOTES

1. "The Case for Radion Automatic: A New Brand in the Lever Portfolio," in *Advertising Works 6*, Paul Feldwick, ed. (Henley-on-Thames: NTC Publications, 1991), pp. 209–222.

2. "Croft Original 'One Instinctively Knows When Something Is Right'," in *Advertising Works 6*, Paul Feldwick, ed. (Henley-on-Thames: NTC Publications, 1991), pp. 26–43.

3. Simon Broadbent, "Modelling with Adstock," *Journal of the Market Research Society*, Vol. 26, No. 4 (October 1984), pp. 295–312, and "Modelling Beyond the Blip," *Journal of the Market Research Society*, Vol. 32, No. 1 (January 1990), pp. 61–102.

4. Raj Sethuraman and Gerald J. Tellis, "An Analysis of the Tradeoff Between Price and Price Discounting," *Journal of Marketing Research*, Vol. 28 (May 1991), p. 167.

5. Laurence N. Gold, "Let's Heavy Up in St. Louis and See What Happens," *Journal of Advertising Research*, Vol. 33, No. 6 (November–December 1992), pp. 31–38.

6. For a detailed discussion of sales response functions, see Dominique M. Hanssens, Leonard J. Parsons, and Randall L. Schultz, *Market Response Models: Econometric and Time Series Analysis* (New York: Kluwer, 1990), pp. 29–73.

7. Fred S. Zufryden, "How Much Should Be Spent for Advertising a Brand?" *Journal of Advertising Research*, Vol. 29, No. 2 (April–May 1989), p. 26.

8. Russell I. Haley and Allan L. Baldinger, "The ARF Copy Research Validity Project," *Journal of Advertising Research* (April–May 1991), pp. 11–32.

9. Beth Lubetkin, "Additional Major Findings From the 'How Advertising Works' Study," Marketplace Advertising Research Workshop, New York: November 6–7, 1991.

10. Frederick W. Winter, "Match Target Markets to Media Audiences," *Journal of Advertising Research*, Vol. 20 (February 1980), pp. 61–66.

11. Cost, circulation, and other media data are published monthly by Standard Rate and Data Service, Inc. The numbers used in the examples are from *Consumer Magazine and Agri-Media Rates and Data*, Vol. 75, No. 9 (September 1993), pp. 274–276, 488–489.

12. Jeremy Green, "How Repetition and Consistency Build Mental Connections," in *People, Brands and Advertising* (London: Millward Brown, 1992), pp. 47–48.

13. "The Ultimate Success Story," in *Advertising Works 6*, Paul Feldwick, ed. (Henley-on-Thames: NTC Publications, 1991), pp. 44–66.

14. Alan Kuritsky, Emily Bassman, John D. C. Little, and Alvin J. Silk, "Development, Testing, and Execution of a New Advertising Strategy at AT&T Long Lines," in *Proceedings:*

9th *International Research Seminar in Marketing* (Aix-en-Provence, France: IAE, 1982), pp. 451–492.

15. Joseph O. Eastlack, Jr., and Ambar G. Rao, "Modeling Response to Advertising and Pricing Changes for 'V-8' Cocktail Vegetable Juice," *Marketing Science,* Vol. 5 (Summer 1986), pp. 245–259, and "Advertising Experiments at the Campbell Soup Company," *Marketing Science,* Vol. 8 (Winter 1989), pp. 57–71.

16. David A. Aaker and James M. Carman, "Are You Overadvertising?" *Journal of Advertising Research,* Vol. 22 (August–September 1982), pp. 57–70, and Gert Assmus, John U. Farley, and Donald R. Lehmann, "How Advertising Affects Sales: A Meta-Analysis of Econometric Results," *Journal of Marketing Research,* Vol. 21 (February 1984), pp. 65–74.

SUGGESTED READING

Achenbaum, Alvin A. "Reversing the Advertising Productivity Crisis," *Marketing Management,* Vol. 1, No. 3 (1992), pp. 22–27.

Gold, Laurence N. "Let's Heavy Up in St. Louis and See What Happens," *Journal of Advertising Research,* Vol. 33, No. 6 (November–December 1992), pp. 31–38.

FURTHER READING

Bell, Stephen S. *Evaluating the Effects of Consumer Advertising on Market Position Over Time: How to Tell Whether Advertising Ever Works.* Report No. 88-107. (Cambridge, MA: Marketing Science Institute, July 1988).

Broadbent, Simon. *The Advertising Budget* (Henley-on-Thames: NTC Publications Ltd., 1989).

Feldwick, Paul. *Advertising Works 6* (Henley-on-Thames: NTC Publications Ltd., 1991).

Forker, Olan D., and Ronald W. Ward. *Commodity Advertising: The Economics and Measurement of Generic Programs* (New York: Lexington Books, 1993).

Jones, John Philip. *How Much Is Enough? Getting the Most from Your Advertising Dollar* (New York: Lexington Books, 1992).

Millward Brown International Plc. *People, Brands and Advertising* (London, 1992).

Randazzo, Sal. *Mythmaking on Madison Avenue* (Chicago: Probus, 1993).

Rijkens, Rein. *European Advertising Strategies* (London: Cassell, 1992).

Stewart, David W. "Speculations on the Future of Advertising Research," *Journal of Advertising,* Vol. 21, No. 3 (September 1992), pp. 1–18.

QUESTIONS

1. Many in the advertising industry have sent out loud warnings that companies are endangering their brands by selling on price instead of image or performance. Others say that this claim is just a ploy devised by the advertising industry to gain its share of the marketing dollar. What do you think?

2. The 1992 South Coast Newspaper Advertising and Consumer Products Survey released by the University of California–Santa Barbara's Economic Forecast Project shows that most people don't remember any specific ads in the newspapers they read. Does this mean that you should not advertise in newspapers?

3. Some U.S. lawmakers have proposed that alcohol ads on television and in newspapers should carry warning labels about the dangers of drinking. What do you believe?

4. Outdoor advertising has undergone a technical revolution. Images can now be painted by computers, allowing a more uniform, accurate look. Advertisers can also control the lighting of their ads through a satellite system. Outdoor advertising is becoming easier, faster, and more responsive to advertisers' needs. Nonetheless, it is facing competition from new out-of-home media ranging from shopping cart displays to blimps. Construct a campaign to help the Outdoor Advertising Association of America tell its story to advertisers.

5. Some critics of advertising have argued that advertising creates unwanted demand. What do you think?

6. *Advertising Age* regularly reports on the movement of an advertiser's account from one agency to another. There is a saying in the advertising industry for such moves: "It's the second-oldest story in the world—new management wanted a new agency." Is this a good reason for an agency shakeup? When should you change agencies?

7. Wrigley dominates the world of chewing gum with the number one brand, Doublemint, and a host of other popular brands, such as Juicy Fruit, Spearmint, Extra, Freedent, Big Red, and Hubba Bubba. It has a 48 percent share of the U.S. retail market, nearly twice that of its biggest competitor. To grow, it needs to expand primary demand. The biggest impediment to gum sales is social stigma. Some people consider gum chewing in public bad manners. Can Wrigley use advertising to convince people that it is all right to chew gum? If so, how?

8. How should you allocate an advertising budget between short-term calls to action and long-term brand building?

9. What type of positioning is represented by each of the following statements?
   a. Cereal: "Kix. Kid-tested, mother approved."
   b. Telecommunications: "BellSouth. Everything you expect from a leader."
   c. Credit card: "American Express Optima. You have your own approach to tradition."
   d. Porcelain tableware: "Fabergé for the table . . . inspired by legend."
   e. Car: "More than 98 percent of all Chevy trucks sold in the last 10 years are still on the road."
   f. Sneakers: "Keds. They feel good."
   g. Baby food: "Gerber adds sugar. Beech-Nut doesn't."
   h. Motor oil: "Valvoline. It's the No. 1 choice of Indy 500 chief mechanics."

Chapter 15

Sales Promotion and Public Relations

Most short-term promotional decisions are really undertaken as a response to weaknesses in other elements of marketing strategy.

LEONARD LODISH

Each element in the basic marketing mix is supplemented by a group of marketing instruments whose main purpose is to induce immediate buying behavior by strengthening the basic mix element for a short period of time. This group of instruments is called the *promotion mix*. Specific support activities are often classified as either sales promotions or public relations. *Sales promotions* have been defined as "action-focused marketing events whose purpose is to have a direct impact on the behavior of the firm's customers."[1] Sales promotions involve such activities as specialty advertising, rebates, couponing, temporary price reduction labels, bonus packs, sampling, premiums, point-of-purchase material, trade allowances, sales and dealer incentives, trade shows, exhibits, and demonstrations. *Public relations* are actions that promote goodwill between a firm and its customers. They involve activities such as customer service, crisis management, consumer education, publicity, special events, and sponsorships.

Although you might believe that most of a company's promotion budget is spent on media advertising, the various sales promotion activities taken as a whole involve much larger expenditures. Product marketers in the United States spend about 25.1 percent of their promotional budgets on media advertising, 49.5 percent on trade promotions, and 25.4 percent on consumer promotions.[2] Trade promotion passed media advertising as the leading category in 1984. The relative importance of some components of promotion is indicated in Figure 15-1. Sampling, particularly in-store sampling, continues to grow in popularity. We begin by discussing the promotion mix in more detail.

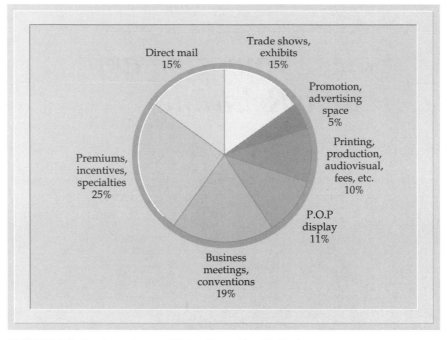

FIGURE 15-1 Importance of Sales Promotion Methods

PROMOTION MIX

The promotion mix can be described in the same terms as the marketing mix. The instruments that support each element of the marketing mix are shown in Table 15-1.

Product

The main type of product promotion is the *sample.* A sample is a free trial of a product. The sample is usually smaller than the regular product. About 90 percent of sampling is for new products.

There are a variety of ways to deliver a sample: in the store, via direct mail, on doorknobs, and in plastic bags along with newspapers. The most effective way to get product trial is to mail or distribute free samples directly to customers' homes. Research has shown that 75 percent of homeowners try the free samples, and 25 percent of these go out and buy the product. Up to 20 percent more users can be obtained by including a coupon with the free sample. Sampling should be used if the product exhibits demonstrable superiority, if the concept is difficult to convey by advertising, if a sizable budget is available for a broad usage category, or if product class dominance is sought. Sampling can be expensive, but it does ensure that people will try the product and it has proved to be one of the most powerful promotional devices available to marketing managers.

TABLE 15-1
Promotion Mix

Mix Element Supported	Instruments Used
Product	Samples, bonus product, premiums
Price	Coupons, temporary discounts, temporary price reduction labels, refunds, slotting fees, temporary favorable terms of payment and credit, end-of-season sales
Distribution	Trade promotions, point-of-purchase materials
Communications	
Personal selling	Temporary demonstrations, trade shows, exhibitions, sales force contests
Mass	Customer contests, sweepstakes
Publicity	Special events, press bulletins, press conferences, tours by journalists

Source: Based on Walter van Waterschoot and Christophe Van den Bulte, "The 4P Classification of the Marketing Mix Revisited," *Journal of Marketing*, Vol. 56, No. 4 (October 1992), pp. 83–93.

Blockbuster Entertainment rents videotapes. Each month, Blockbuster serves 40 to 50 million people who have incomes of more than $45,000 and above-average discretionary income. One Fourth of July weekend, it distributed 4 million "Blockbuster Bonus Boxes" at 2000 stores to customers renting three or more videos. The boxes contained $10 worth of samples from companies such as Keebler, General Mills, and Procter & Gamble. Blockbuster supported the promotion with spot TV and radio ads. Blockbuster's view of this promotion was that "it's a traffic building vehicle, but it is just as important to us as a value add."[2] Reebok put brightly colored kiosks in 200 participating malls to allow prospects to try their shoes. Reeboks then directed them to nearby Foot Locker stores. A follow-up survey found that 15 percent of those who tried on the shoes bought them within two weeks. Lego samples via co-promotion with children's foods. About 20 million packages of Fruit Loops, Apple Jacks, and Snacks 20 ready-to-eat cereals offered free Lego sets for one UPC code.[3]

Sampling is one of the most expensive promotion methods. The Blockbuster Bonus Box had a cost per thousand (CPM) of $70 to $150, considerably higher than a mass-media buy. However, the *cost per customer converted* (see Marketing Tools box 15-1) is much lower for sampling than that of any other promotion because there is no barrier to trial.

Another product promotion consists of giving all persons making a purchase a free gift. For example, Frito corn chips has employed a promotion in which it attached flower seeds to packages of the product. A classic novelty promotion was run some years ago that involved giving gasoline customers a small plastic ball, resembling the "76" signs used to identify Union Oil stations, to mount on their radio antennas.

A variation on the gift idea is the offer of merchandise at low prices to customers who send in labels from packages. *Premiums* are one of the least expensive of all promotional devices because the revenue derived from customers usually covers most of the costs of the promotion. This "self-liquidating" feature results from vol-

---

MARKETING TOOLS 15-1

COST PER CUSTOMER CONVERTED

The Warner-Lambert American Chicle Group found these results for two alternative sampling methods:

Promotion	Free product coupon	Sample
Number	51 million	5 million
Delivery method	FSI	Direct mail
CPM	$7	$80
Users	367,200	800,000
Cost/converted user	$5.88	$1.69

Source: Terry Lefton, "Try It—You'll Like It," *Brandweek*, May 2, 1993, pp. 27, 28, 30, 32.

---

ume purchases and the elimination of the normally high retail margins on premium-type merchandise. The most desirable premiums are showy items that inspire retailers to build off-shelf displays and encourage usage of the product by the consumer.

Price

The primary consumer price promotion is the *coupon*. Where promotional funds are limited, "cents-off" coupons can be an effective means of getting product trial. The average coupon face value is about 50 cents. Retailers earn an 8-cent handling fee per coupon. Manufacturers of consumer packaged goods distributed more than 350 billion coupons in 1992. The coupons are typically sent by mail or incorporated into magazine and newspaper ads. Thus this approach can be used regionally. The number of coupons returned is one measure of the effectiveness of the promotion.

The typical coupon shopper in the United States is a middle-aged, married, working white woman who has a household income of $29,000 and who knocks $6 off her weekly $74 grocery bill by using coupons. Lower-income families aren't exposed to as many coupons because the vast majority of coupons are distributed through newspapers and magazines and such families spend less than average for reading materials.[4]

Rather than using coupons, you can offer the consumer a package with a special *temporary price reduction label*. A cents-off designation indicates the amount the regular retail price is supposedly reduced during the special promotion. However, although the manufacturer may lower the price to the dealer, there is no assurance that the retailer will pass the savings on to the consumer. Manufacturers have encountered sharp trade resistance to cents-off packs because retailers resent handling problems and duplicate inventories. The inability of the manufacturer to control cents-off promotions adequately makes this technique less desirable than couponing.

Coupons suffer from misredemption problems. Consequently, some manufacturers prefer cash *refunds*. Although these refunds carry higher values, a much lower redemption rate may be expected. Some people buy with the intention of sending in for the refund but never get around to it.

Distribution

Point-of-purchase (POP) displays can increase sales markedly. The key is to get the retailer to use them. For example, Seagram was late entering the wine cooler market long dominated by Bartle & James. Seagram launched its first promotion aimed at 60 million Americans who drink wine and bowl regularly. Store displays were created with a mail-in offer to save $75 on bowling equipment. Seagram went on to sponsor prizes on the professional bowling circuit. It also mounted displays featuring recipe booklets, 100-case fruit stands, Memorial Day sweepstakes, football calendars, $5-per-case rebates, and fireworks themes, along with shelf talkers and bull's-eye cards. This continuous use of in-store displays and promotions helped Seagram seize 33 percent of the wine cooler market and garner the number one position by the end of the following year.[5]

Communication

Manufacturers frequently try to build customer interest and sales volumes with *contests, sweepstakes,* and other games of chance. The idea is to attract consumer attention by offering substantial merchandise and cash prizes to a few lucky winners. Entry blanks and lottery tickets are dispensed at the retail level to tie the promotion to the sale of the product. The main objective of contests is to stimulate sales with in-store displays of the product rather than produce a large number of entries.

The activities that have been discussed represent only a few of the many techniques that can be used in creating a promotional strategy for the firm. The only real limit to the variety of promotions is the depth of the imagination of the managers in charge.

TYPES OF PROMOTION

Promotions can be directed either at intermediaries in your channels, called *trade promotions*, or at the ultimate buyer, called *consumer promotions*. These two kinds of promotions are usually used in concert, especially for new-product introductions.

Trade Promotions

Trade promotions are designed to improve dealer cooperation; they include such things as training sessions for sales personnel to make them more knowledgeable about the goods and services of a particular company. A related procedure is to give dealer salespeople special gifts or bonuses when they push the sale of certain products. Dealer interest can also be improved by providing them with attractive POP materials. As an added incentive, prizes are frequently offered to the merchants who construct the best displays utilizing the product and promotional materials. Perhaps the most popular promotional device directed at distributors is the *deal,* or special reduced-price offer. Deals are short-run discounts designed to build dealer stocks and to stimulate retail sales. They may be expressed in terms of lower prices or as "free" merchandise offered for minimum orders. Another effective promotional technique is a sales contest for distributors. Dealers who sell the most merchandise during a certain period are rewarded with vacations in Hawaii, mink coats, and cash bonuses. All promotional efforts are designed to raise sales, but most dealer programs have the goal of improving relations with those who sell the product to the final consumer. Better dealer relations can increase the number of distributors willing to carry the product, enlarge display areas, and gain acceptance of larger inventories and new items.

Trade promotions have been increasing, reflecting the increasing power of the retailer. A survey of product marketers found that 87 percent implemented account-specific promotions for key retail customers. Information Resources, Inc., analyzes a number of trade promotions annually and finds that very few of them pay out; IRI's estimated payout rate is less than 20 percent.[6] We will return to this point shortly.

Consumer Promotions

Consumer-oriented promotional activities are designed to induce consumers to try products. A proportion of those introduced to a product will become steady customers. Moreover, brand switching is a fact of life for low-cost, frequently purchased products. Your aim is to gain more customers than you lose in this churn. Thus, getting back former customers by encouraging retrial is very important. The relative importance of alternative consumer promotions is shown in Figure 15-2.

Coupon users need an average increase of 40 percent in coupon face value to try products they don't normally buy. For example, if a user redeems a 50-cent coupon for a favorite product, he or she will require at least a 70-cent coupon to try a new or not normally used product.[7] Manufacturers will also often drop coupons to head off a big splash by the competition. Timed to reach consumers in an area just before a competitor launches a product or sponsors a special event such as a concert, coupons effectively knock consumers out of the market by encouraging them to stock up their home pantries.

Price promotions may have a "mortgaging" effect as consumers purchase for inventory. When the brand returns to the regular shelf price, sales may be initially slow as consumers draw down promotion-subsidized stocks.

Retailers use price promotions to build traffic. Because they may not be profitable in their own right but do encourage purchases of profitable products, they are known as *loss leaders.* Retailers also use price promotions to clear inventories of obsolete products.

New-Product Promotions

If a new package good does not establish itself in six months, the lost momentum is hard if not impossible to recover. A comprehensive sales promotion plan is conse-

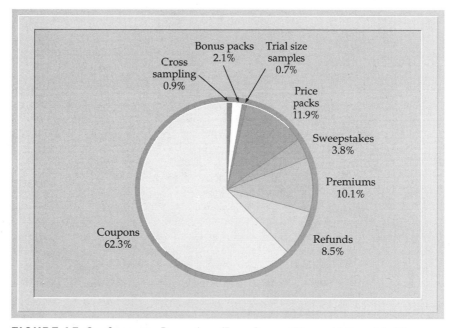

FIGURE 15-2 Consumer Promotions (From Dancer Fitzgerald Sample's "Consumer Promotion Report")

quently a necessity for new-product introductions. New products must first be explained to the company's own salespeople. They should be enthusiastic about the product and convinced that it will be a winner. Second, trade awareness should be built so that when the salespeople arrive, the buyer has some favorable predisposition toward the product. When Gillette launched Earthborn shampoo, every major account was sent a box of dirt before the sales call. Buried in the dirt were three bottles of shampoo.

The presentation to the trade should place its emphasis on the retailer and the consumer's need for the product. The retailer is not about to drop a private label in favor of a branded item. Moreover, the retailer is not interested in simply trading profits with an existing brand. The quantity of buy-in must be decided. An *early-buy allowance* might be used to get a new product into distribution before advertising starts. Such allowances lower the distributor's risk in stocking new brands. Sometimes you do not have a choice. Mass merchandisers charge packaged-goods producers *slotting fees* to carry new products in their stores. These fees may amount to four- or five-figure numbers per item per chain in the United States. Determination of the correct size of the pack for the appropriate stores and the correct size and type of display is also important. Special promotions for new products can be very expensive. Gillette's Silkience shampoo, for example, cost about $40 million to introduce. This included heavy advertising, free samples for 27 million households, and price promotions. The role of promotion in another new-product launch is illustrated in Marketing in Action box 15-1. The practical constraints on promotional efforts include the availability of funds and the need to find some reliable measure of sales effects.

CONFLICTS BETWEEN THE PROMOTIONAL MIX AND THE MARKETING MIX

While the promotional mix is supposed to support the marketing mix, a major concern is that, improperly used, the promotional mix might undermine the marketing mix. This is especially true in the case of price promotions with respect to list price and advertising.

Advertising versus Price Promotion

In boosting list prices and making deep promotional price cuts, consumer goods companies have allowed their focus to be diverted from long-run profits to short-term sales volume and market share. In the process, they have shifted more and more money from consistent theme advertising to consumer and trade promotions. Research from the Promotion Marketing Association of America (not an unbiased source) shows that senior executives believe that promotion is more effective than advertising. These executives have also said that consumer promotion does build brand equity and that trade promotion can do the same. Others believe that price promotions devalue brand image. Managers at Unilever characterize the process as "promotion, commotion, demotion."[8]

On the other hand, consistent theme advertising strengthens a brand's image for the long haul. The resultant brand equity offers some protection from competitive forays. Reductions in advertising expenditures in order to fund price promotions may weaken consumers' perceptions of a brand. Note that price promotion costs vary with volume and permit small regional brands to compete against heavily advertised national brands.

List Price versus Price Promotion

Many manufacturers believe that a high-list, high-deal policy is more profitable than offering a single price to all consumers. This is because it permits them to price-discriminate among customer segments. This is one aspect of *demand pricing*.[9] Consider a brand targeted at two segments: regular customers and deal-prone, price-sensitive customers. Suppose that you face the (linear) demand curves for each segment shown in Table 15-2 and your product has a unit variable cost of $0.80. If you never do any promotion, what price should you charge? The maximum contribution occurs at a list price of $1.60. Suppose, however, that you want to price-discriminate among the segments; what prices should you charge within the ranges given? The best prices would be a $2.00 list price for regular customers and a $1.40 promotion price for deal-prone customers. Demand pricing yields higher profits. You do not want to leave money on the table!

The demand pricing strategy is not without problems. Care must be taken in executing it. Two problems can happen: leakage and slippage. *Leakage* occurs when consumers not targeted for a price promotion manage to take advantage of it. *Slippage* occurs when those who should receive a promotion do not. Table 15-3 illustrates the consequences of these phenomena. For example, with 20 percent leakage, 14 (20 percent of 70) of current list-price segment buyers, plus 3 (20 percent of [85 − 70]) additional list-price segment buyers attracted by the lower price, will buy at the promotional price.

TABLE 15-2
Segment Demand Curves

Price	List-price Segment Units	List-price Segment Contribution	Promotion-price Segment Units	Promotion-price Segment Contribution	Total Market (Both Segments) Units	Total Market (Both Segments) Contribution
$2.00	**70.0**	**$84.00**	00.0	$00.00	70.0	$ 84.00
1.90	72.5	79.75	15.0	16.50	87.5	96.25
1.80	75.0	75.00	30.0	30.00	105.0	105.00
1.70	77.5	69.75	45.0	40.50	122.5	110.25
1.60	**80.0**	**64.00**	**60.0**	**48.00**	**140.0**	**112.00**
1.50	82.5	57.75	75.0	52.50	157.5	110.25
1.40	85.0	51.00	*90.0*	*54.00*	175.0	105.00

Source: Paul W. Farris and John A. Quelch, "The Defense of Price Promotions," *Sloan Management Review*, Vol. 29, No. 1 (Fall 1987), p. 67.

TABLE 15-3

Impact of Leakage and Slippage

	Single Price	Dual Price Leakage = 0% Slippage = 0%		Dual Price Leakage = 20% Slippage = 0%		Dual Price Leakage = 0% Slippage = 20%		Dual Price Leakage = 20% Slippage = 20%	
	List	List	Promotion	List	Promotion	List	Promotion	List	Promotion
Price	$1.60	$2.00	$1.40	$2.00	$1.40	$2.00	$1.40	$2.00	$1.40
Units	140	70	90	56	107	70	72	56	89
Average unit price	$1.60	$1.66		$1.61		$1.70		$1.63	
Unit variable cost	.80	.80		.80		.80		.80	
Average unit margin	.80	.86		.81		.90		.83	
Total number of units	140	160		163		142		145	
Total contribution	$112.00	$137.60		$132.03		$127.80		$120.35	
Promotion admin. (2% of gross sales)	$.00	$6.40		$6.52		$5.68		$5.80	
Net contribution	$112.00	$131.20		$125.51		$122.12		$114.55	
Gain from promotion	—	$19.20		$13.51		$10.12		$2.55	

Source: Adapted from source of Table 15-2.

Trade deals pose further complications.[10] Distributors may not pass on the benefits of a deal to the consumer. Attractive trade deals may also lead distributors to forward-buy or divert goods. *Forward buying* involves purchasing more inventory now than is needed to run a concurrent consumer promotion. The extra merchandise can then be sold at regular prices after the deal period. Enough merchandise may be bought to last until the next deal. *Diversion* involves buying goods in regions where manufacturers are offering unusually deep discounts and moving the goods to regions where the deals being offered are less attractive. Deep-discount stores and warehouse clubs are especially adept at gaining advantage by using these practices. To counteract the advantage of these low-cost retailers, competing chains have demanded that manufacturers sell everything to them at the lowest promotional price offered anywhere the chain operates. This uniform pricing policy limits a manufacturer's ability to engage in regional pricing.

Forward buying and diversion affect a manufacturer's ability to produce in an efficient manner and raise inventory costs throughout the distribution system. Forward buying plays havoc with a firm's manufacturing cycle, creating frantic overtime followed by unproductive lulls. Moreover, deep-discount stores that find these practices attractive are not long-term customers inasmuch as they carry only a few items in any product category and have no commitment to carry any brand regularly.

To try to regain the initiative some manufacturers have begun to emphasize *everyday low prices* (*EDLP*) or *value pricing*. Procter & Gamble has tried to implement EDLP for most of its brands. Some retailers opposed this plan because they were worried about losing promotional flexibility as well as profits. They believed that P&G's plan favored retailers, such as Wal-Mart Stores, that were already following

---

MARKETING STRATEGIES 15-1

GENERAL MILLS ANNOUNCES REDUCTION IN CEREAL COUPONING

General Mills reported in April 1994 that it planned to reduce spending on ready-to-eat cereal couponing and price promotion by more than $175 million annually. Instead, the company cut prices on its top brands by an average of 11 percent. This move was a major departure from standard industry practice among cereal competitors. In the previous 12 months, more than 60 percent of all cereal purchases had been made with some kind of coupon or discount.

Steven Sanger, president of General Mills, noted the tremendous cost associated with printing, distributing, and redeeming coupons. "Because of this inefficiency, the 50¢ that the consumer saves by clipping the coupon can cost the manufacturer as much as 75¢. It just doesn't make sense." General Mills' price cuts affected about 40% of the company's cereal volume and included most sizes of Cheerios, Honey Nut Cheerios, Multigrain Cheerios, Wheaties, Whole Grain Total, Golden Grahams, Lucky Charms, and Trix. The average price of a 15-ounce box of Cheerios was expected to drop to $2.90 from $3.30.

General Mills faced uncertainties about what would happen to its sales. First, customers had been heavily trained to use coupons. Considering that cereal coupons ranged from 50¢ to 75¢, would a 40¢ average drop in the company's prices impress consumers? Second, would trade reaction be favorable? Third, would it be able to stick by its new strategy if competitors continued to coupon heavily?

The practice of pricing up and discounting back has become more and more inefficient for manufacturers and retailers, and burdensome for consumers.

Source: Tim Triplett, "Cereal Makers Await Reaction to General Mills' Coupon Decision," *Marketing News,* May 9, 1994, p. 1.

---

an EDLP approach. Competitors moved in, offered substantial deals, and stole share from P&G in the short run. See Marketing Strategies box 15-1 for another example. The move to a more rational everyday list price system seems inevitable. The question is whether enough advertising and promotional support will be maintained to keep consumers interested in the product category.

PUBLIC RELATIONS

Today more and more customers are taking the time to phone or write companies when they encounter a problem with a purchase. Sophisticated marketers realize that prompt responses to these complaints can help correct problems and retain customers. Managers know that it is a lot less expensive to maintain current customers than to find new ones.

Firms are expanding their customer relations departments because this investment pays off. Most complainers are satisfied with a personal letter and some coupons. Failure to respond to questions, however, can lead to bad word-of-mouth publicity. Inquiries are also a valuable source of information. This approach is detailed in Marketing in Action box 15-2.

Public relations is also responsible for consumer education, publicity, special events, and sponsorships. The idea is that getting attention in a crowded marketplace doesn't have to be expensive. Franklin Sports Industries designed a baseball batting glove of Spandex and English leather to fit around a bat. Most important, the gloves sported the Franklin logo in inch-high letters on the back of the hand. Franklin handed them out by the dozen to every major-league ballplayer. Since then, Franklin's name has shown up on television every time a camera focuses on a batter. It has appeared on batters on the cover of *Sports Illustrated.* As a result, Franklin sells about $65 million worth of all types of sporting goods, yet spends less than $1 million a year on advertising.

Event marketing can be used to lure the customer into the retail outlet to purchase while at the same time building awareness and impacting imagery. During the 1988 Olympics, Seagram Coolers launched a program called ''Send the Families,'' designed to raise money to send a family member to accompany an athlete, all

---

MARKETING IN ACTION 15-2

MAINTAINING CUSTOMER CONTACTS

Two consumers who objected to the bland flavor of a new potato chip alerted Borden to a manufacturing error in one batch. People who inquire about products can be identified and used later in direct mail campaigns. For example, when Campbell decided to roll out a new line of low sodium soups, its customer relations division assembled a list of every customer who inquired about the salt content of its other soups. These customers were then sent a brochure on the new soups as well as some coupons.

The type of response that customers like to receive can be illustrated by two examples. When a buyer wrote to Liz Claiborne to complain about buttonholes unraveling on a dress, the company replied immediately with a letter of apology. The company included instructions to have the dress repaired by any tailor, along with reassurance that reimbursement would be forthcoming. A letter sent to Health Valley Foods complaining about the lack of raisins in a box of cereal prompted a two-page reply from the company president. In addition, the company sent a replacement box of cereal, an Oat Bran Jumbo Fruit Bar, a packet of herb seasonings, and a $1 coupon for cookies or bars. Health Valley doesn't advertise and the company is tickled when people take time to let them know about a problem.

It is simply good business for you to stay in touch with your customers.

Source: Kathleen Deveny, ''For Marketers: No Peeve Is Too Petty,'' *The Wall Street Journal,* November 14, 1990, p. B1.

expenses paid, to Seoul, South Korea. The program involved point-of-sale displays with appropriate literature explaining how consumers could participate, based on purchase, and details about Seagram's contributions. The program was supported by an aggressive public relations effort involving the world's largest greeting card, transported across the country on a flatbed truck and signed by dignitaries and consumers at each stop. Tying all the pieces together was an advertising campaign that conveyed the message about the program and Seagram's support for our athletes.[11]

MEASURING CAMPAIGN EFFECTIVENESS

You have to analyze the effectiveness of any marketing activity you undertake. For example, Colgate-Palmolive applies a strict profit-and-loss formula in measuring the effectiveness of its ongoing cause-related sponsorship of the Starlight Foundation, which grants wishes to seriously ill children. Colgate's effort involves freestanding insert coupons and so is easily tracked. Our ability to track the impact of consumer promotions has been greatly enhanced by the availability of scanner data. The scope of information now available is indicated by a sample page from Information Resources, Inc.'s *Marketing Fact Book* shown in Table 15-4. Using supermarket scanner sales data, Colgate compares product sales in the three weeks following a coupon drop with average sales for the six months preceding it. The difference is then multiplied by the brand's net profit margin, and the event's cost on a per-unit basis is subtracted to find the true incremental profit.

A common criterion used to evaluate the success of promotional activity is plus sales per dollar of company expenditure. This ratio shows how sales respond to the prizes and trips used as incentives and allows comparisons to be made among different types of promotions. Some firms break historical sales data into trend, seasonal, and irregular components so that the plus sales produced by promotional efforts can be measured. This method, called *bump analysis,* adjusts sales for seasonal factors and removes the trend so that the remaining irregular component reflects the impact of the promotion. Figure 15-3 shows the impact of a campaign on sales. Note that the campaign produced losses in volume both before and after the effective dates of the promotion. The reduced volume before the promotion may have been due to the sales force's holding back on deliveries to take advantage of campaign benefits. The drop after the promotion may indicate that the campaign had exhausted the available consumer demand. Total plus sales for the sales campaign were obtained by adding in sales for the two 10-day periods before and after the promotion. If the before and after losses were ignored, the estimate of plus sales in Figure 15-3 would be inflated. Once a reliable figure for plus sales has been estimated, it is divided by the costs of the promotion to get a ratio that can be used to evaluate the results of current and past campaigns.

There is an automated promotion evaluation system called PROMOTER. PROMOTER incorporates concepts from expert systems and contains a knowledge base to recognize and adjust for data irregularities. The system estimates a baseline of what

TABLE 15-4
Scanner Summary Data

Category—Liquid Soap Volume Is Pounds. Annual—Jan to Dec Including Only Brands Purchased by 0.5% or More of All Households	Data Reflect Grocery Store Purchases Only—								% Volume with the Specified Deal						
	Ctgry Volume Volume Share	Type Volume Share	% of Hshlds Buying	Volume per Purch	Purch per Buyer	Purch Cycle (days)	Share Ctgry Rqmts	Price per Volume	Any Trade Deal	Print Ad Featr	In-Store Disply	Shelf Price Reduct	Store Coupn	Man-ufactr Coupn	Avg % Off On Price Deals
Category—liquid soap	689.1*	100.0	31.9%	0.9	2.4	94	100%	2.29	24%	8%	6%	17%	1%	31%	35%
Type—liquid soap	100.0	100.0	31.9	0.9	2.4	94	100	2.29	24	8	6	17	1	31	35
Benckiser Cons Prods	9.8	9.8	5.4	0.8	1.5	97	42	1.96	8	1	2	7	0	12	26
Clean & Smooth	9.8	9.8	5.4	0.8	1.5	97	42	1.96	8	1	2	7	0	12	26
Colgate Palmolive	20.6	20.6	8.5	1.1	1.6	92	52	2.21	39	18	14	24	3	22	34
Softsoap	18.9	18.9	8.0	1.1	1.5	93	50	2.15	40	19	15	23	4	23	35
Softsoap Shower Gel	1.7	1.7	0.8	0.7	2.0	92	33	2.82	29	3	1	26	2	12	29
Koa Corp of Amer	17.1	17.1	8.2	0.9	1.7	93	48	1.86	17	4	2	13	2	35	40
Jergens	10.9	10.9	5.4	0.9	1.5	99	44	1.63	12	2	2	10	1	27	41
Jergens Antibacterial Plus	6.2	6.2	3.7	0.8	1.5	81	34	2.28	26	8	4	19	4	50	39
Minnetonka	3.6	3.6	3.2	0.6	1.3	100	30	2.13	40	8	2	35	1	23	44
Softsoap Country Designs	2.2	2.2	2.1	0.6	1.3	96	28	2.12	44	10	3	36	1	26	47
Softsoap Pastels	0.8	0.8	0.8	0.6	1.2	108	27	2.19	34	1	0	35	0	21	36
Procter & Gamble	17.7	17.7	9.5	0.8	1.6	96	45	2.19	15	4	5	10	1	34	37
Ivory Liquid	8.5	8.5	3.0	1.1	1.9	107	57	1.92	6	2	0	4	1	21	27
Ivory Liquid Accents	2.0	2.0	2.1	0.5	1.3	94	24	2.03	16	5	1	14	1	43	53
Ivory Liquid Classics	1.2	1.2	1.2	0.5	1.3	88	23	2.17	16	6	1	15	0	35	43
Safeguard	6.0	6.0	4.6	0.7	1.3	76	30	2.62	28	6	13	15	1	50	34
The Dial Corporation	22.6	22.6	9.4	0.9	1.8	102	59	2.57	25	6	3	21	1	42	29
Dial	22.5	22.5	9.3	0.9	1.8	101	59	2.56	25	6	3	21	1	42	29
Unilever	3.8	3.8	3.5	0.5	1.5	102	33	3.80	30	11	5	20	2	66	39
Dove Beauty Wash	3.8	3.8	3.5	0.5	1.5	102	33	3.80	30	11	5	20	2	66	39
Private label	1.5	1.5	0.6	1.1	1.4	99	48	1.42	17	0	0	17	0	1	13
Private label	1.5	1.5	0.6	1.1	1.4	99	48	1.42	17	0	0	17	0	1	13

*Category volume per 1000 households.
Source: The Marketing Fact Book. Chicago: Information Resources, Inc., 1992, p. 241.

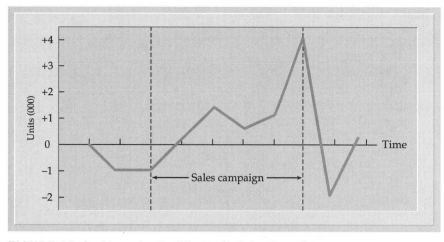

FIGURE 15-3 Measuring the Effects of a Sales Promotion

sales would have been if the promotion had not been run. This is possible because, from 30 percent to 90 percent of the time, a consumer product is not on promotion in a particular store. Thus, using sales data from individual stores, sales from non-promotional weeks can be compared with those from promotional weeks. The incremental impact of the promotion can be measured.[12] Experience with PROMOTER gave rise to a more sophisticated decision support system, PROMOTIONSCAN.[13] Whereas PROMOTER measures total incremental volume for only one brand, PROMOTIONSCAN does so for all brands, including competitors. PROMOTIONSCAN also relates that incremental volume to retailer merchandising variables such as features, display, and price reductions.

The incremental impact of a trade promotion can be seen in Table 15-5. As noted earlier, most trade promotions are unprofitable. The brand is promoted to the trade at a 15 percent discount over a four-week period. Assume that all the stores in the market feature the brand for one week in their weekly newspaper advertising supplement. What's more, half of the stores support the brand with three weeks of in-store display and consumer price reductions, while the other half only reduce the price—but for the full four weeks. You do not usually get such excellent trade support. Nevertheless, the promotion ends up costing 64 cents for each incremental dollar it generates. Unless the product's gross margin is more than 64 percent, the promotion will lose money. The reason is that the manufacturer has to sell a large number of cases at the discounted price to cover the normal sales that would have taken place without the promotion. In addition, the manufacturer must cover the forward buying by the retailer.[14]

A promotion should be evaluated on the basis of the value of new customers attracted in addition to the immediate sales volume it generates. New customers may like the brand and thus may buy it for many years. Therefore, immediate sales may not indicate the real value of a promotion; instead, it will be reflected by the number of new triers and their acceptance of a brand. You must distinguish between gaining triers (the job of the promotion) and gaining acceptance (the job of product development).

TABLE 15-5

Trade Promotion Economics

	Cases	Gross Dollars
Baseline*		
Sales that would have occurred during a four-week promotion period even without promotion.	400	$ 4,000
Incremental sales to consumers[†]		
Due to a one-week feature	100	$1,000
Due to 50% of stores with three weeks of displays and price reduction	250	$2,500
Due to 50% of stores with four weeks of price reduction only	80	$ 800
	430	$ 4,300
Ten weeks of forward buying by retailers	1,000	$10,000
Total sales during promotion	1,830	$18,300
Cost of promotion		$ 2,745
Cost per incremental dollar of sales		$ 0.64

*Assume weekly base sales of 100 cases and a list price of $10 per case.
[†]Based on analysis of single-source data and retailer promotion purchases.
Source: Magid M. Abraham and Leonard M. Lodish, ''Getting the Most Out of Advertising and Promotion,'' *Harvard Business Review,* Vol. 68, No. 3 (May–June 1990), pp. 50–60.

The value of event marketing is often measured by adding up the number of seconds of TV air time or column inches of press clippings that feature a company's name or logo and then multiplying that by the equivalent ad cost. Some research companies make a business of doing such research. Some believe that measures such as ''media equivalencies'' are irrelevant, and that what you should measure are favorable impressions of your brand that last for a while. Thus, researchers recruit event spectators and conduct follow-up telephone interviews several days later to measure sponsor recall and consumers' intent to purchase sponsors' products.

SUMMARY

The promotion mix allows you to fine-tune your marketing mix. A review of the literature finds these reasons for promotions:[15]

- Enables you to adjust to variations in supply and demand without changing the list price.
- Allows you to price-discriminate among consumer segments.
- Rewards consumers.
- Secures distribution for new products.

- Induces consumer trial of new products.
- Encourages use of different retail formats (e.g., shoppers' clubs).
- Permits smaller regional brands to compete against nationally advertised brands.
- Adds excitement at the point of sale to mature products.
- Defends shelf space against existing and anticipated competition.
- Clears inventories of obsolete products.

Thus, the promotion mix gives you flexibility to address specific marketing situations.

You must approach the consumer with an integrated marketing communications package—sales force, direct marketing, advertising, sales promotion, and public relations—all at once. As one observer puts it: "An ideal integrated marketing communications program combines media advertising to build awareness, sales promotion to generate an inquiry or response, data-base marketing to capture customer or prospect information, and ongoing direct marketing to specifically target customer needs and personalize, perhaps even customize, the communication to achieve measurable results."[16]

NOTES

1. Robert C. Blattberg and Scott A. Neslin. *Sales Promotion: Concepts, Methods, and Strategies* (Englewood Cliffs, NJ: Prentice-Hall, 1990), p. 3.
2. *Advertising Age,* April 12, 1992, pp. 3, 53.
3. Terry Lefton, "Try It—You'll Like It," *Brandweek,* May 2, 1993, pp. 27, 28, 30, 32.
4. Richard Gibson, "Recession Feeds Coupon Habit," *The Wall Street Journal,* February 20, 1991, p. B1.
5. *Marketing News,* October 10, 1988, p. 22.
6. Beth Lubetkin, "Additional Major Findings from the 'How Advertising Works' Study," Marketplace Advertising Research Workshop, New York, November 6–7, 1991.
7. "Coupon Users Need Incentive," *Marketing News,* May 25, 1992, p. 1.
8. John Philips Jones, "The Double Jeopardy of Sales Promotions," *Harvard Business Review,* Vol. 68, No. 5 (September–October 1990), p. 149.
9. Paul W. Farris and John A. Quelch, "The Defense of Price Promotions," *Sloan Management Review,* Vol. 29, No. 1 (Fall 1987), pp. 63–69.
10. Robert D. Buzzell, John A. Quelch, and Walter J. Salmon, "The Costly Bargain of Trade Promotion," *Harvard Business Review,* Vol. 68, No. 2 (March–April 1990), pp. 141–149.
11. Arthur Shapiro, "Advertising versus Trade Promotion: Which Is Which?" *Journal of Advertising Research,* Vol. 20, No. 3 (June–July 1990), pp. RC-13–RC-16.
12. Magid M. Abraham and Leonard M. Lodish, "PROMOTER: An Automated Promotion Evaluation System," *Marketing Science,* Vol. 6 (Spring 1987), pp. 101–123.
13. Magid M. Abraham and Leonard M. Lodish, "An Implemented System for Improving Promotion Productivity Using Store Scanner Data," *Marketing Science,* Vol. 12, No. 3 (Summer 1993), pp. 248–269.

14. Magid M. Abraham and Leonard M. Lodish, ''Getting the Most Out of Advertising and Promotion,'' *Harvard Business Review*, Vol. 68, No. 3 (May–June 1990), pp. 53–64.

15. Farris and Quelch, ''The Defense of Price Promotions,'' and Buzzell, Quelch, and Salmon, ''The Costly Bargain of Trade Promotion.''

16. Neil M. Brown, ''Redefine Integrated Marketing Communications,'' *Marketing News*, March 29, 1993, pp. 4–5.

SUGGESTED READING

van Waterschoot, Walter, and Christophe Van den Bulte. ''The 4P Classification of the Marketing Mix Revisited,'' *Journal of Marketing*, Vol. 56, No. 4 (October 1992), pp. 83–93.

FURTHER READING

Abraham, Magid M., and Leonard M. Lodish. ''Getting the Most Out of Advertising and Promotion,'' *Harvard Business Review*, Vol. 68, No. 3 (May–June 1990), pp. 50–60.

Abraham, Magid M., and Leonard M. Lodish. ''An Implemented System for Improving Promotion Productivity Using Store Scanner Data,'' *Marketing Science*, Vol. 12, No. 3 (Summer 1993), pp. 248–269.

Blattberg, Robert C., and Scott A. Neslin. *Sales Promotion: Concepts, Methods, and Strategies* (Englewood Cliffs, NJ: Prentice-Hall, 1990).

Buzzell, Robert D., John A. Quelch, and Walter J. Salmon. ''The Costly Bargain of Trade Promotion,'' *Harvard Business Review*, Vol. 68, No. 2 (March–April 1990), pp. 141–149.

Farris, Paul W., and John A. Quelch. ''The Defense of Price Promotions,'' *Sloan Management Review*, Vol. 29, No. 1 (Fall 1987), pp. 63–69.

Jones, John Philips. ''The Double Jeopardy of Sales Promotions,'' *Harvard Business Review*, Vol. 68, No. 5 (September–October 1990), pp. 145–152.

Schreiber, Alfred L. *Lifestyle & Event Marketing* (New York, McGraw-Hill, 1994).

Shapiro, Arthur. ''Advertising versus Trade Promotion: Which Is Which?'' *Journal of Advertising Research*, Vol. 20, No. 3 (June–July 1990), pp. RC-13–RC-16.

QUESTIONS

1. Minorities in the United States redeem coupons at rates 60 percent below those of whites. Minorities don't use coupons for a variety of reasons. One key reason is that not many subscribe to Sunday newspapers, which carry most coupons in the form of freestanding inserts (FSIs). How would you reach minority consumers?

2. Diet Pepsi sent, by UPS, 24-packs of its drink to 1 million frequent buyers of Diet Coke who had been identified through supermarket research. Each case was accompanied by a brochure featuring Ray Charles, the brand's national spokes-

man. Pepsi spent about $50 million on its month-long promotion. Was this a good use of Pepsi's promotional dollars? When should you use a sampling tactic such as this?

3. Coca-Cola came up with a new, exciting, and unique promotional tool—the MagiCan. The idea was simple. You just pop open the can and, instead of Coke coming out, money would appear. The MagiCan promotion had attractive characteristics. It was self-contained, tied directly to the brand, and easy to handle in the channels. With the big summer selling season coming and having something that Pepsi didn't, Coca-Cola rushed through a limited spring test market and brought out the promotion. Unfortunately, the promotion was a disaster. Despite massive advertising, many consumers were unaware of the promotion. When they heard something inside the can besides Coke, they were afraid that the product had been tampered with. Where did Coca-Cola go wrong? What should have been done next?

4. One way of calculating the amount spent for price promotions is to use the highest price charged as the list price. The method is as follows: the discount offered per unit from the list price is multiplied by the number of units sold on promotion. To this figure are added the costs of implementing the promotion, such as printing coupons, manufacturing special packages, and, in some cases, advertising the promotion. Summing these costs for each trade and consumer promotion yields the total amount allocated to price promotions. Make this calculation for the zero leakage, zero slippage case in Table 15-3. What may be a better measure of list price? Redo the calculation using this measure.

5. American Airlines introduced a value-pricing plan in April 1992. It shunned special offers and gimmicks that had been prevalent in the industry and allowed only four tiers of fares based on the level of service and how far in advance the tickets were bought. On May 29, 1992, Northwest began offering a free ticket to an adult flying with a paying child. The next day American cut the price of all advance-purchase tickets by 50 percent. After a vicious fare war in which every major airline matched or undercut every other's deep discounts, American abandoned value pricing in the fall. Northwest and Continental airlines subsequently brought an antitrust action against American charging predatory pricing. Why is promotional pricing widespread in the airline industry? What do you think of American's actions?

6. Sponsorships do not compete with advertising on a cost per thousand basis. Not only do you have to pay a sponsorship fee, but you have to spend money to make the sponsorship pay off. When, if ever, should a company sponsor an event?

7. In the computer industry there is a complaint that "Microsoft gets too much attention." Research based on about 78,000 documents from almost every computer publication and newsletter indicates that this assertion is true. Table 15-6 shows that Microsoft does get an inordinate amount of free publicity. What explanation can you offer for this finding?

8. Levi Strauss & Company, the jeans maker, revoked contributions to the Boy Scouts of America because of the organization's refusal to accept homosexuals

TABLE 15-6
Company Mentions

Company	Annual Sales ($ billion)	Media Citations*
IBM	62	15,125
Digital	14	8,043
Motorola	11	1,806
Apple	7	7,946
Tandy	5	497
Compaq	3	2,575
Microsoft	2	15,115
Dell	2	1,582
Intel	1	5,757
Data General	1	512
Lotus	0.8	4,694
Novell	0.7	5,521
Borland	0.5	2,568
Symantec	0.2	956

*A company may be mentioned more than once in any article; however, it counts as only one citation.
Source: *PC Magazine,* April 27, 1993, p. 95 (based on Computer Select's January 1993 CD-ROM).

or to allow them to serve as scoutmasters. Levi announced the following year that it was cutting ties to China due to what it called "persuasive" human rights violations. Should companies take stands on controversial issues? Where does public relations come in?

9. As part of its campaign for its new Cinquecento car, Fiat mailed anonymous love letters to 50,000 young Spanish women. The letter smothered each recipient with compliments and invited her to indulge in a "little adventure" after "we met again on the street yesterday and I noticed how you glanced interested in my direction." Fiat considered it an amusing campaign aimed at the independent, modern working woman. What is your assessment of this campaign?

Chapter 16

International Marketing

Free trade, one of the greatest blessings which a government can confer on a people, is in almost every country unpopular.

LORD MACAULAY

No economies today prosper without international trade. Indeed, some of the strongest (Germany and Japan) regularly sell more abroad than they import. Even the United States exports 20 percent of its industrial production and sells two out of five acres of its farm produce abroad. Today one-third of U.S. corporate profits is derived from foreign trade, and this proportion is sure to increase in the future. When you travel abroad, you notice signs for Coke, Pepsi, McDonald's hamburgers, and Caterpillar tractors. These firms have learned how to operate in international markets, and it is now time for the rest of America to become part of the new global economy.

Successful international trade is based on the *law of comparative advantage.* This principle states that countries are better off producing items where they have inherent advantages and buying from others products where they have handicaps. The United States has comparative advantages in the production of agricultural products and airplanes, which it exports, and is at a disadvantage with newsprint and oil, which it imports.

A second factor supporting international marketing is opportunity. Today the United States represents less than 25 percent of the world market for goods and services. Almost all firms that have achieved national distribution in the United States must become international to continue to grow. For non-U.S. firms the potential outside the home country is even greater. Although the Japanese market is large, the potential market outside Japan is 85 percent of worldwide demand. Our discussion suggests that international markets present tremendous opportunities for growth. This chapter will analyze the special character of international trade and present some aggressive marketing strategies for operating in this arena. An example showing how Volvo has taken advantage of international marketing is described in Marketing Strategies box 16-1.

MARKETING STRATEGIES 16-1

THE VOLVO 850

The Swedish automobile manufacturer Volvo first introduced its new front-drive 850 to the United States in the fall of 1992. Volvo faces a limited market for its cars in Sweden and sells most of its 300,000-unit production in other countries. One of its most important markets is the United States, where it sells more cars than it does in Sweden. Volvo has succeeded in the United States because its cars are viewed as safe, comfortable, and durable. However, Volvo is a small manufacturer and has been slow to innovate in the areas of style and special features.

The 850 was designed to appeal to the sports sedan market both in Europe and in America. This new model included many features that were not popular or needed in Europe but are essential for success in the United States. These include air conditioning, automatic transmissions, front wheel drive, dual airbags, tilt/telescopic steering wheel, memory driver's seat, fold-down rear seats, heated power mirrors, CD changer, remote keyless entry, traction control, child booster cushion in the rear armrest, headlight wiper/washer, sun roof, leather upholstery, and a security system. The 850 also had a powerful 20-valve, 5-cylinder, 168-hp engine and a side-impact protection system. The net result was a compact yet roomy, high-performance sports sedan priced at an economical $24,100.

Volvo's ability to produce a car so well adapted to the U.S. market showed that it understands international marketing. Although the engine and other major parts were made in Sweden, the car was assembled in Ghent, Belgium. Sweden had not been a member of the European Economic Community (EEC), and the Ghent plant allowed it access to the EEC without paying extra duties. Also, Ghent is a seaport that simplified the shipment of parts from Sweden and the delivery of finished cars to America and Europe. The Volvo 850 qualified as a world car, as 70 percent of the parts were bought from outside suppliers in such countries as Germany, the Netherlands, France, and Belgium. Also the four-speed automatic transmission was made in Japan. With the introduction of the 850, Volvo showed that international production and marketing is the new standard for automobile firms in the 1990s.

Manufacturers who cater to the needs of their international customers are more likely to succeed.

Source: Guide to the All New Volvo 850 GLT, *Road and Track Special Series*, 1992, 97 pages.

ENVIRONMENT OF INTERNATIONAL MARKETING

International trade provides attractive opportunities for sales increases, but it also carries a number of risks. Part of your job as marketing manager is to know how to balance revenue gains from trade against the possibility of financial losses. Some of the most serious problems include fluctuations in exchange rates, foreign trade regulations, unstable foreign governments, and piracy of trade secrets by outsiders. Perhaps the most difficult issue is what to do about governmental trade restrictions.

Trade Barriers

Economists all agree that trade among countries increases wealth. However, politicians have found that regulations that protect domestic industries from outside competition are popular with the people. Production workers, for example, view foreign trade as a threat to their jobs. They believe imports close factories rather than provide a source of low-cost merchandise. Thus, while trade clearly helps an economy as a whole, many people see only the negative impact on high-cost local producers.

An example of the politics of trade barriers is shown by Japanese restrictions on the importation of rice, citrus fruits, and beef. Japan runs a huge trade surplus with the United States and could easily afford to buy more American agricultural products. However, Japanese farmers are unusually strong politically and have long been favored with tight import rules. The result is that Japanese consumers pay exorbitant prices for rice, beef, and oranges, although their economy would be better off buying these items from abroad. Politically, it is easier to protect jobs in the short run than it is to maximize wealth.

Tariffs and Quotas   There are basically two types of restrictions that countries use to keep unwanted products out and protect domestically produced goods. The more common one is a tariff, or tax on imports. Tariffs are usually expressed as a percentage of the value of the good and are added on to get the selling price. Tariffs range in size from nuisance taxes of 2 percent to prohibitory values of 50 percent or more designed to stop the importation of certain items. For example, a few years ago, European countries slapped stiff tariffs on chickens imported from the United States to protect their own expanding chicken business. The United States responded by slapping a 25 percent tariff on imported trucks, which at that time were primarily coming from Europe. This "chicken" tax continues to this day to protect the U.S. manufacturers of pickup trucks. The net result is that pickups are much more profitable than automobiles, and margins run to $6000 per vehicle. Although the 25 percent tariff has helped U.S. firms in the short run, Toyota has introduced a larger pickup truck to challenge U.S. firms. If this truck sells as well as expected, Toyota will start to produce it in the United States to avoid the 25 percent tariff. Thus U.S. manufacturers can expect much tougher domestic truck competition as the result of the chicken tariff.

A second type of import restriction is the quota. This is an absolute limit on the number of certain items that can be imported. Italy, for instance, has had an annual quota of only a few thousand Japanese cars for a number of years. Although the low quota has helped to protect Italian car manufacturers, there is some question about whether the Italian economy is better off as a result. Germany has no quotas on cars, and the Japanese have a significant share of that market. The Germans, in turn, have the largest share of imported-car sales in Japan. We argue that the absence of German and Japanese auto quotas leads to greater trade and wealth for these two countries.

Another example is the informal U.S. quota on imported Japanese cars. This quota of 1.6 million cars has kept the price of Japanese vehicles high and has allowed American manufacturers to raise prices as well. From 1984 to 1988, GM, Ford, and Chrysler earned $25.2 billion. Unfortunately, instead of plowing the money back into new models and more efficient factories, they invested the cash outside the U.S. auto industry. Meanwhile, seven Japanese manufacturers opened factories in the United States and now assemble 1.4 million cars a year. A second consequence of the quota was a Japanese shift to upscale imports. To maximize profits on each car shipped, the Japanese decided to export more expensive automobiles. U.S. manufacturers now face direct competition from Acura, Lexus, and Infiniti dealerships on sales of their most profitable big cars. As a result, U.S. firms lost $10 billion on their North American business in 1991. The billions of dollars the Japanese have invested in their U.S. operations are a monument to the auto protectionists. In the long run, the trade barriers have failed to protect U.S. firms or to encourage them to rationalize their production processes.

Another class of trade restriction that can cause problems for export-minded firms is the nontariff barrier. This often takes the form of technical specifications or inspection procedures that make it difficult or impossible to move goods across borders. For example, at one time the French required all videocassette recorders (VCRs) coming into the country to pass a customs inspection at a small interior community. This forced the Koreans and the Japanese to route all shipments through this isolated town. In addition, not enough customs inspectors were assigned to this community to handle the work, so the number of VCRs admitted to France declined sharply.

Recent Trends   Despite the periodic imposition of tariffs, quotas, and nontariff barriers, there has been a gradual loosening of trade restrictions in the world economy in the past 60 years. The General Agreement on Tariffs and Trade (GATT) is one international agreement that has reduced the level of tariffs throughout the world on several occasions. The trend toward free trade is gathering momentum in the European Economic Community (EEC). Trade barriers among EEC members have been eliminated, and nonmembers are scrambling to gain access to this huge market. Also, the United States, Canada, and Mexico created a free trade zone in North America. The Uruguay Round, Maastrict, and the North American Free Trade Agreement (NAFTA) have become part of the public consciousness.

When business firms encounter unfair trade restrictions, they can ask their governments to appeal to GATT to impose sanctions to stop the offending practices. In addition to sanctions such as countervailing tariffs and antidumping fines, governments threaten retaliatory action. For example, not long ago, the EEC said it would no longer accept U.S. beef that had traces of growth hormones. This would have drastically reduced the amount of U.S. beef shipped to Europe. The United States countered by saying it would impose tariffs on an equivalent amount of EEC food shipped to the United States. Since neither side wanted trade to decline, there was a strong incentive to compromise on this issue. Most people in business and government agree that the extremely high U.S. tariffs of the 1930s contributed to and helped to perpetuate the Great Depression, and no one wants to relive those frightening years.

Currency Exchange Problems

International marketing is complicated because each country has its own currency. Thus, when you sell products in England, you are apt to be paid in pounds. Since the exchange rate between dollars and pounds changes hourly, you may receive fewer dollars than you expected. The possibility of serious exchange losses is so high that some small firms avoid foreign trade altogether. More experienced companies have learned to hedge their financial positions in the futures markets to reduce currency exchange problems.

The impact of realignments among currencies can seriously damage a firm's sales and profits. For example, the value of the U.S. dollar relative to the currencies of other industrialized countries fell sharply in 1991 and 1992. This meant that U.S. goods were relatively cheap for others to buy, and our exports expanded rapidly. However, it also meant that the goods sold in the United States returned less value in the home currency. This caused many companies that were exporting to the United States to sacrifice profits to keep the valuable U.S. market. One British construction equipment maker realized that all of its competitors produced locally in the United States and that it couldn't raise prices. In contrast, Sweden's Saab-Scania group believed that luxury products were immune from adverse effects of price increases and boosted the price of its Saab 900 Turbo sedan by 31 percent during the same period. Sales plunged. Companies can avoid the sales effects of currency fluctuations by building plants in major foreign markets. Examples showing how a weak dollar helped three small U.S. firms export their products are described in Marketing Strategies box 16-2.

An even more serious problem occurs when you want to trade with a country whose currency is not readily convertible. This has been a problem in doing business with the Russians. The ruble has no value outside the country, as the Russians have few products that outsiders want to buy. Thus companies that do business in Russia often have to work out complex barter arrangements to extract their profits. PepsiCo, for example, has converted rubles into Russian Stolichnaya vodka for the past 20 years and shipped the vodka to the United States, where it is sold for dollars. Recently, PepsiCo entered a joint venture with three Ukrainian companies to sell $1 billion worth of ships to foreign firms. Some of the proceeds will be reinvested in the shipbuilding venture, and some will be used to buy bottling equipment and to build five Pepsi bottling plants in the Ukraine. The rest will finance the opening of 100 PepsiCo-owned Pizza Hut restaurants in the republic. This example shows the complex financial deals that are needed to get around currency exchange problems and to help Pepsi protect its market share in the Ukraine from inroads by Coca-Cola.

One solution to the exchange problem is for the seller to accept payment only in dollars or other hard currency. However, some countries have limits on the amount of these currencies that are available to pay for imports. Thus, when you trade with countries with foreign exchange restrictions, you have to be imaginative in arranging for payment.

Unstable Governments

When the governments of trading partners change frequently, there is a greater risk of business losses. New governments often modify the rules that determine how business is conducted. The most extreme action is nationalization of the property of foreign firms. Other drastic actions that can cause trouble are restrictions on the transfer of currencies and revisions in tariffs or quotas. When you have to deal with

MARKETING STRATEGIES 16-2

WEAK DOLLAR SPURS EXPORTS

To take advantage of a weak dollar and counter slow sales at home, three small U.S. firms have turned to exports. The Torel Company of Yoakum, Texas, started by attending a leather trade show in Germany. They found that European buyers wanted a gaudier product than Americans such as embossed belts with white stitching and big buckles. The company then teamed up with a U.S. leather distributor based in Germany to call on retail shops. This revealed that men's wallets needed coin purses. Now Torel wallets for Germany have coin purses and are deeper to hold German bills. Overseas sales are now $1 million a year and the product labels read "Made in Texas."

Brooklyn Brewery started out in 1988 to manufacture a premium-priced local beer. The product became a hit with New York yuppies and caught the attention of a Japanese trade agent based in New York. He introduced the company to a huge Japanese distrib-

utor, Hiroga Ltd. Hiroga proposed sending the beer by air freight to Japan, dating it, and selling it as "fresh from the brewery" for a higher price. Foreign sales now account for 10 percent of the brewery's $2 million in annual sales.

In six years Quicksilver Enterprises has become one of the hottest makers of ultra light airplanes. Because of the weak dollar, Quicksilver has rung up half of its $4 million sales of the 250-pound planes from foreign customers. Recently, it entered a joint venture with a Nebraska maker of liquid-spray equipment to make ultra light crop dusters. Now many Third World farmers use these $18,000 machines in place of standard crop dusters that cost $100,000. All of the new machines are sold overseas, as they are not licensed for sale in the United States.

Even small firms can sell overseas.

Source: Mark Robinchaux, "Three Small Businesses Profit by Taking on the World," *The Wall Street Journal,* November 8, 1990, p. B2.

unstable foreign governments, there is a strong incentive to export rather than risk direct investment.

Historical examples of countries where nationalization of industry caused serious problems for foreign firms include France with banks and autos, Mexico with petroleum, England with transportation, and Italy with cars. In each of these cases, nationalization has led to monopolies for the government firms and losses for foreign competition. Once governments own business firms, they routinely protect them with tariffs and quotas. Thus countries with a history of nationalization are not good environments for foreign investment. One way you can compete in these countries is to form joint ventures in which capital is raised locally and the outside firm provides technical and marketing expertise. While there are still risks with this arrangement, the chances for massive capital losses are reduced.

Cultural Factors

Successful international marketing demands that you pay close attention to the special needs and customs of your buyers. Foreign customers often have different concepts of time, space, and etiquette. Thus, before you create a marketing plan for overseas business, you need to find out how these customers think about and use your products. Examples showing the impact of cultural differences on marketing plans include the following:

- An American firm lost floor wax sales in Brazil because a change in the formula made the product less effective as a lighter fluid to ignite Sunday barbecues.
- Germans prefer salad dressing in a tube.
- Kellogg's Pop Tart failed in Europe, as many homes do not have toasters.
- PepsiCo's Mountain Dew soft drink is difficult to pronounce in Portuguese, and sales have been slow in these markets.
- Two-liter pop bottles failed in Spain because refrigerators were too small.
- Although 89 percent of Americans agree that everyone should use deodorant, only 53 percent of Australians agree with this statement.

Although these examples suggest that you should adapt products to local cultural norms, it is possible to go too far. Some imported products are successful *because* they are different, and drastic changes can destroy their appeal. For example, when Disney was designing a theme park for Japan, its local partners insisted that nothing be changed from what was available at Disney World in Florida. They cautioned that customers did not want an Americanized Japanese park; they wanted the "real" Disney creation. This means that you must study the needs of each country to determine what portions of the product and marketing program need to be changed and what should be left alone. Some recent research on the impact of cultural factors on international marketing is reported in Marketing Strategies box 16-3.

WHICH MARKETS TO ENTER

Selecting foreign markets for expansion resembles the process of segmentation. First, you want to be sure that there are enough people in the new market to make the project worthwhile. Also, it is important that your product or service have distinct competitive advantages. Finally, you need to consider the higher risks that accompany foreign trade because of cultural differences and the possibility of government restrictions. For example, many international firms consider South Korea to be a difficult market to enter because of excessive government red tape and the difficulty of bringing additional capital into the country. However, disposable income there is rising rapidly, and South Korea is the second largest consumer market in Asia after Japan. Also, the population is well educated, and the number of two-income families is rising. This makes convenience foods and higher-quality products that are popular in the West more attractive among South Koreans. Ralston Purina saw milk con-

MARKETING STRATEGIES 16-3

IS THE EUROPEAN WOMAN DIFFERENT?

With the decline in trade barriers in the European Common Market, marketing managers are scrambling to learn more about cross-cultural differences among countries. A recent study of 1000 women from 26 European countries focused on identifying views on work, relationships, and advertising. What they found was a virtual lack of significant differences among women throughout Europe.

The study did point out some opportunities to exploit characteristics that European women have in common, especially family bonds. More women are having babies without being married. Family values are strong but the family unit is fragmented. Advertising in Europe rarely takes this into account. Indeed, European women say that advertising relies too much on stereotypes like the "sexy bimbo" or the "expert housewife" and doesn't include other dimensions of their lives. Only one in six women classified themselves as housewives, and they feel working is essential for a full life.

European women viewed spending money as a treat or a way of pampering themselves. Also the once-sacred European trait of daily shopping trips has been replaced by weekly excursions. With less time and fewer shopping opportunities, women are less willing to experiment with brands, tending to purchase the tried and true. Surprisingly, the top role models for European women were Americans. For instance, Meryl Streep was liked for her femininity, modesty, and balanced approach to life. Although Europeans look across the ocean for role models, they do some things differently than U.S. women. Women in Europe don't diet and they don't exercise. The highest percentage of exercisers was in Denmark and that was only 17 percent. Also the survey revealed that 50 percent of European women smoke, a much higher figure than for the United States.

Although women do not differ much across European countries, they don't always go for American products and services.

Source: *Marketing News*, August 17, 1992, p. 13.

sumption rising—the consumption of breakfast cereal closely tracks milk consumption throughout the world—and jumped in. It built a $10 million plant to make Chex cereal, and sales are growing rapidly. Purina's success in South Korea was helped by the absence of strong local cereal manufacturers.

Another way to control risk is to enter markets that are nearby and that share a common cultural heritage. American businesspeople have followed this advice; Canada is our largest trading partner and an important area for investment. Not only do we share a language with English-speaking Canada, but most Canadians live near the border. This makes it easier to deliver merchandise and facilitates cross-border promotion by radio and television.

The ultimate test of the foreign market viability involves a financial analysis to determine the potential return on investment. As a first step, you need a good measure of potential demand. Then you must estimate the costs of making your goods and services available in a foreign country. If you are exporting, you must predict transportation costs, tariffs, and dealer margins. If you are locating production facilities in the new market, the costs of labor, raw materials, and taxes have to be considered. Sometimes the availability of raw materials is a serious problem in less developed economies. McDonald's, for example, learned a great deal about local conditions while developing its first fast-food restaurants in Russia. This market appears to be a tremendous opportunity for McDonald's. The population is large, and there is need for high-quality, quick-service restaurants. However, the limited supply of food in the grocery stores that ensures success of the restaurants also means that it is difficult to get the needed raw materials. Currency exchange problems limit the amount of food that can be imported, and McDonald's has had to work with local suppliers to bring them up to the required quality standards. This takes time; it will be years before McDonald's has a significant market share in Russia.

The last step in your evaluation of export marketing is to calculate the ROI for each prospective country. These ROIs should be compared and adjusted for different levels of risk. Remember that a high ROI is less attractive if there is a strong chance for property expropriation and restricted profit transfers. Obviously, the presence of a stable and friendly host agreement makes international marketing much more attractive.

MARKET ENTRY STRATEGIES

Once you have selected a foreign market for development, you have to decide on the best way to proceed. A variety of entry strategies can be employed to present your products to foreign customers. The main choices are exporting, licensing, joint ventures, and investing in your own facilities (Figure 16-1). These alternatives vary in commitment, risk, and profit potential. Note that these approaches are not mutually exclusive. Different entry strategies can be used at the same time in separate markets. Also, you may want to use more than one strategy to enter a single foreign country. A line of products might be licensed for local production and another line manufactured in a joint venture (country B, Figure 16-1). Each of these approaches will be discussed in the following pages.

The emphasis here is on expanding the market for a product from your home country to foreign markets. You could, of course, acquire brand names that already exist in foreign markets. To expand as a world marketer of fish products, H. J. Heinz (Star-Kist Seafood) established a beachhead in Europe with the acquisition of the Marie Elisabeth trademark from a Portuguese sardine packer. Also, Thomson, the French electronics giant, invaded the United States by snapping up the GE/RCA television brands.

Exporting

The most common way to enter foreign markets is through export (Figure 16-1). Extra production from the home market is simply shipped overseas using established

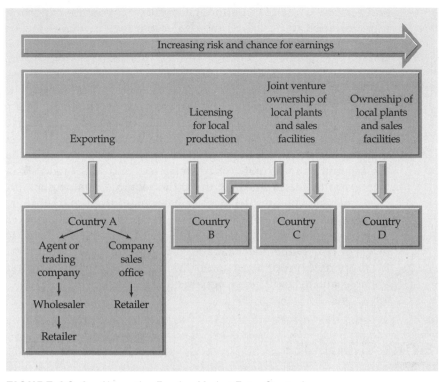

FIGURE 16-1 Alternative Foreign Market Entry Strategies

distribution channels. This approach only requires transportation and payment of duties, so there is little financial risk. A slightly more expensive approach is to make modest adjustments in your product to adapt it to the special needs of overseas customers. These changes may include modification in the size of the product or package, a new name, foreign language instructions, and special colors.

There are several levels of organizational arrangements that can be employed to assist exporting activities. Often, the first step is to hire a special agent or trading company from your own country to help you contact foreign customers. These people are paid on commission and handle all the paperwork involved in overseas selling. The second step is to set up an export department in your own organization. This is staffed with an export sales manager and clerks to handle the necessary documents. A third level of commitment involves hiring foreign-based distributors or agents. In exchange for exclusive rights to sell your products, these people provide invaluable access to local buyers. Marketing Strategies box 16-4 describes how Michelin used Japanese agents to sell tires in that country. The highest level of export investment involves setting up your own foreign-based sales branch. This requires higher fixed costs for salespeople, facilities, and inventory, but it gives you more control over the foreign marketing effort. Your choice of export arrangements depends on the size of the opportunity and the amount of money you have to risk on this venture. A summary of key considerations in developing an international dimension to your business is given in Table 16-1.

MARKETING STRATEGIES 16-4

EXPORTING TIRES TO JAPAN

France's Michelin started selling tires in the Japanese market through a Japanese general trading house. Fourteen years later it established a Japanese sales subsidiary. Currently, Michelin has 8 percent of the entire Japanese auto tire market. This success encouraged Michelin to build a Japanese tire plant in 1992. Michelin has a reputation for quality products, and this enables it to focus on higher-valued product lines with corresponding higher margins. This fits in well with the Japanese preference for prestigious, status-oriented products. For original equipment customers, namely Honda, Michelin quotes a delivered price at the automaker's assembly plant in yen. A nationwide warehouse system allows it to maintain sufficient inventories to meet Honda's just-in-time delivery requirements. In addition, all the non-Japanese staff are proficient in the Japanese language.

You don't have to build a plant initially to enter foreign countries, but you do need to know the language and maintain local inventories.

An example of how to make money exporting bicycles is provided by Cannondale, a U.S. manufacturer of high-priced racing and mountain bikes. Cannondale sells over 30 percent of its $77 million bike volume in Europe and other countries. Its initial distribution channel in Japan was through Mitsubishi, a large trading company. Mitsubishi insisted that Cannondale add another layer of traditional bicycle wholesalers to sell to retailers (see Figure 16-1, country A). This raised costs, and since the wholesalers handled several manufacturers, they provided less attention to any one brand. Cannondale did not like the service it was receiving, so it terminated Mitsubishi and set up its own sales office in a small town outside Osaka. Next, it hired two Japanese-speaking American professional bicyclists who lived in Japan to promote its bikes. The two raced Cannondale bikes every weekend, gaining a lot of free publicity in the bicycle press. On weekdays they make sales calls on bike dealers. Working directly with the dealers has revealed that Japanese prefer smaller bikes in flashier colors—feedback the company never got from Mitsubishi. In the first year of the new program, Cannondale tripled the number of dealers carrying its bikes and sales quadrupled to $2 million. Despite the startup costs of opening its own sales office, Cannondale Japan earned $60,000 in profits in its first year of operation.[1] These results show that exporting can be profitable.

Licensing

Once you get your feet wet with export marketing, you may want to license organizations in foreign countries to produce goods and services to expand market coverage. With this approach, a licensor signs contracts with licensees for the use of a manufacturing process, trademarks, or trade secrets for a fixed royalty percentage. These royalties typically run 2 to 4 percent of sales but sometimes amount to 10 percent or more. The licensor gains exposure in new markets without having to risk

TABLE 16-1
Marketing Dos and Don'ts for New Exporters

- **Do develop a marketing plan before you begin.** You must have clearly defined goals and objectives and know how to reach them. Don't take this crucial first step without competent advice.
- **Do secure top management commitment for the long haul.** It takes time and money to establish yourself in any new market, particularly one with which you are unfamiliar.
- **Do select overseas representatives with care.** Evaluate personally the people who will handle your account, their facilities and resources, and how they work.
- **Do establish a base for orderly growth.** Concentrate on one or two overseas markets and build them up before expanding worldwide.
- **Do modify products to comply with rules and the local culture.** Local regulations and preferences cannot be ignored. Make necessary product modifications at the factory.
- **Do print sales, service, and warranty data in the local language.** Be sure to *use an experienced translator.* Don't cut corners here—the results can be disastrous.
- **Do consider using an export management company.** If you don't want or can't afford an export department right now, consider appointing an export management company.
- **Don't neglect export business when domestic sales rise.** Letting exports slide when domestic sales boom discourages your overseas agents, turns off your customers, damaging your reputation abroad, and leaves you without recourse when domestic sales fall.
- **Don't treat export business like a stepchild.** If you regularly boost domestic sales through advertising, discount offers, sales incentive campaigns, and preferential credit and warranty protection, apply these same incentives to overseas markets.
- **Don't assume that the same marketing technique works everywhere.** Cultural preferences and taboos must be respected. Your overseas representative should be able to advise on effective local marketing.
- **Don't fail to support your product with service.** All products need servicing at some point. If you fail to provide it, your product will acquire a bad reputation that blights further sales.

Source: U.S. Department of Commerce.

local investments. Since very little investment is required, the ROI on licensing agreements can be extremely lucrative.

Licensees gain production or management knowledge of well-known products without having to spend money on R&D. In addition, licensees benefit from advertising and promotion expenditures by the parent organization designed to build worldwide demand. Coca-Cola and Pepsi both used licensing to expand their business internationally. With the reunification of East and West Germany, Coke moved quickly to license beverage organizations in eastern Germany to bottle and distribute Coca-Cola. Coke advanced $140 million to help its licensees upgrade bottling machinery and vending machines. As a result of such aggressive moves, international sales now account for 80 percent of the company's soft drink profits. Coke and

Pepsi maintain control over their foreign licensees by supplying them with the concentrated syrup that provides the flavor for the soft drinks.

Although licensing can be very profitable and can allow you to expand rapidly, it does carry some serious risks. You have very little control over a licensee's marketing efforts. Loewenbrau, one of Germany's best-known makers of beer, licensed the Miller Brewing Company to make its beer in the United States. While sales were initially good, they have subsequently dropped by almost a third. Consequently, Loewenbrau is considering direct export of its beer to the U.S. market. Another example of the perils of licensing is described in Marketing Strategies box 16-5.

MARKETING STRATEGIES 16-5

THE PERILS OF LICENSING

Recently a number of international firms have ended long-standing partnerships with Japanese companies. These associations provided foreign firms with easy entry for their products, but they often lead to problems. Borden ventured into Japan in 1971 with a licensing agreement with Meiji Milk, Japan's biggest dairy company. Initially the agreement worked well, as Borden got access to Meiji's vast distribution network and local production assured prompt delivery of fresh products. Together, Borden and Meiji created a large market for premium ice cream. Their Lady Borden brand secured 60 percent of an eventual $125 million market. Lady Borden, priced at $4.18 a pint, became a synonym for upscale ice cream, usually sold in fancy department stores. However, liberalization of milk product import rules has allowed the entry of Häagen-Dazs and Breyer's Grand Ice Cream from the United States. Lady Borden's market share has slipped from 60 to 50 percent and Meiji has been slow to respond to the competitive challenge.

Borden tried to renegotiate its agreement with Meiji to gain more control over the marketing of Lady Borden. Unfortunately, a change in management at Meiji delayed the implementation of new arrangements. Borden decided to break its ties with Meiji and set up their own sales subsidiary. Meiji agreed to continue to promote Lady Borden for 14 months until its licenses expired. Since Meiji had learned a great deal from Borden about ice cream manufacture, they decided to protect their position in the market by introducing two new premium brands of their own in the interim until the licensing agreement with Borden expired. One brand, Aya, stresses Meiji's Japanese roots with a bold calligraphy brush stroke in the middle of the label. A second brand, called Breuges, is similar in price and content to Lady Borden. Borden did not believe it was fair for Meiji to introduce new brands while it was committed to promote Lady Borden and threatened to sue to stop their distribution. In addition, the loss of local production capacity meant that Borden had to import ice cream all the way from Australia and New Zealand. What appeared to be an attractive deal for Borden in the short run turned out to be a public relations and financial disaster.

Licensing works well for entering markets quickly but often creates problems in the long run.

Source: Yumiko Ono, "Borden's Messy Split with Firm in Japan Points Up Perils of Partnerships There," *The Wall Street Journal,* January 28, 1991, p. B1.

In addition to reducing control over marketing activities, licensing exposes you to potential losses of trade secrets and production technology. To make licensing work, you have to show outsiders how production processes work. This means that you may be training competitors to enter your market when the licensing agreement ends. For example, Quicksilver Enterprises was unable to sell its ultralight airplanes in Brazil because of steep import duties. So the U.S. firm licensed a local firm to build and sell its planes in Brazil. However, six months after Quicksilver's engineers taught the concern how to build, fly, and fix the planes, the royalties stopped. The Brazilian company claimed that it had changed the design, and Quicksilver was out $100,000 in royalties and lost all sales in Brazil for several years.

Another problem is that royalties are paid on the basis of sales reported by your licensee. This means that it is to the licensee's advantage to understate volume to reduce the size of royalty payments. Obtaining an accurate audit of sales figures may be difficult in a foreign country, and signing up trustworthy business partners is critical to the success of a licensing program.

Since 1976, Polo/Ralph Lauren has had good results with a licensing agreement with 14 Seibu department stores in Japan. Polo did not have to put up any money, and it obtained good distribution in prestige outlets. However, it had to give up control of how merchandise was displayed and sold. Some people believe that Western apparel companies that own and license brands successfully in Japan probably regret that they didn't invest in their own subsidiaries five or ten years ago.

Joint Ventures

The objective of joint ventures is to find local partners to share the risks and profits of foreign market expansion. This can be done by buying an interest in an existing local business or by starting up a new venture with a resident business. Teaming up with a local partner cuts the size of your investment and allows you to gain valuable assistance in regard to customers, labor availability, raw material services, and distribution channels. The outside partner often provides the technical and production expertise, and the inside partner provides marketing connections.

Gillette, for example, has signed an agreement with a Leningrad (Saint Petersburg) firm, Leninets, for a joint venture to make razor blades, shaving systems, and disposable razors. While Gillette has exported razor blades to Russia for years, this is its first move toward local production for that market. The agreement with Leninets includes a factory with an annual capacity of 800 million units. Because shaving products are in short supply in Russia, the venture should be quite profitable. Gillette will provide mainly technical assistance and retain majority ownership in the $50 million joint venture.

Joint ventures are also attractive when the outside firm does not have the financial reserves to start a wholly owned operation or wishes to limit the financial risk of market expansion. Sometimes joint ventures are the price host governments exact when they allow access to their markets. Politicians often view joint ventures as a way to generate jobs, train workers, and reward local business interests.

The main problem with joint ventures is disagreement on how to manage the business. Outside firms often prefer to be majority stockholders in joint ventures so that they can control the operation to minimize the chance of losses. After all, outside partners usually provide the technology and production support for the project and have the most to lose if the project goes bad. Local partners may be more concerned with extracting current profits rather than with long-term success. The control issue is complicated further by rules in some countries that local people must own 50 percent or more of the stock of joint ventures. This has been the case in China until recently. Currently, six Japanese firms are negotiating a joint venture for a $4 billion petrochemical plant with two Chinese firms. The plant will be located in Liaoning, China, will have a refining capacity of 2 million metric tons, and will produce 450,000 metric tons of ethylene a year. Ethylene is in short supply in China, and the project looks promising to the Japanese. To protect themselves, the Japanese firms have negotiated a 51 percent stake in the project.

An example of the kinds of problems that can develop with joint ventures is provided by the experience of the Coca-Cola Company in India. Coke first entered the Indian market in 1950 with a joint venture. In 1977 the Indian government ruled that foreign companies couldn't own more than 40 percent of their Indian subsidiaries. In addition, Coke was required to turn over the secret formula for its syrup concentrate to its Indian partners. Coke was reluctant to do this and closed down its operation in India. PepsiCo noted that the 800 million people in India were drinking only three bottles of name brand soft drinks a year. This huge potential market prompted Pepsi to announce a complex $17 million joint venture to sell Pepsi and export food in 1988 even though it was allowed only 39.9 percent ownership. Coke responded by proposing several ingenious proposals that would allow it to maintain the secrecy of its formula while permitting Coke concentrate to be made available to Indian bottlers. The complicated joint venture arrangements needed for India are not unusual. You must be prepared to make similar deals if you expect to crack other foreign markets.

Ownership of Facilities

You can obtain the most control over international marketing activities by constructing your own factories in host countries. Local manufacturing provides significant savings on transportation costs, and resident labor is often cheaper than home market workers. Also, host governments often provide lucrative financial incentives to attract outside manufacturers.

Ownership also gives you a better image with customers because you are creating jobs for residents. In addition, ownership of facilities allows you to learn more about local demand so that you can tailor your products, advertising, and distribution plans to host country needs. Sometimes the operation of factories in foreign countries is the only way to get around tariff barriers and contain political pressures against imported goods.

The main problem with local manufacturing is that you expose yourself to a higher risk of serious financial loss. Foreign facilities are frequently damaged by war, nationalized by governments, or hamstrung by inflation or local currency exchange problems. In addition, foreign governments typically have stiff requirements on severance pay that make it expensive to close down overseas operations.

Some of the factors influencing decisions on foreign ownership of facilities are demonstrated by Japan's experience in selling cars in Europe. Over a period of years, Japan was able to increase its market share to 11 percent of the European market by exporting cars from home. This is an excellent record considering that Italy, France, Spain, and Portugal are protected markets. However, by 1992 all European bilateral barriers had been replaced by one broad trade umbrella. The Japanese were concerned that they might be limited by new import rules to only 10 percent of the EEC's car sales. Thus the Japanese have chosen to build production facilities in Europe to get around the new rules.

Toyota, for example, invested $1.09 billion in a new plant in England. This location was chosen because of its relatively low labor costs and a strong invitation from the British government. England has also attracted auto plant investments by Nissan and Honda. The British car market is dominated by Ford, an American firm, and the government has no domestic firms to protect. France, on the other hand, has two large domestic producers in Peugeot and Renault and has not been receptive to bringing in more auto competition. By building cars in England, the Japanese firms save $1200 per car on transportation, as well as the duties they paid to get the cars into the country. After 1992, the Japanese expected to be able to sell their British-made cars in all EEC countries, without tariffs or other border restrictions of any kind. However, the EEC commissioners have ruled that Japanese cars manufactured in Europe are still considered to be imports and are subject to a quota. Thus, in this case, local production did not provide the free-market access that normally would be allowed. Hindsight suggests that the Japanese should have resolved the issue of import status before they invested billions in EEC factories.

GLOBAL VERSUS LOCALIZED MARKETING

An ongoing controversy is whether firms should pursue a global or localized strategy in their foreign marketing activities. Global marketing emphasizes selling the same product with the same ads all over the world. This approach implies that the world is becoming homogenized and everybody wants the same things. One reason global marketing is working today is that global communications networks are opening access to more markets. CNN now reaches 78 million households in 100 countries, and MTV has an audience of 310 million in 78 countries. Localized marketing, on the other hand, implies that customers' needs are different in each country, and that you should adjust your product and your ads to meet local market conditions.

Both sides in this controversy have their advocates and a rationale.[2] Global marketing can save money and increase profits. Colgate-Palmolive, for example, introduced its tartar-control toothpaste in over 40 countries using only two ads. For every country that used the same ad, the firm saved $1 to $2 million in production costs alone. Colgate has saved millions more by standardizing the look and packaging of certain brands and reducing the number of factories that make them. Levi Strauss used to shoot separate, and not necessarily cohesive, commercials in each of its international markets. Now it saves money by shooting all of its global jeans ads in Los

Angeles in two weeks each summer. Another example of successful global marketing is described in Marketing Strategies box 16-6.

Problems with Global Marketing

Although global marketing is becoming more popular, it does not always work. Procter & Gamble, for example, took a sexy soap commercial that worked well in Europe and tried to use it in Japan. The Camay soap ad was based on the premise that women want to be attractive to men. In the ad a Japanese woman is seated in a bath tub when her husband walks into the bathroom. The woman starts telling him about her new beauty soap, but the husband, stroking her shoulder, hints that suds aren't on his mind. Japanese saw this ad as rude and intrusive, and it was withdrawn. P&G concedes that it would not have made the mistake if a Japanese woman had been running the campaign there. When a woman was put in charge, a successful

---

MARKETING STRATEGIES 16-6

WHIRLPOOL TRIES PAN-EUROPEAN MARKETING

While politicians are uniting Europe politically, marketing managers are searching for the elusive Euro-consumer. The fall of EC trade barriers has not eliminated all the cultural differences among European buyers. One company that has had some success with Pan-European marketing is the American Whirlpool Corporation. Whirlpool first entered the European appliance market via a joint venture with the Dutch firm Phillips Electronics NV in 1989. Since the name Whirlpool was unknown in Europe, they bought into Phillips' appliance business so that the well-known Phillips name would introduce people to Whirlpool. In 1991, Whirlpool bought all of Phillips' appliance business and the right to use the Phillips name until 1998.

Whirlpool wanted to build up its own image with a campaign that would work across the barriers dividing Europe's households. Not only are kitchen appliances different from country to country, but buyers react differently from one country to the next. Competitors and even its own ad agency were concerned that a Pan-European campaign would fall on its face. After reviewing 20 proposed campaigns, the ad team agreed on the slogan ''Phillips and Whirlpool bring quality to life.'' The ads feature a cool, bluish dream world of dryers and dishwashers emphasizing high technology and the universal desire for more free time. Customer response has been good, and polls show that more and more consumers are aware of Whirlpool and have positive views of its products. This has allowed Whirlpool to drop the Phillips name in England, Ireland, the Netherlands and Austria, and they expect to do the same with the rest of Europe long before 1998. Also, while industry sales have been flat, Whirlpool has increased its market share in Europe.

Using one advertising program across several countries can work to build market share.

Source: Mark M. Nelson, ''Whirlpool Gives Pan-European Approach a Spin,'' *The Wall Street Journal*, April 23, 1992, p. B1.

ad showing a beautiful European woman, alone, in a European-style bath was created for the Japanese market.

A review of 17 global marketing programs has identified five pitfalls that can lead to failure: insufficient research, overstandardization, poor follow-up, narrow vision, and rigid implementation.[3] Problems created by each of these deficiencies will now be discussed.

Insufficient Research Half of the global marketing programs studied included no research before startup. Lego A/S, the Danish toy company, had greatly improved its penetration of the U.S. market by employing "bonus" packs and gift promotions. Encouraged by this success, Lego decided to transfer these tactics unaltered to other markets, including Japan. The promotions failed, and subsequent research revealed that customers considered them wasteful and expensive. When research was done first, two-thirds of the global programs succeeded; when it was skipped, two-thirds of them failed.

Overstandardization When global marketing programs are burdened with too many rules, local inventiveness and experimentation dry up. Often local innovation is exactly what a global program needs to keep itself updated and responsive to market conditions. These local deviations in execution don't distract from the common mission; rather, they strengthen the effort by focusing local expertise on the details.

Poor Follow-Up Splashy kickoff meetings for global marketing programs are useful, but momentum is often lost when they are not followed by lower-key promotional activities that extend throughout the campaign. What is needed is careful monitoring of progress, coordinating meetings among local sales managers, and periodic messages of support from top management to ensure that the projects get priority treatment by subsidiary officials. All too often, global programs fail because they do not get the continuous attention necessary for success.

Narrow Vision Two mechanisms used to control the implementation of global marketing programs involve either headquarters staff or a "lead market" subsidiary. Both approaches suffer from narrow vision and are not open to inputs from local managers. In addition, they do not provide a forum for discussion and sharing of solutions to common problems. Local managers view headquarters or lead market decisions as narrow, top down, and dictatorial. A better approach is shown by Unilever's European Brand Group, made up of headquarters and local subsidiary executives. This team was able to develop and launch a lemon-scented version of Vif liquid cleaner across Europe in only a few months. Vif beat out P&G's Mr Clean in the race to every single country.

Rigid Implementation Standardization in global marketing programs is one of the key features that leads to cost savings. However, excessive standardization can be self-defeating. Forced adoption of global programs and inflexible program management have led to program failures. When Nestlé successfully introduced its cakelike

Yes chocolate bar in Europe, the British subsidiary said it would not sell in England. Subsequent market tests showed that the British did not like the soft chocolate concept, and forced adoption would have produced a disaster.

Another case involved Lego A/S, which had pioneered standardized marketing of its toys in more than 100 countries. Lego sold its toy blocks in elegant see-through boxes worldwide. When the American competitor Tyco began selling blocks in plastic buckets that could be used for storage after play, headquarters refused requests by its American subsidiary to package the blocks in buckets. The excuse was that buckets would cheapen Lego's image and would be a radical change from the company policy of standardized marketing. After two years of massive market share losses, the American subsidiary was finally allowed to package blocks in buckets. Soon buckets were outselling boxes, and the worldwide adoption of buckets was a smashing success.

Think Global but Act Local

The examples we have discussed suggest that global marketing often works and can save money. Perhaps the best approach is to think global but act local. This means that you should have global objectives but should not ignore local market conditions. While Colgate toothpaste is available worldwide, for example, the company also makes a spicy toothpaste especially for the Mideastern market and sells a baby soap named Cadum only in France. Similarly, PepsiCo allows offices in other countries to edit and dub its global ads and to plan their own promotional activities. The extent of decentralization of marketing planning is shown by surveys indicating that host country marketing managers make up to 86 percent of advertising decisions, 74 percent of pricing decisions, and 61 percent of channel decisions. However, product design decisions are usually reserved for the parent organization.[4] Global marketing is alive, but the trend seems to be to adjust plans to meet the special needs of particular customers in foreign countries.

In addition, a substantial marketing effort is needed to establish a brand franchise worldwide. Development work is needed to increase brand awareness and to build a quality image. Even Coca-Cola, the world's best-known consumer product, still has room for improvement. For example, surveys of European consumers have shown that they rank Coke first in brand familiarity but only sixty-sixth in product quality. There is also variability in familiarity within Europe. While Coke achieved a 61 percent level of awareness in Norway, it achieved only 25 percent in Britain.[5] Market development requires a long-term commitment.

Strategies for Localized Marketing

A set of strategies for adapting to local conditions is shown in Figure 16-2. Strategy 1 is a global marketing approach that sells the same product in all countries with the same promotional appeals. This strategy has the advantage of low costs and seems to work best for business products such as airlines, computers, and machine tools. Strategy 2 sells the same product in different markets but changes the message for each set of customers. An example is the motor scooter that is sold as primary trans-

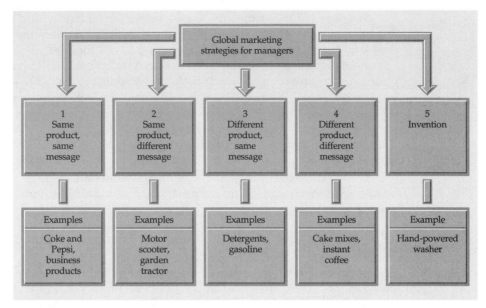

FIGURE 16-2 Global Marketing Strategies (Adapted from Table 21.1 in Warren Keegan's "Five Strategies for Multinational Marketing," *International Marketing Strategy*, rev. ed. Hans Thorelli and Helmut Becker, eds. [New York: Pergamon Press, 1980], pp. 191–198.)

portation in less developed countries and as a recreational vehicle in the United States. Strategy 3 focuses on adapting the product to meet local conditions but uses the same advertising message in all countries. Detergents and gasoline are routinely adjusted to meet weather and water conditions in each market area and are sold with standard promotional campaigns.

Strategy 4 in Figure 16-2 adapts both products and communications for each market entered. When Nestlé tried to break into the British instant coffee market, it found that coffee preferences were more American than European. This forced Nestlé to prepare a lighter blend of instant coffee for the British market. Because coffee is not as popular as tea in England, Nestlé had to use more aggressive advertising to catch the attention of potential customers. Strategy 5 is to invent something to meet the special needs of a local market. This is apt to be an expensive and risky approach to global marketing. To boost the sale of detergents, one manufacturer invented a hand-held plastic washer to sell to customers in underdeveloped countries who were still washing clothes in streams and buckets. Although the strategies shown in Figure 16-2 do not cover all possible market situations, they do provide a useful set of approaches for many localized marketing problems.

SUMMARY

Every day the world becomes smaller because of improvements in transportation and communications. One result is that international marketing is becoming more important to the success of business organizations. Part of your job as marketing manager is to understand the environment of international business and to select the best markets for foreign expansion. This involves calculating the expected rate of return on investment for each country and balancing it against the risk of loss. Next, you must decide on the most appropriate method for entering foreign markets. In some situations, exporting is the best approach; in others, you may want to use licensing, joint ventures, or direct investment.

A common problem with international marketing is deciding whether to adapt your products and advertising to the special needs of individual countries. Some organizations have been successful with a global approach where the same products and promotions are used throughout the world. Others have had more luck tailoring their products and advertising to the preferences of each foreign market.

NOTES

1. Andrew Tanzer, "Just Get Out and Sell," *Forbes,* September 26, 1992, pp. 68–69.

2. Theodore Levitt, "The Globalization of Markets," *Harvard Business Review,* Vol. 61 (May–June 1983), pp. 92–102; and Joanne Lipman, "Marketers Turn Sour on Global Sales Pitch Harvard Guru Makes," *The Wall Street Journal,* May 12, 1988, pp. A1, A10.

3. Kamran Kashani, "Beware the Pitfalls of Global Marketing," *Harvard Business Review* (September–October 1989), pp. 91–98.

4. Subhash C. Jain, "Standardization of International Marketing Strategy: Some Research Hypotheses," *Journal of Marketing,* Vol. 53 (January 1989), p. 76.

5. Lyn S. Amine, "Europe in '92 and the Problem of the Not-So-Global Brands," *AMS News* (April 1989), p. 3, and "Brand Awareness Slips When It Crosses International Border," *Marketing News,* November 21, 1988, p. 16.

SUGGESTED READING

Kotabe, Masaaki, and Eli P. Cox. "Assessment of Shifting Global Competitiveness," *Business Horizons* (January–February 1993), pp. 57–64.

Maruca, Regina F. "The Right Way to Go Global," *Harvard Business Review* (March–April 1994), pp. 134–145.

FURTHER READING

Cateora, Philip R. *International Marketing,* 7th ed. (Homewood, IL: Richard D. Irwin, 1992).

Hall, Edward T., and Mildred Reed Hall. *Hidden Differences: Doing Business with the Japanese* (Garden City, NY: Doubleday, 1987).

Jain, Subhash C. *International Marketing Management,* 3rd ed. (Boston: PWS-Kent, 1990).

Jeannet, Jean-Pierre, and Hubert D. Hennessey. *Global Marketing Strategies,* 2nd ed. (Boston: Houghton Mifflin, 1992).

QUESTIONS

1. P&G agreed to buy out its South Korean joint venture partner for $31 million. The unprofitable partnership sells disposable diapers, soap, and toothpaste manufactured by P&G and exported to South Korea. Its market share of disposable diapers is only 15 percent compared to the 50 percent share held by Kimberly-Clark. A $90 million diaper plant is under construction. Why did the South Korean partner want to get out of the joint venture? Why is P&G planning to stay?

2. The EEC has imposed antidumping duties on 15 Japanese makers of computer printers for selling at prices below those charged in its domestic market. The growing European printer market is estimated to be $1.75 billion a year, and Japan's share has grown from 49 percent to 73 percent in three years. Is the EEC really concerned with the evils of dumping, or does it have some other agenda? Are European buyers better off paying the higher prices that the new duties will require? How are the Japanese likely to respond to the new duties?

3. When 3M enters foreign markets, it typically begins by exporting products from the United States and selling them through company-owned foreign subsidiaries. As volume increases, 3M ships semifinished goods, such as huge rolls of tape, and uses local workers to cut and package the material. The next step is to move into local manufacturing. Why does 3M use this approach instead of licensing or joint ventures?

4. American-style shopping is coming to Europe. Europe's retail industry is characterized by high prices, snobbish service, and shoddy surroundings. Because of category killers and factory outlets, goods in the United States often sell for half their European price. In the United States, the typical factory outlet shopper is a woman driver. Market research shows that two-car families are far from the norm in France. There are also proportionally fewer female drivers in France than in the United States. Indeed, the findings show that French women enjoy being chauffered to the shops by their men. What does this tell American retailers? What is the long-run implication for car manufacturers if the American retailing concepts take hold?

5. The Chinese have agreed to lower barriers to U.S. exports ranging from cigarettes to refrigerators. The agreement averted a trade war in which the United States threatened to impose 100 percent tariffs on $3.9 billion worth of Chinese imports. Products covered by the agreement include chemicals, computers, integrated circuits, medical equipment, autos and auto parts, telecommunications equipment, fruits, grain, and edible oil products. Why was it to the advantage of China to lower its barriers to American imports?

6. Novus, Inc., is a U.S. firm that sells a unique technology for repairing automobile windshields. When the company started exporting, it did not patent its system in every foreign market because of the enormous legal costs. What do you suppose happened? How would you have solved the problem?

7. General Mills and PepsiCo formed a joint venture to sell snack foods in Europe.

Why is it to their advantage to work together in Europe even though some of their products are direct competitors in the United States?

8. Procter & Gamble entered the Japanese diaper and detergent market, and during the following decade it lost $200 million. Today P&G sells its products in 140 countries, and overseas sales account for 36 percent of total revenue. Why did P&G have so much trouble breaking into the Japanese market, and why is it so successful overseas today?

9. General Motors increased its sales in Japan 7.4 percent in 1992 with a campaign of comparative newspaper ads. They claimed that the Cadillac Seville matched Nissan's Infiniti on fuel economy and that the Grand Am was as big as Mitsubishi's Diamante. Why did the campaign increase sales, and what does this say about global marketing programs?

10. Daimler-Benz is a German manufacturer and a world leader in commercial trucks. Rather than export trucks from Germany, the company has 42 factories spread across five continents. Why has a global strategy of shipping parts among its plants helped it succeed?

11. Avon recently opened a plant to manufacture cosmetics and cleansers in the Guangzhou province of China. It currently has a direct sales force of 8000 women selling its products. Why is Avon interested in China?

12. Canada and the United States have the world's largest bilateral trading relationship, valued at $173.4 billion. All tariff barriers between the two countries are being eliminated. Canada has a population of only 26 million compared to 250 million in the United States. Some people have speculated that certain small Canadian businesses will suffer because of the trade agreement. As a marketing person, explain how the new pact will actually help some small Canadian companies.

13. Japanese drive on the left side of the road compared to the right side in the United States and Germany. Because of the small size of the Japanese imported car market, the Mercedes, BMW, and assorted American cars shipped to Japan have their controls on the left side. Does the fact that the steering wheels are on the "wrong" side explain the poor sales of imported cars in Japan?

Chapter 17

Marketing Planning and Implementation

A good plan, violently executed today, is better than a perfect plan tomorrow.

GENERAL GEORGE S. PATTON

One of your most important jobs as marketing manager is the preparation of marketing plans. Research has shown that organizations that plan for the future are more likely to survive.[1] Marketing plans are normally developed on an annual basis and often include actions that take place over several years. A marketing plan is a formal statement that explains where each product or service is today, where you want it to be at the end of the planning horizon, and how you intend to get there. Once marketing plans have been prepared, they are used to guide field marketing activities for the planning period. You must influence others—some of whom you have no formal authority over—to carry out your plans. As the planning period unfolds, you must monitor marketing performance and compare results with the goals set in the marketing plan. Not everything will go as planned; you must *act and adapt*. The objective of this chapter is to show you how to prepare and implement a marketing plan.

BRAND MANAGER AS PLANNER

The most common place for marketing planning to begin is in the offices of brand or product managers. You need to understand the position of these executives in the firm before we go into the details of the planning process. Figure 17-1 shows how product managers fit into the organizational life of a large business. Note that brand/product managers are staff specialists who operate alongside the line field sales organization. Product managers usually report to either a category manager or a group marketing manager (Figure 17-1). Group managers have responsibility for products in more than one product category. Category marketing managers focus on items in one category. This allows for better coordination of strategic and marketing efforts.

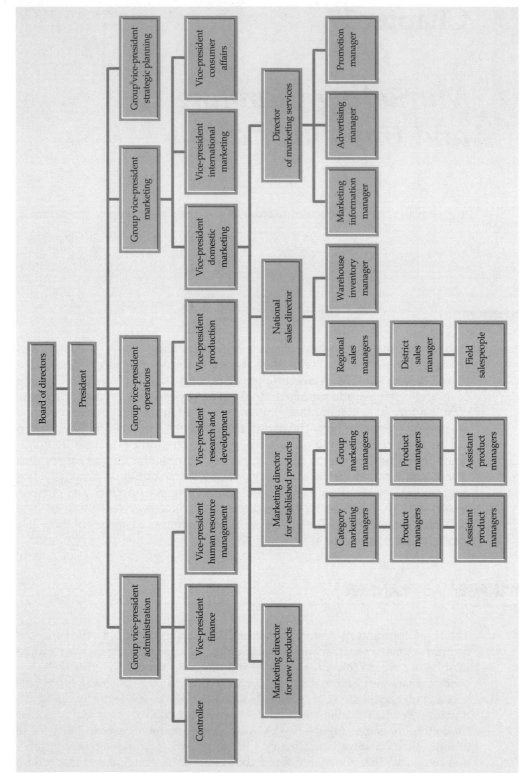

FIGURE 17-1 A Contemporary Organizational Structure

Colgate-Palmolive has category marketing managers for heavy-duty detergents and oral hygiene products and group product managers for hard-surface cleaners and toilet soap categories and for shaving products and first-aid categories. SmithKline realigned its management structure by category to expand health products on a global basis (Marketing in Action box 17-1). In some companies, managers may be organized around customer segments rather than products.

Brand and product managers operate as independent entrepreneurs, with responsibility for generating revenues and profits on the goods and services under their supervision. They create the marketing plans that attract customers, and they

---

MARKETING IN ACTION 17-1

CATEGORY MANAGEMENT AT SMITHKLINE

SmithKline Beecham Consumer Brands put in place a worldwide structure to expand its major healthcare brands ranging from Tums antacid to Contac cold medicine to Oxy acne medication into global over-the-counter (OTC) products. Six key marketing and research areas—OTC gastroenterological, OTC upper respiratory, health drinks, oral care, pain/feminine hygiene, and dermatological/vitamin supplement—are headed by a VP-category management director. These executives are responsible for developing ways to expand existing brands and for offering new concepts to brand groups around the world. Under its old structure, brand groups operated independently in each country.

SmithKline observed that OTC around the world isn't a globalized business, and they believed it should be possible to globalize it. The company has been moving in this direction for years. For instance, SmithKline's German subsidiary developed a successful flexible-head toothbrush called Dr. Best. The product, strategic positioning, and packaging were introduced under the Aquafresh name in the United States and other countries where Aquafresh is sold. The company even used the same advertising.

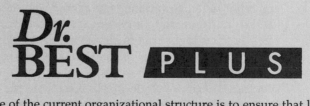

The purpose of the current organizational structure is to ensure that local ingenuity is encouraged even more and not stifled. Now local marketing teams have the benefit of a corporate category team with R&D capabilities who act as a communications point to bring them knowledge from other parts of the world. The globalization of ideas should produce faster product introductions.

A global category management system allows for streamlined global products by offering strategic positionings, advertising, and packaging concepts that can be used worldwide with local adaptations.

Source: Patricia Winters, "SmithKline Realigns by Category," *Advertising Age,* March 8, 1993, p. 17.

TABLE 17-1
Primary Activities of Product Managers

Prepare marketing plans for the following year, including merchandising, advertising, and selling activities to reach sales and profit goals.

Recommend prices, discounts, and allowances.

Forecast sales and set sales quotas with the sales manager.

Analyze sales results, share of market, competitive activity, and brand profits and adjust plans where necessary.

Request market research when necessary.

Initiate product improvements in anticipation of, or in reaction to, shifts in customers' requirements, advances in technology, or actions by competitors.

Continually appraise product performance, quality, and package design.

Recommend products to be eliminated.

---

function as the key decision makers in the day-to-day management of groups of products. The assignment of planning to product managers is essentially a bottom-up procedure. Plans prepared by product managers go up the organization before they are sent back down to be executed by the sales organization (Figure 17-1).

Brand managers also coordinate pricing, promotion, distribution, and research activities on a daily basis. Some of the duties assigned to product managers are listed in Table 17-1. A new assistant brand manager typically starts out developing coupon and promotion programs, examining costs, and getting involved with production and advertising. Brand managers must be brand stewards and assume responsibility for the environmental impact of their products, processes, and packages.[2] The job of a product manager covers almost all the elements of the marketing mix and is one of the most challenging occupations in the business world.

A key problem at both the product management level and the category level is keeping the same people in place so that they become true experts. There is often too much churning, with the average tenure in a position being only about 18 months. As a result, continuity becomes lost.

BUILDING THE MARKETING PLAN

Marketing plans provide a comprehensive statement of what you expect from each brand or service in the future. Plans are prepared on an annual basis, and include both historical data and recommendations on how to improve performance. The plan

TABLE 17-2
Sample Marketing Plan Headings

1. *Executive Summary:* Short review of the facts and recommendations.
2. *Table of Contents:* List of headings and page numbers.
3. *Company Situation:* Current sales, net income, market share, strengths, weaknesses.
4. *Environment:* Competitive plans, opportunities, threats, laws, regulations.
5. *Target Markets:* Who your customers are, where they are, and how much they will buy.
6. *Objectives:* Where the firm is going in terms of sales, market share, ROI, distribution, technology, and quality.
7. *Strategy:* Market development, cost reduction, differentiation, penetration, diversification.
8. *Action Programs:* Specific activities and tactics, individual assignments, timetables, and completion dates.
9. *Anticipated Results:* Projected profit and loss statement and cash budget by month and quarter, break-even analysis.
10. *Contingency Plans:* What to do if sales, profit, and other goals are not met.
11. *Appendices:* Supporting exhibits and tables.

combines a set of marketing strategies with a timetable for action so that specific financial goals can be achieved. An annual plan should include such sections as an executive summary, current company situation, business environment, target markets, objectives, strategy, action programs, anticipated results, and contingency plans (Table 17-2).

Executive Summary

An executive summary is a one- or two-page review of the main facts and recommendations contained in the marketing plan. The idea is to highlight the most important parts of the program for top management. This allows executives to gain an overview of the plan quickly without wading through the whole report and the supporting exhibits. Managers who need more detail than is provided in the executive summary can use the table of contents to go directly to the sections of the marketing plan that include the required information. Executive summaries are designed to make marketing plans more usable, and they are one of the last elements of the plan to be prepared.

Company Situation

The section of the marketing plan dealing with the company's situation sets the stage for the rest of the report by telling the reader where the company stands. The situation analysis reviews historical data accumulated for each product. This section includes information on sales, earnings, market shares, ROI, cash flow, and other variables for the past several years. Often this information is presented in chart form to make it easier for executives to grasp trends and relationships.

In addition to providing basic financial data, the company situation should describe briefly current marketing mix variables, such as product quality standards and communication themes, to help show the way to tomorrow. You must know your strengths and weaknesses. You cannot plan for the future unless you know what is going on in the present.

Environment

This section describes the external environmental factors that influence business planning. These include shifting customer demands, technological change, competition, governmental regulations, and availability of labor and materials. New customer wants and needs and advances in technology open opportunities for new markets and products. Competition is a constant threat to business success, and you need to know who the major domestic and foreign rivals are. You also need data on competitive strategies, pricing, cost structure, and distribution channels. Governmental regulations and court decisions also set limits on what marketing managers can do in particular situations. Thus you must be aware of what is allowable in the areas of the environment, employee rights, and competitive practices in pricing and advertising. Sometimes marketing plans are constrained by the availability of skilled labor and raw materials or uncooperative labor unions. You must be aware of trends in these areas. For example, what is considered environmentally sound keeps evolving with new information. Once, being "green" in the aerosol business meant switching from CFCs (chlorofluoro carbons) to HCFC-based propellants; in restaurants, it meant replacing paper with polyfoam clamshells to save trees. Today these solutions are obsolete. You must know your opportunities and threats. Strengths and weaknesses, and opportunities and threats, are often displayed together in a four-quadrant diagram.

Target Markets

The target market section of your marketing plan provides a detailed explanation of who your intended customers are. The plan should define your market in terms of demographics (age, income, education), geographics (location), and lifestyle. Be sure to include a discussion of the size of each intended market segment. In addition to size, you need to know how fast the target groups are growing and what product or service features customers are looking for. Knowing who your customers are, how much they buy, and when they buy makes it easier to design marketing plans to meet their needs.

Objectives

The objectives section of the marketing plan is a short statement on where you intend the product or business unit to go in the future. These objectives must be in agreement with the overall objectives of the firm, but they do not have to be the same for each line of trade. Thus, the objective for a question mark product might be to build market share, whereas with a cash cow you might prefer to lose market share rather than waste money trying to save a lost cause.

Company objectives, for example, might call for 20 percent sales growth, a 15 percent pretax profit margin, and a 25 percent ROI. Products in attractive markets would be expected to match or exceed these goals, and businesses in more competitive or mature environments would have lower expectations. The idea is to push each business to do as well as it can in the light of differences in potential.

Strategy

The strategy section of the marketing plan provides a summary statement showing how the business will achieve its objectives. The statement indicates the areas the firm will emphasize in its drive for victory. Effective strategies usually tell management what paths to follow for several key operating variables. For example, you can build a sustainable competitive advantage through brand identification, product differentiation, niche marketing, or low costs. Businesses that need to improve profitability could pursue a strategy of raising prices. This strategy, in turn, could mean selective price increases for high-demand items or across-the-board increases on all products. Cost-cutting strategies can involve a variety of areas both within the marketing department and in other parts of the firm. One popular cost-cutting strategy is to drop low-profit items and to restrict the number of product variations offered to customers. Other cost-saving strategies might include reductions in corporate image-building advertising and temporary cuts in sales training activities.

Action Programs

The next step in the planning process is to translate broad strategy statements into specific actions and tactics. This can be helped along by setting up timetables to show the starting and completion dates for each activity. In addition, it is useful to assign responsibility to one individual to see that each project is completed on schedule. For example, a program to identify products for elimination might be given to a group product manager. These managers oversee the work of several product managers, and they have the experience needed to pick items for divestment. The group product managers could also farm out some of the elimination decisions to subordinates who monitor the day-to-day activities of each brand.

The specific actions called for in this section are exemplified by a building products company that had been losing money for two years. For the coming year, sales were expected to decline from $11 million to $8 million because of a construction slump. This new level of sales translated into a projected $450,000 loss for the firm unless an effective cost-cutting strategy could be implemented. In addition, if the company expected to make its standard 20 percent return on invested capital, it needed another $440,000 in margin. The $890,000 objective was attacked with selective price increases that raised $230,000; then $50,000 was cut from the advertising budget, and a $60,000 annual consulting fee to a former owner was renegotiated. Other actions taken to cut costs included laying off 15 people, reducing executive salaries 10 percent, and subletting spacious corporate offices and moving into quarters at one of the company's plants. The company also talked its bank into converting $35,000 of interest due on a loan into principal. As a result of these action programs, morale improved dramatically, and the company started making money despite severe economic conditions.

Anticipated Results

Once the specific tactics have been selected, managers are in a position to forecast the results of the new marketing plan. These are usually presented in the form of break-even charts, projected profit and loss statements, and cash flow budgets. Anticipated unit sales and total revenues are shown for each model and time period. When price changes are expected to occur during the planning horizon, they are factored into the revenue calculations and are shown in the profit and loss statement as net realized price. Costs are broken into fixed and variable categories for planning and control purposes. Production and physical distribution costs are subtracted from revenues to give estimates of gross margins in dollars and percentages. Next, gross margins per unit are divided into fixed costs to give break-even volumes at different prices. Then budgets are set for the sales force, advertising, sales promotion, market research, product development, and administrative expense categories. The difference between these expenses and the gross margin available is the profit for the planning period.

After the projected marketing budget has been approved by top management, it is used to monitor results. Actual sales and expenses recorded in each period are compared with the projected figures on a monthly and a year-to-date basis. Significant differences between the planned and actual results provide signals for remedial action.

Contingency Plans

The contingency section of the marketing plan tells management what to do if expectations and the real world fail to agree with one another. This section asks a series of "what if" questions about possible events in the marketplace and then answers them. For example, what if the market grows faster than forecast levels? A trigger point for action might occur when new orders are 30 percent above the long-range forecast. At this point, the firm could run into capacity limitations, although excess capacity might be available elsewhere in the industry. Possible responses in this situation might be to go to a three-shift production schedule operating seven days a week, advance the timing of capacity additions, be selective in accepting orders, and provide leadership in raising prices. Other contingency plans would be formulated to combat price-cutting by competitors and failures to meet sales goals. The main advantage of contingency plans is that they force management to think about a broader range of problems than might occur when strategies are designed only to meet immediate company objectives. Also, contingency plans that have been thought out ahead of time can be implemented quickly if the need arises. As a former chairperson of General Motors has said, "I don't like people running into my office saying, 'Jeez, this just happened. So what do we do next?' I want to have a plan for just about everything."

Appendices

This section contains supporting documents and exhibits. Make sure that they are numbered correctly and appear in a logical order. Remember that well-designed charts with three-dimensional shading and color are easier to read and understand. Attractive graphics are also useful if you are called on to give an oral presentation of your marketing plan.

A MARKETING PLANNING EXAMPLE

A useful example of marketing planning occurred a few years ago with a small manufacturer of quality sliding glass doors. The objectives of the company were to increase sales 20 percent a year, to achieve a 20 percent return on net worth, and to strengthen its position in the building field. The firm was operating at capacity, with 90 percent of its sales coming from sliding glass doors and 6.6 percent from window-wall units. It had a strong distribution network and was well known for the superior design and construction of its doors.

The company believed its goals could be achieved either by introducing a new low-priced door to compete in the mass market or by expanding its efforts to sell window-wall panels. Low-priced doors looked particularly attractive because industry sales of sliding doors were expected to grow 50 percent in the next three years, and 80 percent of this volume fell into the low-priced category. Wall panels, on the other hand, were made to order, and required extensive direct selling and advertising to convert architects to the new design concept. Although the potential market for wall panels appeared to be large, there were some doubts about whether sales of this item could be developed fast enough to meet their growth objectives.

Competitive Factors

Competition in the low-priced sliding door market consisted of 300 smaller manufacturers who sold directly to local contractors at prices 40 percent below those of the market leaders. The door market was easy to enter because the aluminum extrusions were simple to work with, and the smaller firms copied the designs of larger companies. The wall panel market had few direct competitors, and each product was sold on the basis of its own design characteristics. There were no significant legal, raw material, or social problems associated with either of the product alternatives under consideration. This business analysis prompted the firm to adopt a product line extension strategy and to select the low-priced door as the best possible product alternative.

The most attractive market segment for low-priced doors appeared to be the 5 percent of the contractors who built 70 percent of the new homes. The marketing strategy devised to sell to contractors emphasized a superior product at a competitive price. Because the contractors selected doors on the basis of bid prices, it was important to deliver the new door to distributors at $200. At this price, the firm would have very little promotional money and would have to rely on the distributors to push the product. The manufacturer believed that its reputation for quality merchandise would help it gain orders from contractors despite the absence of promotional efforts. Low-priced doors were typically handled by different distributors, and the firm had to add several new dealers who specialized in these items. On the basis of the mix of marketing activities, the firm estimated that sales of 3000 units a month would allow it to break even within two years at the selling price of $200. This appeared to be a reasonable sales goal because it represented only 4 percent of the low-priced door market. The addition of the new doors seemed to be a logical product-line extension for the company. Money invested in the project would be returned in two years, and the larger facilities would allow expanded production of window-wall units. The firm decided to go after the low-priced door market and invested several hundred thousand dollars in new facilities, equipment, and inventory.

The move into low-priced doors turned out to be hasty and ill-advised. Local competitors, operating with almost no overhead, immediately began to cut prices to keep their share of the business. Because the firm was the high-cost manufacturer, it could not compete on price and was left with a large inventory of unsold merchandise. The resulting financial strain was so severe that the company was forced to sell out to a larger firm.

What Went Wrong?

Why did the company fail to anticipate the reactions of the smaller firms? Part of the problem was that the company was production oriented and did not understand the marketing concept. This lack of marketing sophistication led the company to assume blindly that its reputation for quality was enough to give it a slice of the low-priced door market. A closer examination of customers' needs would have revealed that price was the only factor contractors considered in buying doors for tract houses. Anyone entering this market had to be prepared to beat the prices offered by local competitors. Also, the firm did not prepare contingency plans so that it would be ready to counter the adverse affects of low sales on cash flow.

In this case, the company was so eager to reach its unrealistic sales and profit goals that it ignored the factor of risk. The company completely misjudged the response of its smaller competitors and failed to see that the new product would put a strain on working capital. Management should have realized that although window-wall units offered lower immediate sales, they fit in well with the quality image of the firm and represented a substantially lower risk. Even after the firm decided to go into low-priced doors, it could have salvaged the situation by trying to sell a few doors in a limited geographical area before going into national distribution. This test market could have shown the price-cutting reaction of competitors in time for the company to kill the project before any permanent damage was done. This case shows that it is important to have access to reliable market information.

GATHERING PLANNING INFORMATION

Effective marketing plans are based on detailed information on customers, competitors, and the marketing environment. Part of your job as marketing manager is to

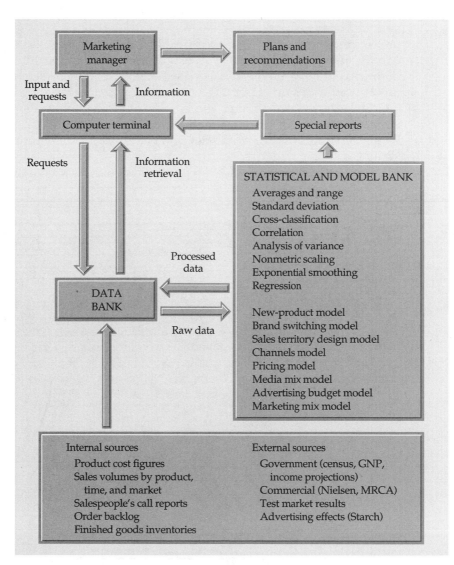

FIGURE 17-2 Marketing Information System Components

assist in the collection and processing of these data. The mechanism for gathering needed data is called a *marketing information system (MktIS)*. The basic components of an MktIS can be described as a structured set of persons, machines, and procedures designed to generate timely data, collected from both intra- and extrafirm sources, for use in planning and decision making.

MktIS typically includes a data bank, a set of analytical tools, and a communication network. An example showing how managers interact with these components is given in Figure 17-2. Notice that MktIS allows managers to retrieve selected historical figures from data files, process raw data with standard statistical programs, and test alternative strategies against complex planning models. Executives may also call on MktIS to generate a variety of routine and special reports to help them in their day-to-day decision making. MktIS can be used for developing marketing plans and then later to help control the programs after they have been implemented. The impact of MktIS at one firm is illustrated in Marketing in Action box 17-2.

Marketing data banks draw most of their historical records from internal sales figures, call reports, and external materials published by research firms and government agencies (Figure 17-2). The popularity of scanners in store checkout lanes has greatly increased the accuracy and amount of product movement data available for planning purposes. The value of environmental information in the creation of marketing programs has led to the development of special environmental information systems.

Once needed data files have been accumulated, a variety of analytical tools can

MARKETING IN ACTION 17-2

MktIS at Ito-Yokado's 7-Eleven Japan

The key to success for the 7-Eleven convenience-store chain is its centralized computer system that links its approximately 4,000 stores nationwide. Rather than simply logging sales data, 7-Eleven Japan uses the computer to chart trends. When they went to the system, they found for the first time that they had to change the range of products they had for every single store, not just by region or size of the store. Outlets near schools need a large stock of boxed lunches, while stores in residential areas sell more groceries.

Sales data are coordinated with the chain's computerized delivery system. Consequently, 7-Eleven stocks some stores three times a day, keeping inventory small and ensuring that the sandwiches and rice balls are fresh.

Data on deliveries help 7-Eleven spot potential new business. Noting that many convenience store shoppers were young, single Japanese doing their shopping after banks were closed, the stores started accepting payment of gas and electric bills. They also handle overnight delivery packages and accept insurance forms for mopeds.

MktIS keeps you on top of your customers' purchase behavior.

Source: Yumiko Ono, ''Japanese Chains Setting Sights on U.S. Market,'' *The Wall Street Journal,* April 13, 1990, p. B1.

be employed to process and summarize the information. These include simple statistical programs for means, standard deviations, cross-tabulations, and more sophisticated programs that study correlations among data. These programs also allow relationships and decision alternatives to be evaluated by means of statistical tests. A recent trend has been an expansion in the use of simulation models to evaluate the impact of alternative marketing plans.

TESTING THE MARKETING PLAN

To help reduce risk, many marketing managers test their marketing plans using computer simulations. This approach saves time and money compared with field test markets or regional market evaluations. The use of simulations also provides secrecy and prevents your competitors from auditing your tests, stealing your ideas, or sabotaging your plan with special advertising gimmicks.

How Do Simulations Work?

Simulation is the use of a model to replicate the operation of a real system over time. Marketing simulations, for example, feed price, promotion, advertising, and distribution values into a model to estimate the sales volumes or market shares the products might have at the end of a time period. The main advantage of marketing plan simulations is that they allow you to bring together and study the interaction of several marketing variables at the same time. In addition, you can test various combinations of marketing factors without having to spend money to take the risks associated with making changes in the real world.

An example of how simulation is used by managers might be described as follows:

INTERVIEWER: Do you make regular simulation runs for assessing the marketing mix for a new product?

ANALYST: Oh, yes.

INTERVIEWER: Do you implement the results?

ANALYST: Oh, no!

INTERVIEWER: Well, that seems odd. If you don't implement the results, perhaps you should stop making the runs.

ANALYST: No, no. We wouldn't want to do that!

INTERVIEWER: Why not?

ANALYST: Well, what happens is something like this: I make several computer runs and take them to the brand manager. He is responsible for this whole multi-million-dollar project. The brand manager looks at the runs, thinks about them for a while, and then sends me back to make a few more, with conditions changed in various ways. I do this and bring them back in. He looks at them and probably sends me back to make more runs. And so forth.

INTERVIEWER: How long does this keep up?

ANALYST: I would say it continues until finally the brand manager screws up enough courage to make a decision.

Simulation thus encourages manager–model interaction to improve understanding of the business environment and to help make better plans. When you do not agree with the simulation results, the input data can be reexamined and tests run to see how sensitive the results are to changes in parameters. This process of interacting with a model allows you to learn more about your problems without giving up control to the computer.

Simulation Examples

Simulations have been used to test marketing plans in a variety of firms. It is common, for example, to run alternative advertising schedules through simulation models to find which media give the best customer exposure. One new product model is used to evaluate the impact of alternative package sizes, coupon schedules, and promotions on the sales of newly introduced items. This program has proved to be so valuable that it is often run over 400 times in a single month.

Simulation can help you build better marketing plans by employing models that replicate the operation of real-world systems. Simulation is not a cure-all; it is merely one of several tools available to simplify complex marketing problems. The main problem with marketing simulations is that usually so many variables are involved that it is often difficult to find optimum solutions. One approach is to make a series of simplifying assumptions, but this can lend an aura of unreality to the recommendations. A better approach is to restrict the number of marketing variables included in each simulation project. For example, Figure 17-3 shows the results of a simulation designed to find the optimal product mix and prices for an individual firm. This simulation involved a search across 20 product alternatives and preferences of 60 consumers divided into eight market segments. The lines at the bottom of the figure represent combined utility curves for the eight segments. Note that the utility curves rise to ideal points and then decline across product alternatives. In this case, a profit-maximizing solution was found in less than a minute, using appropriate heuristics and a desktop computer. Complex simulations that take hours to run on a mainframe computer are not much help to marketing decision makers.

The solution recommended in Figure 17-3 suggests marketing the three products shown by the dark price bars. Profit maximization raised prices so that segments 1 to 3 were shut out of the market. Segment 4 chose product 4, and segments 5 to 7 chose product 10. Segment 8 selected product 17. The beauty of this simulation approach is that it allows marketing managers to quickly evaluate a variety of price and product mix alternatives. Common applications of simulation in marketing have been to (1) help develop alternative marketing strategies, (2) provide inexpensive

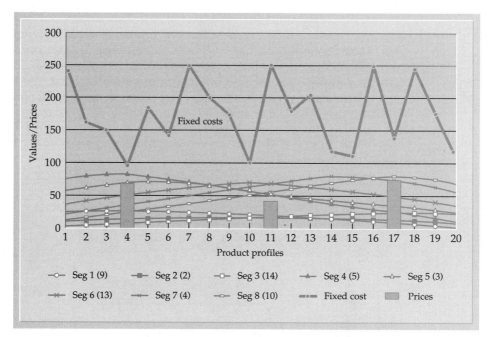

FIGURE 17-3 Using Simulations to Optimize Product Mix and Prices for Eight Market Segments (From Gregory Dobson and Shlomo Kalish, "Heuristics for Pricing and Positioning a Product Line Using Conjoint and Cost Data," *Management Science* [February 1993], p. 170)

test markets to evaluate strategies, and (3) help control the implementation of marketing programs.

IMPLEMENTATION AND CONTROL

The success of marketing plans frequently depends on the level of execution that is achieved by the salespeople, dealers, and advertising agencies that implement programs in the real world. Even the most brilliant plan will fail if it is not implemented correctly. Effective implementation converts marketing plans into individual assignments and makes sure that they are executed on time. Business firms must have a system of control that quickly points out execution errors and helps managers take corrective action. An important first step is to decide what factors will best explain the success or failure of an individual marketing plan. Depending on business conditions, a firm might emphasize market share, dollar volume, unit sales, dollar profit, or ROI. Marketing control is basically a set of procedures that allows managers to compare the results of marketing plans with predetermined standards so that corrective action can be taken to ensure that objectives are met. Effective control requires an MktIS that gathers data on market conditions and places them in the hands of executives who can make adjustments in plans and operating procedures.

A flow diagram that highlights the basic elements of the marketing control process is presented in Figure 17-4. The first few steps involve planning and are usually performed on an annual basis. Objectives are adopted; price, promotion, advertising, and distribution strategies are selected; and performance standards are set for sales quotas, selling expenses, and other control variables. Next, the marketing program is implemented over a span of time, and periodic measurements are taken to record

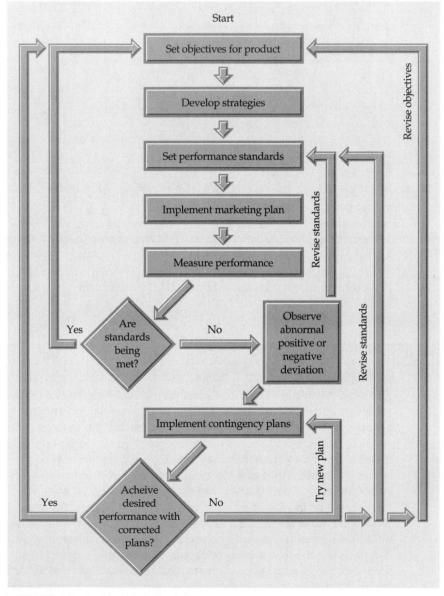

FIGURE 17-4   Marketing Control Process

the reactions of customers and competitors. The basic aim of the control process is to see whether the predetermined performance standards are being met. If they are, the successful results are fed back to the starting point and used to set the objectives for the next planning period (Figure 17-4).

When significant deviations from performance standards are observed, the manager has the choice of changing the standards or implementing contingency plans to attempt to correct the problem (Figure 17-4). For example, suppose that a new product, expected to attain a 3 percent market share after six months, actually captured 10 percent of the market. This suggests that the original estimate was low, and the manager should probably raise the annual forecast to 8 percent or more so that the production, advertising, and distribution efforts can be adjusted to reflect realized demand.

In the more typical situation in which sales fail to reach desired levels, managers can try a variety of short-run strategies to get the product back on target. These may take the form of cents-off coupons, new advertising themes or media, deals for retailers, changes in ad schedules, increased advertising, contests for salespeople, or simple changes in packaging or product specifications. If these tonics fail to do the job, the manager may have to revise the standards or objectives for the next planning period (Figure 17-4). In addition, managers can initiate special market research studies to determine why products do not reach long-run sales goals. These efforts may result in entirely new products, major changes in existing items, new channels, realignments in selling efforts, or a decision to drop the offending products entirely.

Setting Standards

Performance standards are planned achievement levels for selected marketing variables that the firm expects to attain at stated intervals throughout the year. Managers do not have time to watch all dimensions of the marketing plan; they must select the most important performance factors to be monitored on a regular basis. In addition to traditional dollar sales, profit, and market share goals, most firms set standards for selling and advertising expenses. These are often expressed as a percentage of sales to simplify comparisons with past performance and the experience of other firms in the industry. For example, a company could measure the efficiency of its sales organization by setting a standard of 10 percent of revenue to cover branch office overhead, salaries of salespeople and sales managers, travel, commissions, bonuses, and customer entertainment. Other marketing factors that can be used for control purposes are shown in Table 17-3. Most firms employ several marketing variables to control their operations because reliance on a single factor can be dangerous. For example, one San Francisco department store got into trouble by setting rigid standards for markdowns as a percentage of sales. Managers easily met the standards by failing to cut prices and clearing out leftovers at the end of each selling season. This caused the departments to accumulate a lot of old, unsalable merchandise, and eventually the store went out of business. It was not enough just to control the markdown percentage; the managers also had to worry about the age of their stock and about maintaining an inventory of merchandise to meet customers' needs.

TABLE 17-3
Performance Measures Used for Control Purposes

Customers	Awareness levels
	Inquiries
	Complaints
	Number of returns
	Warranty expense
Product	Rate of trial
	Repeat purchase rate
	Cannibalization rate
	Price relative to those of competitors
	Coupon redemption rate
Distribution	Average order and delivery time
	Percentage of stores carrying the product
	Months of inventory in dealers' hands
	Distribution costs per unit
Sales and advertising	Advertising cost per unit sold
	Turnover rate of sales force
	Sales calls per day
	Number of new accounts opened
	Sales per order
	Number of accounts lost

Measuring Performance

MktISs provide the basic data used by control systems to compare planned performance with real-world results. A control system should permit assignment of responsibility for differences between planned and actual performance. Managers rely on a variety of special MktIS reports to point out deviations between standards and actual operations so that corrective action can be taken. One way that managers can be alerted to problems is through the use of control charts. Figure 17-5 shows a chart used to monitor selling expenses over time. Although the planned level of expenses was 15 percent, random events caused this ratio to vary between 13 and 17 percent of sales. If selling expenses fell within this range in 90 out of 100 periods, then corrective action would not be needed. Only when expenses fell outside the normal range would the manager be alerted to the possibility of a selling-expense problem. The application of a "management by exception" policy saves executive time and is quite popular in the business world.

When expenses fall outside control limits, the manager must decide whether it is just a chance event or evidence of a real change. For example, the low expense ratio in period 3 (Figure 17-5) appears to be just random variation and probably can be ignored. The two high values observed in periods 12 and 14, however, suggest an unfavorable trend and should be investigated. This example indicates that the

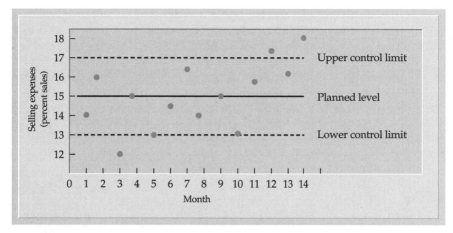

FIGURE 17-5   Control Chart for Monitoring Deviations from Plans

importance of violations of control limits for marketing processes, unlike manufacturing processes, is asymmetrical. The fact that selling expenses are too high is much more worrisome than that they are too low. Other types of graphic control devices that can be used to monitor marketing programs include Gantt charts, PERT diagrams, histograms, and flowcharts.

Example of Marketing Control

An example showing how a marketing control system operates is provided by the U.S. food company H. J. Heinz. The product, in this case, was a frequently purchased item found in supermarkets. It was sold in several different sizes, and one size or another was promoted to the trade every four to six weeks. The impact of promotion on market share appeared to vary by container size and across sales districts. To study these effects, Heinz built some response functions for 27 market areas.

Newspaper features were the primary promotional tool used to draw customers' attention to the product. Heinz kept track of the number of features run, the share of the market of the retail chain, the size of the feature ad, and the percentage discount offered by the feature in relation to the average level of discounting to which the customers had become accustomed. These analyses revealed that there was little evidence of any relationship among promotional spending and either the number of newspaper features or market share. The number of newspaper features for competitive products, as well as those for the product, did influence Heinz's market share.

Additional calculations suggested that most promotions were, on average, unprofitable. Accordingly, the number of promotions in most districts was decreased, and those promotions that were conducted were adjusted to include package sizes that seemed to be most effectively promoted within a given district. During the first year in which these actions were taken, the total number of promotions was reduced by 40 percent, yet market share increased by more than three share points.

A marketing control system was designed to monitor Heinz's promotional activities. Each month the newly available data are entered into the system, and the current effectiveness of the promotions is evaluated. The purpose of the marketing control system is to detect changes in the effectiveness of any particular type of promotion. Heinz was concerned that rapidly rising prices in the general economy might make the consumer less loyal and more price conscious. As a result of the system, Heinz found that sometimes promotions for a particular size that had been successful in the past became ineffectual. Moreover, some promotions that had always been ineffective in a district became successful. The marketing control system thus accomplished its purpose in revealing changes in customers' habits.

Building an Ethics Program

Marketing implementation should be conducted in an ethical and legal manner. The marketing control system should not simply look at marketing performance but should also take into account broader issues. Your firm should act responsibly in a systematic way.

The moral climate of a business reflects the words and actions of its top executives. If management tolerates unethical behavior, then there is little a member of the organization can do about it. Most executives believe that top management has the primary responsibility for setting the ethical tone of a company. The general feeling is that the strongest positive influence on ethical behavior is having an ethical boss. Superiors set the moral climate and provide the constraints within which business decisions are made. Thus, the best way for you to build a strong sales ethics program is to get the backing of the board chairperson and the president of the company. When this support is not available, there are sure to be ethical violations.

Once you gain the support of top management, the next step is to prepare a written marketing ethics policy statement that indicates to employees that the company believes in playing fair with customers and competitors. Surveys have shown that executives believe that codes of ethics are the most effective way to encourage ethical behavior. A written policy allows you to be explicit about what activities are permissible and what actions violate company standards. This can be useful when customers or suppliers ask employees to participate in unethical activities. If your company has a code of ethics, they can reply, "I'm sorry, but company policy forbids that," and graciously end a conversation about a shady deal.

You should remember that publishing a marketing ethics code does not guarantee that it will be followed by marketing employees. More and more companies are offering classes to make sure that employees know what to do in morally ambiguous situations. A recent survey revealed that 35 percent of the respondents had formal ethics training programs.[3] These programs bring groups of employees together with an instructor to find solutions to simulated moral dilemmas. By working through a number of scenarios, employees learn how to recognize problems, assemble facts, consider alternatives, and make decisions. They can also pick up some tips on how the company expects them to operate. At one session a salesperson asked, "When I check in at a motel, I get a coupon for a free drink; can I use it?" The correct answer was that it would be acceptable to use the coupon, but it would be wrong to accept $50 to stay there in the first place. The idea behind ethics training is to make sure that employees are equipped to handle real-world issues they are apt to encounter.

THE MARKETING AUDIT

Marketing planning is not complete unless it includes periodic reviews of the entire marketing effort of the firm. These reviews, called *marketing audits,* are designed to point out the strengths and weaknesses of the marketing objectives, organization, personnel, and operating procedures employed by the organization. The idea is to appraise the overall condition of the marketing program so that the firm can capitalize on its strengths and improve areas that are weak.

Areas to Be Audited

The marketing audit is not concerned with measuring past performance; instead, it looks to the future to see how well the firm's resources are being used to exploit market opportunities. The auditor first looks at marketing objectives to make sure that they are sufficiently broad so that the firm is not trapped with an obsolete product line. For example, an abrasives company would be advised to state its objective as improved sales of metal polishing and removal services rather than just as improved sales of grinding wheels. This approach allows the company to offer a variety of ways to solve customers' problems without restricting itself to the sale of a single product.

The audit should also include an appraisal of the structure of the marketing organization. Does the chief marketing officer have enough power to control all relevant marketing functions? Are the channels of communication open among sales, advertising, promotion, and product development executives? Do the managers of each marketing function have the skills, training, and experience needed to perform their jobs successfully? Should new-product development be handled by a committee, venture teams, or a separate department? These are only a few of the many questions that need to be asked to evaluate the organizational arrangements used to structure marketing activities.

In addition, marketing audits must evaluate the procedures that are used by the firm to implement marketing programs. This means that the auditor must consider how well the product line meets the needs of the perceived market segment. In addition, the auditor reviews the coverage of the sales territories and checks the speed of delivery provided by the warehouse and the transportation network. Auditors should also speak with dealers and customers to find out how they view the marketing operations of the firm. One thing auditors look for in judging operating efficiency is balance across elements of the marketing program. It would be foolish, for example, to spend lavishly on trade promotion unless salespeople are available to make follow-up calls. In another case, an auditor found a large proportion of a pharmaceutical manufacturer's ad budget devoted to billboards. This is an unusual way to promote prescription drugs. The selection of billboards as an advertising medium had been made years before, and had become such a sacred cow that no one in the company questioned its efficiency. Fortunately, the auditor convinced the company to drop billboard advertising in one area, and sales remained constant. Thus, in this case, a single operational change saved the manufacturer more than enough to pay for the marketing audit.

Implementing the Audit

Marketing audits should be conducted in healthy firms as well as in those that are in trouble. Audits can help fine-tune successful programs, in addition to identifying problem areas in companies with declining markets and low profits. To achieve the maximum benefit from a marketing audit, you will probably find it best to hire someone from outside the organization to direct the investigation. Outside consultants are likely to be more objective and can devote their full time to the project. In addition, consultants often have a breadth of experience that allows them to see problems with current practices and recommend improvements.

SUMMARY

This chapter has shown why marketing plans are needed to help guide field marketing activities. In addition, we have explained who prepares marketing plans and how they are organized. The development of effective marketing programs depends on timely data collected by MktISs. MktISs are also used to prepare special reports that highlight sales force productivity, realign territories, measure price elasticity, and calculate marginal responses to advertising.

The success of marketing planning in the real world frequently depends on how well the various elements of the marketing mix work together. Enlightened managers are now able to pretest the interactions of marketing variables by running examples through special business simulations. These simulations are developed from data supplied by MktISs and from subjective inputs provided by executives. These simulations allow the manager to test combinations of marketing factors without spending the money or taking the risks associated with making changes in an actual competitive environment.

Computers can also be used to help monitor the implementation of marketing programs. The basic control process is a check for differences between desired performance standards and actual results. When negative deviations occur, simulation can be employed to determine what has gone wrong with the marketing plans and help develop new strategies. The primary data used to highlight problem areas are provided by control charts and special profit reports prepared by the MktIS.

In addition to monitoring current operations, you must prepare yourself for the future. This means that marketing programs should be audited periodically to make sure that the firm has the right products, personnel, and channels of distribution to fill customers' needs and meet the challenges offered by competitors.

NOTES

1. *The Wall Street Journal,* February 14, 1988, p. B1.
2. Jacquelyn Ottman, "Brand 'Stewards' Will Guide Environmental Planning," *Marketing News,* April 13, 1992, p. 15.
3. *The Wall Street Journal,* July 14, 1986, p. 21.

SUGGESTED READING

Jaworski, Bernard J., Vlasis Stathakopolos, and H. Shanker Krishnan. "Control Combinations in Marketing: Conceptual Framework and Empirical Evidence," *Journal of Marketing,* Vol. 57, No. 1 (January 1993), pp. 57–69.

FURTHER READING

AMA Marketing Toolbox. *Marketing Planning: Preparing the Marketing Plan* (Chicago: American Marketing Association, 1993).
Goetsch, Hal. *Developing, Implementing, and Managing an Effective Marketing Plan* (Chicago: American Marketing Association, 1992).

QUESTIONS

1. When using category management, should you group products according to their similarities to each other or according to how consumers buy them?

2. Why is there such a diversity in marketing organizational structures (e.g., Procter & Gamble emphasizes category management, Warner-Lambert and Campbell key-account management, and Black & Decker channel management)?

3. How many layers of management should be assigned to deal with product planning and marketing strategy? For example, at General Motors there are marketing planners at corporate headquarters in Detroit, in the giant car-building groups, and at vehicle-selling divisions. Does GM have redundant staff?

4. Artists, dancers, musicians, and actors enrich our lives. Yet most arts organizations are perpetually in debt. They may possess a great product, but they cannot attract enough customers. They seem to have fallen prey to the old adage that "If you build a better mousetrap, the world will beat a path to your door." Explain how arts organizations can become more marketing driven.

5. Marketing planners must build on market research studies. The problem is that conflicting information, whether it is about the popularity of brands, the viability of green products, or the demographics of a market segment, often leaves them

exasperated and wondering who to believe. For example, in a poll by Opinion Research Corporation, 75 percent of the 500 women surveyed said that they were willing to pay more for products that were environmentally correct. However, a study by the Hartman Group found that while 70 percent of the participants in its study expressed environmental concerns in general, only 50 percent said that they would make green purchases. Yet another study, by Gerstman and Meyers, found that 80 percent of adults said that they were willing to pay a 5 percent premium for environmentally safe packaging, but only 38 percent said that they would be willing to pay a price that was 15 percent higher. What might explain the disparities? How would you decide what data to believe?

6. With marketing planning requirements, sophisticated MktISs, and massive amounts of customer data, how do you avoid "analysis paralysis"?

Appendix

THE CASE METHOD

The objective of the case method is to introduce a measure of realism into business education. A case approach forces you to deal with problems as they actually occur in a for profit or a not-for-profit organization. Each case is simply a written description of the facts surrounding a particular business situation. With the case approach, it is your responsibility to develop solutions to the problem. Instructors, for example, may set the stage for the case discussion by providing background material or by helping you gain insight into the problem. They may also act as devil's advocates and as critics to test arguments and proposals that you put forth. Finally, they evaluate your performance, assign grades, and make suggestions for improvement.

BENEFITS AND LIMITATIONS

The case method becomes an effective teaching device when students are encouraged to analyze the data presented and to formulate their own sets of recommendations. Because each case is different, the solution that is developed for one case cannot be randomly applied to another. This raises the question of what you actually learn by working with business cases. One obvious benefit is that preparation and discussion of case studies helps you improve your skills in oral and written expression. In addition, the case method provides an easy way to learn about current business practices. Perhaps the most important advantage of the case method is the experience it provides in thinking logically about different sets of data. The development of your analytical ability and judgment is the most valuable and lasting benefit derived from working with business cases.

Most cases, including those in this book, are drawn from the experiences of real firms. The names and locations may be disguised to protect the interests of the companies involved. In addition, final decisions are usually omitted to enhance the problem-solving orientation of the cases, thus permitting you to reach your own conclusions without being forced to criticize the actions taken by others. The case method departs from the typical business situation in that the business executive usually does not have the facts presented as clearly and as neatly as they are in casebooks. Problem solving in business usually involves extensive data collection, something that has been essentially completed for you.

A FRAMEWORK FOR ANALYSIS

You can approach the analysis of business cases in many different ways. Each instructor has his or her own ideas on the number and nature of the steps involved. We believe the following six-step procedure is a logical and practical way to begin.

1. Define the problem.
2. Formulate the alternatives.
3. Analyze the alternatives.
4. Recommend a solution.
5. Specify a plan of action.
6. Prepare contingency plans.

Defining the Problem

Once you are familiar with the facts of the case, you should isolate the central problem. Until this is done, it is usually impossible to proceed with an effective analysis. Sometimes instructors provide questions to help you start your analysis. You should look at questions as guides for action rather than as specific issues to be resolved. All cases should be considered as problems in the management of the marketing mix, not as specific issues concerned only with some narrow phase of management.

We use the term *problem* loosely and employ it to indicate a state of nature that may involve either a negative situation possibly requiring corrective action or simply a situation needing opportunity assessment. You must distinguish between problems and symptoms of problems. Declining sales, market share, or profits are symptoms of more fundamental underlying problems that are their cause. Any business situation may pose multiple problems. The key to solving unstructured problems is to identify the one that must be solved first, the one whose solution will either eliminate other problems or permit their solution. We are usually interested in solving the most immediate critical problem. For example, we may have problems with the introduction of a new product, problems that have been created by a poor new product development process. Our immediate concern, however, is with addressing the difficulties of the newly launched product. We may well recommend an evaluation of the firm's new product development process, but we will leave that for future study. Note that the central problem is a state of nature. A statement of it should not contain any action verbs (i.e., *to do* is part of the plan of action). Nor should it contain the words *or* and *and*, which are, respectively, part of the statement of alternatives, and an indication of compound problems and lack of identification of *the* central problem.

Selecting the Alternatives

The second step is to define possible alternatives available to resolve the problem. Some of these alternatives may be obvious from the material supplied in the case and from the statement of the main issue. Others may have to be supplied from your own review of the situation. You should be careful to limit your analysis to a reasonable number of alternatives. Three or four al-

ternatives are usually sufficient for a typical case. One alternative that should always be considered is the maintenance of the status quo. Sometimes doing what you have been doing is the best course of action.

Analyzing the Alternatives

The heart of the case method is the analysis of alternatives. To analyze is to separate into parts so as to find out the nature, proportion, function, and underlying relationships among a set of variables. Thus, to analyze is to dig into, and work with, the facts to uncover associations that may be used to evaluate possible courses of action. Your analysis should begin with a careful evaluation of the facts presented in the case. You should be sensitive to the problem of sorting relevant material from that which is peripheral or irrelevant. In reviewing a case, you must be careful to distinguish between fact and opinion. You must also make sure that the facts are consistent and reliable. Some cases may contain errors, and the instructor may prefer to remain silent.

You are expected to base your analysis on the evidence presented in the case, but this does not mean that other information cannot be used. You should utilize facts that are available to the trade and information that is general or public knowledge. You should incorporate relevant concepts from other disciplines, such as accounting, statistics, economics, psychology, and sociology. The criterion in using outside material is that it must be appropriate to the particular situation. For example, do not use census data for 1990 to make decisions in a case dated 1987. For this book we have attempted to select cases that provide you with enough information to complete the analysis. In some situations, however, you may wish to collect additional materials from the library.

Sometimes the most important facts in the case are buried in some chance remark or seemingly minor statistical exhibit. Be careful to sift through the data to uncover all the relationships that apply to the alternatives being considered.

This means that the quantitative information must be examined using a variety of ratios, graphs, tables, or other forms of analysis. Rarely are the data supplied in the case in the form most appropriate to finding a solution, and instructors expect students to work out the numbers.

Marketing analyses are usually based on incomplete information. Assumptions must be made.[1] However, they should be made only when necessary and must be clearly labeled as such. Moreover, a rationale should be given for any assumption made. For example, a retail chain stops carrying one of your product lines but continues carrying another. You are interested in what your sales of the dropped product line would have been. You might note that over the past few years the ratio of the sales of the two product lines had been relatively constant. You could assume that the ratio would have remained the same for the current year as well, and multiply this ratio by the current year's sales of the continuing product line to estimate sales of the discontinued line in that chain. Or perhaps you would calculate the lowest and highest ratios over recent history to calculate conservative and optimistic estimates of lost sales. In any case, at the end of any decision-making exercise, you always want to review your assumptions to see how dependent your conclusions are on the assumptions made. (At one extreme, you could assume away the problem!) You should make contingency plans in the event that major assumptions do not hold.

You should realize that a complete analysis is not one-sided. A review of a business situation is not sound unless both sides of important issues are examined. This does not necessarily mean that every point must be mentioned, but major opposing arguments should be addressed where possible. You will find it helpful to explicitly list the pros and cons or advantages and disadvantages of each alternative.

Making Recommendations

After you have carefully analyzed the data and alternatives, you are in a position to make recommendations. Sometimes more than one course of action will look attractive. This is not an unusual situation, as most cases do not have a single right answer. Still, you must come up with a concrete proposal. To arrive at a solution, you should judge the relative risks and opportunities offered by the various alternatives. The optimum choice is the one that provides the best balance between profit opportunities and the risks and costs of failure. Make a clear-cut decision, and avoid qualifications and other obvious hedges. Instructors are much more concerned with how a particular decision was reached than with what alternative was selected.

Students sometimes review the facts and decide that they do not have enough information to reach a decision. They recommend that the decision be postponed pending the results of further research. Usually, "get more information" is not an acceptable solution to a business case. Decisions cannot wait the length of time necessary to conduct good research. In addition, it is unlikely that you will ever have all the information you think you need. Because of the cost of research and the penalties of delay, business decisions are almost always made under conditions of uncertainty.

Specifying a Plan of Action

Having made your decision, how are you going to implement it? You should suggest, in as much detail as the case allows, what actions you would take, when they would be taken, and how much they would cost. You may want to provide Program Evaluation and Review Technique (PERT) charts, pro forma income statements, and other relevant supporting material. Once you have proposed your actions, you would do well to reflect on the potential market reactions to them, espe-

---

[1] In most large companies, a corporate planning group provides certain forecasts, assumptions, and planning premises so that everyone in the company is using the same numbers, for instance, on future inflation rates. These tend to be long documents and are not included in casebooks.

cially competitive reactions. These possible reactions might lead you to modify your actions.

If you judge that collecting additional information is the only feasible means of solving a case, you must provide support for this decision. First, you should state exactly what the research will show and how this information will be used. In addition, you should indicate the research methodology to be followed and the anticipated cost of the study. After you have completed these tasks, you will be in a better position to decide whether additional research is needed. Remember, managers should have a predisposition to act and then adapt, rather than to procrastinate.

Preparing Contingency Plans

When you make a decision, it is based on the facts at hand, as well as on your expectations about the future that you hold at that point in time. Since the future does not always unfold as we expect or wish, we must be prepared for any significant alternative future scenario. You must ask yourself what you will do if the market does not respond to your marketing actions as you anticipate, if competitors take actions that deviate from their usual behavior, if the economy is different than economists have forecasted, and so on.

WRITING THE REPORT

We believe that students who prepare written reports do a better job of analyzing business problems. Writing a good report takes a certain skill, and we would like to suggest a few ideas that may be of help.

When instructors read reports, they check to see whether students fully understand the situation and whether student interpretations of the facts are reasonable. They also like to see papers that are objective, balanced, consistent, and decisive. Perhaps the most common error made by students in writing case reports is to repeat the facts that have been provided. Instead of analyz-

ing the data in light of alternatives, students frequently repeat statements that appear in the cases, with no clear objective in mind. Nothing upsets an instructor more than reading a paper that devotes several pages to explaining what he or she already knows about the case.

Another deficiency often observed in writing reports is lack of organization. Students who make this error begin with the first thought that enters their minds and continue, in almost random fashion, until they run out of ideas. The end result is a paper that has no beginning and no end, and often consists of one long paragraph. To avoid this problem, some instructors require that reports be presented in outline form. However, the condensed nature of such reports sometimes makes them hard to follow. Therefore, we prefer the more readable narrative approach.

There is no optimal length for a written case analysis. It depends on the amount of data provided, the preferences of the instructor, and the number of case reports the student turns in during the course. The report should be long enough to cover the subject adequately. It is fairly obvious that written reports must be neat, legible, and free of grammatical and spelling errors. Business professors are not hired to teach English composition, but they do expect certain minimal standards of performance in written expression. Their standards for written work reflect what the business community expects from college graduates.

SUMMARY

Case analysis is designed to give you an opportunity to develop a productive and meaningful way of thinking about business problems. The case method helps train you to use logic to solve realistic business issues. Remember, however, that solutions are worthless unless they can be sold to those who are in a position to act on the recommendations. The case approach provides you with practical experience in convincing others of the soundness of your reasoning.

SAMPLE CASE: COOK, INC.

Bill and Gayle Cook founded Cook, Inc., in Bloomington, Indiana. They started the firm with a capitalization of $2500, and their apartment was the company's first home. Cook, Inc., was initially engaged in the development and manufacture of medical instruments used in cardiovascular diagnosis. Since blood vessels and the heart do not show up on X-ray film, it is necessary to inject radiopaque dye so that they can be seen. This allows physicians to observe abnormalities such as blockage of vessels or inadequate heart valves so that corrective action can be taken. Most of the products manufactured by Cook, Inc., are related to cardiovascular dye injection.

Cardiovascular catheterization was first accomplished in 1929 by a German physician, Werner Forssman. However, it was not until a Swedish physician, S. I. Seldinger, perfected the technique that cardiovascular catheterizations became a practical method of diagnosis. The use of the procedure became popular in the 1980s because it eliminated exploratory surgery for many patients. Catheterization is begun by inserting a sterile plastic tube into an upper arm or thigh vessel and manipulating it to its destination with a wire guide. The physician observes the movement of the catheter on a fluoroscope, and then dye is injected so that X-ray pictures can be taken of the illuminated vessel or organ.

PRODUCT LINE

The four basic products used in cardiovascular catheterization are manufactured by Cook, Inc. These include (1) the plastic catheter, (2) the spring-shaped wire guide, (3) a needle to help

*This case was prepared by Douglas J. Dalrymple of Indiana University.

insert the catheter and wire guide through the skin and into the vessel, and (4) injector instruments to hold the radiopaque dye and provide the pressure necessary for rapid injection. Cook also manufactures bulk medical tubing, biopsy needles, intestinal and bronchial intubation sets, vascular dilators, retriever sets for recovering foreign objects, and rotating X-ray grids. The sales of Cook, Inc., have grown rapidly over the years.

The company is profitable and has sufficient access to capital from internal and external sources to cover the costs of new product introductions.

As Cook, Inc., grew in size, the company began to diversify its operations. To expand market coverage, a plant was opened in Denmark to serve the European cardiovascular products market. Sabin Enterprises was established as a subsidiary to supply plastic tubing and molded parts to Cook and outside customers. Another firm, called Anthony Products, was set up in Indianapolis to sell otological (ear) supplies. A recent addition to the Cook family is Morgan Guaranty Insurance Company. This firm specializes in product liability and casualty insurance for Cook and other companies.

DISTRIBUTION CHANNELS

At first, Cook, Inc., distributed its cardiovascular products through independent sales agents who called on doctors and hospitals. These agents worked on commission and handled several lines of medical supplies from different manufacturers. The sales agents also helped prepare promotional literature and catalogs for distribution to customers, and they worked at booths set up at medical conventions. Since the sales agents performed almost all the services of a sales department, they received a higher commission than regular independent sales representatives. Cook used only a limited amount of advertising in trade journals and relied mainly on direct contacts of field salespeople to sell their products.

As sales approached $4 million a year, Bill Cook suggested to the executive vice-president, Miles Kanne, that offering a fixed 25 percent commission to sales agents was an expensive way of distributing catheters. To help reduce distribution costs, Cook, Inc., began to hire its own field salespeople and to pay them salaries. Cook now has 15 full-time salespeople selling their products to doctors and hospitals in the United States. This change reduced selling expenses to 6 percent of sales, increased control over the salespeople, and improved the dissemination of information on Cook's products to doctors and other customers.

NEW PRODUCT DEVELOPMENT

Cook was constantly looking for new types of catheters and related items to add to its product line. Miles Kanne had recently learned about a new product from one of his salespeople. The product had been developed by Dr. Everett Lerwick, chief of surgery at the Missouri Baptist Hospital in Saint Louis. A common problem for vascular surgeons is the removal of material that builds up on the inside of arteries and restricts the flow of blood. Bypass operations can move blood around blocked sections of arteries, but these techniques do not restore blood circulation to the area fed by the blocked artery. Dr. Lerwick developed a machine that helped the surgeon remove the material from the artery so that circulation through the collateral vessels would be restored.

A picture of the Lerwick endarterectomy oscillator is shown in Exhibit 1. The patented device consists of a small 120-V motor that produces rotational power through a torque cable to a handpiece. The handpiece then converts the rotation of the motor into an oscillating motion, which is

EXHIBIT 1
Lerwick Endarterectomy Oscillator

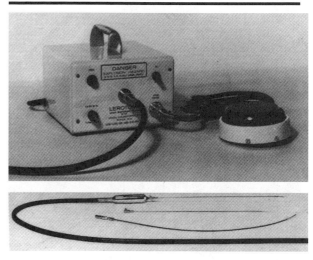

transmitted to a loop attached to the end of a shaft. A variable-speed foot control is provided so that the surgeon can regulate the speed of the motor. The cable, handpiece, rod, and loop are all designed for sterilization in an autoclave.

An example of how the oscillator is used to remove core material from a leg artery is given in Exhibit 2. First, an incision is made in the artery, and the medial core material is transected. The core is passed through the loop of the instrument, and the loop is advanced to the point where the core is still attached to the wall of the artery. Then the motor is turned on, and the oscillating loop is advanced up the artery. The instrument oscillates through an arc of 120° and has a maximum speed of 8000 oscillations per minute. Once the core material and collateral spicules are loosened from the wall of the artery, the intact core is removed through the incision. Next, a debriding catheter is attached to the handpiece to remove intimal and medial debris. Normally, a postoperative X-ray (using Cook cardiovascular catheters, perhaps) is taken on the operating table to be sure that the artery is clean and that no pieces of material are left behind.

Dr. Lerwick had performed 90 successful op-

EXHIBIT 2

Using an Endarterectomy Oscillator to Remove Material from a Femoral Artery

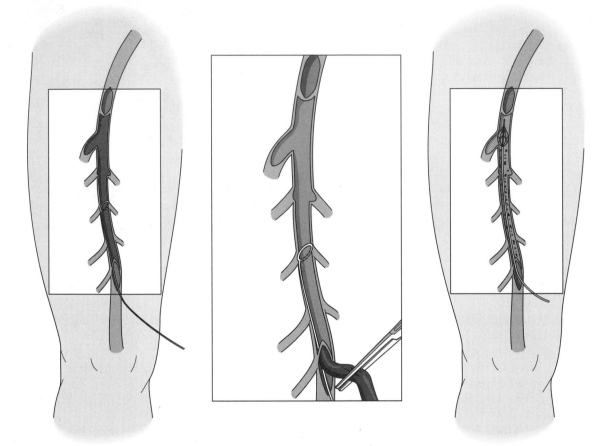

erations with the endarterectomy oscillator. Results had been quite satisfactory in terms of the long-run survival of the patients. Five-year follow-up data were available on several patients. These results showed that the opening of the collateral vessels with the oscillator contributed to a more normal flow of blood to the extremities. Dr. Lerwick felt that the use of the oscillator had considerably more to offer than bypass procedures using vein grafts or synthetic tubes.

Miles Kanne believed that the endarterectomy oscillator offered a number of possible benefits to Cook, Inc. First, Dr. Lerwick was a leading vascular surgeon, and his endorsement and use of the product would make it easier to sell it to others. Also, the product had been tested successfully in 90 operations over a period of 5 years. Another advantage was that the oscillator was closely related to Cook's present line of cardiovascular catheters. In fact, both products were normally used in the same operation. Furthermore, the manufacture and sale of the oscillator would show that Cook, Inc., was an innovative leader in the cardiovascular industry. Finally, the proposed product would fit Cook's channel of distribution and would help boost the sales of the firm.

MARKETING PLANS

Before new products could be approved for production at Cook, Inc., detailed marketing plans had to be submitted to the president of the company. Miles Kanne knew that the president, Bill Cook, would want to know how much profit they were going to make on the oscillator and what marketing techniques would be employed to gain acceptance of the new item. Estimates of the potential size of the endarterectomy oscillator market depended on several assumptions. Kanne knew from experience that about 2500 surgeons in the United States could use the oscillator in their work. However, only a small number of these physicians would actually purchase an oscillator for their own use. Cook, Inc., would first have to sell the surgeons on the product, and it would then request that the hospitals purchase the oscillators. Kanne estimated that only 3000 hospitals performed the type of vascular surgery in which endarterectomy oscillators would be of value. On the other hand, some of these hospitals scheduled vascular surgery in several operating rooms at the same time and would purchase more than one unit. The oscillators were durable, and the replacement market was expected to develop slowly.

Dr. Lerwick provided Cook with a sample oscillator that the production department could use for sourcing parts and calculating costs. The production manager estimated that purchased parts, labor, and materials would run about $450 for each oscillator. The product did not present any unusual technical problems, and the production manager indicated that the oscillator could be produced with existing labor and equipment. Also, the production schedule had enough slack to allow for the manufacture of the oscillators without the use of overtime.

Kanne believed that Cook, Inc., had two basic pricing alternatives if it chose to introduce a new product. One option was to set a high skimming price to take advantage of the patent protection on the oscillator and the absence of direct competition. Another approach would be to set a low penetration price to gain quick access to the market. The final price for the oscillator would have to reflect a royalty payment of 10 percent of gross sales to Dr. Lerwick and any special marketing expenses that were incurred.

The standard procedure for introducing new items at Cook, Inc., was to include them in the catalog, show them at medical conventions, and have the sales force talk about them with doctors. Kanne was not sure this would provide enough push to get the proposed endarterectomy oscillator accepted in the market. One problem was that the oscillator would sell for a much higher price than the catheters, which were reordered on a regular basis. The Cook salespeople were on salary and were not apt to spend a lot of time selling the expensive new oscillator when they could more easily sell large quantities of the low-value catheters. A suggestion had been made that Cook could boost the interest in the new product by offering an extra 10 percent commission to the salespeople for each unit sold. Another promotional tool that could be used was a series of direct mail brochures sent to vascular surgeons. Kanne estimated that each time a brochure was sent to a doctor, it would cost Cook $2 for printing, postage, and handling. Kanne also thought that some initial trade journal advertising might help acquaint physicians with the new item. Full-page ads in the surgical journals cost about $2000 for each insertion. Three insertions in the same journal were available at a cost of $4800. If the oscillator were displayed at medical conventions, Cook could expect incremental expenses of $2800 for each show. This would cover the cost of a larger booth than would be needed for just the catheters, extra sales help, special posters and display materials, and the cost to bring Dr. Lerwick to the conventions and pay his expenses.

As Miles Kanne sat in his office on South Curry Pike, he realized that some decisions would have to be made soon on the endarterectomy oscillator. Bill Cook was expecting a report in three days stating whether Cook, Inc., should proceed with the new product. If the recommendation were to go with the oscillator, then a detailed marketing plan would have to accompany the report.

SAMPLE CASE WRITEUP FOR COOK, INC.

CENTRAL PROBLEM

The central problem is that Cook has an opportunity for diversifying its line of cardiovascular catheters and related accessories. Although Cook is growing, it has the production capacity and marketing resources to expand into other areas. Specifically, the company has an opportunity for the introduction of a new endarterectomy oscillator that can be used to clear blocked arteries.

ANALYSIS

Alternatives

1. The status quo; do not introduce endarterectomy oscillators, and continue with current products.
2. Add endarterectomy oscillators to the product line.

Current Situation

Cook, Inc., is a small but rapidly growing medical supply manufacturer. The company makes a profit selling cardiovascular catheters directly to hospitals and clinics. Cook is currently selling catheters throughout the United States with a staff of 15 field sales representatives. Although the company has been successful, its resources are not unlimited.

Market Potential

The current market potential for endarterectomy oscillators appears to be good. At the present time, artery blockages have to be treated with complex bypass surgery. The endarterectomy oscillator would replace the need for surgery and encourage collateral blood flow in surrounding tissue. If each hospital qualified to do this type of procedure bought only one oscillator and 20 percent of the cardiovascular surgeons purchased as well, total market potential would be 3500 units. This estimate is conservative because many of the hospitals have more than one operating room where cardiovascular surgery is performed. Thus, many hospitals would need more than one unit. If 30 percent of the hospitals bought two units, then total demand would be 4400 units.

A reasonable assumption in this case with respect to the expected life cycle of the oscillator would be about 10 years. This means that 10 percent penetration of the market each year would generate sales of 440 units. If Cook sold each oscillator for $1500, sales revenue would be $660,000 per year. These are substantial revenues that could be added to Cook's sales receipts. Given the strong patent position on the oscillator, the market potential is attractive.

Product Design

The endarterectomy oscillator has been carefully developed and tested by Dr. Everett Lerwick, a leading vascular surgeon. The product has been used in 90 successful operations over a period of 5 years. In addition, the long-run survival rate of patients has been encouraging. Lerwick's oscillator has proven to be durable, and Cook could expect continued sales of replacement loops and debriding catheters to go along with each machine.

In terms of design, the endarterectomy oscillator is fairly simple. The device has an electric motor whose circular motion is converted to oscillations in a 120° arc up to 8000 times per minute. The oscillations are transmitted through a handpiece with special loops that clear the material from the patient's arteries. Speed of oscillation is controlled by a foot pedal. This mechanical device has proven to be reliable, and there are few areas for product failure. All indications suggest that the endarterectomy oscillator is an excellent product that is ready to go to market.

Promotion

Extensive promotion will be needed to help acquaint surgeons with the new oscillator. Several rounds of direct mail are appropriate at a cost of $5000 each. In addition, six journal ads would help prepare the doctors for calls by the Cook sales force. Displays at four trade shows would seem to be a minimum to demonstrate to doctors how the new machine operates. These shows seem expensive ($2800), but they will require Cook to rent extra space and pay Dr. Lerwick's expenses. Trade shows are cost effective because large numbers of surgeons can be contacted in one location.

Distribution Channels

The use of the present distribution channels for the oscillator presents a number of problems for Cook. First, the product sells for a much higher price than the current line of catheters that are purchased for $5 or $10 and then thrown away. The oscillator will require time-consuming personal sales calls to allow for demonstrations and closing. Moreover, the current salespeople are paid a salary and can sell large volumes of catheters much more easily than they can sell the new oscillator. In addition, the purchase of equipment is likely to be handled separately from supplies, and Cook will have to call on different people than those interested in catheters.

Sales force interest in the oscillator could be improved by offering a 10 percent sales commission, but this would reduce the profit potential. Another solution would be to assign one of the current salespeople or hire someone to be an oscillator specialist. This would raise fixed costs but probably could be justified by the strong market potential. Another possibility would be to manufacture the oscillator and then get an outside firm to sell it along with other products. If independent reps could be recruited to sell the oscillator for 10 to 15 percent of sales, then Cook would be advised to consider this channel of distribution. The problem for Cook is that independent reps are not interested in new products until it is clear that they have caught on in the marketplace. Reps do not want items that take a lot of time to build market acceptance. In addition, if development work has to be done, the reps will demand a margin of 30 to 40 percent of sales. If Cook has to pay 40 percent to the reps and 10 percent to Lerwick, then there will be very little profit unless a high price is charged.

Pricing

Pricing is a key decision because price will help determine the ultimate profitability of the product. Because the product is patented and hospitals are not expected to be sensitive to the price of this item, a skimming price is indicated. In this case, hospitals could easily charge off the cost of the oscillator to surgical patients over the course of a year. A skimming price of three to five times the cost would suggest selling prices between $1350 and $2250. Although these prices seem high, they are within the realm of possibility.

Because both fixed and variable cost elements are present, a multiple breakeven analysis is appropriate with selling prices of $1350, $1800, and $2250. Three different scenarios for sales force effort can also be considered. They are: (1) give salespeople no added incentive; (2) give salespeople an additional 10 percent commission; and (3) add an oscillator specialist. The resulting set of breakeven calculations are shown in Exhibit 3.

With a selling price of $1350, the breakeven is less than one sale per week even when sales force effort is encouraged with a 10 percent commission. Adding a specialized salesperson increases the breakeven to about two sales per week at the same selling price. By increasing fixed costs, the addition of a salesperson increases the risk.

EXHIBIT 3
Multiple Breakeven Analysis

Give Salespeople No Added Incentive

Price	$ 1350	$ 1800	$ 2250
Royalty (10%)	135	180	225
Net revenue	1215	1620	2025
Variable production cost	450	450	450
Margin/unit	$ 765	$ 1170	$ 1575
Promotion	30,800[a]	30,800	30,800
Breakeven volume	41	27	20

Sweeten with 10% Commission

Price	$ 1350	$ 1800	$ 2250
Royalty (10%)	135	180	225
Net revenue	1215	1620	2025
Variable production cost	450	450	450
Commission (10%)	135	180	225
Total variable costs	585	630	675
Margin/unit	$ 630	$ 990	$ 1350
Promotion	30,800	30,800	30,800
Breakeven volume	49	32	23

Add a Salesperson

Price	$ 1350	$ 1800	$ 2250
Royalty (10%)	135	180	225
Net revenue	1215	1620	2025
Variable production cost	450	450	450
Margin/unit	$ 765	$ 1170	$ 1575
Promotion	30,800	30,800	30,800
Salesperson	50,000	50,000	50,000
Total fixed costs	80,800	80,800	80,800
Breakeven volume	106	69	52

[a]6 ads (@ $1600)	$ 9,600
4 conventions (@ $2800)	11,200
5000 direct mail brochures (@ $2.00)	10,000
	$30,800

DECISION

Introduction of the oscillator has a number of advantages for Cook. First, the market potential is strong, and the product is patented to keep competition at bay. Second, the oscillator fits in well as a product line extension for the current line of catheters. Indeed, both the oscillator and Cook catheters can be used in the same surgical procedures. Furthermore, the product will be easy to manufacture with existing tools and labor. In addition, the oscillator can be sold with the same distribution channels used for the catheters. At prices over $1000, Cook makes good margins and the breakeven point is low. The key issue, however, is risk. Cook has spent nothing to develop the oscillator. In addition, production of the oscillators does not require new tooling, new equipment, new plant, or new technology, and promotional costs are modest. Thus, the risk to Cook if it takes on the product and it fails is very low. On the other hand, if the oscillator succeeds, profits will be good because Cook has so little money tied up in the project. The benefits of introducing the oscillator outweigh the risks: add the oscillator to the product line.

PLAN OF ACTION

1. Set an introductory price of $1350.
2. Sell extra dissecting loops at $65 each and charge $90 for the debriding catheter.
3. Sell the oscillator with the existing field sales force.
4. Promote the oscillator with direct mail and trade shows.
5. Avoid journal ads and special sales commissions.

CONTINGENCY PLAN

If the oscillator is selling at a rate of less than one per week at the end of the first year, discontinue selling it.

SEQUEL

Cook introduced the oscillator at a price of $1050, using direct mail and its own sales force. The oscillator was sold with two vessel dissecting loops, but the debriding catheter was sold separately for $75. Extra dissecting loops were sold for $50 each. At these prices, Cook would have made a good margin on the supplies. However, sales of the oscillator were slow, and the item was discontinued. This item was one of very few product failures at Cook, Inc.

Discussions with Cook executives revealed that the oscillator did not fail because of lack of a need for the product, too high a price, or a lack of personal selling by the company sales force. The product proved to be dependable, and Cook experienced no product failures or patient injuries. The main problem was that it turned out to be much harder than the company expected to get surgeons to switch to a new approach and a new machine. In addition, Dr. Lerwick did not help train other surgeons in the use of the new device, as Cook had anticipated. Dr. Lerwick did not go to conventions and give speeches about the oscillator, and he did not write articles for medical journals on the results of his own experience with the oscillator. Although Dr. Lerwick had data on the results of his operations, they were never summarized in a form that Cook could use in its promotional material. Without Dr. Lerwick's help, the job of introducing the oscillator became much more difficult. Hindsight suggests that Cook should have done a much more thorough job of field testing before introducing the product to the regular sales force. It should have placed a number of units in hospitals to get some support from other doctors to make up for Dr. Lerwick's lack of interest. The oscillator is an industrial product, and you have to do more than tell the surgeons it is better; you have to show them in actual operations.

Despite Cook's disappointment with the oscillator, other firms have successfully introduced products similar to the Lerwick oscillator. This suggests the existence of a real demand for this product. You may also be interested in knowing that Cook has successfully diversified into ureteral catheters and heart pacemakers and has become a highly profitable $200 million firm.

Subject Index

Photo Credits

Chapter 1 Page 15: Courtesy BMW.   **Chapter 2** Page 34: Courtesy Kodak. Page 38: Courtesy General Motors/Saturn Division.   **Chapter 4** Page 79: Courtesy Signode Corporation. Page 82: Courtesy Royal Appliance Manufacturing. Page 84: BARBIE and © 1994 Mattel Inc. Used with permission.   **Chapter 5** Page 98: Courtesy ConAgra. Page 105: Courtesy Office Depot. **Chapter 7** Page 169: Courtesy of Luigino.   **Chapter 8** Page 188: Courtesy Boeing. Page 195: Courtesy Dr Pepper/Seven Up Co.   **Chapter 9** Page 219: Seth Resnick. Page 227: Courtesy Hertz.   **Chapter 11** Page 268: Courtesy of Dell Computers.   **Chapter 12** Page 298: Courtesy of Loctite Corporation. Page 302: Courtesy Information Systems of America. Page 315: Courtesy Real World Corp.   **Chapter 13** Page 334: Courtesy 3 Com. Page 341: D. Forster/ Courtesy America 3 Foundation.   **Chapter 14** Page 365: Courtesy Van Heusen.   **Chapter 16** Page 402: Courtesy of Brooklyn Brewery. Page 409: Courtesy of Borden.   **Chapter 17** Page 423: Courtesy Smith Kline.